Introduction to Marketing Communication

Introduction to Marketing Communication:

An Integrated Approach

John Burnett
University of Denver

Sandra Moriarty
University of
Colorado–Boulder

Prentice-Hall
Upper Saddle River, New Jersey 07458

Acquisition Editors: Donald J. Hull and Gabrielle Dudnyk
Director of Development: Steve Deitmer
Development Editor: Charlotte R. Morrissey
Associate Editor: John Larkin
Editorial Assistant: Jim Campbell
Vice President/Editorial Director: James Boyd
Marketing Manager: John Chillingworth
Associate Managing Editor: Linda DeLorenzo
Managing Editor: Dee Josephson
Production: GTS Graphics, Inc.
Manufacturing Supervisor: Arnold Vila
Manufacturing Manager: Vincent Scelta
Design Manager: Patricia Smythe
Interior Design: Amanda Kavanagh
Cover Design: Cheryl Asherman
Cover Illustration: JW Stewart

Copyright © 1998 by Prentice-Hall, Inc.
A Simon & Schuster Company
Upper Saddle River, New Jersey 07458

Library of Congress Cataloging-in-Publication Data

Burnett, John
    Introduction to marketing communication: an integrated
approach / John Burnett, Sandra Moriarty.
      p.   cm.
    Includes bibliographical references and index.
    ISBN 0-13-269085-3
    1. Communication in marketing.   2. Advertising campaigns.
  I. Moriarty, Sandra E. (Sandra Ernst)   II. Title.
HF5415.123.B87   1997
658.8—dc21   97-38237
                                             CIP

Prentice-Hall International (UK) Limited, London
Prentice-Hall of Australia Pty. Limited, Sydney
Prentice-Hall Canada, Inc., Toronto
Prentice-Hall Hispanoamericana, S.A., Mexico
Prentice-Hall of India Private Limited, New Delhi
Prentice-Hall of Japan, Inc., Tokyo
Simon & Schuster Asia Pte. Ltd., Singapore
Editora Prentice-Hall do Brasil, Ltda., Rio de Janeiro

Printed in the United States of America

10 9 8 7 6 5 4 3 2 1

BRIEF TABLE OF CONTENTS

TABLE OF CONTENTS

TABLE OF CONTENTS FOR INTERNATIONAL COVERAGE, FEATURES, AND EXAMPLES

TABLE OF CONTENTS FOR TECHNOLOGY COVERAGE, FEATURES, AND EXAMPLES

Pick up a magazine, navigate the Web, watch TV, or drive to the shopping mall; marketing messages will bombard you. In today's information-filled world, marketers have to fight to grab and hold consumer attention. To do so, they must use effective *marketing communication*—the process of communicating marketing messages to promote products, services, and ideas. This text introduces students to the marketing communication tools, techniques, and media that practitioners use to promote their products. It also gives special emphasis to *integrated marketing communication* (IMC)—a strategy of coordinating and combining messages for maximum impact. Some text highlights follow.

- *Balanced coverage of all marketing communication tools.* Unlike other texts that devote the bulk of their coverage to advertising, we balance our coverage of the key marketing communication areas throughout the entire text.
- *Integrated international, ethical, and technology coverage.* Rather than treat the international, ethical, and technological aspects of marketing communication as isolated topics, the text demonstrates how these topics relate to many issues with integrated coverage.
- *Current examples from all types and sizes of businesses.* The current examples used in the text discussion, opening vignettes, features, and end-of-chapter materials show students how marketing communication concepts apply to a wide spectrum of business practice.
- *A focus on key marketing communication concepts and applications.* By eliminating excess detail, instructors and students have more opportunity to cover the basics well. Two unique chapters demonstrate our superior text organization:
  - Chapter 14 (Marketing Communication that Crosses the Lines)
  - Chapter 19 (Campaign Planning).
- *An integrated learning system.* Our learning system helps students move progressively from recall to mastering concepts to critical thinking. This system is used in end-of-chapter questions, the test bank, and our Web site to strengthen students' learning experience and skill development.

BALANCED, CONSISTENT COVERAGE

The text emphasizes how the various marketing communication areas work together to create a cohesive message. As a result, it does more than define and explain the various marketing communication areas and their comparative strengths and weaknesses (Chapters 9–14). It also stresses how to best "mix" marketing communication tools in a strategic, integrated plan (Chapters 1–4); how to plan for and use media in all marketing communication areas (Chapters 15 and 16); and how to budget and evaluate programs for all those areas (Chapters 17 and 18). The book closes with a chapter that integrates all parts of the text as it shows students how one business planned, budgeted for, executed, and evaluated a marketing communication campaign that is still ongoing (Chapter 19). The benefit of this complete coverage? Students will learn from start to finish how to plan, execute, and evaluate a marketing communication program and message strategy that is effective and efficient.

INTERNATIONAL, ETHICAL, AND TECHNOLOGY COVERAGE

Introduction to Marketing Communication recognizes the importance of how the global community affects marketing communication practices. The international discussion occurs seamlessly in the text through examples and discussion where it is most relevant, with particular emphasis in Chapters 6 and 7 in Part II (The IMC Context). For easy reference, a separate table of contents shows exactly where international themes and examples are covered in the text.

The ethical implications of marketing communication are covered in Chapter 7 and are also infused throughout the text in You Decide features. These features highlight ethical concerns and pose questions that force students to wrestle with issues that are rarely black-and-white. For instance, we examine how Odwalla, Inc., a small, natural juice producer, coped with consumer backlash when it distributed apple juice contaminated with *E-coli* bacteria. Because the aim of these features is to sensitize students to situations that can and do arise in practice, each You Decide feature uses a real-world situation as the teaching tool.

Technology is altering many marketing communication practices. Direct marketing databases, sophisticated media tracking, and the use of the World Wide Web to communicate with consumers are only a few examples. We weave technology coverage throughout the text, features, and end-of-chapter materials. Notably, 16 chapters have Internet projects so that students can learn about the strengths and weaknesses of this medium. A separate technology table of contents is included for your convenience.

CURRENT EXAMPLES FROM ALL TYPES AND SIZES OF BUSINESS

This book demonstrates how companies use IMC. In fact, examples abound, not only in the text discussion but also in opening vignettes, IMC in Action and Profile features, and in end-of-chapter cases. The examples and stories bring the theory to life, showing students the relevance of what they are reading. We make the examples vivid, current, and varied. They range from Fortune 500 companies such as Procter & Gamble and Gillette to smaller, privately-held businesses such as Biofoam (a supplier of edible, biodegradable packing materials) and clothier Hanna Andersson. We also focus on international companies of all sizes, ranging from Ecover (a small manufacturer of toxic-free detergents) to Bennetton Group SpA.

We have selected the most powerful examples to demonstrate the concepts with an eye towards currency. For instance, Chapter 1 spotlights how Tiger Woods' prowess on the golfing greens translates into marketing communication success stories for Nike and Titleist. Chapter 17 describes the budgeting strategy for Toyota's RAV4, the 1997 utility vehicle of the year.

Learning is not always about success stories. Snapple, for instance, although originally an example of the effectiveness of IMC and relationship building, lost its way when it was acquired and eventually sold by Quaker. Diagnosing problems and failures is an important aspect of critical thinking, and such examples are introduced to challenge students to learn from others' mistakes and better manage real-world problems.

A CLEAR, EFFECTIVE ORGANIZATION

Time is a precious commodity for instructors and students. Market feedback revealed that instructors want an introductory marketing communication text that 1) covers the basics well and 2) omits unnecessary detail. Careful selection of topics, appropriate depth of coverage, and concise writing helped us meet those two objectives. Instead of the typical 22–25 chapters, *Introduction to Marketing Communication* offers 19 chapters of manageable length.

Introduction to Marketing Communication is divided into five parts—Understanding IMC; The IMC Context; The Tools of IMC; IMC Media; and IMC Appropriation, Evaluation, and Campaign Planning. We briefly describe each part next.

- **Part I, Understanding IMC:** Chapter 1 explains the concepts of marketing communication and integrated marketing communication. Chapter 2 reviews the marketing mix but not in the traditional way. It focuses on the communication dimensions of the marketing mix and how marketing mix decisions drive the marketing communication strategy. The third chapter describes how companies organize marketing and marketing communication teams—internally through departments and externally with agencies. Chapter 4 presents ways to develop marketing communication strategy and the planning process.
- **Part II, The IMC Context:** This section focuses on the marketing communication context, including the effects of the internal and external environment on those who communicate and receive marketing messages. Chapter 5 reviews the sociocultural environment and Chapter 6 explores how consumers make decisions. Chapter 7 examines the legal, ethical, and global environment of marketing communication. Chapter 8 looks at the communication process.
- **Part III, The Tools of IMC:** Part III surveys different areas of marketing communication—advertising (Chapter 9), sales promotion (Chapter 10), public relations (Chapter 11), direct marketing (Chapter 12), and personal selling (Chapter 13). Chapter 14, the final chapter in this part, is unique to this text. It covers marketing communication areas that are hard to categorize because they combine various communication tools—for instance, a sponsorship of a sporting event might require the use of public relations, advertising, and sales promotion. Other topics in this chapter include cause marketing, merchandising,

packaging, and marketing services such as trade shows and exhibits, marketing support services, and customer service.

- **Part IV, IMC Media:** Chapters 15 and 16 deal specifically with media and other message delivery systems, the means used to carry integrated marketing communication messages (such as TV, radio, the Internet, and so on). Unlike other texts, this part describes how practitioners can combine media to create synergy.
- **Part V, IMC Appropriation, Evaluation, and Campaign Planning:** Chapter 17 examines the appropriation and budgeting methods for an entire marketing communication plan. Chapter 18 describes how to measure IMC performance. We close the book with a unique chapter on campaign planning. This chapter shows students how a real company (Saturn) planned, implemented, budgeted, and evaluated its IMC campaign in the planning and product launch stages and how it continues to do so now.

HELPFUL PEDAGOGY

To reinforce learning and build business skills that students can use on the job, we introduce several features that no other marketing communication text offers. Our comprehensive learning system helps students master material quickly and thoroughly. Some features of that system include *opening vignettes, performance-based learning objectives,* and *chapter summaries that link directly to the learning objectives.* We also include the following features that distinguish us from other texts:

- **Concept Reviews** help students grasp the material as they move through the chapter. This learning device recaps the major points of the previous section so that students can review what they've just read to check for understanding of the major issues.
- **You Decide** and **IMC in Action** features foster critical thinking by posing real-world scenarios and questions that have no right answer. The You Decide features highlight ethical issues. IMC in Action boxes spotlight in-depth marketing communication business examples.
- **IMC Concept in Focus** features showcase key or emerging IMC concepts. Examples include such topics as consumer-based media planning, the importance of relationship marketing in business-to-business marketing communication, and zero-based budgeting.
- **Profiles** spotlight young executives from a variety of functional areas and job titles working in different countries. These practitioners describe their jobs, their career paths since college, and their views on how to get ahead in marketing communication. The profiles offer a real-world view of the range of careers available in this incredibly diverse industry.
- **End-of-Chapter Exercises** move students through three levels of learning— 1) fact, recall, and definition; 2) understanding concepts; and 3) applying concepts to new situations. This three-tiered learning system is also incorporated

in the test manual and the Prentice Hall Web site so that instructors can better evaluate the level of understanding that students have mastered.

- **Team, Communication, and Internet Projects** challenge students to learn how to learn outside the classroom. Business practice is demanding. Workers must be able to collaborate in small groups, communicate effectively, and master new technology. Suggested projects at the end of every chapter allow students to practice these skills.
- **End-of-chapter Case Studies** foster critical thinking. Students are given actual business scenarios that stress several concepts found in the chapter. End-of-case questions encourage students to spot issues, analyze facts, and solve problems.
- **Roma's Lite Integrative Case Questions** in each chapter link to a detailed marketing plan for Roma's Lite Pizza in an end-of-text Appendix. As students move through the book they work individually and in teams on case study questions that encourage them to apply what they have learned in the chapter. The result? They build their own integrated marketing communication campaign plan. This skill-building, integrated case teaches students the how-to of campaign planning—a skill that they can use on the job.
- **End-of-part Video Case Studies** are case studies that integrate concepts from several chapters in each text part. The cases use a supporting video as the springboard that allows students to see how concepts interrelate.

INSTRUCTOR RESOURCES

The goal of *Introduction to Marketing Communication* is simple: to make teaching and learning marketing communication successful experiences. We designed each supplemental resource to work hand-in-glove with the text and to add extra value to instructors and students alike.

Instructor's Resource Manual (IRM)

The *Instructor's Resource Manual* contains over 400 pages of course-preparation materials. This handy lecture tool, developed by Dr. Jim Dupree, provides a chapter overview, detailed chapter outline, chapter objectives, a summary of all features, and suggested answers to critical thinking questions posed in the chapter. It also includes lecture tips, discussion guidelines, key figures and tables, a chapter summary, answers to all end-of-chapter exercises, a case analysis, and guidelines for integrative case question answers.

Test Bank

The test bank, prepared with the assistance of Dr. Jim Dupree, provides a file of approximately 2000 questions. The question types include multiple choice, true/false, and essay. Many of these questions target issues from chapter features such as You Decide and IMC in Action. Importantly, the test questions incorporate the

three-tiered learning system used in the end-of-chapter exercises. That way, instructors can assess how well students are mastering each level of learning—recall, conceptual, and application of concepts to new situations.

Prentice Hall Custom Test: DOS, Windows, or Mac Versions

Based on Engineering Software Associates top-selling, state-of-the-art test-generation software program, *Prentice Hall Custom Test* allows complete flexibility. First, you can customize tests to suit your course needs—from simple pop quizzes to multiple versions of a comprehensive exam. With its user-friendly test creation and powerful algorithmic generation, tailor-made tests can be developed quickly, simply, and without error. Whether you work on Macintosh, Windows, or DOS, you can administer your exams traditionally or online, evaluate and track students results, and analyze the success of the exam—all with a click of the mouse or push of a button.

Color Transparencies and Electronic PowerPoint Slides

We offer 100 four-color acetates taken from the text photos, tables, and figures. In addition, we offer over 150 PowerPoint full-color electronic presentation screens that are original, rather than taken from the text. This visual package gives instructors a complete array of helpful presentation aids.

Video Package

We offer one tape of videos containing the ABC and *Wall Street Journal* news clips that tie to the integrated end-of-part cases in the text. Support for those videos is provided in the IRM. We also offer the New York Festival Videos of award-winning commercials and an accompanying instructors video guide.

Internet Faculty and Student Support through PHLIP

PHLIP *(Prentice Hall's Learning through the Internet Partnership—http:/www.prenhall. com/phlip)* allows adopting faculty to sign in with a user name and password and download lecture aids, including lecture notes and outlines, PowerPoint presentations, exercise and case solutions, and updates. The *PHLIPping through the News Internet Service* gives students and faculty access to a learning environment, complete with news stories directly linked to the text, and lists of additional resources and related Internet links.

ACKNOWLEDGMENTS

A book like this is a major undertaking. It would not have happened without the help of a great many significant others. Special thanks go to Prentice Hall and

David Borkowsky for having faith in this project at the outset and Acquisitions Editor Gabrielle Dudnyk who carried it out. Thanks also to Editor in Chief Natalie Anderson and Editorial Director Jim Boyd for their support. Our appreciation also goes to Assistant Editor John Larkin, who handled the supplements process with great care, and Editorial Assistant Jim Campbell who managed many important details with speed and aplomb.

The hard work of two other teams was essential to this text. First, the development team of Steve Deitmer, Director of Development, and Charlotte Morrissey, Senior Development Editor, provided ample elbow grease when and where needed. Second, the production team of Linda DeLorenzo, Joanne Jay, Arnold Vila, Pat Smythe, and Heather Stratton and Margaret Pinette of GTS Graphics made sure that the design and production value of the text were second to none.

Kudos to Senior Marketing Manager John Chillingworth, John's assistant Laura Kelley, and Director of Marketing Brian Kibby who practice what we preach, and whose input and effort played a key role in planning and defining a message strategy for this text. Thanks also to the crack marketing communication team led by Janet Ferrugia, Eve Adams, and Sheila Lynch.

Various people in the industry have participated in the development of this book. In particular, we would like to thank Greg Martin, Director of Corporate Communications at Saturn, Chris Wright-Isaak at Young and Rubicam, David Bell at the American Association of Advertising Agencies, branding expert Larry Light, Ian Beavis, formerly Group Account Director, Saatchi & Saatchi Pacific, and Mr. Irv Griffin, Vice President of Sales and Development, Lexus Divison, Toyota Motor Sales. A very warm "thank you" to the marketing communicators we profiled. Your time and effort made a difference!

This book has been through an extensive review process. The reviewers who have looked at several drafts of this manuscript and made thoughtful and important suggestions deserve special accolades. Most notably, we would like to thank Dr. Jim Dupree for his assistance on the manuscript, the instructors resource manual, and the test bank. Your eagle eyes are second to none. Thank you also to Professor Mark Green for his scrutiny of the international, technology, and case coverage. We also wish to thank the following people:

Avery Abernathy, *Auburn University*
Ruth Clotley, *Barry University*
Barbara T. Conte, *Florida Atlantic University*
Bill Fisher, *Columbia College–Chicago*
Jon Freiden, *Florida State University*
Pat Kennedy, *University of Nebraska–Lincoln*
Bart Kittle, *Youngstown State University*
Rita Larkin, *Temple University*
Tina Lowery, *Rider University*
Peter McClure, *University of Massachusetts*

Martha McEnally, *University of North Carolina at Greensboro*
Stephen Neulander, *Columbia College–Chicago*
Joel Reedy, *University of South Florida*
Scott Roberts, *University of Texas at Brownsville*
Dennis Sandler, *Pace University*
Denise Schuenbachler, *Northern Illinois University*
Susan Spiggle, *University of Connecticut*
Anne Swartzlander, *Mississippi State Tech Community College*

On a personal level, we would like to thank Nancy Burnett and the Burnett children—Laura, Michael, and David—who are saints for putting up with the disruption in their lives created by such a project. We would also like to thank Tom Duncan, director of the IMC graduate program at the University of Colorado, who has done much of the theory building in this area. Many of our ideas have been enriched by or built on his work. And as a spouse, he also gets thanks for enduring the chaos and tribulations that book deadlines create for families.

DR. JOHN BURNETT

John Burnett holds a D.B.A. degree in Marketing from the University of Kentucky. He is a Professor of Marketing at the University of Denver. Dr. Burnett is the author of *Promotion Management,* now in its third edition, and a co-author of *Advertising Principles and Practices.* In addition, he has had numerous articles and research papers published in a wide variety of professional and academic journals.

In addition to his teaching, writing, and research activities, Dr. Burnett is an active marketing and marketing communication consultant for a wide range of industries. He has worked, for instance, as a consultant for AT&T, the Dallas Mart, the AAFES organization, and Scott & White Hospitals. Dr. Burnett has also won several teaching awards and serves as faculty advisor for student chapters of the American Marketing Association.

DR. SANDRA E. MORIARTY

Sandra Moriarty holds a B.J. and M.S. in journalism from the University of Missouri and a Ph.D. in instructional communication from Kansas State University. She started her career as a government information officer. Dr. Moriarty has owned her own public relations and advertising agency, worked as a copywriter, done public relations consulting, and directed a university public relations program. She has also taught at Michigan State University and the University of Kansas. Currently, Dr. Moriarty is a professor at the University of Colorado–Boulder where she teaches in the Integrated Marketing Communication graduate program.

In addition to an extensive list of articles in both scholarly and trade journals, Dr. Moriarty has authored or co-authored eight other books, including *Driving Brand Value: Using Integrated Marketing to Manage Profitable Stakeholder Relationships; Creative Advertising; Advertising: Principles and Practices;* and *The Creative Package.*

chapter

Marketing
Communication

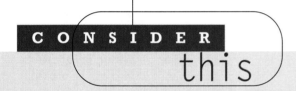

CONSIDER *this*

Microsoft Points the Way

Selling products to today's savvy consumers can be tough. Businesses must learn what consumers need, create products that meet those needs, and effectively market those products to consumers. Microsoft, the dominant player in computer operating systems and productivity software, has been able to market its products successfully around the globe because it sends a consistent marketing message in every way possible.

Take the Windows 95 launch and its Internet products as an example. In the early 1990s Microsoft learned that its customers wanted a faster, more powerful, and more user-friendly Windows operating system. It spent more than three years developing the Windows 95 program. But not without some problems. Despite the fact that Windows 95 was the most tested program in history (400,000 beta testers helped Bill Gates and crew flush out the bugs), initial in-

troduction was delayed nearly two months, partly because of program problems, the difficulty of shipping systems to thousands of retail outlets, and the problem of training retail sales staffs.

Microsoft's marketing program sales objective for its Windows 95 product was ambitious: Persuade 85 million customers worldwide to move *en masse* to a new operating system technology. With such a goal, Microsoft's marketing team realized that the company could not just rely on traditional advertising, such as TV commercials, newspaper and magazine ads, and billboards. Instead, Microsoft opted to communicate its marketing message through as many avenues as possible.

Microsoft started its marketing campaign months before the actual August 24, 1995, launch date. Computer software experts—both private citizens and paid professionals—conducted product tests. Computer manufacturers such as Compaq Computer Corp. and chip designers such as Advanced

Micro Devices, Inc., were brought on board the Windows 95 bandwagon. Bill Gates and associates gave hundreds of interviews, and Gates appeared on all the major talk shows. All publications aimed at the computer and software suppliers (the "trade market") were contacted and given demonstrations along with free computers and software. By launch time customers were literally lined up at the doors of the 29,000 retailers stocked with Windows 95.

The product was introduced starting at midnight in New Zealand, moving time zone by time zone around the world. Microsoft used every marketing scheme imaginable, ranging from TV and print ads to infomercials to publicity stunts. TV commercials were aired in 23 countries, starting with a spot featuring the Rolling Stones' "Start Me Up." An eight-page ad was run in both *USA Today* and the *Wall Street Journal*. Magazine ads were run in business, computer, and consumer titles. A week later ads were run on World Wide Web sites, such as Hot Wired. Those ads linked people to Microsoft's home page. In addition, the Empire State Building was bathed in Microsoft colors, free pizza was distributed at retail stores, and $95 American Airlines and $90 MCI savings coupons were given to buyers. Also, Microsoft designed a companion product, MSN (Microsoft Network) and provided upgrades of several of its most popular software programs to hit the store shelves at the same time as the Windows 95 operating system. MSN is an online interactive service that provides Internet access, e-mail capability, and a connection to Microsoft to ask technical support questions and obtain Windows 95 updates.

Microsoft's Windows 95 marketing communication strategies produced startling results. Industry analysts estimate that within the first year Microsoft sold 62 million units and about 81 million units by the 1996 year-end.

The next year Microsoft changed focus. It cut its global TV budget by $50 million to shift more advertising to the Internet. Why? Microsoft planned to become omnipresent on the World Wide Web. All the marketing messages continued the Windows 95 campaign theme ("Where do you want to go today?") and colors (green, yellow, blue, and red). Billboards, print ads, TV spots, and Internet banners used computer graphics, such as a hand that points the way to one of Microsoft's interactive information and Internet access products. That product line includes MSN, currently the third largest commercial online service; MSNBC, a cable channel venture with NBC that provides free news to MSN subscribers; *Slate,* an interactive magazine on the Web; and Explorer, Web browser software. Microsoft offered these Web-based products as part of its operating system and Microsoft Office software updates to allow the desktop to function as a television-like multimedia system, putting all kinds of new information at customers' fingertips. Microsoft has pointed the way. So far, millions have followed.

Sources: Laurie J. Flynn, "Disney Will Charge Fee for Children's Web Site," *New York Times,* 3 March 1997, C5. John Markoff, "Microsoft and the Web: Making Critical Mass Pay," *New York Times,* 29 July 1996, C1, C2; "Technology Power 50," *Advertising Age,* 1996 Annual Power 50 Report: Internet; Bradley Johnson, "Windows95 Opens with Omnimedia Blast," *Advertising Age,* August 28, 1995, 1, 32; Alice Z. Cuneo, "Apple Gets Gnarly over Introduction," *Advertising Age,* August 28, 1995, 32; Michael J. Himowitz, "Windows95: Do You Need the Most Overhyped Product of the Decade?" *Fortune,* September 18, 1995, 191–96; Katie Harner, "Should You Do Windows?" *Newsweek,* August 21, 1995, 38–42; Amy Cortese and Kathy Rebello, "Windows95: Can Microsoft's New Software Live Up to Expectations?" *Business Week,* July 10, 1995, 94–106; "Another Win–Win95 Proposition," *Business Week,* September 18, 1995, 56.

CHAPTER OVERVIEW

Consumers are skeptical of many marketing efforts, so getting and holding their attention is extremely difficult. Even market leaders such as Procter & Gamble, General Motors, and Microsoft are no longer secure in their market dominance. To ensure a product will sell successfully, businesses must do more than produce the best product, charge the lowest price, or place the product in the best or largest number of stores. Companies must market their products with creative, informative, and interesting messages that show how the products meet the needs and wants of consumers. A key factor in marketing a product is *communication,* as illustrated by the opening vignette.

This text explains the basic concepts of marketing communication. We begin this chapter by examining what marketing is. Next, we define and describe integrated marketing communication and explain the reasons for its use in business. Finally, we conclude with a framework that shows how integrated marketing communication fits into a firm's marketing program.

MARKETING COMMUNICATION

Marketing communication is the process of effectively communicating product information or ideas to *target audiences.** No business can operate in every market to satisfy everyone's needs. Instead, a company succeeds when it targets a market of those people most likely to be interested in its marketing program. A **target audience** is a group of people who receives marketing messages and has significant potential to respond to the messages. Even mass-marketers like Coca-Cola Enterprises and Pepsico target audiences to promote their products. For example, the target market for Diet Coke consists of all diet-conscious soda drinkers. Diet Coke, then, targets an audience of those who are most likely to be diet conscious—12- to 24-year-olds of both sexes and women ages 25 to 45.

To communicate a marketing message effectively, companies must realize that everything they do can send a message. For instance, outfitting a car with a CD-player and leather upholstery sends a strong message about the car's quality. The

"Diner": *Pepsi-Cola via BBDO Worldwide*

This Pepsi-Cola ad targeted an audience of older consumers that enjoy a non-diet soft drink.

---

*Note that here and throughout the text, the word *product* refers to a good, a service, or an idea.

price of a product can also communicate to an audience—a 99-cent pen is probably not going to be as durable or luxurious as a $50 pen. A company that distributes its product only through discount stores tells the consumer a great deal about the status of its product.

Product, price, and distribution can communicate market information to audiences. These three marketing activities—price, product, and channel of distribution—combined with marketing communication, make up the **marketing mix.** Marketing communication is the element of the marketing mix used to showcase important features of the other three to increase the odds the consumer will buy a product. If marketing communication is based on a comprehensive, well-conceived marketing plan, it will produce a "Big Idea" that is persuasive to the target audience. For instance, Microsoft's Big Idea is giving customers the information they want at their fingertips. The application of the idea in its Internet product marketing efforts is the slogan "Where do you want to go today?" and the graphic hand that points to a Microsoft product is the answer to the question.

Marketing communication and the other three marketing mix elements are the four categories of strategic decision making in a marketing plan. A **marketing plan** is a document that analyzes the current marketing situation, identifies market opportunities and threats, sets objectives, and develops action plans to achieve objectives. Each of the marketing mix areas has its own set of objectives and strategies. A pricing objective and strategy, for example, might be to increase sales in a certain geographical market by pricing a product lower than a competitor. Marketing communication presents the overall marketing strategy to target audiences, sending messages about product, price, and distribution to excite interest or make a convincing point. Figure 1.1 shows how the marketing plan and the marketing mix relate.

Next, we discuss five factors found in all marketing communication: persuasion, objectives, contact points, stakeholders, and various types of marketing communication activities.

Persuasion and Information

All marketing communication tries to persuade the target audience to change an attitude or behavior or provides information. For example, Kraft wants consumers to believe that its cheese is the best value compared to all other cheese brands. Hallmark wants purchasers to think of its cards "when you care enough to send the very best." Marketers can persuade in many ways. They can provide information, reasons, and incentives. They can also listen actively to the concerns of people in the market. In fact, Pampers' 800 number is one of its most important marketing communication tools because new mothers can find the number on the package and feel comfortable calling the company with their questions and concerns.

Objectives

All marketing communication is goal directed. Marketing communication objectives are the goals of the communication program. Generally, those objectives are to create brand awareness, deliver information, educate the market, and advance a positive image for the brand or company. The ultimate goal of the marketing communication strategy is to help sell the product to keep the company in business.

FIGURE 1.1

The Marketing Plan and the Marketing Mix

Contact Points

Successful marketing requires managing and coordinating marketing messages at every contact point the brand or company has with its target audience. Contact points can range from the store where the customer sees the product, the hotline the customer calls for information, or the living room where the TV airs a commercial. Marketers can plan formal contacts, such as an advertisement, however, many contacts are unplanned. The unplanned contacts can communicate informal messages that audiences infer. For instance, a store's design can send a message that it retails inexpensive products. Or an unhelpful salesperson can send a message that the company doesn't care about customer service. To persuade audiences most effectively, the company must think about all contact points as important in a marketing program. Successful marketing requires that messages at every contact point work together to persuade consumers.

Stakeholders

The target audience includes more than the target market of potential consumers. A **stakeholder** is anyone who has a stake in the success of a company or its products. Stakeholder audiences include all those who might influence the purchase of products and the success of the company, such as employees, retailers and distributors, suppliers, the local community, the media, and government regulators, as well as customers.

Diet Coke's target market consists of diet-conscious consumers. An example of one of Diet Coke's stakeholders is the Food and Drug Administration (FDA) because it regulates foods and drinks sold to the public, such as Diet Coke. Other stakeholder audiences might include Diet Coke retailers and distributors because they can influence how and when the product reaches consumers, financial analysts who influence the company's shareholders, and local communities where Diet Coke plants are located.

The idea that stakeholders other than consumers may be important in a marketing program is gaining importance in business. Houston-based Men's Wearhouse, a men's clothing chain with 260 stores and annual sales of more than $430 million, credits its success with its emphasis on the people side of its business. In a list of important stakeholders, its top priority is its employees. After that its priorities are its customers, suppliers, the community, and shareholders. The company believes that a commitment to employees will ensure better customer service.[1]

Competitors can even be important stakeholders. IBM and Apple, for example, have combined to develop a computer that reads both platforms. These partnerships are becoming more common as companies agree to work together to protect their market shares. In Asia, for example, Cathay Pacific, Singapore International Airlines, Thai Airways International, and the Malaysian Airline Systems introduced a cooperative frequent flyer program to protect themselves from the large international carriers that fly into their markets and offer such programs.

Government regulators often can have an important say about the success of a business or industry, even those as dominant as cigarette manufacturers or Microsoft. In introducing various products Microsoft found it needed special messages for both regulators and competitors who fear its monopoly potential.

Marketing Communication Messages

Hundreds of different communication activities can deliver messages both formally through explicit marketing communication programs and informally though the marketing mix and other corporate contact points. As depicted in Figure 1.2, the two key types of messages used to reach marketing communication goals are planned and unplanned messages.

Planned messages are delivered through the following marketing communication tools:

- **Advertising**—Any paid form of communication by an identified sponsor that promotes ideas, goods, or services. Although some advertising (such as direct mail) is directed at specific individuals, most advertising messages are tailored to a group and use mass media such as radio, television, newspapers, and magazines.
- **Sales promotion**—Marketing activities that add to the basic value of the product or service for a limited time and directly stimulate consumer purchasing (for example, coupons and product sampling), the cooperation of distributors, or stimulate the effort of the sales force.
- **Public relations**—A coordinated attempt to create a favorable product image in the mind of the public by supporting certain activities or programs, publishing commercially significant news in a widely circulated medium, or obtaining favorable publicity on radio, television, or stage that is not paid for by the company selling the product.
- **Direct marketing**—An interactive system of marketing that allows the consumer to access information, purchase the product through a variety of media, or both. Examples include direct mail, catalogs, and online catalog services.
- **Personal selling**—An interpersonal communication with one or more prospective buyers for the sake of making sales. Examples include sales calls to

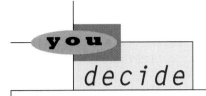

decide

Stakeholders Rein in the Microsoft Juggernaut

Microsoft has a large file in the Antitrust Division at the Department of Justice. First, the Justice Department sued Microsoft to block its $2 billion acquisition of Intuit Inc., makers of the popular Quicken software program that enables its users to pay bills, balance the checkbook, and do taxes by computer. The trustbusters at the Justice Department complained that a combined company would give Microsoft an unfair advantage in the emerging world of electronic commerce, hurting banks, credit card companies, and other financial institutions. Banks, in particular, worried that their plans to launch online financial services would suffer as a result of such a powerful union. Microsoft did not acquire Quicken, but instead developed Microsoft Money, a direct Quicken competitor.

Second, competitors of Microsoft's online and Internet access service, MSN, claimed that bundling MSN with Windows 95 violated antitrust rules. Microsoft's rivals complained to the U.S. Department of Justice that the program could create a monopoly: With a click of a mouse, all Windows 95 users could sign up for Internet access, giving Microsoft a sharp advantage over other commercial online service companies, such as America Online, CompuServe, and Prodigy.

In addition, some MSN critics charged that the initial release version of MSN either destroyed or disrupted the Internet links of rival products, such as Quarterdeck's Internet Suite. Microsoft dismissed such claims, stating that the problem was just a bug that was fixed once discovered.

To further complicate the issue,

Microsoft admitted that it "encouraged" business allies to lobby the Justice Department to keep it from filing suit against the computer software giant before the MSN launch. Their concern was that a lawsuit would delay the launch of Windows 95. The outcome of the investigation? Microsoft admitted no wrongdoing but signed a consent decree stating that it wouldn't use its dominance in the operating system market to give the company an advantage over rivals in other niches of the software market.

The next year the Justice Department started investigating Microsoft's sales activities in the market for Internet browser software. Microsoft is battling for a dominant spot in that market, which is led by Netscape Communications' Netscape Navigator. Netscape accused Microsoft of illegal practices such as using its market dominance to force personal computer users to give Microsoft's browser, Explorer, a more prominent place on new computer screens than Netscape Navigator; and discounting Windows 95 software if PC-makers gave prefer-

ence to Explorer over Netscape.

Microsoft's response to its complaining competitors? It says its products sell better because they are superior, not because of Microsoft's market dominance. Its response to Justice Department inquiries? Microsoft cooperates by disclosing information. Clearly, it would be unwise to burn bridges with regulators who can influence product development and distribution.

You Decide

1. Imagine you worked at Microsoft and had just learned of the Netscape complaint. Craft a brief memo to the Justice Department that defends your company's best interests.

2. What message, if any, do you think the company should send to its customers when an antitrust complaint is lodged with the Justice Department?

3. What different marketing messages do you think Netscape sent to its target audience when it filed an antitrust complaint against Microsoft? Are those messages helpful or harmful? Explain.

Sources: Joshua Cooper Ramo, "Winner Takes All," *Time,* September 16, 1996, 62; Steve Lohr, "Justice Department in New Inquiry into Microsoft," *New York Times,* 20 September 1996, C1, C6; "Justice Eyes Windows 95 and Way It Blocks Rivals," *Boulder Daily Camera,* 5 December 1995, 3; Stephen H. Wildstrom, "Justice Peers at Windows 95," *Business Week,* September 11, 1995, 6; Richard A. Shaffer, "Who Wins Home Banking?" *Forbes,* August 14, 1995, 163; Dan Freedman and Marcia Stepanek, "Microsoft Admits It Urged Allies to Seek Justice's Favor," *Denver Post,* 10 August 1995, C1; Kathy Rebello and Paul M. Eng, "Microsoft's On-line Timing May Be Off," *Business Week,* July 10, 1995, 101; Catherine Yang, "A Grudge Match with Microsoft?" *Business Week,* May 15, 1995, 6.

a business by a field representative (field selling), in-store assistance of a sales-clerk (retail selling), a representative calling at homes (door-to-door selling), or a sales call made via telephone (telemarketing selling).

- **Point-of-purchase or merchandise materials**—Materials that deliver marketing communication messages at the point of sale that facilitate the consumer's likelihood to purchase. These materials, such as in-store coupons, remind the consumer of the product, deliver a selling message, or inform the consumer of a special reason to buy.

- **Packaging**—Both a container for a product and a display for a marketing communication message. As a result, packaging concerns product designers and marketing communication planners. It is the last marketing message a consumer sees before making a product purchase decision and thus has an extremely critical role in the persuasion process.

- **Specialties**—Free gifts used as reminder items because they carry the brand or corporate identification.

- **Sponsorships**—A company's financial support of an event or cause in exchange for an affiliation with the organization or event sponsored. Sponsorships can create goodwill and positive associations that companies can feature through other communication tools such as advertising. Examples include sponsoring a tennis tournament, volunteering to work for Easter Seals, or donating 10 cents of every dollar in sales to the Jerry Lewis MDA Telethon.

- **Licensing**—The practice of selling the right to use a company's character or logo (product symbol) on another company's products. When your university makes it possible for a sweatshirt manufacturer to produce a sweatshirt with your school's logo on it, the university will control such use through a contract that licenses the right to use the logo to the manufacturer.

- **Customer service**—An important part of marketing communication is "aftermarketing," that is, dealing with customers after they have bought the product. Customer service programs are designed to deal with customers' ongoing needs. Other tools that attempt to make the aftermarketing experience positive are warranties and guarantees.

Unplanned messages include all the other elements associated with the company or brand that are capable of delivering implicit messages to consumers. For example, dirty delivery trucks or unsafe parking lots, unfriendly receptionists, antiquated buildings, angry employees, and busy telephones all deliver negative messages that may have more impact than all the planned marketing communication messages such as advertising or public relations. All customer service representatives and other employees may deliver unwanted or unintended messages if they have not been trained to consider the communication impact of their actions and words. Although these unplanned company messages are not always considered the reponsibility of the marketing communication team, those in charge should anticipate and eliminate messages inconsistent with the communication strategy and reinforce the consistent ones.

The marketing mix activities may be either planned or unplanned messages, depending on the circumstances. Marketing mix decisions, such as where the product is sold, how reliable the product is, and whether a fair price is being charged strongly affect the consumer's level of interest in the product. The marketing mix is in the hands of the marketing manager, so in that sense mix decisions are controlled. Marketing mix decisions are not, however, always considered from the communication viewpoint, and the marketing communication team may not be involved in planning the marketing mix. In cases where the marketing communication team does not help plan the marketing mix and consider its message effects, then that mix is considered an unplanned message. In cases where the marketing communication team does help plan the mix and its message effects, the marketing mix is viewed as a planned message.

As Figure 1.2 shows, planned and unplanned communication messages deliver all the messages consumers and other stakeholders receive. Clearly, both types of communication are crucial. Ideally, they work together and deliver a unified story. Advertising and public relations, for example, inform and persuade consumers so they enter the store equipped with brand awareness, product information, and a positive attitude. Sales promotion provides an extra incentive to buy. Then the product and store attributes—such as packaging, merchandising signs, cleanliness of the store, and the friendliness of the sales staff—take over. All work together to influence the consumer's decision to buy the product.

In the Windows 95 launch discussed in the opening vignette, Microsoft used many different marketing communication tools to send planned messages to the

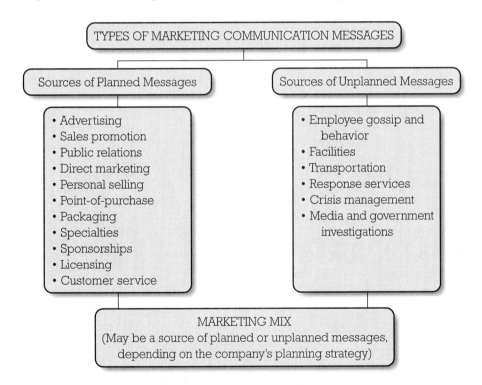

TYPES OF MARKETING COMMUNICATION MESSAGES

Sources of Planned Messages
- Advertising
- Sales promotion
- Public relations
- Direct marketing
- Personal selling
- Point-of-purchase
- Packaging
- Specialties
- Sponsorships
- Licensing
- Customer service

Sources of Unplanned Messages
- Employee gossip and behavior
- Facilities
- Transportation
- Response services
- Crisis management
- Media and government investigations

MARKETING MIX
(May be a source of planned or unplanned messages, depending on the company's planning strategy)

FIGURE 1.2

Marketing Communication Messages

target audience, including advertising, personal selling, public relations, sales promotion, direct marketing, and packaging. Table 1.1 outlines the tools Microsoft used in its Windows 95 launch, the marketing communication objectives, and the target audience for each activity. The IMC in Action feature that follows explains exactly how some of those tools were used.

TABLE 1.1

Marketing Communication Objectives, Tools, and Audiences for the Windows 95 Launch

Advertising

Objectives: Announce new product; inform prospective customers of product features; build high level of awareness

Audience: Current Microsoft Windows users; prospective users who might be more interested in an easier-to-use version of the software; trade (retail and distribution) partners

Media: Cooperative advertising jointly sponsored with suppliers and vendors in magazines; 2-hour QVC infomercial; a 30-minute prime-time television "info show"; entire press run of the *London Times* with a special Windows 95 advertising supplement; TV campaign showing how the program fits into customers' lives with documentary-style footage played to the Rolling Stones' "Start Me Up"; the Windows 95 logo and "Start button" consumer print ads tying each of the logo's four colors to reasons to upgrade, followed immediately by the "Where do you want to go today?" print campaign with different executions for different product features; rolling billboard trucks moving from computer store to computer store on the night of the launch; Windows 95 plastic bag wraps for local newspapers on August 24

Public Relations

Objectives: Lead the launch by exciting pre-launch interest; maximize coverage of the launch-day activities; intensify the news value of the launch events

Audience: Media, industry leaders, general public

Media: Cover and feature stories in most every business and computer publication and many general interest magazines; kickoff interview with Bill Gates on CNN's *Larry King Live;* joint appearance by Bill Gates and *Tonight Show* host Jay Leno at the launch party; in the Phillipines the first package of Windows 95 was given to President Fidel Ramos in a media ceremony; live Q&A session with Bill Gates in Spain taped for TV news broadcast; live online coverage of the launch on the Internet (www.windows.microsoft.com)

Consumer Sales Promotion

Objectives: Intensify interest in the Windows 95 software; stimulate trial

Audience: Users, retailers

Tools: In-store posters, banners, and other displays and signs; 10 million demo disks given away before the launch; free Microsoft Money for Windows 95 software offered via the Internet in a promo dubbed "Free Money"

Trade Sales Promotion

Objective: To drive industry acceptance of the new system

Audience: Supplier and vendor partners, distributors, and retailers

Marketing communication can create positive impressions that enhance the buyer's satisfaction and thus add to the real value of the company's product. For instance, for many consumers buying a pair of Levi's means a lot more than buying just any pair of denim jeans because Levi Strauss & Co. creates a quality image through its advertising and merchandising. But even great marketing com-

Tools: Discounts as high as 40 percent on Windows 95–related cooperative print ads; licensing fee breaks for supporting the logo; special Windows 95 pavilion in the PC Expo in New York; booths offering previews

Tie-In Promotions

Objectives: Extend the impact and broaden the reach
Audience: Users and prospective users, TV viewers, readers of industry materials
Media: Special run of Cracker Jack boxes with Windows 95–related prizes; special price deals on the products of four PC-makers that offered Windows 95 installed; 450 Windows 95–related books in bookstores; NBC and Microsoft's special section in *USA Today* promoting the network's fall lineup and Windows 95; $95 American Airlines and $90 MCI savings coupons; 10 free hours of America Online

Special Events

Objective: Drive high levels of participation
Audience: Supplier and vendor partners, consumers
Media: Invitation-only launch party and carnival in Redmond, Washington, with 120 companies as cosponsors; launch parties in 40 other cities; the Windows 95 logo painted on fields in Britain for aerial viewing; Windows 95 colors projected on Empire State Building; in Australia a four-story Windows 95 box sailed into Sydney Harbor; Microsoft took journalists in Poland down in a submarine to show them what it is like "to live in a world without windows"; in Toronto the phrase *Windows 95* was built letter-by-letter from August 14 through 24 on Canada's tallest building

Sales and Retail

Objective: Drive retail participation
Audience: Retailers and their customers
Tools: Sales kits; bags with logo; "Midnight Madness" program where retailers opened for 95 minutes to sell the first copies of the software along with free pizza, doughnuts, and coffee, and 95-cent printer paper packs and mouse pads; special promotions offered locally varied but included such things as a $19.95 Windows 95 video, a free Windows 95 Bonus Book, and $195 off any computer system

Specialties

Objective: Remind consumers of the product
Audience: Consumers, industry, supplier and vendor partners
Tools: T-shirts and polo shirts with the logo; coffee cups, keyboards, mice, and mouse pads with the Windows 95 logo

Microsoft's Tool Kit

The Microsoft Windows 95 marketing effort used almost every marketing communication tool available, ranging from ads developed in cooperation with personal computer manufacturers to specialty items to talk show interviews to special events.

Microsoft held launch events in some 40 U.S. cities. Examples included a party for 2000 at the Las Vegas Luxor Hotel to an all-day festival for 4000 at the Great America's theme park in Silicon Valley. In Chicago Microsoft created a World's Fair atmosphere at Navy Pier with pavilions, carnival games, and a special run of 5000 Cracker Jack boxes containing key chains and coupons for free PCs.

An elaborate online event was also held for computer techies. And Microsoft developed a $5 million prime time "info show" featuring Windows users from around the United States, *ER*'s Anthony Edwards, and Microsoft Chairperson

Bill Gates. The event was cosponsored by Coca-Cola, Kodak, Compaq, and CompUSA.

The complexity of the launch was underscored by the fact that it was marketed internationally in 23 countries. In Britain Microsoft painted fields with giant Windows 95 logos for aerial viewing. In Paris it threw a party for 7400 in the Palais des Congres. In Toronto it unfurled a 300-foot Windows 95 banner down the city's tallest building.

Microsoft also used specialty items and sales promotions to tout its new operating system. In the six months preceding the launch, Microsoft gave away 10 million demo disks of the program and conducted product testing with some 400,000 customers. As an example of tie-in promotions by Microsoft's partners, four major PC marketers—Compaq, IBM, Digital Equipment Corp., and Hewlett-Packard Co.—announced price cuts days

before the launch in order to be on the top of consumers' minds when the software's big day arrived. Even retailers got involved with a "Midnight Madness" program that opened retail stores at midnight on August 23 for 95 minutes to sell the first copies of Windows 95.

TV ads by the Wieden & Kennedy agency featured documentary-style footage celebrating the ways PCs fit into lives with the Rolling Stones' "Start Me Up" playing in the background. Print ads picked up on the TV subtitles with double-page photographs accompanied by the same subtitles command, "Start creating . . . Start doing . . . Start exploring." Launch consumer print ads tied each of the Windows 95 logo colors to rational reasons to upgrade. All ads concluded with the tagline, "Where do you want to go today?"—which continued as the theme for other products after the Windows 95 launch campaign was over.

Concept ✓ Review

MARKETING COMMUNICATION

A key part of any marketing program is communication.

1. Marketing communication is the process of effectively communicating product information to target audiences.
2. Planned marketing communication message sources include advertising, sales promotion, public relations, direct marketing, personal selling, point-of-purchase/merchandising, packaging, sponsorships, licensing, and aftermarketing customer service.
3. Unplanned marketing communication messages include all the other elements associated with the company or brand that are capable of delivering implicit messages to consumers.
4. The marketing mix may be either a planned or unplanned message source.

The way you top it is with a direct link to the Internet. That way, you have the best of both worlds—the 3D graphics, video, and audio of a CD-ROM, plus built-in access to timely and relevant information located on the Internet. It's called a hybrid, or connected, CD-ROM. And the wonderful thing about it is that it lets you experience

For example, say you were using Fommer's Interactive Travel Guides San Francisco 96® CD-ROM to plan a vacation. It would let you take a cable car tour, reference a map of Fisherman's Wharf, and even check out some of the nearby beach. The Internet link could then connect you to those

CD-ROMs give you a rich multimedia experience you can't get anywhere else.
So how do you top that?

true, interactive multimedia. That's because the data-intensive work, such as processing the CD-ROM's rich audio and vision, is being handled on your PC by the powerful Pentium® processor. Then through the connected CD-ROM's ability to link to the Internet, you can get additional up-to-date information from related Web sites

hotels with a Web site so you can book your actual room reservation. The connected CD-ROM is just one more example of how advanced technologies combined with powerful Intel microprocessors are adding new dimensions to your PC experience. But this is only a taste of what it's all about. To learn more about connected CD-ROMs, check out the Intel Web site

intel
The Computer Inside™

150

The Intel trademark identifies a brand that has set a standard of quality, reliability, and innovation.

lent of a Pearl Jam concert with hordes of fans stationed at the entrances to auditoriums waiting for the doors to open.

Food for Thought

1. Why do you think Microsoft used so many marketing communication tools to promote Windows 95?
2. Review the tools listed in Table 1.1. Are there any that you think were unnecessary? Are there others that might have been used? Explain your answer.

Its public relations success can be counted in the number of cover and feature stories appearing in most every national and local business publication and broadcast media. According to a Medialink Public Relations Research analysis, the Windows 95 launch received 345 U.S. television news stories—which rivaled the amount of coverage given during the same period to the war in Bosnia.

Newsweek described the launch as the computer industry's equiva-

Sources: John Markoff, "Microsoft and the Web: Making Critical Mass Pay," *New York Times,* 29 July 1996, C1, C2; Michael J. Himowitz, "Windows95: Do You Need the Most Over-hyped Product of the Decade?" *Fortune,* September 18, 1995, 191–6; Bradley Johnson, "Windows 95 Opens with Omnimedia Blast," *Advertising Age,* August 28, 1995, 6; Kathy Rebello and Mary Kuntz, "Feel the Buzz," *Business Week,* August 18, 1995, 31.

munication cannot save a bad product. In fact, the fastest way to kill a poor product is with a good communication program. Such a program will quickly expose the weakness of the product to its target audience, the people who count the most.

IMC: A BLUEPRINT FOR SUCCESS IN MARKETING COMMUNICATION

Here's a quiz: Which battery product features a pink rabbit beating a big drum? Almost half of the consumers who answer this question say Duracell. Wrong! The correct answer is Energizer. For all the money spent on the Energizer bunny campaign, many consumers have had a hard time associating the campaign with Energizer, particularly in the early years of the campaign. One of the main reasons for the difficulty is that for many years the pink bunny was strictly an advertising campaign: The bunny wasn't used in sales promotion, packaging, or in-store promotions until much later. Once it became an integrated communication strategy, then the brand association scores began to increase.

What Is IMC?

One of the most important communication trends of this decade is a shift to **integrated marketing communication (IMC),** which is the practice of unifying all marketing communication tools—from advertising to packaging—to send target audiences a consistent, persuasive message that promotes company goals. According to marketing experts Don Schultz, Stanley Tannenbaum, and Robert Lauterborn, IMC is "a new way of looking at the whole, where once we saw only parts such as advertising, public relations, sales promotion, purchasing, employee communications, and so forth." IMC realigns marketing communication "to look at it the way the consumer sees it—as a flow of information from indistinguishable sources."[2]

An example of a successful IMC strategy is the RCA campaign for its television products. By bringing back the familiar image of RCA's white and black dog, teaming it with a new puppy, and juxtaposing them against newer, more advanced products and more lively graphics, RCA was able to appeal to younger consumers yet retain the older users who still remember the original RCA image. Print and television ads, point-of-purchase materials, and packaging all sent the same message—RCA's long-term commitment to the entertainment industry guarantees quality and innovation. The message strategy worked and continues to do so because advertising, sales promotion, point of purchase, and packaging work together to send messages to various age groups.

As discussed earlier in this chapter, the marketing mix of product, price, distribution, and communication sends planned and unplanned messages to target audiences. Marketing communicators use tools to send planned messages and attempt to anticipate and control unplanned messages. In companies that do not use IMC, the marketing communication tools, such as advertising and public relations, are not used together for maximum impact. In companies that do use IMC, marketing communicators coordinate all the tools to create *synergy,* which means each tool has more impact working jointly to promote a product than it would working on its own. That is, the whole is greater than the sum of the parts.

To create synergy, marketing communicators must understand how each tool works best and how they work together. Each tool can reach audiences in different ways, some of which complement one another and reinforce each other's efforts. Furthermore, marketing communicators must understand what each activity can do best and what its strengths and weaknesses are. For example, advertising is capable of reaching a mass audience simultaneously and repeatedly. It is also good at informing customers about new products or new product features and reminding customers about positive past experiences with a product. Public relations is effective at creating highly credible messages. Sales promotion may be most effective at stimulating an immediate response, such as when a company offers an incentive to try a new product.

The important thing to remember is that all these tools have strengths and weaknesses, such that different tools can accomplish different objectives. In an integrated marketing communication program such as Microsoft's, marketing communicators plan how each tool can work with all the others to accomplish a complex set of marketing communication objectives.

Reasons for IMC

Although some critics say that IMC may be a fad, more and more businesses are using it with success. According to a study conducted on behalf of the Promotion Marketing Association of America, 60 percent of the 100 leading senior-level marketing executives surveyed rated IMC as the most important new factor in devising a marketing strategy.[3] Table 1.2 shows the survey results.

What is driving integration? With heightened global competition, technological advances, and more informed consumers, businesses demand more efficiency, stronger customer loyalty, an image that can be transmitted globally, and a more powerful impact. In the marketing context, this means that businesses want better results from the marketing communication plan and budget. IMC is a cost-effective practice because it carefully coordinates and communicates each part of the marketing mix. This is especially true for smaller, cost-conscious companies that can't afford to gamble all their marketing communication dollars on a single ad campaign.[4]

For instance, in its early days in the 1970s, Southwest Airlines used an integrated marketing communication campaign because it could not afford advertising. Playing off the name of its home base, Love Field in Texas, it promoted the airline with attendants wearing hotpants and go-go boots; flight schedules, print ads, and employees' buttons said, "How Do We Love You? Let Us Count the Ways." The airline served drinks called "Love Potions." Everything Southwest did sent the message that the company loved to serve its customers and save them money. Though the company has grown over the last 20 years, its marketing communication program is still integrated—the message of no frills, low fares, the fun of flying, and (more recently) freedom of choice—is sent through all contact points, from TV ads to flight attendant attire to the snacks served on the plane.[5]

Factor	Importance Rank (%)
Integrated marketing communications	60
Consumer lifestyle changes	55
Economic trends	45
Everyday low-pricing strategies	32
New retail formats	29
Integration of consumer and trade promotion	27
Globalization	26

TABLE 1.2

Factors Influencing Marketing Strategies

Source: NPO Group. Reprinted with permission from *Advertising Age,* March 22, 1995, 2. Copyright, Crain Communications, Inc. 1993.

Next we discuss the four main reasons for the growth of IMC: greater efficiency, stronger customer loyalty, international marketing, and added impact.

Efficiency

In the last decade new data-gathering technology, such as scanners and relational databases, have allowed businesses to attract and predict consumer buying behavior with ever-increasing accuracy. As a result, firms can segment and target their audiences more efficiently using new message-delivering technologies instead of spending huge sums on a mass-marketed advertising campaign. These technologies range from interactive media to digital TV to the Internet.

At the same time, companies are demanding greater efficiency from their marketing communication programs. Integrated marketing communication is "the most cost-effective means for achieving marketing goals because it carefully evaluates each component of the marketing mix."[6] Through strategic, careful planning and management of all messages, companies can expect more impact from the marketing communication program.

Two important events occurred in the early 1990s that reflect the intensified client concern for efficiency. The first was the formation of Pentacom, a free-standing media buying service, by the BBDO advertising agency for its client Chrysler. (A media buying service is an organization that buys media time and space for its clients' advertising.)

Though Pentacom operates as a subsidiary of BBDO, it handles all the media buying for the three other advertising agencies involved in the Chrysler account. Before Pentacom was created, each of Chrysler's advertising agencies would buy media separately. Combining all Chrysler media buys gave Pentacom stronger bargaining power. It achieved greater efficiency through lower unit costs, higher discounts because of larger volume media buys, and greater impact from the media budget.

The second development was Coca-Cola's appointment of the Creative Artists Agency (CAA), a Hollywood talent agency. Coca-Cola found it could use its advertising budget more efficiently once it partnered with CAA. Why? CAA had a stable of movie and television stars, film directors, producers, and writers. It became Coca-Cola's one-stop shopping place to find everyone it needed to create fresh, intriguing commercials.

As advertising budgets have decreased, however, firms have increased their spending on other marketing communication tools, especially in areas such as direct marketing and sales promotion.

How to Build Stronger Customer Loyalty

Businesses and marketers alike are concerned about the decline of brand loyalty due to the quantity of products available and the growth of sales promotion. Marketing analyst William Weilbacher claims that the explosion of new brands causes consumers to drown in "unfathomable and largely insignificant product differences" and that is making it more difficult, if not impossible, for advertising to create the psychological value embodied in the great brands of the past—such as Kodak, Coca-Cola and Green Giant.[7]

The indiscriminate use of sales promotion conditions even the most loyal customers to wait for special deals and reduced prices. With some products with little perceived difference in quality, customers only buy a product when it is on sale. The overuse of sales promotion makes it difficult for companies to maintain brand loyalty because price becomes more important than brand preference.

The interesting change, however, is that marketing communicators are learning to use diverse marketing communication tools, including sales promotion, to help build brand loyalty. A sophisticated brand marketing program may not use as much advertising as in the past, but it is likely to use more public relations, direct marketing, event marketing, and, yes, even sales promotion, to build loyalty.

The concerns about brand loyalty decline are justified. The advance in database technology has identified a very demanding consumer rather than a passive audience, a consumer who wants relevant content, extra incentives, and signs of company commitment to things that matter, such as health and ecology. Most of all, this new consumer wants to be in touch with companies and brands on his or her own time and has very little patience with intrusive communication forms such as advertising.

The North American consumer's skepticism is mirrored in the attitudes of some governments on other continents that so distrust advertising and other forms of marketing communication that they actively discourage their use. Some East Asian and Muslim countries tightly control the content of advertising. Germany has strict laws about selling information about consumers for use in direct marketing. Whether the distrust lies with the consumer or government, intrusive marketing communication faces an increasingly hostile audience.

New technology is opening up new opportunities for two-way communication, communication that involves a dialogue between company and customer and communication that can be initiated by the customer. These types of communication will supplement or substitute for the mass forms of communication used exclusively in the past.

To combat the decrease in brand loyalty, many firms are emphasizing **relationship marketing**—a type of marketing that builds long-standing positive relationships with customers and other important stakeholder groups. Relationship marketing identifies "high value" customers and prospects and bonds them to the brand through personal attention.[8] Most executives focus marketing communication on the needs, wants, and desires that are personally relevant to customers. The best way to manage the whole process is through a database that stores critical information about customers and their interactions with the brand or company.

As author Terry Varva explains, "Treat your customers and clients as you would have other marketers treat you."[9] Many companies think of sales transactions as isolated events rather than steps in lifelong relationships with customers. Furthermore, because many businesses haven't accounted for the lifelong value of a customer relationship, companies think that a bad experience just represents the cost of a simple sale. Varva believes that the value of organizations' relationships with their current customers and other important constituencies leads to more intensified customer loyalty. Indeed, research has found that the average dissatisfied customer tells nine to ten people about the experience; 13 percent of dissatisfied customers spread the news to more than 20 people, so the damage may be far greater than a single lost sale.[10]

Andersen Windows Showcases Relationships

In tiny Bayport, Minnesota, Danish immigrant Hans Andersen and his company have marketed windows since 1903. (Unlike Microsoft's, these are the kind you can see through.) The secret of Andersen Windows' success is based on long-term relationships with suppliers, vendors, employees, retailers, and customers. Marketing relationships, often called partnerships, can exist both *upstream* in the marketing channel (suppliers, vendors) and *downstream* (retailers and other distributors, customers). By partnering with these important stakeholders, Andersen captured 15 percent of the window market with nearly $1 billion in annual sales, surpassing its three largest competitors combined. An international marketer, Andersen serves customers in Canada, Japan, England, and the United States.

Windows aren't an impulse buy, and many consumers are unfamil-iar with such a purchase. In Andersen's case, the product line includes more than 1100 different sizes of vinyl-clad windows, patio doors, and skylights in many fashionable styles. To establish a brand identity and educate consumers, Andersen uses a variety of marketing communication devices to teach consumers about its products and help them through the buying process.

First, to find interested buyers before the purchasing process begins, Andersen uses direct response TV and print ads in home magazines like *Better House and Gardens*. These ads pull in more than 300,000 responses each year. Respondents provide their names, addresses, phone numbers, and information about their building or remodeling plans. All that information goes into a database.

Respondents are then sent the *Andersen Window & Patio Door Factbook*, a brochure full of window design ideas and a copy of *Come-Home* magazine, Andersen's in-house publication. The magazine also has a survey card that queries prospects about their needs and offers other publications such as a "Residential Product Guide," a "Window and Patio Door Installation Guide," or "Patio Door Guidebook." For a price, they can also receive "The Enlightened Remodeling Guide." These publications are also available from the local retailer that carries Andersen products. The magazine is seen as a tool to open the dialogue with potential customers and to allow them to express interest.

These contacts also encourage the potential customers to check the local Yellow Pages for their nearest dealer. Andersen then supplies retailers with the names of those who have responded to its various TV and print ads for follow-up and other information about when customers plan to begin

Many relationship marketing experts believe that it represents a major change in the philosophy of marketing and marketing communication.[11] Relationship marketing is relevant to IMC because a relationship program needs more than just mass media advertising. It needs a totally integrated communication process that manages every type of message and every aspect of a brand or company's communication and moves the communication as close as possible to one–on–one communication. As you read through this text, you will see how this process can be accomplished in a marketing communication program. The IMC in Action feature shows how Anderson Windows has relied on a relationship approach.

International Marketing

Another factor driving the need to integrate marketing communication efforts is the continued growth of international or global marketing efforts. Not only do

their projects. In addition, the Anderson home page (www.andersencorp.com) has been an important source of consumer contact with the company. Customers can order information brochures, locate the nearest Andersen dealers, and learn some basic information about Andersen products.

Recently, as Andersen has moved more into customized, made-to-order windows and doors, it found that its distributors and retailers were being overwhelmed by the number of choices it offered. Andersen solved that problem with its "Window of Knowledge," a computer-based point-of-sale kiosk that can be located in retailers' stores.

By integrating advertising, brochures, information, and the Web site, Andersen has established an integrated way of meeting, educating, and communicating with prospects throughout their buying cycle. Everything ties together.

Another factor that has a powerful effect on customer loyalty is Andersen's dedication to long-lasting relationships. After more than 90 years, Andersen still resides in its original home town where nearly 4000 employees own 27 percent of the company. Its hardware supplier dates to 1932; its screen supplier to the 1950s; and its advertising agency, Campbell-Mithun Esty, to 1933. In fact, Andersen was the ad agency's first client. Many distributors have been selling Andersen products for decades. Andersen's devotion to these long-term relationships has helped it maintain tremendous control over the quality of its products, the way products are distributed, and its marketing communication.

Food for Thought

1. Do you think focusing on relationships is always good marketing communication strategy?

Explain your answer. If you think it is, then why do you think some companies don't use it?

2. Imagine you were hired as an outside consultant to evaluate Andersen's marketing communication program. What strengths and weaknesses do you think the program has?

3. Now suppose you were an Andersen competitor. What strategies would you suggest to your company's marketing communication director to combat Andersen's success?

Sources: Justin Martin, "Are You as Good as You Think You Are?" *Fortune,* September 30, 1996, 142; "Integrated Interactive Advertising Campaign Brings Leading Manufacturers Together on Multicom's Latest Home Remodeling CD-ROM," *Business Wire,* August 13, 1996; Susan E. Peterson, "Window of Knowledge," *Minneapolis Star Tribune,* 1 May 1995, 1D; Mollie Neal, "Anderson Takes Great 'Panes' to Build Relationships," *Direct Marketing* (April 1993): 28–30, 68.

the companies have to deal with departments, divisions, and brand management responsibilities, they also have to manage across regions, countries, continents, and the globe. This scope complicates the objective of delivering a consistent image and message.

The international communication challenges focus on questions of what to standardize and what to localize. In international advertising, for example, the campaign strategy is often globalized—the company uses the same product positioning and target audience in every country—but the individual ads may be produced locally to allow for different language, setting, culture, and physical appearance.

Finding the best blend of standardization and localization is crucial for effective message communication. REI, a clothing manufacturer, works hard to standardize the quality of its products all over the globe. The company, however, uses both different clothes sizes and local clothing models in ads to promote its clothing line in countries around the world.

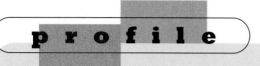

profile

Lisa Rohe
Creative Services Manager, *Variety Inc.*

Lisa Rohe is creative services manager in the marketing department for *Daily Variety* and *Variety,* the world's leading entertainment trade publications. Founded in 1905, *Variety* is the top weekly trade paper covering the entertainment and telecommunication industries worldwide. *Daily Variety* was launched in 1933 and is geared mainly toward the Hollywood entertainment market.

In her role as creative services manager, Rohe oversees the design of *Variety*'s marketing communication efforts for the publications. Among Rohe's primary responsibilities is scouting new artwork from studios, networks, and other industry sources for use in upcoming sales materials. She also works closely with the production department to coordinate the placement of promotional ads in both publications.

Rohe acts as a liaison for the paper and its clients and has worked with the offices of prolific TV producer Aaron Spelling and the late George Burns on cover art for *Variety* specials on their respective careers. She also worked with legendary film producer

Robert Evans to produce an ad for his autobiography, "The Kid Stays in the Picture," which ran in *Variety.*

Rohe attends several film and television industry events each year, such as the Academy Awards or the Cannes Film Festival. "Attending major industry events is important—it helps me understand my audiences better so that I can select the best image for the ads that we do. Plus, it's fun to attend the Emmy Awards or the Cannes Film Festival for your work." As an outgrowth of attending these events, Rohe conceptualized, pitched, and now runs creative marketing services for the daily papers *Variety* produces in France at the Cannes Film Festival. Rohe's background mix of French language study, design, and production skills are key to producing publications in a foreign country.

Academic Background

Rohe received a B.A. in French Commercial Studies with an emphasis in marketing from the University of Illinois in 1987. She also spent a year at the Sorbonne

Impact

Impact involves more than just cash savings. In message design knowing what to say at the right time to the right person can be more effective than mass broadcasting a general idea. Furthermore, the same idea repeated from a variety of different sources can intensify its memorability. For instance, Creative Artists Agency's Coca-Cola campaign targeted each of Coke's market segments differently. Even though Coca-Cola is a mass-marketed product, Coke's marketing managers recognized that many different types of people buy Coke—from teenagers to senior citizens—and you don't talk to them all with the same message, an approach often

University in Paris, where she fine-tuned her language skills.

In 1991 Rohe earned her M.A. in advertising at the University of Colorado with a minor in art history. Her fluency in French landed her an assistantship with the university's French department, and she taught French for three years while completing her degree in the School of Journalism and Mass Communication. Her master's project was a visual communication study to evaluate the cultural sensitivity of symbols and colors. This approach evolved into a systematic research methodology and an article on the research titled "The Cultural Palette," which appeared in *Journalism Educator.*

She continues her education by taking classes in Excel, Powerpoint, and Quark Express, as well as a copywriting course at UCLA. She's weighing whether to embark on an executive MBA degree while continuing to work full-time at *Variety.*

Career Track

Rohe's first job after graduate school was as graphic designer at the *Vail Daily* newspaper in Vail, Colorado. While there, she got her first taste of advertising production under the deadline pressure of a daily paper. To use her language skills, Rohe also taught French at Colorado Mountain College in Vail and then spent a summer leading bicycle tours through France. On relocating to Los Angeles, Rohe worked as a graphic designer at a cosmetics company and at an engineering firm before joining *Variety* in 1992.

Starting as a graphic designer in the advertising department, Rohe quickly moved to the marketing department as marketing and promotion coordinator, where her duties ranged from design and production of marketing communication materials to the reorganization of the computer system. In 1994 she was promoted to her current position as creative services manager.

Advice

One of Rohe's most useful experiences in graduate school was her experience as a teacher because she learned how to organize and present material. The public speaking requirements of a teacher have proven invaluable to Rohe as a marketing executive. Techniques from the classroom have been used to sell her ideas and present information in a meeting in a clear, convincing manner. She says, "Presentation is the key—both verbal and visual. No matter how much information a person may know, if it is not presented effectively and professionally, the message will not come across clearly."

Other suggestions include: Learn to negotiate. She advises taking a class at the business school if it's available because "this is the one skill that is very difficult to learn by experience, and being a good negotiator is really to your benefit."

Another suggestion is to not write off *any* job if you can learn something from it. For example, Rohe worked in a bike shop for three months and through it got the opportunity to lead luxury bicycle tours through France.

Finally, she advises learning to think long term. A slightly lower salary at a company with growth and learning potential is better than a higher-paying dead-end job.

referred to as a "same voice" or "one look" strategy. Although the varied advertisements used different styles and tone of voice, they were unified by a consistent campaign theme, "Always Coca-Cola," the logo, and the Spencerian script brand name. It was a highly successful experiment in creating diverse messages with a consistent core theme. The company claims the experiment has had tremendous impact.

IMC creates more impact than traditional marketing programs because it eliminates message conflict. The more consistent the message, the greater the impact. People who perceive various messages automatically try to integrate them into some kind of central thought or idea. If the messages are consistent and work together, as the various marketing communication vehicles did for Microsoft's products, then the integration leads to more impact than any one message by itself. If they do not work together, then the messages can lead to confusion and irritation. An effective IMC program, then, works with and not against the natural process of perception.

In many companies a lack of coordination creates a consistency problem. The public relations team, for example, may be communicating good citizenship or quality whereas other teams, such as advertising and sales promotion, may be communicating about a new product feature or price reduction. How do all these different messages add up to a coherent image or position for the company or brand?

A fragmented approach does more to destroy a corporate or brand image than it does to reinforce the image, especially when corporate and brand messages conflict. For example, a company that tells shareholders that this will be a banner year and tells employees that there will be no salary increases because of higher production costs could easily lose credibility with both audiences. Integrated marketing communication provides a mechanism for identifying such message conflict, which is important because stakeholder groups often overlap. An employee may also be a shareholder, a community leader may also be a supplier that does business with the company, and so on. This overlap makes it likely that people in an audience group may receive a message intended for another group.

IMC strives to manage or respond to all the messages sent to or by all the various stakeholders. This message management involves tremendous coordination and cooperation within the company across all divisions, not just the traditional marketing communication areas that will be discussed in Chapter 2. As more people are trained to use IMC, however, planning across the company will become easier.

The IMC Model

The model shown in Figure 1.3 depicts the IMC process presented in this text. It incorporates the marketing communication messages from Figure 1.2 and illustrates how they relate to the marketing plan. Marketing communication is determined by the overall marketing plan and its objectives. In a traditional marketing plan, four areas—marketing communication, distribution, price, and product—make up the marketing mix. In the IMC plan, however, message planners recognize that the marketing communication element of the mix is not the only one that can send a message. In fact, the other three elements also communicate messages that can be more important in consumer decision making than the planned marketing communication messages. In our IMC model we show communication as supporting the other three areas. In other words the marketing communication element ties together the other elements of the marketing mix. The second half of the model details the marketing communication plan. That plan, however, takes an IMC approach, which includes planned and unplanned marketing messages.

Figure 1.3 shows a basic model for marketing communication that identifies the critical elements of a dynamic marketing program, one that is both strategically sound and flexible enough to accommodate the demands of a changing marketplace.

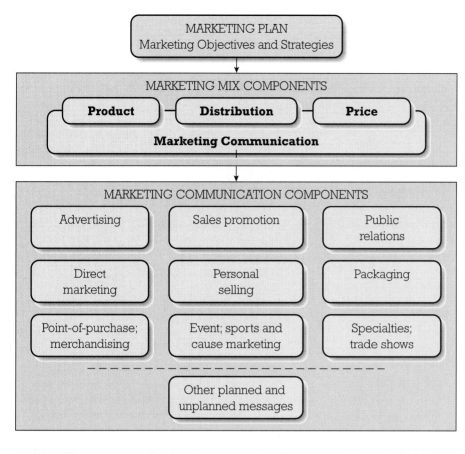

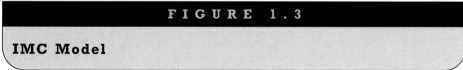

FIGURE 1.3

IMC Model

Concept

Review

IMC: A BLUEPRINT FOR SUCCESS IN MARKETING COMMUNICATION

1. The IMC goal is to create *synergy*, which means that coordinating market-ing communication tools creates more impact than the tools would have without such coordination.
2. Integration promises more efficiency, customer loyalty, and impact for the marketing communication program and helps maintain consistency in global marketing programs.

A CLOSING THOUGHT:
REVOLUTION AND EVOLUTION

Marketers know intuitively that communication coordination is a good idea, but the problem continues to be how to do it. IMC is a revolutionary concept in marketing communication in one sense because, as we see later in the text, it calls for tearing walls down between departments. In another sense it is evolutionary because IMC makes it possible to truly implement marketing objectives that lead to long-term relationships. Why? Those objectives are based on more targeted communication with consumers and other stakeholders. Regardless of how much is revolution and how much is evolution, IMC represents a major change in marketing communication that is gaining momentum both in industry as well as in education.

SUMMARY

1. Explain what marketing communication is and how it is used to promote a product.

One of the four elements of the marketing mix, marketing communication is the process of effectively communicating product information to target audiences. It uses persuasion to target audiences at all points that audiences might come in contact with the company or brand. The marketing communication plan sets objectives, analyzes unplanned messages, and uses marketing communication tools to communicate the marketing message.

2. Describe the types of messages that are used in marketing communication.

Two main types of messages communicate with the target market and stakeholder audiences: planned and unplanned. Planned messages are those that marketing communicators intend to send to target audiences via such activities (or tools) as advertising, direct mail, personal selling, sales promotion, and public relations. Unplanned messages are those that audiences infer. Unplanned marketing communication message sources include all elements associated with the company or brand that are capable of delivering implicit messages to consumers, ranging from the courtesy and knowledge of a salesperson to the condition of the company parking lot. In a traditional marketing program, the marketing mix typically sends unplanned messages. In an IMC program, the marketing mix is part of the communication plan, so it is a planned message strategy.

3. Define integrated marketing communication.

Integrated marketing communication (IMC) is the practice of unifying all marketing communication tools—from advertising to packaging—to send target audiences a consistent, persuasive message that promotes company goals.

4. Discuss the benefits of integrated marketing communication (IMC).

IMC creates synergy by coordinating all marketing communication activities to send a consistent message that target audiences will perceive and remember. This synergy is more efficient because combined, consistent messages have more impact than independent or inconsistent messages. It creates more customer loyalty by focusing on long-term relationships with customers and other stakeholders. It helps with internationalization because it helps control the consistency of messages being delivered in a variety of countries. Finally, it offers tremendous impact because it eliminates message conflict. As a result, the consistency of the message works with the natural process of perception so that audiences are more likely to remember and appreciate that message.

5. Describe how integrated marketing communication relates to marketing.

The company's marketing plan and its objectives determine the integrated marketing communication plan's strategies and objectives. The IMC plan recognizes that all marketing mix elements—product, price, distribution, and marketing communication—can communicate messages, though the marketing communication element provides the foundation for such messages.

POINTS TO PONDER

Review the Facts

1. In your own words, define marketing communication and integrated marketing communication.
2. What is relationship marketing?
3. What is a contact point?
4. What is a stakeholder?

Master the Concepts

5. How do traditional marketing communication and integrated marketing communication differ?
6. Explain the difference between planned and unplanned messages.
7. Why do you think there is a decreasing emphasis on advertising? Explain.
8. How does relationship marketing fit in an integrated marketing communication program?
9. Explain how the demand for efficiency has affected integrated marketing communication.
10. How does internationalization complicate a company's efforts to maintain strategic control over its messages?

Apply Your Knowledge

11. Explain the components of the integrated marketing communication model used in this chapter. Does this model make sense to you? How would you refine it if you were the marketing director for a medium-sized business and the CEO asked you to develop a model of your company's marketing communication?
12. Develop an analysis of all the stakeholders for your university or school. If you were the public relations director for your school, which stakeholders would you consider to be the most important? Explain.
13. Assume you were asked to plan Microsoft's product launch of Windows 2002, which includes updated versions of Microsoft's Internet products. What would you do to improve on the Windows 95 campaign? Don't forget to analyze the marketing mix elements of product, price, and distribution in your analysis.

SUGGESTED PROJECTS

1. If you were to go to work for General Motors, how would you begin to analyze all the places where coordination in message strategies are needed? How does the auto industry, and this company in particular, work in terms of all the various functions, departments, and divisions that are communicating messages?

2. Choose your favorite brand of any product, and collect or research all the different types of marketing communication for that brand that you can find. What tools does the company seem to rely on most? Do the different tools deliver consistent messages? Are there any message conflicts?

3. (Writing Project) Assume your university or school became embroiled in a high profile scandal in which two high-level administrators were charged

with diverting $500,000 earmarked for minority academic scholarships to athletic scholarships. Building on your stakeholder analysis in Points to Ponder question 12, craft a brief memo that outlines the contact points key stakeholders might have with the school and how the school could send messages from the contact points to influence stakeholders' perceptions.

4. (Internet Project) Visit the Southwest home page (www.iflyswa.com) or the Andersen Windows home page (www.andersencorp.com). Follow the links in the site and make a list of the audiences the Web site seems to target. Then assess the messages the site tries to communicate to its audiences. Are the messages effective? Consistent? Explain your conclusions in a 1- to 2-page paper.

CASE 1: TIGER IS A SUCCESS STORY FOR NIKE AND TITLEIST

Golfer Tiger Woods made marketing communication history when he arranged two sponsorship deals worth a cool $40 million before he had started touring as a professional. Sports apparel company Nike and golf equipment company Titleist agreed to pay him an estimated $40 million over three years, plus an additional $20 million after the three-year term expired.

How could a 21-year-old command such startling fees? His athletic skill is extraordinary, but his appeal—according to many—exceeds his mastery of golf. Phil Knight, chairperson of Nike, summed up Tiger's potential. "He is one of a handful of special athletes who transcend their sports, the way [Michael] Jordan has done in basketball and McEnroe did in tennis." Sports agent Leigh Steinberg claimed that Tiger ". . . could have the most profound impact both inside and outside of sports of any athlete since Muhammed Ali."

Why the fuss? In large part it's due to his superb talent. Tiger is the first person of color to ever win the Masters, golf's premier tournament. He is also the youngest person to win the Masters—and he won it with a record-breaking score of 72. But Tiger is not only youthful and talented. The story of his upbringing is unusual for a golfing hero. Golf is traditionally the bastion of wealthy, white males. Tiger came from a middle-class family and has mixed racial heritage. (According to his mother he has Thai, African, American Indian, and European blood.) His relationship with his parents seems imbued with mutual respect, loyalty, and support. In sum, his story represents a hero's tale of breaking through formidable barriers—in his case, the caste system of the country-club golfing greens.

How have Nike and Titleist benefited from this golfing hero? First, Tiger has generated tremendous exposure for his sponsors by wearing Nike apparel and using Titleist golf balls and equipment. For instance, at the Masters, Tiger wore a shirt and hat that prominently displayed the Nike "swoosh," the company's logo. Nike staffers determined that the corporate logo was on the air for more than sixteen minutes during the final round of the Masters—the equivalent of $1,685,000 of purchased air time.

Second, Tiger has generated unprecedented amounts of publicity. In October 1996 he was named Person of the Week on ABC's *World News Tonight.* *Sports Illustrated* named him "Sportsman of the Year" for 1996. He has also appeared on the cover of general-interest and business magazines such as *Newsweek* and *Fortune.* The magazine stories all discussed his background, his athletic achievements, and his future star potential. In addition, most magazine stories had photos of Woods using Titleist equipment, wearing Nike apparel, or both.

Third, Titleist and Nike launched ads that focused more on Tiger's image and appeal than on their products. Titleist print ads claimed the company was proud to have Tiger as "our newest ambassador." Nike print ads showed a collage of children of all races, each claiming "I am Tiger Woods." Nike TV ads ended with the statement, "There are still golf courses in the United States that I cannot play because of the color of my skin. I'm told I'm not ready for you. Are you ready for me?"

Fourth, both Nike and Titleist Web sites have links to information about Tiger Woods, including press releases, statistics, photos, and links to related sites. At the Titleist Web site, for example, viewers can find out why Acushnet Company (parent to Titleist and Cobra) signed a sponsorship deal with Tiger. ". . . Tiger Woods, both as a golfer and a person, represents the promises of quality, excellence and leadership. These are common characteristics shared with our brands. . . . [He] is a man of the next millennium."

Fifth, Tiger has created the Tiger Woods Foundation, a nonprofit agency designed to attract urban children to golf and to support other organizations that aid these children, such as child-abuse prevention clinics. Though Woods is the primary donor, both Nike and Titleist plan to help market and support his organization and its special events.

The message from all these activities is that a modern-day hero is in the making who will help others follow in his footsteps. Nike and Titleist want to associate their products with Tiger's qualities and prominence. Few doubt that Nike and Titleist got a great bargain when they invested millions in sponsoring Tiger.

Case Questions

1. What other marketing communication tools could Nike or Titleist use to send its message? Would these tools be effective?

2. In the chapter, we discussed coordinating marketing messages so that they do not work at cross purposes. What steps should Nike take to create a uniform message strategy? Titleist?

3. Assume you have taken over the role of Tiger's agent. Lucrative offers for endorsements have been pouring in from many companies. Make some general recommendations about the types of products, services, and worthy causes that Tiger might consider endorsing and those he should avoid. Pay close attention to activities that would send messages that might hurt his public image.

Sources: Roy S. Johnson, "Tiger! The Sky's the Limit for Gold—the Game and Business," *Fortune,* 12 May 1997, 72–84; Bruce Horovitz, "Tiger Takes Place Among Ad Masters," *USA Today,* 15 April 1997, 1B; "Acushnet Announces Tiger Woods Signing," *Titleist Press Release,* 10 October 1996, Internet (www.cobra.com); John McCormick and Sharon Begley, "How to Raise a Tiger," *Newsweek,* 9 December 1996, 52–59; Jeff Jensen, "Woods Hits Golf Jackpot," *Advertising Age,* 2 September 1996, 6. Karen Alan, "Advertising Blitz to Introduce Woods to World at Large," *USA Today,* 29 August 1996, 11C.

ROMA'S LITE INTEGRATED CASE QUESTIONS

(Review Roma's Lite Marketing Plan in the Appendix at the end of the text before answering these questions.)

1. Does your review of the marketing plan suggest that relationship marketing is important in the launch of Roma's Lite Pizza? Identify all the different stakeholders who should be considered in this launch. Explain their importance and then rank them in order of their critical impact on the success of this new product.

2. List all the ways customers and other stakeholders might come in contact with Roma's Lite Pizza or the New Roman Food Company. Prioritize the list in terms of those contact points that are most important to this new product launch.

3. (Team Project) You are on the marketing communication team for the launch of the new Roma's Lite Pizza line. How many different areas of marketing communication might be involved in this launch? Explain what each one could do to contribute to the successful launch of this new pizza.

chapter

2

The Marketing Mix and IMC

CHAPTER OBJECTIVES

After completing your work on this chapter, you should be able to:

1 **Explain the marketing concept and outline how the business plan, marketing plan, and marketing communication strategy interrelate.**

2 **Identify the product mix elements and explain how they affect the marketing communication program.**

3 **Describe the distribution mix elements and explain how they influence marketing communication.**

4 **List the price mix elements and analyze how they affect marketing communication strategies.**

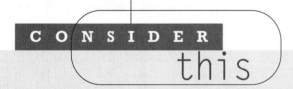

CONSIDER this

Hanna Andersson—A Quality Mix and a Mission Drive the Message

Hanna Andersson is an upscale mail-order company in Portland, Oregon, that specializes in high-quality, 100-percent cotton children's clothing. Established in 1984 by Tom and Gun Denhart at their kitchen table, this company reported about $50 million in sales in the mid-1990s. This growth record can be attributed to the company's dedication to its mission statement, a well-planned marketing mix, innovative direct marketing, a socially responsible promotion program, and the tremendous loyalty of its stakeholders—customers, employees, and the community.

Hanna Andersson limits waste, is sensitive to the needs of the less fortunate, wants its employees to find meaning in their work, and recycles used clothing to the needy through an innovative program called "Hanna-

downs." The company, named after Gun Denhart's grandmother, is built on Swedish values and American business ingenuity.

The Denharts' philosophy permeates the corporation's day-to-day activities and is embodied in this mission statement:

- To supply high-quality children's clothing at the best possible price and to provide superior, informed customer service
- To maximize benefits not only for ourselves and our families, but the customer who makes it all possible, and the community at large which supports us

These words are the reason why it has become one of the most reputable children's clothing lines in the United States. Reputation is the key word here—not image. The firm is known largely through its good deeds and quality reputation rather than advertising. Its advertising is handled

29

exclusively through direct-mail catalogs, its products are distributed through mail order, and the campaign is promoted through its home page on the World Wide Web (www.hannaandersson.com). In an attempt to deal with problems caused by increased mail-order competition, it opened a flagship store in White Plains, New York, and is making a major effort to market in Japan.

Message consistency in an integrated marketing communication program requires that all messages sent by an organization work synergistically to create a coherent image or, in this case, a reputation platform. The company's most important message is sent by the quality, design, and construction of the clothing itself. Hanna has control over this message by ensuring that its fabrics are softer and its clothes' durability outlasts competitors. Simply put, its products deliver its corporate promise.

Although its pricing may be perceived by some as higher than competitors—particularly the low-end children's market—the value is greater because of the durability. Knees don't wear out and seams don't rip under normal usage. In this way, the company uses its product to gain consumer trust and a reputable image by living up to their expectations of "high-quality children's clothing at the best possible price."

Another important product message is delivered through the Hannadowns program. Through this program, customers who return clothing in good condition receive a credit, valued at 20 percent of the original retail, to use on their next purchase. The Hannadowns program then recycles the clothing by donating it to charities. The company has issued more than $1 million in credit to its customers under this program and distributed more than 240,000 items of quality used clothing. This operation reflects the company's mission statement by emphasizing the idea of a more socially engaging moral vision, and it epitomizes the philosophy of maximizing the benefits for "the community at large which supports us." The program not only underscores the message of durability, it also strengthens consumers' relationship to the firm because they can participate in a socially responsible activity, benefit from that activity, and help the company fulfill its mission.

Service messages are also an important part of the Hanna Andersson story. With direct mail, a company only has two opportunities to make an impression on the consumer: 1) through its catalog and 2) through personal contact with consumers on the phone. If either message is an unfavorable experience, then the direct marketer will likely lose a customer. Hanna's mission statement stresses the importance of "superior, informed customer service."

Customer service representatives are instructed to do everything possible to answer customers' questions when they call. To help with this, the phone room is decorated with every article of clothing from the most recent catalog. If a question arises that a phone representative cannot immediately answer from the information in the computer, she or he can examine the article itself and log in any discrepancies between the article, the customer's questions, and the catalog description. This keeps the customer service representative up to date at all times.

Sources: Paul Miller, "Big Shakeup at Hanna Andersson," *Catalogue Age Weekly* (January 11, 1996): Internet (mediacentral.com/Magazine/CatalogueAge/Weekly); "About Hanna Andersson," Hanna Andersson home page (November 11, 1996): Internet (www.hannaandersson.com); "Best Oregon Businesses: Employee Benefits," (January 1996): Internet (www.oregonbusiness.com/Channe104/companies/best019); Heather Burandt, "Hanna Andersson: A Case Study of Integrated Marketing Communications in Practice," unpublished report, University of Colorado, 1994; James Hill, "Portland Clothing-makers Join Kids' Drawstring Ban," *Oregonian*, 8 July 1994, C1; Julie Gallego, "Mail-order Firms Hope Consumers Buy into Social, Political, Environmental Causes," *Chicago Tribune*, 30 August 1993, 5.

CHAPTER OVERVIEW

Many firms, driven by a need to better communicate with their customers and other stakeholders, recognize that marketing "is not a specialized activity at all. It encompasses the entire business. It is the whole business seen from the customer's point of view."[1]

Every aspect of the marketing mix—the product, channels of distribution, price, and marketing communication—affects customers' response to a product. And as we discussed in Chapter 1, the product, price, and distribution affect the marketing communication program. In this chapter we review how the marketing communication program fits into the firm's corporate strategy and its overall marketing strategy. Then we explore how the product type, product life cycle, and product mix affect marketing communication. We also consider the distribution of products, both goods and services, and see how different distribution channels influence marketing communication. Finally, we examine how pricing strategies affect marketing communication.

THE MARKETING CONCEPT

The American Marketing Association defines **marketing** as "the process of planning and executing the conception, pricing, promotion, and distribution of ideas, goods, and services to create exchanges that satisfy individual (customer) and organizational objectives."[2] The *marketing concept* is a business philosophy that defines marketing as a process intended to find, satisfy, and retain customers while the business makes a profit. Central to both of these definitions is the role of the customer and the customer's relationship to the product, whether that product is a good, service, or idea.

The success of a marketing effort, however, depends on whether a firm can convince consumers that the product has a competitive advantage. Consumers believe a product has a **competitive advantage** when they believe the product satisfies their needs better than a competitor's product. A human **need** is a state or feeling of deprivation, such as hunger, the need for affection, knowledge, or self-expression. These needs can be rational or irrational. Harley-Davidson sells a great many motorcycles in Japan because the product's rough-and-tumble image and its power satisfy an emotional rather than a rational need.

When you shop for a particular style of shirt and you find one that you like, you typically purchase it for a sum of money. In marketing, this act of obtaining a desired object from someone by offering something of value in return is called the **exchange.** Moving consumers to make such an exchange requires a great deal of marketing know-how and effort.

The Business and Marketing Plans

Businesses exist to accomplish goals. These goals, known collectively as the company's "mission," define why the company exists. They embody the organization's core beliefs and values. Take a close look at the Hanna Andersson mission statement in the opening vignette, for instance, and you will see that it states that company's core values.

Once a business has established its goals, it then creates a **business plan**—a long-range plan that outlines the objectives and specific actions the organization will take to reach its goals. The business plan objectives are usually measurable. Hanna Andersson might, for example, state that it plans to increase its market share in the toddler clothing market segment by 5 percent over the next two years. To be effective, the business plan should be consistent with the company's goals.

After the business plan has been developed, those in charge of marketing create a marketing plan. Recall from Chapter 1 that the marketing plan analyzes the marketing situation, identifies a target market, states clear and measurable objec-

This UPS ad touts transportation speed as a competitive advantage that its business audience is likely to appreciate.

tives, develops strategies to achieve those objectives, and specifies the activities (through the marketing mix) to implement these strategies. The marketing plan should be compatible with both the company mission and its business plan. The marketing communication plan, in turn, must be compatible with the marketing plan. Figure 2.1 outlines the entire planning process.

The problem is that the compatibility between the corporate mission, business objectives, marketing objectives, and marketing communication objectives can sometimes break down at the implementation stage if not carefully managed. For example, Volvo AB had a long historical commitment to honesty and consumer concern as part of its mission and its business and marketing plans. Unfortunately, a few years ago Volvo's ad agency was caught rigging a product demonstration where a monster truck drove over several automobiles and only the Volvo 240 survived. Evidence showed that producers at the commercial shooting had cut the roof supports of the other cars and reinforced the Volvo 240. All the parties associated with the commercial denied blame, but in the end Volvo fired its ad agency

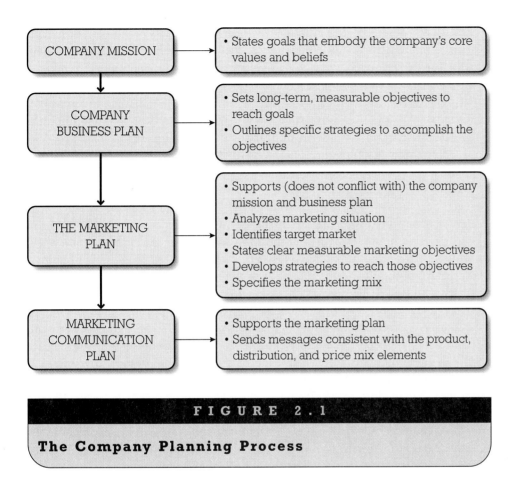

FIGURE 2.1

The Company Planning Process

of 24 years, Scali, McCabe, Slones; and Volvo's reputation may never recover completely. The business and marketing plans were not implemented correctly in the advertising.

Similarly, a blow-up at Texaco Inc. over discriminatory hiring practices reflected the conflict between the company's mission and its employment practices. The charges were widely reported in the media and affected Texaco's relationships with a variety of stakeholders such as its dealers (boycotts), investors (decreased share prices), and employees (lawsuits).[3] An unplanned message, it had much more negative impact on the company's business than any amount of advertising or public relations could counter.

The Marketing Mix

Generally, a company's marketing mix includes product, distribution, price, and marketing communication (the mix was originally referred to as the 4Ps of product, place, price, promotion). Marketers use the marketing mix as the means to reach marketing goals. Each mix element has many dimensions. In fact, each element has its own mix of strategic decisions—the product mix, distribution mix, and so on.

For instance, we introduced many marketing communication activities (also called marketing communication tools) in Chapter 1, such as direct marketing and sponsorships. Those activities combine to form a marketing communication mix. Likewise, components of the product—product design, features, packaging, maintenance, and warranty—create the product mix. The distribution mix involves where, when, and with whom a company places a product to make it accessible to customers. The price mix establishes the terms of the marketing exchange, which might include the dollar price on the package, a trade-in, a discount, or a rebate. In this chapter we discuss the product, distribution, and price mixes and explain how their planning and management communicate messages that impact the company's marketing communication program.

IMC recognizes that every element in the marketing mix delivers a marketing message. For the best chance of success, all these messages should be integrated so they are consistent, because every facet of the marketing mix communicates. The question is how to manage all the mix decisions so the marketing messages are unified.

Not only are the various components of the marketing mix integrated, they are also message carriers. The design of the product says something about its quality, the price carries a message that establishes the product's value, and the store where the product is displayed says something about convenience and status. Because the marketing mix elements communicate, however, firms must be careful that the mix doesn't conflict with the overall company or brand communication strategies.

Some marketing experts claim that the idea of IMC cannot be separated from the way a firm defines its business and the customers it elects to serve. Ideally, what requires coordination, then, is not just marketing communication, but the entire communication of a business.[4] A business must grasp the interrelationship among marketing communication programs and the other three components of the marketing mix.

Concept Review

THE MARKETING CONCEPT

Three basic concepts help us understand why marketing communication should be integrated with the other marketing mix elements.

1. Marketing focuses on customer wants and needs. Communication helps customers see how a product will best serve their needs.
2. The marketing plan must be compatible with the company's mission and business plan. In turn, the marketing communication strategies must support, not conflict with, the marketing plan.
3. The marketing mix involves strategic decisions about the product, its pricing, distribution, and its marketing communication. Because all marketing mix elements communicate, marketers should be sure all mix elements deliver a consistent message.

THE PRODUCT MIX

A good product is at the heart of marketing. (Remember, we use the word *product* in its broadest sense to refer to goods, services, and ideas.) The term *product* refers to the bundle of attributes and features—both tangible and intangible—

A Do-It-Yourself Mix-Up

The design of the product sends a message about quality, the price carries a message about the product's value, and the store where the product is displayed can signal convenience, accessibility, and quality. Because the marketing mix elements communicate, firms must be careful that the mix doesn't conflict with the overall company, product, or brand communication strategies.

A company that learned how important it is to coordinate marketing communication with its overall communication strategies is Black & Decker, a leader in the do-it-yourself tool market since the 1960s. In the early 1990s the Towson, Maryland, company began suffering erosion in its professional tool line, caused by fierce competition from Makita, a Japanese manufacturer, and cannibalization from its own consumer brand. As one Black & Decker employee explains, "It's tough selling a $130 cordless drill to professionals when the same brand name appears on a $30 drill to do-it-yourselfers."

Black & Decker marketed its professional products under the DeWalt brand name, not the Black & Decker brand name. The company had assumed that professionals would not connect Black & Decker products targeted at do-it-yourselfers to its DeWalt products. Instead, professionals saw the ads and products for do-it-yourselfers and found them confusing.

Black & Decker made the decision to relaunch the DeWalt line to professionals in a manner easily distinguishable (beyond just price) from the consumer product line. Products were reassessed, distribution was limited to retail outlets where professionals shop (not Kmart), and a separate pricing strategy was devised in line with its major competitors. Finally, Black & Decker communicated key information about DeWalt products, price, and distribution in print ads in professional magazines, demonstration videos, and through a toll-free number that currently logs over 2000 calls a week. Recognizing how the marketing mix elements of the DeWalt line were undercut by the consumer product line marketing mix helped Black & Decker increase its sales.

Food For Thought

1. Many big companies are marketing brands that sound homespun and disguise the name of its parent company. RJR Nabisco, for instance, promotes cigarette brands under the name Moonlight Tobacco Co. Given the Black & Decker experience with its DeWalt line, do you think this is a good idea? Explain your answer.

2. Gillette creates and markets both Waterman and Parker pens. Do you think that these brands are easily distinguishable? What marketing mix strategies do you think Gillette uses effectively or ineffectively to distinguish the two brands?

Sources: Norton Foley, "Back from the Dead," *Sales & Marketing Management* (July 1995): 30–1; David W. Stewart, "The Market-Back Approach to the Design of Integrated Communications Programs: A Change in Paradigm and a Focus on Determinants of Success," American Academy of Advertising Special Conference on Integrated Marketing Communication, Norfolk, Va., March 1995.

offered by a firm. It includes the elements supporting the physical product (for example, package, warranty, colors) as well as its emotional components (for example, brand loyalty, status, self-esteem, security, convenience).

To effectively manage the message the product sends, marketing communication managers must become passionately involved with a product as shown in the following ad. Their involvement should start early and continue throughout the process of product design and delivery. These managers must assess how the types of products they market affect their marketing communication strategies. They must then examine the product's life cycle and plan the strategic components of the product mix.

Products are the heart and soul of marketing. How does this Ginsana ad convey passion for the product?

Product Classifications

Many different types of products exist. To plan a successful marketing communication program, marketers must know what type of product they will be marketing because the classification often dictates very different communication strategies. There are two main product classifications: the nature of the product (goods, services, or ideas) and the market to which the product is sold and used (consumer or industrial products).

Goods, Services, and Ideas

Products may be classified as a good, service, or idea. **Goods** are tangible products such as toothpaste, cookies, cars, and bicycles. **Services** are intangibles and are represented by activities of people. Service product examples include insurance, barber shops, health care, banks, entertainment, and education. Both goods and services are intended to satisfy the needs of customers. *Ideas* can be marketed—such as donating to a good cause, participating in recycling programs, or voting for a particular candidate—and are "sold" through persuasive communication. The objective of marketing ideas is to shape or change opinions.

Goods and services, however, are the focus of most marketing programs. An overlap often occurs between goods and services. Goods are frequently supported by services and vice versa. In automotive marketing, the service, repair, or financing departments are integral parts of the product. Conversely, in a service industry such as restaurants, tangible products (hamburgers, pizzas, and tacos) are served. To classify whether the product is a good or service, look at its dominant characteristics (Wendy's may provide hamburgers, which are tangible, but its primary role is to serve ready-to-eat food quickly, as shown by its drive-in window, its standardized menu, and its staff. Its dominant characteristics show that it is a service.) Service products are commonly distinguished from goods products by the four characteristics that are listed in Table 2.1.

Of particular relevance to the marketing communication effort is the notion

TABLE 2.1

Product Characteristics that Distinguish Services from Goods

Characteristic	Description
1. Intangibility	Service products cannot be tasted, felt, seen, heard, or smelled. Thus the communication program, especially personal selling and advertising, must describe the benefits derived from the service. Mass advertising can stimulate demand through the use of testimonials and other techniques that show service products' appealing benefits. For example, a hotel chain might highlight symbolic representations of the product such as an easy check-in process or the spectacular view from the room.
2. Inseparability	For many services, the product cannot be created or delivered without the customer's presence. Examples include haircuts and medical care. As a consequence, the marketing communication must convince the consumer that the feeling gained from the service is worth buying it. For example, a sporting event such as a college football game is promoted by focusing on the excitement of the event and the enthusiasm of the spectators.
3. Heterogeneity	For many services, it is virtually impossible to standardize the service product, nor is it easy to predict the quality of the service delivered as it can vary from one time to another and from one service provider to another. That's why training is so important in service industries. McDonald's has trained its staff to comply with standards so that customers have the same experience no matter which McDonald's they visit. Similarly, Holiday Inns advertises that there are "no surprises" when you stay at its motels.
4. Perishability	Service products, such as seats on a scheduled airline flight, cannot be stored, and the demand level is difficult to forecast. Marketing communication, therefore, attempts to encourage consumers to use it in a more predictable pattern. Airlines accomplish this through sales promotion techniques, such as frequent flyer programs and lower prices if customers are willing to fly at certain times of the day, days of the week, or certain times of the year.

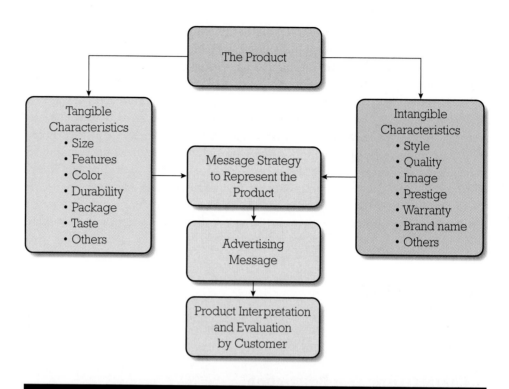

FIGURE 2.2

Tangible and Intangible Product Characteristics

of tangibility. Every product has both tangible and intangible characteristics. A John Deere tractor has obvious tangible features, but it also has intangible elements, such as the warranty, ease of maintenance, available financing, and brand reputation. A goods product tends to have *more* tangible elements than intangible. This does not mean, however, that the consumer values these tangible elements over the intangible. For example, in the United States some car buyers perceive automobiles made in Germany as offering superior quality and cars made in Japan as offering better gas mileage, less costly service, and higher levels of durability than cars made in the United States. Thus, the intangible, symbolic attributes of these foreign-made automobiles may be more important than tangible ones such as four wheels, seats, brakes, and a steering wheel. Figure 2.2 illustrates the interplay between these tangible and intangible product characteristics.

The goods or services classification provides specific implications for the message strategy. In general, the challenge is to make dull tangible features exciting and to make vague, hard-to-visualize intangible features clear and concrete. Consider the packaged cookie. An intangible feature that would need to be made more concrete could be a reputable brand name, such as Pepperidge Farm, that guarantees consistent quality. A marketing message might say, "Every Pepperidge Farm cookie contains ingredients you would have picked yourself if you had the time." The tangible features include the sugar, flour, chocolate, and baking powder used to make the cookie. However, these ingredients are too far removed from the real benefits that interest the consumer—such as "tastes like homemade" or "rich double-chocolate flavor." Because taste and quality are the benefits the consumer wants to learn about, the marketer needs to focus on this information.

The goods or services classification has other marketing message implications. For instance, many service firms depend heavily on personal selling because of the difficulty the customer often has understanding service products. The travel, banking, entertainment, and educational industries all employ many individuals who act as salespersons, explaining the intangible benefits of the service product, answering questions, and prompting action.

In the case of goods products, such as television sets or clothing, the consumer has access to product specifications and can test or try on the product. The salesperson, then, may simply take the order and ring up the sale.

Marketers of service products often rely heavily on public relations. Because service products cannot be readily experienced, consumers tend to trust word of mouth and expert opinions to gauge quality. Restaurants, concert promoters, and Hollywood all rely on critics to give positive reviews. Similarly, banks and utility companies offer free seminars to existing and prospective customers. All of these efforts try to create a positive image for an intangible product.

Consumer and Industrial Products

Products may also be classified according to who uses them. Products purchased for personal or family consumption with no intention of resale are **consumer products.** Products purchased by an organization or an individual that will be used to make another product, distributed to an industrial customer for a profit, or to meet some other business objective are called **industrial** or **business-to-business products.**

Goods such as raw materials used in construction and the services of professionals who use these supplies to make or do something, such as building a home or cleaning an office, are industrial products. When a company or an entire industry expresses a viewpoint about something that affects the way it does business, such as the cigarette industry promoting commercial free speech or self-regulation, it is participating in industry idea marketing.

The distinction between consumer and industrial products has marketing communication implications, as shown in Table 2.2. Because the decision to buy industrial products is usually made by professional purchasing agents or committees that

Marketing Communication Emphasis	Consumer Products	Industrial Products
Advertising	✓✓✓	✓✓
Sales promotion	✓✓✓	✓✓✓
Public relations	✓✓	✓
Personal selling	✓	✓✓✓✓

TABLE 2.2

Marketing Communication Emphasis: Consumer versus Industrial Products

place great importance on cost, marketers assume the decision is based mainly on factual information rather than emotional appeals. Thus, the marketing communication effort for industrial products often includes, in order of emphasis: 1) personal selling, 2) sales promotion, especially if presented by salespeople, and 3) trade advertising that uses print media filled with product information and a toll-free telephone number or Internet address that allows customers to request additional information.

Generally, marketing communication aimed at consumers uses a more emotional appeal. Often the focus is on mass selling through television and print advertising, sales promotion at the point of purchase, and public relations to provide credibility and remind the consumer about the product's positive image. Personal selling becomes relevant when the consumer product is expensive or technically complex and needs demonstration and explanation. The industrial product ad from SAS highlights a trait of business product advertising.

Product Life Cycle

The concept of the product life cycle (PLC), introduced by Harvard Professor Theodore Levitt, is based on a metaphor that treats products as people and assumes

This SAS ad promotes computer software. The ad is targeted to a business market and provides detailed information to help sell the product.

products move through predictable stages in their lifetimes.[5] From birth to death, products exist in different stages and different competitive environments. The product life cycle is typically divided into four stages: introduction, growth, maturity, and decline. The length of each stage and the entire life cycle vary among products. Furthermore, not all products go through the four stages. Marketing communication for a product depends in part on the stage of the product life cycle because a different communication mix is often needed.

Introductory Stage

In most cases new product stories are built on new ideas, new product features, or a new formulation—some innovation that is worthwhile for the customer. The marketing communication program stimulates *primary* rather than *secondary* demand, particularly if it has no competition. That is, it emphasizes the type of product rather than the brand. The problem with new product launches is that often the bugs aren't worked out and the company must be prepared to handle customer complaints. This was certainly the case with the Windows 95 launch discussed in Chapter 1.

A company often launches a new product with a high price to recover as much cost per unit as possible, and therefore it must support the high price with extensive marketing communication. It may take an enormous amount of mass advertising and personal selling to convince the market of the product's merits at the premium price level. A high level of sales promotion serves to accelerate the rate of market penetration because sales promotion is particularly good at stimulating trial. For example, when Gillette introduced its Sensor shaving system, it spent a spectacular $175 million on an integrated marketing communication campaign that included mass media advertising, couponing, point-of-sale displays, product sampling, and public relations that stressed the new technology of the razor. The product grabbed more than 3 percent of the market within three months of introduction—making it one of the most successful new product launches in history.

Growth Stage

By the time the good or service has reached the beginning of the growth stage, its market acceptance has been assured. Previous purchasers continue their purchasing, and new buyers enter in even larger numbers as word gets out. The success of a new product attracts competition. However, these firms require time to introduce their own versions of the product, so there is a short time during which the new product owns the market and can establish its dominance. As technology makes new product innovation easier and easier, the window of time decreases. To stay ahead of the pack, firms may add new product features and refinement to their products quickly to address the needs of the market.

During the growth stage, companies maintain their marketing communication expenditures at the same or slightly higher level to meet competition and to continue educating the market. The aim of advertising shifts from building product awareness to creating brand loyalty and securing repeat purchases. Finally, as more competitors enter the market, the role of personal selling changes. Now the salesperson must deal with distributors more aggressively. Shelf space is at a premium, and a variety of trade deals is common. As the ultimate consumer is inundated with choices, sales promotion tools such as discounts, coupons, and rebates may become more important in the consumer decision process. The across-the-board price reductions of several cereal manufacturers in 1996 and 1997 are indicative of this type of response.

Maturity Stage

In the maturity stage of the PLC, sales increases may continue although the rate of the increase is slowing down and profits may start to decline. Competitive effort is spent on generating small changes in market share. Marginal producers drop out of the market as price competition becomes increasingly severe. Coca-Cola and Pepsi products are in this stage in most countries. The products are still selling well, but both companies must fight harder to retain market share. Keep in mind, increasing market share by one percentage point for Coke in the U.S. market is equivalent to almost $1 billion. (Coke and Pepsi are both entering new markets as they continue to expand globally. In those markets, they find themselves back in the new product stage.) It is also during this stage that manufacturers fight constantly to retain distributors and shelf space, and even more of the budget is allocated to trade deals and consumer sales promotion. This shift to satisfying the retailer rather than the consumer occurs because the consumer has either become brand loyal, in which case promotional efforts are unnecessary, or views the various brands as interchangeable and is therefore affected by how the retailer promotes the brand at the point of purchase.

Over time it becomes more difficult to identify important product features that can be effectively featured in marketing communication. Essentially, all the competitors have the necessary technology to match one another, thereby creating commodity products that are substitutable in the mind of the consumer. The only point of difference, then, becomes the imagery communicated by marketing communication. This imagery may help broaden the brand's position. Miller Beer, for example, was introduced as "the champagne of bottled beer" but was later promoted with a more macho image to build market share in a male-dominated market.

Decline Stage

A product enters the decline stage when it faces severe competition or the market changes as consumer demand decreases, such as the market for eight-track tapes or record albums. This stage highlights why firms should continue to develop new products. It is better to lose sales of an older product to one's own new product than lose sales to competitors. As the market declines, the marketing communication budget and selling efforts decrease. The decline stage does not affect all products. Some long-time products, such as Ivory soap and Campbell's soup, for example, have never entered the decline stage.

One of the most common reasons for decline is a market change. An example is the Cray computer, a huge computer system prized by large users such as weapons engineers, rocket scientists, and government purchasing agencies.[6] In the 1980s and 1990s, the end of the Cold War, combined with the arrival of cheap and powerful microprocessor chips that transformed the computing world, dramatically decreased demand for big systems like Cray. The Cray supercomputers became obsolete, and Cray was not able to keep pace with these market changes.

Sometimes marketers are able to resuscitate a dying product with a take-off strategy. They may redesign the product, improve features, quality, or value; or they may appeal to new markets. Harley-Davidson did all three when Harley management, determined to stay in business in the face of fierce competition from Japan, redesigned its product line, produced advertising that emphasized a "made in America" appeal, and used public relations to place supportive stories in *Fortune* and *Business Week* and on *60 Minutes*. Market share doubled in the first year after the campaign. Anderson Consulting (formerly known as Anderson Accounting) also realized that its survival required that it expand its consulting expertise. Several hundred new employees were hired, especially individuals with computer and strategic planning skills. Today its future looks very bright.

In summary, the product life cycle is a very useful planning tool for marketing communication. Although it tends to be product-specific, Figure 2.3 shows the general communication strategies that should be emphasized as we move from introduction to decline.

MARKETING COMMUNICATION

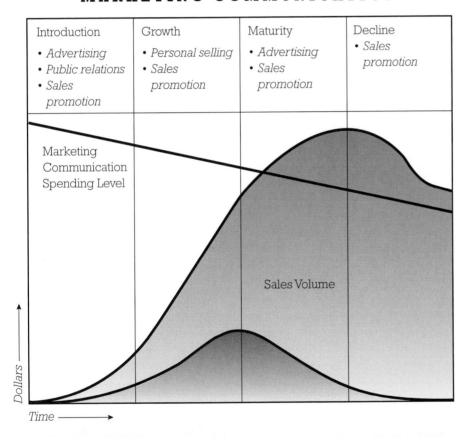

Introduction	Growth	Maturity	Decline
• *Advertising*	• *Personal selling*	• *Advertising*	• *Sales promotion*
• *Public relations*	• *Sales promotion*	• *Sales promotion*	
• *Sales promotion*			

Marketing Communication Spending Level

Sales Volume

Dollars ———▶

Time ———▶

FIGURE 2.3

Marketing Communication Emphasis over a Product's Life Cycle

Strategies for Product Mix Communication

For every product, regardless of where it is in its life cycle, marketers must make certain strategic decisions. The key product mix decision-making areas include research and design, product features, packaging, branding, and support services. In many organizations, these decisions are made by the product manager who uses extensive research to carefully assess the relative importance of these product-related elements in the minds of the customer or potential customer. For computer customers, the key elements are features and compatibility. For Boston's Children's Hospital, it is reputation and availability of skilled physicians. For Armani, the brand name may take precedence over features.

Product Design

The opening story about Hanna Andersson's durable children's clothing underscores the importance of product design and how the design can drive a marketing communication program. In a marketing-driven organization, research and development (R&D) must work closely with marketing to determine consumer needs and product design features that will be most useful to potential customers. Engineers and marketing researchers should partner with strategists. In well-integrated companies, these groups work closely together, often in teams.

Ford Motors is an example of a company that is market driven. The 1996 Taurus was in design planning nearly five years and involved virtually every division of

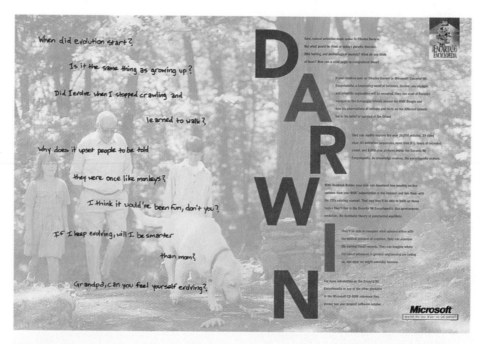

Microsoft's electronic encyclopedia, Encarta, was an interesting design challenge for computer graphics whiz Bill Flora, who had to develop an easy-to-use navigation system that would let novice computer users move easily through complex files of information.

Ford, although marketing led the way. Even kids serve on marketing panels as consultants to companies that are trying to serve their needs. Microsoft meets with preteens regularly to evaluate the performance of its Magic School Bus software series.[7]

Good design may not sell if the concept is not carefully integrated with other marketing mix factors. One of the winners of the 1995 *Business Week/Industrial Designers Society of America* annual awards, for example, was a Hewlett-Packard document-conferencing product that was taken off the market after nine months because of poor sales. *Business Week* described the product's failure as an example of price defeating design excellence.[8] Another product design story involves the conversion of an encyclopedia to an electronic format—Encarta. Product designer Bill Flora had to design the product so that users could navigate their way through complex electronic files. He also knew that the Encarta product instructions had to be consumer-friendly.

Product Features

Product features for goods include form, color, size, weight, texture, and materials. For service products, the features include expertise, physical surroundings, and people. Features create unique qualities, benefits, and appeals that can be used in marketing communication. For example, a new car offers many features—some critical to consumers and some trivial, some better than competitors' and some not. All automobile manufacturers offer safety features such as seat belts, reliable tires, bumpers, and safety windshields. Consider the product features of a service: First Baptist Church of Salem, Oregon, for example, offers a beautiful new building, an award-winning music program, services four times each week, a diverse congregation, and van transportation for the elderly and disabled.

Marketing communication managers analyze what product features will say to an audience. A car that has anti-lock brakes, for example, communicates safety and top quality. Next, the manager must decide how to communicate the features to the target audience and how to do that with an integrated, consistent message. Armstrong Floors, for instance, sends the same message to both consumers and industrial users—durability and variety at a fair price. Its sales promotion effort includes sample sheets, videos demonstrating the various floors, and an iron-clad guarantee. Walk into a store selling Armstrong Floor products and you will find a salesperson thoroughly trained and responsive to customer needs. The Public Relations department also gives millions of dollars of flooring away to groups and institutions that cannot afford this high-quality product.

The complexity of the product also suggests specific communication strategies. When products are complex, companies may rely on personal selling and other sales promotion tools that inform such as printed brochures, demonstrations, and point-of-purchase displays. Salespeople and product demonstrations allow consumers to experience the product and ask questions. To get across simple ideas or to make consumers aware of a product that does not have complex features, firms usually use image advertising—advertising that focuses on one or two general ideas about the brand. Similarly, many businesses commonly use advertising for products that are familiar to consumers, such as Coca-Cola, to make them aware of or remind them of the product.

profile

Bill Flora
Creative Director—Microsoft's Encarta

As creative director, Bill Flora is lead designer for Microsoft's Encarta, an electronic encyclopedia. He is involved in both art direction and product design. His goals are to invent new ways for people to navigate through complex sets of information, make an attractive and visually fascinating product, and develop a useful program for people who have only minimal computer experience.

Bill's job responsibilities include the following:

- Directing the art content of the encyclopedia
- Managing a team of up to five other interactive designers
- Understanding the customer, the market, and the technology
- Designing the functional elements of the product—such as the product's organization
- Designing the interface —that is, developing the look and feel of the product
- Proposing and prototyping design solutions to communication problems
- Applying new styles of information presentation and learning adapted from such activities as interpretive museum exhibits, film documentaries, and new data visualization techniques

An interesting aspect of Flora's work is that the product is redesigned every year to keep up with content changes. For instance, the Encarta 95 edition made major changes to the product's user interface for several reasons. "We wanted to improve it, make it easier to use, less intimidating, and more integrated." The second and more important reason is that "we wanted a new visual appeal—more approachable, more fun, and in our case more sophisticated." Flora notes, "Our main goal was to create an 'experience,' and to make that experience engaging."

Flora explains how his design team solved the clutter problem on the screen. "We wanted to reduce the overwhelming interface that many applications have. In the main screen of Encarta 94 there were over 30 buttons. Usually a user responds with the question of 'Where do I start?' By prioritizing these buttons and hiding the less important ones in menus, we eliminated the screen clutter and distraction and gained precious screen real-estate." He spells out the designer's problem: "The trade-off is having all the options up front with a very busy screen versus fewer options up front with a more approachable, less cluttered screen."

The success of the Encarta 95 program led to coverage of Flora's work in a number of trade and general interest magazines. His string of awards for Encarta include the Industrial Design Society of America (IDSA) Design Excellence Silver Award, an

Packaging

Traditionally viewed as the container that holds the product, packaging is primarily a concern for a goods product, although a service product can also be "packaged" in the way it is presented to the customer. For example, Avon's customer contacts are well packaged—the phone call appointment, the door hangers left when potential customers are not at home, and the leave-behind product

Honorable Mention for Encarta 95 in *ID Magazine,* and *Communication Arts'* Interactive Multimedia Award.

Academic Background

Flora graduated from the University of Colorado with a B.S. in Business in 1987. During that time he worked as advertising director for the *Campus Press,* the School of Journalism's campus newspaper. Flora feels his best school experience, aside from his degree program, was working on the campus newspaper. He values the sales, organizational, and people skills that he acquired during that job. He feels that sales experience is especially handy now because he must sell his ideas and build consensus.

For a year after graduation, he lived and worked with artists and designers in Cologne, Germany, then returned and attended the Art Center College of Design in Pasadena, California, where he got a B.F.A. in the Graphic Design and Packaging program and graduated with honors in 1992. His focus in design school was on publication design, an outgrowth of his journalism background, and he experimented with nontraditional magazine formats. The next obvious step was multimedia—such as magazines with movement and sound. He explains, "It is all about communication for me, and I think computers are the best medium for this now."

His most helpful course in design school was Typography—how to use type for effective communication and beautiful and engaging composition. Color Theory was also useful because a mastery of color and type underlies all of his design problem solving. Finally, he values his instruction in conceptual thinking and creative problem solving.

Career Track

After graduation from the Design Center in 1992, he was offered a position with Microsoft in Redmond, Washington, in its Visual Interface Design Group. He has been at Microsoft since then and has advanced to the position of Microsoft Encarta lead designer.

Typical Day

Flora says a typical day begins with reading e-mail, checking voice mail, and solving any immediate problems. He meets with his designers and reviews their work. Then he turns to his own work: "Usually I have many design tasks and problems to solve—some of which I work on myself and others I oversee." A lot of his time is taken up with meetings with editors, programmers, and program managers to define and refine tasks and get design feedback. He spends a lot of time trying to keep current with other design work outside Microsoft, and he meets as often as possible with other Microsoft designers to share work and ideas.

Day by day, he moves through the annual Encarta product development process:

- Studying the current version and user feedback
- Integrating the feedback and new research data into design refinement proposals
- Initiating new feature ideas
- Prototyping new features; getting feedback on them
- Prioritizing features and changes to be developed
- Communicating and specifying new features to programmers
- Reviewing programmers' final versions and suggesting refinements
- Producing and shipping the product

catalog. When we speak of packaging, we are primarily referring to goods and the physical containers that not only protect the products but deliver an important selling message at the point of purchase. Packaging is so crucial in some product categories—toothpaste, detergents, food products—that the phrase "package goods" is often used to refer to these products. British marketers call such products "fast-moving consumer goods" (fmcg).

Packaging serves three purposes: functional, informational, and persuasive. The functional features of packaging include convenience, safety, and preassortment—that is, placing the product in an individual or a grouped unit, such as a four-pack of Snapple. Easy-open spouts, safety lids, recyclable packaging, and oven-proof paperboard are all examples of package functions that move beyond protecting the product to a marketable product feature. Information can be conveyed through a listing of product ingredients, special instructions, price, and so forth. A package can persuade if the design incorporates a special offer, contest announcement, or perhaps a testimonial.

Conversely, packaging—particularly wasteful over-packaging with multiple wrapping—may provide environmentally concerned consumers with a reason to avoid buying the product. The "long-boxes" that packaged some CDs generated consumer resistance because they were wasteful.

Branding

A **brand** is the name, design, symbol, or any other feature that identifies the good, service, institution, or idea sold by a marketer. The **brand name** is that part of a brand that can be spoken, such as words, letters, or numbers. MCI and TCI are both brand names. The **brand mark,** also known as the logo, is that part of the brand that cannot be spoken. It can be a symbol (Nike's swoosh), picture (Green Giant's jolly green giant), design (United's blue and red U), color combination (IBM's use of blue), or distinctive lettering (the distinctive Spencerian script used to write the Coca-Cola brand name). When a brand name or brand mark is legally

Coca-Cola is one of the most powerful brands in the world. The 750 million daily points of contact with its package provide the experiences that build brand loyalty.

protected through registration with the Patent and Trademark Office of the Department of Commerce, it becomes a **trademark.** The process of developing and selecting brand names, brand marks, and the supporting marketing campaign is called a **branding strategy.**

The power of a brand name recently has been demonstrated by a number of companies. Eastman Kodak used its name and package design to enter the battery business, even though it does not manufacture the batteries it sells. Kodak buys the batteries from suppliers and then gives them the company's familiar yellow "trade dress" found on most of its film products. By the end of the first year, the battery line had won between 5 and 10 percent of the $5 billion worldwide market. Similarly, the name of the clothing retailer, the Gap, has achieved superstar brand status. A Gap label is sewn into every garment sold to raise the store's name to the personality of a brand in customers' minds.

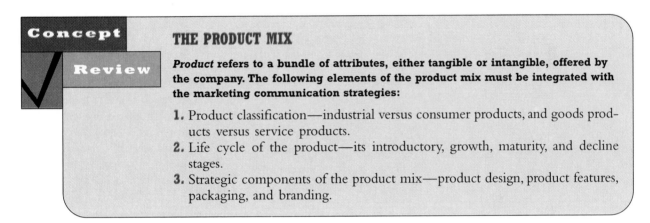

Concept

Review

THE PRODUCT MIX

Product refers to a bundle of attributes, either tangible or intangible, offered by the company. The following elements of the product mix must be integrated with the marketing communication strategies:

1. Product classification—industrial versus consumer products, and goods products versus service products.
2. Life cycle of the product—its introductory, growth, maturity, and decline stages.
3. Strategic components of the product mix—product design, product features, packaging, and branding.

THE DISTRIBUTION MIX

All products, whether goods or services, have a channel of distribution through which the product is delivered to customers. A **channel of distribution** includes all the institutions, processes, and relationships that help the product from the manufacturer to the ultimate buyer, either industrial or consumer. For example, if a manufacturer uses direct mail to distribute products, then the distribution strategy revolves around the design of a system for taking orders and delivering the product to the consumer, for receiving payment, and for handling returns. In contrast, the distribution strategy of a manufacturer of machine parts focuses on identifying wholesalers or brokers who will locate retail outlets and retailers who will sell the product to customers and make sure it is delivered and serviced. Wholesalers, brokers, and retailers are collectively called **resellers.** Managing a product's channel of distribution—also called channel management—is a complex area of marketing that can sometimes raise ethical questions, as the accompanying You Decide feature explains.

Distribution and Communication Strategy

A marketer must constantly consider how its channel of distribution conveys a message. For example, the image of a possible retail outlet can negatively or pos-

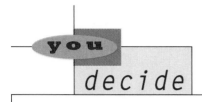

Channel Warfare

Conflicts may arise between people who distribute products through different channels. For example, a group of Long Island retailers, newspapers, and professors have declared war on catalog merchants. Working with a local ad agency that offered its services pro bono (free), the coalition created a newspaper ad headlined, "If these Catalogues Do Their Job, It Could Mean She Loses Hers." The illustration showed a stack of catalogs as high as a retail salesclerk who stood nearby holding a pair of jeans.

Using figures compiled by a Hofstra University professor, the ad claimed that $1.5 billion in retail sales goes outside Long Island each year to mail-order merchants, depriving the local economy of jobs and retail dollars. An editorial in *Direct Marketing* challenged this campaign, pointing out that catalog marketing is a small percentage of total retail sales, in the neighborhood of 3.8 percent, and thus national catalogs have little impact on the Long Island economy. There is also the issue of freedom—just because a business outside a region is doing well inside that region, it

does not constitute a reason for banning the outsider. The catalog channel, by definition, must operate in markets far from its headquarters to be successful. Still, the concern of local retailers is understandable.

In another case, the retail pharmaceutical industry is fighting with prescription drug companies that sell by mail. Many retail drugstores are displaying a counter card with an illustration that depicts a druggist in a white coat and a black blindfold. The headline reads: "A Mail Order Pharmacist Can't See Anything Wrong With You." It's designed to frighten consumers, particularly the elderly, from saving a few bucks by buying their regular medicine from mail-order suppliers, such as the AARP.

Mail catalogers also complain, mostly about the post office. However, they are now facing inroads from the Internet. Some experts predict it will only be a matter of time before catalogers realize that it is much cheaper to "publish" their merchandise online and avoid the printing and postage costs. Such a change will have a

major effect on the production side of the catalog industry.

You Decide

1. Are such campaigns opposing competitive resellers socially responsible or are they a waste of money? What other options are available to retailers who are competing with catalogers and mail-order companies? Would those options send a more effective message to consumers?

2. Do you order from catalogs? If so, what type of merchandise? Does that take business away from local retailers? Should you care about supporting local businesses?

3. Review the Hannah Andersson opening story and consider the distribution issues. Do you feel the company should move into retailing more aggressively and open more stores? Explain your answer.

Sources: James R. Rosenfield, "Bad Targeting Can Sometimes Be Overcome by Good Process," *Direct Marketing* (February 1996): 19–21; Henry "Pete" Hoke, Jr., "Editorial," *Direct Marketing* (March 1995): 80.

itively impact on a brand image. The store's image depends on the consumer's attitude toward the retailer's communication strategy, its services, convenience, layout, exterior and interior appearance, location, personnel, and product mix. The strategy is to match the image of the store to the image of the marketer's product. Therefore, Rolex would not expect Kmart to implement its upscale marketing communication strategy. Likewise, Timex realizes that Nieman Marcus is unlikely to carry its watches because the Timex marketing communication strategy does not match the upscale image of that store. To ensure marketing mix consistency, Nieman Marcus would be a better channel for distributing Rolex watches and Kmart would be better for Timex.

The communication and distribution elements of the marketing mix are becoming increasingly indistinguishable.[9] In some cases, as in direct response marketing, the distribution channel and the communication activity are one and the same. A catalog such as Brooks Brothers', for example, is both the primary mechanism for purchasing the product and the main communication vehicle, listing products along with descriptions, prices, and so forth. Still, traditional channel members such as wholesalers and retailers provide the primary means for purchasing products.

Wholesalers and Retailers

A **wholesaler** is a channel member who receives products from a manufacturer or other wholesaler and distributes them to a retailer or another wholesaler. Wholesalers tend to act as "middlemen" and typically don't deal with ultimate users. If we consider the marketing communication mix, the greatest strength of wholesalers is personal selling. As much as 80 to 90 percent of their marketing communication budget goes to this activity. Wholesalers often use other communication techniques such as direct mail, trade publication ads, product catalogs, and trade shows (a meeting of people in the industry where businesses set up booths to demonstrate or distribute information about products). However, these are usually intended to support the activities of the sales force. Trade shows, for example, are a primary source for sales leads.

Retailers are those who receive products from wholesalers, or possibly from manufacturers, and then sell that product to ultimate users. Without retailers many manufacturers would not have profitable access to customers. The marketing communication activities of retailers are broader than those of wholesalers. At one end

This page from the Brooks Brothers' catalog communicates product and price information, promotes the product, and allows customers to buy the product through its 800 number.

of the continuum is a company such as Sears, which has the capacity to match the communication efforts of the largest manufacturer. At the other end is an individual operating a shoe repair shop, whose entire marketing communication strategy is providing good customer service and placing a small ad in the Yellow Pages.

Regardless of size, every retailer should consider some questions when designing its communication strategy. First, what types of products are carried by the retailer? If the products are indistinguishable and price is the major selling attribute, price should be featured prominently in advertising and, perhaps, store coupons should be made available. Second, what market does the retailer target? For example, if the target market is concerned with quality at any price, such as Montblanc pens, then retailers use image advertising, personal selling, and elaborate point-of-purchase displays. Conversely, a price-conscious target market would prompt communication strategies that emphasize price and sales promotions (sales prices, rebates, coupons). Third, is the manufacturer willing to supplement the retailer's advertising, either financially or through technical expertise—a practice known as **cooperative advertising**? If so, the advertising program may be more extensive and sophisticated than that supported by a retailer that has no such cooperation.

Retail advertising is often focused on price. This Radio Shack ad creatively blends product and price information by focusing on favorable financing terms.

Service Providers

Service product marketers also use a channel of distribution for the product. A hospital, for example, moves the consumer (patient) through a channel that may include an admissions stage, an assessment stage, an action stage (the treatment), a recovery stage, and a follow-up stage. Each stage requires different expertise and communication objectives. Hospitals also use other service and goods marketers to support their efforts, such as ambulance services, pharmacies, and in-home nursing services.

Marketing communication strategies for service-product channels attempt to stress the tangible elements of each channel. For instance, hospitals often allow prospective patients to make a "dry run" that includes introduction to facilities and personnel they will meet later. If the perceived risk of taking a dry run is high, or if it is unrealistic to do so, the marketing communicator tries to reduce the risk with additional information, incentives, and personal attention. These are intangible channels for service distribution. Take, for example, an international vacation: It would be too expensive to offer a dry run. Instead, travel agencies such as American Express Tours assign a trip counselor to each traveler to make sure the client has all information possible. Videos can also be used to simulate the experience.

Because the service channel frequently relies on other resellers, these related services have to be translated by the service provider into a benefit for the consumer. American Express Tours is at the mercy of airlines, hotels, bus drivers, and tour guides to provide services for their customers. To ensure quality, the company provides service by negotiating all these arrangements with each service channel member and monitors their delivery.

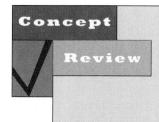

Concept Review

THE DISTRIBUTION MIX

The channel of distribution is the marketing mechanism used to present, deliver, and service the product for customers. The channel of distribution for goods and services affects the product's marketing communication efforts.

1. A goods product is distributed by wholesalers, retailers, or both. Each distributor uses different marketing communication activities. Wholesalers typically rely on personal selling and sales promotion, whereas retailers usually rely on advertising and sales promotion.
2. Service product marketers rely on intangible channels and communication efforts to create tangible benefits for each channel element.

THE PRICE MIX

Superficially, price is easy to define. **Price** is the value assigned to the product by the seller and the buyer. However, a price has different meanings for sellers and buyers. For the seller, it is a series of cost components and an expected profit margin. Most companies cannot operate successfully unless their price guarantees a specific profit. For the buyer, it is a calculation of the historical price of the product, the competitive price (or the price for comparable products), the expected price, risk, and the perceived need for the product. That is, a business like Procter & Gamble makes sure that the price charged for its laundry detergent covers the cost of research and development, materials, marketing, and other costs, and generates a profit. Consumers purchasing detergent, however, don't care about the company's costs and profit margins. Instead they look at how the current price compares to last week's, what other stores are charging for the same product, and what other brands of laundry detergent cost.

Marketing communication must present price from the consumers' perspective, and all the elements of the price message must be consistent. To illustrate, an ad for a $75,000 BMW would be remiss to use poor photography or improper grammar. The ad should focus on the value of the car (such as, "The safest, most luxurious ride ever") and anticipate reaction to a high price. Often, car companies justify price increases indirectly by pointing out new features, such as a newly designed style or engine.

Pricing Strategies

Firms use pricing strategies for three reasons: to stay competitive, to shape consumer attitudes, and to create brand differentiation. First, a firm remains competitive when it offers comparable satisfaction at lower prices. When marketers decide to use price as a competitive weapon, they should show how their price matches or beats competitors' prices. Price can also be used to counter a competitive move. For example, when The Walt Disney Company announced that it planned to enter the cruise industry with 2400-passenger "mega-ships," the four biggest lines—Carnival, Royal Caribbean, Princess Cruises, and Norwegian Cruise Line—all announced price discounts to encourage early bookings on their ships. If the marketing communication does not accurately reflect this relationship between price and performance, then the pricing strategy could fail.

Second, the price helps shape attitudes toward a product. For marketing communication to be effective, the message sent by both the price and the communication must be consistent. For example, a luxury item must have a high enough price to signal high quality. Running a sale or offering a rebate on an Armani suit undercuts the elite image of paying top dollar for a status product.

Third, a high price is often accompanied by heavy advertising that creates brand differentiation. In the case of high-priced products, brand differentiation justifies the price. Intelligent marketers create brand differentiation only if they know how consumers perceive the brand, the price being charged, the prices charged by the competition, and how consumers feel about price reductions and increases.

Price Communication

Information about pricing is probably the most important message that can be transmitted to consumers. The price information on the package, signage, point-of-purchase materials, coupons, and advertising all deliver price messages. Advertising that touts price as the dominant marketing mix element is referred to as **price copy advertising.** Supermarket retailers often use this type of advertising because their customers usually view price information as the most important factor in their product choice.

Pricing information is often a key factor in motivating consumers to act. Price discounts, rebates, and coupons are all price adjustments intended to spur purchase. Industrial buyers are also responsive to price changes. In fact, negotiating for a lower price, rebates, and other price deals are quite normal in many industries. For both consumers and industrial buyers, **price bundling**—the practice of selling multiple units of a product or combination of complementary products for a lower total price than if sold separately—is also common.

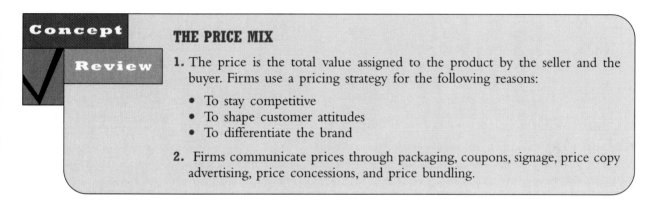

Concept Review

THE PRICE MIX

1. The price is the total value assigned to the product by the seller and the buyer. Firms use a pricing strategy for the following reasons:

- To stay competitive
- To shape customer attitudes
- To differentiate the brand

2. Firms communicate prices through packaging, coupons, signage, price copy advertising, price concessions, and price bundling.

A CLOSING THOUGHT: YOU CANNOT *NOT* COMMUNICATE

The purpose of any product or service is to meet the needs and wants of target markets. This purpose cannot be satisfied, however, without a product that benefits consumers, a distribution program that delivers a product that is accessible to customers, a pricing strategy that clearly determines the worth of the value of the product to customers, and a communication program that tells customers how the product meets their needs and wants. Thus, the linkage between the product, the distribution, the price, and marketing communication is critical.

Why is this link so critical? Every marketing mix element communicates. Furthermore, in any marketing situation, you cannot *not* communicate. The notion of a *mix* of marketing tools and programs challenges any planner to make the product, price, and distribution decisions work together strategically to communicate the same message. It is an extremely important—and difficult—management task.

SUMMARY

1. Explain the marketing concept and outline how the business plan, marketing plan, and marketing communication strategy interrelate.

Marketing focuses on satisfying customer wants and needs. The goals in the company's mission and business plan determine the marketing plan objectives and strategies, and the marketing plan must be compatible with both. In turn, the marketing communication plan must support, not conflict with, the marketing plan. The marketing plan outlines the marketing mix of product, distribution, pricing, and marketing communication.

2. Identify the product mix elements and explain how they affect the product's marketing communication program.

The term *product* refers to a bundle of attributes, either tangible or intangible, of a good, service, or idea offered by a company. The product mix consists of three main elements. The first element is product classification. Is it a good or a service, and is it a consumer or industrial product? The second element is the life cycle of the product. Is it in the introductory, growth, maturity, or decline stage? The third element is the group of strategic product mix components—research and development, product features, packaging, and branding. Each of these elements must be integrated with the marketing communication strategies because all marketing mix elements communicate. Marketers should be sure all mix elements deliver a consistent message.

3. Explain the distribution mix elements and how they influence marketing communication.

Marketing communication planners must understand the informational needs and communication capabilities of the channels of distribution. For goods products there are two primary types of resellers: wholesalers and retailers. Wholesalers communicate the benefits of the manufacturer's product to retailers primarily through personal selling and sales promotion. Retailers communicate product features and store services through mass advertising and sales promotion, especially point-of-purchase displays and price discounts. Service providers are also retailers and rely on other intermediaries to help them provide their services.

4. List the price mix elements and analyze how they affect marketing communication strategies.

Price, a crucial factor in the marketing mix, helps consumers estimate the value of the product. The three purposes of price are to stay competitive, shape consumer attitudes, and differentiate the brand. Pricing is communicated through such elements as the package, store signage, point-of-purchase materials, coupons, and advertising. A price that is too high given the product quality or the distribution channel sends a conflicting message that will confuse consumers. Conversely, a price that is too low given the other mix elements will also send a conflicting message.

POINTS TO PONDER

Review the Facts

1. What is the marketing concept?
2. How does the notion of exchange help explain a marketing focus?
3. What are the four stages in the product life cycle? Give an example of a product in each of the stages.
4. Define a product.

5. Explain branding and what it contributes to the marketing strategy of a product.
6. What is price bundling? Identify three examples.

Master the Concepts

7. Describe how the marketing concept relates to integrated marketing communication.
8. Discuss why the company's mission and business

plan, the marketing strategy, and the marketing communication strategies should all be in harmony. How can a firm ensure that such coordination happens?

9. The marketing of services is receiving more attention since consumer spending on services has risen. How does the promotion of services differ from the promotion of goods products?

10. Describe how marketing communication for industrial products differs from that of consumer products.

11. Outline the role of advertising and personal selling in the various stages of a product life cycle.

12. Discuss a situation in which pricing would be easy to promote and one in which it would be difficult.

13. Explain how the company's mission statement comes alive in Hanna Andersson's business practices and how its marketing mix communicates the brand message.

Apply Your Knowledge

14. You are the marketing director for Coca-Cola in India. The company has only recently received government approval to begin selling the product in this very large market. How would your marketing strategy differ from that of your colleagues in various European countries where the product has been selling for years?

15. As competition moves into the upscale children's clothing direct-mail market, Hanna Andersson is already feeling the pressure, particularly on price. How can the company improve its marketing mix and marketing communication strategies to stay competitive? How does an innovative company like this stay ahead of the market?

SUGGESTED PROJECTS

1. (Writing Project) Select two products in your supermarket that are at opposite ends of the product life cycle. Collect marketing communication material supporting each product. In a brief memo, compare and contrast the information about the marketing mix found in these promotions. How does the information differ? How is it the same? How does the marketing communication information you found compare with the product life cycle discussion in the chapter?

2. (Oral Communication) Interview the managers of three types of retail stores. Determine what types of marketing communication they use and ask them to assess the relative success of each type.

How do their assessments compare with the discussion of retailers' marketing communication strategies in this chapter? If you were introducing a new product that would be distributed through these stores, what type of marketing communication program would you recommend to get the most retailer support?

3. (Internet Project) Visit the Johnson & Johnson home page on the World Wide Web (www.jnj.com). Find the company mission statement, also called its "Credo." Now research some of the company's products, pricing, distribution, and marketing communication strategies. Do they seem consistent with the company's mission statement?

CASE 2: CAN SNAPPLE BOUNCE BACK?

Who isn't familiar with Wendy, the "Snapple Lady"? This former receptionist at Snapple became famous through her TV and radio spots, during which she opened mail from devoted Snapple drinkers and involved fans in everything from special promotions to product design. This approach, which led to an almost cult-like group of highly loyal customers, is a classic example of relationship marketing.

Snapple's unique approach to product development reflected its customer relationship strategy. Unlike most companies, it implemented product suggestions from its customers. A new flavor launched in 1995 was named "Ralph's Cantaloupe Cocktail" after Yonkers, New York, resident Ralph Orofino, who was the inspiration for the new flavor. Snapple even featured Ralph in its advertising for the cantaloupe drink.

Wendy the receptionist became so popular that she eventually managed a consumer affairs unit of six, personally read 200 or more letters out of an average of 2000 per week, visited schools, dined with loyal fans, and even attended a prom (her first) as the date of a New Jersey fan.

When Quaker Oats Company purchased Snapple in 1994 for $1.7 billion, the market believed that Snapple was a winner—especially because of its marketing communication strategy—although its distribution was limited to health stores and other small "mom and pop" retailers. Donald Uzzi, president of Quaker's North American beverage business, noted that Snapple's marketing communication was "brilliant" at building consumer loyalty through product involvement, and the company was convinced it could fix the distribution problems. After a promising start in the early 1990s, however, Snapple sales dropped 6 percent in 1994, lost $100 million in 1995, and continued to be an embarrassment for Quaker into 1996. In March of 1997 Quaker sold Snapple for $3 million to the Triarc Companies in what some analysts termed a fire sale. What happened?

The Quaker acquisition appears to be a classic case of corporate miscalculation, a deal that turned into a contentious mismatch rather than a happy marriage. Quaker's stumble with Snapple is hard to believe. After all, Quaker increased Gatorade's sales from $100 million to $1.3 billion in little more than a decade. Like Gatorade, Snapple is a flavored, noncarbonated drink—so how different could the product lines be?

Very different. Quaker's production and distribution of Gatorade were state of the art. The company's computer talked directly to the computer system of its largest customers and automatically filled orders to keep the supply chain full—but not overflowing— with Gatorade. At the same time, the Gatorade brand was backed by a relentless marketing campaign that cost several hundred million dollars a year and included highly successful ads featuring Michael Jordan. Gatorade, in other words, was a highly promoted product with wide distribution and relatively low mar-

gins (the amount of money the manufacturer and retailer made on every sale).

In contrast, Snapple's order fulfillment was slow and inefficient compared with others in the industry. However, the small retailers who were its core customers were happy to handle the brand because of its high margins. They were less happy to be offered Gatorade, no matter how efficient its distribution, because of its relatively lower margins. And large mainstream retailers didn't have space to accommodate Snapple's huge line of flavors.

Marketing plans for Snapple under Quaker continued to be haphazard as the parent company searched for new strategies to revitalize the brand. First, Quaker discontinued the quirky campaigns for which Snapple was known. Quaker stopped advertising the brand in the summer of 1995, a key selling period for the brand and a major factor in its declining sales that year.

In 1996 new marketing programs failed. In an effort to aid distributors, Quaker reduced the time to get Snapple orders from bottlers to distributors from two weeks to three days. Quaker also introduced new packaging and sizes of Snapple, and new flavors designed by Quaker's chemists. Finally, its advertising began to focus on the brand's hope of becoming America's favorite "third choice in soft drinks," behind Coke and Pepsi. Quaker also developed a huge free sampling program to gain a better understanding of Snapple's market.

When these changes in product, distribution, and marketing communication failed to generate a modest profit, Quaker put the Snapple line up for sale. Some claim that Quaker lost so much money on Snapple because it didn't understand the nature of the brand's personality and the importance of its critical relationships.

Case Questions

1. What elements of the marketing mix made Snapple such a successful product in the pre-Quaker days?
2. Is it possible to take Snapple into a more mainstream marketing program and grow the brand as Quaker did with Gatorade?
3. If you were the Snapple brand manager for Triarc, what would you recommend to revitalize the brand and help it live up to its promise? Outline the highlights of your next year's marketing plan and marketing communication strategies.

Sources: Barnaby J. Feder, "Quaker to Sell Snapple for $300 Million," *New York Times,* March 28, 1997, C1, C16; Scott McMurray, "Drumming Up New

Business," *U.S. News & World Report,* April 22, 1996, 59, 62; Judann Pollack, "Quaker Sell-off Could Boost Snapple," *Advertising Age,* March 18, 1996, 3, 5; Greg Burns, "Will Quaker Get the Recipe Right?" *Business Week,* February 5, 1996, 140–5; Gerry Khermouch, "Quaker Gets Back to Snapple Roots Via Product with Personal Touch," *Brandweek,* May 22, 1995, 42; Julie Liesse, "Quaker Ups the Ante by Buying Snapple," *Advertising Age,* November 7, 1994, 4.

ROMA'S LITE INTEGRATED CASE QUESTIONS

(Review the Roma's Lite Marketing Plan in the Appendix at the end of the text before answering these questions.)

1. (Writing Project) One of the chapter themes is that all marketing activities communicate. In a brief memo (no more than 2 pages) explain how that theme affects the marketing communication plan for frozen pizza.

2. How does the Roma's Lite Pizza product life cycle stage affect its marketing communication strategy?

3. Review the marketing plan in the appendix and explain the proposed strategies for product, distribution, and pricing.

4. (Team Project) Assume you are in charge of marketing communication for the Roma's Lite Pizza new product launch team. Develop a proposal for maximizing the communication impact of the product, distribution, and pricing. What would you suggest to management about these elements and their impact on the launch? What might be done to make their impact stronger?

chapter

Organizing for Integrated Marketing Communication

CHAPTER OBJECTIVES

After completing your work on this chapter, you should be able to:

1 **Explain how the organization of a business affects marketing communication.**

2 **Distinguish between integrated marketing and integrated marketing communication.**

3 **Discuss the development of integrated marketing and why some firms have trouble implementing it.**

4 **Describe the typical organizational elements in a marketing communication program.**

5 **Outline the characteristics of an IMC organization.**

C O N S I D E R
this

Kraft Gets Its Act Together

In the 1980s, Philip Morris Incorporated, parent company of Kraft, bought General Foods Corporation to create a food giant, Kraft General Foods, Inc.. Philip Morris formed Kraft General Foods thinking the newly combined food conglomerate would have more marketing synergy and savings than either company had separately. Combined, the companies should have had stronger purchasing power and been able to cut costs through staff reductions. But because Kraft and General Foods maintained headquarters in different states, and the two had vastly different corporate cultures, Philip Morris was unable to take advantage of potential synergies. One marketing executive explained that each division "had its own structures and priorities: it was very difficult to make things happen."

However, under the leadership of a new CEO, the synergy at Kraft General Foods began to sizzle. In a symbolic move, the CEO decided to drop General Foods from the company name, calling the company Kraft Foods. Then the CEO took a major step to unify both Kraft's operation and its corporate culture by combining the Kraft and General Foods sales forces. The sales force integration eliminated internal competition and reduced duplicative sales activity. The 3500 sales representatives now work in integrated sales teams that are responsible for entire product portfolios —which include such brands as Jell-O, Louis Rich lunch meat, Maxwell House, Post and Nabisco cereals, Tombstone Pizza, Kool-Aid and Crystal Light, Entenmann's, Kraft products, and Oscar Mayer.

The company's next major step was to consolidate the marketing communication programs so that the marketing messages for all Kraft Food

61

products are consistent. Those messages range from sales promotion coupons to the Kraft Interactive Kitchen Web site, an Internet food site that offers product information, recipes with Kraft products, and shopping tips. The result of the consolidation has been greater impact, lower marketing costs, and more efficiency.

The lessons for Philip Morris? A company's organization can affect its success. And the way a company is organized can have tremendous implications for its marketing communication program.

Sources: Glenn Collins, "Make Room in the Kitchen for Yet Another Appliance," *New York Times,* 16 September 1996, C6; Kate Fitzgerald, "Kraft Goes 'Universal' as Others Refigure Couponing," *Advertising Age,* June 24, 1996, 9; Julie Liesse, "Kraft Retires General in Reorganization," *Advertising Age,* January 9, 1995, 4.

CHAPTER OVERVIEW

This chapter explores the role of marketing communication within a company. We begin with a big picture discussion of integrated marketing before exploring the role of IMC in a company. Then we investigate how firms organize the marketing communication staff, particularly for an IMC program. Next we explore various marketing communication tools and how they fit or do not fit in a marketing program, as illustrated by companies such as Kraft Foods. Finally, we examine how firms may choose different approaches to implement an integrated marketing communication program.

IMPORTANCE OF THE ORGANIZATION'S STRUCTURE

The success of any business strategy often depends on whether the company has the appropriate structure to support its activities. This is no less true for marketing communication strategies, which can require a large cadre of experts and support staff to implement the communication objectives. Every business must determine whether the existing organizational structure is adequate to reach objectives or whether reorganization is necessary.

Many companies spend millions of dollars assessing the quality of their organization. U S West, Inc., for example, has a company policy that requires a complete reorganization every five years. Consultants are brought in for months before the reorganization to evaluate every facet of the business and the implications of making specific changes.

To create effective marketing communication, firms must understand how to organize their marketing communication teams and decide whether to make any other changes in the firms' structure. The dynamics of moving to integrated marketing communication, for instance, often requires changes in the organization of the business. Some firms may choose to integrate all marketing and management activities from the CEO level to managers to employees. This is a rare organization. Other businesses may integrate their functional areas, such as marketing, finance, and human resources. The most effective way to integrate marketing communication is to start by integrating the entire marketing function.

INTEGRATED MARKETING AND IMC

Integrated marketing communication works best when all the marketing mix elements, and other operating divisions within the company, work together under a common philosophy of customer-focused marketing. **Integrated marketing** is a process of understanding the needs of the customer (and other stakeholders), orienting the firm's manufacturing and sales processes to meet those needs, and applying integrated thinking to all marketing and management decisions. At the corporate level, all managers share a corporate vision as well as an organizational structure that makes it possible for departments and divisions to share information and participate in joint planning.

That approach represents the direction in which many companies, including Kraft and Disney, are moving. To be truly integrated, every decision at each level should support decisions made at all the other levels. To illustrate, let's say that the corporate goal is to maximize profit. A marketing plan objective to increase sales by marketing new products matches that goal. A marketing communication strategy to promote the new products supports the business and marketing objectives. If all objectives support all others, then integration is much easier to manage.

From a communication perspective, integrated marketing focuses on coordinating all marketing activities to reach the marketing objectives and control or influence the messages they send. In Chapters 1 and 2, we investigated how all marketing activities—from the appearance of the store to the price, design, or packaging of the product to the advertising—could send messages to target audiences. Planning and integrating all those activities, then, means the marketing communication messages have more impact and efficiency and lower cost than those sent through a traditional marketing communication program.

Integrated marketing tries to coordinate *all* company-based marketing messages—those sent by the marketing mix, the unplanned messages (such as a dirty parking lot), and planned messages sent through marketing communication. In contrast, *integrated marketing communication* refers only to the strategic coordination of the planned marketing communication areas identified in Chapter 1 such as advertising, sales promotion, public relations, direct marketing, packaging, telemarketing, event marketing, and so on. IMC is the focus of this text, but it is useful to understand the bigger picture of integration at the corporate and marketing levels. Although integrated marketing is still more an ideal than a practice, companies such as Disney suggest it is catching on successfully.

Evolution of Integration

Although the concept of integration is nothing new, growing specialization in all business areas, including marketing and its various specialties, leads to internal competition for resources and much more isolation between departments. Admittedly, specialization is important—there will always be a need for experts in the various marketing communication areas. However, specialization becomes dysfunctional when it leads to what marketing and management experts call "silos." Communication experts Michael Hammer and James Champy note, "Companies today consist of functional silos, or stovepipes, vertical structures built on narrow pieces of processes."[1] A University of Colorado study found that the number one

Disney as a Product and a Channel

The Disney empire is built on more than just a good product. The movie side of the Disney business, as well as its theme parks, are classic examples of an "integrated marketing" company. We say that because its product (entertainment) is also a distribution channel (movies, theme parks) and an embodiment of the company's mission—wholesome entertainment for all ages. Because the company owns the message and the medium through which it is delivered, Disney may also be referred to as "a seamless company."

And the phenomenon is global. Not only do tourists travel to the United States to visit the theme parks, Disney's investment in international parks such as the ones in France and Japan is taking the company's business approach to all parts of the world. The result has been an astounding decade for the world's biggest entertainment company with revenues shooting up nearly sevenfold between mid-1980 and mid-1990 to more than $10 billion, with a hefty $1.1 billion in profits in the mid-1990s.

Not only does Disney create movies and national and international theme parks, it also has a spectacular merchandising instinct. Kids snuggle to sleep between their Pocahontas and Lion King sheets, dress in the morning in the underwear of their favorite characters from *Hercules* and *Beauty and the Beast,* and cart their lunches and books to school in lunch buckets and bags emblazoned with their favorite Disney heroes. Children and other satisfied customers are Disney's best distributors of product information by word of mouth to friends and family. Given such a magic touch, the company increased its consumer product revenues from $110 million in the mid-1980s to $1.8 billion in the mid-1990s.

And with its purchase of Capital Cities/ABC in 1995, Disney now becomes a supplier as well as a distributor in the new 500-channel, multimedia industry. The purchase gives Disney control over not only the ABC network but also ABC-owned ESPN. The philosophy of the Disney deal with ABC can be summed up with the IMC magic word—synergy.

For example, TV specials on the Disney Channel like "The Making of 101 Dalmations," which helped heighten anticipation of the film, can now be beamed into nearly every household in America. Disney Daily Blast, an online service, features games and stories with Disney characters, an ABC News report for children, and sports scores and highlights from ESPN. Disney envisions high-tech ESPN sports bars in the theme parks that will generate new business for both the network and the parks. Capital Cities also owns 37.5 percent of the Arts and Entertainment cable channel that provides an out-let for Disney's films, including Touchstone, Miramax, and other films that Disney already owns.

Only a company with integrated marketing, such as Disney, would take a children's movie, *The Mighty Ducks,* parlay it into a professional hockey team, broadcast games on its own station, and generate revenue from Mighty Ducks' jerseys sold in 400 of its own stores.

Disney is a brand, a product, and a distribution channel with a very clear sense of corporate mission that comes across in its activities. "I think we wrote the book on synergy," says Judson Green, president of Walt Disney attractions.

Food for Thought

1. In how many different ways is Disney an integrated company? Explain.
2. Retailers have also tried to apply the Disney model to their operations. If you worked for a local bookstore or a national bookstore chain and your boss asked you for some ideas on how to become more integrated like Disney, what would you recommend?

Sources: Laurie J. Flynn, "Disney Will Charge Fee for Website," **New York Times,** 21 March 1997, C5; Warren Cohen and Katia Hetter, "Disney's All Smiles," **U.S. News & World Report,** August 14, 1995, 32–49; March Magiera, "Disney: TV Shows are Brands," **Advertising Age,** June 4, 1990, 38; Christopher Knowlton, "How Disney Keeps the Magic Going," **Fortune,** December 4, 1989, 111–32.

problem with implementing integration was "turf battles" as specialists in their functional silos tried to protect their budgets and activities from encroachment by other marketing communication professionals.[2] Breaking down the walls between departments is a serious challenge in any marketing program. Integrated marketing (IM) and integrated marketing communication (IMC) are both attempts to do just that.

At least one reason for the growing acceptance of integrated marketing communication has been the emergence of **reengineering,** a process that businesses use to break down rigid, departmentalized structures to create more fluid and flexible organizations that can respond quickly to marketplace challenges.[3] In spite of criticisms of the downsizing that has been associated with reengineering, the practice has become so common that firms like Arthur Andersen and Co. have built marketing communication campaigns that tout how their companies handle reengineering, as shown in the ad that follows. Even with reengineering to help change the organizational structures, however, integration still may not be easy.

Small companies, particularly new companies, have found that they have a real advantage in gearing up for integration because they are usually not as bound by

Organizational topics such as reengineering are in the headlines in the press and even in advertisements, as in this ad for Arthur Andersen.

tradition or inertia. Oticon Holding A/S is a Danish hearing aid company that has turned its performance around and become a company on the fast track in a flat market by abolishing the traditional organization.[4] The work is organized around projects, not functions or departments. Everyone has a small office or "workstation" on wheels that they can move to create work teams so that cross-functional planning is much easier. Oticon's R&D leader explains that this approach also avoids turf battles and jealousies because employees learn to respect what other people do. "It's hard to maintain 'enemy pictures' in this company—they're not 'those bloody fools in marketing.' " Instead, marketers are part of the team.

A manager's background and expertise may pose a problem if they chain the manager to a limited viewpoint. The lack of understanding and appreciation for the strengths and weaknesses of all the communication areas may make it difficult for a manager to make effective strategic decisions. The management of an integrated communication program requires the skills of a generalist rather than a specialist, and the ability to adapt to and feel comfortable with changes.

Another problem for agencies trying to offer integrated marketing communication services is the difficulty of organizing for integrated planning. Many advertising agencies and other marketing communication organizations, such as those in public relations and direct marketing, acquired related firms to position themselves as integration experts. However, no matter how many services an organization can offer, if its IMC program is not planned cohesively and the strategies implemented according to the plan, the program will probably not be integrated.

A successful IMC agency meets the needs of its customers and plans and implements marketing communication programs in a unified manner. Seiko Time Corp. vice president for advertising, Cheri McKenzie, praises the Martin Agency of Atlanta as an example of an agency trying to become an integrated marketing communication firm. McKenzie observes that: "They look at what is the right marketing communication solution for our needs. . . . They not only develop our ad campaigns, but they do all our marketing communications work—direct marketing, promotional programs, sponsorships; they act as creative consultants in trade show booth design and design our displays. And Martin Public Relations is our PR agency. They are part of virtually every facet of our business."

Corporations may also initiate IMC. At AT&T, for example, independent marketing and advertising departments were consolidated into one department. At IBM, G. Richard Thonan, the senior vice president in charge of the PC division, not only learned about product and image advertising, he immersed himself in product development and operations. His goal was to change the customer's "out-of-the-box" experience with the computer.[5] NEC Corp. also recently announced a sweeping plan to coordinate advertising, logo, and product design, packaging, and point-of-purchase materials.

Although the acceptance of IMC has come a long way during the past decade, it still represents a small percentage of the marketing communication industry. Serious problems serve as major deterrents for many companies, which we explore next.

Difficulties in Integration

Integration, whether at the marketing level or the marketing communication level, faces certain problems that make implementation difficult. Three basic problems that haunt integration include information sharing, leadership and infringement issues, and integrity.

Information Sharing

Communication across divisions is a problem in any organization and a serious obstacle for companies trying to implement integration.[6] Some even argue that organizational integration only exists to the extent that there is a continuous exchange of information between the units.

In a company with a strong information culture, an increased communication flow promotes information exchange as shown in the Xerox ad. Organizations with greater levels of communication also have fewer problems with the "not-invented-here syndrome." This refers to the tendency of a department or division to ignore communication that was initiated somewhere else in the organization.

Information sharing is the ideal, but not all companies practice it. For instance, when Chemical Bank merged with Manufacturers Hanover, the Chemical Bank

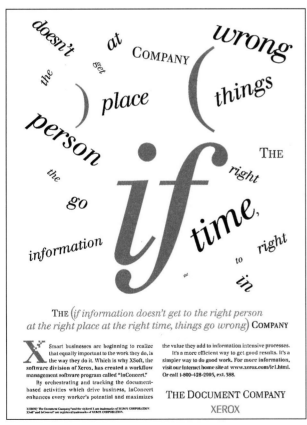

The notion that flow of information is critical to efficient operation of an organization is captured in this ad by Xerox.

The walls between departments are caused not only by specialization but also by inadequate communication systems that don't permit people to talk to one another. This ad by Lotus Development Corp. describes how electronic communication can break down these walls.

managers quickly learned that Manufacturers Hanover's culture differed greatly from their perspective.[7] Chemical shared information across departments and product groups. MH believed that each group owned its information and could choose not to share it. To help integrate bank operations, senior executives created a basic set of information management principles, a process that allowed managers of both banks to discuss these policies and the different meanings they used in referring to categories of information. The information management principles weren't magic, but creating them hastened the integration of the two banks.

Another example of the importance of information sharing in new organizational structures is the story of VeriFone Inc., an international company that provides the hardware and, increasingly, the software through which retailers "swipe" credit cards to receive authorization from a credit card company.[8] The company has no corporate headquarters, although it's officially registered in Delaware. It generates more than one-third of its revenues and stations more than one-half of its workers outside the United States. As a global company, its workday is 24 hours long, and business management is moved from one office to another around the globe as it follows the sun. A customer problem that can't be solved by the close of day in one time zone, for instance, is sent to an earlier time zone so that the problem can be worked on nonstop. The only way such a company can operate is through extensive use of e-mail and information systems. Everyone in the company, including the one-third of the workforce that is traveling at any moment, are all in touch with each other, senior management, and the company's information system.

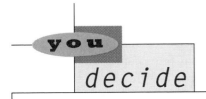

Maintaining Integrity in the Face of Disaster

Odwalla, Inc., manufacturer of some 30 fresh juice, vegetable, and other health drinks, has a mission of respecting the earth as it nourishes the body. The company's secret was fresh juice with no preservatives, no processing, and no pollution. The socially responsible darling of the environmental community, Odwalla was regularly honored for its recycling, organic cultivation, community investment, and financial management strategies.

Then in late 1996 the company got squeezed when customers in Seattle complained of an *E. coli* bacteria–related illness they associated with drinking Odwalla's fresh apple juice. (Pasteurizing kills such bacteria.) The company voluntarily recalled its apple juice and other juices that might possibly have been contaminated with the bacteria. The Food and Drug Administration immediately announced a thorough investigation.

Greg Steltenpohl, the company's founder and chairperson, visited families of the ill people, offered to pay medical expenses associated with illnesses related to its juices, and met with trade partners and health officials in Seattle and Denver. The company also set up a Web site to answer questions about the recall and two 800 numbers, one for consumers and the other for trade partners. CEO Stephen Williamson established a Nutrition and Safety Council, a council of experts to advise the company on the production and distribution of fresh juice products.

Odwalla was founded in 1980 as a company with a strong sense of integrity. Its core values include such things as honesty, empowerment of the individual, personal responsibility and accountability, and ecological leadership and sustainability. Its philosophy of business was seriously tested by this contamination scare and it reassessed its pasteurization decision, ultimately deciding to pasteurize its products rather than risk causing health problems.

You Decide

1. Identify the steps taken by Odwalla to preserve its reputation and integrity. What other actions might be considered by management in this kind of position?

2. Do you feel Odwalla will be able to maintain its reputation in the face of this crisis?

3. If you were the marketing communication director for Odwalla, what would you advise the management about its policy of not pasteurizing the fresh juices? How would you decide if the risk is worth the benefit of freshness?

Sources: Christina Waters, "Pulp Non-Fiction," *Metro* (January 11–17): Internet (www. metroactive.com/papers/metro/01.11.96/ Odwalla-9602); Ricardo Sandoval, "Odwalla Execs Say Performance Counts More than Pay," *San José Mercury News* (June 24, 1996): Internet (spyglass.sjmercury.com/business/salsur/ odwalla.com); "Odwalla, Inc.," Odwalla home page (April 7, 1997): Internet (www. odwallazone.com).

This example points to the need for companies to identify types of information and policies about sharing certain information to aid integration. The more this is done, the more likely integration will be successful.

Leadership and Infringement

Any time an organizational structure changes, there are questions about who will be in charge, who will lose power, and who will lose resources. The problem is how to structure an organizational environment in which all the people, with their various interests and skills, will be most productive. However, the attitude problem—one function is better than the other, or one function should lead and the others should follow—continues to be a hindrance in implementing integration. The Lotus SmartSuite ad illustrates the way many organizations are organized into boxes and silos.

Two areas where a negative attitude can be a problem is in integrating marketing communication budgets and public relations. Many turf wars exist over who gets what. That is, many managers evaluate their success and power in terms of budget size. Integrating communication functions brings up a host of budget-related questions. How is the budget divided? How do you charge for services provided? Who is charged for unexpected expenses? IMC scholar Tom Duncan proposes *zero-based communication planning* as a possible solution. With this type of planning, the marketing communication budgets are built annually on the basis of what needs to be done and which activities will make the strongest contributions to achieve that year's marketing communication objectives. Rather than using last year's plan as a starting point for this year's, zero-based planning means starting with a blank sheet. This year's plan may be entirely different from last year's or next year's.[9]

Infringement issues also arise in an IMC program, particularly with public relations. Some public relations practitioners and academics feel that marketing communicators are focused exclusively on customers and selling and don't understand the wider range of stakeholders that public relations must address. Additionally, these PR managers view IMC as an attempt to encroach further into their territory on the part of advertising agencies.[10] Fortunately, many public relations practitioners understand that the driving purpose behind IMC is to better integrate all communication messages and reach a much broader set of stakeholders, regardless of whether the messages have a PR or advertising focus.

Integrity Problems

Ethical behavior is critical to the success of any marketing program because actions speak louder than words. That is, any lapses in a company's ethical behavior overshadow messages in advertising or public relations and therefore directly affect the company's reputation. People working in marketing and marketing communication are aware of how difficult it is to manage their people and programs so that ethical problems are minimized. Integration introduces many strangers into the people mix so that controlling for such miscues appears next to impossible. It also means that errors in judgment that occur in one part of the integrated organiza-

---

Concept **Review**

IMPORTANCE OF THE ORGANIZATIONAL STRUCTURE

The structure of a company has a strong effect on its marketing communication program.

1. Integrated marketing is the process of coordinating the entire marketing function, such as all marketing mix elements and all unplanned and planned marketing messages.
2. The evolution of integration has been slow and difficult due to the business trend of increased specialization and the creation of organizational silos. Integration requires that businesses break down these silos.
3. The difficulties associated with integration include problems with information sharing, leadership and infringement, and integrity.

tion are attributed to everyone. The You Decide feature on page 69 identifies how an integrated marketing program must take seriously its accountability for any business problem or risk damaging its image.

One expert suggests that when there is a focused mission and a sense of common direction, it is easier to handle crises and potential ethical problems because everyone understands what the company stands for and how it approaches such issues. It is less likely that an integrated organization will make ethical mistakes if it understands how this behavior affects the entire organization.

MARKETING COMMUNICATION AND THE ORGANIZATION

Before we look at the organizational requirements for implementing an integrated communication strategy, it is helpful to discuss the general organizational structure and terminology that marketing communication managers may encounter.

A company may be a manufacturer, service provider, retailer, or nonprofit organization. A company creates a product—a good, a service, or an idea—to make it available to, or sell it to, a target audience. Usually the company's objective is to create a profit, although in nonprofit organizations the emphasis shifts to raising money to provide goods and services, enlisting volunteers, or increasing membership. All organizations, then, create something of value and offer it to others in exchange for some kind of funds (money, barter, donations, dues).

Managers control the marketing strategy that helps achieve the company's objectives. They manage all decisions about the marketing mix and allocate budgets to the various marketing teams. The top executive in charge of the marketing effort may have the title of **vice president of marketing** or **director of marketing.** The marketing director may also oversee a department of people, called **marketing services,** that specializes in managing various marketing communication tools, such as advertising and sales promotion. An external or outside agency that aids a firm's marketing communication efforts may refer to the company's marketing team as "the client" or "the account."

A multiple-brand, consumer-products company may divide marketing responsibility by brand—that is, each brand is the responsibility of a brand or product manager. The **brand manager** is the business leader for that brand and has ultimate responsibility for coordinating sales, product development, budget, profits, and marketing communications. For example, the brand manager of Cheer laundry detergent (a brand of Procter & Gamble) must coordinate product distribution, sales territory allocation, mass advertising, coupon programs, public relations activities, and packaging changes, to name but a few assigned activities. As marketing services expertise has developed in larger companies, brand leaders often manage a cross-functional team consisting of research and development, manufacturing, human resources, financial planning, marketing, distribution, international operations, and so forth.

In cutting-edge companies, particularly business-to-business, that team is customer focused rather than brand focused. A customer-focused organization makes sure that all team members are doing what they need to do to satisfy the needs and wants of the customer. In other words, a company may be organized by customer group and by how they use the company's products, rather than by brand.

Figure 3.1 illustrates the various levels of administrative responsibility in a medium-to-large company. In a small company, one person may handle some or all of the responsibilities shown. At the corporate level, senior management sets corporate objectives and strategies. The marketing department sets marketing objectives and strategies that dovetail with the corporate business plan. The marketing plan sets strategies and objectives for each of the marketing mix elements—product, distribution, pricing, and marketing communication (including how suppliers, consultants, and the internal staff or team members plan and implement marketing communication strategies).

Organizing Marketing Communication Activities

Marketing communication activities can be organized in a variety of ways. A company may control all the activities internally through **departments** (the advertising department, the sales department, the public relations department, and so on) or through in-house agencies. An *in-house agency* is staffed by corporate employees who have the responsibility for creating an advertising campaign, special event, or other communication activity. An **external agency,** such as an advertising or public relations agency, is an organization that helps the client company with marketing communication activities, usually because the company feels the agency has greater expertise or can perform the activity more efficiently. Some companies

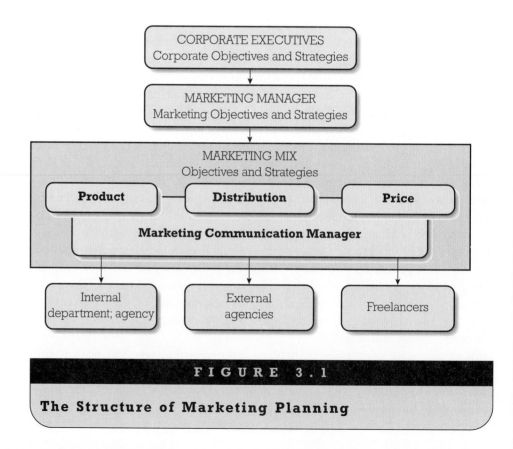

FIGURE 3.1

The Structure of Marketing Planning

use a combination of both internal departments and in-house agency work for some activities and use external agencies for major activities that demand more expertise or personnel than is available internally.

Although the terms **marketing communication manager** or **marketing communicator** are used throughout this text, in many companies the person with the title of director of marketing or director of advertising is the one person responsible for planning and implementing marketing communication. In a small organization, the owner or manager may perform all of these tasks or might have one person or a small staff that manages all the marketing communication activities.

Individuals who are in charge of marketing communication have a variety of responsibilities, some of which they accomplish themselves and some of which they may delegate to external agencies or freelancers. These duties are outlined in Table 3.1.

The larger the company, the more likely each of these activities will be managed by different specialists. The more specialized the team, the more likely problems with turf battles and lack of communication between team members will arise.

To understand how companies coordinate their marketing communication teams, let's look at three types of staffing arrangements in more detail: internal departments and in-house agencies, external agencies, and freelancers.

Internal Departments and In-House Agencies

Often a specialist working for the company manages a part of a firm's marketing communication strategy, such as an advertising manager, sales promotion manager, or special events coordinator. These experts produce, support, and supervise work in their areas of expertise. The advertising manager, for example, is usually

TABLE 3.1

Marketing Communication Manager's Responsibilities

- Decide what products, institutions, or ideas to promote
- Develop the marketing communication plan, including how to use the marketing communication tools
- Identify target audiences, basic message strategies, and message objectives
- Allocate the budget for the various marketing communication tools
- Decide whether to conduct the marketing work internally or hire specialists externally
- Give directions to internal staff, external agencies, and freelancers as needed
- Review, approve, and help develop programs created by internal staff, external agencies, and freelancers
- Pay the bills
- Evaluate all work to make sure it is integrated, consistent, and accomplishes communication objectives

responsible for approving advertising ideas before those ideas undergo preliminary testing with consumers. The advertising manager may also hire an outside ad agency who will create the ads, allocate the budget, pay the bills, and determine whether objectives have been reached.

Typically, the larger the marketing communication budget, the larger the marketing communication staff, and the more likely it is that the business will seek outside expertise to ensure the highest possible quality of work. Size of program, however, generally varies with the type of marketing program. Business-to-business marketers, for instance, usually have much smaller marketing staffs than package goods manufacturers, because they rely more on personal sales.

An **in-house agency** is a group of internal marketing communication specialists that operates as its own profit center and handles all the marketing communication work for its primary client—the company to which it is affiliated. In-house agencies may also handle outside work, particularly for suppliers, vendors, and distributors who work with the company. Many retailers have in-house agencies (such as Pier 1 and Nieman Marcus) that specialize in retail advertising. Retailers tend to operate with small profit margins and find they can save money by doing their own advertising. Also, retailers must develop and place their ads under extremely tight deadlines. There is seldom time to work with an outside advertising consultant. Finally, retailers often receive advertising materials either free or at a reduced cost from manufacturers and trade associations, such as free creative and production assistance.

Table 3.2 summarizes the pros and cons of using an in-house agency.

TABLE 3.2	Pros	Cons
The Pros and Cons of an In-house Agency	**Savings**	
	Saves money because the in-house agency isn't trying to make a profit off its client	Size of external agency may result in bigger savings due to economies of scale
	Technical Specialization	
	In-house agencies allow individuals to become technical experts on the product(s) being promoted	Creative individuals with varied experiences may provide fresh insight and approaches to communicating about a technical product
	Priority Service	
	The in-house agency works only for the client and gives priority to the client's needs	Total commitment to one task may mean other tasks, with greater importance, are not considered
	Minimum Staffing	
	In-house agencies use minimum staffing, employing freelancers when appropriate	Freelancers may not be available when needed, or the quality of those available may be inadequate

External Agencies

A business may choose to use outside professional services for the marketing communication programs ranging from advertising and public relations to package design to special events and direct marketing. Companies use external agencies (communication experts that provide services for a contractual fee) that have more expertise in marketing communication tools than an internal department or in-house agency can provide. Some companies partner with such agencies for a very long time, establishing a familiarity and level of trust comparable to a good marriage. Other client-agency relationships are short term, requiring that the agency perform a very specific task. Agencies that specialize in organizing sporting event promotions, for instance, may only work with a client for a few weeks or months.

Freelancers

Self-employed specialists are called **freelancers.** Marketing communication freelancers include copywriters, art directors, computer graphic experts, photographers, cartoonists and other illustrators, Web-page designers, broadcast producers, casting directors, commercial directors, and researchers.

Typically, freelancers work alone, although they may be a part of a network of other freelancers with whom they partner as the job demands. A copywriter and art director, for example, may team up on an advertising assignment for either the advertiser or an advertising agency that handles the account. From a company's standpoint, freelancers are used when it needs highly specialized people who are not on the company's payroll. They are also used to help with an overload of work that can't be handled by the regular staff or if schedules can't be met.

Concept ✓ **Review**

MARKETING COMMUNICATION AND THE ORGANIZATION

Several organizational features and terms help us understand marketing communication.

1. Typically, the manager responsible for marketing communication is titled vice president of marketing or director of marketing, although in a multiple-brand company, a brand manager may be in charge.
2. Marketing communication may be controlled through departments or through in-house agencies. External agencies may also have primary responsibility for marketing communication. There are specific reasons why one form of control should be used instead of another.
3. Self-employed specialists, called freelancers, often are used to assist with the marketing communication effort.

ORGANIZING TO USE MARKETING COMMUNICATION ACTIVITIES

The next section will briefly review how key marketing communication functional areas organize their activities. We examine the organization of the following areas: advertising, sales promotion, public relations agencies, direct marketing companies, sales departments, event organizers, and packaging and design firms.

Advertising Departments and Agencies

Advertising is a big business in terms of both dollars and complexity. At one extreme, a single individual may create, approve, and place ads in the media. At the other extreme, a business may retain a full-service advertising agency to create and make the media buys. **Full service** means the agency provides creative services, media planning and buying, market research, and all other planning services.

Advertising Agencies

The most important reason for using an external advertising agency is to have access to the talented people employed there. A full-service agency is staffed to provide highly specialized services that clients can rarely afford to provide for themselves, such as research statisticians and people who negotiate with networks. Only large agencies with many accounts can afford to employ such specialists full time.

Most advertising agencies have five main departments: account management, creative services, media buyers and planners, research, and traffic. **Account managers,** also called **account executives,** are liaisons to the client's marketing communication manager. They work out the strategy and the details of the assignment with the client and bring that information back to the agency staff. **Researchers** and **account planners** conduct consumer research and analyze consumer trends and buyer decisions. The **creative staff**—the copywriters, art directors, and broadcast producers—design and produce the advertising for media. The media department consists of **media planners,** people who decide what media mix best fits the client's marketing strategy, and **media buyers,** people who actually negotiate the deals for media time and space. **Traffic managers** are those who schedule and track an ad as it is produced and hire production specialists, such as freelance artists and photo retouchers.

There are also the usual business functions. Human resource managers handle training, staffing, and other personnel issues. The finance and accounting staff monitors budgeting, cash flow, and other monetary activities.

Creative Boutiques

Creative boutiques are small agencies that concentrate entirely on preparing the creative elements for a client. They are generally a small group of individuals—both copywriters and art directors—and are frequently organized as a partnership. Creative boutiques are often hired by companies that do a lot of marketing communication management in-house and only need outside specialists to help develop and execute creative ideas.

Media Buying Agencies

Media buying agencies, as mentioned in Chapter 1 in the Chrysler/Pentacom discussion, have emerged as a result of large agencies attempting to make all their departments separate profit centers and because many clients feel they save money and get better results when media is handled separately. Take Pentacom as an example. It is an independent subsidiary of BBDO that buys all the media for the client Chrysler Motors. Pentacom handles the media planning and buying for all the agencies that work for Chrysler, thus creating synergy and cash savings.

Harris Drury Cohen, an advertising agency in Ft. Lauderdale, Florida, shows its passion for advertising in this New York Festival award-winning promotion.

Media Suppliers

Media suppliers—the broadcasting stations, cable networks, newspapers, magazines, and so on—play a major role in the advertising industry. Each media supplier has its own sales staff to call on agencies and advertisers to persuade them to spend more money with that particular media provider. To encourage business, media suppliers often offer ad writing, design, and production help to advertisers. Media suppliers, then, often hire a professional advertising staff that specializes in producing ads for that medium.

Sales Promotion Organizations

Because of the complexity of sales promotion, many people may be part of a sales promotion organization. In a sales promotion department or agency, **consumer sales promotion specialists** are those whose role is to understand how and when to use price deals such as sales, coupons, samples, contests and sweepstakes, refunds and rebates, loyalty programs, and premiums or gifts that encourage purchase. **Trade promotion specialists** are specialists who know how and when to use point-of-purchase displays and other in-store merchandising materials, dealer and salesperson contests and sweepstakes, and trade shows and exhibits. They also specialize in negotiating trade incentives such as **trade deals,** which are allowances, discounts, goods, or cash given to a retailer in return for handling a special promotion.

Sales promotion managers are people who set objectives and budgets and evaluate the success of promotions. Outside specialists are usually hired to handle the specific details of programs such as sampling, product demonstrations, rebates, contests and sweepstakes, and coupon distributions. Each of these promotional activities may require special expertise. A manufacturer's coupon promotion, for example, needs a procedure for distribution—advertising, mail, inserts in newspapers and magazines, and so forth—arrangements with stores for honoring the coupons, plus a coupon redemption procedure. Specialists are involved at each step in the process and most are hired from outside the client company.

Public Relations Departments and Agencies

Unlike advertising where most professionals work for an advertising agency, most public relations professionals work for the client, though public relations agencies exist and handle big assignments for major companies. Internally, a public relations department may counsel management about public opinion, crisis management, or employee relations. It may also prepare information and publicity materials about the company for an external audience. Almost every organization, firm, or nonprofit company, if it is any size at all, will have a public relations professional on staff to deal with company news, prepare brochures about the company or brand, and produce newsletters to keep all the company's key stakeholders informed. Companies that have their own public relations staff may also consult with public relations agencies about special problems or projects.

Public relations specialists may manage such areas as *corporate public relations, crisis management, media relations, financial relations* (communicating with the financial community), *public affairs* (working with government and the local community), and *marketing public relations* (MPR), which focuses specifically on publicity and other public relations activities for products. Specialists for these areas may be on a company's staff or they may be hired by outside general public relations agencies or agencies that specialize in areas such as financial relations.

Public relations, particularly MPR, plays a key role in an integrated communication program, so public relations professionals should be consulted and involved in IMC planning. These professionals often understand the importance of stakeholders and relationships more fully than other marketing professionals and thus contribute a great deal to a total communication program. Furthermore, because of their sensitivity to relationships and issue management, they are often effective change agents and can provide invaluable assistance to a company trying to organize for a more integrated communication program.

Direct Marketing Companies

More and more businesses have moved to direct forms of communication with their customers. As a result of advances in computer technology and electronic communication systems, direct marketing can occur through mail, video, telephone, and computers. In any of those media, a business can send a marketing message, sell, and deliver its products directly to the buyer without an intermediary reseller or retailer. In this respect direct marketing is more than just a marketing communication tool because it combines channels of communication with channels of distribution. However, it relies on other marketing communication tools such as advertising and direct mail, so it is usually discussed as a marketing communication activity.

Direct marketing specialists have copywriting, graphic design, and research skills that enable them to design a compelling offer powerful enough to move people to immediate action. These specialists manage mail order and broadcast offers through advertising and *infomercials* (longer advertisements that tell a more in-depth product story). They may also manage telemarketing, e-mail, and Internet offers. Finally, direct marketing experts also understand how to manage a system for fulfillment of an order.

Another type of direct marketing expert is one who can create and manage a sophisticated database. **Databases** are files of information that include names, addresses, telephone numbers, e-mail addresses, and demographic and buying behavior data. These files make it possible for a marketer to engage in a dialogue with those people thought most likely to be in the market for a certain product.

Historically, direct marketing was the first area of marketing communication to adopt the integrated philosophy. In fact, we could refer to this activity as *integrated direct marketing* because it uses other marketing communication tools to deliver its messages. Instead of treating each medium separately, integrated direct marketing seeks to achieve precise, synchronized use of the right medium at the right time with a measurable return on dollars spent.

An advertisement, for example, may be used to tell consumers how to obtain a company's catalog and to provide either an order coupon or a toll-free telephone number. Once the customer receives a catalog, that mailing may also contain a toll-free number that puts the consumer in direct contact with a salesperson who can answer questions or take an order. A phone call that follows a mailing or telephone inquiry is an effective step to increase response rates dramatically. Our example only integrates five forms of contact—an advertisement, a coupon sales promotion, a catalog, personal selling, and telemarketing—but shows how various forms of marketing communication can be combined for more effective direct marketing.

Sales Departments

Historically, many companies manage the sales and marketing departments separately. Even though personal sales is an extremely important part of a company's total communication package, rivalries often exist between marketing and sales. Sales representatives are separated from marketing and promotion staff not only by organizational charts but also by different viewpoints.

On the organizational chart, sales and marketing may report to top management through entirely different people. In such a situation, the only way that personal selling will be integrated with other aspects of marketing communication is through the concerted efforts of top management. The differing viewpoints often stem from the direct client contact that sales representatives have. An over-

p r o f i l e

Mike Hurt
Assistant Brand Manager for Coors Light
Coors Brewing Company

As assistant brand manager for a major billion-dollar brand, Mike Hurt participates in the development of almost all types of marketing communication for Coors Light. He participates in the development of television and radio commercials, print ads, outdoor advertising (such as billboards and transit promotions), new package designs for the brand, point-of-sales materials, and specially targeted communication programs such as Hispanic advertising. He also manages event marketing programs, such as sponsorships of NASCAR, Women's Pro Beach Volleyball, the U.S. Pro Ski Tour, and the Silver Bullets profes-

sional women's baseball team. He works with an outside marketing communication agency to develop new promotional concepts.

In addition to his marketing communication activities, Hurt is also responsible for coordinating many regional programs with the field sales group. Another challenging assignment is to develop new products and line extensions.

Academic Background

Hurt received his undergraduate degree in Business Administration/Marketing from Fort Lewis College in Durango, Colorado, in 1991. His minor was in mass

statement or inaccuracy in a marketing communication message (an ad promises delivery of products by December 1, but they don't arrive until December 21) or failure to support a sales effort puts the sales and marketing teams at odds. Why? Salespeople take the heat from clients for what clients perceive to be a marketing mistake.

Obviously the two functions complement each other and should work closely together. For example, salespeople work on the front line so they can find out what customers need and want in a more personal way than marketing research can. This information should be shared with the marketing people. The marketing people, in return, provide the information and sales materials (product literature, consumer research data, brand profile information) used by the sales representatives. If the materials don't work, then salespeople need to inform marketing. For the most effective marketing and selling, both groups need to share information continually at the planning and implementation stages.

The different types of salespeople include clerks in retail stores, door-to-door sales representatives such as Avon salespeople, business-to-business sales representatives, and salespeople such as those who operate both "upstream," selling sup-

communication/journalism. During his undergraduate days he worked as sports director for a radio station, giving play-by-play coverage of football and men's and women's basketball, and worked as a disc jockey on a weekly radio show. In addition, he gave ski lessons, did some construction work, and worked in a restaurant.

He entered the University of Colorado Integrated Marketing Communication (IMC) master's program, graduating in 1993. During his graduate work, the experience that contributed most to his career search was an IMC project that he completed at Coors as part of his graduate studies.

Career Track

Hurt's first full-time job after receiving his master's degree was with Coors as a marketing assistant. He used market research and data analysis skills in addition to his brand management responsibilities. He was named assistant brand manager in 1995.

Advice

"Get any type of experience you can—work, internships—any type of exposure to the workplace will help tremendously when trying to land that first job." Hurt explains, "A college degree guarantees you nothing today. It doesn't guarantee you a standard of living, a salary, or even a job. A college degree is nothing more than the cost of entry into the workplace." His final point is that, "while it is important to know where you want to go, it is also important to have fun getting there."

Typical Day

In Hurt's words, "A typical day revolves around one activity: problem solving. Not only are we trying to solve problems in the marketplace, but we're trying to solve internal problems too. People in brand management need a wide breadth of knowledge and are 'generalists' rather than 'specialists.' It is not uncommon to have days where you not only deal with an outside agency developing programs and evaluating creative work, but you may also spend significant amounts of time with any number of departments—legal, finance, pricing, forecasting, consumer research, operations, packaging, research and development, logistics, scheduling, customer service, and sales. As a result, someone in brand management has to have a working knowledge of these areas to add value and to help solve the problems that inevitably occur."

plies *to IBM,* for instance, and "downstream," selling IBM products *to their customers.*

Retail salespeople are employees of a retail business who sell products to customers and are trained and managed by the retailer. Salespeople at the Gap are an example. Often retail salespeople work on commission, receiving a percentage of the sales they bring in. The commission system is thought to motivate salespeople to work harder. More recently, however, companies like Saturn have moved away from commissions to focus on pleasing customers whatever their needs rather than making the highest priced sale possible. This shift has taken a lot of the "pushiness" out of the customer-sales relationship and made it more possible for the sales representative to be a consultant.

Business-to-business companies operate with either a salaried sales staff that works for the company or independent salespeople who sell the product on behalf of the company, such as independent insurance agents. Independent agents may offer a full line of products and sometimes the products may compete. Obviously an in-house sales force is easier to manage from a communication standpoint than is an outside sales team.

Either way, sales representatives who cover territories away from headquarters are constantly challenged to keep up with information about products and the company's marketing communication programs. Often, regional sales managers are used as intermediaries to help with coordination. An organization in which a sales representative reports to a regional sales manager who in turn reports to a director of sales at headquarters is referred to as a *line organization*.

Multi-brand companies further complicate the communication problem. In some large companies, sales representatives report both to brand sales managers (usually at headquarters) and geographic managers (country, district, or regional), who are in charge of sales in their areas. This arrangement is referred to as a *matrix organization*.

In addition to managers and sales representatives, large sales organizations may also have support staff such as researchers and market forecasters, people who manage leads generated by the sales staff and by others in the company; database experts, people who specialize in developing sales presentation materials; and trainers. These support personnel will usually be located at headquarters but may spend a lot of time on the road visiting regions or districts.

Integrating personal selling with the rest of the marketing communication program is difficult for a number of reasons, including the separation between sales and marketing. The task and the problems of personal selling primarily involve interpersonal relations and communication between salespeople and their customers, salespeople and their supervisors, and salespeople and other departments in the organization.

Because salespeople have the most direct and personal contact with customers, they must understand and buy into the company's communication objectives, or the company runs the risk of an ineffective marketing communication program. This understanding and belief is especially critical in industrial selling, where sales is the key method of marketing. A roundtable of high-level business executives concluded that marketing and sales must be more integrated or companies would "pay the price in the 21st century."

Event Organizers

Event marketing involves both consumer and trade participation. Trade members help produce and promote events, and consumers attend the events as do some trade members. In fact, many companies use event sponsorships as a way to develop reward systems for their employees who are invited to attend free if they reach certain goals, such as sales goals or customer contacts.

Events are often planned as part of some other program, such as a sales promotion or a public relations campaign. For that reason special events and event marketing overlap with other areas. For example, a special event such as an open house almost certainly will be handled by public relations. In contrast, a company-sponsored competition, such as José Cuervo's sponsorship of one-on-one volleyball, might be handled by either the marketing or sales promotion department.

Regardless of who is in charge, the problem is the same—details, details, details. Event management companies that have developed systems for running complex activities are often hired to plan and manage the event. The event companies, in turn, may hire agencies or freelancers to handle the event advertising and other services such as security, catering, and publicity. The tasks of finding locations, negotiating with other sponsors, producing and receiving registration materials, arranging for equipment needed at the event, handling crowd control, and arranging for prizes can be handled internally though many are farmed out.

Packaging and Design Firms

Major companies rarely maintain their own designers, though they often use design firms. The most important corporate design element is the company's **logo,** which is the imprint that is used for immediate identification. Many thousands of dollars are spent creating and revising logos. In addition to logo design, corporate stationery and signage are also the focus of designers who try to make a company's appearance dovetail with its mission and corporate culture. Even delivery trucks and physical spaces like lobbies are part of the total corporate design package. Usually a company will turn to external agencies that specialize in corporate design and logo design for these kinds of projects.

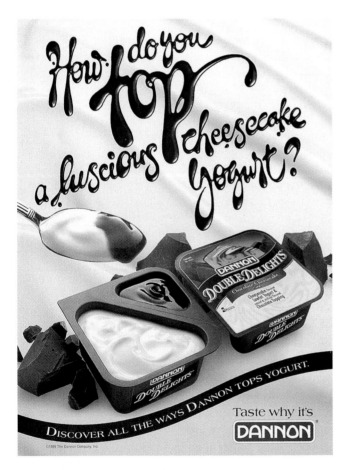

This Dannon dessert package container does more than protect the product. It offers an enticing image of chocolate cheesecake—without the crust—and suggests that an elegant, indulgent experience awaits those who eat this chocolate yogurt blend.

Another important graphic design area is the product's *package*. We mentioned in Chapter 2 that packaging can serve two functions: 1) containing and protecting the product and 2) communicating a marketing message to consumers at the point of purchase. Most companies prefer to use packaging design firms instead of keeping packaging specialists on staff. External design consultants keep busy creating, refining, and redesigning product packages for many different clients because packages are constantly changing.

Concept Review

ORGANIZING TO USE MARKETING COMMUNICATION ACTIVITIES

There are a number of ways to organize marketing communication tools.

1. Advertising agencies that are full-service include account managers, researchers and account planners, creative staff, media planners and buyers, and traffic managers.
2. Sales promotion people plan and implement programs for consumer and trade audiences.
3. Public relations is usually organized as a department within a business, though outside agencies exist. The PR staff can counsel management or communicate about company issues to an external audience, such as the government or financial stakeholders.
4. Direct marketing uses a variety of methods to deliver messages and fulfill orders, a fact that makes it one of the first marketing communication areas to adopt an integrated organizational strategy.
5. Personal sales is often managed by departments separate from marketing, which is one reason why it is hard to integrate the efforts of the two.
6. Events are handled both by marketing and public relations staffs, as well as by people and companies who specialize in handling all the details involved in producing events.
7. Packaging and design staffs are concerned with the physical presentation of the brand, the product, and the company.

THE IMC ORGANIZATION

You now have reached a point where you should understand the concept of integration, problems incorporating it into the structure of an organization, and the elements of traditional marketing communication organizations. Let's look now at the organizational dimensions of a business that uses IMC.

Integrating marketing communication usually begins with a system-wide restructuring of marketing communication activities. This restructuring is based on the observation that most internal activities (employee relations and customer service, for example) are not usually considered part of the marketing communication mix. Author Dan Logan has proposed that IMC is a process of understanding the targeted customer and applying IMC to all marketing functions.[11] In other words, integration requires participation by all parts of the company that affect the customer. At this level, integration must reflect a shared corporate vision as well as an organizational structure that makes it possible for all departments and divisions to share information and strategies.

IMC firms have experimented with two ways to organize for IMC—top-down management and cross-functional teams. Some experts proposed that a "communication czar," who has the power and authority to control various marketing communication programs, manage the integration. This approach is referred to as **top-down management.** Although this is one way to organize for a tightly controlled program, research by experts such as Anders Gronstedt have focused on approaches that involve various stakeholders in partnerships or teams, an organizational approach referred to as a **bottom-up approach.**[12] Gronstedt found that the most effective communication management took place in companies using a bottom-up approach where managers were in close contact daily with customers and other stakeholders and where cross-functional teams were used to coordinate across functions or boundaries. **Cross-functional management,** also referred to as *boundary spanning,* is a process by which teams oversee "horizontal functions," such as PR, sales promotion, packaging, and so forth. In employing IMC, for example, maintaining brand image, corporate reputation, and product quality could be cross-functional objectives.

A problem with using an outside agency to manage an IMC program is that most agencies don't have expertise in all the areas of marketing communication tools that must be integrated. One solution to the specialization problem is to adopt a **general contractor** approach, a solution pioneered by the Interpublic Group. For a fee, an Interpublic agency will develop an overall strategy and retain outside specialist agencies needed to carry out the plan.[13] BBDO used a similar approach with its Gillette account, both in the introduction of the "Best a Man Can Get" slogan and repositioning campaign and in the launch of the Sensor razor. BBDO acted as a general contractor and worked in partnership with its sister agencies, Porter/Novelli, the public relations specialist, and Rapp & Collins for the direct marketing program.

Smaller agencies without the resources of giant conglomerates like Interpublic can compete for IMC business through strategic alliances. **Strategic alliances** are agreements between firms of different marketing specialties to complement each others' services and provide referrals. Experience with strategic alliances at the Price/McNabb advertising agency has taught agency chairperson Charles R. Price, Jr., "that we need to have established relationships with more than one specialist company in a field." Of all the approaches to IMC, the general contractor approach is the most common.[14]

Concept Review

THE IMC ORGANIZATION

An IMC organization often requires system-wide restructuring through the following three tactics:

- information sharing
- cross-functional management
- organizational alliances

A CLOSING THOUGHT: PUTTING THE PRESS ON BAD PRESS

Errant departments and divisions can create marketing communication problems. Public relations personnel are particularly concerned about the damage that advertising and promotional planning errors can cause. Sales promotion, for example, can sometimes set up poorly planned programs that harm the company's image. To illustrate, Kraft's sales promotion division held a sweepstakes contest in which a printing error on the entry forms led to many thousands of winners. The company had to endure bad press plus a substantial cost to buy out unhappy winners.

This incident reflects sloppy planning, but it also reflects a lack of coordination from one marketing unit to another. Public relations professionals are skilled at identifying potential crisis situations and should be involved in all these planning sessions to help avoid unwanted negative repercussions. In many companies lawyers have taken over this role, but even though they are very much concerned about legal liability, they seldom concern themselves with the negative communication impact of poorly designed marketing communication programs.

SUMMARY

1. Explain how the organization of a business affects marketing communication.

The structure of an organization can have tremendous implications for marketing communication because the dynamics of moving to integrated marketing communication often require changes in the organization of the business. The most effective way to integrate marketing communication is to start by integrating the entire marketing area and all the communication functions in cross-functional teams.

2. Distinguish between integrated marketing and integrated marketing communication.

Integrated marketing means that all managers share a corporate vision and an organizational structure that make it possible for departments and divisions to exchange information and participate in joint planning. Integrated marketing tries to coordinate *all* messages sent by a company or brand. In contrast, *integrated marketing communication* refers only to the strategic coordination of the planned marketing communication areas such

as advertising, sales promotion, public relations, direct marketing, packaging, telemarketing, event marketing, and so on.

3. Discuss the development of integrated marketing and why some firms have trouble implementing it.

As businesses rely on more specialists, organizational structures must encourage coordination. Problems that make implementation difficult include turf battles and fear of encroachment.

4. Describe the typical organizational elements in a marketing communication program.

The organizational components that are part of most marketing communication typically include internal departments, in-house agencies, external agencies, and freelancers. Each marketing communication activity, such as public relations and sales promotion, requires people with different skills who can plan, implement, and evaluate their communication.

5. Outline the characteristics of an IMC organization.

Generally, organizations that have integrated communication programs either use a top-down approach with a communication coordinator to oversee the efforts or a bottom-up approach that involves people in cross-functional planning and monitoring teams. The bottom-up approach is more common. IMC agencies tend to operate as "general contractors," working directly with the client and hiring specialist agencies to work as part of the marketing communication team under the direction of the IMC agency.

POINTS TO PONDER

Review the Facts

1. Identify the different levels in a company where coordinated planning needs to occur.
2. Who typically manages the various marketing activities in a company's marketing program? What are their job titles and what do they do?
3. What does reengineering mean? How does it relate to integrated marketing communication programs?
4. What is infringement, and why does it create a problem for organizations trying to move into IMC?

Master the Concepts

5. How does cross-functional management differ from top-down and bottom-up management approaches? Do you think one management approach is more effective than the other? Explain.
6. Explain the different models discussed here for managing external agencies.
7. What are the primary problems encountered in reorganizing a marketing communication program? Can you think of any other problems that might arise? Explain.

Apply Your Knowledge

8. Find an organizational chart, either in a textbook or from a company that you have connections with, and analyze whether it looks like the company is using a top-down or bottom-up approach to organization.
9. Find a company that uses cross-functional management teams and interview people who have worked in that environment. Find out what those people think about planning and decision making in this type of organization. Do they view the cross-functional approach as more or less effective than a traditional organization?
10. Interview a person who works in sales. How does the sales department work with the company's marketing department? Are the relationships good or are there problems in the coordination of these two functions?

SUGGESTED PROJECTS

1. (Writing Project) Interview a senior marketing manager in a company to discuss who is involved in marketing and what they do. Be sure to find out what really happens, not what's supposed to happen according to the business organizational chart. Based on your interview, draw a map of the organization showing where marketing and marketing communication fit in the company structure. Also, write a brief memo that explains who is responsible for marketing communication and what that person does.

2. (Oral Communication) Interview a senior manager in some type of marketing communication agency and determine if the agency is involved in any cross-functional activities. If so, what are those

activities? Also, what type of organizational model does the agency represent? Prepare a brief (five minute) oral presentation of your findings for the class.

3. (Internet Project) Visit the sites of at least two marketing communication companies. Search the sites to see whether the company is organized for or engaged in integrated marketing communication. Two sites that you may want to visit include:

Saatchi & Saatchi Ltd.	www.saatchibuscomm.com
J. Walter Thompson	www.jwtworld.com

CASE 3: DIVERSIFIED SERVICES

Many advertising agencies have developed alliances with other professional agencies specializing in areas such as sales promotion and direct marketing. London-based Saatchi & Saatchi, for example, bought a number of specialized companies in the United States in the 1980s in an attempt to set up a broad-based consulting system. Unfortunately, in the face of continued economic downturns, Saatchi had to sell off many of its associated firms.

One company that has managed to construct an organization system is Omnicom Group's Diversified Agency Services (DAS) unit. Omnicom is a holding company that includes a number of large advertising agencies and a group of marketing services firms that specialize in other marketing communication areas. DAS was created as an afterthought in the mid-1980s as a mix of marketing service companies and small agencies. Lacking any serious commitment from the holding company, DAS almost went under during those initial years.

Now generating $650 million annually, DAS is Omnicom's largest domestic unit, bigger than any of the advertising agencies in the group such as BBDO, DDB Needham, TBWA, and Chiat/Day. This is in keeping with estimates by financial analysts that 67 percent of all marketing dollars now go to marketing services, called "below-the-line" companies and operations, and only 33 percent for the high-profile media advertising. The new director of DAS, John Wren, assumes the role of a corporate diplomat in working out the turf battles and rivalries within Omnicom. Although DAS is the fastest growing unit, 70 percent of Omnicom's business still comes from the advertising agencies, and Wren admits that "we are still a premier advertising company."

No one would have predicted such success for DAS, a division many had written off after its formation in 1986. At that time, there was a lot of duplication within the company and it was seen as a place for operations—and people—"that no one knew what to do with," according to one of the agency presidents. That all changed in 1990 when the Omnicom CEO also became chief executive of DAS and threw the weight of his support behind the struggling DAS operation. Of the 26 companies at the time, 15 were divested or folded into other parts of Omnicom.

Since then, DAS has been rebuilt with a mission. The division now has 21 operating areas, comprising 45 companies. Its five largest companies are direct marketer Rapp Collins Worldwide, PR firm Porter/Novelli, recruitment advertiser Bernard Hodes, a health and medical communication group, and the Thomas A. Schutz merchandising specialist firm. In addition, DAS includes special integrated agencies designed to handle premier accounts, such as Focus GTE which handled its GTE account. Other DAS-shared accounts include Gillette and Hyatt.

Described by *Adweek* as representing the future of advertising, DAS is able to create integrated and interactive marketing programs that support and may some day supplant traditional mass media–based advertising. But organization and management of such an operation are very much still in the learning stage. DAS, however, is leading the curve.

Case Questions
1. How does DAS differ from traditional advertising companies?
2. What changes had to be made to make DAS a success?
3. Why do you believe DAS is the fastest growing business unit in Omnicom?

Source: Noreen O'Leary, "The Successor," *Adweek*, July 24, 1995, 30–36.

ROMA'S LITE INTEGRATED CASE QUESTIONS

(Review the Roma's Lite Marketing Plan in the Appendix at the end of the text before answering these questions.)

1. Outline an organizational structure for the marketing department that will manage the launch of Roma's Lite Pizza as an integrated marketing effort.

2. Would you recommend that the company handle the advertising for Roma's launch through an in-house agency or through an outside agency? Explain and justify your reasoning.

3. How should the marketing communication effort be organized for the Roma's Lite Pizza launch?

chapter

4

Marketing Communication Strategy and Planning

1 **Describe the critical decisions determined through strategic planning.**

2 **Explain the elements of the marketing plan and how they reflect marketing strategy.**

3 **Analyze the hierarchy of effects models and relate them to marketing communication planning.**

4 **Describe the marketing communication plan and the marketing communication planning process.**

5 **Evaluate the strategic implications of IMC planning.**

CONSIDER this

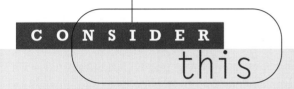

Healthy Choice Based on a Healthy Strategy

Research, planning, and implementation—a healthy strategy for a healthy company. In the ten years since its inception, Healthy Choice has grown to close to $1.5 billion in annual retail sales, expanded its product line from 14 to more than 300 products, and has 80 percent consumer awareness. Its Web site (www. healthychoice.com) has more than a million page views a week from consumers who want information or free product coupons. In 1996 alone, Healthy Choice introduced Healthy Choice Microwave Popcorn, Healthy Choice Bread, Hearty Handfuls (six hot pocket sandwiches), Healthy Choice Special Creations (10 ice cream flavors), Healthy Choice Breakfast Sausage, line extensions that include five frozen meals, and a new line of cookies in collaboration with Nabisco Brands, Inc.

How did the Healthy Choice low-calorie, sodium-controlled frozen food line become so prominent? After the heart attack of Mike Harper, chairperson of food industry leader ConAgra, Healthy Choice was developed to counter the cholesterol problems. It also hoped to draw a health-conscious market of people who had few good-tasting choices in the frozen food market. The decision to introduce Healthy Choice, however, was not based on the whim of the CEO. Research conducted in 1985 to 1988 showed a clear opportunity for a new growth segment. According to the research, 20 percent of Americans were restricted dieters, and a surprising 30 percent were so-called health-conscious eaters.

Research also showed that Healthy Choice had to taste good to succeed. "The product needed to deliver on taste to make it mainstream," explains Mike Trautschold, president, ConAgra Brands, Inc. Extensive test-marketing of the entire line in 18 test markets and careful strategic positioning ensured the product would be perceived as food that tastes good as well as food that lowers the risk of heart attacks.

A public relations campaign set the stage for Healthy Choice's rapid national rollout. Public relations agency Hill and Knowlton exhibited Healthy Choice at health conventions and sent mailings to dietitians informing them of the new product's benefits. The PR agency staged a national press conference in New York, where Mike Harper talked about his heart attack and how his wife was able to make his sodium-controlled diet interesting. By the time it achieved national distribution, word of mouth was rampant. The PR campaign was backed with carefully targeted advertising.

Although plagued by tight freezer space, food stores either enlarged their frozen sections or dropped poor sellers to add the new line. ConAgra's suggested price points—two dinners for five dollars and entrees under two dollars—were accepted by the trade and successful with consumers.

ConAgra hoped to get 5 percent to 7 percent of the frozen-dinner segment during the first year. Within seven months of its introduction, the green-boxed 14-item line grabbed a 25 percent share. Trautschold sums up the reason for this initial success as follows: "Every detail was thoroughly planned. We were on strategy at all times. Our packaging, advertising, and communication defined us as a unique new product, and the retail community was very aware how health conscious the consumer has become."

Sources: "ConAgra Products Named the Best of 1995," *PRNewswire,* May 2, 1996; "What's on the Menu at the Healthy Choice Web Site," *PRNewswire,* December 21, 1995; "Healthy Choice 'Sea of Green' Makes New Waves with Popcorn and Bread," *PRNewswire,* October 25, 1995; Pamela Ellis-Simons, "One from the Heart," *Marketing and Media Decisions* (March 1990): 32–6.

CHAPTER OVERVIEW

The Healthy Choice example demonstrates that a good idea, supported with effective planning and strategic implementation, greatly increases the chances of success. In this chapter we will discuss strategic planning in a marketing program as well as strategic planning for marketing communication. Then we will review the nine steps in marketing communication planning and the specific dimensions of IMC planning that distinguish it from other types of marketing communication planning.

STRATEGIC PLANNING

Marketing communication managers know that marketing communication is just one piece of the larger business plan. Careful business planning is a crucial survival tool, and the quality of the marketing communication plan can be no better than the quality of the business plan and the strategic planning that guides it. **Strategic planning** is the process of developing and maintaining a viable fit between the organization's objectives, its resources, and its changing market opportunities. The purpose of this process is to produce satisfactory profits and growth, given the company's mission.

In general, strategic planning guides three critical types of decisions: It identifies *objectives* (a statement of what the plan is intended to accomplish), decides on *strategies* (an outline of how to accomplish objectives), and implements the *tactics* (the short-term decisions about specific, tangible tasks that make sure strategies are realized).

To illustrate, consider the Healthy Choice objective to establish and then increase its market share in the specialty food market. To achieve that objective, its strategic plan was to introduce five new types of low-fat cookies in a joint venture with Nabisco Brands, Inc. The tactics included decisions to price the cookies at $2.49 per package, start with five flavors, introduce the product in the northeast, maintain the familiar green packaging, develop several TV commercials to announce the cookies, distribute coupon inserts in Sunday newspapers, and develop special point-of-sale material.

MARKETING RESEARCH

Marketing research is essential for informed strategic decisions. Planning is based on information; information is collected through formal research and informal scanning of the environment. **Marketing intelligence** is information from internal or external sources that is useful in developing the marketing strategy.

A systematic research process is used to collect **secondary information** (information that already exists, such as census data) and **primary information** (information collected for the first time) about the market environment, the consumer, and how the consumer responds to elements of the marketing mix. Determining the positive and negative opinions and attitudes of consumers is crucial. For instance, Biofoam, a young Phoenix-based company that produces an all-natural biodegradable packing material, used research to learn about consumer

Biofoam learned that consumers were concerned about polystyrene packing material and developed an ecologically safe alternative. Such responsiveness can only happen if the company has a research program in place to capture consumer comments, attitudes, and behaviors.

attitudes, though its research took an unexpected turn. The founders were researching new snack foods for the Hispanic market when they stumbled on this "puffed," ecologically safe packing material that competes with foam peanuts made of polystyrene. The packing material is even edible!

Concept ✓ **Review**

STRATEGIC PLANNING AND MARKETING RESEARCH

1. To be successful, every business must engage in strategic planning, which is the process of developing and maintaining a viable fit between the organization's objectives, its resources, and its changing market opportunities.
2. Strategic planning forces decision makers to determine objectives, strategies, and tactics.
3. Marketing research is essential to strategic planning. Market researchers collect market intelligence—information that is useful in developing the marketing strategy.

THE MARKETING PLAN

The marketing plan has to be consistent with and support the company's overall business plan and mission. Recall from Chapter 2 that the business mission states the company's overall core goals, as well as the type and scope of its business. The business plan, which guides the marketing plan, is based on an in-depth understanding of the firm's market environment—the industry, the economy, and society—with special focus on competitors and customers. The business plan deals primarily with projecting sales and profits and indicates alternative actions if projected sales are less than actual sales.

Let's look again at Biofoam. A key part of Biofoam's mission is to succeed in the marketplace with a product that allows customers to be environmentally responsible about their use of packing material without having to pay more or sacrifice convenience. Biofoam's business plan projects sales revenues of $80 million by 2000 (up from $2.5 million in 1996), and pretax profits of close to 30 percent.[1] The Biofoam company mission and business plan dovetail—the plan projections indicate that the business will succeed because of its biodegradable packing product.

At some point in the strategic planning process, the company's director of marketing meets with the chief executive officer to offer input about what business goals are relevant to the marketing team. Such goals as increasing sales or market share or moving into a new market require marketing involvement. For example, to increase the speed with which Biofoam is available (and therefore increase sales), the company installs production equipment at large customers' business locations so the Biofoam materials can be manufactured on site. This distribution strategy required marketing's input.

Once it is determined that marketing is crucial to reach certain corporate goals, the marketing director's next task is designing a marketing plan. The **marketing plan** is the central instrument for directing and coordinating the marketing effort.

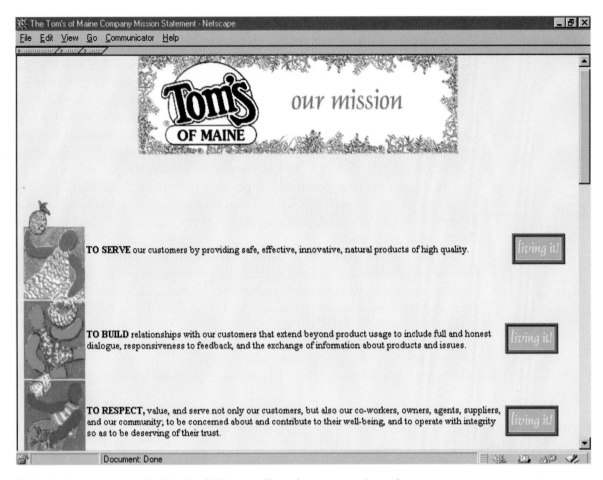

This mission statement for Tom's of Maine outlines the company's goals.

It consists of a situation analysis that summarizes research into the marketing environment, basic decisions on marketing objectives, the marketing mix strategy and implementation tactics, and the total marketing expenditures and marketing allocations. As shown in Figure 4.1, the seven steps in the marketing planning process parallel the stages used to develop the overall business plan.

FIGURE 4.1

Steps in the Marketing Planning Process

Situation Analysis

Managers use research findings to develop the **situation analysis,** a section of the marketing plan that identifies and appraises all environmental factors that affect the marketing program. Table 4.1 summarizes the major parts of the situation analysis, such as an analysis of the company's strengths and weaknesses; the competitive situation; an assessment of the behavior of consumers in choosing and using the product; and environmental factors, including the economy and the political situation. ConAgra, for example, spent three years researching the trends in health awareness before the company began the Healthy Choice product development. Customers' complaints and suggestions identified the market opportunity. For example, hundreds of male consumers told ConAgra researchers that none of the existing so-called healthy frozen entrees tasted good, and that their choices were very limited.

The point of analyzing the marketing situation is to determine how it positively or negatively impacts strategy. A technique for this analysis is called a **SWOT analysis** (Strengths, Weaknesses, Opportunities, Threats). Let's look again at Biofoam and see how it might conduct a SWOT analysis. Biofoam's strengths and opportunities include a demand for an environment-friendly packing product of high quality. Also, Biofoam's product, unlike competitors' biodegradable packing products, is as cost effective as traditional foam peanuts. In fact, it is currently the only "green" alternative to foam peanuts that competes on price. Some weak-

---

TABLE 4.1

Parts of the Situation Analysis

In general, the situation assessment contains the following types of information:

The Market Situation:

descriptive information about the target market(s), changes in those markets, and anticipated changes

The Product Situation:

information on the sales, prices, profit margins, and market share of each product

The Competitive Situation:

descriptive information about all major competitors and potential competitors, including size, sales, market share, profitability, growth, and so forth

The Distribution Situation:

information that describes each channel of distribution used, especially information that relates to sales and profitability

The Macroenvironment Situation:

information about broad macroenvironment trends—demographic, economic, technological, political, legal, sociocultural—that bears on the product's future

nesses and threats in its market include the efforts of the polystyrene industry to be more environmentally responsible by setting up peanut recycling programs. Also, Biofoam is a relatively small company compared with most competitors who are heavy-hitters—such as oil companies and chemical producers. Its competitors, then, can afford to be aggressive. In fact, Warner-Lambert sued the company for patent infringement. In response, Biofoam claimed the suit was an attempt to intimidate customers and drive the company out of business.[2]

Marketing Objectives

Delineating specific marketing objectives is really a two-step process. It begins with the company's financial objectives. Profitability, return on investment, and cash flow are the most common elements. The financial objectives are then converted into marketing objectives. For example, if a company wants to earn a profit of $1.5 million and has a profit margin of 10 percent, the company must earn $15 million in sales revenue ($15 million $\times$ 0.10 = $1.5 million). If the price of each product is $200, it must sell 75,000 units—a 5-percent market share.

All these numbers reflect explicit marketing objectives, but they also suggest implicit objectives. For example, to achieve these goals the company determines it will need 8-percent growth from the target market. Based on experience and the situation analysis, the marketing director knows such growth will require a 12-percent expansion of channel outlets. Of course, in turn, all of these goals have implications for marketing communication objectives.

Marketing Strategies

When considering a strategic plan, we must realize that a strategy is not a standardized, fixed path that all marketers follow. **Marketing strategy** is the process of evaluating the options for achieving the marketing goals. An 8-percent growth in sales, for example, might be accomplished by reducing the price, offering coupons, increasing outlets, or increasing mass advertising. By looking at the options for attaining each objective, the marketing manager can identify the major strategy alternatives.

As a first step in developing a marketing strategy, however, marketers need to develop a **market strategy**—a strategy that identifies how the marketers will approach the market. A **market** is an aggregate of people who, as individuals or organizations, have needs for products and have the ability, willingness, and authority to purchase the product. Consumers in a market are seldom uniform and often have different needs and wants. Consequently, marketers must decide whether to treat their market as **homogeneous**—that is, as a single, large unit—or as **heterogeneous,** a market composed of separate, smaller groups known as *segments.*

Deciding that the market is homogeneous leads to a **market aggregation strategy** in which marketers promote a single product through a single marketing program designed to reach as many customers as possible. At one point in its history, Coca-Cola viewed the entire U.S. cola soft drink market as homogeneous. It only made one flavor and communicated one message. Today, Coca-Cola has changed its view and expanded its product line to include new flavors, with varying caffeine and sugar content. It also uses different communication strategies for each market segment.

profile

Mary Breslin
Assistant Product Manager on Iced Tea
Celestial Seasonings

Mary Breslin is responsible for the $2 million budget to promote, advertise, and market Celestial Seasoning's Iced Tea line. Marketing this line involves the following:

- Developing and executing marketing communication plans
- Evaluating and managing vendors, including negotiating contracts
- Forecasting regional market product lines and channel mix
- Preparing and presenting monthly market analysis to upper management based on information from consumption and shipment databases
- Managing the Iced Tea Team, which includes managers in sales, finance, operations, and R&D
- Developing and executing the creative strategy

Academic Background

A native of the Chicago area, Breslin graduated from Barrington High School in 1987. She did her undergraduate work at the University of Kansas, graduating with a B.S. in Journalism/Advertising in 1991. She then attended the University of Colorado, where she received a Masters in the Integrated Marketing Communication (IMC) program in 1993.

Internships were an important part of her training. While attending the University of Kansas, she worked during her sophomore year as a paste-up artist for the Sunflower Group in Kansas City. This experience allowed her to become proficient in the print production process and gave her a better understanding of layout and design.

After graduating from the University of Kansas, she had an internship at Leo Burnett Advertising in Chicago. She worked in the art-buying department, which hires the talent needed to produce advertisements. She would locate portfolios, models, voice narrators, painters, or illustrators and make a recommendation to the art director.

Few examples of homogeneous markets exist. Even utilities such as electricity, gas, water, and telephone have different strategies for consumer and business customers. Often a company takes a homogeneous approach simply because it does not have the resources to create a number of different strategies.

A more common approach to the market is to assume it is heterogeneous, which leads to a **market segmentation strategy**—a strategy in which marketers divide the market into several market segments. From these segments, the marketer identifies, evaluates, and selects target markets based on similarities of needs. Deciding that the market is heterogeneous also leads to what is called **niche marketing,** an approach that assumes market segments exist that require customized strategies. For example, when Procter & Gamble decided to enter the juice drink market with Citrus Hill, strategists realized that juice drinks have sev-

The last semester of her graduate school at the University of Colorado, she competed for a highly sought-after internship in the marketing department of Celestial Seasonings, Inc., in Boulder. She worked 20 hours a week while finishing her graduate studies. She reported to the director of marketing for iced tea and assisted him with the launch of a new iced-tea line. After graduating, she continued in the internship position for another four months until she was offered a permanent position as marketing assistant.

Career Track

Breslin's first full-time job at Celestial Seasonings grew out of her internship. After a year as a marketing assistant, she became the national sales promotion manager. In this job she was the liaison between the outside sales force and the company. She was responsible for providing the sales force with everything they needed to sell products. After six months in that position, she was transferred back to the marketing department and was named the assistant product manager on iced tea, her current position.

Typical Day

Breslin has found that she never really has a typical day because she is continuously working with differ-

ent people on ever-changing products. But an example might look something like this:

- Today I worked with the creative department most of the morning proofing all of the sales materials on layout, composition, grammar. I also checked product specifications.
- I had lunch with a young woman who came to see me for an informational interview.
- I conducted an Iced Tea business review with my boss for the vice president of marketing.
- I worked on the new Iced Tea forecast and then attended a tea-tasting of our new iced-tea products.
- I spent the last few hours of my day returning e-mail and voice mail messages and getting ready for the next day.

Advice

In Breslin's view, internships are the best way to take a "test-drive" with a company. Not only can the company judge whether you are a valuable investment, but you can also see if the company is a "right fit" for you. Getting a good internship, however, requires that you be persistent and have a good attitude. She says, "If you work hard, ask questions and maintain the highest ethical standards, you can do anything you set your mind to. Don't listen to any negativity from people. Set your goal, get focused, and make it happen!"

eral segments including the sports segment, the kids segment, the health–conscious segment, and so forth. The 300 products now produced by Healthy Choice suggest that they have also followed a segmentation strategy.

Segmenting and Targeting the Market

There are lots of ways to segment a market. Perhaps the easiest way is to segment based on the reason the customer buys the product. The **consumer segment** buys the product for its own personal or household use. The **business segment** buys the product to use in its business or to make products. For instance, Biofoam sells in-plant manufacturing systems to a business market and sells the Biofoam product to both the business market and to the general public consumer market.

Both categories can be further segmented. Consumer segments, for instance, may be segmented by geography (regions such as the northeast or southern California), demographics (age, income, number of children), and usage level (heavy, moderate, light, non-user). Larger marketers also segment consumers based on perceived product benefits and *psychographics.*

Table 4.2 is a classic example of **benefit segmentation,** which groups consumers of toothpaste according to the benefits they seek from a product. This is a particularly useful approach because it leads to marketing communication strategies based on perceived benefits. Benefits, what a product can do for a user, are important pegs for communication strategies, but a communication planner must be able to identify which ones are most important to the consumer and which ones the product features. The intersection of the consumer's most important benefits with the product's most important features should be the focus of the marketing message.

Psychographics is segmentation based on clusters of shared human characteristics for a group of consumers. Those clusters may focus on lifestyle traits, attitudes, interests, and opinions or perceptions of product attributes. Generally, marketers who use psychographics produce a profile that combines several characteristics. Duncan Hines cake mixes, for example, offer the "time-conscious" segment a benefit with mixes that just add water, whereas the "quality-conscious" segment is attracted to the "supreme" mixes.

Industrial markets are further segmented by type of industry (metal mining, anthracite mining), end use (steel can be used for bridge construction, automo-

---

TABLE 4.2

Market Segments Based on Benefits Sought

Segment Names	Principal Benefit Sought	Demographic Strengths	Special Behavioral Characteristics	Personality Characteristics	Brands Disproportionately Favored
The Sensory Segment	Flavor, product appearance	Children	Users of spearmint-flavored toothpaste	High self-involvement	Colgate
The Sociables	Brightness of teeth	Teens, young people	Smokers	High sociability	Gleam/Ultrabrite
The Worriers	Decay prevention	Large families	Heavy users	High hypochondriasis	Crest
The Independent Segment	Price	Men	Heavy users	High autonomy	Brands on sale

Source: Adapted from Russell I. Haley, "Benefit Segmentation: A Decision-Oriented Research Tool," *Journal of Marketing* (July 1968): 33. From *Journal of Marketing,* published by the American Marketing Association. Reprinted by permission of the American Marketing Association.

biles, and building construction), size of purchase (dollars, units, weight), size and structure of the firm, or purchasing method (purchasing agents, buying centers, or committees). More will be said about industrial markets in Chapter 6.

One of the primary values of segmenting is that it reduces the waste associated with trying to reach the entire market. For example, ICI Australia is one of the leading agrochemical companies. Its products are sold through a network of distributors and resellers who have depended on traditional media advertising, especially radio in rural areas, to reach their prospects. ICI determined that this strategy was not effective in reaching its target market: farmers using over $3500 of chemicals annually. Instead, ICI decided to use direct marketing. The company wrote to more than 5000 farmers, asking them to tell ICI about themselves so that ICI could develop chemical products that would best serve their needs in the day-to-day running of their farms. Included in this letter was a free subscription to a magazine that ICI developed for the benefit of the farming market. The response rate to this letter was 30 percent, a staggering result in an industry where 2 percent is the norm.

One-on-One Marketing

In the extreme a strategy of market segmentation may develop a different marketing program for each potential customer. In a one-on-one strategy, companies develop custom products—from concierge services to prescription eyeware to specialized utility trucks—that are developed for one customer. For example, to satisfy Hallmark's demand for quality production, a German company specially designed its presses to meet Hallmark's specifications. Thanks to new technology, especially customer databases, it is both possible and profitable to create a marketing mix for an individual customer. A bicycle company in Japan, for example, custom builds its line of bikes to the physical specifications of each customer. The bikes are assembled and delivered within days after the customer places the order. Capitol Concierge, a Washington, D.C., service, sets up concierges in office-building lobbies. The concierges provide personal and business services to each of the building's clients.

Target Market Selection

Not all market segments are viable target markets. In the ICI example, the target market was a rural farmer using $3500 or more chemicals each year, not just every farmer. In evaluating different market segments, marketers must find answers to several questions, as identified in Table 4.3.

Competitive Strategies

Regardless of whether marketers follow a homogeneous approach or a segmentation approach, or have one or several target markets, they must differentiate their products from those offered by the competition. In this section we will look at product differentiation, product positioning, and branding as general strategic approaches that help a company separate itself and its products from the competition.

Product Differentiation

The process of creating a difference in the mind of the consumer for your product compared to other products is called **product differentiation.** Product differences may be tangible elements such as color, size, choices, or quality of

T A B L E   4 . 3

Evaluating Target Market Segments

- Is the potential market segment the right size and does it have the necessary growth characteristics?

- Does the segment have sufficient long-term profitability? Considerations include: the threat that the segment has too many competitors, the threat of a new competitor, the threat of substitute products, the threat that the power of buyers becomes oppressive, or the threat that the power of suppliers becomes oppressive.

- Does the segment correspond with the company's objectives and resources?

- If selecting more than one segment as target markets, are these segments complementary in respect to cost, performance, and technology?

Source: Philip Kotler, *Marketing Management: Analysis, Planning, Implementation, and Control*, 8th ed. (Englewood Cliffs, N.J.: Prentice-Hall, Inc.), 1994, 281–283.

materials or services. The problem with differences based on tangible elements is that, as new technologies emerge, competitors can copy or imitate tangible features easily and cheaply. Thus, marketers increasingly try to create intangible differences in the mind of the customer. Mass advertising, especially television commercials, are an excellent means to create intangible differences through the use of images, spokespeople, testimonials, and product demonstration.

Even in the case of homogeneous markets, such as industrial chemicals where the government dictates that the products must be identical, marketers compete on the basis of intangibles such as speed of delivery, maintenance, warranties, and return policy. Siemens, the largest utility company in Western Europe, is famous for its "7-day-a-week–24-hour-a-day" customer service. These intangible product elements are also referred to as **value-added** components. Sales promotion is an ideal way to deliver added value through coupons, rebates, product sampling, discounts, and toll-free numbers.

Product Positioning

A **position** is the image that the product projects relative to images presented by both competitive products and other products marketed by the same company. The consumer behavior discussion in Chapters 5 and 6 will describe many factors that provide the basis for positioning decisions.

Stated simply, positioning is how you want the customer to view your product compared to the competition. **Product positioning** is the process of identifying the most important beliefs, attitudes, and product-use habits of the customer; assessing how the marketer's product is perceived relative to these factors; and then placing the product in its most advantageous light.

A positioning strategy incorporates what is known about the environment, the target market, and the product differentiation. In the case of Rolls Royce, the position is created through elegant showrooms, knowledgeable salespeople, exceptional service, print advertising in very upscale magazines, little talk of price, and a very high-priced car. Kmart maintains a good-value-for-money position through

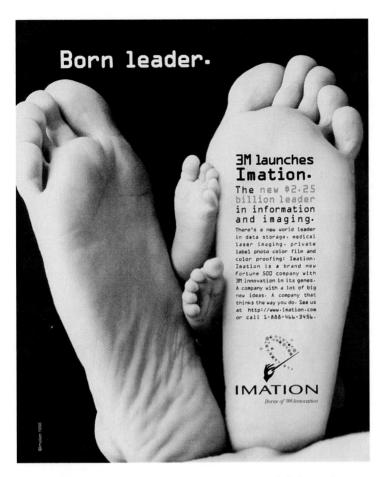

This Imation Corp. ad introducing the company's information and imaging products and services ran in 21 languages in countries around the world. The ad clearly positions the company—a spin-off of several 3M technology, publishing, and imaging divisions—as a worldwide industry leader.

mass advertising that emphasizes low prices for name-brand merchandise. A great many of the intangible elements representing a product's position are delivered through the marketing communication effort. Jell-O tells us that "Jell-O is fun"; Allstate Insurance insists that "You are in good hands with Allstate."

Before a product position can be determined, the marketer must identify the consumer's key attitudes and perceptions toward the attributes of a particular product relative to competitors. Positioning is only as good as the research on which it is based. Based on research results, the marketing manager can determine strategic issues, such as where the test product is positioned relative to the competition, whether that is an advantageous position, whether repositioning is necessary or possible, and how best to communicate the brand's distinctive position.

A repositioning strategy is used to change an existing position. An interesting example of a challenging repositioning strategy is the way Harley-Davidson now positions its motorcycles as a rebellious—but not too much—bike that is ridden, not by outlaws, but by iconoclasts. The bike had to be repositioned from its former

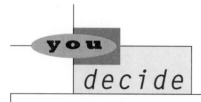

decide   Positioning "Buy" the Book

Michael Treacy and Fred Wiersema, consultants for an international consulting firm called CSC, developed an aggressive scheme to position their book, *Discipline of Market Leaders,* on the *New York Times* best-seller list. The thesis of the book urged companies to dominate their markets by narrowing their focus and disciplining themselves to do well at what they do best. Clearly, the authors took their thesis to heart, and may have taken it too far.

An investigation by *Business Week* found that Treacy and Wiersema used an "over-energetic marketing scheme" to inflate the sales of their book. First, they researched how to ensure best-seller status on the *New York Times* book list. They contacted a number of prominent booksellers to gather ideas on marketing the book and found, according to *Business Week,* that to become a best-seller, massive book purchases had to be spread nationwide among certain bookstores. The purchases had to be carefully spaced so as not to alert the *Times'* computers, and the purchases could not be traceable to the authors.

Next, they spent an estimated $250,000 on bogus purchases from bookstores to inflate book sales. CSC, clients, and friends bought 40,000 copies of the book in quantities of 25 to 1000 from bookstores all over the country. Dozens of bookstores unwittingly filled orders for multiple copies that were sent directly from the publisher to various corporate addresses in San Francisco, none of which were traceable to the authors or CSC. To what end? Aside from the royalties from actual book sales, the authors knew that having a *New York Times* best-seller would open up new, lucrative consulting contracts and speaking engagements.

No one knows if any laws were broken, but there are some real questions about the ethics of phony sales to manipulate the lists. The idea of planning purchases to distort the actual demand for a book outrages many people in publishing who see buying their way onto a best-seller list as misleading to buyers and sellers. Treacy and Wiersema admit that they aggressively and energetically marketed the book. "Did we cross the line?" asks Treacy. "No way we did anything unethical."

You Decide

1. Do you think their marketing strategy was ethical? Explain.
2. What positioning did the authors seek to create by the inflated sales? What position do you think they may have achieved as a result of the publicity?

Sources: Willy Stern, "Did Dirty Tricks Create a Best-Seller?" *Business Week,* August 7, 1995, 22–5; Willy Stern, "The Unmasking of a Best-Seller: Chapter 2," *Business Week,* August 13, 1995, 41.

outlaw image to attract rich folks who can afford to buy these $20,000 bikes and other products.

Marketers have tended to follow four approaches to establishing a position, focusing on: 1) the consumer, 2) the competitors' strategies, 3) social responsibility, and 4) image strategies. **Consumer-focused positioning strategies** emphasize the target market, the type of appeal they respond to, and how and when they use the product. Diet Coke and Diet Pepsi, for example, clearly follow a positioning approach directed toward young adults who care about weight gain.

Competitive positioning strategies relate to claims made by other brands, thus providing a frame of reference for the consumer. Long-distance telephone companies AT&T, MCI, and Sprint have all tried to create a competitive position based on cost savings. Sprint does not make direct comparisons with AT&T and MCI, but instead focuses on its dime-a-minute long-distance rate as presented by Candice Bergen. AT&T and MCI go head-to-head and make direct comparisons on a rate basis, with AT&T focusing on the ease of its savings plan.

A **social accountability position strategy** tries to establish goodwill by positioning the organization as a good community citizen. Through proper positioning, an organization such as Ben and Jerry's, Xerox, or Biofoam can be perceived as socially accountable—as a company that cares about the environment, people, the community, and social problems. This positive position gives the customer another added value and a reason to buy the product.

An **image positioning strategy** focuses on the tangible and intangible characteristics of the product that cannot be duplicated easily by competitors. This need to paint a picture of the product usually requires a great deal of marketing communication. The ad for Sony, for example, creates an image of excitement and adventure.

Branding Strategies

Perhaps the most effective technique for establishing a strong position is through a powerful brand, a topic discussed in Chapter 2. Think of brands such as

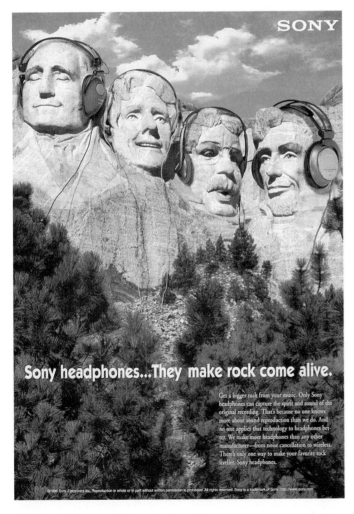

In this ad, Sony positions its headphones as a new experience in music listening.

Marlboro, Swatch, Kodak, and Club Med, and certain images emerge. Branding does several things: It identifies the product, it anchors a position, and it establishes an image or personality for the product that makes it distinctive, liked, and valued. Once established clearly in the mind of the customer, the brand serves as a cognitive shortcut. It may connote quality, convenience, strong values, and excellent service, to name a few possibilities. The Hershey's brand, for example, is made up of a multitude of impressions and values that coalesce, as the slogan says, into "the all-American candy bar."

Powerful brands have strong market shares by virtue of their category dominance that are often extended into a global presence. Examples of such brands include Sony, Nestlé, Pillsbury, and Mercedes-Benz. A well-known brand name is a promise of quality and consistency, and that makes it possible for a respected brand to maintain its sales at a price relatively higher than the competition. The importance of a branding strategy is evident in the visibility and longevity of the brand. If a company can create a memorable brand name, such as Healthy Choice, and then produce quality products that are associated with that name, the result is extremely powerful. For the seller, a brand name means that a product can be distinguished from its competition. For the buyer, branding implies consistent quality, enhances shopping efficiency, and calls attention to new products. Brand names also make it easier for customers to remember and find products. Brands are created primarily through the imagery conveyed by advertising and reinforced through packaging and in-store promotions and merchandising materials such as signage and location in the store.

Implementation Tactics

The implementation section of a marketing plan outlines the critical product, price, distribution, and marketing communication decisions that come together as the marketing mix. For example, the pricing strategy developed for Healthy Choice had to consider the initial costs to manufacture and distribute the product, how these costs would change with various levels of sales, the typical price charged for a product of this type, the price strategy retailers distributing the product used, the importance of price to the sales force and to consumers, and so forth. Similar decisions have to be made about the product design and its distribution. For marketing communication managers, the marketing mix decisions are particularly important because they have communication implications, and, in some cases, such as price, they may be the focus of a communication strategy.

Just as with the business plan, the *implementation* of the marketing plan can be difficult. Making sure that the product reaches the warehouse at the right time for an advertised sales promotion, that ads run on schedule, and that salespeople receive the right support materials are just a few examples of implementation problems. For instance, ConAgra made the introduction of Healthy Choice even more complex because the company decided to make changes in its other frozen food product lines at the same time. Banquet Foods and Armour Dinner product lines were cut back. Armour Dinner Classic Lite underwent a complete restructuring. These changes meant that meetings had to be scheduled with every supermarket chain to negotiate that the freezer space given up by Banquet and Armour reductions would be allocated to Healthy Choice rather than a competitor.

An important part of the implementation program is the development of the marketing budget. Resources have to be allocated to all the various components of the marketing mix, and the budget levels have to be compared with estimated revenue to see if the returns justify the expenditures. Another part of the implementation plan is the schedule. Because of the interaction of various marketing activities, such as the need to have the product in the warehouse before the advertising runs, the schedule is very complex, and timing is critical to the effectiveness of the plan.

Evaluation

As in the business plan, the last step is to evaluate the effectiveness of the marketing plan while it is being implemented and afterward. Tracking studies are often done to monitor the progress of the plan as it unfolds. Afterward, the marketing plan accomplishments are compared with its objectives to determine if the effort was effective. In addition, an analysis of the returns on the investment is conducted to see if the effort was worthwhile given the costs.

THE MARKETING PLAN

The marketing plan is similar to the business plan although it contains important decisions about the target market and budget. The key sections are

1. Situation analysis: an assessment of the environmental conditions and an interpretation of the findings to identify strengths, weaknesses, opportunities, and threats.
2. Marketing objectives: examining explicit and implicit objectives.
3. Market strategy: whether to approach the market as heterogeneous or homogeneous.
4. Target market selection: determining market segments.
5. Competitive strategies, such as:

   - Differentiating the product
   - Positioning the product
   - Branding

6. Implementation tactics: how the marketing mix comes together.
7. Evaluation: before and after marketing plan implementation.

HIERARCHY OF EFFECTS MODELS

Before discussing the specific steps in marketing communication planning, we first consider the hierarchy of effects models, which provide a general framework for analyzing the impact of communication. Although we discuss communication processes and theories in more detail in Chapter 8, we present these models here because they are relevant to marketing communication planning.

Communication models are useful in planning message strategies. These models, referred to as hierarchy of effects, assume that consumers move through a step-by-step process as they receive marketing information and move toward a decision.

An advertisement, for example, is considered effective when it helps move the consumer a step further in the buying decision process. We examine three hierarchy of effects models: the traditional AIDA model, the think-feel-do model, and the domains model.

Hierarchy of effects models help analyze message impact and provide a structure for setting communication objectives. One classic approach, the **AIDA model,** describes the effect of marketing as beginning with *awareness,* then moving to *interest,* then *desire,* and finally *action.*[3] A variation of AIDA is the DAGMAR model (Defining Advertising Goals for Measured Advertising Results), which begins with *awareness,* moves to *comprehension,* then *conviction,* and ends with *action.*[4] In both models the initial effects are easier to create than the ones at the end of the process. The use of cute pups, kittens, and babies are surefire methods for gaining attention, but getting customers to take action is another story.

The **think-feel-do model** of message effects[5] presumes that we approach a purchase situation using the following sequence of responses: we (think) about the cue, then we form an attitude or opinion about it (feel), and finally we take action and respond to it (do). As illustrated in Figure 4.2, the think-feel-do model parallels the AIDA model. The think-feel-do model is also called the high-involvement model because it depicts the responses typically found with consumers who actively participate in the process of gathering information. These consumers are "active" thinkers considering high-priced, high-risk, or complex product categories where there is a need for information. Advertising for these types of products usually provides many product details and is very informative.

The Foote, Cone, and Belding ad agency's (FCB) model[6] is an adaptation of the basic think-feel-do model except that it accommodates both high and low involvement. It creates a matrix with four types of responses, product categories,

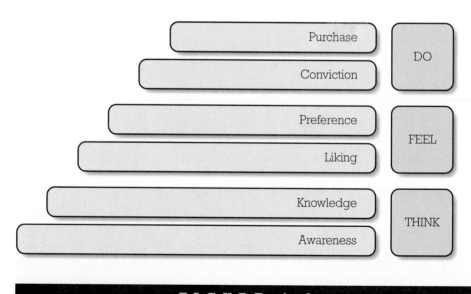

FIGURE 4.2

The Think-Feel-Do Model

	Thinking	**Feeling**
High Involvement	1. Informative (thinking) *Model:* think-feel-do *Products:* car, house *Creative:* demonstration, specific details	2. Affective (feeling) *Model:* feel-think-do *Products:* jewelry, cosmetics *Creative:* execution impact
Low Involvement	3. Habit formation (doing) *Model:* do-think-feel *Products:* liquor, household items *Creative:* reminder	4. Self-satisfaction (reacting) *Model:* do-feel-think *Products:* cigarettes, liquor, candy, gum *Creative:* attention

FIGURE 4.3

The FCB Model

and situations that are characterized by different orderings of "think-feel-do," as shown in Figure 4.3. For instance, when there is little interest in the product—such as an impulse buy—or a minimal difference between products, the FCB model shows that consumers try a product and then form an opinion—that is, consumers "do-feel-think."

Communication objectives can also be built on domains of effect. The **domains model** in Table 4.4 is based on the idea that changing perceptions, providing education, and persuading consumers are the primary objectives for marketing communication.[7] The model recognizes that marketing communication affects many different areas of the heart and mind simultaneously rather than sequentially. Marketing communication planners, then, must select the factors that are most important to consumers and focus on that part of the message. Table 4.4 explains what kinds of effects are measured in the areas of perception, education, and persuasion.

Concept Review

HIERARCHY OF EFFECTS MODEL

Before examining the steps in the communication plan, marketing communicators should consider the hierarchy of effects model to determine the potential effects of their communication plan on their audience. The main versions of the hierarchy of effects model include:

1. The AIDA model
2. The think-feel-do and FCB models
3. The domains model

TABLE 4.4

The Domains Model Measures Effects in Perception, Education, and Persuasion

Perception	Education	Persuasion
Attention	**Learning**	**Emotion**
• Product, brand, ad awareness	• The amount the claim, features, and selling premise registers	• Response to appeal
Interest		**Attitudes**
• How much concern, excitement generated	• The amount of product association with logo, slogan, theme, key visual, jingle, lifestyle, image, mood	• Positive or negative disposition to product
Memory		• Positive or negative evaluation of features, claims, views
• Recognition of ad, image, slogan, logo, copy points, position	• Whether product position or reposition and selling premise understood	• Brand preference
• Recognition of brand, product	• Whether features, claims are differentiated	**Argument**
• Recall of ad, image, slogan, logo, copy points, position		• Acceptability of claim
		• Persuasiveness of reason, promise
• Recall of brand		• Whether false impression has been corrected
		• Whether consumers challenge position, claim, viewpoint
		• Whether counter facts exist
		Behavior
		• Traffic increases
		• Stimulation of inquiries, trial, purchases, repurchases

THE MARKETING COMMUNICATION PLAN

The marketing communication plan evolves from the marketing plan. In the marketing communication plan, however, the objectives are to make the most effective use of all marketing communication functions—advertising, public relations, sales promotion, direct marketing, personal selling, and packaging—and to control the communication impact of the other marketing mix elements. Each function will have its own section in the marketing communication plan. That section explains how the functional area plans to accomplish marketing and communication objectives and details its implementation activities. The overall marketing communication plan identifies the most efficient and effective combination of activities, media, and messages. Let's consider how that plan is built by examining the nine steps in the marketing communication planning process.

The Marketing Communication Planning Process

A nine-step planning process guides the development of a marketing communication plan. These steps, similar to the business and marketing planning steps, can also be used to create a plan for a specific communication function, such as sales promotion or advertising.

Step 1: Determine a Problem or Opportunity

An analysis of problems and opportunities is derived from a comprehensive situation analysis, discussed earlier. Marketers rely on research, past experience, and a competitive analysis to identify problems and opportunities relevant to the communication plan. The SWOT analysis of the marketing plan may also be reapplied at this stage. Here, of course, the concern is for problems and opportunities that affect marketing messages. Marketing communication can only solve message-related problems such as image, attitude, perception, and knowledge or information. It cannot solve problems related to product price or availability, but it can refocus consumer perceptions and identify problematic messages sent by the marketing mix or other areas that undermine the marketing communication strategy.

Say, for instance, that the marketing plan identifies the product's high price or limited distribution as a weakness. The marketing communication plan may focus on both quality and value to justify price, and exclusivity to justify limited distribution. In an IMC program, a cross-functional team would have worked on the price and distribution decisions together at the marketing planning stage and hammered out the communication implications.

Step 2: Determine the Objectives

The statement of marketing communication objectives evolves directly from the marketing objectives and the problems and opportunity analysis. For example, take Kodak's launch of its disposable camera. Kodak's marketing objective was to gain 50 percent market share for the "novice" photographer. However, the price of the product ($8.95–$15.95) created a serious problem in the minds of consumers. The marketing communication objectives therefore emphasized the use of mass media to reach a broad range of consumers, a focus on convenience and picture quality, and an attempt to diminish the high price through product sampling and coupons.

Communication objectives can be planned using the hierarchy-of-effects models as a basis for identifying how the plan will affect consumers. Marketing communication objectives generally fall into five categories: 1) creating awareness, 2) creating understanding, 3) creating changes in attitudes and perceptions, 4) creating changes in behavior, and 5) reinforcing previous decisions and attitudes. Certain marketing communication tools are better than others in achieving a given objective, which is an important factor in developing the marketing communication mix in step 4.

Step 3: Select the Target Audience

A message delivered to the wrong audience is doomed to fail. In marketing plans, *target markets* are identified as groups of people who are in the market for a product or service; in marketing communication plans, *target audiences* are identified for special communication efforts. There is a subtle difference. For example, the target market for children's toys is primarily children. In contrast, the target audiences

ALTHOUGH THE McCOOEY BROTHERS AND THEIR SISTER HAVE ALWAYS BEEN REMINDED OF THEIR STRIKING SIMILARITIES, IT IS THEIR DIFFERENCES THEY HAVE ALWAYS INSISTED ON. IT IS NO WONDER THEN, THAT EACH OWNS A DIFFERENT WATERMAN PEN. FOR WHILE STYLE IS KEY, INDIVIDUALITY IS STILL EVERYTHING.

WATERMAN

Advertising that works must make clear its target audience and what the benefits are to that audience. In this ad, the Waterman line of pens is targeted to a relatively upscale audience, as shown by the clothing the models wear. The message, however, relates different pen designs to different family members, who are representative of different target audience segments.

might include parents, grandparents, various government agencies concerned with the product safety of children's toys, and consumer activist groups, as well as children. In this case the target audience is much greater than the target market.

The opposite is also possible. The target market for long-distance telephone service for small businesses is all businesses that spend between $150 and $1000 a month for long distance. Yet MCI may design a "win-back" (former customers) sales promotion campaign targeted only at Sprint customers.

To properly identify the appropriate target audiences, marketing communication managers need detailed information about the product and the market, who produces and sells the product, who uses the product and how it is used, who influences purchase decisions, and the perceptions of consumers.

Targeting is particularly complex in an integrated marketing communication program. In IMC planning, a set of stakeholder audiences may be targeted because they all need to know about or be involved in a company's new product or promotion, such as sales staff, resellers, employees, and the financial community for publicly held companies. Because the audience may be much larger than customers, IMC planning is often more complicated than traditional marketing communication planning that targets only the consumer audience.

The launch of a new product, for example, demands a complex list of target audiences other than consumers and messages that need to be directed to those audiences. Overall the marketer must provide a central message about the value that this new product offers. Shareholders may want to know about the research and development costs and how the new product will affect shareholder returns. The local community will be interested in whether the new product means more jobs and plant expansion. Employees must be notified because some will help with production, so their support will aid quality. Furthermore, they are often sources of information for family and friends. The media—local, national, trade, and financial—will be interested in news aspects of the product development that affect the community. Suppliers and vendors will want to know what opportunities they will have for providing new resources and services to the company. Retailers will need to be informed and motivated to provide space in their stores for the new product.

Step 4: Select the Marketing Communication Mix

One of the most important functions of the marketing communication plan is to determine the marketing communication mix. A 1996 survey identified the most common marketing communication mix activities used in consumer marketing. Figure 4.4 shows the results according to percentage of sales. The survey respondents spent an average of 2.25 percent of sales revenue on marketing communication and 1.65 percent on personal sales. This pattern contrasts with business-to-business marketing, which spends most of its marketing budget on personal sales.

The activities (or tools) used to achieve the marketing communication objectives make up the **marketing communication mix.** After the target market

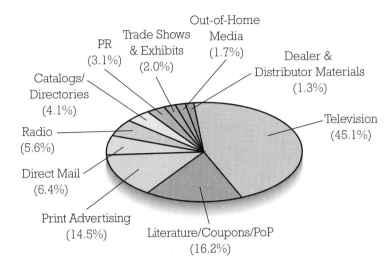

Catalogs/Directories (4.1%)
Radio (5.6%)
Direct Mail (6.4%)
Print Advertising (14.5%)
Literature/Coupons/PoP (16.2%)
PR (3.1%)
Trade Shows & Exhibits (2.0%)
Out-of-Home Media (1.7%)
Dealer & Distributor Materials (1.3%)
Television (45.1%)

FIGURE 4.4

Consumer Marketing Spending on Marketing Communication

Source: From *Marketing News,* 11 March 1996. Reprinted by permission of the American Marketing Association.

---

and audience are selected, the marketer customizes and refines the marketing communication mix to fit the target audience as precisely as possible. The mix will be different for different segments and problem situations. Industry and consumer audiences, for instance, demand entirely different messages. Table 4.5 identifies some general strengths and weaknesses of the most important marketing communication tools.

In IMC planning, the strengths of the various tools are matched against the problems and opportunities to decide which ones are best able to meet the marketing communication objectives. Despite the advantages and disadvantages associated with each tool, several tools may be able to accomplish the same objective. The flexibility of being able to choose among tools is important because it allows managers to match the objective and message needs with budgets.

Step 5: Select the Message Strategy

Determining exactly what to say to the targeted audience groups is a difficult and important process. Message strategies depend on the nature and extent of the opportunity, as well as strengths, weaknesses, and threats identified in the situation analysis. For example, it is always more effective to promote a product that satisfies a consumer trend. ConAgra, for instance, has followed the health-oriented trend. The Pork Association, "Pork: The Other White Meat!," and the American Beef Council, "Beef! It's What's for Dinner," illustrate message strategies that are contrary to that trend.

Although different target audiences have different message needs, messages must be consistent with the company, brand, or product's overall message. This message

TABLE 4.5

Marketing
Communication
Tools–Strengths and
Weaknesses

Tool	Strengths	Weaknesses
Advertising	Creates awareness of a product and informs large mass audiences about a product, service, or idea	Is intrusive, operates in a very cluttered environment, and is expensive
Sales Promotion	Not only does this tool stimulate immediate response by adding incentives and creating tangible extra values, it also creates excitement, increases repeat behaviors, motivates industry support	Can add to communication clutter, creates expectations of lower prices, and may undercut brand image and long-term loyalty
Public Relations	Can create goodwill; can place messages in the media that benefit from the media's credibility and focus on newsworthy information; monitors attitudes to assess a company or brand image; understands and communicates with many stakeholder audiences, a key to an effective IMC program	Effectiveness is hard to measure; does not usually trigger sales directly
Direct Marketing	Can be highly targeted; excellent for reaching small or niche audiences; economical with small audiences; and can create one-on-one communication because it can be personalized, offers a means for customer feedback and self-selection	Effectiveness often depends on accurate database; often disregarded due to clutter; expensive if large audience
Personal Selling	In business-to-business products, it is the most personalized tool and delivers the most informative and persuasive messages	The most expensive form of marketing communication; can be irritating if the customer does not appreciate the sales call
Event Sponsorhip	Can be highly targeted and self-selecting; creates the highest level of participation and involvement; if philanthropic, it also contributes to the corporate good citizen image; and creates news opportunities	Rarely reaches a large audience; does not allow marketers to repeat their messages often; has a high cost given the number of impressions created
Packaging	Makes a strong visual statement about a product; a low-cost reminder message; highly targeted because it is the last message seen before a purchase decision is made	May cause environmental problems; must stand out in a cluttered environment; reaches a small audience
Cause Marketing	Creates positive feelings about the company by associating the business or brand with a philanthropic gesture	If cause does not concern a large audience, or if too many sponsors support it, the effort may get lost; may be seen as self-serving

The "Best" message—no matter what the language—reminds consumers of Gillette's image and quality, as it does in this product display in Shanghai.

or central theme focuses the marketing effort and provides consistency, such as Marlboro's tough, rugged cowboy, an image that is effective today because smokers often view themselves as individualists, given society's growing intolerance for smoking.

Step 6: Select the Message Delivery Systems or Media

The media planner is the person who figures out how to reach the target audiences at their most important contact points. The development of the media strategy works hand-in-hand with the development of the message strategy and the budget analysis. A planner can't create a strategy for a television commercial, for instance, if there is no budget for TV advertising. If direct marketing is used, what media will carry the messages—TV or print advertisement, or materials mailed directly to the home or office, or over the Internet? The message strategy differs for each medium, so writers and media planners must coordinate their actions.

To plan the media delivery system, media planning tools (discussed in Chapter 16) include a disciplined analysis of the media options and a rating system that makes it obvious to others how and why various media vehicles were selected. A pie chart is used to show how the media budget is split up, and a balance sheet is used to show what the various elements cost and how they add up. Typically, a flow chart is used to demonstrate the scheduling strategy.

Step 7: Determine a Budget

One key factor that determines which and to what extent each tool will be used in the marketing communication mix is the budget. Ideally, the budget should not enter the planning process until after the major strategic decisions have been

Zero-Based Planning

In integrated marketing communication planning, there is one important thing to remember: The plans for the functional areas should start with a "zero base." Many firms build plans based on last year's plan because it is simple to do so. Starting with a zero base means that the firm starts from scratch. The plan depends solely on *this* year's situational analysis,

objectives, strategies, marketing communication mix, and budget. Although starting with a zero base requires more time and effort than revising last year's plan, the zero-base method ensures that the firm will use the best tools to solve a problem or seize an opportunity.

Zero-based budgeting, discussed in Chapter 3, is often part of zero-based planning. Starting

with a clean balance sheet and building the budget based on the marketing communication tools that will most effectively implement the plan's strategies is the best approach for a constantly changing marketplace.

Source: Tom Duncan, "A Macro Model of Integrated Marketing Communication," American Academy of Advertising Annual Conference, Norfolk, Va., March 1995, 118.

made. For this reason, we list budget determination seventh in the planning process. In reality, however, the budget is often a given as it is allocated in the marketing plan, so that a marketing communication manager would be told that the marketing communication budget is $3 million next year, and the plans are made accordingly. This process of arriving at a budget figure is described in more detail in Chapter 17.

Once the overall marketing communication budget is set, then a percentage of it is assigned to each tool. For example, the initial promotional mix for Ralston Purina Puppy Chow might look something like this: 40 percent advertising, 30 percent sales promotion, 25 percent personal selling, and 5 percent public relations. Each category would then be broken down into smaller, more specific budget allocations. The advertising component, for example, might be allocated as follows: 30 percent network television, 25 percent magazines, 15 percent newspapers, 10 percent radio, 5 percent outdoor. Another 10 percent might be used for direct mail advertising and 5 percent for specialty items.

An important step after the budgeting stage is to estimate the dollar amounts to be spent on each planned marketing communication activity. How much does advertising during each network television program cost? What does it cost to produce and distribute 500,000 product samples or to produce a sweepstakes campaign? How much does a mailing list cost? To answer this lengthy list of questions, marketing communicators must consult people inside and outside of the organization who can estimate such costs with accuracy. The final budget estimate is often much greater than the amount the company planned to spend. That difference usually spurs plan revisions to cut back activities, adjust the budget, or both.

Step 8: Implement the Strategy

The success of any marketing communication strategy is largely a function of how well it is implemented. Implementation involves three separate stages. First, the marketing communication manager must make specific decisions about all the elements of the plan, including types of media, dates, times, sizes, talent, photographers and artists, and production schedules. Next, the manager must make sure all these decisions can be implemented and that there are people assigned to each task. Finally, the manager must monitor the activities to make sure all decisions were implemented correctly.

A successful implementation coordinates the efforts of all the specialists involved. The advertising program consists of a series of related, well-timed, and carefully placed ads. The sales materials have to be planned and produced so they are available when the ads are shown or published. The salespeople also have to be fully informed about the advertising part of the program—the theme, media used, schedule of ad appearances, and so on. The salespeople then inform resellers and retailers about this marketing communication program and convince them to incorporate the merchandising materials, point-of-sale displays, signage, and sales promotions into their marketing efforts. Personnel responsible for physical distribution activities should ensure that adequate stocks of the product are available in all outlets before the start of the program. People working in public relations should also be alerted to new product stories, product demonstrations, new product applications, special events, and so forth.

Marketing communicators should provide enough lead time in all of these areas so the materials and activities are all available on schedule and do not conflict. Conflicting activities overload the trade and the sales staff, who may have to push two different campaign efforts at the same time. Timing and scheduling considerations affect all stakeholders. Usually employees need to know about new programs first, then investors, later the community and the media, and then consumers. If the new program or product design involves government regulators, the company might need to consult the regulators first.

Step 9: Evaluate the Results

After the implementation step, the marketing communication manager must determine if the promotional effort met the stated objectives. External agencies often perform this evaluation because they have greater expertise with marketing communication measurement techniques.

Three tasks must be completed to measure the results of a marketing communication program. First, marketing communication managers must develop standards for effectiveness so that the planners, those who implement the plan, and evaluators understand exactly what the promotion reasonably should have accomplished. The standards should be as specific and measurable as possible. Second, the marketing communication managers must monitor actual promotional performance against the objectives, often through consumer surveys. Third, the manager must compare performance measures against the standards to determine if the performance was effective and efficient.

Once the firm evaluates a marketing communication strategy, the planner is then able to identify deficiencies and prescribe any needed corrective action. Also, the planner can use insights gained from the evaluation as guides for the next planning effort.

THE MARKETING COMMUNICATION PLAN

The marketing communication plan provides the framework for the communication effort. The nine steps in the marketing communication planning process include:

1. Determine problems or opportunities
2. Determine the objectives
3. Select the target audience
4. Select the marketing communication mix
5. Select the message strategy
6. Select the message delivery systems or media
7. Determine a budget
8. Implement the strategy
9. Evaluate the results

STRATEGIC IMC DECISIONS

The goal of IMC is to coordinate all long- and short-term marketing communication efforts. In addition, effective integrated communication programs must consider all messages stakeholders receive each time stakeholders come in contact with a company. The following section identifies the dimensions of IMC that have the strongest effect on planning.

Coordinated Planning

The leaders of each marketing communication area, such as the advertising and sales directors, should plan the marketing communication program together. Coordinated planning efforts should lead to consistent marketing communication efforts. A recent advertisement for NBC's "Dateline" and *People* showed how coordinated marketing efforts can be effective. The ad featured the show and the magazine and reminded consumers that the two team up to "tell some of America's most compelling stories."

In contrast, suppose a hospital's marketing plan calls for cost containment, but its medical education seminars stress the use of costly new procedures. What are the hospital's clients, the health maintenance and managed care programs, to make of such conflicting messages? Coordinated planning can reduce this conflict. A seminar could focus on how to use new technology to keep costs down, for instance, but that kind of planning can only occur if the seminar director participates in the marketing communication planning discussions. Such coordination is often difficult to manage in large organizations like hospitals.

Managed Contact Points

As mentioned briefly in Chapter 1, there are a variety of message opportunities, or *contact points,* through which people receive important messages about a brand or company. A coordinated communication program will either control or influence as many of these communication opportunities as possible.

For any product or service, a marketing communication manager can draw up a long list of ways in which people come in contact with the brand or company.

The common contact points may include those made through formal marketing communication, such as advertising, articles in the press, sales promotion activities, and in-store merchandising. But informal contact points deliver messages that may speak louder than the formal marketing communication messages. For example, if you manage a hand-lotion brand, then consumers will probably see the product in advertisements and on store shelves. However, the product may also be seen in restrooms, doctor's offices, and in friends' houses. These other locations serve as an informal testimony for the product.

The point is that every contact sends a message—the delivery truck and its driver, the company's plant, the receptionist who answers the phone, and the person who demonstrates the product in the store. Any good IMC plan should include an analysis of all possible contact points and evaluate their importance and impact.

Varied Stakeholder Messages

In a sophisticated integrated communication program, you don't just say the same thing to everyone to maximize consistency. Instead, you tailor the message to each market segment you target while staying consistent with the central themes of the marketing communication program. This is the heart of **strategic consistency.**

After analyzing all contact points, IMC planners should evaluate what kind of communication the various stakeholder audiences need to participate in and prioritize the importance of each audience to the company, brand, or product. Specifying and prioritizing the range of possible target audiences help planners decide which communication specialists should address each target market and with what type of message and with how much effort. This process ensures that each stakeholder group is reached in the most effective and efficient manner and that opportunities are created for stakeholders to initiate contact with the company.

It is important for IMC planners to understand that what customers and other stakeholders need is not necessarily one-way communication directed at them by the company. The new era of electronic communication recognizes that two-way communication can be more effective than one-way because it deals with real feedback. As marketing scholar David Stewart explains, "There remains a persistent belief that marketing communication has a powerful influence on consumers. However, what was once a captive audience is increasingly free and increasingly in control of the information flow." He suggests that IMC planners recognize that "consumers will be addressable only to the extent that they choose to be. Marketers may manage and coordinate, but they cannot make consumers attend to, process, or integrate communications."[8]

Concept Review

STRATEGIC IMC DECISIONS

Employing an IMC approach toward marketing communication planning requires certain adjustments in the planning process.

1. Strategies must be carefully coordinated.
2. All contact points must be managed.
3. Strategic consistency means that careful consideration must be given to the needs of stakeholders.

A CLOSING THOUGHT: EVERY COMPANY IS A COMMUNICATOR

Many years ago someone coined the phrase, "Nothing happens until somebody sells something." This statement signifies how crucial marketing communication activities are to business today. Marketing requires more than developing a good product, pricing it fairly, and making it readily available. These facets of marketing are insufficient to generate enough sales and profits for the firm to survive. Without marketing communication, potential buyers would never become aware of, or be persuaded by, the merits of the product. Why? Competition is so fierce and the marketplace so dynamic that the company must develop a comprehensive and effective program of communication. Every company must communicate. The only choice companies have is to decide how well they will communicate.

SUMMARY

1. Describe the critical decisions determined through strategic planning.

The three most important decisions that are determined by strategic planning include setting objectives, identifying strategies, and developing implementation tactics.

2. Explain the elements of the marketing plan and how they reflect marketing strategy.

Similar to a business plan, a marketing plan includes a situation analysis, objectives, market strategies, the target market, competitive strategies, implementation, and evaluation.

3. Analyze the hierarchy of effects models and relate them to marketing communication planning.

Hierarchy of effects models identify the effects of communication. Marketing communicators use these models to assess how communication efforts may affect their audiences and to help define communication goals. The AIDA model describes the effect of marketing communication as a four-step sequence (awareness, interest, desire, and action). The think-feel-do model assumes a three-step sequence of communication responses: We (think) about the cue, then we form an attitude or opinion about it (feel), and finally we take action and respond to it (do). The Domains Model assumes we respond simultaneously in many ways

to communication and identifies three categories of effects: perception, education, and persuasion.

4. Describe the marketing communication plan and the marketing communication planning process.

The marketing communication plan focuses on producing an effective IMC strategy using elements such as advertising, sales promotion, public relations, personal selling, direct marketing, and packaging. The marketing communication planning process consists of nine critical steps: 1) determining a problem or opportunity, 2) determining the objectives, 3) selecting the audience, 4) selecting the marketing communication mix, 5) selecting the message strategy, 6) selecting the delivery systems or media, 7) determining the budget, 8) implementing the strategy, and 9) evaluating the results and taking corrective action.

5. Evaluate the strategic implications of IMC planning.

In an integrated marketing communication plan, the strategies must also consider coordinated planning, strategic consistency even with messages that are designed to speak to the individual needs of stakeholders, and the various contact points at which messages about a company or brand are delivered.

POINTS TO PONDER

Review the Facts

1. In your own words, describe strategic planning.
2. What is a market strategy and how does it differ from a marketing strategy?
3. What is a market segment?
4. Explain a product position and why positioning strategy is important.

Master the Concepts

5. Explain why strategic planning must begin with a business mission.
6. Compare the elements of a marketing plan and a marketing communication plan. How are they similar and how are they different? Why are there differences?
7. Describe the basic competitive strategies and explain how they can affect a marketing communication program.
8. Distinguish among the major strategic marketing decisions—marketing aggregation and segmentation, product differentiation, positioning, and branding. Now think of your favorite fast-food service provider and identify the strategic marketing approaches it seems to use: market aggregation or segmentation, how it differentiates its product, its position relative to competitors, and its branding strategy.

Apply Your Knowledge

9. Your company markets microwaveable dinners. Your research suggests that 40 percent of your customers use coupons. What additional information would you need from your research division to determine whether this percentage is a potentially profitable market?
10. Assume that you own a small manufacturing business that produces men's knit shirts. For your business, develop the following: a set of at least three marketing communication objectives and a strategy for each one. Use one of the hierarchy of effects models to structure your objectives.
11. Find ads from three companies that depict a clear positioning strategy and three companies whose positioning strategy is unclear from the advertising. Explain how the positioning strategy is working (or not working) in each ad.
12. Cite examples of how either advertising or some other form of marketing communication led you to purchase a product. What need did it satisfy? Could any other form of marketing communication also lead you to the purchase of this product?

SUGGESTED PROJECTS

1. (Oral Communication) Contact two local businesses and determine through at least one interview what kind of planning they use at the corporate or business level, the marketing level, and the marketing communication level. Is the plan for each level formal (written) or informal (most of the information is in someone's head)? How does the interviewee feel about the usefulness and the success of planning? Prepare a five-minute class report on your interviews.

2. (Writing Project) Identify two ads that appeal to unique target audiences and explain what audience segment(s) you think have been targeted

and why you think they are successful in targeting those segments. Now rewrite the two ads to demonstrate how the product might be aimed at a different target audience. Explain your new targeting strategy.

3. (Writing Project) Assume that the top management of General Electronics has hired you to determine if a promotional opportunity exists for a new technology that lets consumers record their own compact discs. Where would you begin your investigation? What marketing factors would be most important in developing a strategic marketing communication plan for this product? Outline

the key decisions you would need to make in the marketing communication plan to launch such a product.

4. (Internet Project) As this chapter explains, planning requires research. The Internet can be an excellent research tool. Suppose that you decide to conduct some Internet research to assist you with the launch plans described in Project 3. Explore at least two different search engines (searching devices that sort through databases of information) to find out more about new compact disc technology. Some free search engines that you might want to visit include the following:

Alta Vista   altavista.digital.com
Excite   www.excite.com
HotBot   www.hotbot.com
Lycos   www.lycos.com
WebCrawler   webcrawler.com
Yahoo   www.yahoo.com

For each engine, try a search that combines the terms "compact disc technology." (Note that each search engine has different search rules. For instance, Excite requires that you put quotes around search terms to link the words together. HotBot requires that you search for "the exact phrase" by selecting that option from a menu of search options. If you do not link the terms, the search engine will find sources that contain *any* or *all* of the terms.)

Review the list of sources from each search and explore the sources you feel are most relevant. Which search engine provided you the best information? Why? In a brief memo, explain your conclusions.

CASE 4: CLEANING HELPS ECOVER CLEAN UP

Doing the laundry, washing dishes, cleaning the windows—these mundane activities are a $20 billion industry in North America alone—and one of the worst sources of environmental damage. Enter Ecover, a small company from Belgium that is challenging big package goods manufacturers such as Procter & Gamble and Lever Bros. Co. Ecover makes all kinds of cleaning supplies, everything from laundry powder and dishwashing liquid to shampoos and car wax. The difference is that its products use only natural soaps and renewable raw materials such as vegetable extracts, sugar derivatives, and natural oils.

Ecover's sales are around $30 million a year and increasing dramatically, but its impact far exceeds its size because it is helping to shape the debate worldwide on the future of one of the world's dirtiest industries. Its ecologically sound factory has become a biodegradable tourist attraction drawing activists from all over the world. A huge grass roof keeps the factory cool in summer and warm in winter. The water-treatment system operates on wind and solar energy.

The company is not relying on its "green" image to find a position in the market. The fact is there isn't a mass consumer revolt against cleaning products even though one-third of all household pollution comes from

cleaning products. It is competing head-to-head with industry giants in terms of pricing and other product features. However, it beats the industry on cleanliness. Not only does its soap clean as well as Tide, it is 6000 times less toxic. And Ecover products are more healthy. Thirty percent of U.S. families have members with skin problems; Ecover is betting that chemical-based detergents and soaps are a big factor.

The company's strategy has been to roll out its products in European countries whose consumers are environmentally aware and health conscious, such as the Netherlands and Switzerland. It even developed a specially formulated detergent for Amsterdam that is designed to work with the city's water. The product has the city's coat of arms on the package. It now sells products in 34 countries and in 15,000 retail outlets. It is also targeting the business market, primarily office buildings and hotels, which Ecover identifies as "industrial society's great silent polluters." It has limited distribution in the United States and sells through a few environmentally concerned retailers, such as Ecowash in New York City.

Ecover is also a pioneer in marketing communication. In Antwerp the company bought numerous billboards that carried ads for competitors. Then it sponsored a contest for artists to recycle the boards—tear them apart, reassemble them, and create billboards for Ecover. The recycled billboards were colorful, cheerful, provocative, and artistic. Then the company organized walking tours and asked people to look at the billboards as if they were an art exhibit.

Not only is the company reinventing the cleaning business, it's also reinventing marketing communication.

Case Questions

1. Develop an outline of what you think Ecover's marketing plan would look like. Start with what you think Ecover's mission statement would say.

2. You are director of marketing for Ecover and your senior management is considering making a major entrance into the U.S. market. What would the marketing research need to include to help you decide if the time is right for this move?

3. Ecover's billboards have been a marvelous marketing communication opportunity. If you were in charge of planning the company's marketing communication, what would you recommend for the next innovative marketing communication effort?

Sources: "Save the Planet: Getting Clean, Staying Green," *Glamour* (October 19, 1996): Internet (www.ecomat.com/Glamour_mag.html); "Gunter Pauli Cleans Up," *Fast Company* (November 1993): Internet (www.fastcompany.com).

ROMA'S LITE INTEGRATED CASE QUESTIONS

(Review the Roma's Lite Marketing Plan in the Appendix at the end of the text before answering these questions.)

1. From the Roma's Lite Pizza marketing plan in the appendix, explain how research was used in the situation analysis.

2. (Writing Project) What segmentation, differentiation, and positioning strategies were made in this case? Do you believe these decisions are justifiable? Explain in a 1 or 2 page memo.

3. (Team Project) As the planning team for the marketing communication program for Roma's Lite Pizza, proceed through the nine strategic planning steps and draft a proposed marketing communication plan. (Assume you will be given the budget figure.)

4. (Team Project) As the planning team for the marketing communication program for Roma's Lite Pizza, brainstorm about different ways customers and other stakeholders might come in contact with this brand. Group the contact points into high, medium, and low priorities. Now identify and prioritize what you want to say to key stakeholders and what their message needs are.

video case

Mission, Marketing, and Messages: Are Wal-Mart's Low Prices Due to Sweatshop Labor?

Sam Walton, Wal-Mart founder, opened his first stores in Arkansas and Missouri in 1962. Today Wal-Mart is the world's top retailer with stores around the world and sales exceeding $82 billion. Wal-Mart's mission is to reflect the values of its customers; and offer friendly, efficient service and low prices on a wide range of merchandise. Sam Walton outlined the company mission in loftier terms when he accepted the Medal of Freedom from President George Bush in 1992. He stated: "[W]e'll lower the cost of living for everyone, not just in America, but we'll give the world an opportunity to see what it's like to save and have a better lifestyle, a better life for all."

Wal-Mart's marketing strategy focuses on low prices, quality brand-name and private-label merchandise, state-of-the-art distribution systems, and a sophisticated marketing communication program that costs close to $130 million a year. Its advertising emphasizes Wal-Mart's position as a low-price leader, complete with prices visibly "falling" in some ads. Sales promotion bolsters Wal-Mart's price position, especially because Wal-Mart relies on creative ways to offer customers savings. For instance, it uses co-marketing ventures with well-known brands, such as Valvoline oil, Windex cleaner, and Champion batteries. How can the retailer

offer rock-bottom prices on these brands? The package goods brands pay all or most of the tab for marketing communication—Wal-Mart doesn't.

Wal-Mart also enhances its image through public relations and cause-marketing events. For instance, its Web site touts Wal-Mart's community outreach programs. These include college scholarships for high school seniors, environmental education, fundraising efforts for children's hospitals, encouraging American companies to bring offshore manufacturing operations to the United States, and sponsoring the Buy American program.

The marketing communication program sends the message that customers get top quality for low prices from a retailer that cares about community. However, adverse publicity from the Kathie Lee Gifford clothing line sent an unplanned message that triggered consumer outrage. Wal-Mart's low prices for that clothing line seemed to come at the expense of exploiting children in Honduras. The unplanned message sent a powerful signal that Wal-Mart might not be the good corporate citizen it professed to be.

What was the flap about? Wal-Mart and celebrity Kathie Lee Gifford partnered to market a moderately priced apparel line that became a success. In one

year, Wal-Mart earned $30 million in profits from the product line; Lee earned $9 million. In late 1996, Charles Kernaghan of the New York–based National Labor Committee testified before Congress that Kathie Lee garments were manufactured by underage girls (some as young as 13) in Honduran sweatshops. Kernaghan stated that the girls work 15-hour shifts under armed guard and earn 31 cents an hour to make clothes that are sold under a label that claims "a portion of proceeds from the sale of this garment will be donated to various children's charities." Testimony from a Honduran girl employed in the sweatshop reported beatings, intimidation, and other mistreatment. One month later, the New York *Daily News* profiled a sweatshop in New York where 50,000 Kathie Lee blouses were made. Workers were paid less than minimum wage and were owed back pay.

Though initially unresponsive when she learned of the Honduran sweatshop from the National Labor Committee, Gifford eventually appealed to Wal-Mart executives to develop a plan for monitoring working conditions. Ultimately, Wal-Mart severed ties with the Honduran factory that paid its workers 31 cents per hour.

The negative publicity grossly contradicted the squeaky-clean image of Kathie Lee and Wal-Mart.

Many of Wal-Mart's customers are concerned citizens who, as Rep. George Miller of California asserted, "have a right to know that the toys and clothes they buy. . . . are not made by exploited children." The revelations also seemed inconsistent with Wal-Mart's support of children's causes and its mission to help people around the world have a better standard of living.

Though retailers point out that in many cases they do not own the factories where goods are made, the threat of negative publicity is providing a wake-up call. Executives realize that it may simply be good business to monitor working conditions no matter where their location or who owns them. As Columbia University professor Elliot Schrage notes, "Many companies are being forced to examine their labor practices around the world by consumer pressure or fear of consumer backlash."

In April 1997, a White House task force that included Kathie Lee Gifford and representatives from unions, human rights groups, and the apparel industry announced a voluntary code of conduct. Those who signed the accord agreed to comply with three main provisions concerning industrial production outside the United States: limiting the number of hours worked per week, paying wages at least equal to the minimum wage, and banning the use of child and prison labor at factories that make apparel and athletic shoes. Any company claiming to comply with the code can label its products accordingly. But as Stephen Coats of the U.S./Guatemala Labor Education Project told *The Wall Street Journal,* "It strikes me that this would not be truth in advertising. Just signing on to a code of conduct doesn't guarantee anything." Roberta Karp, co-chair of the task force and general counsel for designer Liz Claiborne, disagreed. "I can absolutely tell you that working conditions will improve. There is nothing cosmetic about this."

Another lingering question remains: If improved working conditions lead to higher prices, will consumers rebel?

Discussion Questions

1. Do you think that the Gifford publicity caused much harm for Wal-Mart? Explain. Would your answer differ if sales figures showed that the Kathie Lee Gifford product line sales dropped sharply for the three months during the heaviest publicity but then rebounded? Explain your answer.

2. Gifford took action to rectify the harm to her public image, working with the Secretary of Labor to publicize substandard working conditions in this country and working on the White House task force on apparel industry labor standards. Other than severing ties with known sweatshops, what additional steps, if any, would you have recommended that Wal-Mart take in this case if you were the marketing communication director?

3. If you were planning Wal-Mart's marketing communication program for next year, what steps (if any) would you take to avoid negative publicity such as that generated by the Gifford sweatshop issue? Be sure to focus on the issues of planned and unplanned messages (discussed in chapter 1), price communication (chapter 2), coordinating messages (chapter 3), and the nine steps of the marketing communication planning process outlined in chapter 4.

Video Source: "Celebrity Endorsements, Exploited Workers," *Nightline,* 19 June 1996. *Additional Sources:* Wendy Bounds and Hilary Stout, "Sweatshop Pact: Good Fit or Threadbare?" *Wall Street Journal,* 10 April 1997; "The Wal-Mart Story," Wal-Mart Web Site, April 17, 1997 (Internet: www.wal-mart.com/corporate/wm_story); Eyal Press, "Kathie Lee's Slip," *The Nation,* 6 December 1996 (Internet: www.thenation.com/issue/960617/0617edt); Steven Greenhouse, "Accord to Combat Sweatshop Labor Faces Obstacles," *New York Times,* 13 April 1996, 1, 15; "1995 Power 50—Retail," *Advertising Age,* Special Edition 1996 (Internet: www.adage.com/ns-search/news_and_features/special-reports/power50/retail); Judann Pollack and Pat Sloan, "ANA Told: Remember Consumers," *Advertising Age,* 14 October 1996 (Internet: www.adage.com/news_and_features/199661014/article)

c h a p t e r

5

The Sociocultural
Environment

CHAPTER OBJECTIVES

After completing your work on this chapter, you should be able to:

1 **Describe how culture and sub-culture affect marketing communication.**

2 **List and explain demographic factors that influence marketing communication.**

3 **Discuss the role that social class plays in a culture.**

4 **Summarize how social groups can influence and are influenced by marketing communication.**

CONSIDER this

Changing Levi's

Over the last five years, Levi Strauss & Co. underwent a transformation to cope with world changes—more fickle and demanding customers, more numerous and dispersed suppliers, a more cluttered marketing environment, and sales revenues that grew more slowly than costs. In response to the changes, Levi Strauss & Co. revamped its operations to become a more integrated, process-oriented company. As part of that revamping, it retooled its marketing efforts to target younger audiences both at home and abroad. Some efforts have succeeded; others haven't fared as well.

For instance, Levi Strauss & Co.'s merchandising and marketing strategies for Dockers, first launched in 1986, show how the company is targeting younger consumers. First, it relaunched

the Authentics part of the Dockers line. The Authentics products resemble the classic khakis popular in the 1960s. Although the khakis were popular in the 1980s and early 1990s with 24-to-30-year-old males, Generation Xers did not respond as well. To push Authentics more aggressively, Levi redesigned the line and now requires that retailers feature Dockers Authentics separately in a free-standing display instead of mixing Authentics with other Dockers products. These Authentics "boutiques" are positioned with other mid-price collections or in the young men's section of department stores, competing with the likes of Calvin Klein. The displays have appeared in 150 stores in 43 metropolitan markets nationwide. Initial sales results indicate this merchandising strategy is more successful.

Levi also introduced the Dockers' "Nice Pants" marketing communication campaign.

127

The offbeat spots have the kind of edge that usually appeals to younger viewers. In one ad, a guy on a crowded subway spots a beautiful woman. The subway doors close before he can reach her, but she mouths the words "Nice Pants" as the train pulls away. According to an Ad Track poll, the campaign was not well received by its target audience.

For the venerable 501s, Levi Strauss & Co. tried to interest a younger crowd of 15-to-19-year-old males, a segment that research has shown is less brand loyal and less interested in classic tight jeans. For instance, Levi Strauss & Co. opted for a youthful marketing communication program. Instead of relying on traditional outdoor billboards, Levi Strauss & Co. used outdoor lighting technology that projects high-quality still and motion pictures on buildings and other large surfaces, similar to the images shown at large rock concerts. For the first time in 12 years, Levi Strauss & Co. launched print and television campaigns that updated and stressed brand image to ward off the Gap, JNCO, and other private labels that distribute denim products. Once again, Levi Strauss & Co. stressed the features and quality of the 501 line. The worldwide TV campaign entitled "Clayman" was an animated spot featuring the music of Shaggy. The PR team supported the strategy by creating free rock concerts in city streets, giving an MTV-like spin to the brand.

Did the change in the 501 communication strategy work? It didn't receive the acclaim other Levi branding messages garnered in times of old. An executive who worked on the Levi's account called the brand campaign "reactionary, defensive." "Levi's used to be the coolest thing going," he lamented. What was more successful with the youth market was the introduction of and marketing communication campaign for a wide-leg version of Levi's silver and red tab jeans.

Sources: Jennifer Steinhauser, "Squeezing into the Jeans Market," *New York Times,* 14 March 1997, C1, C15; Dottie Enrico, "AD Track: Dockers' Pants Ads Don't Appear to Have Legs," *USA Today/Louis Harris Poll* (21 July 1996): Internet; David Shef, "Levi's Changes Everything," *Fast Company* (June-July 1996): Internet (fastcompany.com/fastco/issues/third); Alice Z. Cunes, "Levi Strauss Dons New Approach for Attracting Men," *Advertising Age,* April 24, 1995, 10.

CHAPTER OVERVIEW

External influences affect consumer decision making. One external element is the marketing mix, discussed in Chapter 2. Another powerful element is the sociocultural environment. The **sociocultural environment** reflects those factors outside the individual—the person's world. As shown in Figure 5.1, the sociocultural environment consists of four main factors: *culture and subculture, demographics, social class,* and *groups that influence.* In this chapter we explore these four factors and how each affects the marketing communication program.

The sociocultural environment is dynamic. As consumers' culture, demographics, social class, and family values change, their reactions to products and market-

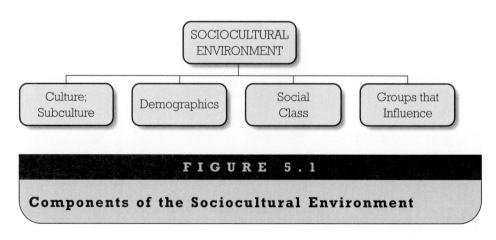

FIGURE 5.1

Components of the Sociocultural Environment

ing communication programs change also. Levi Strauss recognized these changes and decided it had to react to stay on top. "You change when customers say you have to change," says Thomas Kasten, a Levi vice president.[1] Marketing communication managers must constantly track sociocultural changes to understand how consumers make decisions. We begin our discussion with the broadest factors, *cultures* and *subcultures*.

CULTURES AND SUBCULTURES

All of us are part of a cultural fabric that affects our behavior, including our behavior as consumers. **Culture** is the sum of learned *beliefs, values,* and *customs* that regulate the behavior of members of a particular society. Through our culture, we are taught how to adjust to the environmental, biological, psychological, and historical parts of our environment.

Beliefs and values are guides for behavior, and customs are acceptable ways of behaving. A **belief** is an opinion that reflects a person's particular knowledge and assessment of something (that is, "I believe that. . . ."). **Values** are general statements that guide behavior and influence beliefs and attitudes ("Honesty is the best policy"). A value system helps people choose between alternatives in everyday life.[2] **Customs** are overt modes of behavior that constitute culturally approved ways of behaving in specific situations. Customs vary among countries, regions, and even families. In Arab societies, for instance, usury (payment of interest) is prohibited, so special Islamic banks exist that provide three types of accounts: nonprofit accounts, profit-sharing deposit accounts, and social services funds. A U.S. custom is to eat turkey on Thanksgiving Day. However, the exact Thanksgiving Day menu may depend on family customs.

Values and Consumer Behavior

Cultural values influence consumer behavior. Because it is more time- and cost-effective to gather information about cultural values instead of personal values, marketers are forced to concentrate on cultural values.[3] Marketers track trends in cultural values and target their efforts to address the values. For example, virtually all cable television providers are tracking the trend of viewers spending more time watching TV alone and whether one of the reasons for this behavior is having hundreds of viewing choices.

Dominant cultural values are referred to as **core values;** they tend to affect and reflect the core character of a particular society. For example, if a culture does not value efficiency but does value a sense of belonging and neighborliness, few people in the culture will want to use automatic teller machines.[4] What do Americans value? Clearly, a catchall phrase such as the "Protestant Work Ethic" no longer captures the whole value system. As shown in Table 5.1, there are many American core values, and each has implications for consumer behavior and marketing communication.

Among private research firms that monitor values and look for groupings and behavioral patterns, Stanford Research Institute (SRI) is famous for its values and lifestyles systems (VALS), which categorize people according to their demographics and values and then identify associated consumer behaviors. VALS 1,

TABLE 5.1

**Summary of American
Core Values**

Value	General Features	Relevance to Consumer Behavior
Achievement and success	Hard work is good; success flows from hard work	Acts as a justification for acquisition of goods ("You deserve it")
Activity	Keeping busy is healthy and natural	Stimulates interest in products that are time-savers and enhances leisure-time activities
Efficiency and practicality	Admiration of things that solve problems (e.g., save time and effort)	Stimulates purchase of products that function well and save time
Progress	People can improve themselves; tomorrow should be better	Stimulates desire for new products that fulfill unsatisfied needs; acceptance of products that claim to be "new" or "improved"
Material comfort	"The good life"	Fosters acceptance of convenience and luxury products that make life more enjoyable
Individualism	Being one's self (e.g., self-reliance, self-interest, and self-esteem)	Stimulates acceptance of customized or unique products that enable a person to "express his or her own personality"
Freedom	Freedom of choice	Fosters interest in wide product lines and differentiated products
External conformity	Uniformity of observable behavior; desire to be accepted	Stimulates interest in products that are used or owned by others in the same social group
Humanitarianism	Caring for others, particularly the underdog	Stimulates patronage of firms that compete with market leaders
Youthfulness	A state of mind that stresses being young at heart or appearing young	Stimulates acceptance of products that provide the illusion of maintaining or fostering youth
Fitness and health	Caring about one's body, including the desire to be physically fit and healthy	Stimulates acceptance of food products, activities, and equipment perceived to maintain or increase physical fitness

Source: Leon G. Schiffman and Leslie L. Kanuk, *Consumer Behavior,* 6th ed. (Englewood Cliffs, N.J.: Prentice-Hall, 1996), 433.

introduced in 1978, contains nine categories. VALS 2 divides people into three basic categories: those who are principle-oriented, status-oriented, and action-oriented. Then it estimates the resources consumers can draw upon, such as education, income, health, energy level, self-confidence, and degree of consumerism. The result is eight subcategories. Figure 5.2 shows how the VALS 2 categories and resources interact.[5] The questionnaire asks people to agree or disagree with such statements as "My idea of fun at a national park would be to stay at an expensive lodge and dress up for dinner" and "I could stand to skin a dead animal." These responses are statistically combined to create psychographic profiles—profiles that cluster a group of commonly held attitudes.

Note in Figure 5.2 that the three main categories and subcategories are arranged in a rectangle. They are stacked vertically by amount of resources (minimal to abundant) and horizontally by principle-oriented, status-oriented, and action-oriented. We see from Figure 5.2 that principle-oriented consumers are guided by their views of how the world is or should be; status-oriented consumers, by the action and opinions of others; and action-oriented consumers, by a desire for social or physical activity, variety, and risk taking.

The two principle-oriented segments, for instance, are **fulfilleds** and **believers.** Fulfilled consumers are mature, responsible, well-educated professionals. Their leisure activities center on their homes, but they are well-informed about what goes on in the world, and they are open to new ideas and social change. They have high incomes, but they are practical, value-oriented consumers. Believers have more modest incomes. They are typically conservative and predictable consumers who favor established brands. Their lives are centered on family, church, community, and the nation. Do you know anyone who would be in either of these VALS groups?

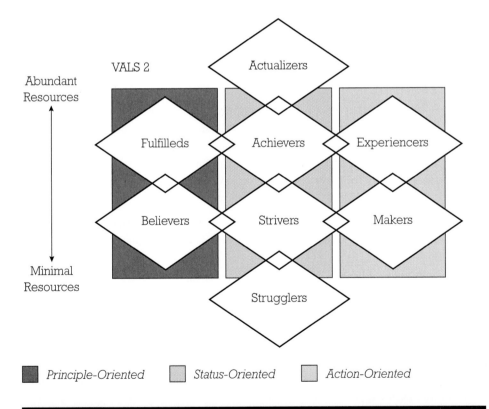

FIGURE 5.2

VALS 2: A Method for Classifying Consumer Values

Source: Martha Farnsworth Riche, "Psychographics for the 1990s," *American Demographics* (July 1989): 26. Reprinted with permission. Copyright © 1995, *American Demographics,* Ithaca, New York.

An annual subscription to VALS provides businesses with a range of products and services. Businesses that do market research can include VALS questions in their own questionnaires. SRI will analyze the results, and businesses can then tabulate the rest of their market research according to VALS classifications.

The VALS 2 system is used by various companies, including Mercedes-Benz, Chevron Corporation, Eastman Kodak, and Ketchum Communications. Chevron, for example, uses the VALS 2 classifications to categorize all its consumers into types that are then combined with information about the size of the market and geographic distribution. Chevron uses the results to target its sales promotions.

Another firm, Yankelovich & Partners, conducts its annual Monitor Series to assess American values. The annual report tracks 41 cultural values, such as "antibusiness," "mysticism," and "living for today," and gives the percentage of people who share the attitude as well as the percentage who are opposed to it. Yankelovich also looks at general trends in the values of America, such as "the need for security."

Core values are slow and difficult to change. Consequently, marketing communication strategies must accurately portray and reflect these values.

Secondary values also exist in any culture. Secondary values are less permanent values that can sometimes be influenced by marketing communication. In addition, secondary values are often shared by some people but not others. These values serve as the basis for subcultures.

Subcultures

A natural evolution that occurs in any culture is the emergence of subcultures. Core values are held by virtually an entire culture, whereas secondary values are not. A **subculture** is a group of people who share a set of secondary values. Examples include Generation X and environmentally concerned people. Many factors can place an individual in one or several subcultures. Five of the most important factors that create subcultures follow:[6]

- *Material culture.* People with similar income may create a subculture. The poor, the affluent, and the white-collar middle class are examples of material subcultures.
- *Social institutions.* Those who participate in a social institution may form a subculture. Examples include participation in marriage, parenthood, a retirement community, the army, and so on.
- *Belief systems.* People with shared beliefs may create a subculture, such as shared beliefs in religion or politics. For example, traditional Amish do not use several types of products, including electricity and automobiles. A whole set of factors has also been correlated with whether a person is a Democrat, Republican, independent, or socialist.
- *Aesthetics.* Artistic people often form a subculture of their own associated with their common interests—including art, music, dance, drama, and folklore.
- *Language.* People with similar dialects, accents, and vocabulary can form a subculture. Southerners and northerners are two traditional categories.

To illustrate, let's examine a subculture that has received a great deal of attention during the last decade—the gay and lesbian community. For many marketers

profile

Ronald Gorlick
Director of New Business for Custom Research
Yankelovich & Partners

At Yankelovich I am the Director of New Business for custom research. I am responsible for research projects for new customers and for conducting qualitative research (focus groups and one-on-one interviews) for a variety of clients and prospects. My research topics vary—I might do research on corporate crisis/image management, employee relations research, product development, or advertising campaign strategy.

Academic Background
I graduated from college in May 1984 with a B.A. in English Literature. After a year working in the New York Theater District, I realized that theater production was not what I wanted to do with my life. Fortunately, I met a market researcher through theater contacts who recruited me to join a research firm, ASI Market Research. At that job, I analyzed and wrote focus group reports for a variety of clients. In 1988 I returned to school to earn an M.B.A., which I received in May 1990 from Washington University in St. Louis.

In the summer between my two years at grad school, I interned at Chiat/Day Advertising in New York. After graduation, I took a job in Strategic Services (research) at Ammirati & Puris Advertising in New York. After two years, I joined KRC Research & Consulting, where I had my most valuable experience as a focus group moderator and researcher for a wide variety of clients. I left when the company was purchased by a New York PR firm, as did most of my colleagues. In May 1995 I joined Yankelovich & Partners in the custom research area.

Typical Day
On a typical day I return calls from or meet with prospective clients to discuss their research needs. I might also design a research proposal for a potential client, present a proposal in a formal meeting, follow up on a proposal, or conduct some research.

My focus group research allows me to talk to many different types of people around the country on a wide variety of topics. One week I might be in St. Louis and San Francisco discussing the impact of large discount stores on small towns' shopping districts. The next week I might be in Seattle talking to young women about why they don't drink milk. Variety keeps my work interesting.

Advice
My career advice to new graduates or the soon-to-be-graduated: Try to pick the firms you join well and stay at least 2 to 3 years at each job. Switching jobs strategically, of course, can mean large jumps in responsibility and money, but you must plan a move carefully.

For anyone interested in a career in business, especially in marketing, I think marketing communication is an excellent place to start. Not only will you work with bright people, you will be exposed to various businesses and job functions. You can apply this experience in many different ways should you decide that marketing communication is not for you.

Remember, businesses seek people who communicate well verbally and in writing. Be sure you take coursework that prepares you to communicate effectively.

the gay and lesbian market represents an untapped gold mine. Because many gays are highly educated and often have no dependents, they have high levels of disposable income. Geographic concentration and a strong word-of-mouth network make them easy to reach.[7]

Still, a great deal is not known about this subculture, and they cannot be researched in traditional ways. For example, estimates of the size of the gay community range from 5 to 10 percent of the U.S. population.

Currently, limited research exists to provide insights about product or media usage in the homosexual community. However, Simmons Market Research Bureau has linked readership of gay publications with purchase behavior. Readers of gay magazines and newspapers are more likely to buy many discretionary items, from sparkling water to consumer electronics and health club memberships. This upscale profile indicates a level of affluence borne out by linking readership with demographic characteristics. Seven percent of readers of gay publications have doctoral degrees, compared with less than 1 percent of the general population. Median household income for this group was $51,300, compared with $30,050 for all U.S. households. This figure may actually underestimate the spending power of gay men because only one-third live with a partner. The drawback to measuring consumer behavior through gay publications, however, is that lesbian women don't tend to read them.[8]

More firms are targeting this growing subculture with separate marketing communication efforts, such as *OUT* magazine.

Understanding Other Cultures Around the World

Adjusting to cultural differences is perhaps the most difficult task facing marketing communicators who operate in other countries. Before entering a foreign market, a company must decide to what extent it is willing to customize its marketing effort to accommodate each foreign market. Naturally, the more the company standardizes its effort, the less trouble it incurs and the greater the assumed profitability. But is some customization inevitable?

Theodore Levitt, a Harvard professor, has argued against customization. In "The Globalization of Markets," he suggested that world markets are being driven "toward a converging commonality" in which people everywhere are motivated by two common needs: high quality and reasonable price. Therefore, the "global corporation sells the same thing in the same way everywhere."[9] He uses McDonald's as one example. Furthermore, segmenting markets by political boundaries and customizing marketing strategies on the basis of national or regional preferences are not cost-effective. Levitt urges companies to adopt a "global orientation" by which they view the world as one market and sell a global product. Companies that do not become true global marketers will perish, says Levitt.[10]

Critics argue that Levitt's assumptions are not realistic. Products and strategies must be adapted to the cultural needs of each country. Philip Kotler, a professor of marketing at Northwestern University, champions the tried-and-true method of selling: tailoring to the local culture. Each national market is different, hence products and promotional strategies must be designed to fit the local culture. He cites several examples to support his position, including M&M/Mars' attempt to enter

OUT magazine is among the brand-name publications that target the lesbian and gay community in print and online.

the European market by creating versions of its candy bars with a better grade of chocolate to compete with Swiss Nestlé and Cadbury Schweppes.[11]

Are there global markets? The answer is yes. Many countries have market segments with similar demands for the same product. Timex, for example, has sold standard products in similar fashion worldwide for decades. Does the world represent a global market? Hardly. There will always be obstacles to standardization, including cultural, political, economic, technological, and other environmental factors. McDonald's restaurants in Hawaii and Japan offer sushi; those in Germany serve beer. In India, a culture that holds the cow sacred, McDonald's offers beefless patties and calls its Big Mac the Maharaja Mac.[12] Levitt's assumptions are not realities yet, and perhaps they never will be.

One study indicates that consumer goods companies are taking globalization seriously. Sixty-one percent of nonfood companies said they were working toward a global strategy on existing brands. When asked their opinion of global new product development for the future, about two-thirds of the executives believed that more and more companies would eventually adopt the global approach touted by Levitt.

TABLE 5.2

A Sampling of Cultural Variations

Country-Region	Body Motions	Greetings	Colors	Numbers	Shape, Sizes, Symbols
Japan	Pointing to one's own chest with a forefinger indicates one wants a bath. Pointing a forefinger to the nose indicates "me."	Bowing is the traditional form of greeting.	Positive colors are in muted shades. Combinations of black, dark gray, and white have negative overtones.	Positive numbers are 1, 3, 5, 8. Negative numbers are 4, 9.	Pine, bamboo, or plum patterns are positive. Cultural shapes such as Buddha-shaped jars should be avoided.
India	Kissing is considered offensive and not seen on television, in movies, or in public places.	The palms of the hands are placed together and the head is nodded for greeting. It is considered rude to touch a woman or to shake hands.	Positive colors are bold colors such as green, red, yellow, or orange. Negative colors are black and white if they appear in relation to weddings.	To create brand awareness, numbers are often used as a brand name.	Animals such as parrots, elephants, tigers, or cheetahs are often used as brand names or on packaging. Sexually explicit symbols are avoided.
Europe	Raising only the index finger signifies a person wants two items.	It is acceptable to send flowers in thanks for a dinner invitation, but not	Generally, white and blue are considered positive.	The number 3 or 7 is usually positive.	Circles are symbols of perfection.

Whether a company assumes a standardized or a customized posture toward foreign markets has a direct bearing on the marketing communication effort. Standardization means taking the existing marketing communication strategy, making sure that everything is translated properly, and otherwise using it unchanged in a foreign country. Customization has far greater implications and makes marketing communication very complex. Extensive research is conducted on a country-by-country basis. Separate agencies may be hired for each market, and separate strategies are developed, as shown in Table 5.2.

What may be more likely to happen is a modularized approach to international marketing communication. A company may select some features as standard for all its communications and localize some others. Campbell Soup Co., for instance, maintains its well-known package and logo on all its ads, but customizes copy and visuals for each country.

Country-Region	Body Motions	Greetings	Colors	Numbers	Shape, Sizes, Symbols
Europe continued	When counting on the fingers, "one" is often indicated by thumb, "two" by thumb and forefinger.	roses (associated with sweethearts) or chrysanthemums (associated with funerals).	Black often has negative overtones.	13 is a negative number.	Hearts are considered favorably at Christmas.
Latin America	General arm gestures are used for emphasis.	The traditional form of greeting is a hearty embrace followed by a friendly slap on the back.	Popular colors are generally bright or bold yellow, red, blue, or green.	Generally, 7 is a positive number. Negative numbers are 13, 14.	Religious symbols should be respected. Avoid national symbols such as flag colors.
Middle East	The raised eyebrow facial expression indicates "yes."	The word "no" must be mentioned three times before it is accepted.	Positive colors are brown, black, dark blues, and reds. Pink, violets, and yellows are not favored.	Positive numbers are 3, 7, 5, 9, whereas 13, 15 are negative.	Round or square shapes are acceptable. Symbols of six-pointed star, raised thumb, or Koranic sayings are avoided.

Sources: Philip R. Harris and Robert T. Moran, *Managing Cultural Differences,* 3rd ed. (Houston Gulf Publishing Co., 1991), 345–50; James C. Simmons, "A Matter of Interpretation," *American Way* (April 1983):106–11; and "Adapting Export Packaging to Cultural Differences," *Business America,* December 3, 1979, 3–7.

Culture, Subculture, and IMC

Understanding the culture and subculture in which you are marketing has important implications for integrating marketing communication. Most notably, all communication must be accurate and consistent within the particular culture or subculture. To communicate a message on a birth-control device in France, you must consider the values and attitudes the French hold toward such technology. However, the communication might be adjusted in Switzerland, where French, Italian, German, and Swiss subcultures exist. Cultures and subcultures represent the starting point for research that serves as the foundation for IMC.

Concept
Review

CULTURES AND SUBCULTURES

1. A culture is the sum of learned beliefs, values, and customs that regulate the behavior of members of a particular society.
2. Values are thought to shape behavior, but no researchers can identify and agree about a set of core values in the North American culture. Searches for general core values have been conducted by research firms such as SRI International (VALS 2) and Yankelovich & Partners (Monitor).
3. Subcultures are based on secondary values. Five factors influence the formation of subcultures:
   - Material culture
   - Social institutions
   - Belief systems
   - Aesthetics
   - Language
4. Marketing in foreign subcultures typically requires major adjustments.

DEMOGRAPHIC CHANGES

Whereas beliefs, values, and customs describe the characteristics of a culture and subculture, **demographics** describe the observable characteristics of individuals living in the culture. Demographics include our physical traits, such as gender, race, age, and height; our economic traits, such as income, savings, and net worth; our occupation-related traits, including education; our location-related traits; and our family-related traits, such as marital status and number and age of children. Demographic trait compositions are constantly changing, and no American, Japanese, or Brazilian is typical anymore.

There is no average family, no ordinary worker, no everyday wage, and no traditional middle class. Still, marketing communicators must understand consumers intimately. Often, the best they can do is take a snapshot and try to understand what is happening in our culture in the final years of this century. As we see next, some trends are old; others are new. For instance, the aging of the population has been going on for several decades, but births and birth rates in recent years have been much higher than expected. Immigration is also greater than predicted, and so is the backlash against it. Interstate migration to the south and west are old trends. What is new is heavier movement from the northeast than from the midwest and rapid growth in the mountain states. Next, we examine nine demographic changes and how they affect marketing communicators.

1. *Households are growing more slowly and getting older.* About half of all households are aged 45 and older and growing at an annual rate of 1 percent compared with nearly 2 percent in the 1980s. Marketing communicators must plan for a greater number of middle-aged households, consumers who are experienced and have a better understanding of price and value. These consumers should have an interest in high-quality household goods and in-home health care.
2. *The demise of the traditional family.* Married couples are a bare majority of U.S. households. Only one-third of households have children under 18, and nearly

one-fourth of households are people who live alone. However, married couples dominate the affluent market as the vast majority of very high income households are married couples. The long-term trend of high growth in non-traditional types of households and lack of growth among married couples can only mean further segmentation of an already segmented marketplace. Figure 5.3 shows the distribution of households by type.

3. *The continued increase in education.* Most adults in the United States still have not completed college (approximately 67 percent), but that number continues to decline. More and more people have attended some college or have an associate or technical degree. More skilled workers mean more knowledgeable and

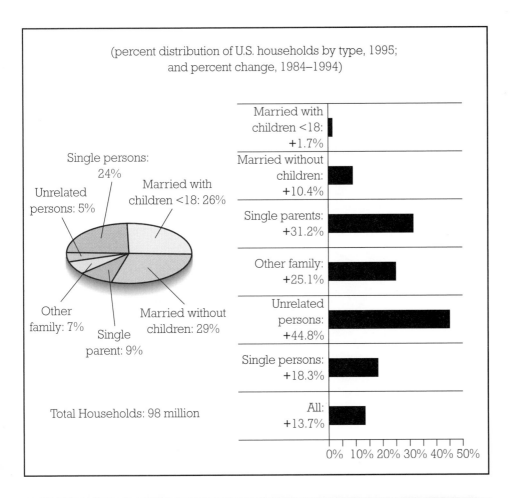

(percent distribution of U.S. households by type, 1995; and percent change, 1984–1994)

Single persons: 24%

Unrelated persons: 5%

Married with children <18: 26%

Other family: 7%

Single parent: 9%

Married without children: 29%

Total Households: 98 million

Married with children <18: +1.7%

Married without children: +10.4%

Single parents: +31.2%

Other family: +25.1%

Unrelated persons: +44.8%

Single persons: +18.3%

All: +13.7%

0% 10% 20% 30% 40% 50%

FIGURE 5.3

Distribution of Household Types

Source: American Demographics' calculations based on Census Bureau surveys.

sophisticated consumers who expect more information about product attributes and benefits before making a purchase.

4. *Nonphysical jobs keep growing.* As illustrated in Figure 5.4, jobs that don't require physical strength keep growing in number. Virtually all job growth during the next ten years will take place among service providers, especially in health care and social services. Because providing services requires little investment compared with producing consumer goods, we can expect continued high growth in small businesses, sole proprietorships, and other entrepreneurial activity. Also, the extremely high cost of employee benefits suggests that the use of temporary workers and independent contractors will continue to grow. Marketing communicators must assess whether consumers who do not have corporate benefits will become more risk averse because they lack the safety net of

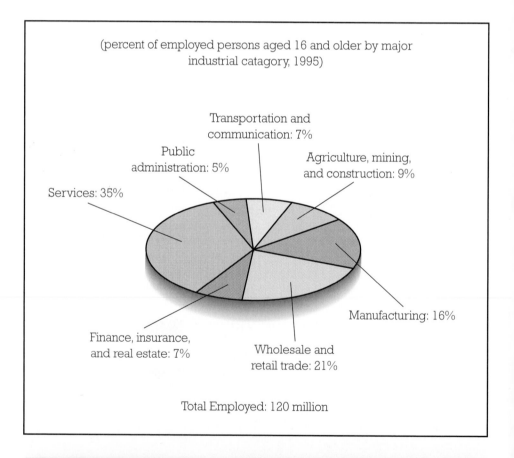

(percent of employed persons aged 16 and older by major industrial catagory, 1995)

Transportation and communication: 7%

Public administration: 5%

Agriculture, mining, and construction: 9%

Services: 35%

Manufacturing: 16%

Finance, insurance, and real estate: 7%

Wholesale and retail trade: 21%

Total Employed: 120 million

FIGURE 5.4

Jobs by Industry

Source: American Demographics' calculations based on Census Bureau surveys.

We Can Help You Run Your Empire.

(All 1900 Square Feet Of It.) If you have your

own business, you should have a MasterCard BusinessCard.

It's accepted at three times as many places

as the American Express' Corporate Card, to meet more of

your business needs. Plus, you'll get

primary car rental insurance and

medical coverage with a MasterCard

BusinessCard. (Amex won't give you

that.) But the best part is, when your bill comes, you decide how

much of it you're going to pay off that month. Hey, you're the boss.

MasterCard. It's more than a credit card. It's smart money.™

For more information, call MasterCard International at 1-800-727-8825, ext. 2.

MasterCard, proud sponsor of world class golf events.

This ad targets the small-business owner. Do you think it does a good job highlighting issues that might concern its target market?

company-provided pension plans and medical insurance. If so, consumers may seek money-back guarantees or other product features that reduce risk. Marketing communicators must also see whether people who work for themselves or for small firms are more time-conscious.

5. *Growing faster than expected.* About 262 million people live in the United States. This is an increase of 13 million since 1990, and most of the growth has resulted from an unforeseen boom in births. The United States had about 20.4 million births between January 1990 and December 1994. This was more than in any five-year period since the last five years of the legendary baby boom (1960 to 1964), and 6 percent more than in the late 1980s. The United States also experienced the highest five-year immigration total (4.6 million) since the turn of the century, an increase of 31 percent over the previous five years. The annual influx of nearly 1 million new residents has led to an increasingly diverse consumer marketplace, particularly among young people.

6. *The growth of minorities.* Although white non-Hispanics have been the biggest contributors to the U.S. population growth in the 1990s, Hispanics have been

"The trunk space is
bumongous."
Larry Carter
Former Chrysler Owner

"You fit in it no matter
what size you are."
Rachael Alexander
Former Caravan Owner

"It's bigger on
the inside than it looks."
Steve Schlief
Former Acura Owner

THERE'S PLENTY OF
ROOM TO TALK.

STARTING AT
$18,545*

FORD TAURUS
THE BEST-SELLING CAR IN AMERICA.

• SPACIOUS INTERIOR WITH PLENTY OF LEG ROOM • AVAILABLE SIX-PASSENGER SEATING
• 15.8 CUBIC FEET OF CARGO CAPACITY • SAFETY CELL CONSTRUCTION • SIDE DOOR BEAMS
• 24-VALVE, DOHC DURATEC V-6 ENGINE** • www.ford.com
*'97 Taurus G MSRP. LX shown w/PEP 210A MSRP $23,870 Tax, title extra. **LX model only

HAVE YOU DRIVEN A FORD LATELY?   *Ford*

Ford recognizes that it must cultivate a diverse customer
base. Do you think this ad has diverse customer appeal?
Why?

a close second. The number of Hispanics in the United States increased from
22 million in 1990 to 26 million in 1995. That number is nearly twice as many
new residents as were added by African-Americans and Asians. If each minority segment keeps growing at current rates, Hispanics will outnumber African-
Americans in ten years. This trend will be particularly important for marketing
communicators that target certain regions, because Hispanics and Asians are
more geographically concentrated than African-Americans. As indicated in the
IMC in Action feature, those who are not from the ethnic group must understand how to communicate with that group or risk inept communication.

7. *Baby boomers become middle-aged.* More than half of Americans are aged 34 or
older, and the oldest baby boomers are now aged 52. The largest ten-year age
group, people aged 38 to 47, has been growing as it absorbs the younger half
of the baby-boom generation. But the number of people in this segment will
reach a peak in 2000 and then decline. The fastest-growing age group is middle-aged people aged 45 to 54—the age at which income and spending peak.
Middle-aged people are also the least likely of all age groups to change their

residence. This combination of high growth, high income, and low mobility will provide considerable lift to discretionary spending, particularly in the categories of home furnishings, education, and insurance.

8. *People are moving south.* More than half (54 percent) of U.S. residents live in the ten largest states, and more than half of U.S. population growth between 1990 and 1995 occurred in these ten states. New York had the largest population of all states in 1950, but in the 1990s fast-growing Texas pushed the barely growing New York to number three. One reason for the explosive growth in the southern states is the influx of people from other countries. More than half of the four million immigrants that located in the United States between 1990 and 1995 moved to California, Texas, or Florida.

9. *The middle class gets hammered.* According to the U.S. Census Bureau, the share of aggregate household income earned by the middle 60 percent of households has shrunk from 52 percent in 1973 to 49 percent 25 years later. Meanwhile, the share of such income earned by the top 20 percent (average income

As the middle-age group of consumers grows, discretionary spending on home furnishings is likely to increase. This Crate and Barrel ad is aimed at people who want to "cocoon" in their homes in comfort and style.

New Folks to Talk To

With few exceptions, companies do not market to the Iranian, Israeli, Polish, Russian, Ukrainian, Arab, Korean, or Vietnamese ethnic groups within the United States. According to the U.S. Census, almost 2.7 million households speak a language from one of these groups. Partly, the reluctance of U.S. marketers to target these untapped markets is based on a lack of understanding. There is also the perception that learning about these segments is too difficult.

To a degree, this perception is true. For example, making sweeping statements about Chinese-Americans is, at best, risky. In effect, there are at least three broad groups of Chinese-Americans who are quite different from each other in terms of their attitudes and behavior:

1. Second, third, and fourth generation Chinese-Americans whose ancestors came to the United States in the 1800s and early 1900s
2. Recent immigrants from mainland China
3. Recent immigrants from Taiwan and Hong Kong

The financial and consumer behavior of Chinese-Americans from the first group are most similar to other U.S. groups. The husband and wife usually share in financial and purchase decisions. Recent immigrants from mainland China are much more traditional, with the husband ostensibly making all major purchase decisions. However, the wife actually has a good deal of influence over her husband's final decisions, which she exercises by "suggestion." For all practical purposes, she manages the money on a day-to-day basis.

Recent immigrants from Hong Kong and Taiwan, particularly those attending college in the United States, behave much more like Americans, sharing financial and purchasing decisions with a spouse. Most newer Chinese-American immigrants read and watch media in their native language, even though they speak and understand English. So-called "ABCs" (American-Born Chinese) still speak and understand their mother language but don't know how to write in Chinese. About half are now returning to Hong Kong, Taiwan, or China to learn to read and write Mandarin.

This problem of communicating in another language is difficult to solve. Experts suggest that when trying to reach emerging foreign language markets in the United

$98,600) increased from 44 percent to 48 percent. In other words, the total purchasing power of the top 20 percent of U.S. households now equals that of the middle 60 percent.[13]

DEMOGRAPHIC GROUPINGS

In addition to understanding general demographic trends, marketing communicators must also recognize demographic groupings that may turn out to be market segments because of their enormous size, similar socioeconomic characteristics, or shared values. We examine three examples of demographic groupings by age that have or will become dominant market segments: baby boomers, Generation X, and the baby boomlet. Their relative size and projections are illustrated in Table 5.3 on page 146.

The Baby Boom

The baby boom occurred from 1946 through 1964. During this 19-year time frame, 76.4 million babies were born in the United States. Today, approximately 70

States, marketing communicators should ask the following questions:

1. How much English is or isn't spoken?
2. Is there just one language for each emerging market?
3. What cultural values of the target market are changing?
4. How do political changes in the countries of origin or the relationships between these countries and the United States affect how the target market spends money?
5. How strong are ties to the country of origin?
6. Is there a cultural distrust of the media that must be overcome?
7. Why did the group members leave their homelands, and what do they hope to find in the United States?
8. What is important to them? How do they dress, eat, pray, work, raise their children, and entertain themselves?

"The Asian-American market offers tremendous opportunities for marketers," notes Eliot Kang, president of K & L Direct, a direct response agency that specializes in the Asian market. "If you keep in mind the cultural sensitivity of each group, there is no secret in how to talk to the Asian market, except that it be in the most appropriate way possible."

If marketing communicators don't take the time to learn the nuances of each ethnic group, they will irrevocably brand themselves as outsiders. The marketer who speaks the unique blend of old and new for each of these immigrants will win their acceptance—and their business.

Food for Thought

1. This feature suggests marketing communicators should adjust to communicate with different ethnic groups within the United States and answer certain questions. Which of those questions should marketing communicators ask when trying to communicate with U.S. citizens living in different regions of the country?
2. Which questions should be asked when trying to communicate with people living in a large city versus a small town?
3. Locate a print ad that targets Chinese-Americans and assess how it is unique.

Sources: Elaine Santoro, "East Meets West: Uncovering the Asian Market in America," *Direct Marketing* (October 1996): 34–9; John Steere, "How Asian-Americans Make Purchase Decisions," *Marketing News,* March 31, 1995, 9; Yuri Radzievsky, "Untapped Markets: Ethnics in the U.S.," *Advertising Age,* June 21, 1993, 26.

million of these baby boomers are still alive. They represent about one-fourth of the total population. Because of their numbers and buying power, baby boomers have and will continue to influence the marketing mix for the services and products businesses offer and how those services and products are offered. For example, the majority of baby boomer women work full time and view their job as a career. This trend has implications for child care, fashion, automobiles, travel, and fast-food marketing. Health concerns will also grow as baby boomers age.

Generation X

Generation X, also known as the "baby busters" or the "shadow generation," is the group of people between the ages of 18 and 29. This group has been labeled with a "slacker" stereotype. Imagine, 45 million humans that are characterized as culturally illiterate, apathetic, and directionless. From a marketers' perspective, they have a total disposable income of $125 billion. In tune to the newest rages, Xers—highly steeped in a culture of sound bytes—seem to know instinctively what they want. And, importantly, what they don't.[14]

TABLE 5.3

A Guide to the Generations

Today, baby boomers are three in ten Americans. In 30 years, they'll be two in ten.
(age range, numbers in thousands, and percent distribution of population by birth cohort, 1995-2025)

AGE	Total	Post-Boomlet*	Baby Boomlet*	Baby Bust	Baby Boom	Pre-Boom
1995	—	—	under 19	19 to 30	31 to 49	50 and older
2005	—	under 10	10 to 28	29 to 40	41 to 59	60 and older
2015	—	under 20	20 to 38	39 to 50	51 to 69	70 and older
2025	—	under 30	30 to 48	49 to 60	61 to 79	80 and older
NUMBER						
1995	262,754	—	72,176	44,603	77,587	68,389
2005	286,324	38,241	76,135	46,364	76,476	49,247
2015	310,370	82,280	78,126	46,788	72,744	30,430
2025	334,216	129,872	79,820	45,452	64,740	14,330
PERCENT OF POPULATION						
1995	100%	—	27.5%	17.0%	29.5%	26.0%
2005	100	13.4%	26.6	16.2	26.7	17.2
2015	100	26.5	25.2	15.1	23.4	9.8
2025	100	38.9	23.9	13.6	19.4	4.3

*Assumes that baby boomlet ends in 1995

Source: Cenus Bureau Data presented by Diane Crispell, "Generations to 2025," *American Demographics* (January 1995):4.

Unfortunately, the more marketers learn about this group, the less it appears to be a market segment. For example, Xers' lifestyles range from the 10 million who are full-time college or postgraduate students to the 15 million who are married. They are also the most racially diverse generation in history. Yet their opinions about life in the United States mirror those of the general population. For instance, 52 percent of Xers believe that "quality of life" is good compared with 53 percent of the entire population, and 64 percent of Xers are more "stressed about money this year" compared with 58 percent of the general population.

The media habits of the Xers are as diverse as the people within the group. "Generation Xers are extremely sophisticated about media, and no one in that age group is a consumer of a single medium," says Karen Ritchie, executive vice president–managing director of General Motors Mediaworks.[15]

Steven Grasse is a Gen Xer who owns the advertising firm Gyro Worldwide, which targets Generation X. He offers the following advice when communicating with Gen X. "First, create an aura of coolness. . . ." He points to his agency as an example. It is decorated like a dorm room, complete with tasteless jokes taped to the toilet in the unkempt bathroom. "[S]econd, know your audience: Generation X will buy cigarettes and alcohol, as well as clothes and music."[16]

Given the diversity of Generation X, what are the possibilities that an integrated marketing communication strategy can be targeted at this group? The key will be finding subsegments within this 45-million-person group. For example, level of education might be a point of distinction. Those in college or with a college degree are likely to be computer-literate and can be reached by online media. Their optimism and general concern for a simpler life suggest that noncondescending marketing messages through public relations or cause-related activities would prove effective. Ultimately, marketing communication managers would be wise not to make assumptions about Generation Xers and to conduct primary research instead.

The Baby Boomlet

Just like the baby boomers, the group of 72 million children of the baby boomers, called the "baby boomlet" or the "echo boom," is creating new waves of change. This group spans 1975 to the present. In 1995 the boomlet had 72 million people under age 19. It is 60 percent larger than the baby bust. Even if 1995 is the final year of boomlet births, this generation will grow through immigration for

This ad from Jhane Barnes is targeted at Generation Xers. What subsegment of that group do you think this ad is trying to target?

Show your character.

Sanrio touts gifts that customers can personalize, an appealing feature for an audience of baby boomlets.

several more decades. By 2015 the baby boomlet will outnumber the aging baby boom.[17]

The baby boomlets will acquire their own attitudes, often shaped by new technology and global changes. Global conversations on the Internet will change their outlook on the world. AIDS will change their attitudes toward relationships, marriage, and family. Real-time information and the customization of the information will produce a consumer who is very discerning. Finally, their attitude will also be shaped by defining events. For instance, it will be a generation that expects terrorist acts, such as the Oklahoma City bombing and the bomb at the 1996 Olympics. Memorable events will have a lasting effect on their outlook.

In this section we investigated how demographic changes and groupings can affect marketing communication. In the next section we explore social class and its influence on marketing communication.

SOCIAL CLASS

Social class refers to position on a social scale based on criteria such as occupation, education, and income. These characteristics define the prestige or power of the individual and, therefore, his or her position. Members of the same social class may never meet or communicate, but they are likely to share certain values, attitudes, and behavior because of similar socioeconomic characteristics. Unlike the rigid social caste system found in India, the social class system in the United States is an *open* system because people can move from one class to another.

Although there are a number of techniques available to place an individual in a particular social class, these results are uncertain. For the marketing communication manager, the traditional **lower, middle,** and **upper class** is sufficient for planning purposes. The assumption that can be made is that to some degree, people within these three social classes develop and assume different patterns of behavior.

For example, time patterns differ sharply by social class. People in the upper social class perform most daily activities an hour or so later than people in the lower social class. The use of language and symbols also differs. Middle-income people use more subtle and complex forms of expression than lower-income people. Simile and analogy are considered more meaningful to middle-class people than to lower-class people.

Perceived risk also separates the social classes. In general, the lower-class segment sees the world as risky and perhaps dangerous. People without much income may not feel adequate to cope with loss or adversity, they are risk averse, and they value personal security. Upper-class people feel risk implies both danger and opportunity; the degree of negative risk is proportional to the rate of positive return.[18]

In cases where social classes differ in at least some purchasing attitudes and behavior, marketers often use social class variations to design communication strategies. For example, banks that market to different social classes should develop marketing communication strategies that match the spending, saving, and investment strategies for each class. Generally, upper-class individuals save more money than people in the lower class. They are concerned about quick and easy access to funds and the rate of return they will receive from investments. Lower-class consumers often save only to accumulate money for a specific purchase, so they may not be concerned about the rate of return they receive. Credit is used more by upper-class consumers, but for different reasons than people in the lower class. Upper-class consumers use credit cards for convenience, whereas lower-class consumers use cards as a type of investment loan.[19]

A final example, and one of particular interest to communication managers, is the differences in media habits. Lower-class consumers tend to depend more on broadcasting for news and sports, and they are devoted to television for entertainment. The late-night television audience is largely upper class. These viewers also watch public affairs programs and public broadcasting, prefer FM to AM radio, read the daily morning newspaper, and prefer magazines targeted at their class.[20]

GROUPS THAT INFLUENCE

A **group** may be defined as two or more people who interact to accomplish either individual or mutual goals. For marketing communication managers, two types of groups strongly influence others' buying behavior, so they have special relevance: *reference groups* and *families.* We examine these two groups in the following sections.

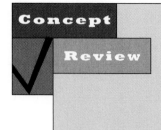

DEMOGRAPHIC CHANGES, GROUPINGS, AND SOCIAL CLASS

1. Demographic changes can strongly influence marketing communication because they often lead to behavioral changes.
2. Demographic groupings based on factors such as size, socioeconomics, age, and values are meaningful to marketing communicators because these groupings often become market segments.
3. Social class is the position an individual has on the social scale, based on objective indicators such as occupation, education, and income, or subjective assessment. When social class differences influence buying behavior, marketing communicators should devise strategies that match the patterns of the target class.

Reference Groups and Their Effects

A **reference group** is defined as any person or group that serves as a point of comparison (or reference) for an individual in the formation of general or specific values, attitudes, or behavior.[21] Although reference groups are normally very specific, for practical reasons marketers classify reference groups into four types: *contractual, aspirational, disclaimant,* and *avoidance.* A **contractual reference group** is a group in which a person holds membership or has regular face-to-face contact with, and that person approves of the group's values, attitudes, and standards (for example, family, friends, neighbors, coworkers). Family and friends serve as the reference group highlighted in many marketing communication messages.

An **aspirational reference group** is one in which a person does not hold membership or have face-to-face contact with, but of which he wants to be a member. This type of group often positively influences the person's attitudes or behavior. Most college students study and attend class because they aspire to be members of the employed reference group. A **disclaimant group** is one in which a person holds membership and does have face-to-face contact with, but she disapproves of the group's values, attitudes, and behavior. For instance, the "Don't drive drunk" campaign encourages teenagers to disassociate themselves from other teenagers who drink. Finally, an **avoidance group** is one in which a person does not hold membership or have face-to-face contact with, and whose values, attitudes, and behavior he disapproves of. For example, many students avoid contact with students who have flunked out.

Although we may belong to many groups, in a particular situation we generally use only one group as a point of reference. For a college student, other college students tend to be the primary reference group. Reference groups have wide-ranging influence on individuals and thus on their behavior as consumers.

Reference groups influence one another through norms, roles, and conformity. Every group has **norms,** which are expectations about what behavior is appropriate. A **role** is a prescribed way of behaving based on the position of the group member in a specific situation. **Conformity** is obedience to these group norms and rules. For example, many colleges and universities are now requiring students

This ad targets a contractual reference group—the extended family (dog included).

to have laptops. Having a laptop, then, is a norm. Having the personal responsibility to buy or lease the laptop when you become a junior is your role. And actually doing this is conformity.

Group Communications Through Opinion Leaders

The reference group influences the communication process. Although information is ultimately processed by an individual, in many cases one or more members of a group filter, interpret, or provide information for the group. Whether people are selecting a restaurant, a lawyer, an automobile, or a brand of cake mix, they seek the advice of knowledgeable friends or acquaintances who can provide information, give advice, or actually make the decision. The individual who provides this service is called an **opinion leader.**

For several years, identifying and influencing the opinion leader have been major objectives of marketing communicators. These tasks have been complicated by the fact that opinion leaders are product specific and tend to be similar, both demographically and in personality, to those they influence. For example, both the opinion leader who shares information about stock investments and the interested investor tend to share many characteristics. However, opinion leaders view or listen to mass media, particularly media that concentrate on their area of leadership. This involvement provides a partial solution to the identification problem. It is logical to assume that people who subscribe to one or more publications on sailing are opinion leaders on sailing. These clues—involvement with sailing, their knowledge, and their subscriptions to sailing publications—signal that they may influence others in this area.

Some product categories have professional opinion leaders who are easy to identify. Examples include auto mechanics, beauticians, stockbrokers, and lawn and garden experts. Martha Stewart and Julia Child are opinion leaders in the culinary field. Perhaps the most prominent opinion leaders as a group are physicians. Not only do they suggest medications and recommend other physicians, but they also may prescribe exercise equipment, wheelchair brands, diets, or vacation sites. Consequently, marketers of medical supplies have long directed their marketing communication to the opinion leader physician rather than the patient, the ultimate user of the product.

Product usage tests, tests of advertising campaigns, and media preference studies are usually conducted on samples of individuals who are most likely to be opinion leaders. It is important that these people not only approve of the marketing mix but feel strongly enough about it to tell others. (The You Decide feature deals with many of the aspects of societal norms and group influences.)

For the marketing communicator, knowledge of reference groups serves several useful purposes. For example, you wouldn't want to use couponing if your target audience viewed coupon clippers as an avoidance group. Likewise, you wouldn't advertise in the *National Enquirer* if your target audience disliked those who read that newspaper. Finally, you would design messages using reference groups that the audience relates to in a positive manner. In this context a reference group is called a **source,** a topic discussed in more detail in Chapter 8.

The Family

The family remains one of the most influential elements in the macroenvironment. Our values, attitudes, and perceptions of life and the world are all formed by our families. The family is a key agent of socialization, the process by which people acquire the skills, knowledge, and attitudes necessary to function in society.

Clearly, purchasing and consumption patterns are behaviors, reflecting attitudes and skills strongly influenced by the family unit. These patterns depend in part on the type of family involved, the stage of the family's life cycle, and the method of decision making used by the family. We explore these factors next.

The American Family

Fifty-two percent of Americans marry and spend the majority of their adult lives as members of a **nuclear family,** which consists of two adults of the opposite sex, living in a socially approved sexual relationship, and their own or adopted children. A nuclear family may be the *family of orientation,* which is the family a person is born or adopted into, or the *family of procreation,* which is the family formed by marriage. The family of orientation is the source of many of our attitudes and values. Although we carry many of these values and attitudes into the family of

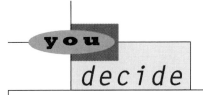

The Problems of Being Ethical

Marianne Jennings, director of the Lincoln Center for Applied Ethics at Arizona State University, shared some concerns about being ethical versus sounding socially responsible.

Business ethics catchphrases typically include no use of animals in product testing, domestic partners' benefits, concern for the rain forest, refusal to do business in China, and so forth. Express full-fledged support of a politically correct agenda and the public cheers.

Many applauded the mission of Anita Roddick's Body Shop: natural cosmetics and "Products for People Tested by People." Readers objected, however, when Jon Entine published articles in *Business Ethics* that exposed the Body Shop's false advertising claims, unfair treatment of franchises, and other ethical slips. Gordon Roddick, Anita's husband, objected, too. His response, however, confirmed some key points—the Body Shop used synthetics to color, perfume, and preserve its products.

Ben & Jerry's Homemade Inc. is often cited as a model of social responsibility. Its ice cream contains all-natural ingredients; its founders donate profits to charity. But the company's self-audit, eventually released to shareholders and the public, showed that the Cherry Garcia flavor contained sulfur dioxide preservatives, and some flavors contained margarine, not butter. Further, due to lackluster financial performance and stiff competition, charitable contributions were decreased.

An ethical business does more than tout its ethics agenda. Once the agenda is set, then, we shouldn't stop asking questions about basic ethical issues. Which is more important—no animal testing or the fair and honest treatment of franchises? Commitment to the rain forests or truth in labeling? Charitable contributions or fairness to shareholders?

Should a business ethics agenda set ethical standards? No one checks to see that firms with commendable social agendas aren't just using them as marketing ploys designed to maximize returns. Stating certain social goals is not the equivalent of acting ethically in business. Though we may want to believe that commitment to social issues is a good measure of ethical conduct, it is not an absolute determinant of fairness and honesty.

You Decide

1. Do you feel that these companies were misleading to position themselves as socially responsible?

2. How should these companies respond to consumers about the conflicts between their images and their actions?

3. Now assume you are a stockholder of these companies. Do your views of their actions change?

Source: Adapted from Marianne M. Jennings, "Confessions of a Business Ethicist," *Wall Street Journal*, 25 September 1995, A14; Marianne M. Jennings, "What's Going On," originally aired on National Public Radio, *All Things Considered*, 18 March 1996. Internet: www.swcollege.com/bef/jennings/br_whats_going_3.18.96.

procreation, lifestyle and purchasing patterns usually shift drastically after marriage. The *extended family* is the nuclear family plus all other close relations—grandparents, aunts, uncles, and cousins. Since World War II, the extended family has become less important to Americans but remains influential in some subcultures.

Within traditional nuclear families in the United States, one important change has occurred: We have become a nation of small families. Lower birth rates mean fewer children per family. Of those families who have children, the mean number is 1.8, down from 3.5 in 1955. Consequently, most Americans are not likely to identify with a portrayal of a large family interacting in a television ad. In fact, the ad might create a negative response. However, for single mothers with even

In Tennessee, Brittany Johnson and her mother, Kathy, attend classes together through Families for Learning, a program sponsored by Toyota.

EVERY YEAR, we help THOUSANDS of people get FROM A to B.

AT TOYOTA, we believe a car company can also be a vehicle for change. That's why for more than 20 years, we've been supporting educational programs that range from kindergartens to colleges to job-training programs and beyond. In the last four years alone, Toyota has invested more than $50 million in worthwhile educational organizations like the National Center for Family Literacy, United Negro College Fund and hundreds of other projects across America. As the fourth-largest manufacturer of vehicles in America, Toyota is committed to helping individuals go as far as they possibly can.

INVESTING IN THE THINGS WE ALL CARE ABOUT. **TOYOTA**

For more information about Toyota in America write Toyota Motor Corporate Services, 9 West 57th Street, Suite 4900-Q26, New York, NY 10019

This ad by Toyota targets an ongoing concern for families. Do you think the ad is effective for Toyota? Why?

a few children, providing a good education is difficult. The Toyota ad addresses this issue.

For decades, some social commentators worried that the traditional family was not only shrinking but actually becoming obsolete, in part because of increases in cohabitation and divorce. But despite increases in cohabitation during the last decade, the Census Bureau estimates that only about 2 percent of all households consist of unmarried people of both sexes, and most unmarried couples live together only a short time before they marry or separate. Divorce is a more significant phenomenon. The number of divorces granted each year has doubled in the last ten years, although most divorces are followed by remarriage.

The result of these remarriages is often an *aggregate,* or *blended, family.* Two divorced people with children remarry, bringing the children of both marriages into the new, expanded family. It is estimated that 25 percent of American children are now or soon will be members of an aggregate family.[22]

Of course, divorce may also create a household made up of just one person or a household headed by a single parent. Recent dramatic increase in the number of single-parent households has had definite marketing implications. Convenience items, day-care centers, and appliances safe enough for young children to use without supervision have all become important to the single-parent family. When and what type of media should be used to deliver the marketing communication message must be adjusted to reach this type of family. Most single parents do not have time to read newspapers and magazines regularly. Nor do single parents watch television until late at night after the children go to bed and the kitchen is cleaned. A message delivered through late-night television or direct mail, then, is more likely to be seen or read.

Family Decision Making

For more than 40 years, marketers have been studying how families make their purchasing decisions. How many members are involved in each decision? How are they involved? How does their influence work on the outcome? And what is the best way to reach each of them?

Table 5.4 shows some consumer roles played by members of a typical family. Decisions about purchases depend in part on which family member takes on which role. Studies of husband-wife decision making usually classify the decisions as being husband-dominated, wife-dominated, joint, or autonomous. These influences are quite fluid and depend on the specific product features under consideration. Consequently, marketing communicators must be sure that they are portraying the husband and wife correctly in various decision-making scenarios.

Children play an important role in family decision making. Researchers in one study observed the interaction between parents and children during the purchase of breakfast foods. In 516 episodes the two most frequent scenarios were (1) the child demands a particular brand of cereal and the parent yields (30 percent), and (2) the parent invites the child to select a brand, the child does so, and the parent

TABLE 5.4 Consumer Roles Within a Family	Role	Description
	Stimulator	First mentions the product or service
	Filter	Regulates the flow of information about consumer goods
	Influencer	Helps shape other people's evaluation of goods or services
	Decider	Makes the decision to buy or consume the product
	Preparer	Converts the goods to a form that can be consumed
	Consumer	Uses or consumes the product
	Monitor	Regulates consumption by other family members
	Maintainer	Services or repairs goods
	Disposer	Discards goods that are no longer wanted or needed

Source: Robert B. Settle and Pamela L. Alreck, *Why They Buy: American Consumers Inside and Out.* Copyright 1986 by John Wiley & Sons. Reprinted by permission of John Wiley & Sons, Inc.

agrees with the selection (19 percent). Regardless of whether the parent or the child initiates the selection, the child seems to direct the brand selection for breakfast food. Recognizing the influence of children, many firms target young children in their promotions. Cereals are often positioned as after-school snacks and include toys and games as part of the package or offer a prize or premium.

The Family Life Cycle

Families, like individuals, move through a series of relatively distinct and well-defined stages that affect their needs and wants. Table 5.5 lists the life-cycle stages and their accompanying purchase patterns. Notice the dramatic shift in the types of products from those purchased by the "young, *unmarried,* childless" to those purchased by the "young, *married,* childless."

For marketing communication managers, changes in the family life cycle offer opportunities to match strategies with particular life stages. A company such as Eastman Kodak uses diverse ads in different media to match the stage of the family life cycle. On the one hand, the "young, unmarried, childless" individual has little money for photography and associates picture taking with pleasurable events

This GE Capital Assurance ad targets older consumers who are interested in financial services that will protect their assets in later years.

TABLE 5.5

Family Life-Cycle Changes and Purchasing Decisions

Phase of Cycle	Financial Condition	Typical Purchase Patterns
Phase 1 Young, unmarried, childless	Both income and expenses are limited, little saving, free spending, beginning use of credit, little financial stress	Apparel, fashion goods, personal care products and services, things related to mating and dating, basic necessities and home supplies, cheap transportation, education, (shared) apartment rent
Phase 2 Young, married, childless	Resources adequate (two incomes), little financial burden, free spending, use of credit, little saving, little stress	Consumer durables, major appliances and furniture, audio and video home entertainment goods, air travel, restaurant meals, spectator entertainment, vacations, apparel, and personal care products
Phase 3 Unmarried, preschool children	Income strictly limited (unmarried new parent), cautious spending, credit not readily available, no savings, high financial stress	If home-sharing, food and housing expenses shared, dependent on Family Life–Cycle phase of others; if nesting, buying patterns similar to those of next phase, appliances, furniture, child-care products and services, including day care
Phase 4 Married, preschool children	Income limited if only one parent is working, few liquid assets, careful spending and credit, little saving, distress and discontent	Purchase and furnishing of first home, durables, especially large and small appliances, child-care products and services, life and casualty insurance, transportation and utilities
Phase 5 Unmarried, grade school children	Income limited, careful spending, credit used if available, little saving, high financial stress, substantial discontent	Rent or mortgage payment, economical appliances and furniture, food, clothing, education, transportation expenses for child, limited personal spending, housekeeping and/or child-care costs, low-cost recreation

Source: Robert B. Settle and Pamela L. Alreck, *Why They Buy: American Consumers Inside and Out*. Copyright 1986 by John Wiley & Sons. Reprinted by permission of John Wiley & Sons, Inc.

GROUPS THAT INFLUENCE

Two main types of groups influence the consumer: reference groups and the family.

1. The reference group serves as a point of comparison for an individual in the formation of general or specific values.
2. The family forms many of our values, attitudes, and perceptions of life and the world.

such as vacations. With this in mind, the Kodak ads in such magazines as *Seventeen* and *Rolling Stone* emphasize the low cost of Kodak cameras and show young people preserving enjoyable times. The "married with preschool children" group, on the other hand, is very involved in picture taking. Network television, direct mail, and print ads in magazines such as *Parents* portray the joy of saving the moments of childhood through photographs.

SUMMARY

1. **Describe how culture and subculture affect marketing communication.**

   Marketing communication strategists who plan to operate in the dynamic marketing environment of the twenty-first century must continuously monitor and evaluate the sociocultural environment. Culture, the broadest element of the sociocultural environment, consists of three components. The first, beliefs, reflects our knowledge and assessment of something. The second component, values, is divided into core values and secondary values. Core values predominate within a culture, whereas secondary values predominate at the subculture or personal level. Both types help us make choices in everyday life. The final component is customs, overt modes of behavior prescribed in a culture.

2. **List and explain demographic factors that influence marketing communication.**

   Demographic characteristics are elements we can observe about the individual. Nine general demographic trends that influence marketing communication are the following: slow growth of households, the demise of the family, the increase in education, the growth of service jobs, the faster than expected population growth, the growth of minorities, the aging population, migration toward the south, and the shrinking middle-class income. In addition, three age-related demographic segments (baby boomers, Generation Xers, and baby boomlets) have communication implications because each responds uniquely to communication.

3. **Discuss the role that social class plays in a culture.**

   Demographic traits are often related to another key element of the sociocultural environment: social class. People in different social classes tend to follow different lifestyles, but the relevance of social class to promotion strategies depends on the product involved.

4. **Summarize how social groups can influence and are influenced by marketing communication.**

   The family and other reference groups shape values, attitudes, and behavior. People tend to conform to the norms and roles established by their reference groups, and they often turn to opinion leaders within these groups for guidance. The most important reference group remains the family, which is the key agent of socialization. Consumer purchases are influenced by the type of household people live in, by their current stage in the family life cycle, and by their methods of family decision making. Changes in families and households, such as recent increases in the numbers of single-person and single-parent households, offer dramatic challenges and opportunities for marketing communication managers.

POINTS TO PONDER

Review the Facts

1. Define the sociocultural environment.
2. What are core values? Secondary values?
3. What is a subculture? Define Generation X.
4. What are norms? Roles? Conformity?

Master the Concepts

5. What factors can be used to distinguish one subculture from others? What does a culture have in common with its subcultures?

6. Outline the major changes in the demographic environment during the 1990s.
7. What are the most significant trends affecting women in the United States?

Apply Your Knowledge

8. Baby boomers were presented as one of the most important demographic groups. Identify three specific marketing communication strategies that would be appropriate for reaching

(1) the older baby boomers and (2) the youngest baby boomers.

9. Describe a marketing communication strategy for a compact disc player that would be appropriate for Generation X.

10. Gold Star is a company that manufactures dual-track video players. It would like to design a marketing communication strategy targeted at the American family. What are the key considerations Gold Star should identify before targeting this group? Is there a typical American family?

SUGGESTED PROJECTS

1. (Writing Project) Trace the baby-boom generation through the year 2020. Graphically show the kinds of goods and services baby boomers will need as they move toward that date. Write a brief memo (1 to 2 pages) analyzing how you arrived at the conclusions shown on your graph.

2. Review the purchase decision-making process your family has followed during the last year. Are purchasing decisions made exclusively by one member of your family? Jointly?

3. (Internet) Find the Internet home page for a favorite product, brand, or company. Analyze the Web site to see what market segment(s) it targets, and be as specific as possible. For instance, what age group(s), socioeconomic group(s), reference group(s), and value(s) does the site seem to target? Write a brief memo to support your findings.

CASE 5: THE POOR AS A MARKET SEGMENT

People tend to think of others as being like themselves. When you hear the phrase "young adults," you probably think of other college students, not of 20-year-olds living in poverty with no job, income, or prospects. This tendency holds true in corporate boardrooms and in advertising agencies, and, because top executives and marketers are generally better off than the average person, many marketing campaigns are pitched at richer customers. As Harvard Business School professor John Quelch puts it, "The marketing community has no aspirations to address the needs of a demographic group of which it is not a member."

S. C. Johnson & Son, Inc., manufacturer of Raid, is an exception to this rule. It all began in 1992 when Lisa Peters, account supervisor at BR & R Communication, Chicago, was faced with the unenviable task of finding new market opportunities for the 40-year-old Raid brand. With the migration of the U.S. population toward urban housing, improvements in insulation, and the popularity of commercial exterminators, the market for home pest exterminator products such as Raid had declined steadily.

After several months of research, Lisa determined that there was one market segment that still had a need for products such as Raid. Her research found that 78 to 98 percent of inner-city urban homes and apartments are infested with cockroaches. Market testing indicated that the current Raid formulation was not effective in dealing with these super bugs.

The lab went to work and produced a new-and-improved version of Raid they named Raid Max. Next, the product was test marketed in several Chicago housing developments—samples were distributed to 1500 families. After 30 days, test families were queried about both the effectiveness of the product and its affordability. The product would prove profitable if a 24-ounce aerosol can could be sold for at least $1.75. Lisa's research indicated that this low-income consumer group could and would pay this amount. The product was launched in the spring of 1993.

The following year the company added a health spin. It seems that in addition to being unsightly, the little devils are the leading cause of asthma and allergies in many urban cities. Johnson hired medical specialists to test people for cockroach allergies and recruited two minority entomologists to answer questions about cockroach asthma and allergies and tell consumers how to control the bugs. At the same time, the company rolled out its Raid Max Roach Bait Plus Egg Stoppers, which uses a special ingredient that the company claims "renders cockroaches sterile."

The company also developed a series of educational brochures. The copy was kept simple and there were a lot of graphics. The company tapped into community leaders to help make the pitch. "We want to be invited in," Peters said. "We don't want to just appear on a billboard . . . . when consumers go into the store,

they remember that the company cared enough to come into the neighborhoods and provided them with something they can use to make a difference."

Case Questions

1. Which sociocultural factors proved most important in the success of Raid Max?
2. How would you evaluate the approach Johnson used in marketing to this consumer group?
3. If you were the marketing communications director with this information, what consistent theme or themes would you use to promote Raid Plus Egg Stoppers? Name three types of marketing communication you would use and explain your choices.

Sources: Jan Larsen, "Fact, Fiction and Homeless," *American Demographics,* August 1996, pp. 14–15; Paula Mergenhagen, "What Can Minimum Wage Buy?," *American Demographics,* January 1996, pp. 32–36; Donald L. Bartlett and James B. Steele, "American Dream Turns Into Nightmare For Many," *The Denver Post,* Sunday September 1996, 31A–32A.

ROMA'S LITE INTEGRATED CASE QUESTIONS

(Review the Roma's Lite Marketing Plan in the Appendix at the end of the text before answering these questions.)

1. Which sociocultural factors will be important in the launch of Roma's Lite Pizza? Explain.
2. List and discuss the demographic factors that would be most important in understanding pizza consumption.
3. (Team Project) Have each team member interview at least two household members about how they purchase pizza. Also, identify (through a questionnaire) sociocultural characteristics unique to each family that would help you better understand this purchase process.

chapter

6

Decision Making in the New Marketplace

CHAPTER OBJECTIVES

After completing your work on this chapter, you should be able to:

1 **Describe how the psychological factors of motivation, learning, and attitudes affect consumer decision making.**

2 **Explain how consumers make complex and simple decisions and how marketing communication can influence this process.**

3 **Contrast organizational and consumer buying behavior.**

4 **Outline the organizational buying process.**

CONSIDER this

Investors and Their Needs

How do you attract prospective clients and retain their business over the long haul? Ask professionals at some of the country's financial institutions, and you're likely to hear one phrase continually repeated: needs-based selling. It means identifying an individual's needs and recommending an appropriate plan to help meet them. This approach enables marketers with numerous products to modify their sales strategies to accommodate the demands of most investors.

William Taylor, a manager with Royal Alliance Associates, Inc., in Marin County, California, uses the needs-based selling approach religiously. "There's no better way to build long-term relationships with investors," says Taylor. "To keep clients, you have to be authentic and human, instead of mechanical and sales-oriented. Address-

ing a client's needs instead of trying to sell a particular product is the best way to accomplish this goal." Some advisers try to build their business by touting their performance record, but Taylor says that's a losing strategy.

Joseph Bombard agrees. Bombard works in the Syracuse, New York, Prudential Securities' office. He designs his business plan to make clients and prospects feel as if they have a partner—not someone who's out to make a commission on every sale. "I do this by analyzing an individual's goals and risk tolerance in person," he says. "Then, using Prudential's select list of money managers, I'll recommend a professional I believe is most appropriate for that individual. If, after a year or two, the manager doesn't live up to our expectations, I'll select another professional who might be more suitable. But we'll do it as a team. I want to create the feeling that we're on the same side of the fence." Bombard admits that building a business through needs-based selling is more time-consuming than selling a product, but he says it's worth it. "I have found that people are more likely to trust you when you take this approach."

If you ask Ed Fitzgerald, a financial consultant with PaineWebber in Iselin, New Jersey, whether he believes needs-based selling is a smart way to do business, he'll tell you: "It's the only way. Without it, you're just trying to push square pegs into round holes." Fitzgerald deals with many investors who put money away for retirement.

Because most believe they'll have enough socked away for their leisure years, he makes sure clients understand that they'll need about 75 percent of their current income to maintain their standard of living in retirement. "In essence, instead of simply uncovering an investor's goals, I'm creating needs for them to consider."

While there are as many ways to practice needs-based selling as there are investment professionals, the bottom line on this strategy is that it's well received by most individuals. And understandably so. Most people respond favorably to those who want to help.

Sources: L. B. Gschwandtner and Gerhard Gshwandtner, "Balancing Act," *Selling Power* (June 1996): 22–9; Dom Dee Prete, "Investment Advisors Identify and Sell to Individuals' Needs," *Marketing News,* June 5, 1995 1, 9; Murray Raphael, "Upgrading Prospects to Advocates," *Direct Marketing* (June 1995):34–7.

CHAPTER OVERVIEW

In Chapter 1 we stressed that to succeed in today's business environment marketers must focus on customers' needs and serve those needs well. Whether the term for this approach is relationship marketing or needs-based selling, the outcome should be the same—a mutual commitment and trust between the marketer and the customer.

Chapter 5 described sociocultural factors—such as culture, social class, and reference groups—that marketing communicators must understand to influence buyer behavior. But marketing communicators must also understand the psychological factors that influence consumer decisions. These factors include motives, attitudes, and personalities.

In this chapter we investigate psychological traits that affect purchasing decisions, the types and process of consumer decision making, and purchase and post-purchase consumer behavior. Most importantly, we see how the psychology of consumer behavior affects marketing communication programs. We also examine how organizations, and the people in them, make decisions and how the psychology of those decisions affects marketing communication programs.

The difficulties in understanding buyer behavior are daunting. People themselves often do not understand why they buy some products rather than others. Countless variations in consumer behavior occur simply because each person is an individual with a unique personality. Predicting consumer behavior becomes even more difficult for companies that are trying to influence the consumer decisions of people from many different cultures. Despite difficulties, businesses must search for common threads so that they can appeal to many people with one marketing communication program.

We start with a model of consumer decision making, as shown in Figure 6.1. Our focus is on answering this question: What does the marketing communication strategist need to know about human behavior to create effective messages? We first examine the psychological characteristics of motivation, learning, personality, and attitudes shown in Figure 6.1.

EXTERNAL INFLUENCES

INTERNAL FACTORS AND PROCESSES

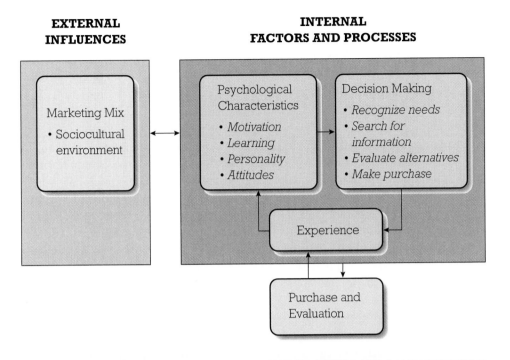

FIGURE 6.1

External Influences and Internal Factors and Processes

This figure focuses on the specific elements that influence a consumer's decision to purchase and evaluate products.

THE PSYCHOLOGICAL BACKGROUND

Although we focus on individual consumers throughout this chapter, all the members of the stakeholder audiences—employees, community members, suppliers, resellers, and so forth—are people who exhibit and are influenced by psychological factors. The buying behavior we explore here applies to all types of audience members, though integrated marketing communication managers may have to adapt their communication strategy to each audience group. For instance, motivating an employee to work harder to prepare more pizza may require a different set of cues (such as financial incentives or more responsibility) than motivating a consumer to purchase pizza, or a cheese supplier to deliver its product to the pizza maker on time.

Regardless of which stakeholder audience group we choose to communicate with, a basic understanding of what makes that person tick is essential. Suppose you were trying to sell lights to a buyer in an industrial plant who wanted powerful outdoor security lights. Trying to sell that buyer decorative lamps would probably get you nowhere. If sellers do not appeal to the right motive, they will likely lose the sale. Similarly, a business that does not accommodate its customers' beliefs, interests, attitudes, self-images, or other psychological characteristics risks losing customers. A business should learn about its customers—why customers do or do not buy their products, where and how they make purchases, and when. Gathering such information may reveal marketing communication opportunities. Next, we introduce three key aspects of consumer behavior psychology: motivation, learning, and attitudes.

Motivation

A **motive** is an inner drive or pressure to act in order to eliminate tension, to satisfy a need or want, to solve a problem, or to restore a sense of equilibrium. A need or desire must be aroused to serve as a motive. The sources of arousal may be internal (biological or psychological) or environmental. Hunger, for example, may be stimulated by a lack of food, by thoughts about food, or by a food commercial that shows a remarkable picture of your favorite meal.

Marketing communication managers need to understand what motives stimulate consumer behavior and how these motives and behaviors are influenced by specific situations. Identifying motives is the first step in this task. Because each individual's personal development is unique, so are each person's motives.[1] For example, if you buy a particular brand of soft drink on a hot summer day, that decision may reflect both your need to satisfy thirst and your need for self-expression. Although marketers cannot control your thirst, they can influence your choice of a soft drink.

The number of possible motives for consumer behavior is vast. Many have attempted to classify these motives, but no one classification is complete or universally accepted. Probably the classification most closely associated with marketing communication divides motives into rational and emotional motives.

Rational motives are supported by a reasoning process that consumers perceive as being rational (that is, acceptable) to their peers. For example, an investor may decide to invest in Ford Motors stock because her father always bought Fords. Whether this reasoning is sound is irrelevant. What matters is that the individual *believes* the motivation is rational. Rational motives commonly include criteria such as convenience, price, risk, performance, endurance, delivery time, and reliability.

Emotional motives are characterized by feelings that may emerge without careful thought or consideration of social consequences.[2] People are often unwilling to admit emotional motives openly. Sometimes these motives—known as **latent motives**—lie below consciousness. It would probably be unwise to emphasize these motives in marketing messages because consumers might not recognize that they are relevant. Motives that people are conscious of but are often unwilling to acknowledge are **manifest motives.** Being afraid of snakes might be an example. A great many emotional motives exist, but generally those most important in marketing include status, prestige, conformity, sex, loneliness, self-esteem, and the desire to be different.

Motives, both rational and emotional, may be stimulated through the use of marketing communication tools that provide product information, extra incentives, entertainment, and so forth. Motorola, for instance, uses a special year-long team event to motivate its employees. The event is motivating because it addresses employees' need to increase self-esteem, improve status, and gain financial reward. The event is called the Total Customer Satisfaction Team Competition. The winning teams, selected by Motorola's top managers, are judged both by how they achieved superior customer service and how that service resulted in bottom-line benefits.[3]

Learning

Learning starts with motivation. Needs and goals stimulate motivation, which in turn, spurs learning. **Learning** is a process of taking in information, processing it along with existing information, and producing new knowledge. Suppose a customer is motivated to begin an exercise program because he is putting on weight and feeling lethargic. A **cue**—in this case an ad for a new health club—persuades the direction the individual will follow to satisfy the goal of losing weight. The message in the health club ad, however, will only serve as a cue if it is consistent with the person's expectations. If he has already tried to lose weight at other health clubs, the ad will not create a response.

How an individual reacts to a cue constitutes her **response.** Learning can take place even if the response is not overt. A positive response to a cue is called **positive reinforcement;** in the future the same cue is again likely to produce a similar reaction. If a past response to a cue produced an unpleasant experience, then **negative reinforcement** has taken place. Note all the cues highlighted in the ad for Geico Insurance.

This Geico Insurance ad highlights several cues that can spur learning, such as savings, convenience, and service. What other cues can you find?

Psychologists distinguish two basic types of behavioral learning: *classical conditioning* and *instrumental conditioning*. In **classical conditioning** a response is learned as a result of the pairing of two stimuli. Assume that Spike Lee elicits positive feelings in members of an audience. If they repeatedly see him and milk together in a commercial, then eventually the sight of milk alone will elicit those positive feelings. In the language of classical conditioning, Spike Lee and milk are stimuli that have been paired. The positive reaction to milk is a **conditioned response** that has been learned as a result of the pairing of the stimuli.

In **instrumental conditioning** a response is learned or strengthened because it has been associated with certain consequences. If buying milk brings the reward of a good-tasting, healthy drink, then the act of buying milk is **reinforced** and is more likely to occur in the future.

Attitudes

Motivation and learning both play a part in forming the third component of the psychological background for consumer behavior: attitudes. An **attitude** is an enduring disposition, favorable or unfavorable, toward an idea, a person, a thing,

The Spike Lee ad for milk is designed to create a conditioned response—those consumers who like Spike should now feel positively about milk.

or a situation. Thus, attitudes toward brands are tendencies to evaluate brands in a consistently favorable or unfavorable way. Each attitude has three components: *cognitive, affective,* or *behavioral.* All three components must be consistent for enduring attitudes to result.

The **cognitive component** includes beliefs and knowledge about the object of the attitude. For example, you might believe that Shell Oil is a major petroleum manufacturer, an aggressive marketer, and is socially responsible. Each of these beliefs reflects knowledge about an attribute of the company. The sum of your beliefs about Shell Oil represent the cognitive component of an attitude toward the company.

If you say "I hate Shell Oil" or "I feel like the gasoline from Shell Oil is better than any other," you are expressing the affective aspect of an attitude. Feelings about the object make up the **affective component** of an attitude.

Actions taken toward the object of an attitude constitute the **behavioral component** of an attitude. Buying a product, recommending a company to friends, or requesting information are examples of behavioral components. Behavior is usually directed toward an entire object and is therefore not likely to be attribute specific.

A great deal of marketing strategy is based on the idea that the cognitive, affective, and behavioral components of an attitude tend to be consistent. Thus, if a company like Intel can change the cognitive component of people's attitudes—that is, change people's beliefs about the firm—their feelings and actions about the company may also change.[4] However, this assumption is more true in certain decision settings than others.[5]

The situation, or consumer attitudes toward the situation, play an important role in how well attitudes predict behavior. For example, suppose a consumer loves thick crust pizza but does not like the fact that the pizza restaurant serving the product allows smoking. Regardless of his positive feelings about the product, the situation precludes the possibility that a purchase will be made.

Similarly, many consumers hold extremely negative attitudes toward doctors or lawyers who advertise. If a large segment of the doctors' or lawyers' target market holds these attitudes, then those professionals should not advertise but should instead send their marketing communication message through other channels.

The Multiattribute Attitude Model

In general, the simple linkage between beliefs, feelings, and behavior has not held up. Instead, attitude research has shown that these three elements are not equivalent. Rather, some components are far more important than others in forming attitudes. For instance, the fact that a ValuJet plane crashed in Florida in 1996 is an event that many consumers will focus on rather than ValuJet's on-time record, cost savings, or clever advertising. A greater possibility that a certain airline's plane will crash is more important than these other factors.

Each element contains a set of attributes relevant to the object considered. Marketing communication managers that know which attitude is most salient can design their message strategy with that attribute in mind. The **multiattribute attitude model** is quite helpful with message strategy in that it systematically predicts individuals' attitudes toward an object by examining their reactions to specific object attributes.[6]

According to the multiattribute attitude model, a person's overall attitude toward a brand can be measured by determining (1) the consumer's evaluation of individual brand or product attributes, (2) the consumer's ideal for those attributes, and (3) the importance the consumer assigns to those attributes. The difference between the evaluation of each attribute and the customer's ideal, weighted by the importance of that attribute, determines the strength of the attitude. This definition may be formulated in the following way:

$$A_b = \sum_{l=i}^{n} W_i[I_i - X_{ib}]$$

in which:

$A_{(b)}$ = the consumer's attitude toward a particular object
$W_{(i)}$ = the importance the consumer attaches to attribute i
$I_{(i)}$ = the consumer's ideal performance on attribute i
$X_{(ib)}$ = the consumer's belief about object b's performance on attribute i
n = number of attributes considered

As an example, suppose that a consumer perceives Crest toothpaste to have the following levels of performance on four attributes:

	1	2	3	4	5	6	7	
Low price		*I*			*X*			**High price**
Good taste			*I*	*X*				**Poor taste**
High cavity prevention	*I*	*X*						**Low cavity prevention**
Good breath freshener		*I*				*X*		**Poor breath freshener**

In this example, as shown by the Xs, the consumer believes that Crest has a fairly high price, has a fair taste, has better-than-average cavity prevention, and is a poor breath freshener. The consumer's ideal toothpaste, as shown by the Is, would be low priced, taste good, prevent cavities, and be a good breath freshener. For each attribute, the consumer assigns an importance weight.

Attribute	**Importance**
Price	10
Taste	20
Cavity prevention	50
Breath freshening	20
Total	100 points

The list shows that cavity prevention is the most important attribute, followed by flavor, breath freshening, and price. Now let's examine each attribute. By taking the difference between the ideal score and the actual score times its weight, we see that the consumer's attitude score toward Crest toothpaste is as follows:

$$
\begin{aligned}
A(\text{Crest}) &= (10)(2 - 5) + (20)(3 - 4) + (50)(1 - 3) + (20)(2 - 6) \\
&= 10(3) + 20(1) + 50(2) + 20(4) \\
&= 30 + 20 + 100 + 80 \\
&= 230
\end{aligned}
$$

Determining whether this attitude score of 230 is good or bad can only be ascertained by computing an attitude index with 0 as the strongest favorable attitude (that is, perceived performance and ideal scores are identical) and the other end of the index reflecting the maximum possible difference between desired and perceived beliefs.

In this example the maximum possible difference is 530. Therefore, an attitude score of 230 suggests a somewhat favorable attitude toward Crest, as it is on the favorable half of the index. A comparison of this attitude score with the scores for competing brands shows how consumers perceive Crest relative to other brands. This comparison might show Crest in a more favorable or less favorable light when compared with competitors.

Influencing Attitudes

How easily can attitudes be changed? The answer depends to an extent on two characteristics of the attitude: its *centrality* and its *intensity*. **Centrality** depends on the degree to which an attitude is tied to values. Note that although personal values influence attitudes, the two are distinct. Values are not tied to a specific situation or object; they are standards that guide behavior and influence beliefs and attitudes. People have a large number of beliefs, a smaller number of attitudes, and even fewer values. The stronger the relationship between an attitude and a person's values, the greater the centrality of the attitude.

For example, for a person who places a high value on thriftiness, social responsibility, and ecology, a favorable attitude toward recyclable containers is likely to have high centrality. If the centrality of an attitude is high, then changing it would create inconsistency between the attitude and a person's values. Not surprisingly, research suggests that the more central an attitude is, the more difficult it is to change.[7]

Intensity depends on the affective component of an attitude. The strength of feeling toward the object of an attitude constitutes the intensity of the attitude. Intense attitudes are difficult to change. Consequently, most marketing efforts are directed at creating minor changes in attitudes—from negative to neutral, from neutral to positive, or from positive to more positive. A person who holds an intensely negative attitude toward a product or idea might best be dropped as a target audience member.

Change in consumers' attitudes is most likely to occur when people are open-minded in their beliefs or when an existing attitude is weak, such as an attitude based on poor information. However, if people have strong brand loyalty, changing their attitudes will be difficult. A marketing communication manager must use highly persuasive communication to change one or more of the three attitude components. For instance, the use of coupons, free samples, or cents-off sales

This ad attempts to change consumer attitudes toward the product by stressing the value of caring for the environment, emphasizing that Saturn recycles and preserves the land on which it operates.

might induce open-minded buyers to change their behavioral component—they may try a new brand. The IMC in Action feature shows how the Australian Airline Qantas attempted to change attitudes through new information and by offering incentives.

Regardless of the efforts to change attitudes, the burning question remains whether this is worth it given the uncertainty of attitudes that predict behavior. The results of a survey conducted by Roper College Track shows how attitudes translate into behavior. The survey asked college students questions regarding their attitudes about food and meals, and what foods they purchased. Essentially, the attitudes of the students indicate that they are willing to trade quality for convenience and speed. Quick and easy meals are most attractive to students, so the microwave is an appliance that plays a major role in students' lives. Cereal is a staple; some college students regularly stock three different kinds of cereals, one for each meal. Far and away the most popular food is pizza, followed by hamburgers. Other highly regarded items are subs, chicken wings, fried mozzarella sticks, onion rings, french fries, Oreos and Chips Ahoy!, Cool Ranch Doritos, Twinkies, Mountain Dew, and Jolt![8] Any of this ring a bell?

The You Decide feature on page 174 details a product category that consumers have changed their attitudes about—credit cards.

Psychographics and Lifestyles

A way of examining the psychology of human behavior in total and is of particular use to the marketing communication manager is through a grouping technique called *psychographics,* or lifestyle analysis, which we discussed briefly in Chapter 4. The origin of the term "psychographics" is a take-off from the more

Lack of Continuity Down Under

Australia has been slow to accept programs that offer points as a bonus for customer loyalty because "third-party" trading stamps like S&H and Green Shield have always been illegal. The recent spate of loyalty program activity may prove that its slow start was a costly gamble.

To compete with international carriers, after the merger of Qantas with Australian Airlines, the "new" Qantas launched Australia's first frequent flier program using a "two-party" approach (the airline deals directly with the customer). The only other national competitor, Ansett, followed simultaneously. Qantas and Ansett now have, between them, more than 450,000 members. After considerable cost,

both companies still share the market almost equally. Existing customers are the winners.

Soon after the airline frequent flier program debut, American Express launched "Membership Miles," linking American Express card purchases to the Qantas frequent flier program. More than 100,000 American Express cardholders have taken advantage of the program, and the program is now the benchmark for other credit card companies' co-marketing plans. The program helped Qantas move ahead in the loyalty program battle.

But the battle continues. Both Ansett and Qantas have opened Web sites that outline their frequent flyer programs and partners.

For instance, Qantas has partnered with British Airways, American Airlines, Canadian Airlines International, USAir, Continental, and SAS. Frequent flyer points count toward increasing privileges and membership status to Blue, Silver, or Gold. With each status upgrade, members earn greater travel privileges, such as priority baggage handling, extra baggage allowance, priority check-in service, and membership in The Qantas Club. Ansett's programs are similarly enticing.

Are the programs capturing new customers and building loyalty? Or are they rewarding existing customers?

Food for Thought

1. Which component(s) or attitudes are changed through this communication strategy?
2. What happens to attitude changes when all competitors offer the same or similar incentives?
3. Imagine you are the marketing communication director for Qantas. Taking the cost of frequent flyer miles redemption into consideration, what steps, if any, would you take to improve the frequent flyer program?

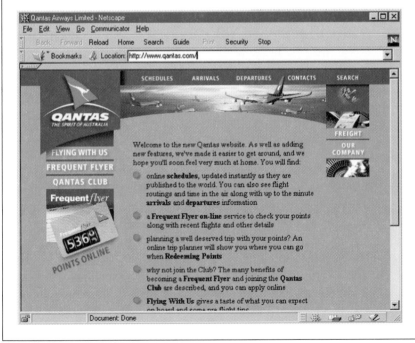

Sources: "Frequent Flyer Membership Programs," Qantas Airlines home page (September 1996): Internet (www.qantas.com); "Ansett Frequent Flyer Travel Services and Membership Levels," Ansett Airlines home page (September 1996): Internet (www.ansett.com.au); Mike DaSilva, "Customer (Dis) Loyalty in Australia," *Promo* (December 1994): 53.

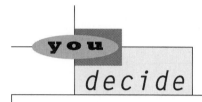

The Curse of Plastic

After a fling with frugality in the early '90s, Americans are back in love with their credit cards—and not just because the economy has improved. Credit card marketers keep offering consumers more reasons to whip out plastic. They're coaxing businesses—from supermarket chains to the family dentist—to accept the cards. And by offering airline miles or rebates, they're providing consumers more incentives to use credit cards in place of cash or checks.

Consumers love rebate products. Credit cards that offer rebates, such as the United Airlines Mileage Plus Visa Card, are known in the business as "co-branded" or "affinity" cards. MasterCard now has 49 million co-branded cards outstanding. Meanwhile, new issues of plain vanilla cards without rebates will increase 5 percent. More people are shopping with more plastic: Anderson Consulting says the average spender held seven cards in 1989. Today, that purse or wallet carries 11.

All the new incentives to use plastic are likely to boost consumer spending, but it's too soon to gauge the exact effect. Of course,

new opportunities to charge also mean new opportunities to sink into debt. But card issuers insist that consumers are getting better at managing debt, and indeed delinquent rates are at low levels. Also, they say, a big chunk of charges gets paid the same month. A study done for Visa, for example, shows that 72 percent of grocery charges are paid by the month's end.

But critics note that most consumers don't use separate cards for food or luxury items. When the economy gets worse, they say, it will be tempting to roll over charges for essentials month after month.

Take, for example, the case of Anne Marie Moss, a 26-year-old who is in her final year in the graduate journalism program at the University of Texas at Austin. Currently, she owes $1200 on her cards and doesn't want to push that amount any higher. "Right now I am just doing the minimum payments," says Moss. "It's just debt paying debt, which is kind of frustrating." Moss turned to plastic last summer for living expenses while serving an unpaid internship at a

magazine in New Orleans. Plastic can be a blessing to a grad student—it can be a source of emergency loans and is convenient—but it can also be a curse.

You Decide

1. Do credit card companies take advantage of our general weakness to spend money we don't have?

2. Is it possible to change the attitudes of consumers who use credit cards irresponsibly? If yes, can you think of any marketing communication strategies you might use to do so? Explain.

3. If you were the marketing communication director for a financial institution and you were asked to target the 17-to-25-year-old consumer market, what would you do to motivate this market to sign up for a credit card with your company?

Sources: Margret Mannix, "Unpaid Debt Can Be a Distraction—and Worse," *U.S. News Online* (April 30, 1996): Internet (www.usnews.com/ Usnews/fair/gbcredit); Russell Mitchell, "Sorry, We Don't Take Cash," *Business Week,* December 12, 1994, 42.

familiar "demographics." We can define **psychographics** as a tool that combines consumer characteristics, such as attitudes and motives, that may have bearing on their response to products, packaging, advertising, sales promotion, and public relations efforts.

Lifestyle variables are often considered the mainstay of psychographic research. Lifestyle research is a sociological concept that studies how individuals choose to allocate their time and energy (and money). Because lifestyle reflects behavior, it is an extremely reliable source of information for the psychographers.

Lifestyle analysis has become popular with marketers as the measurement techniques have become more accurate and the consumer categories that result from this process are easily applied to business strategy decisions. As a result, producers are using psychographic research to target their products and promotions to various lifestyle segments. Black & Decker Corp., for example, designs special programs for the "do-it-yourselfers." Lifestyle analysis tells B & D that people in this lifestyle category often perform home improvements and repairs and are fascinated by electronics and computers. They also have high brand awareness and are willing to give others advice about automobiles, power tools, hand tools, tires, home building products, and home video equipment.

Table 6.1 outlines the components of each major lifestyle dimension. Such *AIO inventories* (activities, interests, and opinions) reveal information about a consumer's attitudes toward product categories, brands within product categories, and user and non-user characteristics.

Lifestyle segmentation studies tend to focus on how people spend their money; their patterns of work and leisure; their major interests; and their opinions on social and political issues, institutions, and themselves. The emergence of the dual-earner middle-class couple has had the greatest impact on lifestyles. For example, dual-income young families are jugglers. With at least one child younger than age six, at least one more of school age (six to seventeen), and two parents with jobs, it is not easy to keep all the balls in the air. It often takes a second income earner to put a young family into the middle class, and that fact explains a lot about this group's values and attitudes. Building IRAs and college funds are important goals for young families. They spend money on family-oriented leisure, educational toys, kids' furniture, bigger homes, and at least two cars. They also like stay-at-home entertainment—such as VCRs and exercise equipment—that the whole family can enjoy.

As indicated in the IMC Concept in Focus feature, people in transition make a very interesting lifestyle challenge.

TABLE   6.1

Lifestyle Dimensions

Activities	Interests	Opinions	Demographics
Work	Family	Themselves	Age
Hobbies	Home	Social issues	Education
Social events	Job	Politics	Income
Vacation	Community	Business	Occupation
Entertainment	Recreation	Economics	Family size
Club membership	Fashion	Education	Dwelling
Community	Food	Products	Geography
Shopping	Media	Future	City size
Sports	Achievements	Culture	Stage in life cycle

Source: Joseph T. Plummer, "The Concept and Application of Life-Style Segmentation," *Journal of Marketing* (January 1974): 34. Reprinted from *Journal of Marketing,* published by the American Marketing Association. Used with permission.

People in Motion

One of the newest lifestyle extensions is known as syncographics. This is the short-term period when something is either about to happen, has recently happened, or is happening in people's lives. This period, generally identified as a lifestyle change—graduating college, getting married, having a baby, buying a home, retiring— qualifies consumers as prime targets for specific products and services. Other changes that may place a person in this lifestyle segment include divorce, death, and disability.

Syncographics identifies people going through demographic changes. The segment has movement; it's not static like others. It allows marketing communicators to hone in on a key niche market and avoid wasting money on mass markets. For example, a woman getting divorced generally wants to take back her name. She wants a charge card with her own name, so credit cards are a natural for this market. People who have been widowed or divorced recently also become more interested in financial services.

Reaching customers experiencing lifestyle changes may cost a little more per contact, but the results typically are much greater. For example, businesses that offer baby products can target a pregnant woman before she gives birth. When she goes to the OB/GYN early in the pregnancy, she often will receive a gift pack filled with samples of diapers and formula. Many businesses place a product sample or coupon in the pack. Still others buy the names of the women who complete an information card distributed in the pack. The information card asks such questions as, "What is your name?", "Is this your first baby?", "When are you expecting?", and "What is your telephone number?" Generally the response rate of pregnant women who fill out the card is high, 20 to 35 percent.

By targeting markets in motion, businesses can zero in on the proper target and spend communication dollars more wisely.

Sources: Tracy Finley, "Targeting 'Consumers in Motion,'" *Marketing News,* August 28, 1995, 7; Paul Mergenhagen, "Seizing the Day," *American Demographics* (July 1995): 22–3.

In this section we discussed the psychological background of consumer decision making. In the following sections we explore the types of decisions consumers make and how they make them.

THE PSYCHOLOGICAL BACKGROUND

Concept Review

1. Three components make up a person's psychological background.
   - *Motive.* The inner drive to take action to eliminate tension, to satisfy a need or problem, or to restore a sense of equilibrium.
   - *Learning.* A process of taking in information, processing it with existing information, and producing new knowledge. Cognitive learning involves thought and conscious awareness. Behavioral learning does not require awareness or conscious effort. It depends on an association between events.
   - *Attitude.* An enduring disposition, favorable or unfavorable, toward an object—an idea, a person, a thing, or a situation.
2. Psychographics and lifestyle analysis group these three psychological variables in a manner useful to the marketing communicator.

The ad for Room Plus appears to be targeting young families that have children at home and who need furniture that can change as their children grow.

CONSUMER DECISION-MAKING PROCESSES

So far we have investigated the psychological characteristics that influence consumer decisions. Our next question is, how does the consumer make decisions? What steps are involved in consumer decision making?

The answer depends on whether the consumer engages in *simple* or *complex decision making*. Figure 6.2 shows the differences between these two processes. Notice in the figure that **complex decision making** requires a search for information and an evaluation of alternatives, whereas simple decision making does not. In **simple decision making** some information search and alternative evaluation may occur, but these activities are minimized. Note further that evaluation after the purchase always occurs with complex decision making. In simple decision making it may or may not occur.

Which type of decision making occurs depends on (1) whether the decision is novel or routine and (2) the extent of the consumer's involvement with the decision.

High-involvement decisions are those that are important to the consumer. Such decisions are closely tied to the consumer's ego and self-image. They also

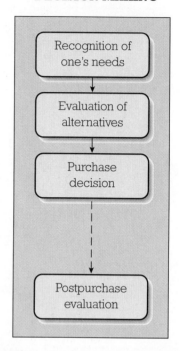

COMPLEX DECISION MAKING

- Recognition of one's needs
- Information search
- Evaluation of alternatives
- Purchase decision
- Postpurchase evaluation

SIMPLE DECISION MAKING

- Recognition of one's needs
- Evaluation of alternatives
- Purchase decision
- Postpurchase evaluation

FIGURE 6.2

The Process of Complex and Simple Decision Making

involve some risk to the consumer—financial risk (high-priced items), social risk (products important to the peer group), or psychological risk (the wrong decision might cause the consumer some concern and anxiety). In making these decisions it is worth the consumer's time and energy to consider product alternatives carefully. A complex process of decision making is therefore more likely for high-involvement purchases, such as a new computer or new car.

Low-involvement decisions are those that are not important to the consumer, such as buying a pizza or pack of gum. Financial, social, and psychological risks are not nearly as great. In such cases it may not be worth the time and effort to search for information about brands or to consider a wide range of alternatives. Consumers who make a low-involvement purchase, then, generally use a simple decision-making process.[9]

When a consumer has bought a product many times in the past, the decision making is likely to be simple, regardless of whether it is a high- or a low-involvement decision. Suppose after much care and involvement a consumer decided to bank at Norwest Bank, was satisfied with the choice, and continued to bank there. The customer's careful consideration of this service product has produced **brand loyalty,** which is the result of involvement with the product decision. Once a consumer is brand loyal, a simple decision-making process is all that is required for subsequent purchases. The consumer now buys the product through **habit,** which means making a decision without the use of additional information or the evaluation of alternative choices. This is a simple but high-involvement decision.

Habitual buying may also reflect low-involvement, simple decision making. If a consumer is not highly involved in the initial decision to buy a product and makes no commitment to the product but simply responds to the positive reinforcement it provides, the person may develop a type of brand loyalty called **inertia.** The consumer thus buys the product passively. An example would be buying the newspaper every morning.

Even when a consumer buys a brand for the first time, if it is an inexpensive, unexciting product that is purchased regularly, such as ballpoint pens, the consumer is likely to exert very little thought or effort in choosing the product. This type of process is a simple, low-involvement decision. Now consider the case of a consumer deciding whether to buy for the first time an expensive, personal, or emotion-laden product such as a car or medical care. It is fairly safe to assume that the consumer will expend a great deal of effort on the process. This process is a complex, high-involvement decision.

In the rest of this chapter, we examine a complex decision process to buy a new product and explore each of the steps outlined in Figure 6.2. We turn next to a consideration of how consumers recognize needs.

RECOGNIZING NEEDS AND PROBLEMS

Every day people face a myriad of consumption problems. Some are routine, such as filling the car with gasoline or buying milk. Other problems occur infrequently, such as searching for a good life insurance policy or a new mountain bike. Whether the problem is routine or infrequent, the process of solving the problem starts when an unsatisfied need creates tension and thus motivation. As discussed earlier, recognizing that a need exists can be prompted by an ad, attractive packaging, or a cause marketing appeal. Whether people recognize a need exists, however, often depends on the information received and how it is perceived. Your roommate's claims that "We're running out of bread!" for three days doesn't become a felt need until you want to make a sandwich and only the heels remain.

Even if people recognize a need exists, whether they act to resolve the problem depends on two factors: (1) the magnitude of the discrepancy between what they have and what they need and (2) the importance of the problem. A young mother with two kids under five must decide whether the need to protect her children by purchasing two new car seats is worth the hassle of going to the mall. She may decide that the car seats she has are good enough.

Every person has his or her own personal hierarchy of needs. For some people, having a cup of coffee first thing every morning is a need with a high priority. This hierarchy varies from person to person, across time, and situations. Some people feel having their own automobile is essential; people living in Manhattan may feel public transportation is fine. For buying to occur, people must be motivated both to acknowledge the need and to do something about it. Furthermore, consumers must define the problem so that they can act to solve the problem.

profile

Erica Wiegel
Strategic Planning and Research
DDB Needham Chicago

Erica Wiegel works as an associate in the Analytical Resources Group in the Strategic Planning and Research Department of DDB Needham Chicago. She works on data analysis, coding, and presentation of consumer research projects. She must have a firm command of statistics, spreadsheet and statistical software (SPSS, Excel, VMS DCL), marketing modeling, and strong communication skills to work effectively.

Career Track

Before working at DDB Needham—with the exception of spending one year as apparel manager of a major discount retail store—I spent most of my years in school. While in school, I gained the majority of my practical consumer research experience by working for professors and doing probono research for non-profit firms.

Advice

To those who are interested in pursuing a career in consumer research, I would recommend getting hands-on experience while you're still a student. When hunting for jobs, I found that experience in conducting and interpreting consumer research is highly regarded and often weighted more heavily than education (though education is still heavily weighted!).

The question students always ask, however, is,

"How am I supposed to get experience when I'm enrolled as a full-time student?" Enroll in marketing, advertising, and consumer behavior research courses and volunteer to help your professors with their ongoing research projects. Getting hands-on experience is a must, and professors are often looking for a dependable helping hand. Take research methods courses which expose you to survey and experimental design, and take your statistics courses seriously. Knowing how to use statistical analysis software (such as SPSS or SAS) will definitely help you get more than your foot in the door. Above all, make sure you are interested in studying consumer behavior!

Typical Day

8:30 A.M.: I arrive at the office after a thirty-minute ride on the bus, during which I'm able to catch up on past issues of *Advertising Age, AdWeek,* and perhaps enjoy a bit of *The New Yorker.* I first check my voice mail, e-mail, and snail mail to see what consumer research issues my colleagues would like me to investigate today. I doublecheck my calendar to make sure I haven't forgotten any meetings I'm supposed to attend, and then I get to work.

9:00 A.M.: I attend a meeting with some members of an account team to try to narrow down the sites we are recommending for next year's Ice Capades tour,

In many cases problem recognition and problem definition occur simultaneously, as happens when a person runs out of toothpaste. But consider a more complicated problem that is involved with status and image—how we want others to see us. Consumers may know that they are not satisfied with their appearance, but because they may not be able to define the problem more precisely, they might not do anything about the situation. Consumers do not usually begin

which one of our clients is sponsoring. We're trying to hit cities where the client has distribution and media, while also trying to visit surrounding smaller, but sufficiently large towns. We've used Claritas' Compass geo-demographic mapping system to help us determine which towns to consider, based on population size and proximity to media markets. This meeting results in a list of markets we recommend as first and second choices.

10:00 A.M. to 12:45 P.M.: I return to my office and begin to address a research question for a new client. This client is interested in identifying segments of the population that are most likely to be interested in its services. Some company personnel have defined some groups they think might be interested in its services, but they want an estimate of the extent to which people in these groups already use those services. Fortunately, Mediamark Research, Inc., (MRI) has included some pertinent product use questions in its last few waves of data collection, so querying MRI is my first plan of attack. This client is also interested in determining each segment's intent to subscribe to the service which it offers, which the DDB Needham Life Style questionnaire measures. So, using my SPSS skills, I delve into the data and retrieve this information for the targets of interest.

12:45 P.M. to 1:30 P.M.: I grab a sandwich from a nearby deli and return to a conference room that doubles as a lunchroom during this hour. Here a revolving group of strategic planners and researchers gathers to talk about fun stuff like the NCAA tournament, who has got tickets to the Cubs' opening day, current events, and what new DDB Needham ads we've seen lately.

1:30 P.M. to 3:30 P.M.: I attend a meeting with some representatives of a market research supplier to discuss coding issues for the recently completed wave of our annual Life Style questionnaire. Since this year's questionnaire hasn't changed drastically from last year's, this meeting flows smoothly.

3:30 to anywhere from 5:30 to 7:30 P.M.: Fortunately, I have the rest of the afternoon to address some of the other requests that have come across my desk, the most urgent of which requires me to analyze some information from a recent fashion study DDB Needham conducted. Part of DDB Needham's efforts to gain new business includes sharing some of our recently collected proprietary data with new business prospects. To this end, a team of DDB Needham representatives has scheduled a number of meetings with representatives of the apparel business community to discuss findings on women's perceptions of competing fashion brands. I'll be assisting with the preparation of these presentations, one of which is early next week. So, for the rest of the day, I familiarize myself with the hosiery brands included in the fashion study, identifying "fans" of specific brands that compete heavily with the company with which we next meet. My primary objective for this presentation is to determine how brand fans differ in their feelings about when and for what apparel hosiery fashion is important.

With the exception of a few phone calls, I am fortunately able to spend the rest of the afternoon concentrating on the presentation. When it's time to go, I pack up, walk a few blocks to the bus stop, and wait for the next bus home.

to solve a problem until it is adequately defined. As we discuss in the following section, marketing communication may help consumers both to recognize a need and to define it in a way that makes a particular purchase likely.

Marketing communication managers become involved in the need-recognition stage in two ways. First, if they know what problems consumers are facing, they may help develop a marketing mix to solve those problems. To measure problem recognition, marketers use market research techniques, including surveys, focus groups, observations, and consumer feedback. Marketing communication managers can use this research to select the best communication tools and messages that address how the product solves a consumer problem.

Second, marketers themselves may activate problem recognition. The cooperative ad for Vanilla Fields and Sears, for example, points out a problem that most of us would like to solve at holiday time.

Marketers can also help define the need or problem. If consumers need a new coat, do they define the problem as a need for inexpensive covering, for a way to stay warm on the coldest days, for a garment that will last several years, for a warm covering that will not attract strange looks from peers, or for an article of clothing that will express a personal sense of style? A salesperson or an ad may shape the answers.

Marketing communication managers can influence need definition greatly in part because people usually experience several motives at a time and usually act based on a mixture of rational and emotional motives. That is, when buying a new jacket, the consumer is probably influenced by rational motives such as price

This ad stimulates our "need" to find the perfect gift and shows how we can do so simply.

and endurance as well as by emotional motives such as a desire for prestige or to look better. Commercials, point-of-purchase displays, and sales presentations often appeal to both types of motives. In fact, when a product inherently appeals to one type of motive, marketing communication managers may find it effective to stress another type of motive. For example, because automobiles and clothing inherently appeal to emotional motives such as self-esteem, it is wise to include appeals to rational motives when promoting these products. This rational appeal allows the consumer to believe that they purchased a product for sound, logical reasons instead of emotional responses. But because the inherent appeal of a lawn mower is probably rational, effective marketing communication is likely to include appeals to emotional motives.

Sometimes needs evolve over time as the culture changes. For example, many homeowners today feel they need protection or security because of a rising fear of crime across the United States. Numerous new products and as many new marketing communication strategies have emerged to fill this need. Among the hottest new home security products are hand-held personal alarms; mace or pepper-based defense devices; video cameras for homeowner surveillance of entry areas; and integrated security, temperature control, and entertainment systems. One of the hottest items is the $200 Electronic Watchdog that growls, barks, and snarls like a real German shepherd when intruders approach.

INFORMATION SEARCH AND PROCESSING

Problem recognition creates a state of tension that causes the consumer to search for information that will help in decision making. The information search is the second step in complex decision making and involves mental and physical activity. The search takes time, energy, and money and can often require giving up more desirable activities.[10] The benefits of the information search, however, often outweigh the costs. Undergoing a thorough information search may ultimately mean saving money, receiving better quality, or reducing risk.

The consumer becomes involved in two types of information search: internal and external. In an internal search, the consumer attempts to resolve problems by recalling previously stored information. For example, people who suffer from allergies can easily recall what they did last year for relief. They may even remember the location of the drugstore where they last bought allergy medication. When problems cannot be resolved through an internal search, people search externally for additional information. The external sources may include family, friends, professionals, government or corporate publications, ads, sales personnel, or displays.

The sources that a person uses may depend on the importance of the decision, past experience, confidence in particular sources, and psychological makeup. Some consumers find it too troublesome to search for information and are willing to rely on the information provided by a salesperson for a minor purchase. But when these same people buy a new car, they may go through an elaborate search that includes writing for information, comparing government reports, driving from dealership to dealership, and talking with knowledgeable people.

When the search occurs, what do people do with the information? How do they spot, understand, and recall information? Marketing communication managers must understand this process so they can affect buyer behavior.

Steps in Information Processing

Assessing how a person processes information is not an easy task. Observing the process can help with the assessment, but because we can't see people's thoughts we have to draw some conclusions. Many theories try to explain the process. Figure 6.3 shows an outline of the information-processing sequence. It includes five steps.

Exposure

Information processing starts with consumer **exposure** to some source of stimulation such as watching television, going to the supermarket, or driving past a particular billboard. To start the process, marketing communication managers must attract consumers to the stimulus or put it squarely in the path of people in the target market. For instance, messages that contain celebrity endorsements or coupons to attract consumers should appear in a media mix that consumers will be exposed to. For instance, Nike, Inc., uses Michael Jordan in TV commercials to attract consumers. The company then runs the commercial twelve times during the NBA Game of the Week to ensure that consumers will see and hear the message.

Attention

Exposure alone does little unless people pay attention to the stimulus. At any moment, people are bombarded by all sorts of stimuli, but they have a limited capacity to process this input. They must devote mental resources to stimuli in order to process them; in other words, they must pay **attention.** Without attention, no further information processing occurs, and the message is lost. Attention is selective. We have neither the cognitive capability nor the interest to pay attention to all the messages to which we are exposed.

Some stimuli are more attention-getting than others. For example, bright colors and movement both attract attention. Contrast (that is, size of the stimulus relative to its background) and intensity (for example, loudness and brightness) also prompt attention.[11] Personal attributes also influence which stimuli will attract attention. People are likely to pay attention to a message when it provides information that is relevant to problems that evoke high involvement and that they are motivated to resolve.[12] People also tend to pay attention to messages that are perceived to be consistent with their attitudes and ignore those perceived as inconsistent.[13]

Several attention-enhancing advertising methods have been identified. For example, ads that are positioned first in a series of ads are more likely to gain attention, as are humorous ads and those that use a sexual appeal.[14] A print ad in

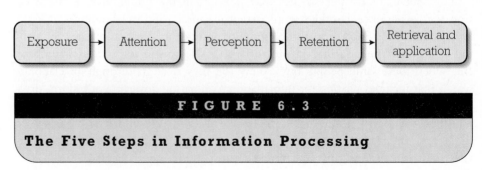

FIGURE 6.3

The Five Steps in Information Processing

a newspaper is more likely to receive attention if it is placed in the center of the reader's optical field. Buying a full-page ad eliminates this positioning problem.

Employing an IMC approach provides a wide variety of tools to create attention. Effective packaging, point-of-purchase materials, special events, free samples, and annual reports can grab the attention of the target audience. Seeing a McDonald's ad on TV, receiving a coupon in the mail, and listening to a story on the radio about how McDonald's donated food to a local fund-raiser all combine to increase the likelihood that you will visit a McDonald's soon.

Perception

Step three in the information-processing sequence is *perception*. It involves classifying incoming signals into meaningful categories, forming patterns, and assigning names or images to them. **Perception** is the assignment of meaning to stimuli received through the senses.

Perceptions are shaped by (1) the physical characteristics of the stimuli, (2) the context, and (3) the individual perceiving the stimuli. The senses transmit signals

This full-page ad uses many attention-getting techniques: the color contrast of a black-and-white photo of Mr. Policy set next to red and gold colors, a well-known sports figure, and a humorous sexual innuendo. Do you think the ad grabs attention?

about the shape, color, sound, and feel of stimuli, but each individual perceives those stimuli within a particular context shaped by the person's own frame of reference. Thus, a person's past learning, attitudes, personality, self-image, and current motivations and emotions shape perception. Some stimuli are perceived totally, some partially, some accurately, some inaccurately. The perceptual process results in a highly personalized mental representation of sensory stimuli.

The actual process of human perception has been well researched. In general, perception is thought to be a three-stage process: selection, organization, and interpretation of stimuli. Although we are not always conscious of it, we select the stimuli we will perceive, depending on our previous experience with the stimuli and our motives. The more experience or familiarity we have with a setting or situation, the more selective we are. A student enters a classroom with a set of expectations about what he or she will see, hear, and smell on entering the room. Given everything is as expected, the student will perceive only those things selected as relevant (for example, an available seat near the door). If expectations can be changed dramatically, it is possible to influence the selection process. This is called creating *contrast,* which is what Infiniti did when the company produced a television ad that did not show the car. Motivation, as discussed earlier, is a somewhat similar phenomenon.

People tend to perceive things they need or want. The stronger the need, the greater the motivation to perceive stimuli that will satisfy their need or want and to ignore stimuli that will not. We tend to organize stimuli into groups and perceive them as unified wholes. This tendency to organize and integrate stimuli into a group greatly simplifies our lives.

Evidence indicates that we automatically group stimuli in a manner that forms a unified picture or impression. We tend to *group* stimuli to facilitate memory and recall. Telephone numbers, social security numbers, and addresses are everyday examples of how we group. Soft drink companies are famous in their attempts to group their products with a positive experience.

We all like to know how an unfinished story, movie, or even joke turns out. This desire reflects our need for *closure,* organizing perceptions so that they paint a complete picture. Even when a message is incomplete, we tend to consciously or subconsciously complete it. Coke told consumers it was "IT," hoping people would interpret "IT" in a positive way. Pepsi used "Uh-huh" in a similar way.

Finally, an individual interprets stimuli according to a set of prescribed criteria. Although this interpretation can be affected by many factors, there are a few general factors that appear to always operate. Clarity of the stimuli is critical. Stimuli that are ambiguous or fuzzy run the risk of being misperceived. A person's past experience also influences interpretation. Prejudice, either racial or some other type, is simply taking certain stimuli and generalizing from experience, whether accurate or inaccurate. Our motives and interests also influence interpretation. We tend to interpret clearly when we are interested in the topic.

Comprehension is part of the perceptual process, but it goes beyond labeling and identification to produce a more thorough evaluation of the perceived stimuli. Our first exposure to a red bicycle simply provides the perceptual reaction: "This is a red bike." A split second later we add to that assessment through comprehension: "Red bikes are best" or "Red bikes are ugly." In general, people comprehend messages in a way that makes them consistent with preexisting attitudes and opinions. People who believe that automobiles made in the United States are best, for instance, tend to discount or distort perceptions that challenge this view.

Without the consumer's ability to perceive, integrated marketing communication would not succeed. That is, if consumers were unable to group a variety of cues in some sort of meaningful manner, they could not see how a number of communication techniques blend into a comprehensive message. For example, if you work part-time at a Pearle Vision optical store, you are receiving messages as an employee, as a consumer, and as an employee receiving feedback from customers. Perception allows you to understand all these messages, group them, and comprehend them.

Retention

Storage of information for later reference, or **retention,** is the fourth step of the information-processing sequence. Actually, the role of memory in the sequence is twofold. First, memory holds information while it is being processed throughout the sequence. For example, for a stimulus to be perceived at all, it must first be held for a extremely brief time in what psychologists call *sensory memory.* Next, memory stores the information for future, long-term use.

Memory itself is a process involving several stages. First is *encoding:* Before a person can remember anything, information must be put into a form the memory system can use. If a person reads a paragraph, for example, she might encode the general meaning of the passage, the image of the printed words, or the sound of the words. Once encoded, information can be stored in memory.

Information can be encoded and stored automatically, without conscious effort, but *rehearsal,* the mental repetition of material, is often necessary to ensure that these processes occur. Rote repetition is sometimes sufficient, but it is not as effective as *elaborative rehearsal,* which involves thinking about the information and relating it to other, already stored information. A person might remember a name if he simply repeats it to himself, but he is more likely to remember it if he also thinks about the name and associates it with something else. Prudential Insurance has used the Rock of Gibraltar as a means of creating an association.

Whenever possible, marketing messages are couched in a way that encourages elaborate rehearsal. Many Kodak ads, for instance, are intended to trigger a stream of pleasant thoughts about milestones in one's life. Black & Decker shows a man having a difficult time assembling a desk in the first part of its television ad and then shows how a Black & Decker portable screwdriver can make the task easier. That ad encourages the neophyte carpenter to think about past negative experiences with building and then offers the Black & Decker product as a solution to these difficulties.

Retrieval and Application

The process by which information is recovered from the memory storehouse is called **retrieval.** Combined with *application* (how we are going to use this information), retrieval represents the final stage in information processing. If consumers can retrieve relevant information about a product, brand, or store, they will apply it to solve a problem or meet a need.

Research findings suggest that the most effective way for marketing communication managers to aid product information retrieval is to provide information about the product's benefits and attributes and then show a strong connection between them. The cereal industry uses this association when it presents the key attribute of high fiber as a means of preventing cancer, a clear benefit. Auto companies that include air bags as standard safety equipment provide a similar connection between the attribute and the benefit—in this case prevention of serious injury in a car crash.

IDENTIFYING AND EVALUATING ALTERNATIVES

Once a need is recognized and defined and the information search is completed, alternatives are identified and evaluated. How people search for alternatives depends in part on such factors as the following:

1. the cost in time and money
2. how much information they already have
3. the perceived risk associated with a wrong decision
4. their predispositions about making choices

Because some people find the process of looking at alternatives to be difficult and disturbing, they tend to keep the number of alternatives to a minimum, even if they do not have enough information to determine that they are looking at their best option. Other people feel compelled to collect a long list of alternatives, a tendency that can slow down decision making.

Once people know their alternatives, how do they evaluate and choose among them? In particular, how do people choose among brands of a product?

To illustrate this decision for one market segment and one product category, let's revisit the Generation Xers and how they buy home furnishings. A recent young adult study from consumer researcher Roger Starch Worldwide found 20 percent of those aged 18 to 29 plan to buy furniture in the next year. Many in that age group have jobs that aren't careers because of the difficulty of finding a first career-track job. As a result, their leisure time is more of an expression of themselves than work is, and they want their homes to be as nice as possible. Style and value are the two most important decision criteria. There is also a need to show that their products fit into their lives.[15]

PURCHASE AND POSTPURCHASE BEHAVIOR

After searching and evaluating, at some point consumers have to decide whether they are going to buy or not. Anything marketers can do to simplify the decision making will be attractive to buyers because most people find it hard to make a decision. Perhaps marketers can suggest in their advertising the best size of a product for a particular use or the right wine or drink with a particular food. Sometimes several decision situations can be combined and marketed as one package. For example, travel agents often package travel tours, combining airfare, ground transportation, and hotels.

To do a better marketing job at this stage of the buying process, a seller needs answers to many questions about consumers' shopping behavior. For instance, how much effort is the consumer willing to spend in shopping for the product? What factors influence where a consumer will shop? Do stores each have an image? If so, is the image important to a shopper when selecting a store? What are the differentiating characteristics, if any, of impulse buyers?

Marketing communication managers can play a key role at the purchase stage. Providing basic product, price, and location information through advertising, personal selling, and public relations is an obvious starting point. Sales promotion, in particular, is critical at this stage. Product sampling, coupons, rebates, and premiums are a few of the sales promotion devices used to encourage the customer to purchase. Communication elements at the point of sale may also be important. Packaging, signage, store appearance, merchandise techniques, and attitude of the sales and management personnel are relevant in closing a sale.

For instance, E-Lab, a small market research and design firm, discovered why Hallmark's Showcase stores weren't generating higher sales. Researchers videotaped customers in the stores to record their behavior. The footage revealed a recurring set of images—shoppers would move slowly through the aisles, appear discouraged, and leave with only a greeting card. The conclusion? Store layout was confusing, signage was unclear, and high-visibility products were hard to find. Based on the research, Hallmark redesigned its stores, signage, and merchandising displays to make them easier and more fun to navigate.[16]

Integrating all these marketing communication tools so they coincide with the decision criteria of the individual can make all the difference. For many purchase decisions, the salesperson is the key. This is particularly true for industrial products and retail sales. In recent years direct marketers have played a prominent role in reshaping the purchasing process of millions of consumers. Because of time constraints and the risks alleviated through warranties and guarantees, purchasing through direct marketing is now an alternative for virtually all consumers. These benefits are highlighted in marketing messages produced by direct marketers. Children's clothier Hanna Andersson (discussed in Chapter 2), for instance, promises a money-back guarantee.

A consumer's feelings and evaluations after the sale are also significant to a mar-

This Lipton coupon is distributed in grocery store aisles both to draw attention and to promote product sales at the moment of the purchase decision.

keter because they can influence repeat sales and what the consumer tells others about the product or brand. Keeping the customer satisfied is what marketing is all about.

Consumers typically experience some postpurchase anxiety after all but routine and inexpensive purchases. This anxiety reflects a phenomenon called **cognitive dissonance.** According to this theory, people strive for consistency among their cognitions (knowledge, attitudes, beliefs, values). When inconsistencies arise, dissonance is created, which people try to eliminate. In some cases the consumer makes the decision already aware of the dissonant elements. In other instances dissonance is aroused by disturbing information received after the purchase.

To avoid or eliminate dissonance, consumers may avoid negative information. They may change their behavior, their opinions, or their attitudes. They may seek information or opinions that support their purchase. Sometimes the consumer's attempt to reduce dissonance can produce dire consequences for the marketer. For example, in the process of convincing oneself that the purchase of a new GE microwave oven was a good decision, the consumer seeks additional information from friends. Unfortunately, the consumer's best friend says she had a terrible experience with her GE microwave oven.

The marketer may take specific steps to reduce postpurchase dissonance. Advertising that stresses the many positive attributes or confirms the popularity of the product can be helpful. Providing personalized reinforcement has proven effective with big-ticket items such as automobiles and major appliances. Salespeople in these areas may send cards or publicity materials or may even make personal calls to reassure customers about their purchase. One company that has done an excellent job of checking on customer dissonance is Xerox Corp. In the mid-1980s Xerox sent mail questionnaires to 40,000 customers per month—broadly targeting decision makers, operaters, and administrators at customer companies. Today Xerox uses phone surveys and goes after decision makers exclusively, conducting about 10,000 surveys per month. It has also gone beyond measuring customer satisfaction to gauging customer loyalty.[17]

CONSUMER DECISION-MAKING PROCESSES

Consumers go through a specific decision-making process to resolve needs. These decisions can be complex or simple. The following steps outline the complex decision-making process.

1. Recognizing needs and problems: Consumers must be motivated both to acknowledge and resolve a need in order for the buying process to proceed.
2. Information search and processing that includes the following stages:
   - Exposure
   - Attention
   - Perception
   - Retention
   - Retrieval and application
3. Identifying and evaluating alternatives
4. Purchase and postpurchase behavior

ORGANIZATIONAL MARKET BEHAVIOR

Those who supply goods and services to consumer markets are themselves in need of goods and services to run their businesses. These organizations—producers, resellers, and governments—make up vast organizational markets that buy a large variety of products, including equipment, raw material, labor, and other services. Some organizations sell exclusively to other organizations and never come in contact with consumer buyers. A common term used to describe these types of exchanges is **business-to-business marketing.**

Despite the importance of organizational markets, far less research has been conducted on factors that influence their behavior than on factors that influence consumers. However, we can identify characteristics that distinguish organizational buying from consumer buying and typical steps in the organizational buying process.

Characteristics of Organizational Buying

Many elements of the sociocultural environment discussed in the previous chapter influence both organizational and consumer buying, but additional forces arise only in the organizational setting. In particular, each organization has its own business philosophy that guides its actions in resolving conflicts, handling uncertainty and risk, searching for solutions, and adapting to change. For example, coal supplier Peabody Coal, which is part of a declining industry, relies on a conservative purchase strategy to maintain the status quo.

Five characteristics mark the organizational buying process.[18]

1. In organizations many individuals are involved in making buying decisions.
2. The organizational buyer is motivated by both rational and emotional factors in choosing products and services. Although the use of rational and quantitative criteria dominate in most organizational decisions, the decision makers are people, subject to many of the same emotional criteria used in personal purchases.
3. Organizational buying decisions frequently involve a range of complex technical dimensions. A purchasing agent for Volvo AB, for example, must consider a number of technical factors before ordering a radio to go into the 740 SL model. The electronic system, the acoustics of the interior, and the shape of the dashboard are a few of these considerations.
4. The organizational decision process frequently spans a considerable time, creating a significant lag between the marketing communicators' initial contact with the customer and the purchasing decision. Because many new factors can enter the picture during this lag time, the marketer's ability to monitor and adjust to these changes is critical.
5. Organizations cannot be grouped into precise categories. Each organization has a characteristic way of functioning and a personality.

The first item in this list of characteristics has important implications. Unlike the consumer buying process, groups making organizational buying decisions must generally follow enforced decision-making rules. The group dynamic greatly complicates the task of understanding the buying process. For example, to predict the buying behavior of an organization with certainty, we need to know who will take part in the buying process, what criteria each member uses in evaluating prospective suppliers, and what influence each member has. We should also understand something not only about the psychology of the individuals involved but also how they work as a group.

Who makes the decision to buy depends in part on the situation. Three main types of buying situations exist: the straight rebuy, the modified rebuy, and the new task. The *straight rebuy* is the simplest situation: The company reorders a good or service without any modifications. The transaction tends to be routine and may be handled totally by a purchasing agent. With the *modified rebuy,* the buyer is seeking to modify product specifications, prices, and so on. The purchaser is interested in negotiation, and several participants may take part in the buying decision. A company faces a *new task* when it considers buying a product for the first time. The number of participants and the amount of information sought tend to increase with the cost and risks associated with the transaction. This situation represents the best opportunity for the marketer because the customer is open to new information and alternatives.

Purchasing Objectives

As you can see in the GA Insurance advertisement, purchasing objectives in the business market for the most part center on rational, pragmatic considerations such as price, service, quality, and assurance of supply. The GA ad assures business pur-

ONLY THE STATE DEPARTMENT HAS MORE TO DO
WITH INTERNATIONAL POLICIES THAN WE DO.

True, we write insurance policies, not peace treaties. But when you're dealing with unfamiliar countries, there are always problems to negotiate. Which is why you need General Accident Insurance. Through a network of offices throughout the world, we've written millions of policies in 44 countries. Our people really know the local markets. So they're always prepared to help, with even the most complex situations.

To learn more about our global commercial insurance capabilities, talk to your agent or broker, or call our International Unit. You'll find we have worldwide assets of over $15 billion. An A+ (Superior) rating from A.M. Best, a well-known insurance rating service. And 25,000 people who are equipped to handle anything with the utmost diplomacy.

General Accident Insurance

1·800·811·0029

This business-to-business ad makes several rational appeals for buying a fleet of Mazdas.

chasers that the company offers an expertise in international insurance, an affirmation it backs up with detailed data about the various resources it employs.

1. *Price.* Buyers in the business arena are more concerned than ordinary consumers with the cost of owning and using a product. Most notably, the large volume of a particular product purchased, or the high per-unit cost, means that businesses spend thousands or millions of dollars with each purchase decision. In evaluating price, therefore, businesses consider a variety of factors that generate or minimize costs, such as: What amount of scrap or waste will result from the use of the material? What will the cost of processing the material be? How much power will the machine consume?

2. *Services.* Business buyers require multiple services, such as technical assistance, availability of spare parts, repair capability, and training information. Thus, the technical contributions of suppliers are highly valued wherever equipment, materials, or parts are in use.

3. *Quality.* Organizational customers search for quality levels consistent with specifications. They are reluctant to pay for extra quality or to compromise specifications for a reduced price. The crucial factor is uniformity or consistency in product quality that will guarantee uniformity in end products, reduce the need for costly inspections and testing of incoming shipments, and ensure a smooth blending with the production process.

4. *Assurance of supply.* Interruptions in the flow of parts and materials can shut down the production process, resulting in costly delays and lost sales. To guard against interruptions in supply, business firms rely on a supplier's established reputation for delivery.

The organizational buying process has eight stages, or key phases, as illustrated in Figure 6.4.[19] Although these stages parallel those of the consumer buying process, some key differences have a direct bearing on the marketing communication strategy. The complete process only occurs in the case of a new task. Even in this situation, however, the process is far more formal for the industrial buying process than for the consumer buying process. Most of the information an industrial buyer receives is delivered through direct contacts such as sales representatives or information packets. It is unlikely that an industrial buyer would use the information provided through a trade as the sole basis for making a decision.

Problem Recognition

Problem recognition begins when someone in the organization recognizes a problem or need that can be met by acquiring a good or service. The recognition can occur due to internal or external stimuli. External stimuli examples include a presentation by a salesperson, an ad, or information picked up at a trade show. Examples of internal stimuli are running out of a product or dissatisfaction with an existing product.

General Need Description

Having recognized that a need exists, the business buyer must add further refinement to the description of the need. Working with engineers, users, purchasing agents, and others, the buyer identifies and prioritizes important product characteristics. The salesperson serves as the primary information source for many industrial

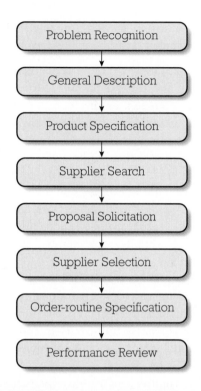

FIGURE 6.4

Stages of Organizational Buying

customers. Armed with extensive product knowledge, this individual is capable of addressing virtually all the product-related concerns of a typical customer. To a lesser extent, trade advertising provides valuable information to smaller or isolated customers. Note the extensive use of direct marketing techniques (for example, toll-free numbers and information cards) used in conjunction with trade ads. Finally, public relations plays a significant role through the placement of stories in various trade journals.

Product Specification

Technical specifications come next. This is usually the responsibility of the engineering department. Engineers design several alternatives, depending on the priority list established earlier.

Supplier Search

The buyer now tries to identify the most appropriate vendor. The buyer may examine trade directories, do a computer search, or phone other businesses for recommendations. Marketing communication managers can participate in this stage by contacting possible opinion leaders and soliciting support or by contacting the buyer directly. Personal selling plays a major role at this stage.

Proposal Solicitation

In this stage the business buyer invites qualified suppliers to submit proposals. Some suppliers will send only a catalog or a sales representative in lieu of a proposal. Others will submit a formal proposal and conduct a presentation. Proposal development is a complex task that requires extensive research and skilled writing and presentation.

Supplier Selection

At this stage the buyer screens the proposals and makes a choice. A significant part of this selection is an evaluation of the vendor. One study indicated that purchasing managers felt the vendor was often more important than the proposal. Purchasing managers listed the three most important characteristics of the vendor as delivery capability, consistent quality, and fair price. Another study found that the relative importance of different attributes varies with the type of buying situation.[20] For example, for routine-order products, delivery reliability, price, and supplier reputation are highly important. These factors can serve as appeals in sales presentations and in trade ads.

Order-routine Specification

The buyer now writes the final order with the chosen supplier, listing the technical specifications, the quantity needed, the warranty, and so on.

Performance Review

In this final stage the buyer reviews the supplier's performance. This may be a very simple or a very complex process.

Concept Review

ORGANIZATIONAL MARKET BEHAVIOR

1. Five characteristics of organizational buying are
   - Multiple-decision making
   - Rational and emotional decision factors
   - Complexity
   - Lengthy time frame
   - Diverse classification of organization types
2. The following eight steps are typical in organizational buying:
   - Problem recognition
   - General need description
   - Product specification
   - Supplier search
   - Proposal solicitation
   - Supplier selection
   - Order-routine specification
   - Performance review

A CLOSING THOUGHT: BUILD OR BREAK CUSTOMER LOYALTY?

If specific behaviors do not always follow attitudes, or if social trends do not always parallel business trends, why do marketing communicators think it still is important to understand consumers?

The reason is simple. The savvy marketing communicator knows that having solid trend information at one's disposal, even with its limitations, is a much more desirable alternative to having no information. Even worse, however, is having "information" that is largely or even partly wrong.

Almost all facets of marketing—including marketing communication, product, packaging, and price—are a form of communicating to a target consumer. The better marketing communicators know their targets, the more effectively they can communicate with them. Information about consumers provides marketing communicators with a much more detailed and thorough understanding of the target market than unaided judgment could provide. And that knowledge can greatly increase the chances for campaigns that speak directly to what is on consumers' minds. This approach to the consumer is the heart of relationship marketing.

Because customers have more options and information, firms must strive to meet customers' needs and wants better than competing firms. To create customer loyalty, businesses must build strong relationships not only with their customers, but with each group that helps the firm serve its customers—suppliers, distributors, resellers, and members of the financial and local communities.

Does relationship marketing work? Iris Harrell of Harrel Remodeling in Menlo Park, California, thinks so. She spends 70 percent of her $17,000 marketing budget on low-cost goodwill efforts that spawn referrals and repeat business. For instance, she sends "Pardon our dust" letters to everyone who lives near a client's remodeling site that ask neighbors to call if they have any complaints. Instead of complaining, many neighbors call to ask Harrell to bid on their projects. She also sends her kitchen remodeling customers gift certificates to a nearby restaurant when the kitchen is about two-thirds completed and a handwritten note of apology for the upheaval. The result? Seventy-two percent of her sales come from repeat or referral business.[21]

What firms do for their current or potential customers with each and every contact helps build or break customer loyalty. In sum, relationship marketing is customer-focused: It aims to build long-term relationships with each customer.

SUMMARY

1. Describe how the psychological factors of motivation, learning, and attitudes affect consumer decision making.

Consumer decision making is influenced by motivation, learning, and attitudes. A motive is an inner drive or pressure to act to eliminate tension, to satisfy a need or want, to solve a problem, or to restore a sense of equilibrium. Learning is a process of taking in information, processing it along with existing information, and producing new knowledge. An attitude is an enduring favorable or unfavorable disposition toward some object. Motivation spurs learning, and both these factors shape attitudes. Understanding these psychological factors can help marketing communicators stimulate consumer motivation and learning and shape attitudes so that consumers are more likely to buy.

2. Explain how consumers make complex and simple decisions and how marketing communication can influence this process.

The two main types of decision making are complex or simple decisions. Novelty of the purchase and consumer involvement influence whether the decision-making process is simple or complex. Complex decision making involves five steps: need recognition, information search, evaluation of alternatives, purchase, and postpurchase behavior. Simple decision making does not require information search or evaluation. This process is based on habit.

The three psychological factors of motivation, learning, and attitudes influence the various stages of complex decision making. The process begins with need recognition, then moves to information search and processing (internal motivation is nec-

essary for this step), continues with identifying and evaluating alternatives, and concludes with purchase and postpurchase behavior. Marketing communicators that understand the complex decision process can motivate buyers to learn about and identify their products as the best purchase choice. They can also influence some postpurchase behavior through planned follow-up and relationship building.

3. Contrast organizational and consumer buying behavior.

Organizational buying behavior differs from consumer decision making in five key ways. First, groups, not individuals, make decisions according to enforced decision-making rules. Second, although the organizational buyer is motivated by both rational and emotional factors in choosing products and services, organizational buying behavior tends to be less emotional and relies on information. Third, organizational buying decisions often involve complex technical dimensions. Fourth, the organizational decision process often takes a long time, creating a significant gap between the marketing communicators' initial contact with the customer and the purchasing decision. Finally, organizations differ in how they function and their personality.

4. Outline the organizational buying process.

The eight steps of the organizational buying process are problem recognition, general need description, product specification, supplier search, proposal solicitation, supplier selection, order-routine specification, and performance review.

POINTS TO PONDER

Review the Facts

1. What is an attitude?
2. List the three elements of the learning process.

Master the Concepts

3. How can marketing communicators influence a person's motivation to take action? How can they facilitate learning?
4. Discuss the components of an attitude. What are the implications for marketing communication?
5. Discuss several reasons why marketers continue to have a hard time understanding, predicting, and explaining consumer behavior.
6. Present a diagram of the consumer decision process. What is the role of marketing communication in each stage of this process? Consider which marketing communication activities might be most effective for each stage.

7. Distinguish between high-involvement and low-involvement decision making.
8. What are the differences between the consumer decision-making process and the organizational decision-making process?

Apply Your Knowledge

9. Based on your understanding of consumer motives, develop some general guidelines or directives for practicing marketing communication.
10. Use the multiattribute perspective to measure your attitude toward two different brands of jeans.
11. Assume you are training a salesperson to sell industrial products. Although this salesperson has a strong track record, she has been selling consumer products. What would you emphasize during training?

SUGGESTED PROJECTS

1. Locate an individual who has purchased a new automobile during the last year. Using the five-step decision-making process, ask this person to indicate how he or she accomplished each step.

2. (Writing Project) Contact ten students. Ask them to list the three primary motives they considered when selecting which university to attend. Ask them whether they would still use these same motives. Have them indicate any new ones. Write a short paper (2 to 3 pages) in which you summarize your findings and address how understanding motives can help marketing communicators understand the decision-making process.

3. (Internet Project) As discussed in this chapter, the Stanford Research Institute's (SRI) Values and Lifestyles Program 2 (VALS 2) can help marketers understand consumer psychographics, determine product positioning, and increase marketing communication effectiveness. Log onto SRI's Web site (future.sri.com) and follow the site's links to the VALS 2 page. What kind of companies have used VALS 2 and for what purpose?

Now determine your own psychographic profile by navigating to the on-screen survey and entering your responses. What is your primary type in the VALS 2 framework?

CASE 6: SO LONG TO THE VAN?

Gerri Gayner traded in her new Plymouth Voyager minivan—at a loss—to reclaim her individuality. A single mother of three, she didn't want to be typecast as a cargo-hauling "mommy." "It's not what I am," says Gayner, an entrepreneur who now drives nothing but convertibles. However, Gayner is planning to marry a man with three children of his own. The engagement entailed "a minivan talk," she says. Well, maybe it wasn't much of a discussion. "I said I would never drive one of those things as long as I live," she recalls. Today, her fiancé is shopping for a Chevrolet Suburban, the biggest sport-utility vehicle on the market. It seats nine, about two more than your average minivan.

What's going on? Americans' love affair with the automobile has crashed into life's practical demands and the evil angst of aging. To some people in their 30s and 40s who feel powerless against the tide of dirty diapers, day-care expenses, and kiddie soccer games, the minivan is starting to look like a good place to draw the line. Students of automotive culture say this rejection of the conventional is predictable behavior. In fact, some believe historians will look back on the minivan as an aberration, a vehicle whose popularity was almost entirely dependent not on its image but on its practicality. "That has not been the major motivating force of this industry," says Michael Marsden, an expert in the role of the automobile in popular culture. "The mainstay has been excitement, fun, liberation, movement—the feeling that destiny is in your own hands and that you are on the open road."

There are more than 6 million minivans on American roads today, and manufacturers expect to sell 1.5 million in 1997. Minivans have become icons of modern suburbia, filling school parking lots across the United States. They are invading Europe, and China wants them to help cart around its 1.3 billion people. But just the same, manufacturers know something is going on image-wise: It shows up in focus groups conducted by market researchers. One research consulting firm asked what minivans represent. The answer from one Californian suburbanite: "Family, family, family. Kids, kids, kids. No fun, no fun, no fun."

Manufacturers know that customers may grasp for alternatives like pricey Volvo station wagons or rugged Jeep Cherokees to escape the stigma, but parents, after all, will always need something to haul kids, pets, and sports equipment. It's just that people can be so cruel. When Jane Osgood announced she was expecting twins, she waited for her phone to ring with warm, congratulatory calls. Instead, her pals needled her about the minivan that seemed inevitably to be in her future. "This is it, you're going to have to get a minivan!" her friends gloated, observing that she would soon have a total of three children and a dog. "They were laughing at me," she says.

Case Questions

1. How are learning, attitudes, and perception affecting the purchase of minivans?
2. Identify places where marketing communication could improve minivan buyer behavior.

Sources: Robyn Meredith, "For Mini-Vans, a Mid-Life Crisis at Age of 14," *New York Times,* 12 May 1997, A1, C4. Keith Bradsher, "G.M. Sales Decline, but Chrysler's Surge," *New York Times,* 2 August 1996, C4; Oscar Suris, "It's Useful, Practical, and No One Can Make Me Drive It," *Wall Street Journal,* 26 February 1995, A-1.

ROMA'S LITE INTEGRATED CASE QUESTIONS

(Review the Roma's Lite Marketing Plan in the Appendix at the end of the text before answering these questions.)

1. What is the difference between consumer and organizational buyers? Develop a plan to target retailers so they will decide to carry Roma's Lite.
2. (Team and Writing Project) Divide into groups of four to six. Your group should design a survey questionnaire that addresses three ideas: (1) How do consumers feel about new food products. (2) How do they feel about pizza?, and (3) How do they feel about low fat products? Distribute your report to the rest of the class and summarize your findings in a brief report. How do these results impact your communication strategy for Roma's Lite Pizza?

chapter

7

The Legal, Ethical, and Global Environment

CHAPTER OBJECTIVES

After completing your work on this chapter, you should be able to:

1 **Identify the government agencies that control the efforts of marketing communicators.**

2 **Assess the major legal issues that affect marketing communication.**

3 **Analyze the social responsibility issues that affect marketing communication.**

4 **Discuss the role of self-regulation in marketing communication.**

5 **Outline the key global factors that affect marketing communication.**

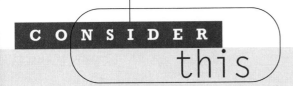

C O N S I D E R this

Stop the Smoking

According to a recent *Advertising Age*/Gallop Organization poll, 68 percent of Americans believe cigarette ads influence children and teens to smoke. A whopping 66 percent of the total—and 60 percent of smokers—believe some cigarette ads are specifically designed to appeal to young people. Two-thirds of Americans, including almost half of all smokers, want the U.S. government to impose greater restrictions on cigarette advertising. For 53 percent, that means a total ban. Fifteen percent said that although they don't support a total ban, they do believe there should be greater restrictions.

Adding to tobacco marketers' worries are the statistics from the Centers for Disease Control and Prevention that show there is a 90 percent chance that a person will not smoke if he or she does not

start by the age of 19. Add that to the *Journal of American Medical Association* article that offers evidence linking advertising to increased consumption by underage smokers, and the situation appears perilous for the tobacco industry.

The link between advertising and teens and young adults certainly appears to apply in the case of Camel cigarettes. In 1986 the brand's market share among 17-to-24-year-olds was less than 3 percent. In 1988 the "Joe Camel" brand image was introduced. By 1989 the Camel brand market share among underage smokers was 8 percent. By 1993 that share had risen to 13 percent. John Pierce, an epidemiologist at the University of California, San Diego, says "Advertising makes people susceptible to experimenting with smoking. But once they're susceptible, advertising doesn't make them want to experiment. Exposure to peers does."

Cigarette marketers have a dilemma. Their industry code says they must aim their sales pitch at adults—but market research shows that nearly all smokers start smoking, and become loyal to a specific brand, before adulthood. Research also shows that the percentage of teen smokers surged in the 1990s. The companies insist that their marketing efforts don't intentionally target teenagers. The $5 billion they spend every year on advertising and sales promotion, they say, is intended to promote their brands among adults who already smoke. However, some cigarette company records contradict those statements. Cigarette companies have left behind a paper trail stating their goals of developing, through clever advertising campaigns, children as customers.

Still, the tobacco industry fights back. R.J. Reynolds Tobacco Co. sponsored a study conducted by Roper Starch on 1117 young people ages 10 to 17. Their findings indicated that: (1) Where 73 percent recognized the Joe character, it was actually the least recognized among advertising symbols, (2) Only 81 percent of those who identified Joe as an advertising symbol knew he was a symbol for Camel cigarettes, (3) Only 3 percent who recognized Joe said they had a positive attitude toward smoking (all of that 3 percent were 16-to-17-year-olds), and (4) Far more teens who were aware of cigarette advertising remembered Philip Morris USA's Marlboro advertising than remembered Joe Camel.

In late 1996 President Clinton signed an Executive Order that gave the Food and Drug Administration (FDA) regulatory authority over cigarettes. President Clinton asserted that with FDA regulation "Joe Camel and the Marlboro Man will be out of our children's reach forever." Perhaps his claim is an overstatement, but the Order has numerous restrictive effects.

The FDA asserts that cigarettes are the delivery system for nicotine, an addictive drug. FDA regulation would drastically restrict cigarette advertising, accessibility, and promotions that could reach young people. Some of the more popular provisions include banning cigarette vending machines, halting distribution of Joe Camel–style paraphernalia, restricting cigarette advertisers to black-and-white text-only ads in magazines with significant teenage readership, and forbidding sponsorship at sporting events.

Initially, industry responses were unfavorable. The industry filed suit in federal court to challenge the FDA's regulatory authority over tobacco products. It also filed suits in state courts that challenged the advertising rules as a free speech violation. "The next thing you know the government will put ice cream on the list of products to regulate because it causes high cholesterol. If tobacco is bad, why not ban it entirely? How can you have something that is legal and yet can't be advertised?" noted Kent Brownridge, general manager of *Rolling Stone.*

However, after a small cigarette manufacturer, Liggit, admitted the harmful effects of cigarettes in exchange for release from civil liabilities, the large tobacco companies began negotiating with the government about abiding by the FDA regulations, agreeing to additional marketing restrictions, and paying a hefty settlement fee.

Sources: John M. Broder, "Two Top Cigarette Makers Seek Settlement," *New York Times,* 17 April 1997: A1, A13; Richard Lacayo, "Put Out the Butt, Junior," *Time,* September 2, 1996, 51; Jeffrey Goldberg, "Next Target: Nicotine," *New York Times Magazine,* August 4, 1996, 23, 36; Ira Teinowitz and Keith Kelly, "FDA Reopens Tobacco Rules," *Advertising Age,* March 25, 1996, 48; Melanie Wells, "Ad Agencies Wary of Tobacco Account Stigma," *USA Today,* 27 July, 1995, B1, D1; Steven Colford, "Hooked on Tobacco: The Teen Epidemics," *Consumer Reports* (March 1995): 142–6; "Teen Smoking and Ads Linked," *Advertising Age,* February 21, 1994, 1, 36.

CHAPTER OVERVIEW

Marketing communicators in the tobacco industry face a paradox. On the one hand, they must convince their clients that the communication strategies they propose achieve objectives, including turning nonsmokers into smokers. On the other hand, they must convince the government and the general public that these same strategies don't affect an underage audience of potential smokers. They must also grapple with the issue of whether it is socially responsible to market a product around the world that is physically harmful.

Marketing communication strategists must work within a tremendously complex legal, ethical, and global environment. The intent of this chapter is threefold:

(1) to provide an overview of legal issues that affect marketing communication, (2) to examine self-regulation in the marketing communication industry, and (3) to consider ethical and global issues that affect marketing communication.

MARKETING COMMUNICATION AND GOVERNMENT REGULATION

Government regulation that protects consumers can take place at the federal, state, or local level. In fact, the first attempt to protect consumers came not from the federal government, but from the states. For example, before the Federal Food and Drug Act was passed in 1939, New Jersey passed the "Seven Sisters" laws that regulated questionable food-processing activities practiced by family-owned businesses. Eventually, the business practice of "caveat emptor" (let the buyer beware) became so prevalent that the federal government became more involved in consumer protection. Both state and federal laws indirectly regulate marketing communication. The key federal laws are listed in Table 7.1.

Next we examine the key regulatory agencies that "directly" affect marketing communication. First, we turn to the regulatory agency of greatest importance to marketing communication, the Federal Trade Commission. Then we briefly look at other groups that shape the marketing communication environment.

TABLE 7.1

An Overview of Federal Laws Designed to Protect Businesses and Consumers that Affect Marketing Communication

Laws Protecting Consumers	
1939	Federal Food and Drug Act
1953	Flammable Fabrics Act
1966	Fair Packaging and Labeling Act
1968	Truth in Lending Act
1971	Fair Credit Reporting Act
1972	Consumer Product Safety Act
1975	Fair Credit Billing Act
1975	Magnuson-Moss Warranty Act
1975	Equal Credit Opportunity Act
1978	Fair Debt Collection Practice Act
Laws Protecting Competition	
1936	Robinson Patman Act
1937	Miller-Tydings Resale Price Maintenance Act
1947	The Lanham Trademark Act
Laws Maintaining a Competitive Environment	
1890, 1914	Sherman and Clayton Acts
1914	Federal Trade Commission Act
1938	Wheeler-Lea Amendment

The Federal Trade Commission

In 1914 Congress enacted legislation, the Federal Trade Commission Act, that declared unfair methods of competition illegal. The legislation established the Federal Trade Commission (FTC), an investigative and regulatory agency that monitored unfair business practices that could harm competition, such as price fixing.

The FTC today has extremely broad authority to regulate numerous business activities. It controls unfair competitive practices and also acts as a consumer protection agency. Specifically, it has been given authority to regulate credit, labeling, packaging, warranties, and advertising. Some of its specific responsibilities include:

- Initiate investigations against companies.
- Regulate acts and practices that deceive businesses and/or consumers and issue "cease-and-desist" orders where such practices exist. Cease-and-desist orders require the practice be stopped within 30 days.
- Fine people or companies that violate either (1) a trade regulation rule or (2) a cease-and-desist order given to an offender or to any other firm in the industry (a cease-and-desist order given to one firm is applicable to all firms in the industry).
- Order public notification of a violation or unfair practice.
- Fund the participation of consumer groups and other interest groups in rule-making proceedings.[1]

Most recently, the FTC has policed health and weight loss business practices, 900 numbers, telemarketing, and advertising that targets children and the elderly.

Other Regulatory Groups

Marketing communication managers must also be aware of the powers of the state attorney general, the United States postal service, and the Federal Communications Commission (FCC). The National Association of Attorneys General, the states' attorneys general, regulate advertising at the state level. For example, in 1990 34 attorneys general urged the FDA to prohibit cereal manufacturers from using advertising that claimed cereal reduced the risk of cancer. Individual attorneys general have also sued companies and advertisers to protect consumers in their prospective states. For example, Robert Abrams, New York Attorney General, brought action to force Coca-Cola to change the artificial sweetener labeling on Diet Coke because he felt the terminology was confusing and misleading.

Although it is not a regulatory agency, the U.S. postal service also controls advertising, both directly and indirectly. Its direct control stems from its right to control advertising that depends on the use of the mails—specifically, direct-mail advertising and mail-order advertising. If the Postal Service judges an ad to be fraudulent, it may take legal action. If a violation has been committed, the local postmaster is directed to stamp "Fraudulent" on the offending party's promotions and to return the mail to the sender. The Postal Service also retains indirect control because it has jurisdiction over advertising carried in any publication that goes through the mails. Its power is based on the power of the Postal Service to grant or revoke second-class mailing privileges. In effect, a revocation of the mailing privilege may punish a periodical that carries a misleading ad.

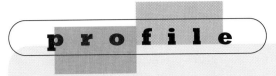

Lisa Cole
Attorney, Federal Trade Commission

Background
I am currently an attorney with the Denver Regional Office of the Federal Trade Commission, specializing in antitrust and merger enforcement. The Denver Regional Office also focuses on consumer protection enforcement in the areas of deceptive advertising, telemarketing fraud, and business opportunity fraud, and also performs consumer education outreach. In addition to attorneys, the Denver Regional Office is staffed by two investigators and a consumer contact representative who answers consumers' questions about the laws that the FTC enforces and assists consumers with complaints they are having against businesses.

Education and Career Track
I graduated from the University of Vermont in 1986 with a Bachelor of Arts in Political Science and the University of Virginia School of Law in 1991. I have worked for the Denver Regional Office since law school graduation. When I attended the University of Vermont, I also worked for the Vermont Attorney General's Office Consumer Protection Division, first as a student intern for academic credit, and later as a paid employee. After I graduated college, I worked for two years for the Arlington County, Virginia, Department of Consumer Protection.

Since my undergraduate days, I focused on a career in consumer protection. At the same time, my course work was very broad. I do not believe you should be disillusioned if you aren't focused on a specific career path because college is the time to learn and explore and have fun. However, I do think it is important to get out of the classroom and get some real-world experience while in college, regardless of the career path you want to pursue.

Typical Day
Working for the government is not easy. My typical work day is nine hours, and I am forced to make do with a lot less than is available in the private sector. However, the upside is that the government is a major employer, and employees tend to be given a great deal of responsibility. The government, including the FTC, is always looking for interns, and I highly recommend this if you are considering a career in government. Because the government is forced to make do with a lot less, it tends to delegate important tasks to its interns, so you'll get excellent experience.

My days are definitely not typical, and vary depending on the type of case I am working on. I spend a lot of time on the telephone interviewing people and becoming familiar with industries that I may investigate due to a merger or other antitrust issues. For example, I spend a lot of my time in the health care antitrust field and gather evidence from hospitals, physicians, and insurance companies. Because antitrust involves detailed economic analysis, a typical day for me could also involve talking to economists and familiarizing myself with economic literature. I also do a tremendous amount of writing and reviewing documents that have been submitted to me by third parties or the parties under investigation. Finally, I often will hold hearings to gather evidence that can be introduced in court, should I challenge a transaction under the antitrust laws. Courtroom work is not a big part of my job, but it certainly is a component. On the consumer protection side, some of my day can involve talking to consumers who want to talk to an attorney or giving speeches to consumers.

Advice
Antitrust and consumer protection are very specialized fields, and if you are interested in pursuing a career path in these fields, I recommend hands-on experience. Becoming familiar with private sector business and how it actually operates is also important.

The Federal Communications Commission exercises power over some advertising. Created by the Communication Act of 1934, the FCC regulates radio and television stations and networks. It is concerned with eliminating messages that are deceptive or in poor taste and has informally brought such advertising messages to the attention of a station. The FCC also has the power to revoke or refuse to renew a station's license if the station repeatedly runs advertising that the FCC considers objectionable. In most cases the FCC refers problems concerning advertising to the FTC.

Table 7.2 summarizes the regulatory agencies that can influence marketing communication.

TABLE 7.2

Specialized Agencies that Affect Marketing Communication

Agency	Effect on Marketing Communication
Federal Trade Commission	Regulates credit, labeling, packaging, warranties, and advertising
National Association of Attorneys General	Regulates advertising at the state level and enforces state consumer protection laws
U.S. Postal Service	Controls advertising by monitoring materials sent through the mail
Food and Drug Administration	Regulates packaging, labeling, and manufacturing of food and drug products
Federal Communications Commission	Regulates radio and television stations and networks
Bureau of Alcohol, Tobacco, and Firearms	Division of the U.S. Treasury Department, regulates advertising for alcoholic beverages
Securities and Exchange Commission	Has the power to ensure truthful, accurate, and adequate advertising of securities sold in interstate commerce
U.S. Labor Department	Regulates advertising by employers and unions in labor-related matters
U.S. Treasury Department	Imposes restrictions on the advertising of currency, coins, bonds, and similar items
Consumer Products Safety Commission	Can require corrective advertising if it finds defects in consumer products
U.S. Department of Agriculture	Regulates advertising of meat products, seeds, and some insecticides
U.S. Department of Transportation	Responsible for approving certain aspects of airline advertising

MARKETING COMMUNICATION AND THE LAW

The federal laws and regulatory agencies discussed so far have a direct impact on marketing communication. We will next examine how five areas of marketing communication are affected by their legal environment: advertising, sales promotion, public relations, direct marketing, and personal selling.

Advertising and the Legal Environment

As noted earlier, the FTC is the primary governing agency over the advertising industry. Its main focus is to identify and eliminate ads that are deceptive or mislead the consumer. An ad that is considered deceptive must have one or more of the following characteristics: (1) a false testimonial or endorsement, (2) an indication that the product possesses certain qualities it does not have, (3) an untrue characterization of the price or deal, (4) nondisclosure about some important aspects of the product, and (5) ambiguous statements that may appear true in isolation but can deceive if taken as a whole.

As an illustration of a deceptive ad, consider a recent ad from *Sports Collectors Digest,* in which Stan's Sports Memorabilia, Inc., offered baseballs signed by the Baltimore Orioles' iron man, Cal Ripken, Jr., for $39.95—less than half what the baseballs cost elsewhere. Ira Rainess, counsel to the Tufton Group (the exclusive licensee for Ripken autographs), could show the autographs were fake. Rainess estimates that sales of fake Ripken collectibles could reach $15 million, compared with just $5 million for the real stuff.[2]

Officially, the FTC gauges an ad to be deceptive if it contains the following three elements:[3]

1. There must be a representation, omission, or practice that is likely to mislead the consumer.
2. The deception must be considered from the perspective of a consumer acting reasonably in the circumstances.
3. The representation, omission, or practice must be a "material" one. The basic question is whether the act or practice is likely to affect the consumer's conduct or decision concerning a product or service. If so, the practice is material, and consumer injury is likely because consumers probably would have chosen differently without the influence of the deception.

This interpretation of a deception creates a heavy burden of proof. The commission must prove that deception was intended and that "reasonable consumers" were misled. In addition, both marketing communicators and legislators remain uncertain about what will mislead a "reasonable consumer." There are a few areas, however, in which the law prohibiting deceptive advertising is fairly clear-cut. These will be discussed next.

Unreasonable Basis for Making a Claim

Before an advertising claim can be made about product performance, the advertiser must have a reasonable basis for making the claim. If the advertiser cannot show that it had proof to support the claim before it developed the ad, the ad is illegal even if the claim is true and the product performs as advertised. Advertising claims that Eggland's Best eggs were low in cholesterol (see IMC in Action feature) is an example of an unreasonable claim.

Every country has its own definition of a reasonable claim. For example, recently the Chinese government banned the unstoppable Duracell battery bunny because the bunny endurance contest broke new rules that ban superlative claims and comparative advertising. Likewise, Budweiser had to quit using their slogan "King of Beers" or provide statistics proving it.

Misleading Demonstrations

A demonstration of a product or product performance on television must not mislead viewers. There are instances, in the case of food products for example, when additives or substitutes can be used legally because hot lights, film quality, and other aspects of the filming process do not provide an accurate portrayal of the product. The issue is whether the demonstration shows the product in a normal way in a normal setting without falsely upgrading the consumer's perception

A Healthy Egg? Or a Misleading Ad?

Eggland's Best, a Pennsylvania company selling eggs in most states, claimed in its advertisements that "even a dozen *Eggland's Best* eggs a week caused no increase in serum cholesterol" in tests as part of a low-fat diet. The appealing claim caught the attention of the Federal Trade Commission. The FTC charged the firm with false and misleading advertising. Eggland's admitted no wrongdoing but settled the case and agreed to modify ads and halt nutrition claims unless it could back them with "competent and reliable scientific evidence." The FTC also ordered the company to label its egg cartons for a year with this message: "There are no studies showing that these eggs are different from other eggs in their effect on serum cholesterol."

Eggland's then issued new ads that made the same claims, and used no new scientific evidence. The company relied on the same two company-sponsored studies it did before the FTC acted. Those studies each followed about 100 volunteers with elevated cholesterol levels. The volunteers maintained low-fat diets for six weeks. Half also consumed two *Eggland's Best* eggs daily, six days a week; the others ate no eggs at all. In one study the results showed that cholesterol levels dropped an average of 8 to 10 percent in both groups; in the other study both groups' cholesterol dropped, but by smaller amounts.

The studies showed the expected results of following a low-fat diet. Importantly, though, studies never compared *Eggland's Best* to other eggs, so Eggland had no evidence that *Eggland's Best* eggs were better at maintaining serum cholesterol than others. Critics said that the new ads implied *Eggland's Best* were better than other eggs. The ads stated that in the test those people who ate *Eggland's Best* eggs, showed no increase in cholesterol levels, and then asked: "How? Simply by enjoying these fresh, delicious eggs. . . ."

Robert J. Fukrman, Eggland's president, insisted the new ads didn't violate the agreement with the FTC. But the FTC disagreed. At issue, noted an FTC official, was whether "reasonable people come away from the ad thinking there's something special about *Eggland's Best,* that you can eat 12 a week and not raise your cholesterol, but that you couldn't do that with other eggs." The FTC's settlement with Eggland's included a civil penalty of $100,000 and a consent order that prohibits Eggland's from violating the terms of the first settlement.

Sources: FTC Press Release, "Eggland's Best Cholesterol Claims Called Deceptive," (March 13, 1996 retrieved via the Internet at www.ftc.gov/opa/9603/egg); "A New Shell for an Old Ad Claim," *Consumer Reports* (March 1995): 134; "A Better Egg?" *Consumer Reports* (January 1995): 131; Steven Colford, "Paper Tiger Litmus Test," *Advertising Age,* December 20, 1993, 2.

of the product. Dropping a truck 20 feet to show its strength but using special reinforcement of the frame would be an example of a misleading demonstration. Demonstrations are usually evaluated by the FTC on a case-by-case basis.

Reinforcement of False Beliefs

Ads that create or reinforce false beliefs are also illegal. Under FTC guidelines, what is critical is how members of the audience perceive the ad and how it affects their opinions and beliefs about the advertised product or service. That is, deception exists if *consumer perception* of the truthfulness of a claim is inconsistent with *actual* truthfulness. The fact that Listerine mouthwash allowed consumers to continue their erroneous belief that the product reduced colds proved to be the reason the FTC found Listerine guilty of deception. Similarly, Lowenbrau beer never corrected U.S. consumers' notion that the beer was imported, though it is made in the United States.

Unfair Comparison Advertising

In narrow terms, **comparison advertising** is the comparison of two or more specifically named or recognizably presented brands of the same generic product or service class in terms of one or more specific product or service attributes.

Although the effect of comparison ads on market share, advertiser image, and competitor image is still uncertain, comparison ads may provide consumers with biased information on the relative importance of two or more brands, and disparage brands either by implication or by direct criticism. Suppose that Tagamet HB created a comparison ad with Mylanta. It would be deceptive if the information shown was inaccurate or Tagamet only selected decision criteria that favored the sponsor.

Bait Advertising

Bait advertising is an alluring but insincere offer to sell a product or service that the advertiser does not really intend or want to sell. Bait-and-switch ads that are impermissible are those that do not represent a bona fide offer to sell the advertised product or those that misrepresent the actual price, quality, or salability of the product.[4]

In one case of a bait ad, Sears, Roebuck and Co. allegedly advertised home appliances but did not intend to sell the advertised items. Customers who shopped at Sears because of the bait ad were instead shown more expensive appliances by the salespeople. Sears was finally ordered to maintain an inventory that was reasonably adequate to meet demand for the sale items and to display a copy of the ad conspicuously in the home appliance department.

False Endorsements and Testimonies

An **endorsement** or **testimonial** is any advertising message that consumers perceive as reflecting the opinions, beliefs, or experiences of an individual, group, or institution. If, however, one can reasonably ascertain that a message does not reflect the announcer's opinion, the message isn't an endorsement. Although any one individual can endorse a product or service, some advertisers use the services of motion picture celebrities, television stars, or sports personalities.

Because consumers rely on expert endorsements to make purchase decisions, it is important that the endorser use the product and be qualified to make expert judgment. When an expert endorses a product, the endorser must use his or her expertise to evaluate the product and must examine it as extensively as would another person with similar credentials. If endorsers compare competing brands, they must also evaluate the selected brands. If an organization makes an endorsement, the organization must use evaluative procedures that will ensure that the endorsement fairly reflects the collective judgment of the organization.

"Free" Bargains

Normally, special promotions or bargains are presented as two-for-one sales, cents-off sales, multiple purchase discounts, or special offerings. Regardless of the language used, these special deals generally suggest to the consumer that something is being offered free of charge or at a discount. If "free" is contingent on the purchase of other products or has additional costs associated with receiving the item, such as handling costs, the FTC might view this message as deceptive. Likewise, a discount must actually be a reduction in the base price of an item, which pre-exists over a given period of time.

FTC Remedies for Deception

The FTC has many remedies for deception. A powerful tool is the cease-and-desist order, an order to halt the deceptive advertising. The FTC may also assess moderate fines for marketers who violate its orders. It may also require the advertiser to run corrective advertising that rectifies the deception. A typical corrective advertising order mandates that the offending company spend 25 percent of its annual

Nike often relies on sports celebrities to endorse its products. In this ad, women's basketball star Lisa Leslie endorses Nike's sportswear. What legal issues do you think Nike had to consider with this ad?

ad budget on corrective ads. Those ads must be approved in advance by the FTC and must state the previous claims and correct the claims in light of the facts.

Affirmative disclosure, such as the warning on cigarettes or on alcohol, is often required of deceptive advertisers, particularly in the food and drug industries. These disclosures are designed to help consumers make objective, informed decisions. The FTC frequently accompanies affirmative disclosure orders with a **cooling-off directive,** requiring the company to give consumers a three-day period to reconsider their product purchase. These directives only apply to sales made at locations other than the seller's place of business.

The FTC also requires firms to submit on demand documentation to substantiate advertising and product uniqueness claims. When the FTC issues a complaint against a company, it is the company's responsibility to show that there is a reasonable basis for the product claims it has made through such means as acceptable, objective, well-documented research procedures.

Sales Promotion and the Legal Environment

Most of the laws related to sales promotion deal with incentives offered to consumers. The FTC has rules that govern what information must be contained on a coupon, what the conditions of a price discount should be, and the conditions under which a customer can keep unsolicited merchandise.

There are also laws that relate to *contests, lotteries,* and *sweepstakes.* A **contest** requires some act of skill that requires a judge to make a relative comparison. A **lottery** involves a payment or other legal consideration in exchange for a chance to win a prize. All three elements—chance, consideration, and prize—must be present, or the promotion is not a lottery. **Sweepstakes** are games of chance that are lawful only if there is no charge or obligation of any kind for participants. The guidelines for stating the chance of winning, the considerations for entering, and the nature of the prize are well developed by the FTC.

The FTC has alleged that three general types of violations with contests, lotteries, and sweepstakes are most common:

1. False guarantees that a consumer has won a prize
2. Misrepresentations about the nature or value of the prize being offered
3. Failure to disclose the conditions necessary to obtain the prize

The courts and legislature have also scrutinized warranties, another sales promotion device. In 1975 a law governing consumer product warranties went into effect that requires a designation of whether the warranty is full or limited. A full warranty must include a statement of the time period during which it will remain operative. A limited warranty must set forth clearly what limitations are included. In 1985 the FTC published guidelines for the advertising of warranties. Any sales promotion practitioner that uses the term *warranty* or its equivalent in a promotion must do so with care and adherence to the FTC guidelines.

Public Relations and the Legal Environment

Marketing communication managers must also be aware of the laws that affect public relations. We discuss four such areas of law: defamation, privacy, copyright, and contract negotiations.

Warranty Information

Harvard Interiors Manufacturing Company warrants its products to be free from defects in workmanship and materials under normal use for a period of fifteen years from the date of purchase except for control mechanisms & pneumatic height adjustment mechanisms which are warranted for five years from the date of purchase; casters and upholstery are warranted for two years from the date of purchase. Normal use is defined as the wear which occurs in an office environment during the course of a normal eight hour work day. Harvard's warranty obligation is limited to the replacement or repair, at Harvard's option, of defective products which, during the warranty period have been reported by the purchaser to be defective in workmanship or material and which are found to be so by Harvard upon inspection. Defective products must be returned, with transportation charges prepaid, to Harvard or one of Harvard's authorized dealers. Returns must be authorized in advance by Harvard.

Customer shall be responsible for all maintenance service consisting of lubrication and cleaning of the product, minor assembly and adjustment, and performing operating checks.

Warranty Limitation and Exclusion:
Harvard will not honor the warranty if the product is subjected to abuse, misuse, negligence or accident or if the customer fails to perform the maintenance service referred to above. Harvard's warranty is limited to the original purchaser of the product, and is null and void if the product is resold.

Disclaimer of unstated warranties:
The Warranty printed above is the only warranty applicable to this product. All other warranties, express or implied, including, but not limited to, the implied warranties of merchantability and fitness for a particular purpose are disclaimed.

HARVARD INDUSTRIES
Harvard Interiors Manufacturing Co.

4321 Semple Avenue, St. Louis, MO 63120
(314) 382-5590 • FAX: (314) 382-8102
1-800-227-3161 (Parts)

P/N 479083

This Harvard Industries limited warranty outlines the warranty terms and exceptions.

Defamation

Defamation is any untruthful communication to at least one other person (other than the person or entity defamed) that tends to damage a reputation. The untruthful communication must clearly identify the defamed party, though not necessarily by name. If the party can be recognized from a description such as "the bald-headed, bearded guy who always sits in the corner of the lunchroom," that identification would be sufficient.

Usually defamation is divided into slander and libel; **slander** is classified as *oral* defamation and **libel** is classified as *written* defamation. However, some cases seem to combine both libel and slander. Take, for instance, a television or radio commentator that makes a defamatory remark while reading from a written script. The commentator in such a case is often charged or sued for libel because when the remarks were communicated to an audience they were spoken.

With the emergence of interactive technology, the issue of defamation has become even more confusing. Computer experts are now able to modify a company's Web site and replace words and pictures to produce derogatory results. The government has yet to decide who is responsible for monitoring this technology, and the courts have not yet issued clear guidelines for defamation in cyberspace.

Public relations practitioners may be involved in libel actions in two ways. One of the practitioners' clients might be libeled, or, more likely, the practitioner could be accused of libel through a news release, speech, or other communication.

Privacy

The rights of privacy do not apply to a public interest news story about a public figure or to information that is a matter of public record. The right of privacy applies only to people, not to organizations, and it takes four forms: (1) intrusion into solitude, (2) portraying someone in a false light (making the person appear to be someone he or she isn't), (3) public disclosure of private information, and (4) appropriation. **Appropriation,** using private pictures without permission, is the violation that causes most public relations problems. Model and photo releases (forms that give the company permission to use the model or photo in advertising) should be obtained to avoid any PR fiascos. For instance, in 1996 an Amazon chief sued Body Shop International because he alleged the company featured his photo in a publicity poster without his permission.[5] As will be discussed in Chapter 11 in more detail, the suit damaged Body Shop's image of a company concerned with the environment and all the world's citizens.

Copyright

PR experts often use written, artistic, or photographic materials as part of their message strategy. In such cases they must be careful to comply with copyright laws when using others' work. Under copyright laws, users of another person's creative works must understand the *fair use* exception to the copyright law. It is the only defense against copyright infringement.

The **fair use** exception allows the use of a part or parts of the work in criticism, comment, news reporting, teaching, scholarship, or research without seeking permission from the copyright holder. What amount of material is allowable is relative, and each case is decided on its own merits. Because so much public relations work is farmed out, public relations freelancers should realize that they don't own works made "for hire"—works that they were paid to produce. The firm that hired them does.

If a work is published without being copyrighted, or if the period of copyright has expired, the work enters the public domain and may be copied freely.

Contract Negotiations

Ordinarily, contracts are drafted with the help of an attorney, but certain documents become so familiar that the users forget they are dealing with actual contracts. When a PR practitioner gives a printer a brochure to print, both parties are entering into a contract. Contract negotiations may be equally informal with many public relations suppliers—photographers, artists, freelance writers, models, typographers, and film producers.

Typically, standard forms are used for such transactions. The forms should include these five elements: (1) names of all parties, (2) consideration specified (something of value exchanged), (3) an explanation of the extent of the use of the work (for instance, a photo is to be used in one brochure only), (4) duration of the arrangement, and (5) an indication of any other important factors. Still, these forms should be evaluated periodically, and legal experts should be employed whenever possible.

Direct Marketing and the Legal Environment

The use of direct-marketing techniques such as telemarketing, direct advertising, direct mail, and catalogs is growing rapidly. The FTC actively monitors and regulates direct-marketing activities. The FTC and the U.S. Postal Service jointly regulate direct-mail companies to ensure that ads are not deceptive or misleading or misrepresent the product or service being offered. Laws prohibit mailing unordered merchandise to consumers and using "negative option" plans whereby a company sends merchandise to consumers and expects payment unless the customer sends a notice of rejection or cancellation. The FTC also encourages direct-mail marketers to ship ordered merchandise promptly (for instance, within 30 days if no time is stated). Companies that do not ship promptly must provide buyers with an option to cancel the order and receive a refund.[6]

Telemarketing regulations are still evolving. In 1995 Congress asked the FTC to develop a set of rules to complement the Telephone Consumer Fraud and Abuse Prevention Act of 1994. Under the new rules, telemarketers must state their name, the company they represent, and the purpose of the call. Companies offering credit or loans or similar services—such as credit repair—can only bill consumers once services have been rendered. The rules prohibit companies from sending couriers to pick up payments and ban calls before 8:00 A.M. and after 9:00 P.M. In addition, the rules also prohibit telemarketers from calling consumers more than once every three months for the same product. Industry protests forced the FTC to soften its original, more stringent rules so that Congress could pass a revised version of the Act in October 1995.[7]

Telemarketers must also be aware of the complex set of rules developed by the FCC in support of the Telephone Consumers Protection Act of 1991. Telemarketers must maintain an in-house list of residential telephone subscribers who do not want to be called. Telemarketers are banned from using automatic dialer machines that contain a prerecorded sales message and from sending recorded messages to emergency phones, health care facilities, and to numbers for which the call recipient may be charged.[8]

The Internet looms as an important and complex direct-marketing medium. The debate over how it should be governed rages as this text goes to press. No one knows exactly whether the Internet will be self-governed or controlled by the FTC or FCC. Internet expert Martin Cohen comments on just one legal Internet issue as it relates to sweepstakes. Consider the standard sweepstakes rule, "enter as often as you like, but each entry must be mailed separately." While it limits entries in a traditional program, if the promotion is offered both on the Internet and via traditional media, the advantage shifts to the electronic entrant. E-mail allows the computer user to forward entries as fast as the fingers can complete the entry form and click "send." To control this, "the rules should include statements limiting the number of e-mail entries, as well as reserving the right to disqualify all entries which violate the limitation."[9]

Personal Selling and the Legal Environment

Historically, personal selling has not been considered an integral part of marketing communication. With the acceptance of an integrated approach to marketing communication, that view has changed. Clearly, the salesperson is often closest to the customer and is the organization's primary communicator. Consequently, the marketing communication manager must be familiar with the laws that impact the salesperson and the sales manager.

Undoubtedly, laws regarding *commercial bribery* are probably most significant. **Commercial bribery** is the act of influencing or attempting to influence the actions of another company's employee, such as a purchasing agent or buyer, by giving the employee money or a gift without his or her employer's knowledge. This practice has become so common in some industries that it is virtually impossible to discover the illegal act. Still, salespeople found guilty of commercial bribery not only face personal legal consequences but also such acts can literally destroy an organization.

Price fixing is the illegal act of setting prices in concert with competitors. Price fixing occurs most often in concentrated industries where several major competitors exist, for example, steel manufacturing. Often, the price fixers are sales managers.

Finally, salespeople are not allowed to engage in tying arrangements. In a **tying arrangement** a seller forces a buyer to purchase one product to obtain the right to purchase another.

Concept ✓ **Review**

MARKETING COMMUNICATION AND THE LAW

1. The FTC evaluates advertisements that have the capacity to deceive. Deceptive ads may have one or more of the following problems: an unreasonable basis for making a claim, a misleading demonstration, reinforcement of false beliefs, an unfair comparison, the use of bait advertising, a false endorsement or testimonial, or "free" bargains.
2. Sales promotion devices such as contests, lotteries, and sweepstakes each has distinct legal problems.
3. Legal issues that affect public relations include defamation, privacy, copyright protection, and contract negotiation.
4. Direct-marketing techniques such as direct mail, telemarketing, and the Internet all have important legal limitations.
5. The salesperson and sales managers are affected by three main legal issues: commercial bribery, price fixing, and illegal tying arrangements.

MARKETING COMMUNICATION'S RESPONSIBILITY TO SOCIETY

In Chapter 5 we discussed the role of values in cultures and subcultures. Values, guidelines for making judgments, include honesty, hard work, and love of family. When the marketing communication activities of a business appear to violate widely held values, the actions become **societal issues.** That is, part of society wants to change the offending actions. Even though such activities are not always illegal, the organization that ignores the underlying societal issues risks losing goodwill or business.

Marketing communication managers must be aware of societal issues and be prepared to adapt their strategy. These issues differ from one culture to another and from one subculture to another. For instance, a message that seems unremarkable in a large city may become an issue in a small town.

Because marketing communication activities are highly visible, widely varied, and difficult to screen, the general public tends to distrust marketing communications, especially advertising. For instance, a recent nationwide survey asked both consumers and advertising executives about their attitudes toward advertising. The findings showed that ad executives are fed up with bad ads produced by their trade—and, importantly, that they're becoming more and more concerned about advertising clutter. "The quality of advertising is really lousy. [Marketing people] feel the bad stuff compromises their work," notes Allison Cohen, president of People Talk, a marketing consulting group in New York.

A large number of consumers in the poll said they "don't care one way or the other" about several types of advertising. Many research experts believe such ambivalence could doom the ad industry. "People care less because there is too much advertising—they're just getting overwhelmed," People Talk's Cohen notes. "They are subject to so much that they tune it out." Perhaps most surprising was the fact that 42.5 percent of the people who work in advertising could not recall an ad seen during the past 24 hours. Only 17 percent of all consumers were able to recall a specific brand name.[10]

It is doubtful that negative attitudes toward advertising will ever disappear, so it is worthwhile to be aware of the social issues facing advertisers. Each of these issues is complex and each involves balancing the public welfare against the right to free speech and freedom of choice. The collective advertising industry, including agencies, advertisers, and the media, has an important stake in how the public and legislators view these social issues.

Consequently, the advertising industry has taken a proactive strategy in defending their image and informing the public about the virtues of the industry. The ad for the advertising industry illustrates the approach being used to enhance their image.

Issues of Social Responsibility

In the following sections we explore six societal issues that affect marketing communicators: manipulation, the right to privacy, puffery, offensive products and appeals, stereotyping, and advertising to children.

Manipulation and Subliminal Messaging

Critics claim that marketing communication manipulates people so that they purchase products and services that they neither need or want. This criticism raises an extremely difficult issue. On the one hand, there do appear to be gullible people who believe everything they hear or read. And some people buy everything they see, regardless of whether they can afford it. Other people—including chil-

WHEN ADVERTISING DOES ITS JOB, MILLIONS OF PEOPLE KEEP THEIRS.

Good advertising doesn't just inform. It sells. It helps move product and keep businesses in business. Every time an ad arouses a consumer's interest enough to result in a purchase, it keeps a company going strong. And it helps secure the jobs of the people who work there.

Advertising. That's the way it works.

INTERNATIONAL ADVERTISING ASSOCIATION

The global partnership of advertisers, agencies and media

This International Advertising Association ad promotes the business benefits of advertising.

dren, the senile, or the poorly educated—may not have the intellectual or physical capabilities to judge good from bad or real from unreal. The extent to which marketing communication influences these people is impossible to determine. On the other hand, no amount of marketing communication is going to make most people do something they do not want to do. Even a smooth-talking, aggressive salesperson cannot *make* the customer sign on the dotted line. Freedom of choice is a right that marketing communication cannot negate.

This same freedom does not exist, however, in the case of subliminal techniques. A **subliminal message** is one that is sent in such a way that the receiver is not consciously aware of receiving it. This usually means that the symbols are too faint or too brief to be clearly recognized. In essence it is a type of brainwashing and is morally wrong.

So, the critical question is whether advertisers engage in subliminal messaging. There is no evidence that they do, or should. First, the risk of engaging in such an underhanded activity is too great compared with possible benefits. Second, the potential benefits are uncertain as well. No evidence supports the claim that symbols subliminally perceived by one person are perceived in the same way by another person. Third, marketing communicators can't predict how, where, and in what context the audience will receive the subliminal message. Because of these factors, the effect of any subliminal message strategy would be, at best, limited and inconsistent—especially when compared with the risk communicators would face if consumers learned the business used such techniques.

DESPITE WHAT SOME PEOPLE THINK, ADVERTISING CAN'T MAKE YOU BUY SOMETHING YOU DON'T NEED.

Some people would have you believe that you are putty in the hands of every advertiser in the country. They think that when advertising is put under your nose, your mind turns to oatmeal.

It's mass hypnosis. Subliminal seduction. Brain washing. Mind control. It's advertising. And you are a pushover for it.

It explains why your kitchen cupboard is full of food you never eat. Why your garage is full of cars you never drive. Why your house is full of books you don't read, TV's you don't watch, beds you don't use, and clothes you don't wear. You don't have a choice. You are forced to buy.

That's why this message is a cleverly disguised advertisement to get you to buy land in the tropics. Got you again, didn't we? Send in your money.

ADVERTISING
ANOTHER WORD FOR FREEDOM OF CHOICE.
American Association of Advertising Agencies

Many consumers have negative perceptions about advertising, some of which are effectively challenged in this eye-catching ad.

Privacy

One basic human right is privacy—the right to be left alone. Critics argue that marketing communication violates our personal privacy. Ads confront us on parking meters, grocery store shopping carts, movie screens, rented videocassettes, and television monitors at airports. Ads are sent to fax machines, and few nights go by without a household's receiving at least one telemarketing or sales call, usually during dinner. Even Channel One, a student news program, offers commercials to students during school.

The criticism of privacy violation appears valid. Marketing communication strategists must find less offensive ways of reaching consumers than bombarding them wherever they go. Doing a better job of identifying consumers who are truly interested in the product is part of the solution. Providing a mechanism for consumers to initiate the communication process—by calling a toll-free number, for example—is also helpful.

Puffery

Consumers do not like to be lied to. But do they mind puffery? **Puffery** is advertising or other sales representations that praise the product or service with subjective opinions, superlatives, or exaggerations, vaguely and generally, stating no specific facts.[11] Statements such as "Nestlé makes the very best chocolate" and "When you say Budweiser, you've said it all" are mild forms of puffery.

Regulatory agencies deal with deceptive messages but have no jurisdiction over those that exaggerate. Critics argue that promotional messages should contain useful information, but not puffery. Defenders suggest that reasonable people know that puffery merely shows enthusiasm for a product and that consumers understand this persuasive type of selling. Clearly, puffery can be risky because overexaggerating can dissuade an audience. Defining puffery and determining whether to encourage, tolerate, or avoid it require the marketing communication manager to make a careful evaluation.

Offensive Products and Appeals

We have come a long way since the 1950s, when an advertising executive coined the term B.O. (body odor) for use in a print ad for a deodorant because consumers would be offended by the word *sweat*. Nevertheless, consumers may still be offended or irritated by certain types of appeals and by promotions for certain products. Feminine hygiene products, hemorrhoid cures, and jock itch are a few products whose advertisements offend some people. Sexual appeals may also offend.

Marketing communication managers who use controversial appeals and promote controversial products argue that their messages are appropriate for the target audience. But managers must be sensitive to the fact that people outside the target audience may also receive the messages. When people feel that marketing communicators have gone too far, they are likely to pressure marketers to change their messages and resellers to stop carrying the products. The You Decide feature describes how consumers who felt Calvin Klein ads were offensive threatened a consumer boycott of Klein's products.

This problem of being sensitive to other people's tastes becomes even more complicated when communicating in other cultures. In South Korea, for example, marketing communicators are not allowed to advertise products such as beer, liquor, and cigarettes. Keeping pet animals used to be regarded as a luxury in Korea, and the government opposed advertising pet-related products on the grounds that it was inappropriate to advertise such products while some families had difficulty feeding their children.

Stereotyping

The portrayal of people, not products, has also become a social issue. Marketing communications are accused of being discriminatory by presenting stereotypes in their promotions. **Stereotyping** ignores differences among individuals and presents a group in an unvarying pattern. Stereotypes of women are one prominent target of criticism. Recent studies have shown that females are more scantily dressed than their male counterparts in the same ad. Ads often depict women as sexualized bodies, with their status based on how they look.[12] The two most prominent images of women presented in ad campaigns, those of the "innocent virgin" and of the "dark lady," pit innocence and romance against knowledge and sexuality. Although there is still concern about sexual stereotyping, more communicators are recognizing the diversity of women's roles.

Racial and ethnic groups also complain of stereotyping in marketing communication. Minorities may be the basis of a joke or, alternatively, consigned to the background. Other critics complain that minorities are underrepresented in

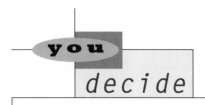

Klein Does It Again

In 1995 Calvin Klein introduced a risqué ad campaign that many media and marketing executives claim went too far. The advertisement in question, produced in-house, promoted Calvin Klein's jeanswear by picturing young men and women in suggestive sexual poses with their underwear showing. Sounds pretty typical for the designer, except that the six-page ad spread ran in *YM* magazine, whose readers are as young as 12 years old.

The ad caused a buzz in the magazine industry, where there is debate about whether a publication that reaches such a young audience should have run the ad. At least one magazine that appeals to a similar audience, *Seventeen,* says it wouldn't have accepted the ad if it had been approached by Calvin Klein. "It's too blatant," says Janice Grossman, publisher of *Seventeen.* "It just isn't right for the market we target. It's too in-your-face and too obvious." Another magazine in the young adult category, *Sassy,* "would take a hard look at whether to run the jeans ad," says Ira Garey, its publisher. *YM* doesn't understand the fuss. "This comes close to crossing the line, but it doesn't actually cross it," says Victoria Las-

don Rose, publisher of *YM.* "We've come to expect a little challenge from Calvin Klein. Most of his campaigns have been on the edge and have stretched the envelope. . . . *YM* readers are quite vocal. They're not afraid to write us and tell us about something they don't like, either editorially or in our ads."

Not all retailers were thrilled with the ads either. Steven Watson, president of Dayton Hudson Corp., which represents Marshall Fields, Dayton, and Hudson stores in nine states, declined to have their store names listed in the ads. Critics like the Catholic League, Morality in Media, and Aqudah Israel of America said the ads represented more than just bad taste. They called the ad campaign "kiddie porn," and they urged a consumer boycott of all Calvin Klein products. Despite Klein's contention that the ads were supported by solid strategy, the designer pulled the plug on this campaign.

To make matters worse, shortly after Klein announced he was halting the campaign, the FBI announced that it was investigating to determine if the ads broke child pornography laws. At least one model was a minor. A Klein

spokesperson said only: "We are confident that we have not violated any laws." Noah Dear, a New York City councilman who wants to ban all sexually explicit advertising from buses and subways, expresses his feelings as follows: "There is no difference between pornographers . . . and advertisers like Calvin. Both are peddling porn, and both should be subject and held to the same laws."

You Decide

1. Do you feel such ads for Calvin Klein are socially responsible?

2. Can you think of strategically sound reasons for such ads?

3. If you were the Calvin Klein marketing communication director, would you try to place sexually suggestive ads in magazines that have an audience that reaches 12 year olds? What about 10 or 11 year olds? Fifteen year olds?

Sources: Rick Hampson, "FBI Probes Jean Ads for Porn," *The Denver Post,* 9 September 1995, 1A, 20A; Judice Glaue, "Calvin Klein Axes Controversial Campaign," *The Denver Post,* Tuesday, 29 August 1995, 9C; Kevin Goodman, "Calvin Klein Ad Rekindles Debate as It Runs in Youth's Magazine," *Wall Street Journal,* Monday, 10 July 1995, B-8.

advertisements. Communication that perpetuates stereotypes can offend society at large and promote biases.

Another group frequently stereotyped is senior citizens. Critics often object to the use of older people in roles that portray them as slow, senile, and full of afflictions. Such portrayals are definitely on the decline.

Advertising to Children

Those who favor regulating children's advertising are concerned that children do not possess the skills necessary to evaluate the advertising message and to make

As life expectancy and quality of life for senior citizens increase, the stereotypes of seniors no longer apply. This V8 ad shows how one senior defies aging, living an active, healthy life.

informed purchase decisions. They also believe that certain advertising techniques and strategies appropriate for adults are confusing or misleading to children.

Advertising to children has been regulated since the 1970s, when experts estimated that the average child was exposed to over 20,000 commercials.[13] Two groups in particular, Action for Children's Television (ACT) and the Center for Science in the Public Interest (CSPI), petitioned the FTC to evaluate the situation.

On October 2, 1990, the House of Representatives and the Senate approved the Children's Television Advertising Practice Act, which restored 10.5-minute-per-hour ceilings for commercials in weekend children's television programming and 12-minute-per-hour limits for weekday programs. The Act also restored rules requiring that commercial breaks be clearly distinguished from programming and barring "host selling" tie-ins and other practices that involve the use of program characters to promote products.

In February 1996 the president signed the Telecommunications Act into law. That act mandates that the broadcast industry develop a program ratings system compatible with the V-chip, a blocking device for programs that are identified as violent, sexual, indecent, or otherwise objectionable for minors.[14] After the passage of the Act the industry worked to develop a ratings system. Advertisers that wish to target children will need to consider the program ratings and should devise commercials that match the ratings.

The Communications Decency Act (CDA), a provision of the Telecommunications Act, regulates obscene or "indecent" material on the Internet. Though some parts of the CDA have been found unconstitutionally broad, advertisers whose messages could be seen by children must be careful to comply with provisions that remain unchallenged (such as a prohibition against obscene material), or face stiff civil and criminal penalties.[15]

SELF-REGULATION OF MARKETING COMMUNICATION

One reason for the heavy regulation of marketing at both the federal and state levels is the long-standing assumption that marketing involves illegal and unethical activities. Marketing communication has unfortunately caught the brunt of this criticism. Consequently, professionals working in marketing communication have developed guidelines and codes of ethical conduct so that marketing communication managers and their companies can both avoid violating the law and can act in a socially responsible manner.

For instance, the alcohol industry (except beer and wine) initiated a self-imposed ban 48 years ago to keep liquor ads off radio and television. The ban lasted for nearly half a century. Then in 1996 Edgar Bronfman, Jr., president and chief executive of Seagram Co. broke the ban by airing a 30-second commercial for its Crown Royal whiskey on an NBC affiliate in Texas. Since then Seagram has purchased advertising time in several markets and has prompted several other distillers to consider breaking the ban. For instance, Hiram Walker & Sons Inc. followed suit, placing ads for Mudslide, a Kahlua–based drink, in 22 local markets. This advertising activity has triggered FCC concern and the attention of President Clinton. Some legal experts believe that the government may step in with regulation that either mirrors the self-regulation or is more stringent.[16] (See the Part II Video Case on pp. 238–239 for more details on this topic.)

The Marketing Communication Clearance Process

In addition to external regulation, most companies, agencies, and media have an elaborate network for reviewing marketing communication efforts. Although this review process tends to differ from company to company, it typically starts with the creative team and ends with the medium that carries the marketing communication, such as TV, magazines, the package, or the Internet.

At each step in the process, the marketing communication piece is critiqued from a number of different perspectives to make sure it meets all reasonable standards of ethics and good taste as well as legal requirements. Lawyers may review the piece at several different stages. The agency often has a set of standards against which it measures and scores all work. The general Creative Code of Advertising Agencies, shown in Figure 7.1, serves as a useful reference point. Marketing communication efforts that receive scores below a certain level are rejected. Figure 7.2 on p. 224 shows one example of a marketing communication review process.

Standards of Practice of the American Association of Advertising Agencies

FIRST ADOPTED OCTOBER 16, 1924—MOST RECENTLY REVISED SEPTEMBER 18, 1990

We hold that a responsibility of advertising agencies is to be a constructive force in business.

We hold that, to discharge this responsibility, advertising agencies must recognize an obligation, not only to their clients, but to the public, the media they employ, and to each other. As a business, the advertising agency must operate within the framework of competition. It is recognized that keen and vigorous competition, honestly conducted, is necessary to the growth and the health of American business. However, unethical competitive practices in the advertising agency business lead to financial waste, dilution of service, diversion of manpower, loss of prestige, and tend to weaken public confidence both in advertisements and in the institution of advertising.

We hold that the advertising agency should compete on merit and not by attempts at discrediting or disparaging a competitor agency, or its work, directly or by inference, or by circulating harmful rumors about another agency, or by making unwarranted claims of particular skill in judging or prejudging advertising copy.

To these ends, the American Association of Advertising Agencies has adopted the following *Creative Code* as being in the best interests of the public, the advertisers, the media, and the agencies themselves. The A.A.A.A. believes the Code's provisions serve as a guide to the kind of agency conduct that experience has shown to be wise, foresighted, and constructive. In accepting membership, an agency agrees to follow it.

Creative Code

We, the members of the American Association of Advertising Agencies, in addition to supporting and obeying the laws and legal regulations pertaining to advertising, undertake to extend and broaden the application of high ethical standards. Specifically, we will not knowingly create advertising that contains:

a. False or misleading statements or exaggerations, visual or verbal

b. Testimonials that do not reflect the real opinion of the individual(s) involved

c. Price claims that are misleading

d. Claims insufficiently supported or that distort the true meaning or practicable application of statements made by professional or scientific authority

e. Statements, suggestions, or pictures offensive to public decency or minority segments of the population.

We recognize that there are areas that are subject to honestly different interpretations and judgment. Nevertheless, we agree not to recommend to an advertiser, and to discourage the use of, advertising that is in poor or questionable taste or that is deliberately irritating through aural or visual content or presentation.

Comparative advertising shall be governed by the same standards of truthfulness, claim substantiation, tastefulness, etc., as apply to other types of advertising.

These Standards of Practice of the American Association of Advertising Agencies come from the belief that sound and ethical practice is good business. Confidence and respect are indispensable to success in a business embracing the many intangibles of agency service and involving relationships so dependent upon good faith.

Clear and willful violations of these Standards of Practice may be referred to the Board of Directors of the American Association of Advertising Agencies for appropriate action, including possible annulment of membership as provided by Article IV, Section 5, of the Constitution and By-Laws.

Copyright 1990
American Association of Advertising Agencies, Inc.

FIGURE 7.1

Creative Code of the American Association of Advertising Agencies

Virtually every major medium has guidelines for acceptable marketing communication. *Reader's Digest,* for example, has a long list of unacceptable product categories and message appeals. The three major television networks probably have the toughest standards. Ads that might air on cable or Fox may not be seen on NBC, CBS, or ABC. Even if ABC finally accepts an edited version of a questionable ad, the network may allow it to be shown only after 9:00 P.M.

Marketing communication managers believe that a vigorous internal review process is beneficial. The risks of allowing an unethical or illegal promotion to be seen or heard by the public are simply too great.

Self-Regulation by Professional Groups

To date there are very few, if any, universal standards by which to judge marketing communication activities. Marketing communicators do not agree among themselves as to what is legal or ethical, and critics apply their own ethical standards. Despite the lack of consensus, uncertainty about what is permissible has decreased during the last two decades. Most of this change comes as a result of

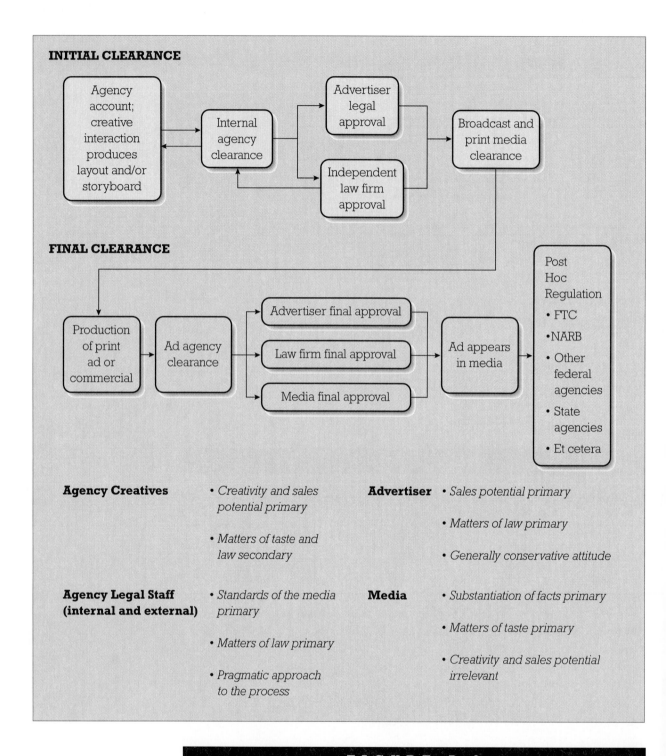

INITIAL CLEARANCE

Agency account; creative interaction produces layout and/or storyboard → Internal agency clearance → Advertiser legal approval / Independent law firm approval → Broadcast and print media clearance

FINAL CLEARANCE

Production of print ad or commercial → Ad agency clearance → Advertiser final approval / Law firm final approval / Media final approval → Ad appears in media → Post Hoc Regulation
• FTC
• NARB
• Other federal agencies
• State agencies
• Et cetera

Agency Creatives
• *Creativity and sales potential primary*
• *Matters of taste and law secondary*

Agency Legal Staff (internal and external)
• *Standards of the media primary*
• *Matters of law primary*
• *Pragmatic approach to the process*

Advertiser
• *Sales potential primary*
• *Matters of law primary*
• *Generally conservative attitude*

Media
• *Substantiation of facts primary*
• *Matters of taste primary*
• *Creativity and sales potential irrelevant*

FIGURE 7.2

Chart of Initial and Final Clearance Process

the activities of independent organizations that impose regulation through public pressure, and codes developed by groups within the promotion industry that are attempting self-regulation. These codes are usually area-specific and deal with topics such as testimonials, personal selling techniques, or couponing.

The National Advertising Review Council (NARC)

Perhaps the most ambitious example of self-regulation occurred in 1971, when the American Advertising Federation, the American Association of Advertising Agencies, the Association of National Advertisers, and the Council of Better Business Bureaus established the National Advertising Review Council (NARC) to implement a program of self-regulation. As an intermediary between consumers and the federal government, the NARC is charged with maintaining high standards of honesty and accuracy in national advertising.

In its first year of operation, the NARC convinced 84 advertisers to withdraw or modify ads. Recently, the NARC was successful in getting Sprint Long Distance to modify three ads; Topps, Co. (a manufacturer of baseball cards) to drop a print ad; American Airlines, Inc., to change the wording in a print ad for its Los Angeles to Hong Kong route; and Glidden Paints to drop an unsubstantiated claim about durability. The NARC has been successful in monitoring false and misleading advertising and in setting a state-by-state precedent for self-regulation.

Complaints regarding the truth and accuracy of ads may be initially submitted by consumers, consumer groups, industrial organizations, or advertising firms to the NARC's investigative staff, the National Advertising Division (NAD). After a complaint is filed, the NAD evaluates the legitimacy of the complaint and, if the complaint is justified, attempts to resolve the problem. If the advertiser or advertising agency is unwilling to change or withdraw the ad, the complaint is appealed to the National Advertising Review Board (NARB). This regulatory group consists of members representing national advertisers, advertising agencies, and public or nonindustry fields. On receipt of the appeal, the chairperson of the NARB appoints a five-member panel to resolve the issue. After reviewing both the NAD's findings and the advertiser's counterarguments, the NARB panel arrives at a decision. If, after exhausting all appropriate remedies, the advertiser is still unwilling to accept the NARB's decision, the federal government is informed of the violation and the appropriate regulatory agency takes over.

The NAD and the Children's Advertising Review Unit

The NAD has a special Children's Advertising Review Unit and has published guidelines on children and advertising. This unit was established in 1974 in response to the special problems of advertising directed to children. Its purpose is to promote truthful, accurate advertising that is sensitive to the special nature of its audience. The areas it primarily investigates include (1) how products are presented to children, (2) the amount of information provided, and (3) the amount of overt pressure to buy.

The NAB and Other Media Groups

The media have attempted to regulate advertising by screening and rejecting ads that violate their standards of truth and good taste. *Modern Maturity* magazine, for example, refuses to carry ads that demean senior citizens in any way. *Reader's Digest* does not accept tobacco or liquor ads. The National Association of Broadcasters (NAB) has separate codes of conduct for radio and television that specify products that cannot be advertised and give guidelines that should be followed in presenting ads or offering contests, premiums, and offers.

As a result of a civil antitrust suit filed against the NAB in 1979 that charged that NAB rules regulating television advertising were anticompetitive and in restraint of trade, the NAB has no formal standards concerning the following:

- The number of commercial minutes per hour
- The number of commercials per hour
- The number of consecutive commercials at each commercial interruption
- The number of products that can be promoted at each commercial interruption
- The purchase of network time for liquor ads
- The actual consumption of beer or wine on television

Many broadcasters, including the major television networks, have a Standard and Practices Division, which carefully reviews all ads submitted for possible broadcasts and regulates the number of ads and the type of products advertised.

Other Agents of Self-Regulation

Self-regulation has also been supported by the Better Business Bureau (BBB), local advertising review boards, advertising agencies, advertising media, and public relations firms. Supported by local businesses, the BBB investigates complaints, attempts to persuade offenders to stop unfair practices, and, if necessary, employs legal restrictions on advertising.

The Better Business Bureau urges businesses to adopt the following three principles of advertising self-regulation:

1. My organization will take primary responsibility for truthful and nondeceptive advertising.

Concept Review

MARKETING COMMUNICATION'S RESPONSIBILITY TO SOCIETY AND SELF-REGULATION

1. Marketing communicators must be responsive to societal issues, especially the following:
- Manipulation and subliminal messages
- Puffery
- Privacy
- Offensive products and appeals
- Stereotyping
- Advertising to children

2. Marketing communicators engage in self-regulation to prevent violation of state and federal laws and to adhere to their social responsibility.
- Each organization has its own process of evaluating its marketing communication
- Industry review boards also exist to evaluate

2. My organization will make available to the media, or the BBB, evidence to substantiate advertising claims.

3. My organization will ensure that the overall impact of its advertising is not misleading, even though every statement may be true when viewed separately.

MARKETING COMMUNICATION AND THE GLOBAL ENVIRONMENT

Just as legal and social issues affect marketing communication, so does the dynamism of the international environment. In this section we explore five key factors that affect marketing communication directly. First, to compete effectively, more industries are locating manufacturing, assembly, or other facilities close to customers in important world markets. Second, the international community has created a forum to resolve disputes between trading partners—the World Trade Organization. Third, established trade blocs such as the European Union are working to lower barriers to international trade. Fourth, with the disintegration of the communist Soviet Union, huge new markets opened as the nations of Central and Eastern Europe embraced democracy and capitalism. Finally, technological breakthroughs have spawned a number of products and services—fax machines, pagers, cellular telephones, and the Internet among them—that have fostered fast-paced marketing communication unlimited by national boundaries.

Counterbalancing the forces that are shrinking the globe, however, is a growing sense of nationalism among citizens who are concerned about losing their national identity in a borderless world. To reach target audiences that have such concerns, marketing communicators must "think global and act local," or risk alienating large markets.

Globalization of Industries

In industries with international customers, failure to develop global strategy can harm a company's competitiveness. To better serve an integrated market, for instance, a company should not limit itself to obtaining raw materials or locating manufacturing facilities, or offering customer services in the home country (the country where the business is based). Examples of industries that have globalized include housewares, automobiles, computers, pharmaceuticals, soft drinks, and telecommunications.

The globalization of industries has a direct impact on marketing communication. For example, automobile manufacturer Toyota no longer simply builds cars in Japan for export to other countries. Toyota has manufacturing and assembly plants worldwide to better serve its markets and to offset a bias against foreign-made products. In its marketing communications in the United States, Toyota stresses the fact that the Camry and other best-selling models are built by U.S. workers using a high proportion of U.S.–made parts. The communication strategy helps U.S. consumers that want to "buy American" overcome reservations about buying Toyota. Toyota must also decide to what extent it will customize its message in the United States versus the rest of the world, what adjustments it will make in its media and sales promotion, and so forth.

Mercedes-Benz and BMW have just begun to invest in manufacturing facilities in the United States. In addition to creating new vehicles that will be targeted at

This Toyota Camry ad emphasizes that Camrys are built in the United States.

a younger demographic, both companies are reinvigorating their marketing communication efforts. Aiming for annual sales of 125,000 vehicles in the United States by 1998, Mercedes' communication plans call for a $40 million ad campaign supporting the launch of its new E-class automobile, a site on the World Wide Web, a direct-mail campaign targeting current and prospective Mercedes owners, and sponsorship of an Elton John concert at New York's Radio City Music Hall.[17]

The World Trade Organization and Trading Blocs

The World Trade Organization (WTO) provides a forum in which international trading partners can resolve disputes related to unfair trade practices and other issues (including advertising, distribution, or pricing disputes). Based in Geneva, Switzerland, the WTO has a Dispute Settlement Body (DSB) that mediates complaints concerning disputed issues among the WTO's 125 member countries. During a 60-day consultation period, parties to a complaint are expected to engage in good-faith negotiations and reach an amicable resolution. Failing that, the party that brings the complaint can ask the DSB to appoint a three-member panel to hear the case behind closed doors. After convening, the panel has nine months within which to issue its ruling. The DSB is empowered to act on the panel's recommendations. The losing party has the option of turning to a seven-member appellate body. If, after due process, a country's trade policies are found to have violated WTO rules, it is expected to change those policies. If changes are not forthcoming, the WTO can authorize trade sanctions against the loser.

The WTO can have a direct effect on international marketing communication activity, as shown by a dispute between Kodak and Fuji film. Eastman Kodak filed a complaint against Fuji Photo Film Co., Ltd., in 1995. Kodak CEO George Fisher charged that Fuji unfairly dominated the Japanese photography market and requested that the U.S. government intervene. Fuji responded with similar charges about Kodak's behavior in the United States. One of Kodak's concerns was Fuji's close links with the four biggest film distributors in Japan, which Kodak alleged prevented it from getting equal access to distribution channels. Fuji denied the charges. Moreover, it claimed Kodak's Japanese problem was the result of poor marketing.

Aside from the fact that the underlying claim involved distribution and other marketing communication issues, not surprisingly, the international dispute generated a great deal of publicity between 1995 and 1997. Even as the WTO took up the dispute, Fuji initiated a marketing communication effort to shore up its image with U.S. consumers. Fuji hired a marketing communication agency to develop a packaging and branding campaign designed to highlight the fact that it has invested more than $1 billion in the United States. Employees at the company's Greenwood, South Carolina, plant perform photofinishing services and produce a range of products including photographic paper and videotape.[18]

Trade barriers in different parts of the world are being reduced or eliminated as countries forge economic agreements with neighbors on a regional basis. One of the most well-known of these trading blocs is the European Union (EU). Member countries include Belgium, France, Holland, Italy, Luxembourg, Germany, Great Britain, Denmark, Ireland, Greece, Spain, Portugal, Finland, Sweden, and Austria. Implementation of the Single European Act at the end of 1992 meant that citizens of the 15 countries were free to cross borders within the Union. Marketing conditions have been improved because content and other product standards that varied among nations have been harmonized. Further EU enlargement has become a major issue. In December 1991 Czechoslovakia, Hungary, and Poland became associate members. The Baltic countries—Latvia, Lithuania, and Estonia—are also hoping to join and thus lower their vulnerability to Russia. There is no doubt that marketing communication in the region should be adjusted to reflect a European audience that, despite cultural differences and a dozen different languages, is becoming more unified.

Developing Nations in the Global Spotlight

Even as the importance of regional trading blocs grows, individual nations are also commanding attention—not all of it flattering. Four Asian countries—South Korea, Taiwan, Singapore, and Hong Kong—are sometimes collectively referred

This billboard in a railway station in Warsaw reminds consumers that Colgate is the "Number 1 Toothpaste in the World." Its image and copy are purposefully simple because Poles distrust ad blitzes and regard Yuppie images as propaganda.

to as "tigers." Fueled by foreign investment and export-driven industrial development, these four countries have achieved stunning rates of economic growth. Another four countries—Thailand, Malaysia, Indonesia, and China—are getting close to the point of industrial take-off. China's population of 1.2 billion offers both a huge potential market for many products as well as a massive low-wage labor force for manufacturing.

However, even as these countries become more fully integrated in the world economy, a number of concerns are surfacing. One is the issue of poor working conditions and the use of child labor in the toy, athletic shoe, and apparel industries. Allegations reflect poorly on both the countries in which abuses occur and the well-known companies whose products are produced in those countries. Increasing numbers of consumers are well informed about where, by whom, and under what conditions their favorite brand-name products are manufactured.

For instance, in May 1996 an explosion of publicity erupted concerning the Honduran manufacture of talk-show host Kathie Lee Gifford's Wal-Mart clothing line. (See Part I Video Case on pp. 124–125 for more details on this topic.) Company executives who fail to address sweatshop issues are asking for a public relations nightmare as they come under increased scrutiny from organized labor groups at home and in developing countries. Some companies are making major initiatives in this regard. Representatives from Levi Strauss, Gap, Reebok International, and other companies regularly inspect labor conditions in developing countries. Reebok recently announced that its soccer balls will carry a guarantee that they were not manufactured by children. Gap has agreed to allow Catholic priests to monitor work conditions in the factories that are under contract to manufacture clothing.

Another problem linked to developing countries is piracy of computer software, videos, recorded music, and other forms of intellectual property. The issue has been a major source of ongoing friction between the United States and China. The International Intellectual Property Alliance estimates that Chinese counterfeiting of copyrighted material alone costs U.S. companies $800 million annually. Experts estimate that 98 percent of the computer software used in China is pirated. Factories in China also produce counterfeit Levi's jeans for about $5 per pair and sell them to people who falsely claim to be legitimate Levi representatives. Chrysler Corporation has even discovered sports-utility vehicles on the streets of Beijing that are nearly identical to Jeep Cherokees. Such revelations reflect poorly on China. Notes Hong Kong businessman Barry C. Cheung, "China lacks skills in public relations generally and crisis management specifically, and that hurts them."[19] Part of the problem stems from the unwillingness of China's Communist leaders to publicly explain their views on these issues, to admit failure, and to accept advice from the West.

Central and Eastern Europe after Communism

According to studies conducted by Freedom House, 117 of the world's 191 nations are now democratic—an increase of 20 percent during the past decade. Democracy's accession is especially striking in Eastern and Central Europe, where 19 out of 27 nations are democracies.[20] In the early 1990s the extraordinary political and economic reforms that swept the region focused the world's attention on a market of more than 400 million consumers. With wage rates much lower than those in Spain, Portugal, and Greece, the countries of Eastern and Central Europe represent attractive locations for low-cost manufacturing. The transition from centrally planned economies to market-based systems has been accompanied by a realignment of regional power. In December 1992 Hungary, Poland, and Czechoslovakia signed an agreement creating the Central European Free Trade Association (CEFTA). The signatories pledged cooperation in a number of areas, including telecommunications, tourism, and retail trade.

Marketing communication will play a key role in promoting economic development throughout the region, although several decades may pass before marketing practices reach a level of sophistication comparable to Western Europe. Having thrown off the yoke of communism, the citizens of the former Soviet bloc must learn about democracy and capitalism and the marketing communication tools that are available in such systems. In Hungary, for example, the practice of public relations was restricted under communism, and there were no advertising agencies or media organizations. However, as a 1991 headline in *The Hungarian Observer* proclaims, "PR is Back: Hungary has to learn how to sell itself all over again." Formed in 1990, the Hungarian Public Relations Association has seen its membership grow dramatically in recent years.[21]

Many consumers in the region are familiar with Western brand names and view them as being higher in quality than domestic products. This situation creates an environment in which marketing communications are likely to be perceived favorably. In Russia, L'Oréal SA, Calvin Klein, and Estee Lauder, Inc., are among the companies moving quickly to tap burgeoning demand for consumer products. Russian editions of well-known Western women's magazines such as *Cosmopolitan, Harper's Bazaar,* and *Good Housekeeping* provide ideal media vehicles for upscale advertisers. Commenting on Russia, George Nikides, director of *Elle,* noted, "This is a major market. The major advertisers are here. Now we're here."[22] Unfortunately, the distribution infrastructure in Eastern and Central Europe remains weak. The wholesale distribution system is underdeveloped; insufficient and unattractive retail space, the absence of self-service, and the three-line system (to select, pay for, and pick up merchandise) make shopping time-consuming and frustrating.

Global Technological Change

Technological change has dramatically impacted marketing communication over the past two decades. Pagers, cellular telephones, fax machines, laptop computers with modems, and satellite television have improved communication throughout the world. In addition to these communication changes, the explosion of Internet access and use means that marketing communicators can operate around the world, 24-hours a day. The World Wide Web portion of the Internet and commercial online services such as America Online offer individuals, organizations, and companies new ways to interact and conduct business with customers throughout the world. Although only 10 percent of U.S. households currently surf the Internet, experts believe that the Web will become a truly global mass communication medium. Predicts CEO Hal Krisbergh of WorldGate Communications, "Just imagine if 60 percent of the population—roughly the number of cable subscribers—has access to the Internet. You'll see a whole shift in communications, shopping—every aspect of how we see the world. It will have a major, universal impact."[23]

The growing popularity of the Internet also creates a number of marketing communication challenges. First, as people spend more time online, they view less television and cut back on reading and other leisure-time activities that represent traditional marketing communication channels. Second, the cost of setting up Web sites can be prohibitive. For example, by 1997 the cost to set up and run a Web site for selling goods and services for one year exceeded $4 million. The third issue is privacy. As more transactions are conducted online, consumers will need guarantees that credit card numbers and other personal information are secure. Besides wanting data protection, some computer users and regulators also want

---

Concept Review

MARKETING COMMUNICATION AND THE GLOBAL ENVIRONMENT

1. The globalization of industries has a direct impact on marketing communication.
2. Two important global organizations include the World Trade Organization and regional trading blocs, such as the European Union.
3. Developing nations affect IMC around the world.
4. New technology has changed global marketing communication.

to block access to certain types of online content—pornography, for instance. In Singapore, government regulators have the authority to censor the content that reaches the country's 100,000 Internet users.[24]

A CLOSING THOUGHT: ALL ACTIONS AND COMMUNICATIONS MUST BE FAIR

If an integrated marketing communication strategy is to work, it is critical that every message, every medium, and every contact point is both legal and ethical. Making a mistake in one area of the strategy may have dire consequences for all the other strategic elements. An unsafe package, an overly aggressive sales force, or a deceptive ad can negate every other element of the marketing communication program. Therefore, marketing communicators should create a review mechanism that considers the *entire* marketing communication program.

To review the program as a whole, marketers may need to reorganize, to change their business philosophy, or to enlist additional resources. The IMC in Action feature illustrates how several companies within an industry violated this integrated approach and confused consumers as a result.

Giving the Consumer a Headache

Talk about splitting headaches. Since the fall of 1995, the two over-the-counter painkiller giants, Johnson & Johnson's Tylenol and American Home Products' Advil, have been giving consumers a migraine with their constant fighting. Somehow, both have lost sight of the fact that their integrated communication strategies are being negatively affected by their public warfare.

The pounding began when Johnson & Johnson launched a television attack ad that soon had the two companies decrying the side effects of each other's products. The confusing charges and countercharges prompted the major TV networks to pull the harshest spots. ABC went so far as to ban all drug commercials that take potshots at rival remedies.

Undaunted, the combatants continued their fight in print, where Advil launched an assault on Tylenol through a full-page ad in the *New York Times* and other papers that featured an open letter written by Antonis Benedi, a former appointment secretary for George Bush, who blames Tylenol for the liver failure that forced him to have an emergency transplant in 1993. Johnson & Johnson was furious, not just about the letter but also at the fact that the newspaper published it without labeling it advertising. Worse, in Johnson & Johnson's view, at the bottom of the ad was a message that Whitehall-Robin's Healthcare was underwriting the letter reprint "as a public service." Not exactly, as it's the unit of American Home Products that makes Advil.

The latest attack led industry watchers to warn that the infighting could become suicidal. "This has exploded out of control," says Paul Kelly, president of Silvermine Consulting, which advises consumer-products companies. "Sooner or later people are going to get concerned about the whole catgory [of painkillers] and stay away." There is evidence that this has taken place. Tylenol's market share has dropped to 31 percent in 1996 from 34 percent in 1995.

Both companies continue to be outstanding strategic marketing communicators who have a clear understanding of how the tools can be synchronized to produce a beautiful melody. They don't seem to understand the risk they take with a sour note.

Source: John Greenwald, "Bitter Ads to Swallow," *Time*, April 1, 1996, 48–9.

SUMMARY

1. Identify the government agencies that control the efforts of marketing communicators.

Marketing communication is the most legislated and scrutinized element of marketing. Because of its visibility, legislators regulate many marketing communication activities. The Federal Trade Commission, the U.S. Postal Service, and the Federal Communications Commission are the primary regulatory agencies that affect marketing communication. Other agencies that regulate marketing communication include the Food and Drug Administration; the Bureau of Alcohol, Tobacco, and Firearms; the SEC; the U.S. Departments of Labor, Agriculture, and Transportation; the Consumer Products Safety Commission; and the U.S. Treasury.

2. Assess the major legal issues that affect marketing communication.

Advertising legal issues involve deceptive practices, such as making false claims, unfair comparisons, misleading demonstrations, bait advertising, false endorsements, and "free" bargains. Legal issues affect each area of marketing communication. Legal issues relevant to public relations include defamation, violation of privacy, copyright violation, and contractual obligations. In conducting sales promotion, managers must pay particular attention to incentives, contests, and warranties. Direct marketers must be cognizant of laws governing direct mail, telemarketing, and the Internet. In personal selling, key legal concerns include commercial bribery, price fixing, and other unfair methods.

3. Analyze the social responsibility issues that affect marketing communication.

The key social responsibility issues that affect marketing communication are manipulation and subliminal advertising, puffery, privacy, offensive products, stereotyping, and responsible advertising to children. These issues must be carefully balanced against the right to free speech and freedom of choice. Marketing communicators must make a reasoned decision about how to send messages in a socially responsible manner.

4. Discuss the role of self-regulation in marketing communication.

Marketing communicators self-regulate to prevent violation of state and federal laws and to adhere to their social responsibility. They may also self-regulate to prevent laws from being enacted that might be more restrictive than the self-regulatory measures. Self-regulation can occur both within the organization and through industry review boards, such as the National Advertising Review Council, that review marketing communication messages. Although the internal review process may differ from company to company, it often starts with the creative team and ends with the medium that carries the marketing communication. At each step in the process, the marketing communication piece is reviewed to make sure it meets all reasonable standards of ethics and good taste and all legal requirements.

5. Outline the key global factors that affect marketing communication.

Several critical issues affect marketing communication. First, numerous industries are becoming international, locating services and plants closer to the customers they serve. Marketing communicators in such industries must strike a balance between thinking globally and acting locally. Second, the World Trade Organization resolves disputes between trading partners, many of which relate to marketing communication issues. For instance, a WTO dispute can result in negative public relations to which marketing communicators must be able to respond. Third, several multicountry blocs, such as the European Union, regulate issues among countries. Marketing communicators must be aware of how these blocs affect their ability to promote products in various regions. Fourth, markets in developing nations are opening up as never before, but companies that do business with such nations must be aware of stakeholder reaction to such issues as human rights and environmental concerns. Target audiences in industrialized nations often react negatively to perceived violations of social standards when dealing with developing nations. Fifth, the opening of markets in former communist countries has spurred new marketing activity. However, because of differences in cultural values, economic systems, and attitudes toward Western countries, marketing communicators must proceed with caution to deliver messages that will persuade audiences in those markets. Finally, technology has affected the pace and reach of marketing communicators around the world.

POINTS TO PONDER

Review the Facts

1. Provide an overview of the most important laws affecting marketing communication strategies and tactics.
2. What criteria does the FTC use to gauge deception in advertising?
3. What is subliminal messaging?
4. What is the role of the World Trade Organization?

Master the Concepts

5. In what ways does the Federal Trade Commission regulate marketing communication?
6. "Corrective advertising has proven harmful to most advertisers forced to engage in the process." Do you agree or disagree?
7. What is being done to develop ethical codes for the self-regulation of marketing communication? Do you think these activities are sufficient? Explain.
8. Why does the development of a marketing strategy or program require an understanding of the legal environment?
9. What advice would you give to a person who is developing a claim for an advertised message?
10. How can the marketing communication manager avoid stereotyping?
11. Should businesses engage in subliminal advertising? Why?
12. Why does the development of a marketing strategy or program require an understanding of the global environment?
13. Why do you think it is important for marketing communicators to think globally and act locally?

Apply Your Knowledge

14. Assume that you are a judge. What factors would you use to determine whether a retailer was indeed practicing bait-and-switch advertising?

15. Suppose you were the marketing communication director for a clothing designer trying to target the teenage to young adult markets. Your creative team devised a series of print ads and billboards using images of notorious criminals, such as Charles Manson. The initial market research suggests that most people in your target audience like and remember the campaign, but some are offended because they feel the ads elevate mass murderers to cult status. Is it socially responsible to run the ads and billboards? Is it a good business decision? Consider the IMC implications. Explain your answers.
16. Catalog and retail company Sharper Image Corp. ran an ad, designed to be humorous, for a night vision lens that showed a leather-gloved hand aiming the lens into the open window of an amorous couple. The ad shows the bare back of a woman whose lingerie has fallen to her elbow as she pulls a man to her, neck arched. The ad copy for the product claims it can be used to "view all kinds of interesting and educational stuff, even in absolute darkness." It gives a price of $398 though "bail is not included." Numerous customers were outraged, claiming the ad was offensive and promoted stalking and voyeurism. As the marketing communication director for Sharper Image, what steps would you recommend the company take, if any, to respond to the complaints?
17. Assume you are in charge of a cellular phone company's new integrated marketing communication program for Central and Eastern Europe. What parts of the marketing communication program would have to differ from the firm's North American and Western European program? What could stay the same?

SUGGESTED PROJECTS

1. Contact your regional FTC office. Ask a representative to send you examples of three advertising-related cases that have been evaluated during the last year. What criteria were considered? What was the final judgment?

2. (Writing Project) Collect three print ads that demonstrate obvious sexual appeals. Ask five students ages 17 to 21 to indicate their response to these ads. Next, ask five students over the age of 21. Analyze the responses in a three-page report.

3. (Team Project) Divide the class into groups of four to six students. Have each person in your group research a different company that offers facilities or services in countries other than the company's home country. The research should focus on the pitfalls and benefits of conducting business in countries other than the home country. Meet in the small group to discuss the research findings. As a group, compile a list of the advantages and disadvantages of locating facilities or services in countries other than the home country, and draw up guidelines for companies that plan to globalize. Be prepared to present your findings to the class.

4. (Internet and Writing Project) You are convinced that a major company is making false claims in its advertising, sales promotion, and Internet direct marketing activities. You want to make a formal online complaint about these activities to the appropriate regulatory agencies. Visit the following sites and write a brief memo (two to three pages) about the online complaint filing process (if any) at each agency, which agencies you feel would be most responsive to your complaint (or certain portions of your complaint), and why.

Better Business Bureau	www.bbb.org
Ad Council	www.adcouncil.org
Federal Trade Commission	www.ftc.gov
Federal Communications Commission	www.fcc.gov

CASE 7: WILL POWER'S SURVEYS LOSE THEIR PUNCH?

Consumers shopping for a car are in a difficult position, especially if they are interested in new models. Dealers, of course, sing the praises of their brands, but other than such things as EPA miles-per-gallon ratings, consumers have very few objective yardsticks by which to measure one manufacturer's cars against another. Many eagerly await *Consumer Reports'* yearly car-buying guide, which indulges the magazine's ratings of new cars and its subscribers' ratings of cars they own. But although salespeople may be eager to tell prospective customers about the magazine's ratings, *Consumer Reports* refuses to let manufacturers use its ratings in advertisements.

The Surveys

So to provide consumers with objective evidence of their products' quality, car manufacturers turn to J.D. Power & Associates. Power publishes four major surveys each year, based on information collected from some 30,000 car owners. Consumers' satisfaction with the buying process is reflected in the Sales Satisfaction Survey. The Initial Quality Survey measures how owners feel after they've had their car three months, the Customer Satisfaction Survey rates customers' assessments of car quality and dealer service a year after purchase, and the Vehicle Dependability Index indicates how owners feel after five years.

Only Good News

Consumer advocates generally approve of the way that Power gathers its information, but some criticize what the company does once it has compiled its surveys; they are, in effect, Power's clients. Until 1986, Power released all its findings, positive and negative. But the manufacturers—also Power's clients—complained that a poor rating from Power could hurt car sales, so now Power makes public only positive ratings. The surveys also rate entire car lines—all Buicks, for instance—rather than individual models, which makes it more difficult for consumers to know how good a particular model is likely to be.

The Bad News

What threatens Power's credibility is the proliferation of ads that use the results of Power's surveys. As many as a dozen different cars may be promoted with Power's rankings at one time. These ads aren't lying; they're just using isolated pieces of the surveys. The major surveys include 20 or more categories, so it is relatively easy for a manufacturer to say that its product was rated "highest in its class" or "tops among American cars in its class," even though the car in question may in fact have done poorly in the overall ratings or when compared to imported models. The Chevrolet Lumina, for instance, was advertised as "the most trouble-free car in its class," according to Power's Initial Quality Survey. What the ad didn't say was that the Lumina had actually scored below average in the survey; it's just that the other cars in the "midsize specialty class" did even worse.

J.D. Power himself, who started his company in 1971, recognizes the risks of his name being overused. In 1986 he began reviewing—for a hefty fee—all ads that referred to his company's surveys. Policing ads for their validity is a good step, critics say, but it alone won't stop the devaluing of Power's survey results. It seems that car buyers may still have to do their own research just to find out what the Power survey results mean.

Case Questions

1. What are the possible legal and/or social problems faced by auto makers who use the J.D. Power survey data?
2. What are some of the long-term risks the marketing communication manager takes in using data provided by J.D. Power?
3. What would you recommend J.D. Power do to maintain the value of its surveys, given the legal and social concerns?

Sources: "Rating J.D. Powers Grand Plan," *Business Week,* September 2, 1996, 75–6; Kim Foltz, "J.D. Power's Big Problem: Popularity," *New York Times,* 17 August 1990, C-5; Barry Meier, "A Car Is Rated Most Trouble-Free, But How Good Is That?" *New York Times,* 13 October 1990, 16.

ROMA'S LITE INTEGRATED CASE QUESTIONS

(Review the Roma's Lite Marketing Plan in the Appendix at the end of the text before answering these questions.)

1. (Team Project) Break into small groups of three to four students. Discuss how deceptive acts and practices can occur and can affect a marketing communication program, such as the launch for Roma's Lite Pizza.
2. Outline the types of marketing communication self-regulation Roma's Lite should consider as part of its IMC strategy.
3. (Writing Project) Prepare a brief memo (1 to 3 pages) that discusses Roma Lite's social responsibilities and how the marketing communication program will help the company meet its responsibilities.
4. (Team Project) Identify and explain the various legal issues that might affect the marketing communication strategy for Roma's Lite Pizza.
5. (Team Project) Identify and explain the various international issues that might affect the marketing communication strategy for Roma's Lite Pizza.

chapter

8

The Marketing Communication Process

CHAPTER OBJECTIVES

After completing your work on this chapter, you should be able to:

1 **Define and outline the communication process.**

2 **List five different types of communication systems and explain why they differ.**

3 **Explain why marketing communicators use persuasive communication.**

4 **Discuss how the source, the message, and the audience affect persuasive communication.**

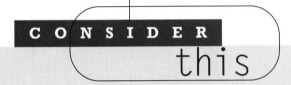

CONSIDER this

The Communication Revolution

Viewers of *Homicide,* NBC's Emmy-winning crime drama, can now watch the show online. The online version, sponsored by NBC Interactive, allows viewers to watch *Homicide* episodes on PC screens, have access to Web content (such as synopses of past episodes), and see interviews with the cast, during which viewers can interact with cast members with the click of the mouse. Welcome to a world where the TV meets the PC.

We've only begun to see how converging technologies may transform the TV medium so completely that it may scarcely be recognized. TV is a one-way viewing device that demands viewers receive the information passively. The TV is morphing into a medium that combines features currently offered via television, personal computers, and the telephone. The medium will no longer offer just one-

way communication, instead offering interactivity, as shown in this Gateway ad.

A dazzling scenario, to be sure, but it is definitely fraught with uncertainty. No one involved has a precise idea of what the new world will be or how audiences will react to it. When TV offers custom selections to suit every narrow interest, will mass-audience programming disappear? What will happen to CNN ratings when the 60 or more cable channels become a million or more on the Web? Will the interactive offerings appeal mainly to a select audience of technical gurus, while the rest of us stick with our regular favorites? What about commercials, local affiliates, and video stores? Will we wind up watching more TV or less?

Some businesses are betting that television will become the main access point, or "on-ramp," to the information superhighway. Electronics manufacturers such as Philips Electronics, Sony Corp., Thompson

239

Consumer Electronics, Bandai of Japan, and Funai Electric Company of Taiwan sell a set-top box and remote keyboards to fit on televisions. The box gives access to the Internet and the ability to receive and send e-mail. But computer companies tend to see television access to the information superhighway as a glorified extension of today's personal computer. They're betting that consumers will access the Web and view their favorite TV shows on big-screen PCs.

Still others are hedging their bets, investing in many different media, and waiting to see what will happen. Netscape, an Internet browser provider, is putting its browser software on almost anything with a screen and a modem—an Internet TV, followed by a $500 network computer, online video gaming machines, and Net-surfing cell phones. Sony, NEC, Nintendo, and IBM are joined in the venture. Microsoft purchased Web TV Networks Inc., a company that delivers Internet information directly to TV viewers. In a venture with Compaq and Intel, Microsoft also plans to develop a digital interactive computer–TV that will use Microsoft's Windows operating system.

No matter what services are eventually offered, consumers will drive the development of the television medium. As the system unfolds, companies supplying the hardware and programming will keep track of which services users favor. If users watch a lot of news, documentaries, and special-interest programming, those offerings will expand. If video-on-demand is popular, that area will grow. If services such as videoconferencing, interactive yellow pages, or electronic town meetings are widely used, these services will spread.

Clearly, technology is changing the nature of how we communicate with one another. Even the experts are unsure how the picture will look five, ten, or twenty years from now. Major communication delivery companies such as NBC, Disney, AT&T, TCI, and a host of others are betting billions of dollars on the possibility that their strategy is best. Still, regardless of the delivery method, audiences still care about the underlying message, the source of the message, and how the message affects their lives.

Sources: John Markoff, "Microsoft Deal to Aid Blending of PC's, TV's and the Internet," *New York Times,* 7 April 1997, C1; Frank Rose, "The End of TV As We Know It," *Fortune,* December 23, 1996, 58–68; Lawrence M. Fisher, "2 Companies to Make TV-Top Internet Links Using Oracle Systems," *New York Times,* 5 November 1996, C4; Joshua Cooper Ramo, "Winner Take All," *Time,* September 16, 1996, 59; Michael Krantz, "Voice of America Upgrades Service," *Adweek,* January 2, 1995, 14; Frederick Elking and Amelia Kassel, "A Marketer's Guide for Navigating the Information Superhighway," *Marketing News,* July 31, 1995, 2–3; George Gilder, "Telecom Angst and Awe on the Internet," *Forbes ASAP,* December 4, 1995, 113–216.

CHAPTER OVERVIEW

The premise of this text is that even a marketer with the best product and lowest price is unlikely to be successful unless there is effective communication with target audiences. With thousands of marketers delivering their stories at the same time, the messages combine to produce a roaring noise that may irritate and confuse listeners. Marketing communication is the way a marketer blends all communication efforts to create an understandable, credible message that addresses the needs and wants of the audience. Marketing communication attempts to convince listeners to prefer the sponsor's brand, idea, or service to other alternatives.

To succeed, marketing communicators must understand how to communicate persuasively. In this chapter we explore the flow and purpose of marketing communication, the communication process, and types of communication. We also analyze persuasive communication. We then examine the communication source, the message, and the audience. Let's now explore the basic marketing communication features.

BASIC FEATURES OF MARKETING COMMUNICATION

The role of marketing communication is to support the marketing plan and help key audiences understand and believe in the marketer's advantage over the competition. As Figure 8.1 illustrates, marketing communication has an *external* and an *internal flow.*

The **external flow** is directed at those outside the business: past, present, and potential customers; resellers, both wholesalers and retailers; other companies; and government agencies, private agencies, and experts in the field. A large, multi-

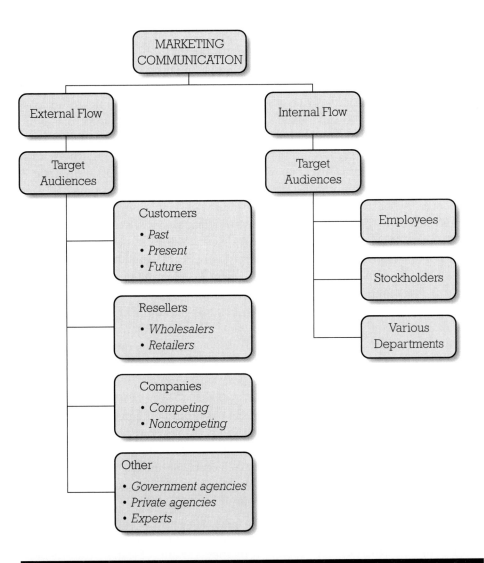

FIGURE 8.1

The Flow of Marketing Communication

national company such as Polaroid Corp., for example, maintains an elaborate network of external communications. It communicates with past customers through advertising and direct mail; with current customers through advertising, warranties, product updates, and material on how to use its products; and with potential customers through advertising, point-of-purchase displays, salespeople, and so on. Through direct mail and its sales force, Polaroid also communicates information about its products, pricing, and promotion to resellers. It exchanges similar information with competitors and with companies that sell complementary products such as photo albums. Finally, Polaroid keeps government agencies (such as the Federal Trade Commission) and consumer interest groups (for example, photography clubs) informed about its efforts.

The **internal flow** of marketing communication is directed at those who are members of the organization. The internal communication may differ according to each internal audience. For instance, employees often need to know what marketing is doing, especially when the organization is introducing new products or deleting old ones, changing prices, or distributing the product in new outlets or markets. By influencing how employees perceive their organization, marketing communication can help shape their morale and performance. If employees feel they are working for an innovative market leader that produces highly regarded ads, for example, they are likely to work harder, stay with the company longer, and become positive opinion leaders in public. Marketing may communicate in more detail with certain departments. Research and engineering departments, for example, share product information with marketing, and vice versa. Through sales forecasts, marketing determines the day-to-day level of production. Stockholders also need to be informed about marketing activities. If they are going to buy stock and recommend the company to other buyers, they must be convinced that the firm's marketing decisions are in their best interest.

Marketing must also communicate with members of the firm in different locations. Making sure that employees in different cities and regions receive the same messages and understand them in a similar way is critical for the cohesion of the organization and for the coordinated implementation of the business strategy. Of course, this task becomes even more difficult when a company must communicate internationally. On an international level the flow of vital intrafirm information can easily be distorted by factors such as cultural differences and physical distance. For example, Snapple found it hard to convince consumers in the United Kingdom to buy a drink that is not served hot or with milk.

Whether the flow is internal or external, effective communication means reaching the right people with the right information through the right sources at the right time. It requires an **integrated strategy,** as follows:[1]

1. *The right information.* Assess the relative importance that audience members place on information. Do audience members want objective information, replete with facts and comparisons? Or do they prefer emotional appeals? What do they already know?
2. *The right people.* Select the best way to deliver information. Which delivery methods do audience members prefer? Do the members turn to different methods for some purposes, such as an expensive purchase?

3. *The right sources.* Gauge where the communicator stands in relation to competing sources. Is the audience committed to a particular source, such as friends or *Consumer Reports*? Is the audience open to new sources? What are they?
4. *The right time.* Provide guidelines to determine what mix of communication techniques to use, when to use them, and how best to allocate funds. These guidelines should be based on the communication objectives and available resources.

Implementing a strategy requires a thorough understanding of the needs and wants of the various audiences, a working knowledge of the available communication techniques and how they blend together, and an awareness of competing communicators, including other companies, friends, the government, the news media, and so forth. In short, a great deal of data must be gathered before the marketer can implement a communication strategy.

The marketing communication strategy is part of the firm's overall persuasive marketing effort. The more that business managers understand about communication, the more they can contribute to a marketing communication program. In the rest of this chapter, we discuss basic ideas about how people communicate and present some keys to effective communication.

Concept ✓ **Review**

BASIC FEATURES OF MARKETING COMMUNICATION

1. The role of marketing communication is to support the marketing plan by helping target audiences understand and believe in the marketer's advantage over the competition.
2. An integrated communication strategy should reach the right people with the right information through the right sources at the right time.

THE COMMUNICATION PROCESS

What is meant by *communication*? To communicate is a process of sharing some idea, attitude, or information. Scholars through the ages have tried to formulate more precise definitions. The communication process has a beginning, middle, and end and is guided by the communication objectives of the participants. In this text we define human **communication** as a process in which two or more persons attempt to consciously or unconsciously influence each other through the use of symbols.

Figure 8.2 illustrates the basic elements of the communication process. Note, however, that these elements are all closely related. In fact, even something as complex as communication within a large factory can be viewed as a single process, with components and interrelationships within it. If one element is changed, each of the others is altered. In other words, senders, messages, and receivers together form a *system of communication*.[2]

First, consider the communicators, a component of every communication system. In traditional communication the two communicators are referred to as the *sender* (or encoder) and the *receiver* (or decoder). The **sender,** or **source** of the

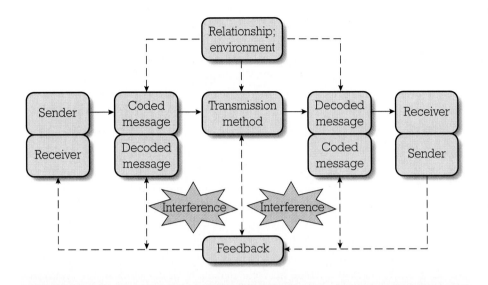

FIGURE 8.2

A Model of Human Communication

message, can be an individual, a group, or an institution that wishes to transmit a message to a receiver (or target audience). The **receiver,** the recipient of a message, can also be an individual, group, or institution.

The sender/source accomplishes the transmission of the message by selecting and combining a set of symbols to convey some meaning to the receiver. The greater the similarity or overlap between the sender and receiver, the more likely that communication will be effective and the less likely that miscommunication will take place. If the sender does not have much in common with the receiver, the sender should learn as much as possible about the receiver to bridge the gap. Successful salespeople, for example, qualify prospective customers to make sure that those customers' needs and wants are understood, so that the correct information is transmitted.

The process of transforming thoughts into a sequence of symbols is called **encoding.** When encoding, the source should consider the characteristics and capabilities of the receiver. The symbols the sender uses should be familiar to and viewed positively by the receiver. Just as important, the message must be delivered through a medium that the receiver uses and at an opportune time. Delivering the same message through two different media can produce very different results. Receiving a message in person versus through the radio is an everyday example. The message received face-to-face will seem much more personal than the radio message.

Possible media may be classified as either personal or nonpersonal. Personal media refers to message-delivery devices that tend to be one-on-one. Examples include word of mouth or personal selling. Nonpersonal media is also called "mass media," and includes broadcast, print, catalogs, and so forth.

Although the receiver does not initiate the communication process, the receiver is just as much a communicator as the sender. The receiver communicates with the sender through **feedback** using the same set of symbols the sender used to communicate. When the receiver provides feedback to the sender, they reverse roles—the receiver is now the sender. Sometimes feedback is explicit: It entails words, pictures, overt signs, or gestures. On other occasions feedback is given implicitly through the use of nonverbal expressions.

Mass communication, especially advertising, often involves implicit, delayed feedback from target audience members. Advertisers, for instance, usually receive feedback in the form of customer reaction, or lack of reaction, to the products or services advertised. When feedback is implicit and delayed, it is difficult to gauge whether the sender has effectively communicated. The nature of the feedback is determined by how well the receiver **decodes,** or interprets, the message delivered by the sender.

Two main factors affect decoding: the communicators' relationship and the environment. The nature of the relationship between the sender and receiver can affect how the message is delivered and how the receiver interprets the message. For instance, a family member could write a short, informal note that another family member could interpret clearly but a potential customer would find confusing. Another factor that can affect decoding is the environment in which the communication takes place. Both the external environment—the weather, time of day, competing messages, and so on—and the internal environment—experiences, attitudes, values, and biases—can often influence the decoding process.

Whenever environmental factors distort the communicators' relationship or the communication process, this distortion is called **interference** (or "noise").[3] For the marketing communicator, one growing source of noise is competing messages. Experts estimate that the typical North American is exposed to more than 12,000 messages each day.

Concept Review

THE COMMUNICATION PROCESS

1. Communication is a process in which two or more persons attempt to consciously or unconsciously influence each other through the use of symbols.
2. In the communication process two or more parties are simultaneously sender and receiver, who encode and decode messages and provide feedback.
3. The decoding process can be affected by two factors:
   - The relationship between the communicators
   - The environment

TYPES OF COMMUNICATION SYSTEMS

Several types of communication systems exist. They vary in complexity, the amount of contact between communicators, the timing of feedback, and the communicator's ability to adjust to feedback. Next, we investigate five types of communication systems: interpersonal, organizational, public, mass, and interactive. Figure 8.3 summarizes the characteristics of each of these systems.

CHARACTERISTICS

TYPES	Complexity	Contact	Timing of Feedback	Adjustment to Feedback
Interpersonal	Low	High	Short	High
Organizational	Moderate	Moderate	Moderate	Moderate
Public	High	Low	Long	Moderate
Mass	High	Low	Long	Low
Interactive	High	High	Short	Moderate

FIGURE 8.3

Types of Communication Systems and Their Characteristics

Interpersonal Communication Systems

The most basic communication system is interpersonal communication. An **interpersonal communication system** is a communication system that may consist of as few as two people and as many as can interact face-to-face so that the participants have the opportunity to affect each other. When the system consists of just two people of two distinct groups, it is called a **dyad.** As the system becomes more complex and more people are added, the **small group** emerges. The upper limit of the small group is usually between 15 to 20 people. If more people are involved, the group must impose artificial regulations on itself, such as parliamentary procedure.

Interpersonal communication is also affected by the use of supplementary message delivery media. That is, a salesperson talking to a customer is engaging in direct communication. The same salesperson who delivers part of the message through less direct media—such as the telephone, letter, fax, or e-mail—changes the nature of the communication and may diminish the benefits of direct interpersonal communication. The close, direct contact between communicators allows the salesperson to customize the sales message to suit the audience, receive immediate feedback, and adjust the message accordingly. The message itself can be complex because explanation is possible.

Unfortunately, communicating interpersonally also brings disadvantages. It is so time-consuming that some members of the target audience will be missed because there is not enough time to call on all customers. Salespeople working for Eli Lilly and Company, for instance, attempt to call on 50 percent of their customers once each month, 25 percent once each six months, and contact 25 percent by letter or telephone two or three times annually.

Organizational Communication Systems

In a bank, factory, retail store, or government agency, communication is much more complex than in an interpersonal system. Each institution has an **organizational communication system,** which is a system composed of a large collection of subsystems organized around common goals. The subsystems all exist as separate entities yet interrelate with each other. Consequently, both a formal and an informal network of communication is often required, making it more difficult to communicate because feedback is often delayed and incomplete.

For example, the marketing communication manager for Kroger-Southwest must inform its resellers of special prices, price rebates, or other deals. The central purchasing office for Kroger may receive several product deals from competing manufacturers during the first seven days of a quarter. Kroger may hesitate to respond immediately because the offers do not include comparable information, they may be waiting to hear from other manufacturers, or they may feel that some manufacturers are willing to negotiate and others are not. Kroger's messages from manufacturers and to resellers will likely be standardized to enhance understanding, thus losing the personal appeal of interpersonal communication. Some problems with organizational communication have been reduced through technology such as e-mail and teleconferencing, which enhances speed and introduces an element of personalization.

To communicate effectively in an organizational system, managers must learn as much as possible about the organizations with which they communicate. Simply using the correct technical jargon is an important consideration. Furthermore, their messages should include important benefits the organization desires. Benefits such as reliability, speed of delivery, and high quality are valued by most organizations.

Public Communication Systems

A **public communication system** usually involves communication from one person to a large group of people, as occurs when a person gives a speech to an audience. Although everyone affects everyone else to some degree in every communication system, in public communication the speaker generally has the strongest effect on the group. The feedback listeners give to the speaker is less obvious and more subtle than the feedback provided in interpersonal and organizational systems. The speaker needs considerable sensitivity to detect this feedback, which is frequently limited to nonverbal cues such as facial expression, body posture, or eye contact.

Certain types of personal selling use public communication. Party selling such as that of Tupperware Home Parties is an example. Company executives also find themselves giving speeches to local groups, stockholders, and congressional subcommittees.

Mass Communication Systems

Compared with public communication, **mass communication** offers even less opportunity for people to interact or to affect one another. Although there is feedback in mass communication (through such means as e-mail, 800 phone calls, letters, and coupon use), the distinguishing characteristics of this system are delayed feedback and no direct contact. In such a system the source of the mass message does not face the audience nor can the source possibly receive feedback from all the people who receive the message.

Marketing communication managers must establish a mechanism to compensate for this lack of personal contact and provide a formal feedback system to gauge audience response. The Titelist sporting goods manufacturer, for example, connects with customers through the use of Tiger Woods as its spokesperson. Feedback is provided through focus groups, phone surveys, and intermittent in-depth interviews. However, as explained in the next section, the need for a formal feedback system may change with the emergence of interactive technology.

Interactive Communication Systems

Interactive communication systems use computer technology that allows the marketing communicator to send persuasive messages while simultaneously allowing the receiver to react, modify, and customize the message and the response. For example, Ford recently ran basic interactive ads on Interactive Channel-Europe. The first 60-second spot was a corporate ad listing various features available in Ford cars. Viewers could use their TV clickers to name how many features were mentioned in the spot. The ad would then congratulate viewers on a correct response. If the viewers answered incorrectly, the ad would tell them so and supply the right answer.

The second Ford commercial let viewers find out more about the new Mondeo model. Again using the clicker, viewers could select one of four commercials: a conventional car commercial, one that stressed the Mondeo's technical specifications, one that listed the model's U.K. distribution, or one that showed various press comments about the Mondeo. As this example shows, interactive technology delivers messages to the masses while providing the benefits of interpersonal communication. Still, it is not face-to-face communication, and the number of options available to the receivers is limited and may not always be what the receiver wants to hear or see.

Experts agree that interactive technology will revolutionize marketing communication. But before this can happen, some problems need to be solved. First, interactive systems need to be established in consumer homes at an affordable rate. Second, they need to be as simple as possible so that people like to use them. Many consumers find PCs too complicated, so developers are trying to design devices that are as easy to use as the TV or telephone.[4] Finally, providing a high level of security is needed. Most experts agree that interactive marketing communication systems won't be available at a significant level for several years, but when they become widespread they will create a new type of communication—two-way mass communication.

Persuasive Communication Systems and IMC

People communicate in many different ways. In integrated marketing communication, however, persuasive communication is paramount. Even if an individual ad or sales promotion piece is intended to deliver information, remind, or build awareness, the explicit goal of the IMC strategy is to persuade. The attempted persuasion may take several forms, including providing believable, accurate information; changing attitudes or beliefs; convincing audiences they need to change

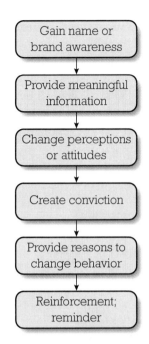

FIGURE 8.4

The Sequence of Persuasive Objectives for Marketing Communication

attitudes or behavior; and motivating audiences to take a particular action. Consider some marketing communication tools to see the forms of persuasion they use. Advertising and PR tend to be most effective in persuading audiences that information is accurate and attitudes need to change, whereas sales promotion and personal selling, by definition, are a call to action.[5]

Recall that in integrated marketing communication, *all* marketing communication mix elements should work together to promote the firm's marketing objectives. Together, the elements should provide sufficient motivation to the audience to prompt a change in behavior. The marketing communication objectives, then, tend to be sequential as shown in Figure 8.4, beginning with name or brand

Concept Review

TYPES OF COMMUNICATION SYSTEMS

1. Several types of communication systems exist that vary in complexity, the amount of contact between communicators, the timing of feedback, and the communicators' ability to adjust to feedback.
2. The five main types of communication systems are interpersonal, organizational, public, mass, and interactive.
3. Persuasive communication is critical in an IMC strategy and may take different forms to accommodate reaching the various communication objectives.

awareness, moving to providing meaningful information, then changing attitudes and perceptions, and ultimately creating conviction and behavioral change. An overtone of persuasiveness permeates all these objectives.

CHARACTERISTICS OF THE SOURCE

The source of a message is the communicator or endorser—the person or business whose message is directed at the target audience. Three types of sources exist. The **sponsor source** is the manufacturer who pays for the message delivery and is usually identified somewhere in the message itself. The ad for Vaseline products not only is a sponsor ad but also includes several integrated components such as an 800 number and sampling.

The **reseller source** is either a wholesaler or retailer who has associated with the message, often through manufacturer products. Ads produced by Sears or Ace Hardware represent a retail and wholesale source, respectively. The **message presentation source** is the person, animated character, or voice-over who delivers the actual message. The Energizer Bunny, Snoopy for Met Life, and the actor-spokesperson (Cliff) for IHOP all represent a presenter source.

This ad features the sponsor source, Vaseline Research.

This ad shows Snoopy, Met Life's message presentation source.

What makes one source more effective in persuasive communication than another? One of the most successful matchups in recent years is Sprint and actress Candice Bergen, who has filmed more than 75 spots since 1990 and who, the company claims, is directly responsible for Sprint's increased market share. Sprint wanted to distinguish itself from AT&T and MCI as the smart, feisty, and irreverent competitor. Candice Bergen (as the star of CBS's *Murphy Brown*) represented that personality. In addition, Candice Bergen had the three characteristics that contribute to persuasiveness: credibility, attractiveness, and power.

Credibility

Credibility is the extent to which the receiver perceives the source to be truthful or believable. Highly credible sources tend to create an immediate change in attitude. Highly credible groups (such as the American Medical Association) are even more effective sources than highly credible individuals.[6]

Credibility depends on two related factors. The first is the expertise attributed to the source. Characteristics such as intelligence, knowledge, maturity, and professional or social status all lend an air of expertise to an individual or group. For example, Pete Sampras could be considered an expert on tennis equipment. The second factor determining credibility is the objectivity attributed to the source. In other words, does the receiver believe the source is willing to discuss the subject honestly? For example, Michael Jordan and Emmitt Smith are highly credible sources for athletic shoes, and former Surgeon General C. Everett Koop was a highly credible source in a public service announcement advising people to stop smoking. Table 8.1 shows how nine celebrities rank as credible sources.

Objectivity seems to be less important than knowledge or expertise, however, perhaps because most people do not expect the sponsor of a message to be objective. Obviously, Michael Jordan is being paid to promote Air Jordans, so he is not completely objective.

Despite the importance of expertise in determining credibility, the source should not be too perfect and should exhibit human flaws. John Madden would be an example. Why? Perhaps the perfect source is too obvious a fabrication, or perhaps perfection detracts from a second source characteristic: source attractiveness.

Attractiveness

The greater the perceived attractiveness of the source, the more persuasive the message. Cindy Crawford, who acts as a spokesperson for Pepsi-Cola, for example, is an attractive source to many audiences. However, it is not just because she is beautiful and wears expensive clothes, although these characteristics may be part of the attractiveness equation. Source attractiveness is the extent to which the receiver identifies with the source. It results from similarity, familiarity, or likability. For many who have watched Cindy for several years, she represents all these components. Of course, Cliff in the International House of Pancakes TV commercials reflects a similar familiarity and likability that would be appealing to baby boomers (and those who don't want to count calories) who find IHOP a good place to eat breakfast, lunch, or dinner.

Research suggests that the more receivers feel that a source is similar to themselves, or how they would like to think of themselves, the more likely they are

TABLE 8.1				

The Celeb-O-Meter

(Numbers indicate the percentages of respondents naming each celebrity as the one they most trust or distrust.)

Most Trusted		Least Trusted	
Michael Jordan	9.1%	O.J. Simpson	12.2%
Candice Bergen	7.6%	Ed McMahon	7.1%
Bill Cosby	3.2%	Candice Bergen	4.2%
Kathie Lee Gifford	2.4%	Dionne Warwick	4.0%
John Madden	2.2%	Bill Clinton	2.8%

Source: "In Celebs We Trust," *Adweek,* January 2, 1995, 17.

to be persuaded. This similarity, or perceived similarity, can be exhibited through ideologies, attitudes, and behaviors. Many political candidates are experts in saying the right things to various audiences to make each audience believe its ideology is similar to the candidate's.

The second source of attractiveness, familiarity, is normally created through past association. People have been seeing Bill Cosby for many years. He appears in concerts, on television, and in charity fundraisers. Children especially relate to him because he is funny and one of the most patient, loving, and unusual fathers ever to appear on television. For Jell-O and its pudding and gelatin desserts, Bill Cosby is the ideal spokesperson. By association, Jell-O is fun too. It is not surprising that this well-established familiarity with Cosby has made him one of the most attractive sources in marketing communication history.

Some people have long idolized fashion models, so these models are frequent spokespeople. Christie Brinkley, for instance, is a likable spokesperson because of her beauty and wholesomeness. The more we like a source, the more attractive that source is to us. Liking, however, is hard to measure and tends to be a transitory feeling that changes quickly. In the end, empirical studies of celebrity spokespersons have yielded mixed results in terms of believability, overall effectiveness, and purchase intention. There are, of course, serious risks associated with using celebrities. Christie Brinkley, for example, became the topic of gossip with her quick succession of marriages and divorces. And Bill Cosby's image suffered when a woman claimed she was his illegitimate child.

Power

In addition to credibility and attractiveness, power can make a source effective. Power depends on the receiver's perception that a source has the ability to administer rewards or punishments. It has three components: perceived control, perceived concern, and perceived scrutiny.[7] For example, salespeople gain perceived control over prospective customers through their knowledge of the product or their ability to offer customers important benefits not otherwise available. Many public relations efforts try to create the idea that the sponsoring company feels concern for members of the audience. IBM asks us to have a positive attitude toward the company because it is concerned with preserving the arts in America. Government agencies, banks, employment agencies, and other organizations attain power through their perceived ability to scrutinize our lives. A letter from the Internal Revenue Service is quickly opened and carefully read.

Word of Mouth: An Indirect Source

Most individuals seek information from a variety of sources outside the sponsoring organization. These external sources may organize formally to distribute such information (for example, articles from the Small Business Administration or *Consumer Reports*), provide information in line with their expertise (for example, reports from doctors, investment analysts, and auto mechanics), or may offer individual opinions that are trusted on a particular topic (such as the opinions of family, friends, neighbors, or coworkers).[8] Experts and trustworthy individuals often provide what is commonly called word-of-mouth information. Unlike the producer, reseller, or spokesperson, **word-of-mouth sources** do not benefit from the acceptance of the message and are not under the control of the sponsor.

Gordon Weaver, executive vice president of Paramount Pictures, claims, "Word of mouth is the most important marketing element that exists."[9] Its importance is well documented. Marketing communicators must therefore attempt to influence those who may create word-of-mouth communication.

Starbucks Coffee Co. certainly followed this strategy when it introduced its product in 1971. Initially it began with a small coffee shop in Seattle's touristy Pike's Place Market, along with free samples doled out to passersby. Spurred by extremely strong word-of-mouth communication, Starbucks started its integrated marketing communication campaign in 1988 with its "Familiarity breeds contentment" campaign on transit and outdoor billboards, which consisted of pictures of drinks with architectural drawing lines to illustrate ingredients. The campaign later expanded to brochures and point-of-purchase displays. The mail-order business, advertised through *The New Yorker,* also began waking up the national taste buds. Today, Starbucks serves over 14 million customers a week.[10]

The impact of negative word-of-mouth communication has also been well documented. When Microsoft faced word-of-mouth criticism for Windows 95, it immediately conducted consumer research, tested the product, and resolved technical problems. Not all problems generate negative word of mouth. When is it likely? Albert Hirschman proposed a model that suggests some answers. According to Hirschman, a dissatisfied customer may make one of three responses:[11]

1. *Exit:* voluntary termination of the relationship
2. *Voice:* any attempt to change, rather than escape from an objectionable state of affairs, by directing dissatisfaction at management or anyone willing to listen
3. *Loyalty:* the customer continues with the dissatisfying product or seller and suffers in silence, confident that things will soon get better

The response a customer selects depends on characteristics of both the individual and the industry. The key individual characteristics are (1) the perceived probability that complaining would help, (2) the costs and benefits of complain-

---

Concept Review

CHARACTERISTICS OF THE SOURCE

1. The source of a message is the speaker, communicator, or endorser. The persuasiveness of the source is affected by three characteristics:
   - Credibility—the extent to which the receiver perceives the message source to be truthful or believable—depends on the perceived expertise and objectivity of the source.
   - Attractiveness—the extent to which the receiver identifies with the source—is determined by similarity, familiarity, and liking.
   - Power of the source is determined by perceived control, perceived concern, and perceived scrutiny.
2. Word of mouth—messages distributed by individuals not under the control of the sponsor—is a powerful indirect source of information.

Word of Mouth Helps Chrysler

To gauge the success of Chrysler Corp.'s test-drive program for the launch of its LH models, all Tom McAlear needed to do was get a haircut. Shortly after Chrysler had community opinion leaders test-drive its LH line of cars, McAlear, Chrysler's Detroit zone sales manager, was shooting the breeze with his regular barber. "He said to me, 'I drove an Intrepid for three days. It's terrific, and I'm going to buy one'," McAlear recalled. "That's the type of great PR we want. A barber talks to a lot of people every day. We didn't just pick CEO's [for the test-drive program]. These cars are not just for them." This chance conversation was the type of positive word of mouth Chrysler hoped for.

The introduction of Chrysler's LH cars—the Dodge Intrepid, Chrysler Concorde, and Eagle Vision—was touted as the most important in company history, and Chrysler wasn't satisfied to rely on only the usual advertising and promotion to get the message out. To spur word-of-mouth support,

Chrysler embarked on the most ambitious example to date of a growing trend in auto marketing: putting consumers into new cars away from the dealership, often for days at a time. From October through January, Chrysler dealers in 25 regions offered an LH model for a weekend to influential community leaders and businesspeople. More than 6000 primary drivers took the automaker up on the offer, and 90 percent of them responded to a survey afterward. Based on survey results, Chrysler estimated the cars received 32,000 exposures in the three months, including secondary drivers and passengers.

The results were "nothing short of phenomenal," said John Damuse, vice president of marketing for Chrysler. More than 98 percent of those responding said they'd recommend the car to a friend, and 90 percent said their opinion of Chrysler had improved.

In January, Chrysler also placed an LH vehicle at 19 different luxury resorts for free use by guests. A

third facet to the Chrysler plan earned further upscale exposure: the Chrysler Concorde Cultural Tour, a sponsorship of charity balls in eight major markets, organized by PR agency Anthony M. Franco, Inc. "People in evening gowns and tuxedos with tails crawled into the cars and kicked the tires," says Peg Tallet, vice president of Fundraising and Corporate Philanthropy at Franco. Tallet estimates more than 7500 people had direct contact with the vehicles, and another 200,000 received information about the car through the foundations involved.

"People are now talking about Chrysler as a luxury car again, something they haven't done in decades," says John Bulcroft, president of Advisory Group. "Word of mouth can make or break a car manufacturer, particularly in the luxury segment."

Sources: Bill Vlasic, "Can Chrysler Keep Up?" *Business Week,* November 25, 1996, 108–20; John P. Cortez, "Put People Behind the Wheel," *Advertising Age,* March 22, 1993, S-28.

---

ing, and (3) the sophistication of the consumer, such as his or her awareness of how to make a complaint.

The industry characteristics are essentially structural. Is the industry concentrated, highly competitive, or a loose monopoly? Negative word of mouth is most likely in concentrated industries and least likely in loose monopolies.[12] For example, a great deal of negative word of mouth exists in the automobile industry (see the IMC in Action feature), but little in the nursery plant industry, where three or four growers control the entire output of houseplants sold in the United States. Hirschman's model has been empirically tested and appears to accurately portray the likelihood of negative word of mouth.

MESSAGE VARIABLES

The specific elements used to communicate an idea and the way these elements are organized constitute the **message variables.** The role of the marketing communication manager is to take marketing information and translate it into the most effective message format. Message variables are divided into two categories: structure and content.

Message Structure

The structure of a message depends on several items: whether the message is a verbal or nonverbal message, readability, ordering effect, repetition, and the presence or absence of counterarguments.

Verbal versus Nonverbal

When we think about delivering a message, we think about using words, or verbals. Verbals can be powerful. They can make us laugh, cry, or feel terrified. Nike tells us to "Just do it!" and Allstate Insurance tells us we're "in good hands. . . ." Still, nonverbals also play an important role in effective communication. Is a picture worth a thousand words? According to a study conducted by Ogilvy and Mather, in a given message the words create 15 percent of the impact, the tone creates 25 percent, and the nonverbals create 60 percent of the impact. In his excellent book, *Nonverbal Communication,* Stephen Weitz develops five categories of nonverbal communication:[13] (1) facial expression and visual interaction (for example, eye contact), (2) body movement and gestures (such as muscle tightening and movement toward or away), (3) paralanguage (for example, loudness, pitch, and tremor of the voice), (4) proximity behaviors (appropriate distance between people for certain activities, for instance), and (5) multichannel communication (simultaneous interaction between various factors operating in a communication, such as people and activity).

For persuasive appeals, the most effective nonverbal cues are facial expressions, paralanguage, and timing of phrases; the message designer clearly controls these elements. More specifically, one study of several nonverbals used in a television commercial found that people who communicated simplicity or single-mindedness were positively associated with persuasion. For instance, nonverbals that correlated strongly with persuasibility included the characters' hands at their sides, the principal character expressing contentment, a likable spokesperson, a humorous mood, a busy setting, and a wink.[14]

Some messages should emphasize words and others should limit words and show pictures. Elizabeth Hirschman concludes that "for product categories (for example, financial institutions, legal services, medical organizations) that generally desire to create an impression of heightened rationality and factualness, the use of all-text or predominantly text would appear best. In contrast, when introducing new products, particularly true innovations, visual images will provide the consumer with perception of greater familiarity."[15] "New and improved" Cheer and its associated campaign used a totally visual message strategy. A man wordlessly hand-washing a dirty handkerchief in cold-water Cheer and displaying the successful results told us all the benefits we needed to know.

Readability

If we concentrate on the verbal elements of a message, it is critical that the message be readable. Readable messages are understandable to the audience and have a very good chance of being persuasive. What makes a message readable? Important factors include its arrangement of words in the core message, word frequency, and sentence length. In addition, the number of ideas used to construct the core message should be kept to a minimum, and these ideas should be restated throughout the message.[16] In a recent Nissan spot, a GI Joe-type character sped over in a toy Nissan sports coupe to win "Barbie" from her preppy boyfriend. Barbie quickly joined GI Joe to take a ride, leaving Ken to watch from the toy house. Then, a quirky Asian man, the Nissan spokesperson, turned to viewers with a smile. The tagline confirmed that "Life's a journey, enjoy the ride." It's a simpler message than discussing features but still understandable.

Sometimes readability depends on the target audience. Different regions of the country have their own colloquialisms, as do groups of people. Figure 8.5 shows slang associated with some of today's teenagers. Some additional guidelines for making messages readable and persuasive are listed as follows:[17]

- Use metaphors, such as Revlon's Redline for Revlon Nail Enamel, "Drop-Dead Nails."
- Use low-intensity language, such as Spray n' Wash's tagline, "Spray n' Wash Gets Out What America Gets Into."
- Choose concrete words to make your point, such as the AT&T tagline, "Your True Voice."
- Select simple words to explain complex topics, such as Pioneer stereo telling us "For a Great Sound in a Space You Can Live With."
- Include rhyme to make your message more memorable, such as the Oscar Mayer bologna song.
- Use common words, such as "Tastes Great" and "Just Do It," that are easy to relate to and grasp.
- Avoid synonyms, homonyms, and negative constructions, such as the Buck cigarette tagline, "Herd of These?"
- Keep your heading length short, with five to eight words being the norm.

Ordering Effect

Should key ideas be presented at the beginning, middle, or end of the message? Research indicates that the earlier the key message points are presented, the better they will be remembered.[18] Specifically, experts suggest keeping the following tips in mind when ordering your message:

1. When contradictory information is provided in a single message by a single source, disclaimers at the end of a message will generally be ineffective.
2. If people already feel a strong need for a product or service, supportive information should be provided first. The Sallie Mae ad demonstrates this point.
3. Points that are most valued by the receiver should be listed first.
4. Unfavorable information should be placed last.

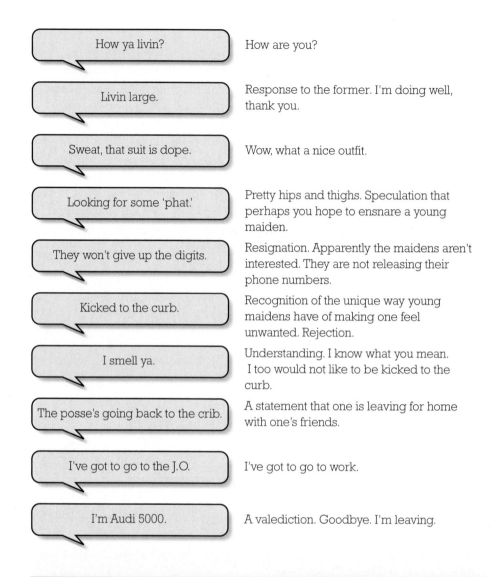

How ya livin?	How are you?
Livin large.	Response to the former. I'm doing well, thank you.
Sweat, that suit is dope.	Wow, what a nice outfit.
Looking for some 'phat.'	Pretty hips and thighs. Speculation that perhaps you hope to ensnare a young maiden.
They won't give up the digits.	Resignation. Apparently the maidens aren't interested. They are not releasing their phone numbers.
Kicked to the curb.	Recognition of the unique way young maidens have of making one feel unwanted. Rejection.
I smell ya.	Understanding. I know what you mean. I too would not like to be kicked to the curb.
The posse's going back to the crib.	A statement that one is leaving for home with one's friends.
I've got to go to the J.O.	I've got to go to work.
I'm Audi 5000.	A valediction. Goodbye. I'm leaving.

FIGURE 8.5

A Guide to the Gab for the Teenage Audience

Source: Helene Cooper "Once Again, Ads Woo Teens With Slang," *The Wall Street Journal,* 29 March 1993.

Repetition

Repetition can take place within a message (repeating a key word or phrase), or it can be the entire message. Research suggests that repeating a message increases its believability, regardless of its content.[19] For audience members who pay attention and understand a message, one exposure is effective. After three repetitions, effectiveness quickly falls. However, in today's world of information overload, no one can guarantee audience attention. Therefore, the number of times a marketing communication manager should repeat a mass communication message is still uncertain.

Sallie Mae provides a great deal of supportive information for an audience with an identified need.

Too much repetition can even be harmful. The results of one study suggested that repetition actually reduced comprehension.[20] Excessive repetition may create **wearout.** In the case of humorous messages, wearout tends to occur much faster than with serious messages.[21] Perhaps this is one reason why the characters delivering the humor in the milk ads change so often. Changing the people and the context makes a tired punchline less wearing.

Repeating a point within a single message also seems to have a positive effect on persuasion. Several studies have shown that repeating the same point in a message aids retention and increases believability. Marketing communication managers must use both judgment and market feedback to balance the benefits of repetition against the possibility of message wearout.

Arguing and Counterarguing

A **one-sided message** presents an argument for the sponsor without mentioning counterarguments. Using this approach is beneficial when the audience is generally friendly, when the advertiser's position is the only one that will be presented, or when the desired result is immediate opinion change. One-sided arguments tend to reinforce the decision of the audience and do not confuse them with alternatives. McDonald's, for example, only talks about its products and benefits in its advertising.

In contrast, a **two-sided message** includes counterarguments. In general, a two-sided argument is useful with better educated audiences, who view counterarguments as more objective and thus more honest. Educated audiences are aware of opposing points of view and expect communicators to acknowledge and refute these views. Also, if an audience member has multiple opinions about topics important to him or her, counterarguments improve persuasibility. AT&T and MCI, for instance, have been arguing and counterarguing for several years.

Message Content

The specific words, pictures, music, and other communication devices, along with the overall appeal, compose the content of the message. We can divide message content into two categories: *rational appeals* and *emotional appeals*. A **rational appeal** tends to be factual and logical. In contrast, an **emotional appeal** is directed toward the individual's feelings and is intended to create a certain mood, such as guilt, joy, anxiety, or self-pride. The rational and emotional distinction is somewhat misleading, however, because emotions and thoughts are not tangible things we can place in locked boxes. When someone appeals to our emotions, our cognitive processes still affect our reactions. And even nonemotional appeals may arouse strong feelings in some people.

To fashion emotional appeals, marketing communicators can use many specific types of content. They might use eerie music to create a mood. They might use funny stories or sexy pictures. The choice of appeals is limitless. No one type of content is always persuasive; each choice brings potential risks and benefits. We discuss the primary appeals in the following sections.

Shown in Table 8.2 is a list of the most popular types of appeals used in television, broken down by gender.

TABLE 8.2	Type of Commercial	% Women	% Men
Get Their Attention	Humor	57	68
	Children	61	44
	Celebrities	39	34
	Real-life situations	34	30
	Brand comparisons	32	23
	Product demonstrations	17	26
	Expert endorsements	17	13
	Company presidents	6	12

Source: Video Storyboard Tests Commercial Break.

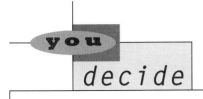

Scared to Health

The image is chilling: a series of menacing bear traps laid out like footsteps. "Is a bear trap snapping shut on a human foot, your foot, a scary thought?" reads the copy. "Good...." A promotion for the latest Hollywood horror blockbuster? How about an ad for the Diabetic Foot Care Centers of Paramus, New Jersey. Now running in newspapers and on radio throughout the area, the campaign is just one example of the growing use of scare tactics by drug and health-care marketers. "It's shock jock advertising, a bit of desperation on the part of marketers who are faced with new challenges," notes Burt Flickinger, manager of consultancy A.T. Kearney, New York.

There are no hard numbers to illustrate the trend, but observers say fear marketing is definitely on the rise. The issues came to a head in California where Abbott Sales' Ross Products division used heavy print and radio advertising to push its Advera nutritional drink for HIV-positive and AIDS patients. The print ad showed a handsome, seemingly healthy young man with a pair of running shoes and a glass of Advera nearby. AIDS groups criticized this ad, saying it used an implicit scare tactic because anyone as healthy looking as the ad's model wouldn't need the product. Dr. John Stansell, director of San Francisco General Hospital's AIDS clinic, calls the ads "disgusting."

Drug and health-care marketers may have a special temptation to use fear marketing because they deal with people when they are most vulnerable. "We've tried positive-type ads in the past and they did nothing," says Dr. Vincent Giacalone, medical director of the Diabetic Foot Care Center. "We've gotten a much greater response from our new ads." But, notes Paul Barthelemy, account executive for McDonald David & Associates, "That kind of approach can backfire. You don't want to terrify. You need to stay as close to the public mind-set as you can."

You Decide

1. What are the potential strategic problems with the fear messaging described?

2. What are the potential ethical problems?

3. Assume you were the new marketing communication director for Advera. Would you recommend that the campaign use or avoid fear tactics? Explain your answer.

Sources: Peter Galuszka, "Humana Heal Thyself," *Business Week,* October 14, 1996, 73–74; Joseph Weber and Nanette Byrnes, "A Fat Pill with a Big Fat Problem," *Business Week,* September 9, 1996, 50; Emily DeNitto, "Healthcare Ads Employ Scare Tactics," *Advertising Age,* November 7, 1994, 12.

Fear Appeals

Intuitively, one might expect that the more fear the message causes, the more persuasive it will be. But research suggests that fear is effective up to a certain level. Beyond that level a "boomerang effect" takes place and negative results occur. As indicated in the You Decide feature, sometimes a fear appeal can go too far.

The relevance of the message to the audience helps determine the impact of a fearful message. For instance, many college students are not motivated to purchase life insurance because death is not that relevant to those so young. However, by the time they hit thirty and have two kids, the fear of death capitalized on in insurance messages will find more accepting listeners.

The effect of fear may also depend in part on whether the message pertains to physical harm (such as sickness, injury, or death) or to social anxiety (such as streaked dishes or body odor). Over the years the most effective "stop smoking" campaign was an ad featuring Brooke Shields, who stated she didn't like the smell of boys who smoked. Again, personal relevance seems to be what matters.

The effectiveness of fear appeals also depends on audience demographics, such as age, sex, race, and education.[22] Personality differences are also significant. For instance, people with high self-esteem react more favorably to high levels of fear than do people with low self-esteem, who are more persuaded by low levels of fear. Similarly, the more vulnerable receivers feel, the less effective a fear appeal will be, particularly if it uses high levels of fear. The appeal may terrify them into inaction. In short, marketing communication managers must keep in mind that effective fear appeals depend on many variables.

Humor

Humor can be expressed visually or verbally through puns, jokes, riddles, and so on. Humorous appeals can create four positive effects.[23] They can enhance source credibility, attract attention, evoke a positive mood, and increase persuasion. Using humor may also increase attention paid to the commercial, reduce irritation at the commercial, improve its likability, and increase product likability.[24]

The use of humor brings risks, however. Not everyone finds the same things funny. Humor also can be distracting. An audience may enjoy a humorous message but may miss the main points of the message, including the name of the sponsor. Humor aids awareness and attention, but it may hinder recall. Finally, humor wears out. Once the audience tires of the humor, they may become indifferent to the message or even irritated by it.[25] For instance, no one knows how much longer people will find the Energizer Bunny amusing.

Despite the risks and uncertainties of using humor, it is likely to remain the favorite strategy of many advertisers. For one thing, humor creates strong memorability, a measure of success that ad agencies consider vital. A 1989 poll indicated that 88 percent of the viewers still remembered Wendy's "Where's the beef?" campaign, which stopped running in 1984. Ad executive Cliff Freeman explains advertising's love affair with humor as follows: "There's an actual physical thing that happens in the body when you laugh. You give off certain chemicals; it's a very positive thing. Therefore, the association with a product is extremely positive. . . . And if your product is good and your advertising is of that nature, it'll really begin to develop an emotional bond between the consumer and the product."[26]

Pleasant Appeals

Most people would rather feel good than feel bad. Taking advantage of this desire is the rationale behind **pleasant appeals,** which create a positive experience and product likability. A pleasant appeal can take several forms. It can use expressions of fun and entertainment, perhaps by showing people dancing, singing, or simply having a good time. Warmth is an emotion considered synonymous with liking. Homecomings, nostalgic situations, and loving relationships all connote warmth. Babies, puppies, and kittens seem to guarantee a feeling of warmth. People cannot resist the Kodak ads that string together heart-warming scenes of childhood, old age, and ordinary family life. These spots are geared to gently jerk a tear or two. "They're very personal and real," says one woman. "They bring you close to life. I always cry." People like being reminded about the bittersweet side of life.

What type of emotional appeal does this Bennetton ad use? Is it effective?

Evidence supporting the effectiveness of pleasant appeals is strong. Warm, entertaining messages are noticed more, are remembered more, increase source credibility, improve attitudes, and create feelings that are transferred to the sponsor. The Ogilvy Center for Research and Development reported a direct link between pleasant appeals and persuasiveness. After showing 73 prime-time commercials to 895 consumers, the center discovered that people who enjoy a commercial are twice as likely to be convinced that the advertised brand is best. "Now we can say likability enhances persuasion and that, at the very least, you don't pay any penalty if people enjoy your ad."[27]

Sex Appeals

Sex appeals in marketing communication range from nudity and obvious double entendres to devices so subtle that it takes a trained observer to recognize them. Kmart Corp. uses a fairly subtle sexual appeal when it presents actress Jaclyn Smith in advertising, at store openings, and as a public relations spokesperson.

Even if the ethical questions raised in Chapter 7 are not considered, the effectiveness of sex as a persuasive device is questionable. There is little doubt that

profile

Shelton Scott
Associate Creative Director—Copywriter
DDB Needham, Chicago

As a copywriter, your job is to write and execute TV and radio commercials, print ads, posters, and so forth. Usually, you work together with an art director to come up with creative selling ideas that will capture the attention of the target audience.

Academic Background and Career Track

I attended the Fashion Institute of Technology in New York and earned an Associate of Applied Science degree in 1979. I then attended New York's School of Visual Arts and graduated with a Bachelor of Fine Arts in 1983.

After graduating, I worked for Backer, Spielvogel, Bates Advertising for four years as a copywriter for several clients, including Hyundai Motors, Miller Beer, and Bailey's Irish Cream Liqueur. I designed and cowrote national newspaper ads and consumer and business-to-business print ads. I also created national television ads and outdoor billboards. Then I worked for a year at Ammirati & Puris Advertising in New York doing newspaper and mag-

azine ads for Chiquita Corporation and Club Med Vacations.

In 1988 I moved to Miami, Florida, to work for Beber, Silverstein Advertising. There I created an entire outdoor campaign of billboards, newspaper ads, and local television commercials for CBS Channel 6 television station and did other copywriting work for the Knightridder Newspaper chain and Floridagold Orange Juice. After two years I joined Crispin & Porter Advertising and developed consumer newspaper campaigns for the *Miami Herald* newspaper. I also created local and regional television commercials and print ads for several clients, including the Lipton Tennis Tournament.

In 1992 I moved to Chicago to work for Burrell Advertising. I worked for several clients' minority advertising campaigns. For instance, I created minority-targeted television and outdoor ads for Coca-Cola Classic, Minute Maid Orange Soda, and Sprite. In 1994 I joined DDB Needham, Chicago as an Associate Creative Director—Copywriter.

sex is an effective, attention-getting device for both men and women. Nevertheless, many people believe that the use of sexual appeals is simply not good marketing. For example, several studies have examined the ability of nudity to enhance brand recall. In every case neutral or nonsexual scenes produce higher brand recall.

Other researchers conclude that sexual appeals in the correct context produce higher attention and recall. That is, there are situations in which the use of a sexual appeal is appropriate, whereas in other instances the use of a sexual appeal is included for its shock value and has nothing to do with the context. Examples

Advice

If you are interested in being a copywriter, I recommend reading a lot about virtually anything and everything because a large reservoir of general knowledge is priceless in this field.

Typical Day

6:30 A.M.: Alarm rings. I get up to work out at home (rowing machine, dumbell curls, sit-ups). I sweat, shower, and get dressed.

9:15 A.M.: Arrive at work. Return phone calls, read memos, and review a sample commercial done for one of our clients. Finally, I turn on my computer to work on TV scripts for a client we are pitching. I'm also preparing to go to a focus group, so I rewrite the statement I want focus group participants to respond to. Now to write a script. . . . Aargh! Okay, let's be funny. Leaving for airport in two hours.

11:23 A.M.: Hmm . . . script's kind of funny. Needs more dialogue and a cool tagline. Junk break! Mmm, Taco Bell Doritos (can't wait for lunch).

12:16 P.M.: Time to print out a script. Hope it's funny. Pack up for trip to airport. Do last minute errands and get taxi. Work on script in cab. Script's getting there, but still needs work (and a cool tagline).

2:00 P.M.: Arrive at airport and grab lunch. Wish I could take a nap. Work more on the aforementioned script. Check in at the gate. Change end joke on script and continue search for cool tagline.

2:55 P.M.: Plane takes off. I fall asleep. Awake as snack cart narrowly misses my knee. Start new script for pitch or maybe work on some beer ads (another project I'm currently working on).

3:40 P.M.: They just announced that we're about to land.

4:30 P.M.: Arrive at focus group center with account executive, Mitch. We discuss groups we're about to observe. We've got an hour to kill before groups start. By the way, a focus group is a research vehicle to help a client and its ad agency learn more about the consumers their products and ads will be aimed at. In this case we will be talking to people about air conditioners and furnaces.

5:25 P.M.: Meet focus group moderator and client representatives. Waiting for groups to start.

5:30 P.M.: First focus group starts. For the next two hours, Mitch and I and three representatives from the client observe as people answer questions and give opinions concerning air conditioners and furnaces. I listen. I take notes. I eat M&Ms. I take a break. It's 7:30. One group is done. We have dinner. Next group arrives. After two more hours of questions, answers, and M&Ms, the groups are finished. We're all tired, but we've learned quite a bit about how our target audience feels about air conditioners and furnaces. After a brief debriefing, we all head to our hotel. It's 9:45 P.M.

10:00 P.M.: I arrive at my hotel room and order a snack from room service. Hmm, wonder what's on HBO?

of correct context are messages that provide fantasy fulfillment (such as travel), functional fulfillment (for example, fashion), or symbolic fulfillment (for example, romantic setting). In sum, sexual appeals in the correct context can produce powerful results; sex outside of this context can be disastrous.

Music

Prominent singers and musicians, background singers and instrumentalists, and jingles have all been used to deliver persuasive messages. The general consensus is that the right music can make a significant difference in the effectiveness of a particular message, but the amount of empirical evidence supporting this assumption is limited. Recent work suggests at least three potential effects of music.

First, music, especially "distinctive" music, can attract consumers' attention. Certain songs and performers immediately spark the attention of different target audiences. Many young people believe that "I Heard It Through the Grapevine" was written especially for the California Raisin ad and have claimed the song as their own. Second, music can influence consumers' processing of the messages. Music can affect learning and persuasion by creating excitement, relaxation, empathy, news, and imagery, and can enhance the perceived benefits of the message.[28] Finally, music can complement other elements in the ad, such as words, color, pictures, background, and so forth. Music can create a mood that encourages certain types of attitudes and behavior.

Concept Review

MESSAGE VARIABLES

1. Message structure factors that influence persuasiveness include the following:
   - *Verbal versus nonverbal:* Verbals should be emphasized when unique, meaningful messages can be delivered about the product.
   - *Readability:* Writing should be clear, concrete, and accessible.
   - *Ordering effect:* Key ideas should be presented first.
   - *Repetition:* The key point of the message should be repeated, though no fixed number of repetitions is best. Too many repetitions may cause wearout.
   - *Arguing and counterarguing:* The effectiveness of the one-sided versus two-sided message depends on the audience and strength of the argument.
2. Message content may consist of a rational or emotional appeal. The content may include fear, humor, pleasant appeals, sex appeals, and music.

AUDIENCE FACTORS

Are some people easier to persuade than others? We all know gullible individuals who will believe anything. Yet there is little solid evidence to support the notion that some personalities are more susceptible to persuasion.

Various personal characteristics, however, can affect persuasibility. William McGuire suggests that personality factors influence persuasibility by affecting the **comprehension** of a message and **willingness to comply** with a message.[29] Self-esteem is an example. For reasons yet to be explained, people with low and high self-esteem differ in their ability to cope with simple and complex information. That is, people with low self-esteem may do better with simple information and people with high self-esteem may handle complex information better.

Gender is the one demographic trait related to persuasion.[30] Women seem more persuadable than men, especially when the source is a female. Some evidence suggests that males and females differ in their information-processing strategies. For example, some studies conclude that females are more sensitive to external cues, with the possible exception of smell.[31] Moreover, it appears that females are willing to take more effort in deciphering complex messages.

As noted in Chapter 7, children are viewed as very vulnerable to the effects of persuasive communication. Children's vulnerability to persuasive communication raises many important questions. Do children pay attention to advertising? Do they understand its purpose and its content? How do children process advertising messages? What is the effect of factors such as age, race, or parental education on these process effects? What is the impact of advertising on children's attitudes and behaviors? What effect does advertising have on the socialization process of children, that is, their learning roles as consumers?[32]

Although the answers to most of these questions remain unresolved, the evidence does suggest that children of all ages are capable of distinguishing commercials from programs, but that young children (preschool age) are not able to discern the intent of commercials,[33] nor do they understand the disclaimers used in many ads. Further, advertising has a moderate impact on children's attitudes toward the advertised product, though the content of commercials does affect children's preferences and choices, as revealed by studies in the area of food advertising to children.[34] Finally, advertising encourages children to request products from their parents, a situation that often leads to child-parent conflict. Parental education, family interaction, and peer integration, however, may reduce these effects.[35]

Are senior citizens more susceptible to persuasive communication? The stereotype of senior citizens who are senile and believe everything they are told seems to suggest they are, but this stereotype is flawed. Senior citizens are not a homogeneous group.[36] The majority of senior citizens are not institutionalized or living under the care of others. As to the persuasibility of seniors, the evidence to date is inconclusive. No clear link has been established between membership in senior citizen market segments and the degree to which individuals respond to the persuasive content of a message.

Persuasiveness reflects interactions between the personality and culture of members of the audience, the situation, and characteristics of the source and message. To be persuasive, a marketing communicator should keep in mind the interests, attitudes, and values of the audience.

Communicating to Foreign Markets

Marketing communication strategies often need to be tailored to specific foreign markets or countries. For instance, the ad copy should be adapted to differences in customers' perceptions and response patterns. For many marketing communicators, adapting has proven quite difficult. Any book or article on international marketing offers numerous examples of how some marketer (usually North American) made a horrible advertising blunder by using a word that translated negatively, a color that connoted evil, or a song that was perceived as too sensual. Every facet of a message—words, tone, pictures, context, spokesperson, and appeal—must be carefully screened. As noted in the IMC Concept in Focus feature, providing an integrated marketing communication approach is more difficult when considering other countries.

Obviously, the marketing communicator must use the language of the country, but the words must be more than technically accurate and perfectly translated. They must reflect the tone and emotion of the language. A key to successful communication in a foreign market, then, is to intimately understand the nuances

Communicating Across Borders

Global advertising campaigns have long romanced the marketing imagination with their seductive promise of "one world" executional elegance. But the logic they are based on—that global campaigns offer economies of scale and consumers the world over are becoming increasingly more homogeneous—is flawed. If the campaign fails, the economies of scale aren't realized. And consumers' tastes, needs, and wants still remain diverse.

Chanel is an example of a company that failed in its attempt to deliver a global message. Its problems stemmed from taking a top-down, manufacturer-centered approach to advertising instead of using a more consumer-oriented approach. Chanel may well market "global" brands, but consumers live, buy, and consume in "local" environments. Unless the marketing communication for a brand is meaningful in the context of the local environment, consumers couldn't care less about a product's global image.

Does this imply that using the same marketing communication concept in diverse multinational markets is impossible? Or that fragrance concepts and advertising campaigns don't travel well across borders? Au contraire! To borrow from Eric Clapton, "It's in the way that you use it."

For Impulse Body Spray, the deodorant-and-fragrance-in-one mass market brand, parent company Unilever uses the same advertising concept (boy meets girl) in almost every market. At last count, the brand was doing quite well in 40 countries—primarily due to the fact that the two-in-one brand concept is unique, and the advertising concept is universally relevant and meaningful, rooted deeply in the human condition.

The moral? Marketers like Chanel run into trouble because they're primarily concerned with standardizing the marketing communication message. But in a world filled with diversity, marketing communicators should instead figure out how people from many cultures and countries respond to products, and use and develop relationships with parent brands and companies.

Sources: Geoffrey Lee Martin, "Ad Doesn't Measure Up to Council's Standards," *Advertising Age International,* January 15, 1996, 16; Ashish Banerjie, "Global Campaigns Don't Work: Multinationals Do," *Advertising Age,* April 18, 1994, 23.

---

of the culture, especially the language, values, and attitudes of its consumers. The process of designing the message must therefore begin with the cultural context, as the following questions show:

1. *Is the product used for the same purpose in all countries?* Campbell Soup Company learned that its soups are used very differently in the United States and in Eastern and Western Europe. Consumers in France, for example, would never consider using canned soup as the base for a sauce.

2. *What is the motivation for purchasing the product?* The same product may be purchased for a mixture of functional, convenience, and status reasons, with a different combination of motivations in each country. In underdeveloped countries, for example, McDonald's provides status rather than convenience.

3. *Who is the key decision maker?* In patriarchal cultures the father makes most purchase decisions. In the case of certain products (for example, cereal, toys, fast food), children take a very active role. However, the influence of children on a product purchase varies a great deal from country to country, and marketing communicators must examine this purchase pattern closely before making any generalizations.

Mars Inc. campaigned heavily in Russia to create brand identity for its Snickers candy bar. Promoting Snickers in Russian billboards, ads, and retail displays resulted in a name recognition increase from 5 percent to 82 percent.

Cultural mores represent a key factor that affects message design. For example, in Germany and France many women do not shave their legs or underarms. Thus, razor blades are positioned as a special occasion purchase. The Japanese view deodorant differently, so Feel Free deodorant described its product as youthful and chic rather than as a solution to odor problems. As noted in Chapter 5, these cultural mores express human values. Values determine how people want to receive product information. Eastern Europeans, for instance, do not trust advertising and want to know only facts about the product.

The presence or absence of market segments also dictates message appeal in foreign countries and represents one of the more successful ways of standardizing promotional strategies. For example, a market segment such as college students is

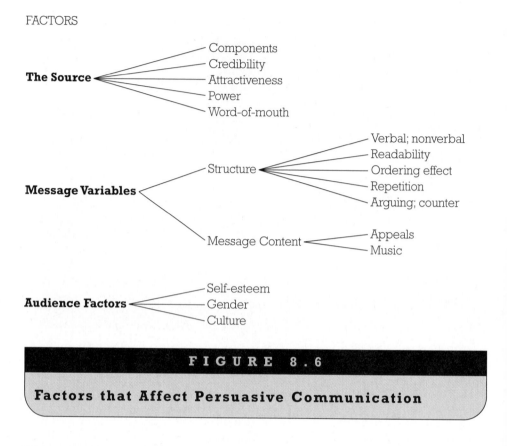

FACTORS

FIGURE 8.6

Factors that Affect Persuasive Communication

fairly similar from country to country. Levi's uses the same basic appeal to the worldwide youth market for its 501 jeans.

International jet-setters respond similarly to appeals for fine jewelry, luxury cars, and expensive cosmetics. Similarly, when countries join together to share economic resources, transportation networks, or technologies, they create common interests that can also serve as the basis for promotional appeals.

A marketing communicator must decide whether to run a message in one or several local languages. For example, some citizens of Switzerland speak mostly German, others speak mostly French, and most speak English. The Snickers billboard illustrates how one U.S. company customized its marketing communication to fit a particular country.

Figure 8.6 summarizes the factors that affect persuasive communication.

A CLOSING THOUGHT: MAKE THE COMMUNICATION RELEVANT

Consumers no longer tolerate irrelevant communication. They demand messages that speak to their needs and wants and are irritated by messages that don't. With the growth of interactive technology, this trend will increase the demand for one-on-one communication. Nonetheless, the fundamental principles of good communication still apply. Although the means and timing of delivery may change, markets capable of delivering a clear, concise, persuasive message will tend to be most successful.

SUMMARY

1. **Define and outline the communication process.**
   Communication is a process in which two or more people try to influence each other, consciously or unconsciously, through the use of symbols. Steps in the process occur simultaneously. The basic elements of the process include the communicators (the sender and receiver), the encoding and decoding of messages, a medium of transmission, relationships between communicators, feedback, the environment, and factors that interfere with effective communication.

2. **List five different types of communication systems and explain why they differ.**
   Five types of communication—interpersonal, organizational, public, mass, and interactive—differ in complexity, form of contact, and ability to adjust to feedback.

3. **Explain why marketing communicators use persuasive communication.**
   Marketing communicators use persuasive commu-

nication to inform, remind, and build awareness so that receivers will change attitudes, perceptions, and behaviors.

4. **Discuss how the source, the message, and the audience affect persuasive communication.**
   Variables that influence the effectiveness of persuasive communication fall into three groups: (1) source factors, (2) message factors, and (3) audience factors. Manipulation of the credibility, attractiveness, and power of the source can affect the ability to persuade. Message variables (that is, structure and content) show little consistency in their effect on persuasiveness. Each message-related factor must be viewed in context. The effect of audience factors is even less predictable, so marketing communicators must use their judgment to send messages that will be relevant to target audiences.

POINTS TO PONDER

Review the Facts
1. Outline the communication process.
2. Define word-of-mouth sources of communication.

Master the Concepts
3. Discuss how the communicator can be both the sender and the receiver.
4. What are the differences between verbal and nonverbal communication?
5. What is the result of interference in human communication? List some ways to reduce interference.
6. Contrast general communication with persuasive communication. What should be the outcome if persuasion is successful?

7. What are the advantages and disadvantages of using music in advertising?
8. Sources can be considered attractive in terms of similarity, familiarity, and liking. Give an example of each.
9. "I really enjoy funny ads. I wish all ads were like that." Comment on these statements.

Apply Your Knowledge
10. Write a 500-word essay expressing why you feel communication must be either intentional or unintentional.
11. Describe the characteristics of a communication source that would appeal to (1) college students and (2) their parents.

SUGGESTED PROJECTS

1. Collect ads from magazines to locate examples of the following: high source credibility, high source attractiveness, nonverbal appeal, high fear appeal, and high humor appeal. Explain the criteria you used in each case.

2. (Oral Communication) Ask two friends to allow you to observe their conversation. Note the kinds of nonverbal cues each person uses. Quiz them afterward as to whether they are aware they use these nonverbals.

3. (Internet and Team Project) Break into small groups of four to six people. Pick a product or service that your group wants to research. Each group member should search the Internet, find three companies that offer the product or service, and visit the home page of each company. (For a list of search engine sites, see Chapter 4, Suggested Project 4, p. 122.) Take notes about how well each company communicates persuasive messages about the product. (Is information easy to understand, memorable, clear, and visually appealing? Is the information static or offered in an interactive format that allows for two-way communication?) Meet as a group to discuss your findings, then select the two best examples of persuasive marketing communication. Choose a spokesperson who will present and explain the reasons for your choices in a five-minute oral presentation to the class.

CASE 8: DONEGHEL SPEAKS UP

Background

The Doneghel Furniture Company is a small, regional furniture manufacturer located eight miles west of Greensboro, North Carolina. During the last 32 years, the company has produced custom-made furniture for consumers living within a 200-mile radius of the plant. Its major customers, however, are large furniture manufacturers that contract with Doneghel to make hardwood components of the larger pieces sold by companies such as Ethan Allen and Thomasville. Until recently, the management of Doneghel had been very satisfied with this arrangement. However, two occurrences have changed the future of Doneghel. First, due to the general decline of the furniture industry, several of Doneghel's manufacturer customers reduced their orders, some by as much as 50 percent. Second, the reputation of Doneghel's custom-furniture line seems to have extended beyond the immediate market. Consumers from as far away as California have written to request catalogs and general product information. Most of this interest appears to stem from positive word of mouth from satisfied customers who have moved out of the region. Doneghel does no advertising.

John Doneghel, president of the company, along with Carol Doneghel, vice president, and their two sons, Jamie and Frank, are faced with the possibility of changing the way they do business. John, Jamie, Frank, and 20 other craftspeople represent the total workforce. Carol takes care of the books and pays the bills. The family loves to work with wood and to create beautiful furniture. Unfortunately, the Doneghels have little experience or interest in doing much else. Last year Doneghel's sales were $1.2 million, of which $200,000 resulted from the custom-furniture business. The only element that even resembled marketing was a ten-page catalog that described the general kinds of pieces Doneghel makes and gave approximate prices. This catalog was mailed only to people who requested it.

The dilemma facing the Doneghel family is obvious. Do the Doneghels maintain the status quo and hope the market for large manufacturers improves? Or do they expand their custom-furniture business and learn all they can about marketing as quickly as possible? After agonizing over this problem for several days, the decision was made to hire a consultant.

The Market

Tony Wingler is a marketing professor at a nearby university. He has conducted research for several furniture manufacturers and is thoroughly familiar with the industry. It is his recommendation that Doneghel pursue the custom-furniture business. Because it would be unprofitable for the company to offer total customization, Doneghel should develop a product line that is somewhat standardized and offer two or three modifications of each piece. Wingler further indicates that the upscale customer (that is, someone whose income is higher than $75,000) should be targeted. This person would be willing to pay the higher prices charged for customized furniture. Finally, Wingler feels that distribution represents the most difficult problem facing Doneghel. Because it is unlikely that Doneghel would be able to place its furniture in stores throughout the country, direct marketing offers a better alternative. Direct mail combined with print ads in magazines such as *Southern Living* and *Town and Country* would represent the primary communication vehicles. Direct mail would also serve as a mechanism for ordering and receiving the furniture.

A meeting was set up with Wilkes Advertising to discuss the marketing communication strategy appropriate for Doneghel. The agency determined that the two main benefits Doneghel offered were excellent craftsmanship and the use of hardwoods. The primary limitations were twofold. First, the public could not experience the furniture firsthand. Would people buy furniture they could not touch? Second, the selection was limited to between 70 and 75 different pieces. Wilkes felt that combating these limitations would be difficult and that many potential customers would be lost because of them.

Case Questions

1. What are the communication problems facing Doneghel if it uses a direct-marketing approach?
2. (Writing Project) Suggest an initial communication strategy for Doneghel, including specific structure and content recommendations. Make your recommendations in a 1 to 2 page memo.

ROMA'S LITE INTEGRATED CASE QUESTIONS

(Review the Roma's Lite Marketing Plan in the Appendix at the end of the text before answering these questions.)

1. Consider what types of communication you could use in the Roma's Lite Pizza campaign. How could you generate positive word of mouth?
2. Distinguish between source characteristics that you control versus those you cannot control in the campaign.
3. (Team Project) Consider the various marketing messages you might use to introduce Roma's Lite Pizza. Develop three general message strategies that vary the source, structure, and content. Develop an ad for the strategy that works best.

video case | The FTC Puts Beer and Liquor Advertising Under a Microscope

In Deember 1996, the Federal Trade Commission (FTC) authorized its Bureau of Consumer Protection to investigate the advertising practices of Stroh Brewing Company and the American subsidiary of Canada's Joseph E. Seagram & Sons. By early 1997, the investigation had broadened to include both Anheuser-Busch and the Miller Brewing division of Philip Morris. At issue was whether the companies were deliberately targeting television advertising at persons under the legal drinking age.

The FTC's investigation came in the wake of a decision by Seagram executives to begin running TV ads for Royal Crown whiskey during the summer of 1996. By taking this step, Seagram broke ranks with a voluntary industry ban that had kept liquor ads off American TV and radio for nearly half a century. According to figures compiled by the Distilled Spirits Council of the United States (Discus), overall sales of hard liquor has fallen 28 percent over a 14-year period, from 450 million gallons in 1981 to 325 million gallons in 1995. Seagram and other dis-

tillers have watched in frustration as the brewing industry spends some $700 million each year on TV advertising; the distillers spend about $225 million annually on print advertising. In November 1996, Discus lifted the television ban, in theory opening the door for other distillers to advertise on TV. However, the Council's action did not affect a separate ban imposed by the television networks; ABC, NBC, CBS, and Fox still refuse to broadcast liquor ads. However, managers at local TV affiliates and radio stations can sell air time to liquor advertisers if they wish to.

Some industry observers complained that the Seagram ads represented the first wave of a new advertising assault on America's children, and negative reaction to the Council's move came from both the government and private advocacy groups. Reed Hundt, chairman of the Federal Communications Commission (FCC), said, "This decision is disappointing for parents, and dangerous for our kids." The FCC is empowered to make sure broadcasters serve the public interest, and chairman Hundt favors some form of restric-

tion on liquor ads. Karolyn Nunallee, president-elect of Mothers Against Drunk Driving, declared that "this will open a floodgate to alcohol ads on TV." George Hacker, director of alcohol policies at the Center for Science in the Public Interest, was more blunt. "This means open season on America's kids," he said.

Discus CEO Fred Meister defended the decision to end the self-imposed ban. "There is simply no justifiable, social, political, or scientific basis for treating spirits differently from other beverage alcohol," Meister said. Responding to critics who accuse distillers of targeting children, Meister noted, "Distilled spirits advertisements will continue to be responsible, dignified, and tasteful messages for adults, and will avoid targeting those under the legal purchase age, regardless of the medium."

Seagram's competitors are adopting a wait-and-see attitude. A spokesperson for Heublein, which markets Smirnoff vodka and Jose Cuervo tequilla, said "[Television advertising] may make sense for some of our brands, but we want to make sure if it's done, that it's done responsibly and tastefully." Some advertising experts have even called into doubt the notion that liquor advertising would substantially increase consumer demand for hard liquor. According to this view, advertising does not persuade nondrinkers to start using alcohol. Instead, advertising helps one brand take market share away from another. Indeed, nearly a decade ago, the Federal Trade Commission issued a report stating that there is "no reliable basis to conclude that alcohol advertising significantly affects consumption, let alone abuse." The report went on: "Absent such evidence, there is no basis for concluding that rules banning or otherwise limiting alcohol advertising would offer significant protection to the public."

The controversy escalated in the spring of 1997. President Clinton asserted that ads for hard liquor on TV will make it more difficult for parents to raise children. The president called upon the FCC to find a way to block television advertising of spirits. Discus, unhappy that the president's remarks did not include beer advertising, proposed that the president call on all liquor, beer, and wine marketers to join with broadcasters in drafting a common code of alcohol advertising on radio and TV. The Beer Institute, a trade and lobbying group representing brewers, immediately distanced itself from the issue. In a statement, the Institute said, "There are obvious differences between beer and hard liquor." Likewise, the National Association of Broadcasters rejected the call by Discus. An NAB spokesperson said, "Talking to broadcasters is a nonissue because virtually all the stations do not accept distilled spirits advertising."

Discussion Questions

1. Given that the legal drinking age in most states is 21, why do you think critics are so quick to complain that liquor ads on TV represent "liquor profiteering at the expense of America's children?" Do you think the argument has merit? What evidence would you point to?

2. Assume that the critics are right: Distillers are targeting youth in their television ads. Now assume that you are in charge of planning a series of TV ads for a distiller. What sociocultural factors would you consider as you planned the ads? What psychological factors would you consider? (Remember to look at motivation, learning, and attitudes and whether this is a complex or simple purchase decision.) Explain how these factors will affect your marketing communication plans.

3. Now take a look at the type of communication process that occurs in the broadcast medium (see chapter 8). How will that process affect your message strategy?

4. Should the FCC forbid the advertising of distilled spirits on TV? Why or why not?

Video Source: "Hard Liquor TV Ads," *Nightline,* 11 November 1996. *Additional Sources:* Bruce Horovitz, "Liquor Industry's Hard Line on TV Ads," *USA Today,* 10 April 1997, 5B; Horovitz, "Distillers Indulge Anew in TV Ads," *USA Today,* 8 November 1996, 1B, 2B; Sally Goll Beatty, "Seagram Again Challenges a Ban on TV Ads Invoked By Industry," *The Wall Street Journal,* 24 November 1996, B12; Catherine Yang, "The Spirited Brawl Ahead Over Liquor Ads on TV," *Business Week,* 16 December 1996, 47; Doug Bandlow, "Liquor Ads on the Rocks," *The Wall Street Journal,* 31 December 1996, 6.

chapter

Advertising

CHAPTER OBJECTIVES

After completing your work on this chapter, you should be able to:

1 **Define advertising.**

2 **Identify the strengths and weaknesses of advertising.**

3 **Explain how advertising works.**

4 **Outline the three phases in creating an advertisement.**

5 **Describe what makes advertising effective and how to evaluate effectiveness.**

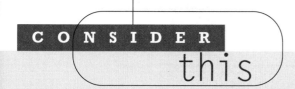

CONSIDER this

Gillette Shaves Its Image

Gillette in the late 1980s faced troubled times. It survived three hostile takeover threats and won a fight among shareholders for control of the company. In addition, Gillette consumer research showed that although older men still thought well of the Gillette brand, younger men did not. For instance, they viewed the Gillette Good News disposable razor, introduced in the 1970s, as "hollow, plastic and blue." This consumer perception spelled trouble for Gillette.

Gillette turned to its advertising agency, BBDO, to create an integrated marketing campaign that would turn its image around. BBDO discovered in consumer research that many consumers still perceived the Gillette brand image positively, equating its image with quality and masculinity. BBDO de-

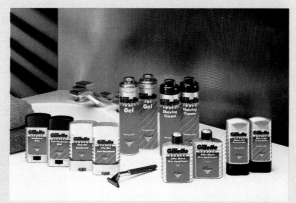

cided to position Gillette as the standard of quality in men's shaving products and to underscore the idea that Gillette understands what it takes to make a man feel better. BBDO's slogan, "The Best A Man Can Get," embodied the BBDO advertising strategy.

The launch of the new international brand image campaign in 1989 with a budget of some $80 million involved employee relations, trade marketing, sports marketing, public relations, sales promotion, direct marketing, building design, stationery, and every form of communication possible, including, of course, advertising. This award-winning campaign has been cited as one of the most successful advertising campaigns ever and provided the foundation for the launch of a variety of new products.

In 1990 Gillette introduced the Sensor, followed by the Sensor for Women, the SensorExcel, the Sensor-

Excel for Women, and the Gillette Series of toiletries (Wild Rain, Cool Wave), again using an integrated strategy managed by BBDO. The Sensor and Sensor for Women launches were incredibly successful—the new products helped bring even more credibility to "The Best" slogan that continued to be used as an anchor for the brand.

The Sensor launch was a classic case study of integrated marketing communication. The advertising focused on the Gillette image of quality and "The Best A Man Can Get" slogan. The launch announcement, how- ever, was handled by the Porter/Novelli public relations firm and generated a huge level of awareness before the advertising campaign began. Following the launch, Rapp Collins Marcoa, a sister agency of BBDO, created an extensive direct-marketing campaign that included a sampling program for young men reaching their 18th birthday.

The "Best A Man Can Get" advertising theme, though developed in the 1980s, is still being used today, as a platform for Gillette's new generation of SensorExcel razors and related products. ▪

Sources: Pablo Galarza, "Nicked and Cut," *Financial World,* April 8, 1996, 39; "Gillette Series to Launch at Retail With Super Bowl Advertising Campaign," *Business Wire,* January 20, 1993; "The Best a Plan Can Get," *The Economist,* August 15, 1992, 61–3; Gary Levin, "Direct Mail Program Helps Gillette Drive Growth of Sensor Razor," *Advertising Age,* October 21, 1991, 24; "After a Close Shave, Cutting Edge Technology," *Inside PR,* September, 1990, 25–6.

CHAPTER OVERVIEW

The Gillette campaign mentions many of the key marketing communication tools we discuss in Part III of the text. In this chapter we focus on advertising, the first of those communication tools. First, we explore advertising basics, including its strengths and weaknesses. Then we investigate how advertising works, focusing on attention, awareness, and memorability. Finally, we examine how marketing communicators create and execute an advertising strategy and how they determine what makes an effective ad.

WHAT IS ADVERTISING?

Michael Jordan tells thousands of American teenagers watching television to stay in school. A flyer on dozens of doorsteps urges consumers to try the new restaurant down the street. Gillette offers consumers a coupon to try the newest version of the SensorExcel razor. A full-page ad in the newspaper announces that a local bank is offering reduced interest rates for home mortgages. Candice Bergen bemoans the fact she is known as the Sprint "dime lady." The U.S. Marines announce that they still need "a few good men." And at Super Bowl time, networks rake in close to $1.3 million for each 30-second television advertisement. Pre- and post-game ads command between $400,000 to $600,000.

This attention-getting ad for Sony uses a twist on the phrase "display your productivity" to grab attention and make consumers aware of its products.

Marketing communication managers must understand where advertising fits in the overall marketing communication strategy. Some large marketers (for example, Case Office Equipment, Hershey's, the Disney theme parks) use very little advertising, and others, such as Procter & Gamble, spend over a billion dollars annually on advertising. Regardless of the emphasis, managers should apply a careful analysis when making advertising decisions that parallels their decisions about other components of the marketing communication mix.

Defining Advertising

Advertising is any paid form of nonpersonal presentation and promotion of ideas, goods, and services by an identified sponsor to a targeted audience and delivered primarily through the mass media. The American Marketing Association has a more expanded definition of advertising: "Paid, nonpersonal communication through various media by business firms, nonprofit organizations, and individuals who are in some way identified in the advertising message and who hope to inform and/or persuade members of a particular audience. Advertising includes the communication of products, services, institutions, and ideas."[1]

The purpose of advertising depends on your vantage point—that is, whether you are a marketer or consumer. Advertising helps identify the meaning and role of products for consumers by providing information about brands, companies, and organizations. To most business managers and marketers, advertising helps sell products and builds company and brand reputation.

The Strengths and Weaknesses of Advertising

Marketing communication managers, like those planning Gillette's advertising, need to keep in mind both the powers and the limitations of advertising. Some advertising is more effective than others in certain situations, and some types of advertising seem to work better with certain types of products. Some consumers will not buy in spite of extensive advertising, and some will buy without any advertising. Many other marketing issues may affect product and institutional advertising success, such as the price of the product and the convenience with which you can buy it. The effect of specific ads may also vary widely from consumer to consumer and from time to time.

Advertising's primary strength is that it reaches a large mass audience to intensify broad-based demand for a product. It can build brand awareness, create long-term brand images and brand positions, and increase brand knowledge effectively. Advertising also serves as a reminder of a product or brand with which a consumer has had a positive experience. Finally, advertising provides message repetition, an important factor in memorability as described in Chapter 8.

Advertising has limits, however. Consumers often perceive it as intrusive. In turn, consumers may avoid advertising by turning the page, changing the channel, muting the sound, or using other technology to screen out an ad. Because of the large number of competing ads in most media, advertising is also perceived as cluttering the media environment, particularly on television where consumers complain about the number of commercials. Another problem with advertising is the opposite of one of its strengths—it may reach a large audience, but many of those audience members are likely to be nonusers of the advertised product. As a result, advertising wastes a large number of impressions.

In the final analysis advertising is only valuable to businesses if it creates easy consumer identification of the advertised brand or institution. Although advertising may help consumers identify the brand they wish to buy, it may also help them identify those brands they wish to avoid because of bad reports or experiences. Ideally, the continued advertising of a particular brand or institution over

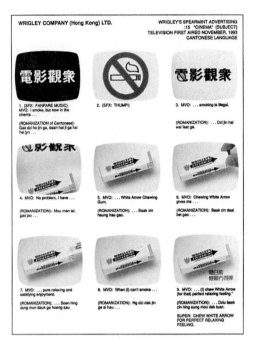

This Wrigley's ad helps remind consumers of a durable, well-known brand.

several years is an implied warranty to the consumer that the product has met the test of quality and that is why it is still being used. The measure of success for any product is repeat purchase.

How Advertising Links to Other Marketing Communication Areas

Advertising does some things well, like build brand images and reach a wide audience through the mass media. It can also help companies screen consumers for more personal marketing, or make it possible for prospective customers to identify themselves to the marketer. For example, when Procter & Gamble developed Cheer Free, a detergent for people with allergies and sensitive skin, it announced the product in magazine ads with a coupon for a free sample. When people returned the coupon, they included their name and address. From that information, Procter & Gamble was able to build a database of interested customers to target in a direct-mail promotional effort, a more cost-effective means of communicating than mass advertising for a niche market.

Advertising's strengths and weaknesses should be analyzed relative to the strengths and weaknesses of the other marketing communication tools. Because marketing communication resources are limited, marketing communication managers must plan a communication mix in which advertising is used to maximize its strengths, not because it's considered glamorous or because the ad agency only wants to do big-budget television commercials. Advertising, in the past, has been seen as the dominant marketing communication area, and that has created some jealousy, as the IMC Concept in Focus feature discusses.

Tensions in the Mix

The adversarial relationship between advertising and the other marketing communication mix components has existed for decades. Because of its high profile, advertising traditionally received all the attention from top management and from those outside the organization. As a result, personal selling, sales promotion, and public relations sometimes took a back seat to advertising. As this situation is gradually changing, advertising is learning to work with these other marketing communication activities, as did BBDO in the Gillette story in the opening vignette.

This change has not been necessarily by choice. Marketers' demand for greater accountability has led to a de-emphasis on image-building advertising; they prefer instead to focus on tools that deliver sales as an immediate result. Price discounts and coupons, for example, give sales a quick, easily measured boost.

As a result of this bottom-line focus, many companies now spend about 70 percent of their marketing communication budgets on sales promotion, leaving just 30 percent for advertising. The link between advertising and sales promotion can be highly successful if they reinforce one another. As the Cheer Free example illustrates, advertising can serve as a vehicle for delivering sales promotions such as coupons, samples, and discounts. Advertising can also serve as a communication device for supporting sales promotion offers such as sweepstakes, special

events, and sponsorships. A similar relationship exists between advertising and public relations (PR). In addition to public relations advertising, which carries PR messages through paid-for media, advertising also carries a variety of PR messages. For example, an event such as a marathon or a parade is announced through advertising as well as news releases. New product introductions often require public relations and advertising to work together in a marketing public relations (MPR) program, which we will discuss in Chapter 11.

Consider the interaction between advertising and public relations that Taco Bell used on April Fools' Day in 1996. The company announced in full-page advertisements that it had purchased the Liberty Bell to help reduce the federal budget deficit. The ad copy noted that the bell would be renamed the "Taco Liberty Bell." More than 2000 calls were made to Taco Bell's customer service hotline. Radio call-in shows all over the country discussed the idea. Later that day, Taco Bell issued a news release confessing to the hoax and announced that it was donating $50,000 to the restoration of the Liberty Bell—creating a positive public image. The results? The company increased sales by $500,000 on April 1 and $600,000 on April 2. According to Taco Bell's PR agency, the publicity had a value of around $22 million.

The most difficult relationship to establish is often between advertising and the sales force. Although

advertising can simplify the job of the salesperson, salespeople often believe that the advertising team doesn't understand their problems or their job on the front line. Conversely, advertising people complain they don't get feedback from sales that would help them plan more effective advertising. When the relationship between advertising and sales is harmonious, the sales force can provide ideas for advertising appeals and copy. In turn these ads help familiarize consumers with the brand and its features, giving the salesperson a distinct competitive advantage. This kind of customer preparation saves the salesperson time and energy, reduces anxiety, and increases the likelihood of a successful sale.

Food for Thought

1. Do you have insights into any company—one where a family member or friend works or where you have worked—where tensions exist between advertising and other marketing communication areas? Explain.

2. How would you recommend a business alleviate any tensions between advertising and other marketing communication areas? Why do you think it is important to alleviate such tensions?

Sources: Stuart Elliott, "Warning: The Merry Pranksters of Madison Avenue Are Out Today," *New York Times,* 1 April 1997, C2; "Taco Bell Doesn't Care If You Didn't Appreciate the Joke—Sales Were Up," *Inside PR,* May 6, 1996, 7.

WHAT IS ADVERTISING?

1. Advertising is the nonpersonal communication of marketing-related information to a target audience, usually paid for by the advertiser and delivered through mass media.
2. Advertising's strengths include its ability to
   - Reach a large mass audience
   - Stimulate broad-based demand
   - Create brand awareness
   - Position a brand or product
   - Increase brand knowledge
   - Provide message repetition
   - Serve as a reminder
3. Advertising has three main weaknesses:
   - It may be perceived as intrusive and, in turn, avoided.
   - It clutters the message environment.
   - It wastes a large amount of impressions because of its mass appeal.
4. Advertising should be used in the marketing communication mix to maximize its strengths, which should be analyzed relative to other marketing communication tools.

WHAT DOES ADVERTISING DO?

Most businesspeople advertise because they expect an ad to create a sale. In the case of direct-action advertising, which uses techniques to stimulate immediate action such as toll-free numbers and coupons, this view may be reasonable. However, most advertising is indirect—that is, it creates demand for a product in the long run through indirect methods. Usually, ads try to change mental states to stimulate consumer awareness and interest. Though the ad may not lead to an immediate sale, it is likely to predispose the audience toward the purchase of the advertised product. Benetton campaigns have achieved high levels of awareness using highly controversial advertising that makes little or no effort to sell a product (see the You Decide feature).

Even though advertising's primary objective is to create demand, establishing the link between a specific ad and a particular sale is often difficult, if not impossible. However, a correlation between money spent on advertising, sales, and profitability does seem to exist. In a study of the relationship between advertising expenditures, sales, and profits, researchers found the following:

1. Businesses with higher relative advertising-to-sales ratios earn a higher return on investment.
2. Advertising expenditures and market share are related.[2]

In addition, other studies show that businesses that do not cut advertising during severe economic downturns have the highest growth in sales and net income. In contrast, companies that cut advertising during downturns have the lowest sales and net income increases.[3]

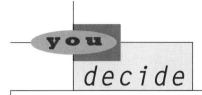

Benetton Shows Its Colors

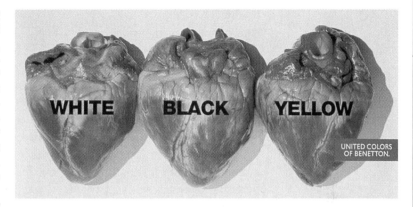

Many companies combine their advertising campaigns with social issues such as the environment, education, and tolerance. But Benetton, the Italian clothing company that targets the international youth market, has moved beyond combining product and issues in an advertisement. It focuses primarily on social issues that range from racism and world peace to AIDS. The ads have aroused strong reactions and controversy.

The controversial advertising routinely attracts more attention than its relatively modest budget would suggest, which shows how advertising and publicity can be interwoven to create high impact. The creative director of Benetton, Oliver Toscani, claims that the purpose of its focus on social issues is to increase worldwide attention on the issues. Toscani has featured pictures of a dying AIDS patient, a human arm tattooed with the words "HIV POSITIVE," a terrorist car bombing, Albanian refugees, a Catholic nun and priest kissing, a bloody newborn baby, pastel condom sheaths, a black woman breast-feeding a white baby, and a bloody soldier's uniform. In contrast, an ad released in 1996 showed three hearts labeled white, black, and yellow—a less obviously controversial ad.

The divisive advertising triggered some consumer and retailer complaints. Arnie Arlow, executive vice president and creative director at TBWA, an international advertising agency, is one of Benetton's critics: "To place a Benetton logo on the picture of [AIDS victim] David Kirby's deathbed is awful. . . ." Advertising critic Barbara Lippert also takes exception to several Benetton ads. She challenged a Benetton print ad that showed a boatload of refugees desperately swarming in the water, claiming that it was "almost pornographic to use such abstract suffering" for commercial gain. Benetton was also sued by several of its German retail outlets who believed that the provocative ads drove away customers. Benetton won the cases.

Some Benetton ads are more traditional and demonstrate that the company can tone down its controversial approach. Toscani, however, believes his provocative photographic work shows the reality of the world. And that realistic, social-issue focused imagery, according to Toscani, is what moves young people today.

You Decide

1. What do you think? Do Toscani's images speak to young people? Do you feel they appeal to Benetton's target audience?
2. Should controversial photos of others' personal suffering be used to build an image of social concern for a company that sells upscale fashions? Do the controversial visuals contribute to a social-concern image?
3. Assume you are the new director of marketing communication at Benetton. What would you advise for its next year's advertising program—the more traditional fashion ads, the more controversial imagery, or something in between such as the three hearts ad?
4. Assuming the controversial ads seem to generate more awareness, leading to high sales, how should businesses balance their responsibility to society versus the corporation and its shareholders?

Sources: Brad Wieners, "Keep Your Bloody Hands Off Benetton: In Praise of the Yuppie Sweater Company's Sensationalistic Ad Campaign," *Media Circus,* Salon Daily Clicks, July 4, 1996; "SOS Racisme International Convention Prepares for World Anti-Racism Day," Benetton press release, Benetton home page (July 10, 1996): Internet (Benetton.21Network.Com/Benetton/pressreleases/SOS Racisme.html); Christina Lynch, "The New Colors of Advertising: An Interview with Luciano Benetton," *Hemispheres* (September 1993): 23–7; Barbara Lippert, "Mixing Politics and Separates," *Adweek,* February 17, 1992, 30; Noreen O'Leary, "Benetton's True Colors," *Adweek,* August 24, 1992, 27–32.

HOW ADVERTISING WORKS

How does advertising work? In the following section we answer this question by examining three basic features of effective advertising: attention, memorability, and persuasion. Understanding how an ad grabs attention and lodges in memory can help you design a persuasive message strategy.

Attention

One of the biggest challenges for advertisers is to get consumers to notice their messages. To have impact, advertising must break through a cluttered environment, consumer distrust, and catch consumers' attention in a positive way.

Few advertisements actually get read or watched. Consumers often scan the stories and ads in the newspaper, but with limited concentration. Less than half of all ads are paid attention to—that is, noticed on a "thinking" level. Perhaps 20 percent are read a little. Very few are read thoroughly.

Once advertising grabs the attention of the audience, it should then create awareness. **Awareness** implies that the message has made an impression on the viewer or reader, who can later identify the advertiser. Ads that grab attention are usually high in intrusiveness, originality, or relevance. Relevant advertising creates awareness because the ad is more involving if it speaks to the audience's wants and needs. Ads can address our wants and needs by providing information about such personally relevant concepts as work, hobbies, roles, and relationships.

Interest helps move the audience from attention to awareness. Different product categories, for instance, might arouse different interest levels. Usually, food and vacations are more interesting to most people than are toilet cleaners. Some products are of interest to specific groups of people. A balding person might look at an ad for Rogaine and avoid an ad for hair spray. An ad for a post-menopause product, Premarin, sponsored by People for the Ethical Treatment of Animals, appeals to two different audiences—post-menopausal women who may be considering using the drug and people who are concerned about animal rights. In addition to the built-in interest of the topic for these two groups of people, the ad's creators intensified the interest level by using a visual parody of a well-known campaign for milk that uses celebrities with a milk "mustache" as shown on the next page.

An interesting message is usually created by one of two things—personal involvement or curiosity. If a message applies to topics that are on your list of interests, then the message has personal relevance. Most people also respond to general "human-interest" items—such as babies and puppies and tragedies and success stories. Ads that open with questions or dubious statements can also build interest and create curiosity.

Attention is the stopping power of an advertisement. Interest is the pulling power of an ad—it pulls readers or viewers through to the end of the message by keeping them involved. Interest is a momentary thing, however; it dies easily

The strong visual coupled with the enticing description of this vacation spot helps create interest and awareness.

as attention shifts. To sustain interest in an advertisement, the message must involve the audience.

Involvement refers to the intensity of the consumer's interest in a product, medium, or message. Recall that high involvement means that a product—or information about it—is important and personally relevant, such as a car commercial when you are shopping for a new car. Low involvement means that the product or information is relatively unimportant. Advertising for high-involvement products provides information about the product. In contrast, an advertisement for low-involvement purchases such as chewing gum, toothpaste, and toilet paper often focuses on simple slogans or memorable images.

Sometimes irritating strategies are used deliberately to intensify attention. Certain product categories—feminine hygiene, jock itch, condoms—are difficult to advertise because the categories are unpleasant and cause consumers to turn away. But there are other types of irritation that are caused by the advertising itself, such as obnoxious characters (used-car salesmen and furniture dealers in some local advertising) and sounds (hammers, buzzers, loud ringing phones) that are used to get attention. Sometimes the strategy itself is irritating, as in negative political commercials.

Mean-spirited product comparisons are another source of irritation and are even outlawed in many European and Asian countries. Though not outlawed in the United States, when Tylenol and Advil moved away from touting their products' potency to attacking each other in 1996, networks refused to run the ads. The reason? The networks claimed the ads overstated the dangerous side effects of each others' products. Marketing experts predicted that if the two didn't stop sniping at each other, people would be too scared or disgusted to buy either product.

Memorability

Whereas attention is a function of stopping power, and maintaining interest is necessary for pulling power, effective advertisements also have locking power—they lock their messages into the mind. If you can't remember seeing the ad, or if you can remember the ad but not the brand, then the sponsor might as well not have created it. Let's say a store advertised a sweater sale for a select brand. When you go to a clothing store, it is important that you remember which brand was on sale. How does that process happen?

Our memories are like filing cabinets. We watch a commercial, extract those parts of it that interest us, and then find a category in our mental filing cabinet to store that fragment of information. The fragment, incidentally, may not look much like the original information because the mind modifies it to fit into our own system of concerns and preconceptions. A week later we may not remember that we have a fragment labeled "sweater sale" filed away, or we may not be able to find it in the file. Most of us have messy mental filing systems. A cue, such as a holiday party invitation, may remind you of the sweater sale because you planned to wear a sweater to the party. Cues trigger memory, pull items out of the file, and place them in the forefront of our memory. When

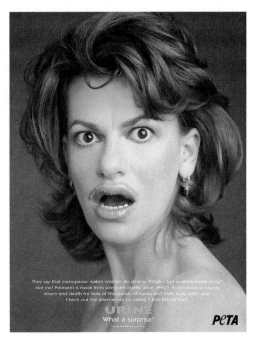

People for the Ethical Treatment of Animals parodied the milk mustache campaign in this ad that shows comedian Sandra Bernhard sporting a yellow mustache. The ad slams Wyeth-Ayerst Laboratories for its post-menopause product, Premarin, which is made from the urine of pregnant horses.

you need batteries, for instance, a copper top reminds you to buy the Duracell brand.

Advertising research focuses on two types of memory—*recognition* and *recall*. **Recognition** means we can remember having seen information about some product creating top-of-mind awareness. **Recall** is more complex. It means we can remember the content of the advertising message. As discussed in Chapter 8, repetition aids recognition and recall.

Several other techniques can enhance message memorability. Jingles and clever phrases are useful because they catch attention and can be repeated without boring the audience. Advertisements use slogans such as "The breakfast of champions" and "The real thing" for brands and campaigns. **Taglines,** which are used at the end of an ad to summarize the point of the ad's message, can be phrased in a memorable way, such as "Nothing outlasts the Energizer. It keeps going, and going, and going." Advertisers that create jingles, slogans, and taglines often use methods to improve memory such as rhyme, rhythmic beats, and repeating sounds. The highlight of an advertising person's career is when a catchy phrase or jingle is picked up and used in popular conversation, such as "Just do it!" from the Nike advertisements.

In addition to verbal memorability devices, many print ads and most television commercials feature a **key visual** that conveys the essence of the message and can be easily remembered. This image is one that the advertiser hopes will remain in the mind of the viewer, such as the finger that gently pokes the doughboy in the stomach at the end of Pillsbury commercials.

Persuasion

Advertising attempts to develop and change attitudes by providing information or touching emotions to persuade consumers to act. As mentioned in Chapter 8, persuasion is the conscious intent on the part of one person to influence or to motivate another through the use of reason, emotion, or both. Advertising that relies on expert opinion also uses reason to persuade. Advertisers often use emotion to intensify the persuasiveness of a message, such as an appeal to joy, nostalgia, or sorrow.

When advertising changes or shapes an attitude, the advertiser hopes that consumers will learn to prefer its product so that a purchase will follow. Advertisers use involvement techniques to intensify preference. Such techniques include anything that involves viewers in doing something either physically or mentally. Starting with a question, for example, is one way to draw the audience into the message. An ambiguous idea or a play on words, as in the Sony display ad shown earlier, may involve people because it tries to figure out the verbal game.

One persuasive advertising technique that has long been controversial is puffery, the ability of advertisers to make bold statements without substantiation, such as Folger's campaign slogan, "The ultimate one cup coffee machine." Such claims can be made by companies without being sued by consumers because the Federal Trade Commission has determined that sophisticated consumers will not

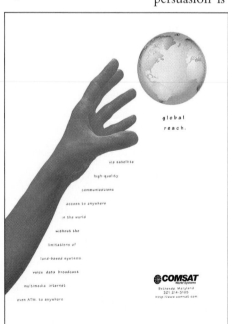

This Comstat ad uses a key visual that highlights its "Global Reach" tagline.

take such exaggerations literally. Usually you see puffery in **adese,** the language of hyperbole used by advertisers to pump up their claims with such terms as "astounding," "stupendous," and "amazing." The *right* of advertisers to use puffery was reaffirmed in late 1995 and early 1996 (although many question the *wisdom* of its use). Proposals for revisions to the Uniform Commercial Code, a legal code that governs commercial activities, would require that consumers prove they have been reasonably misled and harmed by the puffery.[4]

Concept
Review

WHAT DOES ADVERTISING DO, AND HOW DOES IT WORK?

1. The purpose of advertising is to create demand for a product, though it may do so indirectly.
2. Advertising may not lead to a direct sale, but advertising expenditures seem to correlate to profitability.
3. There are three critical elements of effective advertising: attention, memorability, and persuasion.
   - *Attention* means that the target audience notices a message. Awareness, which results from attention, means the message has made an impression on the viewer or reader.
   - Effective advertisements are *memorable*. Recognition and recall are two memory techniques used to lock messages into the mind. Recognition means you can remember having seen something before. Recall means you can remember the information content of the message.
   - *Persuading* through reason or emotion is essential to motivate consumers to act.

CREATING THE ADVERTISEMENT

The three-phase process of creating an advertisement begins with an analysis of the marketing and advertising strategy to plan a specific creative strategy. In phase two, the execution phase, copywriters and art directors execute creative strategy by writing and designing the ads. The final phase is the production phase. We explore each stage of the process in the sections that follow.

Phase I: Strategy

The marketing communication strategic planning process outlined in Chapter 4 is also used for advertising planning. Two of the most important parts of the advertising strategy are stating the communication objectives and identifying the target audience. Both of these decisions guide the advertising plan—from the creative strategy to the media plan.

Advertising objectives specifically state what the advertising is supposed to accomplish. In Chapter 4 we introduced the Domains Model as a guide for developing objectives (see Table 4.4). The model identifies the effects of three marketing communication message strategies: perception, education, and persuasion. Perception leads to attention, awareness, interest, and recall. Education involves learning and comprehension, association, positioning, and differentiation. Persuasion creates emotional responses, rational responses to reasons and arguments, and attitude and behavior change. The advertising objectives must be consistent with the message strategy.

For example, let's assume you are the advertising director in charge of a new product launch of the newest Gillette razor for women. You want to set your advertising objectives so they complement your message strategy of developing audience perception, educating consumers, and persuading them to buy your product. First, to ensure that consumers perceive your advertising message, you identify building product awareness and generating interest as your first two objectives. The advertising, then, could try to spur interest by explaining to women how the engineering pioneered in the men's SensorExcel had been modified for women. Second, to implement your strategy of educating consumers, you set an objective to provide information that teaches the target audience to comprehend and differentiate the new Gillette product from its competition. Finally, to persuade the audience to buy the product, your stated objective is to get interested women to try the product through the use of coupons and other promotional techniques.

Targeting an audience is another critical part of the advertising strategy. Advertising is most effective if it is written to a specific audience. **Copywriters** are those responsible for creating the copy for an ad. **Copy** is the text of an ad or the words that people say in a commercial. Good copywriters not only work from a profile of the targeted audience but also develop a picture in their minds of someone who fits the profile. The more the copy is targeted to a specific individual, preferably someone with whom the copywriter can identify, the more likely it is to be believable and engaging.

From a strategic standpoint, advertising—and marketing communication in general—moves toward tighter and tighter targets as products are designed for niche markets or customized for individuals. That means messages that may have been designed for mass audiences in the past, such as Coca-Cola's "It's the real thing," are now being more tightly targeted by consumer interest and contact points. The "Always Coca-Cola" campaign, for example, had messages designed specifically for the MTV and Generation X audiences, as well as for older consumers. That means every element of the ad's message—tone, style of writing, music, setting, characters, and the storyline—had to be adapted to fit the characteristics of the audience.

Niche markets make it easier to write personal, intelligent copy. Most major advertisers have had special advertising programs in the United States for African-Americans, Hispanics, and, in some cases, Asians. Some even have special campaigns for gays and lesbians. Subaru, for example, made headlines in the advertising trade press in 1996 for a special campaign that it developed to reach lesbians after discovering that they were four times as likely to own a Subaru as the general market. American Express was the first major credit card advertiser to place ads in gay magazines.

A document that outlines the advertising strategy is called a **copy platform,** or **workplan.** The copy platform can vary in format and content. For instance, Karsh & Hagan advertising agency requires that its copy platform answer the following set of questions:

- What is the problem or opportunity?
- What net effect do we want from advertising?

- Who are we trying to reach?
- What is the doubt in the mind of our prospect?
- What or who is the competition?
- What is our key point of persuasion?
- How do we support the above?
- How will we measure effectiveness?
- Are there any obligatory elements to consider?

This copy platform touches on most of the important factors in a creative strategy. Other factors include the product's position, the psychological appeal, the creative approach or "big idea," and the selling premise.

Message Strategy

An agency's creative effort is guided by a **message strategy** (or *creative strategy*) that outlines what type of message needs to be developed. Charles Frazer of the University of Oregon developed an outline of seven advertising message strategies, classified by marketing situation, as shown in Table 9.1. The chart shows that by analyzing the advertising situation, we can determine what type of message strategy to use. To illustrate, until Glass Plus entered the market, Windex owned

TABLE 9.1

Message Strategies

Type of Strategy	Description
1. Generic	Makes no effort at differentiation; claims could be made by any in the market; used in monopolistic situations
2. Preemptive	Uses a common attribute or benefit but gets there first; forces competition into "me too" positions; uses categories with little differentiation, or in new product categories
3. Unique selling proposition	Uses a distinct differentiation in attributes that creates a meaningful consumer benefit; appropriate in categories with relatively high levels of technological improvements
4. Brand image	Uses a claim of superiority or distinction based on extrinsic factors such as psychological differences in minds of consumers; used with homogeneous, low-technology goods with little physical differentiation
5. Positioning	Establishes a place in the consumer's mind relative to the competition; suited to new entries or small brands that want to challenge the market leaders
6. Resonance	Uses situations, lifestyles, and emotions that the target audience can identify with; used with highly competitive, nondifferentiated product categories
7. Anomalous/affective	Uses an emotional, sometimes even ambiguous, message to break through indifference and change perceptions; used where competitors are playing it straight

Source: Charles Frazer, "Creative Strategy: A Management Perspective," *Journal of Advertising* 12, no. 4 (1983): 40.

the market and could use a generic strategy. Glass Plus, however, realized that Windex was being used for things other than just glass, and used a preemptive strategy that focused on all the other uses to undercut Windex.

Selling Premises

Selling premises also affect the advertising creative strategy. In the industry vernacular these are called the "hot buttons," the ideas that touch peoples' lives and feelings. We discuss two selling premises next: *benefits* and *unique selling propositions*.

The most common selling premise is a **benefit,** which identifies the basis on which the product can best serve a consumer or fill a need. To develop a benefit, you must be able to translate an attribute or product feature in terms of what it can do for the user. To illustrate, Du Pont's use of cordura nylon is a feature that benefits users of its backpacks because the nylon allows packs to be light, yet tough. A **promise** is a type of benefit statement that looks to the future and pledges that something good will happen if you use the product. If you use a certain type of toothpaste, for example, then your breath will smell better or your teeth will be whiter.

A **reason why** you should buy something is another form of a benefit statement that explains with logic or reasoning why the user will benefit from a product feature. An ad for Neutrogena Shampoo, for instance, starts with a headline that states, "Why your favorite shampoo will work better if you stop using it for 14 days." The copy explains the reasons why. In many benefit strategies, the reasoning is unstated, implied, or assumed.

Proof is important for benefit selling premises, such as promises and reasons why. For example, Remington wanted to develop a campaign that proved its long-time promise that a Remington electric shaver "shaves as close as a blade or your money back." Remington turned to database company Polk, which collects product registration card data.[5] From the data Remington learned about consumers' previous and current shaving methods and their former and current shaving problems. When Polk examined the data, Remington found that users of other electric shavers were significantly more likely to have complaints than Remington users, and twice as many former blade users had problems with nicks and cuts. Remington users complained much less than those that used other shaving methods. Armed with this information, Remington renewed its claim with convincing proof.

A **unique selling proposition** (USP) is a selling premise based on a product formula, design, or feature that is both unique and important to the user. If some aspect of the product is special, particularly if protected by a patent or copyright, then the advertiser can be assured of uniqueness. That is why a USP is frequently marked by the use of an "only" statement: "This camera is the only one that lets you automatically zoom in and out to follow the action."

To review, the strategy phase of creating an advertisement involves, first, deciding on the advertising strategy; and second, deciding the specific message strategy and the appropriate selling premises. These steps are summarized in Table 9.2. The next step involves the execution of the strategy.

Phase II: Execution

Executing the message strategy is the next step in the process of creating an ad. The execution phase is where the ad is actually written and designed for pro-

TABLE 9.2	**Phase I: Strategy**
Creating the Advertisement	Decide the advertising strategy.
	Decide the message strategy.
	Identify the selling premises.

duction. This phase involves three stages: devising a creative idea, applying that idea so that it is consistent with the creative strategy, and adapting the idea for different types of media. We investigate each of these stages next.

The Creative Concept

To execute the message strategy, advertisers build on a creative idea that is called either the *creative concept* or the *big idea*. The creative people—the copywriter, art director, and other team members such as a creative director or creative supervisor—take the strategy outline from the copy platform and express the strategy in a way that is imaginative, attention-getting, memorable, and persuasive.

This big idea is usually created through a process of brainstorming, a creative problem-solving technique in which ideas are listed as they come to mind. Often one idea leads to another until a large collection are available to sort through. Brainstorming is usually done in a group, but copywriters and art directors also do a form of individual or team-based brainstorming in which they develop thumbnail sketches, which are rough drawings of an ad or key visuals that try to capture the essence of the big idea.

All types of media make different demands on the production of the message and offer different creative opportunities. As a result, the details of the execution—how the advertisement looks, feels, and sounds—depend on the types of media used in advertising.

Copywriting and Art Direction

A writer and art director usually make up the creative team. They devise the creative concept jointly and then the copywriter expresses that concept in words—either for print, broadcast, or other media. Copywriting is an art form of its own. Writers are expected to develop captivating, powerful ideas that are easy to understand; can be presented succinctly; and lock in the mind, such as the "catchy phrases" in Table 9.3.

Some talented copywriters consider copywriting to be a form of accessible poetry. Not only must copy be captivating and succinct, it must speak to people in language they use and a tone of voice they respect. "The Farmers Speak" campaign in Case 9 at the end of this chapter is a good example of writing that is personally relevant and intelligent, despite the potentially dull nature of the advertised product—agricultural insecticide.

The history of Pepsi slogans also gives some insight into how catchy phrases may evolve over time. The most recent Pepsi slogan, "Nothing Else is a Pepsi," replaced "Be Young, Have Fun, Drink Pepsi" (1994–1995). Before that, Pepsi used "Gotta Have It" (1992–1993), "The Choice of a New Generation" (1989–1992),

TABLE 9.3

Slogans and Catchy Phrases

See how many of these phrases—product and campaign slogans, taglines and catchy phrases from ads—you remember. Match the phrase to its brand.

_____ a. "Don't leave home without it."

_____ b. "Where's the beef?"

_____ c. "Builds strong bodies 12 ways."

_____ d. "Melts in your mouth, not in your hand."

_____ e. "How do you spell relief?"

_____ f. "When it rains it pours."

_____ g. "Reach out and touch someone."

_____ h. "Takes a lickin' and keeps on tickin'."

_____ i. "99 44/100 percent pure."

_____ j. "Fly the friendly skies."

_____ k. "Let your fingers do the walking."

_____ l. "You're in good hands."

_____ m. "You deserve a break today."

_____ n. "We bring good things to life."

_____ o. "When you care enough to send the very best."

_____ p. "Good to the last drop."

1. Maxwell House
2. Allstate
3. McDonald's
4. Hallmark
5. United
6. General Electric
7. Yellow Pages
8. Rolaids
9. Wonder Bread
10. Timex
11. AT&T
12. M&Ms
13. Morton Salt
14. American Express
15. Ivory Soap
16. Wendy's

Answers: a. 14; b. 16; c. 9; d. 12; e. 8; f. 13; g. 11; h. 10; i. 15; j. 5; k. 7; l. 2; m. 3; n. 6; o. 4; p. 1.

"Pepsi Now" (1984–1988), and "Come Alive! You're in the Pepsi Generation" (1967–1969). Which ones strike you as the most captivating and memorable? Which ones are forgettable?

The art director designs print ads and other printed forms such as outdoor, collateral materials, posters, and brochures and establishes the "look" for television commercials. **Art** refers to the visual elements, which include illustrations or photographs, the type, logotypes (logos, or brand symbols), signatures (how the brand name is written), and the layout (how all the elements of the ad are arranged) in print.

Because advertising is a highly visual communication form, the visuals are a crucial part of the message design. Pepsi ads, for instance, use a dynamic graphic element—the logo on the can—in its ads to create a visual reminder.

The Effects of Advertising Media on the Creative Process

Often the creative idea will be communicated through a variety of advertising media that require message adaptation. Thus, creative people must know the advertising medium that will be used and its peculiar characteristics before they can

The logo on Pepsi products is designed to be a memory cue. Using the logo in ads creates a powerful reminder.

plan an ad. Let's review the key creative requirements of the more common advertising media.

Print Advertising. Print advertising includes printed advertisements in newspapers, magazines, brochures, and flyers. The key elements of print advertising are copy and art. The copy elements include headlines, subheads, body copy, captions, slogans, and taglines. The use of type in print makes it possible to write a clear and extended explanation. Print advertising tends to be visually intensive, with the message being communicated as much by the pictorial elements as by the words. Visuals that are easy to understand and remember communicate fast and speak to the busy reader who often doesn't want to take the time to read a lot of copy. Copy-heavy advertising, however, is appropriate when there is an interesting story to be told or when the reader is presumed to be interested in acquiring information.

Broadcast Advertising. Ads that are broadcast are heard in one of two formats—radio or television—and they tend to be 15, 30, or 60 seconds in length. This short length means the ads must be simple enough for consumers to grasp, yet intriguing enough to prevent viewers from switching the channel. Interesting and entertaining commercials can hold viewer attention, as evidenced by consumer recall for such commercials as the Mennen Skin Bracer commercial with the tagline, "Thanks, I needed that."

Television is a visual medium of moving images, so action is the component that separates TV commercials from other forms of advertising. Certain types of commercials are particularly effective in television, such as storytelling, demonstrations, sight and sound spectaculars, and real-life situations that touch emotions.

A riveting Mazda ad from the Netherlands, for example, showed a man driving at night on a dangerous two-lane highway when he was clearly fighting to keep awake. At the end of the action in the spot, he deliberately drove off the road and rammed a post. The objective of this curious action was to make his airbag inflate, at which point he went to sleep using it as a pillow.

The components of a television commercial include the **video,** or the images; the **audio,** or the sound; the **talent,** or the people or animals in the commercial; and other stagecraft elements such as props, setting, and lighting. Graphics can be generated on the screen as well. These components of a commercial are held together by **pacing,** the speed at which the action develops.

A growing advertising tool is the infomercial, a program-length television commercial. The infomercial business is currently a $1 billion industry. It is used by such big-name advertisers as Microsoft, Sony, Lexus, Nissan, CBS/Fox Video, Sears Roebuck, Procter & Gamble, and Apple Computer. Fitness products are the leading product category, featuring, among others, Richard Simmons' *Farewell to Fat.* Ross Perot relied heavily on infomercials to deliver his political messages in both the 1992 and 1996 elections. More than 600 infomercials aired in 1995, up from 500 in 1994.[6]

Infomercials are successful because they give consumers more information, more education, and more time to understand the product and its message. Effective infomercials provide how-to information that consumers in the target market are eager to receive. Nissan, for example, produced *The Art of Buying a Car,* an infomercial targeted at female car viewers that delivered many leads, given its total cost. As mentioned in Chapter 1, Microsoft broke new ground with its half-hour program introducing Windows 95 that aired during prime time on network affiliates in the top 50 markets. Long-form commercials are particularly useful for explaining complicated products to consumers, such as Upjohn's Rogaine hair-growth product.

Infomercials can also be used to tie in with other marketing communication efforts. Excedrin, for example, used a trio of direct-response spots—that is, infomercials that gave viewers the chance to call in during the ad and respond to the offer—to generate a database of headache sufferers who then received a free sample, coupons, and a quarterly newsletter.

Radio advertising relies on attention-getting sound effects and highly memorable music. Radio advertising is often called the "theater of the mind" because it depends so much on listeners' imaginations to fill in the missing visual element. Listeners, in other words, are active participants in the construction of the message, and that makes radio a very involving medium. Radio, because it is limited to sound, depends on voices, sound effects, and music to create a story. It is also the most intimate of all media because it usually plays to an audience of one. The use of the human voice adds to the sense of intimacy.

Even though people often listen to the radio while they are doing something else, strategies in radio advertising have found three ways to heighten the impact on the listener. The first is repetition, particularly for jingles that are so simple and easy to remember that they become sing-alongs. A second technique is to present the creative strategy with either music or humor, both of which grab attention and inspire memory. Finally, timing the ad to correspond to an immediate need works well. Restaurant ads, for example, are often played while the listener drives home from work.

Out-of-Home Advertising. Advertising that reaches audiences in their daily external environment is called **out-of-home advertising.** It includes painted walls, telephone kiosks, truck displays, bus benches, shopping mall displays, in-store merchandising, aisle displays, and billboard advertising. Blimps, airplanes, towing messages, and the scoreboards in sports arenas are also types of out-of-home advertising. This type of advertising is a good way to target groups of people with specific messages at a time when they are most susceptible to its impact. Planes towing message banners, for example, are often used at football games to reach sports fans. Out-of-home advertising has enjoyed great success during the 1990s because more advertisers are looking to alternative media to carry their

Swatch hung this eye-catching watch in downtown Atlanta to remind people that it was the official Olympic time-keeper.

messages to more tightly targeted audiences. Entertainment and amusements, travel, media, health care, apparel, and cigarette and liquor advertisements commonly use this medium.

Transit advertising is primarily an urban advertising tool that uses vehicles to carry the message throughout the community. Occasionally you might see trucks on the highway that also carry messages. Transit advertising is of two types—interior and exterior. Interior is seen by people riding inside buses, subway cars, and some taxis. Because such advertising sends messages to a captive audience that has time to read, there is often more copy on the ads. Exterior transit advertising is mounted on the sides, rear, and top of these vehicles, and it is seen by pedestrians and people in nearby cars. Transit messages can be targeted to specific audiences if the vehicles follow a regular route, such as buses. Most of these posters must be designed for quick impressions, and they serve as quick reminders. Transit advertising also includes the posters seen in bus shelters and train, airport, and subway stations. Like interior cards, these posters may be seen by people waiting for transit, and therefore they can be more detailed than messages that are seen quickly by people passing by.

Online or Internet Advertising. For marketers interested in the Internet, figuring out how to make money on the Web is the biggest challenge. Starwave, a suburban Seattle company that pioneers in the new medium of publishing online, is out to find the gold. Starwave runs the main newsroom behind ESPNet Sportszone, which attracts 230,000 visitors a day, making it one of the most heavily trafficked sites on the Web. It is also a leading recipient of advertising dollars among Web sites.[7]

Online advertising may be seen on commercial information online services such as CompuServe, America Online, and Prodigy; on electronic bulletin board systems; and on the Internet, a global network of computer users that allows people to send and receive images and data. The IMC in Action feature gives a number of tips for Internet advertisers.

The commercial services have electronic shopping malls where businesses can offer their products and services to users. Companies can also sponsor conference areas where they are able to participate in dialogues with present and potential consumers. The commercial services also make available space for "banners," lines of copy relating to a product that invite viewers to "click" on the ad to link to more information. These banners run in conjunction with some other page of information that the viewer has consulted. Effective banners must arouse the interest of the viewer who is often browsing through other information on the computer screen. The key is to balance vivid graphics and clear copy. An example is the banner for Tom's of Maine dental products.

Internet banner advertising is developing rapidly as new technologies from companies such as Sun Microsystems' Java, Netscape, and Microsoft make it possible to incorporate sound, animation, and video. For example, the Java-driven ScorePost on ESPNet Sportszone scrolls through sports scores, and as it does so

How to Advertise on the Internet

Home pages are the place where Internet browsers can check out your business, your products, and perhaps be motivated to some kind of action. Computer wizards can help you handle the technical details of getting your site online. Here we explore how to design an Internet advertising message.

The new creative frontier is figuring out how to lure potential customers into your area. First, you must inform people where your site is by promoting it in other areas of the Internet and in other media. Those who abide by Internet etiquette ("netiquette") frown on unsolicited mass e-mailings, so many businesses announce their Web site address in print or broadcast ads.

Assuming you have your home page up and running, how would you write an online ad? To make a

good impression on electronic visitors, a company should consider five tips. First, stop surfers in their tracks. Offer a deal or use an involvement device such as a challenge or contest that offers a discount or a freebie as a prize. Second, change your offer frequently, perhaps even daily. One of the reasons people surf the net is to find out what's happening now. Good ads exploit "nowness" and newsiness. Third, keep your executions short and succinct because most browsers have short attention spans. Graphics make a page slow to set up, so use them sparingly on the home page, although once inside your site, you can offer slow-building graphics to people who have made a commitment to search your cyberspace store.

Fourth, find ways to keep your browsers' attention focused. Ask

provocative questions, make the time they spend with your site worthwhile, give them something even if it is only a new piece of knowledge they can use, or offer a bonus for reading the text. For example, TWA's Web site (http://www.twa.com) makes it possible for visitors to win frequent flyer miles every time they visit and register with the site. Fifth, find ways to use the advertisement to solicit information and opinions. For example, reward browsers for sharing their opinions with you by offering them three free days of a daily horoscope or something else they might find fun or captivating.

Design is the big challenge. When you couple interactivity with the volume of information offered on each home page, advertisers must help people navigate their site. Information design practition-

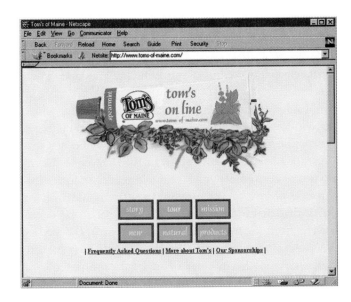

This banner for Tom's of Maine uses vivid colors and copy to capture viewers' interest.

ers help companies design user-friendly sites that people can visit without getting lost.

Examples of successful sites include Pepsi's high-tech tour de force (http://www.pepsi.com). Targeted at young computer whizzes, Pepsi's site is amazingly intricate and took about five years to create. Planet Reebok comes alive in Reebok's Web site (http://www.planetreebok.com). Budweiser's site (http://www.budweiser.com) attempts to bind its viewers to the page with technology that allows visitors to tour the site in 3-D. Nissan Motor's site for its Pathfinder line contains content related to the outdoors (http://www.nissanmotors.com/pathfinder). Toyota's site offers a collection of lifestyle publications on topics like gardening, travel, and sports, with little reference to its cars (http://www.

toyota.com). *Condé Nast Traveler* created a business-travel section for its site in a joint venture with Delta Airlines (http://travel.epicurious.com).

New Balance Athletic Shoes has tips on exercise, diet, running, and events. It even asks the magazines in which it advertises to provide material for the site (http://www.newbalance.com). Ragu uses the Old World personality of a virtual Italian grandmother for its Mama's Cucina site that features recipes and unexpected topics like Italian lessons (http://www.ragu.com or http://www.eat.com). L'eggs offers a lot more than information about hose in its site (http://www.leggs.com). It delivers fashion and career advice, information on government officials, and even a recipe suggestion box. Tambrands has created Troom (http://www.troom.com) as

a place for teens to get advice on many issues in their lives—music, makeup, and menstruation. The site is elaborately constructed to look like a teenage girl's room.

Food for Thought

1. What message do you think advertisers send to stakeholders if their site is hard to navigate?

2. How would you advertise the address for Snapple's home page?

Sources: Denise Caruso, "Digital Commerce: Simple is Beautiful, Especially in a Place as Confusing as Cyberspace," *New York Times,* 16 August 1996, C5; Jeffery D. Zbar, "Blurring the Ad-editorial Line," *Advertising Age,* November 13, 1995, 14; Herschell Gordon Lewis, "Cruisin' Down the 'Hype-er Space' Road: How to Write Copy for the (Gulp!) Internet," *Direct Marketing* (November 1995): 36–7; Larry Chase, "Crossroads: Advertising on the Internet," *Marketing Tools* (July/August 1994): 60–1.

it moves through a series of ads, much like the rotating signs at basketball games. Duracell uses a drawing of a battery breaking through a page instead of a conventional banner. Curious viewers that click on the battery see an image of the back of the page covered with electrical circuits along with the message "Powered by Duracell."

Netscape also can run multiple window-like frames simultaneously, which allows an ad to run in one window while viewers are surfing to other pages. Viewers can read other pages while watching animation or even video ads in a split-screen arrangement. Netscape's "cookies" tool allows a Web server to download ads tailored to specific types of consumers. A 15-year-old teenager, for example, would receive a different style of Levi's ad than would a 40-year-old woman.

Online advertising is so new that methods of evaluation have yet to be developed. AdLab, a tracking service from Competitive Media Reporting, however, reports that the top advertisers use a print magazine format at their Web sites. Its "ad activity index" ranks advertisers on the number of such ads, the size of ads, and the number of active links the advertiser has. In 1996, for example, AdLab reported the following companies as the top ten advertisers in online magazines:[8]

1. Apple Computer
2. Netscape Communications Corp.
3. Saturn Corp.
4. AT&T
5. Internet Shopping Network
6. Oracle Corp.
7. Chrysler Corp.
8. Insight Software
9. Intel Corp.
10. Microsoft Corp.

Other Advertising Media. There are a variety of other ways to reach audiences with advertising, including direct-mail advertising to the home or business. Let's briefly review other forms such as direct-mail, directory, and movie advertising.

Direct-mail advertising refers to ads in print and broadcast media that offer a product and a means to respond to the ad with an order. The copywriting has to be very strong because it has the sole responsibility to motivate the target audience to respond without other assistance such as personal sales or a store display. This type of advertising crosses over between advertising and direct marketing and will be discussed in more detail in Chapter 12.

Directory advertising occurs in books that list the names of people or companies, their phone numbers, and addresses. The most common directories are produced by a community's local phone service. The Yellow Pages is a major advertising vehicle for local retailers. Yellow Pages advertising is described as directional advertising because it tells people where to go to get the product or service they are looking for. Directory advertising's greatest strength is that it reaches prospects who already know they have a need for the product or service. But Yellow Pages are just the beginning of the directory business. There are an estimated 7500 directories available, and they cover all types of professional areas and interest groups.

Most movie theaters will accept filmed commercials to run before the feature. Called **trailers,** these advertisements are similar to television commercials but are generally longer and better produced. In most cases advertisers do not use their regular TV advertising in movie theaters, although Coca-Cola uses some of its commercials for its Fruitopia line in theaters. Coke's strategy is to reach youth at points where they are having fun. In addition, movie advertising also includes **product placements** in films. This is a relatively new medium for advertisers, but they have found that having an easily identifiable product that a character in a movie uses can have tremendous impact on the product's acceptability.

International Strategies

Once a strategy has been developed, then advertisers need to evaluate how to execute it across social, cultural, and political boundaries. Advertising for international clients offers a challenge: How can advertisers develop advertising that will succeed around the globe? In rare cases advertisements may be taken from one country to another, but in most cases there has to be some modification, if only to the language. Usually, the advertising strategy is the easiest to standardize from country to country, followed by the message strategy and selling premises, and finally the executions.[9] In most cases the executions have to be modified for local audiences.

The same considerations apply to multi-ethnic advertising within a country. In the United States, for example, advertisers often develop separate campaigns for African-American and Hispanic audiences. In Malaysia advertisers may adapt their strategies to fit the native Malaysian population, which is primarily Muslim; a large Chinese population; and a smaller Indian population, which is primarily Hindu.

Whether a strategy can be globalized depends on product category. Certain business products, computer products, status products like Rolex and Montblanc, and soft drinks are used the world over. The target audience may also affect whether the advertising strategy may be globalized. Certain types of people are similar in their interests regardless of where they live (business travelers, teenagers, computer techies). Pampers executives have observed, for example, that mothers around the world have similar needs for diapers for their infants. Also, the MTV generation shares a common sense of fashion and music regardless of the language they speak. Ads for products and consumer groups that cut across national boundaries, therefore, can be fairly standardized in their strategies.

Sometimes the creative concept can also carry across borders. One example is the purple raw silk imagery used in Europe as a visual statement for the Silk Cut cigarette. The Marlboro cowboy works even in countries where cowboys are

TABLE 9.4	
Creating the Advertisement	**Phase II: Execution** Develop the creative concept or big idea. Write the copy and design the look of the ad. Adapt this creative approach to all of the areas used in the creative mix: print, broadcast, infomercials, out-of-home ads, transit, online ads, and other advertising forms and tools. Adapt the creative approach to cross-cultural and international marketing situations.

profile

Masaru Ariga
Senior Strategic Planner, Marketing Management Division
Dentsu Inc.

Dentsu is an international marketing communication agency. Masaru Ariga is responsible for planning international marketing communication strategies for Dentsu's client companies. He travels extensively and works with planners in overseas Dentsu offices. He frequently takes charge of marketing communication campaigns on a pan-regional basis, particularly in Asia. He explains, "Coming from headquarters, I consider my responsibility to be identifying what can be used across the countries and what needs to be country–specific."

Ariga is also in charge of developing new marketing methodologies to cope with various timely issues. For example, how can national brands compete effectively against private labels? How to use database marketing? How to implement integrated marketing communication? In this role he has been interviewed as an expert on advertising and marketing communication by such international media as CNN.

In addition to his client-based work, Ariga also gives lectures and writes articles on marketing-related topics. He is a lecturer of marketing at the International University of Japan and, from time to time, is asked to give lectures for such organizations as Japan Marketing Association (JMA) and Japan Advertising Agency Association (JAAA). Some of his articles that have appeared in professional publications include the following:

- "Seven Crucial Viewpoints to Understand Japanese Consumers"
- "Mass Retailing to Japanese Consumers"
- "Changing Marketing Environment and Integrated Marketing Communications"
- "Database Marketing in Singapore"

Academic Background
Ariga graduated with a B.A. in political science from Waseda University in Tokyo in 1985. During the 1981/82 academic year, he earned a scholarship and studied at Macalester College in St. Paul, Minnesota, as an exchange student.

unknown, probably because of the worldwide fascination with the idea of the West and the rugged independence that the character represents. The Snuggles bear also works well in just about every country in the world.

The execution of an ad, which we discuss in the next section, may need to be modified for individual countries to maximize effectiveness. The creative concept for Impulse Body Spray, for instance, uses the image of a man stopping a woman on the street to give her flowers. That idea works almost everywhere, but the ads are filmed locally so the settings and physical characteristics of the people seem familiar.

There are some parts of the world where advertising messages need special care. Some Asian countries are particularly concerned about "cultural imperialism" and resent the incursion of Western values through advertising. Consequently, some countries severely restrict Western advertising. Malaysia, for instance, requires that all advertising be locally produced. Muslim countries forbid advertising for "sin" products (cigarettes, alcohol), and the women's images in the visuals have to con-

In 1991 he returned to the United States to get his master's degree from Northwestern University. He graduated in 1992 from its new IMC program. His graduate education was sponsored by Dentsu, for whom he had been working since 1985.

Advice

Ariga has found that traveling abroad has been his most helpful experience. He had already visited 30 countries before graduating from college and now can claim 40 countries. He explains, "Having visited new places and exposing myself to different cultures at a young age helped me develop diverse ways of looking at things."

Typical Day

0730: Get up, eat a quick breakfast, and take a commuter train to Dentsu's offices in downtown Tokyo. Unfortunately, it is next to impossible to go to work by car as highways in Tokyo during weekdays are notorious for being "the largest car park in the world."

0930–1015: Start off today's business day by going through newspapers of five Southeast Asian countries that are sent by air mail everyday. Go through articles and ads of interest carefully. By doing so, I can keep track of what's going on in those markets.

1030–1200: Meet with the creative director and account executives for an upcoming new product launch in Thailand. Exchange ideas regarding how to define the emerging "urban new middle class," which will be the volume market for the product, with research manager in the local Dentsu office.

1200–1300: Moderate an internal brainstorming session for a marketing campaign. We often hold brainstorming sessions during lunchtime because it is the best time to get busy people together. Also, many talented people can be recruited by the promise of good food.

1330–1600: Go to a client to present the results of a campaign effectiveness measurement research project.

1700–1900: Discuss issues with members of a project based in Vietnam. Today's theme is to develop execution plans that will prevent possible image problems with Western companies.

2000–2200: Join a farewell party for the participants of a training program who came to Tokyo from different parts of the world.

2330–2400: On returning home, make a phone call to Chicago. Doing business with the States is a big headache because of the time difference, which eliminates between 14 and 17 hours. I have to wait until midnight to communicate with my counterparts if I need to talk to them directly over the phone. And that's why I am a firm believer that e-mail is the greatest invention of the past decade. I feel the world is much smaller now than in the era before e-mail.

form to Muslim notions of propriety, which can vary from country to country.

Even major international marketers can sometimes stumble into culturally insensitive practices. Ford Motors of Europe found it had a problem when it reprinted a photograph for use in Poland. The original photo showed European workers of all different races to illustrate the company's diversity. In creating the Polish brochure, all the black and Asian faces were retouched to look Caucasian to appeal better to the predominately white Polish market. The Ford workers depicted in the original brochure were horrified to find that they had been "whitened."[10]

The execution phase of creating an advertisement is summarized in Table 9.4 on page 303.

Phase III: Production

After the creative idea has been developed and executed for the different media, the third phase is to produce the advertisement. The production requirements for print and broadcast ads are entirely different, but both are complex and demand the specialized skills of expert technicians. Brochures, posters, outdoor boards, the World Wide Web, and all other advertising usually requires specialized skills.[11]

Getting a print ad produced, for instance, requires knowledge of the graphic arts industry and specialized information about typography (how the type is chosen and typeset) and art production. Photography, in particular, is difficult to reproduce in printing and demands a number of technical operations to convert a photographic image to a **halftone**—an image that converts a full range of tonal values to a screen pattern that can be printed. Color photographs also need a special conversion process to replicate a full range of color values. The final step in the printing process is page assembly, trimming, and binding. Special treatments such as die-cutting (creating unusual cut-outs or shapes), flocking, and embossing are also done after the printing.

A radio ad is produced by recording the sound effects, voices, and music as detailed in the script written by the copywriter. A television commercial uses audio and video recording techniques. Shooting a TV commercial is a complex event that involves characters, sets, lighting, props, and an audio track. All of these elements are assembled according to a script written by the copywriter and a storyboard drawn by the art director. A **storyboard** is a drawing of the key scenes in the commercial. A producer manages the videotaping and directs the shooting of the script, which usually results in a lot more footage than is actually needed in a typical commercial. A film editor assembles the best footage into a series of scenes that follows the script and lasts the correct length, such as 10, 30, or 60 seconds.

The production phase in creating an advertisement begins after the strategy has been decided and the creative ideas for the ads have been developed. Table 9.5 summarizes all three phases in the process of creating an advertisement.

Concept ✓ Review

CREATING THE ADVERTISEMENT

1. Advertising strategy involves stating the communication objectives and identifying the target audience; the message strategy identifies the strategic creative approaches and the selling premises.
2. In the execution phase the strategy is transformed into concrete ideas for actual ads for all types of media. The creative team does the following:
   - Develops a big idea, writes ad copy, and designs ads that dramatize the big idea
   - Adapts the idea, ad copy, and design to match the needs of the media tools or the form of advertising
   - Considers any adaptions that might need to be made for cross-cultural or international marketing situations
3. Production is a very technical operation for all media that usually requires many specialized skills.

TABLE 9.5

Creating the Advertisement

Phase I: Strategy

Decide the advertising strategy.

Decide the message strategy.

Identify the selling premises.

Phase II: Execution

Develop the creative concept or big idea.

Write the copy and design the look of the ad.

Adapt this creative approach to all of the areas used in the creative mix: print, broadcast, infomercials, out-of-home ads, transit, online ads, and other advertising forms and tools.

Adapt the creative approach to cross-cultural and international marketing situations.

Phase III: Production Phase

Work with experts to produce the materials used in all areas of the creative mix.

WHAT MAKES AN EFFECTIVE AD?

Like most viewers you probably have a love-hate relationship with television commercials. On the one hand, you may have a favorite commercial or campaign; on the other hand, you can probably identify a dozen commercials that you resent so much you change the channel or leave the room when they appear. You might hate the product, dislike the characters, and consider the message insulting. Your evaluation of the ad may be based on personal taste—different people like different things. It may be that you aren't part of the target audience so the message doesn't interest you. Or it may be rational judgment—there are, after all, poorly conceived commercials on television and in print. This simple example demonstrates a key point. There are many ways to evaluate an effective ad. Keep in mind that effective advertising must grab attention, be memorable, and persuade. It must also target its audience and meet the advertising objectives.

Ways to Judge Effectiveness

Is effectiveness based on how much consumers like ads? Video Storyboard Tests, an organization that monitors consumer reaction to ads, determined that the best ad series of 1995 was the "Bud" "Weis" "Er" frog, which made the king of beers the king of commercials, at least for one year.[12] *Time* magazine polls rated the Nissan ads that featured a faux-Barbie and GI-Joe going for a spin in a Nissan sports coupe (leaving Ken to watch from the toy house) as the top ad for 1996.[13] The *New York Times* rated the

This Braun ad persuades its target market with attention-getting devices —a humorous fear appeal and a reminder of the product's benefits.

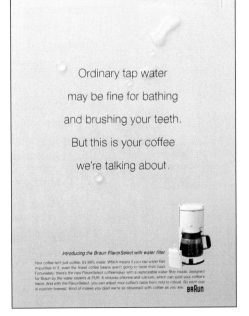

Ordinary tap water

may be fine for bathing

and brushing your teeth.

But this is your coffee

we're talking about.

Introducing the Braun FlavorSelect with water filter.

BRAUN

Levi's wide-leg jeans ad as one of the best commercials of 1996. In that ad a young man and woman in an elevator wonder what it would be like to date each other—but that fantasy becomes a nightmare as they consider the implications of marriage and kids.[14] As opposed to consumer ratings, advertising effectiveness also can be judged through a number of award show programs that consider creative dimensions (the One Show, the Cleos, the Cannes awards) or the ads' sales impact (the Effies).

More recently, advertising effectiveness is being measured using *single-source data,* information gathered by the A.C. Nielsen Co. that compares in-store purchases with exposure to television advertising. In a study based on such data, Syracuse University professor John Philip Jones reported in his book, *When Ads Work,* that it is possible to persuade people to buy a product through single exposure to an effective advertisement.[15] In exceptional cases advertising can actually triple sales. The advertisements that were the most effective in stimulating short-term sales generate six times the amount of sales as the weakest ones. Some of the weakest advertising actually caused sales to fall. Jones also found a strong correlation between advertising and sales promotion when both activities work together. However, the most successful campaigns made advertising more effective and lessened the need for promotions, particularly price promotions.

Public service advertising provides different evidence of advertising effectiveness. Recent examples of successful public service advertising include the United Negro College Fund campaign by Young & Rubicam that has helped raise close to $1 billion for black colleges; a crime prevention campaign from Saatchi & Saatchi that averages over 3000 crime tip calls a week; Leo Burnett's safety belt campaign that the Department of Transportation estimates has saved more than 40,000 lives; and a domestic violence hotline, featured in a new Altschiller Reitzfeld campaign, that received over 22,000 calls in six months.[16]

Evaluation

Advertising can be considered effective only after it has been evaluated in some way. For instance, to better assess advertising effectiveness, General Motors announced that it is developing a standardized approach to evaluate—and learn from—its advertising successes and failures. Its three-part process involves:[17]

1. *Strategic development,* through which creative ideas are tested using a toolbox of techniques such as focus groups, image studies, and positioning studies
2. *Copytesting* using various methods to diagnose the effectiveness and problems of ads as they are being produced
3. *Market tracking,* which will tie the advertising to sales impact

Evaluation research can occur at several points in time. The first opportunity is before the ad has been aired. Pretesting, testing done during concept development, helps assess whether the ad will accomplish what the strategy calls for before making a big investment in production, time, and money. The second point in time, known as posttesting, is while the advertising is running or shortly thereafter. This testing gives real-life feedback about how well the advertising met its objectives and provides information for future ad strategies.

Copytesting is formal evaluation research in advertising used to decide whether an ad should run in the marketplace and to help guide execution decisions. It is focused on persuasiveness, recall (awareness), and message understanding. Advertisers who use copytesting at the concept stage hope that it will provide a valid measure of effectiveness and that it will eliminate the risks and conflicts inevitable when decisions are based on judgment alone.

Copytesting is an important research tool because the stakes in advertising are high. By the time an average 30-second commercial is ready for national television, its production may have cost as much as $200,000. And if it is run nationally, it may cost several million dollars in air time. Ideally, the results of copytesting would be available before large sums of money have been invested in the finished work.

In general, advertisers must use copytesting carefully. Tests that are fast and affordable often have obvious flaws and provide data that may not be reliable. Furthermore, creative people within agencies distrust many copytesting methods because they believe the tests don't really measure the impact of the advertising as it plays out in a real-world situation. When decisions are difficult, research cannot always tell the decision maker what to do, so there is still a need for insight and professional judgment. However, such research can provide information to guide and support the more intuitive judgments of the seasoned professional who understands from experience how advertising works. Copytesting and other evaluation techniques are discussed in more detail in Chapter 18.

WHAT MAKES AN EFFECTIVE AD?

1. Effective advertising is attention-getting, memorable, and persuasive. It also must target an audience and meet stated advertising objectives.
2. Advertising is evaluated at two points in time: before an ad has aired or been published (to test effectiveness before a large investment has been made) and during or shortly after an ad has run (to test impact). The former type of test is a pretest; the latter is posttesting.
3. Most copytesting measures persuasion, recall (awareness), and understanding of key copy points.

A CLOSING THOUGHT: CLUTTER BUSTING

Good creative people know that every advertising message must compete in a cluttered environment for the attention of an indifferent audience. The only way to break through is to express the selling message in an original, fresh way. Though dull advertising can be persuasive, it will rarely get the attention of the audience. Breakthrough advertising should be both persuasive and creative. It can be risky, though, because it is often difficult to evaluate; it doesn't perform like the traditional advertising with which most consumers are familiar.

Another way to break through the clutter is to integrate the advertising with a wide range of other communication tools that reinforce the same message or big idea, as is demonstrated in the "The Farmers Speak" advertising campaign featured in Case 9. When a captivating idea is repeated at different times in different ways, the synergy adds more power to an already strong concept. That is why it is so important in IMC planning to have consistency at the heart of all the different messages stakeholders receive from a company.

SUMMARY

1. Define advertising.

Advertising is any paid form of nonpersonal presentation and promotion of ideas, goods, and services by an identified sponsor to a targeted audience and delivered primarily through the mass media.

2. Identify the strengths and weaknesses of advertising.

Advertising has many strengths. It can reach a large mass audience to intensify broad-based demand for a product, build brand awareness, create long-term brand images and brand positions, and increase brand knowledge effectively. Advertising also serves as a reminder of a product or brand with which a consumer has had a positive experience. Finally, it can enhance memorability through message repetition. Advertising has several weaknesses also. It is perceived as intrusive and as cluttering the environment. It also wastes many impressions, so it may not be cost-effective, especially if the business is targeting a niche market.

3. Explain how advertising works.

To be effective advertising must accomplish three tasks. It must create attention, be memorable, and deliver a persuasive message. Attention, the act of noticing a message, is the first step toward developing awareness, which means the message has made an impression on the viewer or reader. Advertisers use recognition and recall to enhance memorability. Recognition is the ability to remember that you have seen something before. Recall means you can remember the information content of the message. Finally, to motivate consumers to

act, advertisers must persuade audiences through reason or emotion.

4. Outline the three phases in creating an advertisement.

The first phase in creating an advertisement analyzes the marketing and advertising strategy and identifies the message strategy for a particular ad. Advertising strategy focuses on the target audience and the communication objectives. Copy platforms outline the message strategy and selling premises. The second phase is the execution: the development of the big idea, the copywriting, and how to design the ad for the creative mix of different media—print, broadcasting, outdoor, and other types of advertising such as directory, transit, movies, and electronic. The production phase identifies the experts who know how to produce the advertising for a particular medium.

5. Describe what makes advertising effective and how to evaluate effectiveness.

Effective advertising is attention-getting, memorable, and persuasive. It also must target an audience and meet stated advertising objectives. To evaluate advertising effectiveness, businesses may use such research methods as focus groups and image and positioning studies, consumer ratings, or market tracking to test the sales impact of advertising. Copytesting is often used to diagnose the effectiveness and problems of ads in the development stage and during or shortly after an ad has run. Evaluation research before the ad has run is pretesting. Such research during or after the ad has run is posttesting.

POINTS TO PONDER

Review the Facts

1. Define advertising and explain its basic function.
2. What are advertising's primary functions? What are its limitations?
3. Define persuasion and explain how it is used in advertising.
4. Explain the difference between advertising strategy and message strategy.

Master the Concepts

5. Think of two television commercials that stick in your mind. Analyze them to determine why they are so memorable.
6. Find an advertisement that illustrates each of the selling premises described in this chapter.
7. Find a magazine ad that crosses cultures and could be used in international advertising with only minor changes. Also find an ad that you think is culturally bound and could not be used for cross-cultural or international advertising. Explain your reasoning.
8. "Every ad should generate sales." Comment on this statement.

Apply Your Knowledge

9. You are writing ad copy for a new bicycle shop named Pedal Power that will open in a couple of months in your community. Brainstorm with your friends and develop a list of at least ten slogans that the owner might consider.
10. Spend some time on the Internet and find three advertisements that you believe are either highly effective or ineffective. Critique the ads by examining whether they grab attention, are memorable, and persuade.
11. Why might there be conflict between agencies and their clients on the evaluation of advertising ideas?

SUGGESTED PROJECTS

1. (Oral and Written Communication) Assume that you have been charged with organizing an in-house advertising department for a growing consumer products company. The first task is to hire an advertising manager who will have ultimate responsibility for the company's advertising. Interview advertising managers at companies in your community to find out how they perceive their job responsibilities. What responsibilities do you believe should be mentioned in the job description for this position? Write the job description.

2. (Oral Communication) Divide the class in half. Debate the two sides of the following question: "Is advertising worth the money?"

3. (Internet Project) This chapter discussed Benetton's recent print ads. Now explore the company's Web site (www.benetton.com) to see if it sends marketing communication messages that are consistent with the advertising messages. (Be warned: The "Fan and Hate Mail" link posts uncensored letters that may contain explicitly and graphically sexual material.) Explain your conclusions about the consistency between Benetton's print and Web site marketing communication messages in a brief memo. Be sure to support your conclusions with specific references to the Web site's content, design, and accessibility to its target audiences around the world.

Now review the entire gallery of Benetton ads by following the links from the home page to the Advertising Index. Select one ad of your choice—other than one of the ads we discussed in the chapter—and evaluate its effectiveness using the criteria described in this chapter. (For instance, is the ad attention getting, memorable, and persuasive? Does it communicate to its target audience? Does it reinforce or hurt Benetton's image?) Prepare a brief memo of your evaluation criteria and your final assessment.

CASE 9: AMERICAN CYANAMID: THE FARMERS SPEAK

In an unlikely promotional event, the farm news director for KDSN Radio in Denison, Iowa, featured an advertising campaign for American Cyanamid in his newscast. The director aired two 90-second spots plus a five-minute interview with the advertising account supervisor from Atlanta-based Tucker/Wayne/Luckie & Company. The newscast discussed the Cyanamid campaign contrasted with others that treat farmers as though they were idiots or a commodity. "This campaign treats farmers fairly, praising them for their concern for the environment." Copy for the campaign included the following lines:

> *"I am responsible.*
> *For being an active environmentalist. Not an environmental activist.*
> *For answering to God. To the land. To my family. I farm accordingly."*

The Cyanamid ads promoted corn soil insecticide. This type of insecticide typically comes packaged in a bag that can expose farmers to the insecticide when handled. Instead, Cyanamid offered two packaging options: a bag or a self-contained returnable and recyclable Counter Lock 'n Load package that eliminates direct contact with the insecticide.

The objective was to get current Counter Lock 'n Load users to feel good about paying a premium price; entice users of both Counter and competitors' bagged insecticide to switch to Lock 'n Load; and maintain brand leadership—Lock 'n Load commands a 40 percent share of a $250 million market.

The $3.5 million IMC campaign consisted of one 60- and one 30-second TV commercial, six radio spots, two magazine two-page spread ads, "I am responsible" bumper stickers and posters, a video, an extensive direct-mail program, and special events.

The campaign featured a farmer, a farm wife, and a twenty-something farm son—each appearing in separate ads and voicing their feelings on the responsibilities of farming. Their opinions are paraphrased from comments made in focus groups. The objective was to embody every farmer, not use a series of individual testimonials. The idea for the campaign germinated from information culled from 12 years of focus groups. One subject repeatedly surfaced in off-the-cuff comments during the years: Farmers always voiced their concern about how people perceive them. Farmers are well-educated and sensitive to the land and to their image.

The ads were designed to evoke a reflective mood. For example, the TV ads showed a farmer walking through his farmyard under early morning gray skies. He seemed almost contemplative, speaking about his responsibilities—never about Lock 'n Load. After a final pause, a spokesperson delivered the pitch for the product. Far from a hard sell, the ad focused on how Lock 'n Load could help farmers meet their responsibilities through safe, returnable, and recyclable insecticide containers.

The TV and radio spots ran on local stations in such states as Iowa, Colorado, Nebraska, Kansas, and Wisconsin. The print ads ran in farm trade publications, including *Successful Farming, Farm Journal,* and *Progressive Farmer.* All of the ads featured an 800 number for farmers who wanted more information or wanted to locate a dealer.

A heavy dose of direct mail rounded out the IMC campaign. Cyanamid sent five different mailings to a total of 20,000 farmers (from its database of one million). The mailings were segmented based on product usage. For example, one mailing that went to current Lock 'n Load users included a thank-you note, an "I am Responsible" bumper sticker, and a copy of the print ad. The goal was customer retention. Other mailings were sent to users of competitive brands or users of Counter's bagged insecticide to encourage switching to the returnable, recyclable Lock 'n Load package.

The response was outstanding. The 800 number received several hundred phone calls, 90 percent of which were used in the direct-mail campaign. The direct-mail campaign, which offered a videotape of Lock 'n Load, garnered a 30 percent response rate. Cyanamid also received dozens of letters from farmers, farm wives, and agricultural associations complimenting the campaign.

To further demonstrate its commitment to farmers' quality of life, Cyanamid and *Successful Farming* magazine cosponsored the Farm Family Enrichment conference in Des Moines, Iowa. The conference covered such issues as intrafamily relationships and reducing stress.

Addressing the farmers' concern for family and land is an important approach because, even though the Lock 'n Load recyclable packaging system is safer and more environmentally friendly than competitors' brands, its insecticide product is not significantly different from competitors' products. Preserving Cyanamid's identity as a premium brand, then, is critical. According to customer feedback, the advertising strategy caught farmers' attention, was memorable, and highly persuasive.

Case Questions

1. Why do you think the "Farmer Speaks" campaign worked for Cyanamid's Counter Lock 'n Load system?

2. Re-create the copy platform that guided the development of this advertising approach.

3. What elements of the marketing mix fueled this campaign? Analyze how effectively the advertising worked with other marketing communication elements. What other marketing communication areas or tools might you recommend Cyanamid use?

4. If you were assigned to plan next year's advertising campaign for the Lock 'n Load system, what direction would you take in the message strategy? How should this campaign be managed over time? How should it evolve?

Source: Ginger Trumfio, "Fully Loaded," *Sales & Marketing Management* (August 1995): 90–1.

ROMA'S LITE INTEGRATED CASE QUESTIONS

(Review the Roma's Lite Marketing Plan in the Appendix before answering these questions.)

1. What are the strengths and weaknesses of advertising and how do they apply to the launch of a new product?

2. How does advertising work? How can it help with the launch of Roma's Lite Pizza? Build the argument for an intensive advertising campaign for this new product launch.

3. (Team Project) Develop an advertising program for the launch of Roma's Lite Pizza. What would be your objectives, target audiences, and creative strategy? What theme would you use? How would this theme translate into ads for print, billboards, television, and radio?

chapter

10

Sales Promotion

CHAPTER OBJECTIVES

After completing your work on this chapter, you should be able to:

1 **Define sales promotion and discuss its purpose.**

2 **Explain how sales promotion fits in the marketing communication mix and how it can be used in an IMC program.**

3 **Outline how sales promotion strategies differ for the trade and consumer target audiences.**

4 **Compare and contrast the techniques used for and the objectives of reseller, sales force, and consumer promotions.**

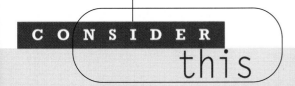

C O N S I D E R this

Color My World

One company that knows how to offer exciting promotions for all ages is Binney & Smith, maker of Crayola products. Take, for instance, its contest to name new Crayola colors. The contest objectives included generating 50 percent awareness in the target market, getting 20 percent of kids ages 3 to 7 to try Crayola's "Big Box" set of 96 crayons, and building a database of 60,000 Crayola consumers of all ages. Here's how Crayola met its objectives.

The contest was aimed at parents and children. Prizes included 16 all-expense-paid trips for four to Hollywood, California, and induction into the Crayola Hall of Fame. The promotion was supported by advertising, in-store displays, and a strong publicity program. A parallel retailer contest offered prizes to retailers who supported and generated the most excitement for the consumer contest.

The color-naming contest was a

huge success. Crayola received more than two million color-name submissions from 122,000 entries. Media coverage resulted in about 1000 print articles and 700 television news stories. Color winners included: purple mountain's majesty, macaroni & cheese, granny smith apple, pacific blue, tropical rain forest, timber wolf, tumbleweed, tickle me pink, robin's egg blue, cerise, asparagus, denim, shamrock, razzmatazz, wisteria, and mauvelous.

Crayola followed the name-the-color contest with the Crayola Big Kid Classic adult-coloring contest, which it announced on its Web site (www.crayola.com). The prizes included $25,000 in silver and gold bullion. In an unusual twist Crayola selected judges for the drawing contest by holding a writing contest in which kids explained why they would make good judges. Crayola chose six judges who were flown to Orlando. A Louisiana woman, Reva Wallace, was the winner from more than 60,000 entries.

311

To support worthy causes and to promote its Web site, Crayola sponsored an Internet auction of crayon and marker artworks created by more than 30 celebrities such as Whoopi Goldberg, Martin Sheen, Mario Andretti, and Phil Collins. In the first two days, the auction generated more than 50,000 visits to the Web site and to the American Council of the Arts Gallery in New York where the works were exhibited. Proceeds were donated to the Very Special Arts, a nonprofit organization that promotes learning through the arts to the disabled.

Crayola's sales promotion efforts continue. In 1997 kids had the chance to win a $25,000 "Room Full of Fun" by collecting four puzzle pieces from specially marked packages of various Crayola products or to win a trip for creating an illustrated storybook. The sales promotions have heightened consumer awareness of Crayola's new products, reminded customers of its old products, and strengthened its brand image of wholesome fun.

Sources: "A Room Full of Fun Contest," Crayola home page (January 1, 1997): Internet (www.crayola:80/roomful.com); "Crayola Goes Crayon-line," *Promo* (August 1995), 12; "Name the Crayola Colors Contest," *Brandweek,* April 4, 1994, 32.

CHAPTER OVERVIEW

This chapter introduces the second element of the marketing communication mix—sales promotion. First we examine the strengths and weaknesses of sales promotion and how it fits in the marketing communication mix. Then we outline a framework for planning promotions. Finally, we examine specific techniques aimed at resellers (including retailers, wholesalers, and distributors), the sales force, and consumers.

DEFINING SALES PROMOTION

Originally, *sales promotion* was used as a support tool that was seen as less important than advertising and personal selling in the marketing communication mix.[1] This perspective is no longer valid. Today, sales promotion can support or complement other marketing communication tools, or it may serve as the main tool.

The Council of Sales Promotion Agencies defines **sales promotion** as a marketing communication tool that offers sales-related incentives to generate a specific, measurable action or response for a product or service.[2] Sales promotions may be targeted at any or all of the consumer and trade audiences. The trade audience includes retailers and wholesalers, distributors, and brokers in the distribution channel. The trade audience can also refer to the sales force and other employees. We can better understand sales promotion by examining what sales promotion can accomplish and its strengths and weaknesses.

Stimulate Immediate Action

The main purpose of sales promotion is to offer consumers and trade members (such as sales staff, resellers) an "extra incentive" to act. Sales promotion stimulates sales by offering an extra, short-term incentive to motivate action as is illustrated in the Shaq Mac Attack box. Although this extra incentive is usually in the form of a price reduction, it may be offered in the form of additional product, cash, prizes, premiums, and so on. The Crayola contest prizes are examples of incentives. This extra motivation is what distinguishes sales promotion from the other marketing communication mix tools.

The Shaq Mac Attack

Though many were sad to see 7′1″, 300-pound Shaquille O'Neal leave Orlando to move to the Los Angeles Lakers, McDonald's breathed a sigh of relief. Why? The McDonald's in Orlando could finally end a special promotion with the Orlando Magic that had turned out to be a nightmare. When Shaquille O'Neal arrived in Orlando in 1993, McDonald's began redeeming home game tickets as a coupon for a free Big Mac or Egg McMuffin every time the team hit 110 points or more. It seemed like a good idea at the time.

In 1995, however, the NBA made it easier for teams to run up big scores. First, the NBA moved the three-point line closer to the basket. Second, it eliminated hand checking, the defensive technique of placing hands—sometimes in an ironlike grip—on an offensive player as he tried to move the ball down the court. The Magic also improved its team by adding Horace Grant from the Chicago Bulls and developing Penny Hardaway into an outstanding point guard. The result? Magic fans wolfed down Big Macs at an alarming rate because

in 80 percent of the 1995 home games, the Magic team scored 110 points or more.

A perfect example of integrated marketing, the ticket became a coupon that highlighted McDonald's and its sponsorship of the team in a positive way. Winning the free Big Mac had all the excitement of a game. From a sales promotion viewpoint, then, the ticket was a coupon, the redeemed Big Mac was a sample designed to encourage repeat business, and the basketball game was a special event sponsorship. For McDonald's bottom line, however, it turned into a loss because that kind of a winning record gave the 16,000 fans 36 chances to trade in their tickets for a free Big Mac. As you can well imagine, the vision of so many thousands of Big Macs leaving McDonald's free gave the company heartburn.

And backing out of the promotion wouldn't have been simple: At one board meeting a board member suggested raising the barrier to 115 points, but others voiced the concern that McDonald's would then appear stingy. Fortunately,

Shaq's departure to the West Coast solved the dilemma.

Food for Thought

1. Assume Shaq had not left Orlando. What sales promotion plan would you have recommended to the Orlando McDonald's?

2. If you were a marketing communication director for the McDonald's in Los Angeles, would you recommend a similar promotion with a 115-point requirement? Explain the advantages and disadvantages of such a promotion.

3. Suppose McDonald's of Los Angeles decided to do a promotion similar to Orlando's and put you in charge of implementation. What should the promotion rules be, and what precautions, if any, would you take before starting the promotion to avoid hurting the company's bottom line?

Sources: "Lakers Sign Shaquille O'Neal," *Starwave Corp and ESPN Inc.* (October 7, 1996): Internet (www.nba.com/Court/shaq_lakers); Rance Crain, "Big Shaq Attack Giving McDonald's Heartburn," *Advertising Age,* January 9, 1995, 14.

Sales promotion is based on the premise that each brand or service has an established perceived price or value and that sales promotion changes this accepted price-value relationship by increasing the value, lowering the price, or both. Thus, sales promotion offers consumers an immediate inducement to buy a product by the simple step of making the product more valuable. Promotion can prompt consumers who know nothing about the product to try it, and it can persuade them to buy again.[3] Unplanned purchases, for example, can often be directly traced back to one or more sales promotion offers.

To entice customers to try a new product, companies such as Del-Monte Corp., Ralph Lauren, and Wilkinson Sword distribute more than 500,000 free samples in Daytona Beach each spring break. To encourage increased spending during the holiday season, Kraft food products and Hasbro toys participated in a joint promotion through a nationally distributed freestanding newspaper insert (FSI) that included cents-off coupons and rebates on toys. In France, Orangina (the tangerine-flavored soft-drink maker) joined forces with a fast-food chain to offer music-related premiums to consumers who ordered the drink in the fast-food stores. Orangina sales rocketed as a result.

Sales Promotion Strengths and Weaknesses

Sales promotion techniques can accomplish certain communication goals that the other elements in the marketing communication mix cannot. For instance, sales promotion can turn around a sales trend in the short term. It can help introduce a new product, reinforce advertising images and messages, and generate positive brand experiences among buyers at many stages of the consumer decision-making process. It can also provide new channels for reaching audience segments, such as in-store merchandising materials and special events.

Research suggests, however, that sales promotion cannot accomplish certain goals. For example, sales promotion cannot create a brand's image, change negative attitudes toward a product, or reverse a long-term declining sales trend. In the following sections we discuss the strengths and weaknesses of sales promotion in more depth.

Strengths

The most important strength of sales promotion is its ability to stimulate people to act—to try or to buy something. It does this by adding extra value through special pricing or some other kind of special deal, a practice called changing the price/value relationship. In other words, in the eyes of the consumer it adds a tangible value to the product, such as cents off or a premium. From the company's perspective, sales promotion is also used to increase purchase frequency and/or quantity.

Sales promotion also offers businesses the flexibility to meet many different marketing communication objectives and to reach any target market. Because of the wide range of promotion techniques, all kinds of businesses—small and large, manufacturers and services, profit and nonprofit groups—can use sales promotion.

Coupons offer money off products and add extra value for consumers, stimulating them to buy products.

A word of caution, however. Although sales promotion is an effective strategy for creating immediate, short-term, positive results, it is not a cure for a bad product, poor advertising, or an inferior sales force. Although a consumer may use a coupon for the first purchase of a product, the product quality is what draws repeat purchases.

Sales promotion activities directed at sales forces and resellers can motivate these important trade members to "push" the product by supporting promotions and giving the product more sales attention. Sales force promotions such as rewards and cash bonuses can motivate the sales team to increase sales contacts and overall sales. For instance, a business might give salespeople with the top three sales revenues a $1000 bonus. Promotions aimed at resellers can offer incentives—such as special price deals and gifts of related merchandise—to encourage the trade audience to provide merchandising support to retailers and to create excitement among those responsible for distributing or selling the product. For example, a special promotion on iced tea might offer all participating retailers the coolers used in the display and retailers with product sales above $20,000 the chance to win a trip to Hawaii.

Finally, sales promotions that require customers to fill in name and address information, such as a rebate or mail-in coupons, enable businesses to build databases of customer information. The database information is useful for tracking consumer behavior and for targeting customers with direct mail. To illustrate, Nabisco built a database of 200,000 cookie and snack purchasers from information collected during a promotion in which consumers sent in proofs of purchase to acquire autographed baseball cards. The company used that database for more individualized direct-marketing efforts.

Weaknesses

Sales promotion activities may have negative consequences. The main weakness of sales promotion is its contribution to clutter. Promotions try to be more creative, shout louder, or deliver ever-increasing discounts to get the attention of consumers and the trade. Another weakness of sales promotion is that repeated use of price-related techniques may reduce the perceived value of the product or brand. In fact, couponing is now so pervasive that some consumers will not buy the product without a coupon. Further, consumers and resellers have learned how to take advantage of sales promotions. Most notably, consumers now wait to buy certain items until they are reduced in price. Resellers may also use *forward buying* (which means stocking up) when the price is low to improve their bottom lines rather than passing on the savings to their customers.

Also, some sales promotion techniques lend themselves to abuse. Many consumers, for instance, redeem coupons for products they haven't purchased. Theft of premiums (special gifts that reward purchase) is also a problem, especially when easily removed from a package. These fraudulent practices cost businesses millions of dollars.

A key weakness of trade promotion is that it is difficult to get busy trade members, including a company's own sales force, to cooperate. There is no guarantee that trade members will participate in events like contests or that they will use sales promotion materials directed at retailers or distributors. Promotion planners, then, should work closely with the trade audience to provide incentives that will inspire cooperation. Even if trade members such as distributors or salespeople cooperate, however, promotional materials may be wasted if retailers refuse to use the merchandising materials.

If not used carefully, sales promotion may also contribute to declining brand loyalty by shifting consumer focus from brand value to price. Procter & Gamble's division manager of advertising and sales promotion, V. O. "Bud" Hamilton, describes the situation as follows: "Too many marketers no longer adhere to the fundamental premise of brand building, which is that franchises aren't built by cutting price but rather by offering superior quality at a reasonable price and

TABLE 10.1

Strengths and Weaknesses of Sales Promotion

Strengths	Weaknesses
Gives an extra incentive to act	Adds to clutter
Changes the price/value relationship	Can set false retail price
Adds tangible value to product offering	Some consumers won't buy unless there is a price deal
Gives sense of immediacy to purchase	
Adds excitement, spectacle	Leads to forward buying by trade members
Stimulates trial	Fraudulent redemption of coupons and theft of premiums
Stimulates continuity of purchase or support, repeat purchases	Can be difficult to get trade cooperation
Increases purchase frequency and/or quantity	Can undercut brand image, create brand insensitivity
Promotes reminder merchandise	
Motivates trade support	
Builds databases	

clearly communicating that value to consumers. . . . The price-cutting patterns begun in the early 1970s continue today, fostering a short-term orientation that has caused long-term brand building to suffer."[4]

Some critics believe that the move from brand-building advertising to trade promotions and couponing has created a brand-insensitive consumer who views all products as commodities. In support of their claim, critics cite the price-cutting strategies followed by Coke and Pepsi as an example of two brands that many consumers now view as interchangeable. On any given weekend, especially holiday weekends, Coke and Pepsi products are located on end-of-the-aisle or in-island displays featuring six-pack prices as low as $0.99. People buy the cheapest brand and stock up with enough six-packs to last until the next sales promotion. The strengths and weaknesses of sales promotion are summarized in Table 10.1.

Concept Review

DEFINING SALES PROMOTION

1. Sales promotion is a marketing communication tool that uses a variety of incentive techniques for consumer and trade audiences to generate a specific, measurable action or response.
2. Its main purpose is to stimulate immediate action—to prompt consumers and trade members to act.
3. The primary strength of sales promotion is that it offers an "extra incentive" for consumers to act. Its primary weaknesses include clutter and the potential to undercut branding.

SALES PROMOTION IN THE MARKETING COMMUNICATION MIX

To use sales promotion effectively, marketing communication managers must understand how the sales promotion strategy relates to the overall marketing communication strategy. In this section we explore how sales promotion can help implement *push* and *pull strategies*. Then we investigate how sales promotion can aid two specific marketing communication strategies: introducing new products and building brands.

In many cases sales promotion is used with other types of marketing communication. For example, trade promotions often augment personal sales, advertising may announce special promotions for consumers, and sales promotions may help build databases for later direct-mailing programs.

Table 10.2 reflects a synthesis of the contributions of the various marketing communication tools. These contributions may become blurred when sales promotion is used with other marketing communication tools, such as advertising, because the combined efforts create synergy. The synergistic effect of sales promotion can be a powerful addition to a marketing communication effort. Note the last row of the table. That row shows the contribution to profitability, which is the ratio between what is spent on a promotion compared with the profits generated by that expenditure. We see that sales promotion has a high contribution to profitability, relative to advertising and public relations.

Stimulate Push or Pull Demand

Promotional strategies can be broadly classified as push or pull strategies, depending on whether the focus is on the consumer or the trade. A **pull strategy** directs most marketing efforts at the ultimate consumer and is usually implemented with large advertising expenditures. It may include additional incentives for the

TABLE 10.2

A Comparison of Sales Promotion with Other Marketing Mix Tools

	Sales Promotion	Advertising	Public Relations	Direct Response (Interactive)	Personal Selling
Time Frame	short term	long term	long term	short term	both
Primary Appeal	both emotional and rational	emotional	emotional	rational	rational
Primary Objective	sales	image/brand position	goodwill	sales	sales relationships
Contribution to Profitability	high	moderate	low	high	high

consumer through the use of coupons, rebates, samples, or sweepstakes. These efforts create consumer demand to "pull" the product through the channel of distribution. Thus, a pull strategy requires little promotional effort from resellers.

In contrast, a **push strategy** directs most marketing efforts at resellers and the sales force to stimulate personal selling efforts. The business "pushes" the product through the channels of distribution by asking resellers to demonstrate products, to distribute in-store promotion devices and merchandising materials, and to sell the product.

A pull strategy is used when demand for the product is high and when there is high differentiation among products' real or perceived benefits. Some markets, such as children, respond well to a pull strategy. Occasionally, a novelty product or fad can create this overt and assertive behavior on the part of the consumer. Healthy Choice frozen dinners is an example of a product that was successfully launched by a pull strategy. However, examples of companies that have solely relied on a pull strategy are rare.

If the product is relatively new, or complex, or if many acceptable substitutes exist, then a push strategy may be more appropriate. Marketers of imported beers often use a push strategy to stimulate reseller support. They do not have large enough budgets to engage in mass advertising.

Most companies use a combination of push and pull. Marketing representatives for Fruitopia call on supermarkets, discount stores, convenience stores, drugstores, and even specialty stores like coffee shops and bakeries. As the sales representatives restock the product, they also announce special promotions, offer trade deals, and negotiate for the best possible position for product displays. The company also spends a great deal of money on a consumer marketing communication program to inspire its customers to ask for their favorite beverage. Figure 10.1 outlines the push, pull, and combination strategies.

In addition to stimulating push and pull conditions, there are two specific areas where sales promotion can contribute to a marketing communication strategy—introducing a new product and building a brand.

Introduce a New Product

One area in which sales promotion is particularly useful is the introduction of new products and services. Suppose we were in charge of introducing a new corn chip named Corn Crunchies. Our first marketing challenge would be to create awareness of this product. Although advertising can often do this effectively, sometimes sales promotion can call attention to advertising and the brand name. Possibilities include a reduced introductory price, in-store sampling, and a special tie-in with a well-known salsa company.

Creating awareness will only take the product so far. Corn Crunchies must also be perceived as offering some clear benefit compared with the competition. We could use sales promotion to enhance the marketing communication message by offering coupons as a means of advertising. The coupons should stimulate product trial—that is, consumers should try the product. We might also mail free samples of Corn Crunchies to households and offer reduced prices in stores. Conducting a contest in conjunction with the product introduction could also

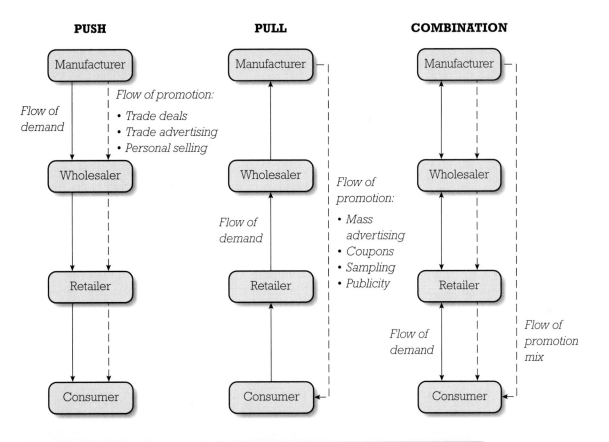

FIGURE 10.1

Push, Pull, and Combination Strategies

create interest and intensify desire. If we successfully implement this consumer strategy, consumers who are convinced of the value of Corn Crunchies will demand that the product be stocked in their favorite stores. By asking for it, they will pull it through the channel of distribution.

Unfortunately, creating awareness and desire means nothing unless the product is available. A push promotional strategy is used to convince members of the distribution network to carry Corn Crunchies. Resellers must be convinced that the product will move off the shelves before they will stock it. Trade advertising directed at wholesalers and retailers can be effective in providing these resellers with important information. In addition, trade sales promotion techniques, especially price discounts, point-of-purchase (P-o-P) displays, and advertising allowances, help to gain shelf space.

After the initial purchase, we want the customer to repeat the purchase, and we also want retailers to allocate more shelf space to Corn Crunchies. To prompt such actions, we must change the advertising copy to remind customers about the positive experience they had with the product and use sales promotion to

This eyecatching P-o-P display helps Gillette gain valuable shelf space.

reinforce customer loyalty with coupons, rebates, and other rewards. For those retailers that carry the product, repeat purchase promotions can also reward them because customers who buy the product are likely to purchase other products while in the store.

Build a Brand

In contrast to the criticism that sales promotion destroys brand loyalty, many sales promotion experts believe it can build brand loyalty. HPD Group, a research firm, conducted a 17-year tracking survey of brand equity in which the results show that loyalty to top brands has been steady since 1987.[5] Marketing communication strategist Michael Schrage notes, "traditional advertising no longer has the responsibility of maintaining brand equity. Product value is no longer created through advertising imagery, it is determined by the price/performance relationship."[6]

Experts in sales promotion respond to the criticism about branding in two ways. First, they argue that the claim that sales promotion destroys brand image is greatly exaggerated. They refer to many cereal brands, rental car companies, airlines, and hotels that have used a variety of well-planned sales promotion strategies to enhance brand image. Marlboro's Country Store, for example, does a big business in *tie-in* merchandising. A **tie-in** is a promotion that links one product to another, so that the marketer can take advantage of the brand strength of another product. Because customers exchange product packages for merchandise, the Country Store promotional program builds loyalty. Second, sales promotion experts acknowledge that continuous promotion—particularly continuous price promotion—does not always work. However, sales promotion can and does work if it is part of a well-executed strategy to build brand trial and familiarity—especially if it is part of an integrated marketing communication plan.

IBM sales promotions for its PC line provide an example of brand-building promotions. IBM uses relatively low-profile promotions, such as giving away a free CD-ROM with lots of software on it to people who buy a new home computer.[7] The company also uses tie-in (or cosponsored) promotions with other marketing partners, such as retailers or suppliers. This type of promotion is designed to help cement relationships with its partners and customers. Its strategy of using high visibility promotions backfired, however, at the 1996 Summer Olympics. The poor performance of its computer systems generated such damaging publicity that those messages outweighed IBM's brand-building messages.

SALES PROMOTION STRATEGY

Recall that sales promotion can be targeted at either consumer or trade audiences. **Trade promotion** is promotion directed at resellers and sales forces; **consumer promotion** is promotion directed at consumers. The target audience dictates both the promotion objectives and the mix of sales promotion tools used.

Objectives

To create sales promotion objectives, planners need to consider two factors: who the audience is and whether the approach will be proactive or reactive. First, different objectives apply to each of the target audiences. Sales promotion is intended to *stimulate* the consumer to act, *motivate* the sales force, and *gain the cooperation* of resellers. Second, sales promotion tends to be either proactive or reactive. The proactive, long-range objectives tend to accomplish the following goals:

1. Create additional revenue or market share
2. Enlarge the target market
3. Create a positive experience with the product
4. Enhance product value and brand equity

TABLE 10.3

Sales Promotion Objectives

Consumer	Trade
• Prompt trial by new users	• Introduce a product to a new distribution area
• Introduce new or improved products	• Reduce selling costs
• Stimulate repeated use of the product	• Improve working habits
• Encourage more frequent purchase or multiple purchases	• Offset competitive promotions
• Counter competitors' activities	• Increase sales volume
• Encourage trade-up in size or cost	• Control inventory
• Keep customers by providing an implied reward	• Stimulate in-store support
• Reinforce advertising or personal selling	• Create a high level of excitement among those responsible for its sale
• Stimulate trade support	

Reactive objectives are responses to a negative or short-term situation. They try to accomplish the following goals:

1. Match competition
2. Move inventory
3. Generate cash
4. Perhaps go out of business

Table 10.3 provides examples of both consumer and trade sales promotion objectives. Identify the ones that seek to accomplish proactive and reactive types of objectives.

The Sales Promotion Mix

Promo, the magazine of the promotion marketing industry, reports that the sales promotion industry is growing rapidly for many reasons. It offers the manager short-term solutions; its success in meeting objectives can be measured; it is less expensive than advertising; and it speaks to the current needs of the consumer to receive more value from products.

The sections that follow describe specific types of sales promotion. Table 10.4 is an overview of some of the common categories of sales promotion activities. The table shows that every promotional activity except couponing and licensing has increased. The areas with the greatest increases include interactive promotions, in-store marketing, and advertising specialties (items such as cups, calendars, pencils, and T-shirts with a company's name and/or logo printed on it).

The most difficult step in sales management is to decide which sales promotion tools to use, how to combine them, and how to deliver them to the two target audiences. Each tool has its own advantages and disadvantages that may change when used in combination with other marketing communication tools.

TABLE 10.4

Promotion Industry Gross Revenues ($ millions)

Tool or Area	1994	1995	% Change
Premium incentives	$20,000.0	$20,800.0	+4.0
P-o-P displays	11,098.0	12,024.0	+8.3
Advertising specialties	7,008.0	8,037.0	+14.7
Couponing	6,995.0	6,950.0	−0.6
Promotional licensing	4,900.0	4,850.0	−1.0
Sponsored events	4,250.0	4,700.0	+10.6
Interactive promotions	1,126.0	1,540.0	+36.8
In-store marketing	828.8	990.4	+19.5
Product sampling	703.9	774.0	+10.0

Source: Adapted from "1996 Industry Report," *Promo* (July 1996): 36.

Sales promotion planners should consider several questions when mixing sales promotions:

- *How should the various sales promotion tools be combined physically?* Will the sales promotion tools be delivered separately or will they be designed as an **overlay**—that is, a sales promotion combined with other marketing communication tools and delivered together? Crayola's "Big Kids" promotion, for example, used a contest to attract people to its new Web site. Will the promotion be a tie-in, a promotion that links one product to another to take advantage of the brand strength of the other product? Kingsford Charcoal, for example, did a tie-in with Armour Hot Dogs by offering a price reduction on the hot dogs with a purchase of the charcoal.
- *Can or should sales promotion be integrated with other elements of the marketing communication mix?* A coupon, for example, is often used as part of an advertising campaign. A final strategic decision is choosing the type of media to deliver the promotion. Coupons are typically delivered through print media such as newspapers, magazines, direct mail, and freestanding inserts (FSIs). FSIs are a separate section of a newspaper that carry coupons.

Contests and sweepstakes are often more exciting if they are announced on television rather than in print. An example is Taco Bell's Double Decker campaign featuring a one-on-one match-up between basketball greats Shaquille O'Neal and Hakeem Olajuwon. The television spots ran for only four weeks but garnered high effectiveness ratings by research company Ad Track—42 percent of those who knew the ads called them very effective. In addition, the competition generated substantial free media publicity.

Next we will discuss the reseller, sales force, and consumer sales promotion tools in more detail.

Concept Review

SALES PROMOTION STRATEGY

1. Sales promotions are directed at consumer and trade (resellers and the sales force) audiences. To set sales promotion objectives, planners need to consider two factors: who the audience is and whether the approach will be proactive or reactive.
2. Consumer sales promotions are directed at the ultimate users of the product so they "pull" the product through the channel.
3. Trade promotion uses a push strategy. Reseller promotions are directed at the distributors, wholesalers, and retailers whose support is needed to "push" the product. Sales force promotions are aimed to motivate salespeople to give products more sales attention and to meet higher sales goals.
4. Planning the sales promotion mix involves deciding how to combine sales promotion tools physically and how to integrate them with other elements of the marketing communication mix.

TRADE SALES PROMOTION: RESELLERS

A reseller sales promotion is a trade promotion directed at resellers who distribute others' products to the ultimate consumers or to the sales force. Resellers (also known as intermediaries) are the 1.3 million retailers and 338,000 wholesalers in the United States who distribute goods and services to other resellers and ultimate users. Manufacturers cannot succeed unless resellers are willing to distribute their products. Manufacturers, then, use sales promotion to gain reseller support. Service providers also use trade sales promotion to push their products. Fast-food companies and hotel companies, for instance, use trade promotions to involve their franchise owners and local employees in push programs.

The actual size and worth of reseller promotions are difficult to determine. Although this category represents 50.7 percent of total promotional spending, expenditures vary by industry and size of business.[8] Moreover, there are millions (or perhaps billions) of promotion dollars that are difficult to trace. Businesses seem to be making a shift, however, from trade promotion (a push strategy) to consumer promotion (a pull strategy).[9]

Reseller spending now averages 12 percent of sales in consumer packaged goods, growing from $8 billion in 1980 to over $130 billion in 1995. It currently represents the largest component of a manufacturer's marketing investment.[10] Some studies show that such spending does little to build brand loyalty. It does, however, build stronger relationships between manufacturers and retailers, a trend described as "co-marketing" (see the IMC Concept in Focus feature).

Many promotional devices can motivate resellers to support a product. Here we examine four techniques: dealer contests, trade coupons, dealer loaders, and trade deals including allowances. These techniques are summarized in Table 10.5.

TABLE 10.5

Trade Sales Promotion Techniques for Resellers

Technique	Objective	Method of Distribution
Dealer contests	Encourage quantity purchases; create enthusiasm; support other marketing communication "big ideas"	Direct mail; trade advertising; sales force
Trade coupons	Increase frequency and amount of purchase; prompt quick trial; promote local store and manufacturer's product	Local advertising; in-store dispensers
Dealer loaders	Reward purchasing at a certain level; reward reseller for supporting a promotion with a gift; create goodwill	Sales force; trade advertising
Trade deals	Reward reseller financially for purchase of product or support of a promotion; stimulate frequency and quantity of purchase; encourage cooperative promotional efforts	Sales force

Co-Marketing

Co-marketing is a process whereby leading manufacturers develop marketing communication programs *with* their main retail accounts, instead of *for* them. Co-marketing programs are usually based on the lifestyles and purchasing habits of consumers who live in the area of a particular retailer's stores. The partnership means that the advertising and sales promotions build equity for both the manufacturer and the retailer. For example, Procter & Gamble and Wal-Mart might develop a spring cleaning promotion directed at Wal-Mart shoppers. The program could feature P&G cleaning products sold at reduced prices in Wal-Mart stores.

Co-marketing is not the same as co-branding, which occurs, for instance, when American Airlines puts its logo on a Citibank Visa card and awards AAdvantage points to Citibank Visa users. In co-marketing ventures manufacturers focus on their brands, and retailers focus on their product categories.

In co-marketing the manufacturer usually initiates the joint venture. In exchange for the manufacturer's brand marketing expertise (consumer knowledge, advertising, sales promotion, and other marketing communication tools), the retailer provides resources, such as personnel and marketing funds, to generate incremental category sales and profits. The manufacturer's brand equity helps drive the promotion. A study of co-marketing strategies found that the two most important requirements were cooperation between partners and a willingness to share information.

Co-marketing usually involves a cross-functional team of people, including such people as a sales promotion agency account manager, the manufacturer's representative, and a representative from the retailer. Companies actively involved in co-marketing ventures include Procter & Gamble, Oscar Mayer, Kraft Foods, Hershey's, Duracell, Keebler, and Nestlé. McDonald's recently made headlines in the trade press because of its co-marketing arrangements with several partners from the ConAgra company to create Contadina Pasta Shops, Nestlé Toll House Cafés, and Healthy Choice Sandwich Shops.

Food for Thought

1. Explain why co-marketing programs are particularly important for companies that have adopted a relationship marketing approach.

2. You're in charge of designing a co-marketing program for your company, Zephyr In-Line Skates, for the store owners who carry the skates. What kind of consumer promotions might you jointly sponsor? What kinds of information do the two companies need to share? Who should be on the cross-functional team that manages the effort?

Sources: Karen Benezra, "McMenu Expands," *Brandweek,* April 22, 1996, 1, 6; "Promotion . . . By the Numbers," *Brandweek,* March 13, 1995, 34; Christopher W. Hoyt, "Co-Marketing: What It Is and Is Not," *Promo* (March 1995): 34.

Other reseller promotion techniques that may be used to support sales promotion programs, such as trade shows and point-of-purchase displays, will be discussed in Chapter 14.

Dealer Contests

Sales promotion practitioners can develop contests and sweepstakes to motivate resellers. Contests are far more common than sweepstakes, primarily because contest prizes are usually associated with the sale of the sponsor's product. A sales quota is set, for example, and the company or individual who exceeds the quota by the largest percentage wins the contest.

To create enough excitement and motivation to galvanize resellers in a crowded

Vanilla Fields Cologne Spray
By Coty. 0.75 ounce.

12⁹⁹

OscoDrug STORE COUPON

UPC# 9426

Vanilla Fields Baseball Cap

FREE!

with purchase of 0.75-ounce Vanilla Fields Cologne Spray and this coupon
($8 Value)

Limit 1 with coupon/
1 coupon per customer

0 00000 09426 9 Good Sun., June 15 thru Sat., June 21, 1997.

This Vanilla Fields promotion, displayed in an Osco coupon booklet, is a sample of a trade coupon.

marketing environment, designers have been forced to devise spectacular contests with impressive prizes and incentives. According to a survey sponsored by *Business & Incentive Strategies* magazine, 46 percent of women and 51 percent of men opt for cold cash, followed by merchandise worth $1000 or more, and travel.[11]

If conducted properly, contests can provide short-term benefits (such as encouraging larger reseller purchases) and can improve the relationship between the manufacturer and the reseller.

Trade Coupons

Retailers redeem consumer's coupons and must wait for reimbursement from the manufacturer who issued them. Trade coupons differ from consumer coupons in that the manufacturer or service provider offers them to the local retailer to be carried in the retailer's ads or fliers. The manufacturer pays for the advertising and gives the retailer an allowance that covers the upper limit of the estimated redemption. The redeemed trade coupons, then, usually do not have to be returned to the manufacturer.

Trade coupons are often used to stimulate trial of new products quickly. Typically, trade coupons must be redeemed within a few days. The time limit is intended to prompt a quick response. Trade coupons can be a cost-effective tool because they offer the retailer an inexpensive way of promoting the store and help marketers move products into new or difficult markets. Trade coupons can increase both the frequency of purchase and the amount of products purchased.

Dealer Loaders

A **dealer loader** is a premium that is given to a retailer by a manufacturer for buying a certain amount of a product. These types of promotions build goodwill with resellers. The two most common dealer loaders are **buying loaders,** typically a gift given for buying a certain order size; and **display loaders,** a display that is given to the retailer as a reward after supporting a promotion. As an example of a buying loader, Budweiser offers store managers a free trip to the Super Bowl if they sell a certain amount of beer in a specified time period. As an example of a display loader, Dr. Pepper built a store display for the July 4th holiday that included a gas grill, picnic table, basket, and so forth. The store manager was awarded these items after the promotion ended. Both techniques can be effective in getting sufficient amounts of a new product into retail outlets or in getting a point-of-purchase display into a store.

Trade Deals

Trade deals, which are usually special price concessions, are the most important reseller sales promotion technique. Retailers are "on deal" when they agree to give the manufacturer's product a special promotional effort. These promotional efforts can take the form of special displays, extra purchases, superior store locations, or greater promotion. In return retailers receive special allowances, discounts, goods, cash, or credit on an invoice.

The money spent on trade deals is substantial. Experts estimate the amount is approximately $8 billion to $12 billion annually.[12] Some industries—such as grocery products, electronics, computers, and automobiles—expect trade deals. In fact, a manufacturer would find it impossible to compete in these industries without offering trade discounts, which often provide the primary incentive for retail support. The requirement to "deal" has become so prevalent that many marketers fear the deal is more important than either the value of the product or the expertise of the manufacturer in determining which products receive the greatest promotion.

There are two general types of trade deals. The first, referred to as **buying allowances,** is a type of trade deal in which a manufacturer pays a reseller a fixed amount of money for purchasing a certain amount of the product during a specified time period. All the retailer has to do is meet the purchase requirements. The payment may be a check from the manufacturer or a reduction in the face value of an invoice. The second category is advertising and display allowances, which we discuss in more detail in a moment.

Buying Allowances

One problem with buying allowances is **forward buying.** This practice, common in grocery retailing, means retailers buy more merchandise at the discounted price than they need during the deal period. They store the extra merchandise and bring it out after the sale period, selling it at regular prices.

Two types of buying allowances include the *slotting allowance* and the *free goods allowance.* The **slotting allowance,** a fee that retailers charge manufacturers for space the new product will occupy on the shelf, has become the most controversial form of buying allowance, as discussed in the You Decide feature. A **free goods allowance** is a certain amount of product offered to wholesalers or retailers at no cost if they purchase a stated amount of the same manufacturer's product. The reseller that buys the required amount of product is given free merchandise instead of money.

Advertising and Display Allowances

The two main types of advertising allowances are standard *advertising allowances* and *cooperative advertising allowances.* Used mainly in the consumer-products industry, an **advertising allowance** is a common promotion technique in which the manufacturer pays the wholesaler or retailer a certain amount of money for advertising the manufacturer's product. This allowance can be a flat dollar amount or it can be a percentage of gross purchases during a specified time period. A **cooperative advertising allowance** is a contractual arrangement between the manufacturer and the retailer in which the manufacturer agrees to pay part or all of the advertising expenses incurred by the retailer.

A **display allowance** involves a direct payment of cash or goods to the retailer if the retailer agrees to set up the display as specified. Why would manufacturers pay retailers for display space? Such space is a scarce resource. One trade publication reported that "it's very expensive real estate, and retailers have learned to use that real estate wisely by getting manufacturers to pay for it."[13]

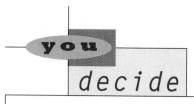

Do Slotting Fees Mean the Big Guys Always Win?

Are retailers ripping off marketers? Manufacturers feel that it doesn't matter anymore how good the product is or isn't. The only way a retailer will place a product on its shelves is if the manufacturer pays a slotting fee. That particularly limits small start-up companies who may not have the financial wherewithal to pay these fees. Manufacturers of all sizes, however, feel they are being held up for ransom by retailers. They also feel the balance of power in the manufacturer-retailer relationship has slipped too far in favor of the retailer.

Retailers argue that they must charge these fees because of small profit margins and product promotion costs. They claim also that introducing new products requires money to redesign shelves and reprogram computers. But grocery manufacturers accuse retailers of peddling their shelf space for extra money—trade deals pay for all the costs of shelving a product. For example, in the grocery industry approximately 60 percent of all manufacturers' sales are accompanied by a trade deal averaging about 12 percent of the manufacturer's recommended price. That amounts to some $27 billion in cash "incentives" marketers pay to get their products in the pipeline.

So how is the money from slotting fees used? One food industry source estimated that 70 percent of all slotting fees go directly to retail-ers' bottom lines. In other words, some retailers pocket the money instead of passing it on as savings to the consumer. Even if untrue, retailers suspected of pocketing the allowance money risk jeopardizing key relationships with resellers, such as retailers and manufacturers. They also risk jeopardizing relationships with customers.

However, the slotting fee problem doesn't just lie with retailers. In 1995 the FBI began investigating New England distribution intermediaries, such as brokers and sales promotion companies, on charges of fraud for bilking manufacturers for nonexistent retail promotions. The investigation resulted in the conviction of five brokers and one promotions supplier. The FBI is still conducting an ongoing investigation of large retailers who may have defrauded such big-name marketers as James River Paper Company, Tropicana Products, Van den Bergh Foods, and Cabot Creamery. The cost of this fraud? *Brandweek* estimates that as much as $4.2 billion in incentive money is "lost" every year.

Marketers are slowly seeking ways to balance power more equally with retailers. Many manufacturers and service providers are putting together promotional programs and pitching them directly to local store managers. Some are also proposing co-marketing programs to foster cooperation with retailers and are trying to manage retailing promotions more effectively. For instance, Procter & Gamble now has managers in charge of coordinating promotions for similar brands, such as Dash and Tide detergents, so that such promotions help retailers generate more business because they are well-timed and don't compete. Maybe the knots in the retailer-manufacturer relationship created by the slotting allowance will diminish through these efforts.

You Decide

1. What do you think? Should retailers be permitted to charge slotting fees? Should manufacturers refuse to pay them?
2. Do you think it's ethical for retailers to use the slotting fees to help their bottom line, rather than to pass savings on to consumers?
3. Slotting fees often stifle smaller, start-up businesses because many of these businesses can't afford to secure shelf space. Do you think that's simply the cost of doing business? Or do you think it's unfair discrimination? Explain.

Sources: Betsy Spethmann, "Trade Promotion Redefined," *Brandweek,* March 13, 1995, 25–32; Judann Dagnolie and Lauri Freeman, "Marketers Seek Slotting-Fee Truce," *Advertising Age,* February 22, 1988, 132; Keith M. Jones, "Held Hostage by the Trade?" *Advertising Age,* April 27, 1987, 18.

Trade deals have several advantages: They are flexible and can be changed from day to day, if necessary. They also can be combined with other promotional strategies to provide great impact. Ultimately, the willingness of retailers to carry and support a manufacturer's brands depends on the combination of the direct incentives offered to retailers and the promotions offered to consumers.

TRADE SALES PROMOTION: RESELLERS

1. A trade sales promotion is directed at resellers who distribute products to ultimate consumers.
2. The most common trade sales promotion techniques include:
   - Dealer contests
   - Trade coupons
   - Dealer loaders
   - Trade deals

TRADE SALES PROMOTION: SALES FORCE

Sales promotion targeted at the sales force is a crucial competitive weapon. It can help businesses introduce new products successfully, gain shelf space, and motivate resellers and sales personnel. Sales force promotions are intended to motivate salespeople to increase overall sales. Short-term goals may include securing new dealers or retailers, promoting sales of new or seasonal items, communicating special deals to retailers, and increasing order size.

In general these activities build enthusiasm. Often they are aimed as much at raising the morale of the sales force as at creating a sale. Why? Enthusiastic salespeople usually work harder at supporting the marketing effort.

Sales promotion activities directed at the sales force are classified into two categories: **supportive programs** that prepare salespeople to do their jobs and **motivational promotions** designed to encourage salespeople to work harder.

Supportive Programs

Supportive programs are used in training or are used to educate experienced salespeople and to equip them with materials for sales presentations. Examples of such materials include sales manuals, portfolios, models, slides, films, videos, and other visual aids.

One of the most common supportive programs is the **sales meeting,** an educational meeting that can bring together a local, regional, national, or international sales force. The meetings mix business and pleasure in varying proportions. Although social elements are important and can motivate people, training and educational elements tend to be more meaningful. In-house publications such as a newsletter are also useful in relaying information about new products, meetings, awards, schedules and deadlines, announcements, and sales ideas.

Sales kits contain sales manuals with background information, details about other elements of the promotional effort, or detailed product specifications. Sales kits are critical promotional tools that educate and assist salespeople with product presentations. Today much sales information is computerized so that sales representatives can access it any time by modem through a groupware software program, such as Lotus Notes, shared by the salesperson and the organization. Computerized sales kits make it possible for the sales representative to custom design presentations for customers.

Motivational Programs

Contests dominate motivational programs. The incentive in a contest is generally a prize or award for those who demonstrate excellent sales performance. Affiliated Paper Company of Tuscaloosa, Alabama, for example, offers as its primary incentive world-class travel—ranging from trips to Disney World, an African safari, or a trip around the world.

Honorary clubs and cash awards may also be used to motivate the sales force. A "sales honors club" may reward teamwork, such as a president's club, which is used in a number of industries to reward sales teams and increase sales. **Push money** is an extra payment given to salespeople for meeting a specified sales goal. For example, a manufacturer of air conditioners might offer a $10 bonus for the sale of model EJ1, $20 for model EJ19, and $25 for model EX3 between April 1 and October 1. At the end of that period, salespeople send in evidence of total sales to the air conditioner manufacturer so they can receive a check for the appropriate amount. Although push money has a negative image because it hints of bribery, many businesses offer it as an incentive to the sales staff and to motivate outside salespeople and resellers.

TRADE SALES PROMOTION: SALES FORCE

1. Sales force promotions are used to support and to motivate salespeople to increase overall sales.
2. Sales force promotions include:
  - Supportive programs that include sales kits and sales meetings
  - Motivational programs such as contests, honorary clubs, and push money

CONSUMER SALES PROMOTION

Consumer sales promotions are directed at the ultimate users of the product. Users can be consumers or businesses. The "Color of Money" case at the end of this chapter, for example, illustrates how sales promotion is used in business-to-business marketing.

Typically, these promotions focus on products used by individuals, especially products sold in the local supermarket and drugstore. Consumer sales promotions are intended to "presell" consumers so that when people visit a store they will look for a particular brand. Table 10.6 identifies some common consumer sales promotions, their objectives, and their methods of distribution. The following section describes some of the key techniques used to encourage people to take action.

Price Deals

A consumer price deal saves customers money when they purchase a product. Price deals are commonly used to encourage trial of a new product, to persuade existing users to buy more or at a different time, or to convince new users to try an established product. They are effective only if price is an important factor in brand choice or if consumers are not brand loyal. For instance, soft drinks, laun-

TABLE 10.6

Consumer Sales Promotion Techniques

Technique	Objective	Method of Distribution
Price Deals		
Price discounts	Stimulate incremental and trial purchases, increase purchases per transaction	Point of purchase, mass media, cents-off deal, bonus pack, banded pack
Coupons	Stimulate trial purchases, increase frequency of purchases, encourage multiple purchases, motivate resellers, encourage consumer trade up	Sales force, direct mail, newspapers, magazines, FSIs, in-pack or on-pack
Refunds and rebates	Stimulate trial purchases, encourage multiple purchases	Sales force, direct mail, mass media, in-pack or on-pack
Contests and sweepstakes	Encourage multiple purchases, enhance brand image, create enthusiasm	Sales force, mass media, direct mail
Premiums	Add value, encourage multiple purchases, stimulate trial purchases	Store premiums, in-pack or on-pack, proof of purchase, container premiums, self-liquidator, continuity-coupon plan, free-in-the-mail premium
Samples	Stimulate trial purchases, encourage consumer trade up	In-pack or on-pack, direct mail, magazines, point of purchase
Continuity programs	Maintain consumer loyalty	Sales force, mass media, direct mail

dry detergents, paper products, and diapers are types of products that use price promotions effectively. We explore three kinds of price deals: price discounts, coupons, and refunds and rebates.

Price Discounts

The two main types of consumer price discounts are *cents-off deals* and *price-pack deals*. A **cents-off deal** is a reduction in the normal price charged for a good or service (for example, "was $1000, now $500," or "50 percent off"). Cents-off deals can be announced at the point of sale or through mass or direct advertising. Point-of-sale announcements include the package itself and signs near the product or elsewhere in the store. The manufacturer, the wholesaler, or the retailer can initiate both types of cents-off deals.

Price-pack deals provide the consumer with something extra through the package itself. There are two types of pack deals: *bonus packs* and *banded packs*. **Bonus packs** contain additional amounts of the product free when the standard size is purchased at the regular price. For example, Purina Dog Food may offer

25 percent more dog food in the bag. Often this technique is used to introduce a new large-size package of the product. A **banded pack** is a pack that offers one or more units of a product sold at a reduced price compared with the regular single-unit price. Sometimes the products are physically banded together. Bar soap, such as Dial, is often offered this way.

Coupons

Legal certificates offered by manufacturers and retailers that grant specified savings on selected products when presented for redemption at the point of purchase are called **coupons.** Manufacturer-sponsored coupons can be redeemed at any outlet distributing the product. Retailer-sponsored coupons can only be redeemed at the specified retail outlet. The primary advantage of the manufacturer-sponsored coupon is that it allows the advertiser to lower prices without relying on cooperation from the retailer.

Up to 77 percent of U.S. households use coupons to some degree, many of them saving as much as $1000 a year.[14] Coupons represent a $96 billion industry. According to a study conducted by the Food Marketing Institute, coupon usage varies:

- Shoppers who live in the East and Midwest are most likely to use coupons.
- One-person households are the most infrequent coupon users.
- The most avid coupon users are those with a high school education or less and those in the $15,000 to $25,000 annual income bracket.
- Only 32 percent of shoppers under age 24 use coupons.[15]

This coupon for Healthy Choice's Hearty Handfuls is a manufacturer's coupon that was distributed in a Healthy Choice product package.

Manufacturer-sponsored coupons can be distributed directly (direct mail, door-to-door), through media (newspaper and magazine ads, freestanding inserts), in or on the package itself, or through the retailer (cooperative advertising). Manufacturers pay retailers a fee for handling their coupons.

The latest trends in retailing are online coupons and in-store coupons delivered from shelf dispensers or on the back of the sales receipt. The receipt coupons often link the consumer's purchases to coupons in related product categories. Online coupon services such as Money Mailer, a company that mails coupons to homes, offer coupon databases. The Money Mailer site, H.O.T! Coupons, contains a database of millions of coupons for local, regional, and national consumer products and services (www.hotcoupons.com).

Marketers are finding ways to target coupons more carefully.[16] In fact, coupons are becoming the cornerstone of some of today's database marketing programs. Using some of the more sophisticated data-tracking programs, marketers can determine who in a given household bought which product when and at what store—and sometimes even which TV commercial prompted the purchase.

There are several disadvantages associated with coupons. Although more than 90 percent of consumer product marketers use coupons, the redemption rate is only 2.3 percent for those delivered through FSIs, and 4 to 6 percent for those delivered through direct mail. Depending on the product category, between 60 to 90 percent of coupons are delivered through freestanding inserts, however insert fees (the fees newspapers charge for inserting FSIs) are increasing dramatically, making coupon distribution very expensive.

Another problem is misredemption (accidentally or intentionally misredeeming coupons) and, finally, fraud (counterfeit coupons).[17] Experts estimate that coupon fraud is a $1 billion a year problem for retailers and manufacturers.

Refunds and Rebates

Simply stated, a **refund** is an offer by the marketer to return a certain amount of money to the consumer who purchases the product. A **rebate** means essentially the same thing as refund. Unlike price discounts, evidence suggests that consumers consider refunds and rebates a reward for purchase. This after-the-fact experience appears to build brand loyalty rather than diminish it. Refunds are attractive because they stimulate sales without the high cost and waste associated with coupons.

Most refunds encourage product purchase by creating a deadline. General information of the refund program may be delivered through broadcast media. Details are usually distributed through print media or direct mail. The refund may take the form of a cash rebate plus a low-value coupon for the same product or other company products, a high-value coupon alone, or a coupon good toward the brand purchased plus several other brands in the manufacturer's line.

The disadvantage of rebate and refund programs is that consumers may view them as a nuisance. In a 1992 survey 85 percent of the respondents stated that they would rather use a coupon valued at $1 than send in for a refund worth $2. Furthermore, only 40 percent had taken the time to mail in a refund over the past year, compared with more than 70 percent who regularly use coupons.[18]

Contests and Sweepstakes

The popularity of contests and sweepstakes grew dramatically during the 1980s and 1990s. These strategies create excitement by promising "something for nothing" and offering impressive prizes. Consumer **contests** are promotions that require consumers to compete for a prize or prizes on the basis of some sort of skill or ability; that is, participants must perform some task. A **sweepstakes** is a random drawing that only requires participants to submit their names for inclusion in a drawing or other chance selection. A **game** is a type of sweepstakes. It differs from a one-shot sweepstakes drawing in that the time frame is much longer. A continuity is established, requiring customers to return several times to acquire additional pieces (such as bingo-type games) or to improve their chances of winning.

A good contest or sweepstakes generates a high degree of consumer involvement that can revive lagging sales, provide merchandising excitement for dealers and salespeople, give vitality and a theme to advertising, and create interest in a low-interest product. If handled improperly, contests and sweepstakes can tarnish a company's image. To illustrate, consider the bad publicity Publishers' Clearing House endured after New York City trash collectors discovered approximately 2000 completed sweepstakes envelopes and entry forms strewn along the railroad tracks in the borough of Queens. The dumping activity prompted Publishers' Clearing House to set up a new facility for opening envelopes and removing entry forms.[19]

Premiums

The toy in the Cracker Jacks box is an example of a premium, a tangible reward for the person who buys the product.

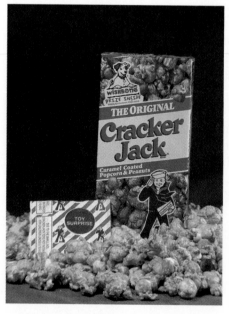

A **premium** is a tangible reward given to consumers for performing a particular act, usually purchasing a product or visiting the point of purchase. The premium may be free. If not, the amount the consumer pays for it is well below market price as was the case in the Pizza Hut promotion featured in the IMC in Action box. The toy in Cracker Jacks and the offer of a free atlas with the purchase of insurance are examples of premiums. Companies spend over $17 billion on premiums, with $6.7 billion devoted to consumer premiums.

Direct and *mail premiums* are the two general types of consumer premiums. **Direct premiums** provide the incentive immediately, at the time of purchase. The four categories of direct premiums include:

1. *Store premiums:* premiums given to customers at the retail site
2. *In-packs:* premiums inserted in the package at the factory
3. *On-packs:* premiums placed on the outside of the package at the factory
4. *Container premiums:* the package is the premium

In contrast, **mail premiums** require the customer to take some action before receiving the premium, such as sending in proof-of-purchase seals. Bausch & Lomb generated trial and purchase of its contact lenses by giving away sunglasses as premium incentives. The company gave eyecare practitioners sunglasses certificates to distribute to consumers who purchased Bausch & Lomb contact lenses. Consumers then sent their certificates to Bausch & Lomb to redeem the free sunglasses.

Pizza Hut Scores Big

Sports is big in the promotion world because it attracts interested sports fans. Pizza Hut used a self-liquidating promotion to leverage its multiyear sponsorship of the NCAA men's basketball championship. The promotion featured a designer Rawlings basketball that had "streetwise" graphics and NCAA logos on the exterior. In one year nearly 4 million basketballs were redeemed at a cost of $4.99 with a pizza purchase (in-store, carry-out, or delivery), making Pizza Hut the country's number one basketball retailer and a winner in *Promo*'s "1995 Top Ten Pre-mium Promotions of the Past Ten Years."

In terms of trade support, each retailer received a free basketball and other incentives, including chances to win NCAA apparel and tournament tickets. On the consumer side, Pizza Hut supported the campaign with point-of-purchase materials, print ads, direct mail, TV and radio spots, and tie-ins with *Sports Illustrated*. But what made the campaign so integrated was its association with the NCAA basketball championship, a special event that has high awareness among Pizza Hut's audience.

Food for Thought

1. Why are consumer promotions so important in sports marketing? Likewise, why do you think sports tie-ins are so attractive for promotional planners?

2. What should Pizza Hut do for its next sports-related promotion? Outline your ideas for a new campaign. Should the company stick with basketball or move to some other sport?

Sources: Jeff Jensen, "Promotional Marketer of the Year: NFL," *Advertising Age,* March 4, 1996, S1–S2; Daniel Shannon, "Turning the Tube On," *Promo* (October 1995): 45–52; Blair R. Fischer, "The Top Ten Premium Promotions of the Past Ten Years," *Promo* (May 1995): 17–21.

A **self-liquidator** is a type of premium that requires consumers to mail in a payment before receiving the premium. Star-Kist Foods, for example, offers a Morris-the-Cat T-shirt. The payment is usually sufficient to cover the cost of the item, handling, mailing, packaging, and taxes, if any. Generally, a self-liquidator costs the marketer very little. The food industry is the largest user of self-liquidating premiums, as are industries that sell detergents, cleansers, toiletries, and beverages.

The **continuity-coupon plan** is another type of mail premium. It requires the customer to save coupons or special labels attached to the product that can be redeemed for merchandise. Cigarette and diaper manufacturers have used continuity-coupon plans.

The final type of mail premium is the **free-in-the-mail premium.** With this type of premium, the customer mails the advertiser a purchase request and proof of purchase. For example, Procter & Gamble offered a premium that was a discount on a down comforter with a proof of purchase of White Cloud toilet paper. An advantage of free-in-the-mail premiums is their ability to enhance an advertising campaign or a brand image by association with a desirable product or brand name.

Sampling

One of the keys to success for many marketers is getting the product into the hands of the consumer. Allowing the consumer to experience the product or service free of charge or for a small fee is called **sampling.** It is a very effective strategy for introducing a new or modified product or for dislodging an entrenched market leader. To be successful, the product sampled must virtually sell itself due to unique features and be able to create a positive impact with minimal trial experience.

Samples can be distributed to consumers in several ways, such as through the mail or door to door. Advertisers can design ads with coupons for free samples, place samples in special packages, or distribute samples at special in-store displays. The Body Shop has taken its health and beauty products on the road with an 18-wheeler containing a miniature Body Shop that traveled across the United States, stopping at college campuses, malls, various socially responsible events like the March of Dimes Walk-a-thon, and various environmental events. Salespeople on the truck gave out coupons and catalogs and did makeovers and massages to demonstrate the products.[20]

In general retailers and manufacturers maintain that sampling can boost sales volume as much as five to ten times during a product demonstration and 10 to 15 percent thereafter. Sampling is generally most effective when reinforced at the same time with product coupons. Most consumers like sampling because they do not lose any money if they do not like the product.

Continuity Programs

The intent of a continuity program is to keep people using a brand by offering ongoing incentives that reward them for their loyalty. A continuity program like the AT&T True Rewards or an airline frequent flyer program requires the consumer to continue purchasing the product or service to receive the benefit or reward. Typically, the higher the purchase level, the greater the benefits.

This ad for AT&T features a continuity program that offers rewards for continuous use of its services.

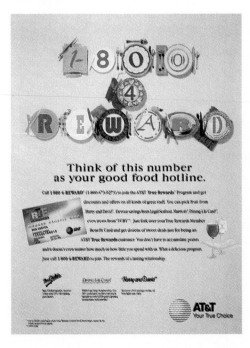

In the 1950s and 1960s, the popular type of continuity program was trading stamps. Today continuity programs are synonymous with the word "frequent." Frequent flier clubs sponsored by airlines are the model of a modern continuity program. They offer a variety of rewards, including seat upgrades, free tickets, and premiums based on the number of frequent flier miles accumulated.

Continuity programs work in very competitive situations where the consumer has difficulty perceiving real differences between brands. For example, in a joint continuity program, American Airlines offered College Savings Bank's College Sure Certificate of Deposit (CD) as a premium for the airline's AAdvantage frequent flier members. The CD, designed to help parents save for their children's college education, has a lower price (about $16,400 per unit, rather than $18,000) and higher yield (minimum interest rate of 5 percent) than the bank's standard CDs (4 percent).[21]

There are other techniques that are sometimes referred to as sales promotions such as specialties, event sponsorship, and licensing. These are cross-over marketing communication methods that are also used as part of other programs, such as advertising or public relations. We will discuss them in more detail in Chapter 14.

Although price deals, contests and sweepstakes, premiums, sampling, and continuity programs can be effective alone, they can also be combined to create tremendous impact. For instance, Nestlé positioned three of its products—Raisinets®, Goobers®, and Crunch™—as the "Home Video Candy" in a promotion where consumers could redeem a mail-in certificate with any VCR movie rental receipt along with proof of purchase and receive a $2 cash rebate. The certificate was available in freestanding inserts and at point-of-purchase displays, and the three candy products were packaged in a take-home pack.

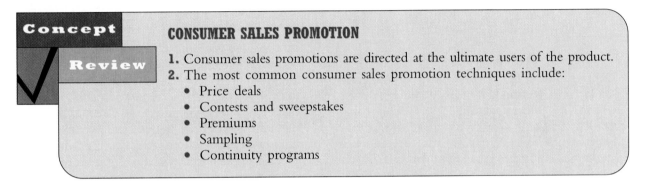

Concept
Review

CONSUMER SALES PROMOTION

1. Consumer sales promotions are directed at the ultimate users of the product.
2. The most common consumer sales promotion techniques include:
   - Price deals
   - Contests and sweepstakes
   - Premiums
   - Sampling
   - Continuity programs

A CLOSING THOUGHT: WORKING THE PROMOTION PUZZLE

Sales promotion is a diverse area of marketing communication. Trying to become an expert on all aspects of sales promotion may be unrealistic, and special skills in certain areas may be best learned on the job. In integrated marketing communication programs, sales promotion skills remain the most difficult for advertising specialists to master. Of course, this difficulty may be due partly to the historical differences in the creative philosophies between the two marketing communication areas. As long as advertisers feel that sales promotion denigrates the brand and steals dollars from them, cooperation and synergy are unlikely. Yet, sales promotion will continue to grow as a marketing communication alternative. Whether it will diminish the importance of advertising is still debatable, but certainly the variety of sales promotion options have changed the marketing communication landscape.

SUMMARY

1. Define sales promotion and discuss its purpose.

Sales promotion is a marketing communication tool that uses a variety of incentive techniques for consumers, trade, and the sales force to generate a specific, measurable action or response. It is designed to offer an extra incentive to consumers or resellers, something that gives the product or service additional value, and stimulates immediate action.

2. Explain how sales promotion fits in the marketing communication mix and how it can be used in an IMC program.

Sales promotion is used in the marketing communication mix to help implement push and pull strategies, to introduce new products, and to build brands. Integrated marketing communicators often combine sales promotion with other marketing communication tools to create a powerful synergy.

3. Outline how sales promotion strategies differ for trade and consumer target audiences.

Sales promotion strategies may be directed at consumer audiences or trade audiences that include resellers and the sales force. Trade promotions designed to build support among resellers and the sales force help "push" the product. Consumer sales promotions directed at the ultimate users of the product are designed to "pull" the product through the channel of distribution.

4. Compare and contrast the techniques used for and the objectives of reseller, sales force, and consumer promotions.

Promotions designed for trade and consumer audiences use different techniques to accomplish different objectives. Techniques used in trade promotions for resellers include point-of-purchase materials, dealer contests, trade shows, dealer loaders, and trade deals of various types. These techniques help garner support for a product and can build a relationship with the manufacturer or service provider. Sales force promotions are intended to increase the productivity of the sales staff through motivation (contests, prizes, and push money) and support for sales force efforts (training, sales meetings, sales manuals, visual aids, newsletters). Sales promotions directed at consumers include price deals (price discounts, coupons, and refunds and rebates), contests and sweepstakes, premiums (direct and self-liquidating), sampling, and continuity programs. The objectives of these promotions are to stimulate trial or repeat purchase, increase the number of purchases, enhance brand image and consumer loyalty, and add value to the product.

POINTS TO PONDER

Review the Facts

1. What is sales promotion?
2. Define trade members.
3. List the main strengths and weaknesses of sales promotion techniques.
4. How do the objectives of trade and consumer sales promotions differ?
5. Describe the various consumer price deals and the role they play in promotion.

Master the Concepts

6. What are the broad goals of sales promotion for each of its target audiences, and how do these goals differ from those of advertising? How are they the same?
7. When should sales promotion and advertising be used in combination?
8. One agency executive was quoted as saying: "Advertising is on its way out. All consumers want is a deal. Sales promotion is the place to be." What do you think this executive meant? Do you agree or disagree?
9. Your promotional strategy professor is covering some sales promotion methods. Your professor explains that when selecting consumer sales promotions, planners must know the brand situation

and objectives before choosing techniques, because some increase product use and others increase new consumer trial. Which methods do you think increase product use, and which increase new consumer trial? Explain.

10. Under what conditions should price deals be used?

11. What types of sales promotion are available to a small manufacturer that must develop a cooperative channel of distribution?

12. Explain the problems associated with slotting allowances. How can businesses avoid paying slotting fees?

13. Which type of sales incentive is best? Explain your answer.

Apply Your Knowledge

14. Allison Wilson is a brand manager for a new line of cosmetics being introduced by Sears called Circle of Beauty. She is about to present her planning strategy to division management. Wilson knows her company has been successful in using sales promotion plans, but she has strong misgivings about following the company trend. "This new line must develop a strong consumer brand identity—and promotion isn't the best way to do that," she thinks to herself. What is a weakness of sales promotion in "developing brand identity"? Should Wilson propose no promotion, or is there a reasonable compromise for her to consider?

15. Alltech Product's sales promotion manager, Mary Lincoln, is calculating the cost of a proposed consumer coupon for March. The media cost and production charges for the freestanding coupon insert are $125,000. The distribution will be 4 million coupons with an expected redemption of 5 percent. The coupon value is 50 cents, and Lincoln has estimated the handling and retailer compensation costs to be 8 cents per redeemed coupon. Based on these estimates, what will be the cost to Lincoln's budget?

SUGGESTED PROJECTS

1. (Oral and Written Communication) Review your local newspaper to identify a retailer who is engaging in cooperative advertising. Interview a store manager for that retailer and determine the specific arrangements that exist between the advertiser and the retailer. What is the attitude of the retailer toward this arrangement? Write a two-page report on the effectiveness of cooperative advertising for this retailer.

2. You have just been named product manager for Puffs toilet paper, a new line-extension product that will be introduced to the market within the next six months. What type of sales promotion strategy would work best for this product? Outline a sales promotion plan for the launch.

3. (Internet and Team Project) Form small groups of 2 to 4 students. Assume your group has been asked to create an online sales promotion strategy for the Puffs toilet paper product mentioned in Project 2.

As background research, you've been asked to examine the H.O.T! Coupons home page (www.hotcoupons.com), the Crayola Web site (www.crayola.com), and at least one other Web site to see how online sales promotion differs from more traditional sales promotion. Each team member should visit three sites to analyze how effectively the businesses use couponing, sweepstakes and contests, and other sales promotion techniques. Meet to discuss your findings and plan a basic online sales promotion strategy.

4. Assume you are a marketing manager for a medium-sized manufacturer of electrical components used in computers. You wish to expand your market from the New England states to the entire eastern seaboard. You have a sales force of six people and will expand it to fifteen. Outline an incentive program that would motivate these new salespeople, as well as the old ones.

CASE 10: THE COLOR OF MONEY

A.B. Dick, a Chicago manufacturer of duplicating machines, used an integrated marketing communication program to launch itself into the full-size printing press market. Its integrated marketing communication program combined every possible tool from sales promotion to specialties to product videos.

The problem was that the company was considered a leader in duplicating equipment, not as a printing press manufacturer. To succeed it had to make its audience aware of its printing press business by changing consumers' perceptions. Change in this market was an uphill battle. A.B. Dick made its move in late 1992 into the new market with its Century 3000 two-color printing press. The company targeted three markets for the Century 3000: small printers moving into color printing, in-plant printers who do printing jobs in-house for their companies, and large commercial printers who wanted a press for short-run color printing. The Century's position was to handle jobs that were either too large for a small printer or too small for a big one.

Using Tucker Chicago, an IMC agency that serves midsize and Fortune 500 business-to-business marketers, the company launched a high-profile campaign. All the pieces shared a creative theme adapted from the Paul Newman/Tom Cruise movie, *The Color of Money.* Why this theme? Tucker president, Bob Tucker, explained that the idea of color ties in with printers who are tremendously concerned about color reproduction. In addition, it carried the timeless business-to-business appeal of making money. The theme promised a product that could generate new revenue streams in return for a relatively modest investment.

In an unusual move the centerpiece of Tucker's integrated campaign was a six-minute video that illustrated the capabilities of the Century 3000. Although Paul Newman didn't star in the video, it did effectively associate the campaign with the movie. The new printing press was introduced to trade reporters at a special *Color of Money* press event and was also introduced to trade audiences at subsequent in-office sales presentations.

Tucker kicked off a two-year trade ad campaign with a two-page spread in industry publications. The ads carried a direct-response form offering the free video. After the product was launched, the print campaign moved to testimonials with printers describing new uses they found for the press. These word-of-mouth success stories were relayed to the A.B. Dick marketing manager by field salespeople.

Direct mail with promotional offers was used to highlight the video. Printers received a *Color of Money* poster the first week of the direct-mail campaign. The next week they got an oversized $100 bill accompanied with copy about making "big bucks." The third week they received the video along with a package of microwave popcorn and a business reply card that read, "The movie was great, but I want to see the Century 3000 in action." Those who replied received a live demonstration from a salesperson. The field salespeople knew when the direct-mail campaign began, and were given copies of each mail piece to take on sales calls. A.B. Dick mailed 12,000 copies of the video during the three-year campaign. At the request of the sales staff, the marketing department also customized direct-mail pieces for targeted individual prospects. For example, one salesperson used a custom mailing to the public schools in his territory and another to churches.

A *Color of Money* newsletter was distributed to salespeople and customers to promote success stories and new uses of the press. In keeping with the movie-inspired theme, A.B. Dick sent out sunglasses to the "star" printers featured in the newsletter and the ads.

The payoff from the continuing *Color of Money* campaign is the development of a sophisticated database of prospect information. The leads come from the reply card on the video and from incoming faxes responding to direct-mail and advertising pieces. These leads were then sent to the telemarketing department where telemarketers called the prospects, asked more about their needs, and identified the key decision makers. This information was entered into the database and then given to the field sales representatives. The loop was closed when the salespeople responded on the status of the leads and fed more specific customer information into the database that could be used to polish the marketing efforts.

What this integrated program all added up to was the color of new money for A.B. Dick's business.

Case Questions

1. Develop a proposal for additional trade promotions that could tie-in with the *Color of Money* theme.
2. What would you recommend as a sales force promotion that would support this *Color of Money* theme?
3. This is a business-to-business case, but it still uses customer sales promotion as part of its integrated marketing communication strategy. What are the customer sales promotions used in this case, and what others would you recommend for next year's campaign?
4. How many different areas of marketing communication are included in this campaign? Which ones are missing?

Sources: "Printing Money," *Sales & Marketing Management* (February 1995): 64–9; Bill Robinson and Alan Maites, "Promotion vs. Direct: Who Should Win?" *Potentials in Marketing* (May 1995): 70–2.

ROMA'S LITE INTEGRATED CASE QUESTIONS

(Review the Roma's Lite Marketing Plan in the Appendix before answering these questions.)

1. What are the strengths and weaknesses of sales promotion, and how could this marketing communication tool apply to the launch of this new pizza product?
2. What type(s) of sales promotion strategies could be used to launch Roma's Lite Pizza? How could they be used in combination with the advertising you proposed to help launch Roma's Lite Pizza in Chapter 9?
3. (Team and Writing Project) In small groups of about 4 to 6 people, develop a sales promotion program for the launch of Roma's Lite Pizza for each of your target audiences. Assign someone to take notes. Have the group draft a memo that describes who your target audiences will be, how your objectives will differ for each audience, and how your strategy will differ. Then detail how the sales promotion program will work with the advertising program.

chapter

11

Public Relations

1 **Define public relations and explain its purpose.**

2 **Identify the strengths and weaknesses of public relations.**

3 **Distinguish between internal and external stakeholders.**

4 **Explain seven types of public relations programs.**

5 **Outline the steps in the public relations research and planning process.**

6 **Discuss the role of public relations in an integrated marketing communication program.**

7 **Describe the tools used in public relations programs.**

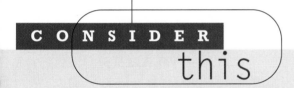

CONSIDER this

Gillette Launches Sensor with an Explosion of Publicity

As discussed in Chapter 9, Gillette is an excellent example of a marketer that understands the effectiveness of integrated marketing communication. Gillette's product launches also illustrate the important role public relations plays in an IMC program. The Porter/Novelli public relations agency leads most Gillette product launch campaigns and works closely with other agencies such as BBDO advertising to establish the market. The coordination between marketing communication agencies coupled with an integrated approach have helped secure Gillette's position as market leader in the shaving industry.

After Gillette succeeded in repositioning its brand under the "Best A Man Can Get" campaign, it continued to have success throughout the 1990s, introducing sev-

eral new products—the Sensor, the Sensor Prestige Series in sterling and platinum, the Sensor for Women, the new SensorExcel, and Cool Wave and Wild Rain men's toiletries. All these products were launched first with public relations campaigns, supported by advertising, and, followed in some cases, by sales promotion and direct-marketing campaigns.

Let's look inside the Sensor launch, which was the pioneering effort, to see how public relations was used to drive a successful integrated international program. After months of joint planning meetings and idea sessions, Sensor was introduced on Super Bowl Sunday in January 1990 with the launch of its advertising campaign. Before that, however, massive publicity generated announcements and special stories on such major programs as *CBS News,* the NBC *Today* show, and the *Tonight Show,* and hundreds of stories in newspapers and magazines around the world and in Europe. The launch was handled simultaneously in 19 countries. The Sensor shaving system had been more than ten years in development and cost more than $200 million to create. Because of Gillette's takeover battles in late 1980, the media covered both the corporate and the new product stories heavily, keeping Gillette and its brands in the public eye.

According to an analyst for Prudential-Bache, the Sensor was "the single most successful consumer non-durable product introduction in the history of the planet." They may sound like hyperbole, but Sensor claimed 6 percent of the market in a little more than six months, selling some 17 million razors in that period, which was twice what the company had forecasted. Gillette stock soared almost 30 percent in the same six months. Surprisingly, the marketing communication had to be cut back because Gillette had trouble meeting demand.

The reason the PR campaign worked so well, according to Bill Novelli, president of Porter/Novelli, was because of the number of different story angles. "The financial media was interested in the corporate story; the marketing press was interested in the marketing story because of the size of the budget and the fact that it was an integrated international launch; the technology writers were interested in the technology because Gillette had taken out 22 patents to make the Sensor work; and the consumer media was interested in the consumer story."

Gillette worked with Porter/Novelli, BBDO, and other Omnicom agencies that specialized in direct mail, sales promotion, packaging, and sales meetings. It also worked with 17 of these agencies' international affiliates. Porter/Novelli's affiliated agency, the U.K.–based Countrywide, headed the European PR launch effort. Such a high level of integration is unusual in corporate communications and is rare in product marketing. The Gillette marketing manager concluded that "PR was a key part of our strategy," but, he says, "we were not really prepared for the level of success it achieved."

Sources: Pablo Galarza, "Nicked and Cut," *Financial World,* April 8, 1996, 39; "To Launch in the United States, European Success Fuels U.S. Introduction," *Business Wire,* October 4, 1994; "The Best a Plan Can Get," *The Economist,* August 15, 1992, 59–61; Gary Levin, "Direct Mail Program Helps Gillette Drive Growth of Sensor Razor," *Advertising Age,* October 21, 1991, 24; "After a Close Shave, Cutting Edge Technology," *Inside PR,* September, 1990, 2; "Gillette Mocks Critics with Sensor Sales, *USA Today,* 12 August 1990, 1B; "Gillette Sensor," campaign handout from Porter/Novelli.

CHAPTER OVERVIEW

As the chapter opener shows, public relations (PR) is a vital element in marketing communication. We begin by exploring what public relations is and the way it analyzes its "publics." Then we examine types of public relations programs, how managers plan an effective public relations program, and PR's role in a comprehensive marketing communication program. Finally, we investigate the many tools of public relations.

WHAT IS PUBLIC RELATIONS?

The concepts of "public" and "relations" are both important to public relations. **Publics** are all the audiences that the marketing communicator targets to receive messages about the company or who are perceived as influencing opinions about the company. The term *relations* signals that these publics are involved in a relationship with the company. That relationship should be positive to ensure an effective business operation.

Most companies are unwilling to leave their corporate image and reputation to chance. Instead, they try to create goodwill and control their image through public relations activities. As Walter W. Seifert, former president of the Public Relations Society of America (PRSA) noted many years ago, "The public relations expert is as necessary as any other firefighter. But long before the fire begins, he is needed to build a backlog of goodwill that minimizes misadventures."[1]

The growth of public relations during the last five decades has been tremendous. Among the top 300 companies in the United States in 1936, only one out of fifty had a full-fledged public relations department. Today, the ratio is three out of four. The number of people in PR work has been estimated as high as 145,000. The number of PR jobs is increasing faster than jobs for any other management function.[2] Growth from 1988 through the early 1990s increased at 18 to 20 percent for the PR industry, compared with 7 percent for advertising.

Although PR agencies noted some downturns during the recession in the early 1990s, revenues have been good in the mid and late 1990s. For the fiscal year 1995, ten of the top 16 PR agencies reported double-digit growth and six of them managed better than 20 percent.[3] The reason for the growth is that public relations is a powerful communication tool because of its emphasis on public opinion, relationships, and corporate credibility—and its cost-effectiveness. The critical issue is no longer whether to do public relations, but how to do it well.

THE ROLE OF PUBLIC RELATIONS

Public relations tells an organization's story to publics to foster goodwill and understanding. Public relations practitioners help shape the company's practices by counseling top management on public opinion and issues, and on the positive and negative implications of certain behaviors. They also determine the concerns and expectations of the organization's various publics and explain them to senior management. In summary, **public relations** is the use and communication of information through a variety of media to influence public opinion.

Monitoring attitudes and public opinion is an important part of PR's role. A survey of American institutions by PR agency Porter/Novelli identified the levels of credibility that different institutions enjoy. The survey also spotlighted a widespread level of public cynicism. Table 11.1 shows the highlights of the survey results.

Another function of public relations is to plan how to handle communication about crises before they occur or how to handle unpredictable crises in a quick and careful way. For example, as discussed in Chapter 4, Odwalla faced serious public relations challenges in 1996 when the *E. coli* bacteria was traced to its apple juice products. It had no plan for dealing with the huge volume of inquiries from customers, retailers, and the media but quickly established a Web site and hotline to respond to questions. It also held informational press conferences and responded carefully and speedily to FDA regulators and to victims and their families.

Strengths of Public Relations

Public relations has a number of strengths. First, public relations targets and manages relationships with important stakeholders. Second, public relations can reach difficult-to-reach audiences, such as opinion leaders and upscale consumers. Many of these people devote time to reading publications and watching or listening to news programs, but they are uninterested in advertising, are highly likely to dispose of direct mail, and have assistants who screen out sales calls. Publicity presented through the news media can more effectively reach this group.

Third, public relations professionals, ever-sensitive to public opinion, can advise clients and companies on the implications of trends and corporate activities.

TABLE 11.1

**Credibility of American
Institutions**

Institution	% Rated Believable
Television and newspapers	46
Consumer advocates	41
Computer industry	37
Internet	28
Pharmaceutical industry	28
Public utilities	26
Food companies	25
Airline industry	22
Chemical manufacturers, oil companies, managed care industry	10
PR firms	10
Government	8
Advertising agencies	6
Tobacco industry	6

Source: "Survey Highlights 'Age of Cynicism' But Finds Most Keep an Open Mind," *Inside PR,* July 15, 1996, 1, 3.

Fourth, public relations specialists can present the company as a good citizen through careful relationship management and monitoring of an organization's reputation and corporate image. Fifth, they can plan how to handle crises, thereby minimizing negative effects on the organization's reputation. Sixth, public relations offers a business more message flexibility compared with advertising and sales promotion because the laws governing news releases are less strict than for those regulating advertising of all forms.

Seventh, PR adds credibility and believability because target audiences usually consider news stories to be more objective than other marketing communications that are developed, presented, and paid for by a sponsor. Eighth, public relations breaks through clutter more effectively than other marketing communication areas because people are more willing to believe a news message than a commercial message. Finally, public relations is relatively cost-effective because news coverage, if warranted, is free.

Weaknesses of Public Relations

Public relations also has three main weaknesses. First is the lack of control over how stories are covered. Business information released to the media may not be

TABLE 11.2

Strengths and Weaknesses of Public Relations

Strengths	Weaknesses
Reaches stakeholders other than consumers—employees, community leaders, legislators and regulators, financial community, and special-interest groups	Lack of control over how the story gets covered
Reaches hard-to-reach targets, such as upscale opinion leaders	Subject to others' approval for news story to run
Can advise company/client on image issues	Bottom-line impact is difficult to measure
Establishes corporate-citizen role	
Proactive—can plan for crises	
More message flexibility due to fewer legal restrictions	
Adds credibility/believability	
Can break through "ad clutter"	
Low costs	

used by the press as the company intended, especially because the press has access to other information sources. Second is the inability to control which stories receive coverage. Editors and producers act as "gatekeepers," which means they decide what gets into the newspaper, magazine, or news program. If editors or producers feel that a story released by a company doesn't have enough news value, they don't have to use it. For instance, on a day during which many newsworthy events happen, the business story may not get covered.

Another weakness of public relations is that it is hard to evaluate its effectiveness. Public relations is monitored in terms of the extent of the media coverage that a story generates, but that doesn't really measure its impact on public opinion or other stakeholder relationships. In short, the problem is measuring its effect on opinions, as well as on the bottomline. Table 11.2 summarizes public relations' strengths and weaknesses.

UNDERSTANDING PR'S PUBLICS

A public exists whenever a group of people, drawn together by specific interests, has opinions about those interest areas or issues. Individuals are frequently members of several publics, which may result in overlapping roles and conflicts of interest. For example, conservative voters considering a school bond might be torn between their interests as parents and their interests as members of a group opposed to higher taxes.

Public relations must be sensitive to two types of publics: *internal* and *external*.

Concept
Review

THE ROLE OF PUBLIC RELATIONS

1. Public relations is used to create and maintain goodwill and control a corporate or brand image.

2. Public relations is the use of information and the communication of that information through a variety of media to influence public opinion.

3. Public relations has many strengths, including its wide reach, credibility, message flexibility, and relatively low costs. Its weaknesses are the lack of control over how and which stories are covered and the difficulty in measuring effectiveness.

Internal publics are the people with whom an organization normally communicates in the ordinary routine of work, such as employees, investors, suppliers, dealers, and regular customers. **External publics** are the people with whom an organization communicates but does not have regular or close ties, such as local community neighbors, government officials, regulators, special-interest groups, media, and the financial community. Table 11.3 lists the internal and external publics. All these groups are referred to collectively as *stakeholders* because in some way they have a stake in what the company does.

Internal Publics

The most important internal audience is employees. As Figure 11.1 shows, companies rely on a combination of downward, upward, and horizontal communication to foster employee relations. Downward communication from management to employees keeps people informed about programs and policies. It is handled through employee newspapers and magazines, video news broadcasts, bulletin

TABLE 11.3

The Publics of Public Relations

Internal Stakeholders
Employees
Shareholders
MPR Publics: Suppliers, distributors, brokers, wholesalers, retailers, dealers
Regular or loyal customers
External Stakeholders
The media
Local community neighbors
Local, regional, state, and federal government bodies and regulators
The financial community
Special-interest groups
Prospective customers, employees, and shareholders

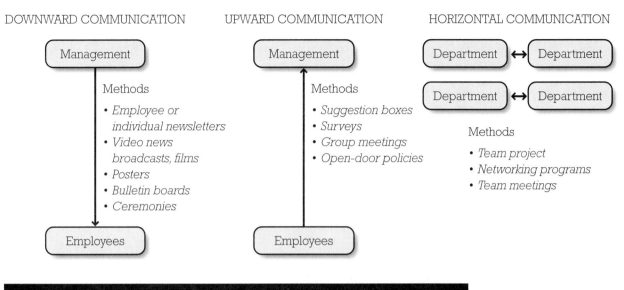

DOWNWARD COMMUNICATION

Management

Methods
- *Employee or individual newsletters*
- *Video news broadcasts, films*
- *Posters*
- *Bulletin boards*
- *Ceremonies*

Employees

UPWARD COMMUNICATION

Management

Methods
- *Suggestion boxes*
- *Surveys*
- *Group meetings*
- *Open-door policies*

Employees

HORIZONTAL COMMUNICATION

Department ↔ Department

Department ↔ Department

Methods
- *Team project*
- *Networking programs*
- *Team meetings*

FIGURE 11.1

Downward, Upward, and Horizontal Employee Relations Communications

boards, posters, films, reading racks, letters, and ceremonies. Upward communication from employees to management is usually much less developed, relying on informal feedback, suggestion boxes, surveys, group meetings, and open-door policies. Horizontal communication across department lines is usually structured through teamwork projects, networking programs, or team meetings.

External Publics

In external relations the first concern is usually with the press because it can have tremendous influence over public opinion. **Publicity** is a tool of public relations that is used to provide the media with information. In publicity, information is disseminated through the media as news stories or mentions in stories. Some people use the term "publicity" as a synonym for public relations. However, the terms are not interchangeable. As we see later in this chapter, public relations includes many more activities than publicity.

Consumers are a large external public. They are reached directly through advertising and sales and indirectly through media publicity. Another important external public is the government. Frequently, governmental interests overlap with consumers, particularly consumer activist groups. Special programs may be necessary to develop positive relationships with activist groups if the company is working in sensitive areas that affect public health, safety, or the environment. If an environmental program had been in place, for example, Exxon Corporation would have been in a better position to deal with the ill will generated by the *Valdez* crisis.

The financial community—investors, stockbrokers, and the financial press—is another important audience for publicly held companies. Financial relations experts must have a basic understanding of business law, economics, corporate finance, and investment practices. They must understand how corporate and external activities affect stock prices and changes in the company's bond rating. These highly skilled specialists develop the company's annual report and handle media relations with the financial press.

There can be interaction and overlap between internal and external publics. The trade, for example, is both an internal public in that suppliers, vendors, and resellers usually work in partnership with a business. However, trade associations and other people in the industry are an external audience because they are not directly involved with the company's business.

The Importance of Stakeholders

IMC relies heavily on the idea of targeting stakeholder publics as part of the marketing communication strategy. This concept of stakeholders radically expands the traditional notion of the customer as the target audience in a marketing communication program.

The task of targeting stakeholders successfully is not easy because many consumers do not believe businesses treat stakeholders well. To illustrate, a Pew Foundation survey found that the public perceives big business to have concern primarily for investor and senior management stakeholders, though it should have more concern for other stakeholders.[4] The survey results show that 46 percent of the respondents believe businesses put investors' interests first; 34 percent believe big business puts executives' interests first; and only 4 percent believe big companies put the interests of their employees first. However, when asked whose interests should come first, 31 percent of the respondents answered customers and 30 percent answered employees. Only 4 percent responded that they thought executives' interests should come first. These findings identify a serious gap in public perception about what does happen and what should happen with stakeholder interests.

In a stakeholder-focused program, all publics associated with corporate communication are important. These publics include financial industry publics, such as analysts, stockbrokers, and the financial media; employees; customers; suppliers and vendors; resellers, such as brokers, dealers, wholesalers, and retailers; the local community, including local officials and neighbors; special-interest groups; and government regulators at the federal, state, and local level.

Why are these stakeholders important? Consider these possibilities. If employees are not part of the team, they can sabotage production, contribute to quality control problems, or conduct a negative word-of-mouth campaign against the firm. If special-interest groups are not listened to and their concerns addressed, they can take legal action that stops production or expansion. If the media are not treated as partners, then the first time the company has a product crisis the media will be more willing to look for irresponsible behavior rather than to explain the company's perspective.

These possibilities become more likely when members of the stakeholder groups overlap. An employee may be an investor, so what a company says to its investors had better be consistent with the messages it sends to its employees. For instance, the financial relations department can't tell investors that it's been a great year while human resources tells employees that costs are so high that staff must be cut. An employee-investor who hears both messages will not only be confused but distrustful. Likewise, local government officials ruling on a company's plant expansion may also be customers or investors. Integrated marketing communication minimizes contradictory messages, which helps organizations to develop more positive contacts with all stakeholders.

Concept

Review

UNDERSTANDING PR'S PUBLICS

1. Internal publics have communication with the organization in the ordinary routine of work. These publics include employees, investors, suppliers, dealers, and resellers.
2. External publics do not have close ties with the organization, but their interests overlap occasionally. Examples include the press, consumers, activist groups, government, the financial community, and trade associations.
3. Stakeholders are all those who have a stake in the activities of a company and who can affect its business. They are important because they can influence the quality of the product and perceptions about the business or product.

TYPES OF PUBLIC RELATIONS

Public relations can perform many functions. In this section we explore seven types of public relations: *media relations, corporate public relations, crisis management, employee relations, financial relations, public affairs* and *community relations,* and *marketing public relations.*

An annual survey of PR agency clients by the Thomas Harris company gives insight into what clients value in a public relations agency.[5] Ninety-seven percent of the client-respondents feel media relations is the most important PR capability, which we turn to first.

Media Relations

The public relations function that is primarily responsible for publicity is **media relations.** Media relations specialists develop personal relationships with the media covering their industry or company. They provide information in the form of story ideas, press releases and other publicity materials, serve as a source or find an expert when reporters need to talk to someone knowledgeable, and train other corporate executives in how to be interviewed and how to handle questions from the media.

The relationship between the news media and the PR professional can be both cooperative and adversarial. The reporter is motivated by the public's right to know, and that sometimes challenges the PR person's loyalty to the client or the organization's best interests. Successful public relations is built on reputation; once this reputation is lost, the PR person cannot function with any effectiveness. Thus the road to media respect is honesty, accuracy, and professionalism. As part of professionalism, the practitioner must understand the news organization's news values.

Corporate Public Relations

Corporate public relations is the term for high-level counseling with senior management about the company's overall reputation, its image in the eyes of its various stakeholders, and its response to issues that may affect the success of the company. The corporate public relations practice of planning a company's response to important issues is called **issue management.** Corporate public relations practitioners help shape their organizations: They determine the concerns and expectations of the organization's publics and explain these concerns to management.

Corporate public relations manages **corporate advertising,** which is advertising used by the company to create positive attitudes and goodwill toward the company. Although a form of advertising, the corporate public relations department usually handles it. Why? Such advertising does not try to sell a particular brand but aims instead to enhance the image of the sponsoring organization. The ad from Prudential describes its Spirit of Community Award program as an example of corporate advertising.

This ad for Prudential demonstrates that the company is actively engaged in honoring kids who make contributions to their community. Do you think this ad enhances Prudential's corporate image?

Advocacy advertising is a type of corporate advertising that expresses the viewpoint of the company on some issue. Oil and cigarette companies, for instance, will sometimes run ads that read like editorials and explain their views on governmental regulation of their industries. On the other side of the smoking issue, both Massachusetts and California health departments have sponsored powerful anti-smoking advertising campaigns.

Crisis Management

Crisis management involves planning how to manage communications during crises or disasters—oil spills, plane crashes, management improprieties, carcinogens in the product, and challenges to other company operations. Sometimes internal corporate public relations specialists prepare the crisis plan, but some businesses, especially large ones, will hire an outside firm that specializes in developing crisis management plans and training staff to prepare for a crisis.[6]

In almost every corporation's life there will be some event that is perceived negatively by the public. In crisis management a public relations staff anticipates the possibility of disaster and establishes a plan for communicating the bad news to various stakeholder groups. That staff designates spokespeople to describe the damage accurately and to answer questions from victims, their families, the media, lawyers, and government officials. The crisis management team assigns someone to make arrangements for space where reporters can work, transportation, phones and computers, and perhaps even food when necessary. Crisis management public relations is such an integral part of doing business that insurance companies, such as National Union Fire Insurance Company, cover the costs of hiring a crisis management PR firm as part of their corporate liability policy.[7]

As one crisis management expert notes, management people don't judge good guys based on whether they've made mistakes but how they've fixed them. Johnson & Johnson took immediate steps to recall Tylenol after contaminated bottles were found. On the other hand, Jack-in-the-Box dawdled after hamburger food poisoning incidents left three children dead and 144 customers hospitalized. Intel tried to avoid the cost of recalling its flawed Pentium chip and denied the problem as the company got flamed on the Internet by worried customers.

One of the most dramatic crises faced by a business was the disaster created by the wreck of the Exxon oil tanker *Valdez*. Exxon may never be forgiven for the damage it did to the environment and wildlife off the coast of Alaska. To make matters worse, Exxon CEO Lawrence Rawl was widely criticized for the way he and his staff handled the crisis. At first, Exxon denied the extent of the catastrophe and responsibility for the cleanup. Later admitting errors in judgment, Exxon provided a great deal of misinformation about the costs of the cleanup. The public response was immediate and dramatic. Over 40,000 Exxon credit cards were cut up by consumers and mailed back to Exxon headquarters.

A crisis doesn't have to destroy a company's reputation. Philadelphia's gas and electric utility, PECO Energy, took "full responsibility" for an early morning explosion that killed two, critically injured one, and destroyed two Norristown homes.[8] The quick action defused negative public opinion. The CEO apologized to the victims' families and told the press that admitting responsibility was the right thing to do both morally and pragmatically. For 18 months prior to the crisis, however, PECO employees had been involved in a values training program that created a corporate culture in which responsibility and accountability emerged as key values.

With careful preparation, a company can weather a crisis with its reputation intact. A crisis plan, however, must anticipate the kinds of crises that the company might face and must detail people's duties in such a situation. Some companies practice dealing with disasters by creating disaster scenarios and acting out their responses as outlined in the crisis plan.

Employee Relations

Employees are key to the success of any business. **Employee relations,** a company's internal communication to its employees, creates programs designed to motivate employees to do their best work. Such programs may be run by human resources or public relations specialists. Employee relations staff are involved in the development of newsletters, bulletin boards, flyers, and video programs. Table 11.4 offers six keys to a successful employee relations program: security, respect, participation, consideration, recognition, and opportunity. If employee relations are effective, companies are much more likely to have high employee morale, motivation, and productivity. All these factors can help improve the company's bottom line because employees also help produce positive relationships with customers and other stakeholders.

Financial Relations

Financial relations is a public relations field in which specialists who understand finance work with the financial community and comply with government financial regulations for public companies. Financial relations specialists manage communication with stockbrokers and investors and the financial press. They also deal with a wide variety of financial information, such as company acquisitions, changes in company policies and how those changes may affect stock prices, and changes in the company's bond rating and stock prices. A primary responsibility of the financial relations staff is the production of the company's annual report, a document that has to follow strict governmental regulations and present the image and position of the company to its investors.

TABLE 11.4

Secrets of an Effective Employee Relations Program

1. Security: How secure is the company and my job within it?
2. Respect: Am I recognized as a person who does something worth doing?
3. Participation: How much do I have to say about the processes of which I am a part?
4. Consideration: Is there an opportunity for me to express my ideas?
5. Recognition: What rewards are given for good and faithful service?
6. Opportunity: Is there a chance to advance?

Porter/Novelli worked with Gillette to sponsor this Gillette Sensor for Women special event for media specialists.

Public Affairs and Community Relations

Specialists in **public affairs,** public relations programs that focus on government relations, work closely with federal, regional, state, and local government agencies. **Lobbying,** activities aimed at influencing policy decisions of government officials, is a type of public affairs activity. **Community relations** involves managing relations with stakeholders in the local community. Community relations officers arrange community events and sponsorships and handle community issues such as the environmental implications of a company's operations.

Marketing Public Relations

The public relations field that seeks positive publicity for products is **marketing public relations** (MPR). MPR is particularly important in the launch of a new

---

Concept Review

TYPES OF PUBLIC RELATIONS

The main types of public relations include the following:

1. Media relations
2. Corporate public relations
3. Crisis management
4. Employee relations
5. Financial relations
6. Public affairs and community relations
7. Marketing public relations

p r o f i l e

Teresa McFarland
Marketing Communications and Public Relations Manager
Mall of America

Teresa McFarland manages two public relations specialists and works with approximately 20 people in the Mall of America marketing department. Minnesota's Mall of America is the largest mall in the United States and a destination for many travelers who visit it as much for its entertainment features as for its shopping experiences.

Her responsibilities include media relations, community relations, and, because of previous experience in the Minnesota Governor's office, public affairs. She acts as spokesperson for Mall of America, spending a great deal of time answering local, state, national, and international media questions. In addition, Mall of America holds hundreds of special events and promotions throughout the year, which the public relations department helps to promote through media coverage.

In the area of public affairs, she works on government issues that affect the mall, such as property tax issues, mall expansion efforts, and organizing meetings and events with state and city officials. To play an active role in the business community and to stay in touch with government officials, she serves on two key committees: the Communications Committee for the Minnesota Chamber of Commerce and the Political Effectiveness Committee for the Minnesota Business Partnership. Not only do these committees help McFarland keep in touch, they also provide a more visible role for Mall of America in the business community.

Her community relations responsibilities involve organizing on-site events and fundraising opportunities. Supporting good causes is important for an organization that wants to be a good citizen, and the mall has worked to develop an affiliation with inner-city community groups.

Academic Background
Teresa graduated in 1987 from the University of St. Thomas in St. Paul, Minnesota, with a degree in journalism and public relations. She credits one professor with teaching her a lesson that has guided her career. He said, "There are do'ers and there are thumbsuckers." The do'ers get into the journalism field and gather as many experiences as they can through internships; the thumbsuckers, as you can imagine, basically do nothing but take the classes they need to graduate. McFarland decided she didn't want to be a thumbsucker and proceeded to find and work hard at several internships that proved to be the best experience during her undergraduate years.

She worked on the college newspaper in her freshman year and on a community weekly newspaper in her sophomore year. In her junior year she enjoyed a year-long internship in the Ramsey County Public Relations Department. From there she moved to an internship in the Communications Office of the Minnesota Department of Trade and Economic Development, where she worked until finishing college.

product, a point illustrated in the Gillette opening story, where the concept of "newness" makes the product newsworthy and thus offers a natural platform for publicity. For instance, a positive review in the newspaper of a new movie, restaurant, or book is an example of successful MPR. But more than that, MPR specialists work closely with marketing people on the design of the product and its strategic posi-

She observes, "Internships allowed me to practice—in the real world—what I was learning in the Journalism School." She explains, "By the time I graduated from college I had a portfolio of clips and projects that looked as though I had actually been in the working world awhile."

Career Track

After graduating, Teresa got a job as a writer for the Minnesota Governor's Office. For three years she worked for Governor Rudy Perpich as a communication assistant and then as a special assistant for the governor. In these positions she wrote articles, speeches, and press releases. She also handled media relations statewide, did advance work for appearances, and traveled with the governor.

After Governor Perpich lost his election in 1990, she moved to Washington to work as Minnesota Congressman Tim Penny's press secretary. After three years, when Congressman Penny decided to retire, she received a call from the Mall of America offering her the position of marketing communication and public relations manager.

Advice

Her advice to new graduates is to establish, early on, that you will go the extra mile to get the job done. She also believes that it's important to have a positive attitude if someone asks you to do something. If you find yourself in a rut in your career or career search, she strongly recommends informational interviews with anyone who will speak to you in the field in which you are interested. Not only does it help you sort things out, it also helps you develop a network. She also notes that gaining experience in both a political environment and the business world helped her expand her horizons.

Typical Day

"One thing I have learned is that there is never a typical day at Mall of America. This is an extremely busy place and therefore a busy job that requires juggling many, many projects at one time." She describes one day as follows:

- I started the day with a 7:30 A.M. meeting on property taxes. We organized the meeting to encourage retailers and businesspeople to join together to lobby the governor and state legislature on the need to lower commercial industrial property taxes.
- Back in the office by 8:50 A.M., I did a half-hour radio interview with a Minnesota station on holiday decor and events at Mall of America, including the mall's yearly economic impact on the state of Minnesota and how we hope to establish a reception area at the mall to help promote other tourism opportunities in Minnesota.
- At almost 10:00 A.M., the public relations staff meets with our outside public relations firm to brainstorm media opportunities and events to promote holiday shopping at the mall.
- Just before lunch I meet with a Mall of America retailer to discuss unique gift opportunities from their store that we will promote during the holiday season.
- After lunch I meet with our tenant services department to talk about key messages to release on retail sales during the holiday months.
- In the middle of the afternoon I'm finally able to answer phone calls from the media and follow up on their questions. I help a local television station set up an interview with a new Mall of America store. I also work with a national radio show that wants to do a story a day from Mall of America the week before Christmas.
- For the rest of the day, I develop a Holiday Media Plan for Mall of America vice president and mall owners and write a memo summarizing the plan.

tioning in the marketplace. In addition, MPR specialists know how to handle the special events used for major announcements and product launches. They may work closely with an advertising team, as Porter/Novelli worked with BBDO on the Gillette new product launches, and other marketing communication specialists such as those in direct marketing, sales promotion, and event marketing.

MANAGING PUBLIC RELATIONS

Like any business endeavor, successful public relations requires a plan. Like all other areas of marketing communication, a plan requires research. Therefore, before discussing the development of a public relations plan, let's examine the goals and techniques of PR research.

Public Relations Research

Before an organization can communicate an image to others, it should correctly identify that image. Research is used to diagnose the organization's image. The general objectives of PR research include probing basic attitudes, measuring actual opinions, identifying opinion leaders, describing the characteristics of various stakeholder groups, testing themes and media, and identifying potentially troublesome issues before they develop.

Figure 11.2 shows the results of an attitude survey by the Roper Group that examined the public's impression of business. Although this reflects general atti-

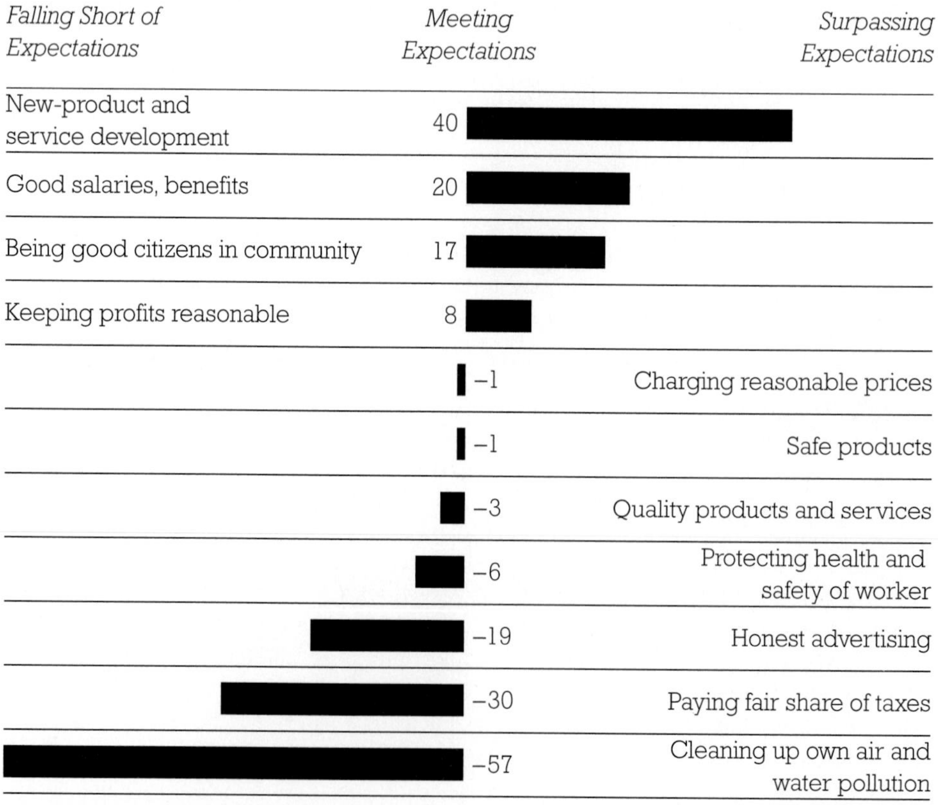

Falling Short of Expectations	Meeting Expectations	Surpassing Expectations
New-product and service development	40	
Good salaries, benefits	20	
Being good citizens in community	17	
Keeping profits reasonable	8	
	−1	Charging reasonable prices
	−1	Safe products
	−3	Quality products and services
	−6	Protecting health and safety of worker
	−19	Honest advertising
	−30	Paying fair share of taxes
	−57	Cleaning up own air and water pollution

Note: *Values are the point difference between perceptions of responsibility and fulfillment.*

FIGURE 11.2

Survey of the Public's Impression of Business

tudes toward business, a similar study can be undertaken for any organization. These results indicate that some consumers generally approve of what business is doing in the areas of developing new products, paying fair salaries, charging fairly, and being good community citizens. Others, however, feel that business is causing environmental problems, not paying its fair share of taxes, and not advertising honestly. The role of PR managers is to intelligently assess such findings, puzzle out the contradictions, and identify the relevance for their organization.

Planning Public Relations

Public relations plans are developed like other business and marketing plans. The plan development consists of the following six steps: (1) an assessment of the current situation, (2) a statement of objectives, (3) selection of target audiences, (4) selection of methods of implementation, (5) a determination of costs, and (6) an evaluation of results.

Assessing the Situation

Research helps organizations assess current situations. A key problem often uncovered in research is a confused or an unfocused corporate image. It takes constant vigilance to maintain a positive image and reputation. As an example, Procter & Gamble made an immediate and expensive public relations response to quell negative word of mouth surrounding the rumors that the origin of its logo was from a satanic cult.

Objectives and Targeting

Once the current situation has been assessed, PR professionals can develop program objectives that are in concert with the marketing communication program. For the most part, PR attempts to change some aspect of public opinion. But public opinion is elusive, difficult to measure, and in constant flux. Because the impact of public relations is often difficult to gauge and may take a long time to appear, establishing meaningful objectives is especially difficult. Most PR objectives relate to attitudes, opinions, information, and feelings. Some, however, relate to behavior. Because researchers can measure how many people attended a company-sponsored event due to event publicity, PR specialists might set an objective of 100,000 attendees at a special event.

Gillette's PR objectives for the Sensor launch were fairly straightforward: to communicate that the Sensor razor was a breakthrough new product, to create anticipation and widespread awareness, to generate trial when the product hit the market, to maximize conversion to the new shaving system, to reinforce the Sensor shaving experience, and to generate trade support.

The potential audiences for a public relations effort should be researched just as carefully as the target audiences for an advertising campaign. The more PR practitioners know about each audience, the better the message design will be. Researchers should be able to answer several questions. Who are the people, institutions, or organizations that need to be reached by the PR effort? Where are they located, and what is the most effective and efficient way to make contact? What do they believe and feel about the company, and what does the organization need to say to them?

Gillette relied heavily on consumer attitude research during planning for the

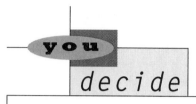

Do Promotion and Publicity Belong in Classrooms?

A number of public relations efforts are aimed at reaching children in school. Some of them offer valuable instructional materials, but others are just promotions masquerading as education. Take, for example, the following:

- Revlon, which sells a line of cosmetics to young consumers, sent a guide to 29,000 teachers of home economics. The exercises included asking students to bring in pictures of themselves on a "good hair day" and a "bad hair day" and to list the three hair-care products they would "have to have" if stranded on a desert island.
- Weyerhaeuser produced a teacher's guide on forestry that poses such pressing questions as "What innovative practices have Weyerhaeuser introduced in recent years?" and "What related companies are part of Weyerhaeuser?"
- Keep America Beautiful, a lobbying association of the bottling industry, produced materials that inform students that "incinerating plastics is a form of recycling."
- A poster from the National Soft Drink Association tells children that "a peach may give you certain vitamins that the soft drink does not, just as the soft drink gives you more liquid than the peach does."

Obviously such self-serving and biased materials need to be edited before being used in a classroom. So why do teachers use such materials? The answer is often money. In many schools that are operating on diminished budgets, the new, slick pamphlets, posters, and videos that companies offer are usually free or cheap, and they lighten up the classroom and bring a more entertaining dimension to instruction.

In addition to teaching materials, a Grab Bag sampling program by Cover Concepts targets some three million kids in grades 1 through 12. And special magazines such as Nike-sponsored *Hey!* follow in the steps of the *Weekly Reader.* Company-sponsored book covers have been used by Coca-Cola, Foot Locker, and Nike. And KIDSNEWS, with sponsors such as Reebok, Coca-Cola, and Universal Pictures, comes out every other month in a video format.

The most dramatic example of commercializing the classroom comes from Channel One, a daily 12-minute, soft news program that at one time reached more than eight million students in 11,700 schools daily. Channel One, developed by Whittle Communications and now owned by K-III Communications, was attractive because subscribing schools received a satellite dish, two videocassette recorders, plus a video monitor for each classroom in return for playing Channel One in class. These gifts were paid for with revenue from the two minutes of commercials included in the news broadcast from such sponsors as Clearasil, Reebok, Gatorade, Pepsi, and other products. Whittle founded Channel One after an education focus group expressed a need for a TV news program for teens. Many cash-strapped schools could not catch up with the electronic revolution on their own. Sponsors, eager to reach the school-age target audience, were willing to help.

Channel One's advertising practices aroused the ire of parents, educators, and social critics—so much so that New York State banned it, and state educational boards in New Jersey and California sought restraints against it. Critics charge that it is unethical to require children to watch commercials in school. Channel One answered by supplying instructional materials designed to teach children how to watch commercials critically and to question the claims of advertisements.

You Decide

1. Should the materials of commercial sponsors and their commercials be allowed in schools?
2. Is it unethical to produce a commercial message specifically for a classroom?
3. You teach a high-school civics class and Channel One offers the possibility of having a daily news program to supplement your textbook discussion of civics and government. Your school is poor and the only way to get televised current event materials into your class is to sign up with Channel One. Would you do it?

Sources: "K-III Enhances Channel One Network Management Structure," *K-III Communications Press Release,* October 18, 1996, Internet: www.K–iii.com/news/96.10.18; Michael F. Jacobson, "Now There's a Fourth R: Retailing," *New York Times,* 29 January 1995, 9; Betsy Spethmann, "Marketers Seek to Reach More Kids in School," *Adweek,* September 27, 1993, 13.

Sensor launch. Based on research that showed Gillette's user imagery was almost identical in the United States, Canada, and seven European countries, Gillette decided to treat the North Atlantic (America and Europe) as one market. It planned to deliver the same message in the same way to virtually every male shaver in the pan-Atlantic region.

Implementation

Once PR planners decide what they want to do and which audiences to target, they must wrestle with how to implement their plans. Implementation includes the choice of specific public relations tools, decisions about the message strategy, and the method and time of delivery of the message.

Although the intention with the Sensor launch was to keep the theme consistent across the North Atlantic, some local adaptation occurred because northern European shaving markets differ from southern European markets. In the south complexions are darker, men have tougher beards, and the Latin countries are more open to a romantic angle. In Scandinavia most men have soft blond hair, a fair complexion, and are less swayed by romantic imagery. Even with the adaptations, the European campaign communicated the quality and breakthrough engineering of the product and the Gillette Sensor "Best A Man Can Get" theme.

The publicity also had to be adapted because techniques such as video news releases worked well in countries like Italy that have flourishing private electronic media but were less effective in the United Kingdom, where a public company, the BBC, still controls access to two of the four channels and avoids commercialization.

Coordinated timing is critical in an integrated PR campaign. In the case of Gillette's Sensor, Gillette decided that the Sensor story could be presented at two different times from two different perspectives. Three months before the product became available, Gillette presented the Sensor as a business story, focusing on the company, the product patents, the development of the product, and the marketing story. Most product publicity (why the shaving system was effective) was timed to take place a few weeks before both the launch and the start of the consumer advertising campaign. This two-step plan made it possible to sustain interest over three-and-a-half months. The amount of actual media coverage far exceeded the goals set for the PR program.

Unfortunately for the Sensor launch, there was so much interest in the story that product information started to leak out to general publications ahead of schedule. In response, Porter/Novelli decided Gillette should hold a press conference simultaneously in six markets two-and-a-half months before the launch. The coverage from that press event was so heavy in the United States that *Fortune* named the Sensor one of its ten products of the year—before the Sensor became available in stores. Despite Porter/Novelli's concern that publicity might have peaked too early, consumer interest in the Sensor continued to grow. When the ad campaign broke on Super Bowl Sunday, Porter/Novelli had another "spike" of heavy publicity to manage.

Budgets and Evaluation

Planners must know—not guess—what things cost. For example, publicity places news stories in the media without a media fee, but it is hardly free. A great many resources are used to prepare a press release and develop the media contacts that result in "free" publicity. The costs of other specific items, such as a brochure, newsletter, video news release, or special event, however, can be estimated. The budgeting question then becomes, What can the business afford? For instance, the most effective way to communicate with a specific audience might be via a prime-time television program, as Hallmark does with its Hallmark Hall of Fame. But the cost of this type of public relations might exceed the budget. To match the needs of the business to the budgetary constraints, PR planners must ask: What can we afford to do to implement the public relations objectives properly?

Despite the difficulty of measuring the results of public relations, a study found that 97 percent of PR executives feel that public relations professionals should routinely measure the impact of their programs.[9] PR is evaluated through both informal and formal research methods. Informal techniques include counting the attendance at an event, hosting informal interviews, or recording the number of requests for speakers.

Formal research methods include focus groups, content analysis, and monitoring public relations activities and public opinion over time. Focus groups can be used to measure the qualitative effects of material or messages on members of a target audience before the material is officially distributed. Content analysis of PR communications can show what is being reported, where, to how many people, over what period of time, in which media, and how the coverage changes over time. Monitoring keeps track of PR activities and public opinion over time. It might include weekly on-going opinion polls or a count of the number of press releases that appear in print.

The Sensor launch was measured by examining sales revenues and monitoring coverage. Gillette's marketing manager estimated the impact of public relations to have added $5 million in publicity to the value of the advertising. The marketing manager based the estimate on the number of PR contacts, which included 403 million media impressions (the number of people seeing the story or mention) that resulted from 840 placements in the media. The continuing success of public relations is highlighted in the IMC in Action feature.

Concept Review

MANAGING PUBLIC RELATIONS

1. Research in public relations is a planned, carefully organized, sophisticated fact-finding effort that focuses on listening to the opinions of others.
2. The six steps in public relations planning are:
   - Assessment of the current situation
   - Statement of objectives
   - Selection of target audiences
   - Selection of methods of implementation
   - Determination of costs
   - Evaluation of results

PR Drives Sales for The Sensor for Women

Given the incredible success the Porter/Novelli public relations firm had with the launch of the Gillette Sensor, it wasn't any surprise when, several years later, Porter/ Novelli was picked to lead the launch of Gillette's new razor for women. Using a similar strategy, Porter/Novelli drove pre-advertising sales to more than 50 percent beyond Gillette's own ambitious forecast and established Sensor for Women as the fastest-growing product in the health and beauty category.

Prior to consumer advertising, more than 600 separate stories appeared in high-profile media communicating to women across North America the breakthrough technology and design of the new product. The strategy was to use credible, third-party editorial coverage to inform women about the benefits of the newly designed razor. Objectives were to establish awareness and achieve trial and repeat purchases.

Activities included a two-day media preview. The first day targeted magazine and newspaper editors that required a long lead time to publish articles. The second day targeted general news media with a press conference. This strategy resulted in two peaks of publicity. The first round of coverage appeared in general news, business, and trade publications; and broadcast outlets through the spring. The second round appeared in the influential women's magazines and in newspaper lifestyle sections during the summer when the product first became available.

For the magazine and newspaper editors that required more lead time, Porter/Novelli created a summer environment on a dreary day in February to get editors thinking about shaving for summer activities. More than 250 feet of tenting, hundreds of azaleas, tulips, jonquils, daffodils, ficus trees, and even a custom-made waterfall transformed the rooftop of New York's Peninsula Spa into a summer garden. The 57 editors attending received an in-depth product briefing and were offered an opportunity to sample the product in the spa. The press materials were contained in a media resource guide that included an 18-month editorial calendar and extensive background information for the development of feature stories.

On the following day, business, financial, and general news media watched the creation of a dramatic photo of Sensor for Women on a seven-story wall of water. They also received samples and product information. At the same time, specially packaged product samples were distributed to 1600 female opinion leaders nationwide. The success of this effort in driving sales demonstrated the power of public relations when used as a strategic marketing communication tool.

Sources: "Gillette Sensor for Women," Porter/ Novelli handout; "Sensor Gets Big Edge in Women's Razors," *New York Times,* 17 December 1992, B1.

This photo shows how Gillette created a summer day in February for press members.

INTEGRATING PUBLIC RELATIONS

Successful public relations efforts depend in large part on how well they are integrated with other marketing communication functions. A survey found that of the companies that use public relations, PR executives believe that 70 percent of management want public relations integrated with other marketing communication. It also found that 90 percent of the PR executives feel that public relations professionals should spearhead efforts to integrate PR with other communication areas.[10] For the most part, companies have failed at this task. Historically, public relations has been physically and philosophically separated from the rest of the organization's marketing communication team and, thus, has not had a role in managing or planning the company's total communication program.

This historical isolation has been partly due to the nature of the work performed by public relations and partly due to the attitudes of the people working in it. Because management often does not see PR as a profit generator and has difficulty verifying the effect PR has on the bottom line, profit-oriented managers may discount its value. This perception is compounded when people working in public relations, often trained as journalists with little background in business, do not view selling or profit generation as a part of their responsibility.

PR expert William Novelli believes these attitudes must change: "All communications can and should stem from common strategies, and the total program should speak with one voice."[11] Another expert, Yustin Wallrapp, suggests: "There must be a real commitment to the legitimacy of PR as a part of the communication mix."[12] For public relations to have an important role in a total communications program, it must be recognized that PR's expertise is in relationship management, which is the heart of a marketing communication program.

Integration is essential, especially in areas where it overlaps with other marketing communication tools. Corporate advertising, advertising for PR purposes, overlaps with advertising and can enhance the advertising message and brand image. Research shows that customers do care about a company's social responsibility, and that information gets factored into their buying decisions.

Furthermore, the problems and crises that PR people have to manage are often linked to other marketing communication activities, such as Kraft's sweepstakes promotion that, because of a printing error, made the company responsible for giving away an unexpectedly large number of minivans. The Big Mac Shaq story in Chapter 10 is another example of a sales promotion that caused public relations problems—McDonald's knew that if it modified the contest to avoid huge losses, the public would have cried foul for changing the game rules.

Concept ✓ Review

INTEGRATING PUBLIC RELATIONS

1. To be effective, public relations should be integrated into a marketing communication program because it overlaps with other communication activities and its specialists are experts in relationship management.
2. Historically, PR has been isolated from other marketing communication areas because many managers don't view it as a profit generator and many PR specialists don't feel responsible for generating revenues.

TOOLS OF PUBLIC RELATIONS

Public relations specialists use many tools to communicate. Some of the most common ones include publicity and news releases, corporate advertising, publications, videos and film, company-sponsored events, lobbying, meetings, and organized social activities.

Publicity

Providing editors and reporters with an organization's story generates publicity. As mentioned earlier, publicity is one of the responsibilities of a media relations program. The credibility of articles in the mass media is much higher than that of advertising because the medium has the choice to run or not run the story and to change it as desired. Publicity often requires massive effort, no matter whether the result is a twelve-page lead story in *Fortune* magazine on the success of Sam Walton and the Wal-Mart chain, a one-sentence mention by Dan Rather on the evening news, or a *plug,* which occurs when celebrities such as Tiger Woods mention a particular product.

Sometimes publicity can deliver impact that no advertising budget can accomplish. Benetton, for example, known for its controversial advertising, rarely runs its ads in the mass media. Most are used in the company's publication, *Colors.* The few times the ads run, however, they generate enormous publicity because their controversial nature creates news coverage, resulting in far more exposure than the ad budget delivers.

Most publicity is delivered in the form of a **news release** that commits a story to paper or video in the style acceptable to the medium for which it is intended. News stories are usually written one way for newspapers and another way for the electronic media. Newspeople appreciate direct, clear-cut explanations because they themselves are experts in concise writing and are usually hard-pressed for time. A single copy, or *exclusive,* is sent to a news editor, section editor, or a specific reporter. Multiple copies can be mailed to a mailing list of editors or put on a news wire, such as Reuters. Table 11.5 provides guidelines for submitting a news release.

To make a significant announcement to representatives of the press, an organization may hold an event called a **press conference.** At a press conference, press representatives listen to the announcement and may also ask questions and interview important people. Busy media will not attend such events unless the announcement is important, such as a candidate announcing that he or she is running for national office. If the news could just as well have been obtained from a prepared release, then the press conference probably should not be held. A collection of supporting materials, known as a **press kit,** provides

This press release from Biofoam's PR agency presents the facts early, includes a contact name and number, and suits the magazine medium for which it was intended.

FOR IMMEDIATE RELEASE

FOR MORE INFORMATION CONTACT
Rhonda Grundemann .... (602) 222-4343
Mullen Public Relations   or direct line (602) 222-4310

ACCIDENTAL DISCOVERY MAY BE NATURE'S ANSWER TO MAJOR ENVIRONMENTAL PROBLEM

All-Natural Packaging Material Promises To Replace Styrene

PHOENIX, AZ -- A few years ago, two Arizona entrepreneurs were trying to develop a tasty snack food for the Spanish market where junk food sells faster than salsa. In their search for the perfect goodie, the businessmen accidentally bumped into an all-natural answer to a major environmental problem that has been haunting environmentalists the world over.

Much of the "puffed" foods on today's food counters are extruded. That is, the ingredients are forced throughout a small aperture and then "exploded" into popcorn-style products. A unique, and different process than the manufacture of styrene plastic packaging material, known as "peanuts" that cling to your clothes and, tragically, linger in the world's landfills forever.

So, in a tiny Phoenix-area laboratory, the snack food was put on hold and Biofoam, an all-natural packaging material, was readied for introduction to the waiting world. Made from grain grown on America's farms, Biofoam is an all-natural, 100 percent biodegradable and ecologically safe material.

- more -

918 South Park Lane, Suite 102, Tempe, AZ 85281 U S A
Phone: 1-602-966-3735 • Phone: 1-800-959-FOAM • Fax: 1-602-966-5659

TABLE 11.5

Guidelines for Preparing a New Release

1. Learn as much as possible about the particular medium being used and what that medium considers newsworthy.

2. Make sure the story is totally accurate.

3. Make sure the story is timely. Old news is of no use to most editors.

4. Keep the story as succinct as possible.

5. Because newspaper readers are skimmers, present the main facts in the first few sentences when submitting to this medium.

6. Proofread carefully. Any typographic or grammatical mistakes will suggest a lack of professionalism on your part and may result in the news release being dumped in the trash.

7. Include a name and phone number of a contact person who can answer questions.

8. Don't expect the news medium to use your news release just because you sent it and it is important to your company. News judgments are balanced against the volume of the news and the editor's feel for the audience's interests.

Corporate public relations is the focus of this State Farm ad that highlights its Good Neighbor award.

photographs, releases, copies of speeches, maps, timetables, and other material that might be of use to reporters. Publicity photos in the press kit are particularly important because the decision to use a story may depend on the availability of a dramatic visual.

Corporate Advertising

As noted earlier, corporate advertising is communication by an organization about its work, views, and problems that aims to gain public support. The emphasis is on the image of the company rather than the sale of a product. Unlike publicity, corporate advertising, including advocacy advertising, is paid for by the organization and enables the sponsor to tell its story when and how it chooses. On the minus side, the audience recognizes that an institutional ad is paid for and self-serving, so audience resistance may be higher. Publicity is not paid for by the sponsor, so it is deemed to be more credible.

Philip Morris used paid ads and a promotional tour to celebrate the anniversary of the Bill of Rights. Unfortunately, the company's underlying message was support for commercial free speech, particularly for cigarette advertising, and that connection irritated many people. The State Farm ad, an example of corporate advertising, speaks out on educational needs and announces an award the company sponsors for innovative teachers. What corporate image do you think the ad creates or reinforces?

Publications

Although no one has taken an official count, experts estimate that about 8000 magazines and newspapers are published for organizations' internal audiences—such as company employees—with a readership of perhaps 20 million people. These publications cost companies about $150 million. They range from a single-page sheet to a large, glossy, four-color magazine.

Although most of these publications target an internal audience, some are also distributed to external audiences. A university magazine, for instance, may target community leaders, donors, legislators, and alumni. Such publications create prestige, goodwill, and an understanding of the organization. They may also provide product information, or promote products and services.

In addition to internal magazines and newspapers, other publications include brochures, flyers, posters, and other forms of printed materials. PR departments, particularly those for nonprofit organizations like hospitals, often produce a variety of brochures that describe specialized programs or products offered by the organizations. Banks, for example, may have a line of brochures that describe their various offerings, investment programs, and financial planning services.

Another type of company publication is the **annual report.** This is an official document required by the Securities Exchange Commission (SEC) for publicly held companies. It contains financial information that the SEC requires. In addition, the annual report, which is sent to all investors and the financial community, is often used as a statement about the company's financial health and market position. It is an important tool in establishing and maintaining a corporate image. Most annual reports are full of glowing facts and quotes. However, one company, Ben & Jerry's, uses its annual report to give a complete picture of its activities. Its annual reports typically review its social performance and may admit that it didn't do as much to help the Brazilian Indians as claimed or that the garbage which was generated by throwing away empty Ben & Jerry's ice cream containers amounts to 15,550 cubic yards of trash.[13]

1995 Annual Report

BEN & JERRY'S
VERMONT'S FINEST • ICE CREAM & FROZEN YOGURT™

Ben & Jerry's takes an unusual approach toward reporting its activities, reporting failures as well as successes.

Videos and Film

Although videos and film are some of the most complex and expensive means of communication, they offer an opportunity to influence viewers in a way that no other medium can match. For instance, businesses may send video news releases to television stations as a type of publicity. Videos can also be used for sales meetings, training, and staff conferences. Some large companies even produce their own news shows that are played for employees during lunch or breaks. **Product placements**—the practice of having a product appear in a news show or movie to generate lots of valuable visibility—is another form of publicity that uses the film medium. *Seinfeld,* for example, highlighted products such as Glide dental floss and Kenny Rogers chicken in select episodes.

There are some limitations to video and film, however. First, people are accustomed to quality images and therefore expect to see video and film that are professionally produced. And that means these materials will be expensive. Second, moving images tend to proceed at their own pace and allow little time for viewers to ask questions, so they do not generate two-way conversations.

Special Events and Company Sponsorships

Special events such as open houses and tours are useful ways to educate people about where people work and what they produce. Tours are usually provided for general consumers but also for special groups such as students, scientists, and members of the trade. Universities often set up tour programs to help with the recruitment and orientation of new students. In one company a new public relations person discovered that salespeople-in-training never received a plant tour to see how products were manufactured. In fact, many veteran salespeople had never been inside the plant. As a result, the PR team developed a plant tour program—which gave salespeople more information about the quality of the products they sold and more motivation.

Company sponsorships of another organization's special events—such as IBM's sponsorship of the Special Olympics—are also an important public relations tool. Companies such as Procter & Gamble, AT&T, American Express, Coca-Cola, and Gillette sponsor events around the world. Virtually every major sporting event now has a corporate sponsor, including college football bowl games. Sponsorship has grown because it provides strong media coverage. Volvo estimates that its $3 million investment in tennis is equivalent to $25 million in advertising because of the extra media coverage it generates. Company-sponsored events are also good for motivating employees who attend or participate in the event.

Lobbying

Lobbying is an area of great sensitivity because it involves contacting government officials with information and persuasive communication. Lobbyists are often former government officers, although some public relations practitioners who are lobbyists work for organizations like the American Association of Retired Persons, the National Rifle Association, or utility companies. Lobbyists work closely with the staffs of federal and/or state elected bodies and regulatory offices. The staff often depends on lobbyists to explain the intricacies and implications of proposed legislation and regulation. Lobbyists use their in-depth information to influence and persuade.

Fundraising

Public relations is important for nonprofit associations who rely on goodwill to stimulate memberships and donations. Fundraising is a specialty that involves public relations. Your campus is probably filled with people or groups who help raise funds, such as the alumni association or university foundation, the athletic department, the library, the museum, and numerous student groups. Professional fundraisers are skilled at developing campaigns that can bring in large sums of money. They know how to make the initial contacts that inspire other people to participate, how to use other marketing communication tools such as advertising, and how to make the best use of special events and public recognition. The National Trust for Historic Preservation ad shows how fundraisers use advertising to promote a fundraising drive.

Fundraising, also called *development,* is a way of life for most universities. Fundraisers understand the importance of jump-starting a campaign with one or more important gifts. A successful contact made headlines when New Jersey businessman, Henry M. Rowan, donated $100 million to Glassboro State College. In return the college announced that it was changing its name to Rowan College of New Jersey in honor of the donor and his wife.

Meetings

Meeting with others to discuss ideas is an often-neglected communication technique in sophisticated communication planning because it seems too simple. Meetings have great power for good or ill because they involve personal, interactive communication rather than the distant, passive communication of a mass media message. Because meetings are limited by the size of the setting, they should be used to communicate with relatively small stakeholder groups. They are often used for such purposes as an annual report meeting for investors, an employee meeting to announce a new policy, a public lecture by a visiting scientist, or the showing of a new movie or play to opinion leaders.

A poorly run meeting can send a message of disinterest or incompetence. To avoid such an image, meeting planners should select the setting with care, plan for audiovisual materials, provide equipment, invite participants in a timely and gracious manner, organize social activities before and after the event, and attend to a hundred other details.

Social Activities

Company picnics, holiday parties, bowling and softball leagues, and golf tournaments are all tools of public relations. Public relations specialists use these events to create a pleasant atmosphere for employees and to convey the impression that management is thoughtful and interested. PR specialists may also use social activities to build relationships with major customers, dealers and retailers, donors, investors, and other important stakeholders.

A CLOSING THOUGHT: FITTING IN PR

For public relations to fulfill its promise, it must be integrated as a key part of a total communication program. The public relations team, then, must work closely with the other marketing communication functions, making it a partner rather than a poor relation.[14] If such a partnership is the future of public relations, it holds important challenges for PR practitioners who must be market savvy and sensitive to the bottom-line concerns of business managers. Many public relations programs and practitioners have moved in this direction. They work with clearly

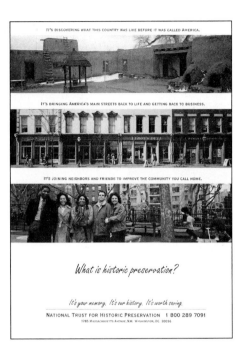

This ad focuses on the fundraising efforts of the National Trust for Historic Preservation.

stated, measurable objectives that dovetail with the company's marketing communication plan.

Meanwhile, companies are likely to place increasing importance on public relations as they become more aware of the critical role that PR has to play in relationship marketing. With consumers who are demanding better information, higher value, and improved service, companies will have to be aware of and learn to manage the images they portray to all stakeholders whenever possible.

TOOLS OF PUBLIC RELATIONS

1. Using publicity as a public relations tool requires the ability to handle media relations, news releases, and press conferences.
2. Corporate advertising focuses on the image of the organization rather than a product.
3. Company publications, another PR tool, can reach both an internal and external audience. They include magazines, newspapers, and newsletters, brochures and flyers, and more formal documents such as annual reports.
4. Videos and film are used for video news releases to television studios, for sales meetings, training, staff conferences, and in-house news programs.
5. Special events such as tours and open houses can communicate a strong, positive message about a company that can motivate stakeholders. Corporate sponsorships often provide strong media coverage and may also improve employee morale.
6. Other tools used in public relations include lobbying, fundraising, meetings, and organized social activities.

SUMMARY

1. **Define public relations and explain its purpose.**
Public relations is a communication activity that tries to change the attitudes and beliefs of stakeholder audiences. It helps build goodwill and strengthen relationships with all stakeholders and develop and maintain a positive company image.

2. **Identify the strengths and weaknesses of public relations.**
Public relations has many strengths. First, marketing communicators can use it to manage many different stakeholder relationships (employees, financial community, media, local community, and so forth) and to monitor issues and public opinion related to the organization's concerns. It can also add credibility and believability to a message when it appears in the media. Weaknesses include a lack of control over how and which messages are covered in the media and the difficulty of evaluating effectiveness.

3. **Distinguish between internal and external stakeholders.**
Stakeholder publics are the groups of people targeted to receive public relations messages. Internal publics are those with whom an organization normally communicates in the ordinary routine of work, such as employees, investors, suppliers, dealers, and regular customers. In contrast, external publics are publics the organization communicates with but does not have regular or close ties, such as local community neighbors, government regulators, special-interest groups, media, and the financial community.

4. **Explain seven types of public relations programs.**
There are seven main types of public relations programs: media relations (working with press representatives and providing them with story ideas and information), corporate public relations (counseling senior management about the company's overall reputation, its image in the eyes of stakeholders, and its response to important issues), crisis management (predicting where and

when disasters will strike and planning how to handle the company's relations and communications in times of crisis), employee relations (keeping the employees informed and in the communication loop), financial relations (keeping analysts, stockbrokers, and investors informed), public affairs and community relations (working on local and government issues that affect the organization), and marketing public relations (the use of publicity and other PR tools to launch and promote products).

5. **Outline the steps in the public relations research and planning process.**
Research is used to help planners become better informed about the issues and attitudes of stakeholders. The planning process, similar to that used in other areas of marketing communication, consists of the following six steps: (1) assess the situation, (2) set objectives, (3) select target audiences, (4) implement details, (5) determine costs and budgeting, and (6) evaluate results.

6. **Discuss the role of public relations in an integrated marketing communication program.**
Public relations contributes to an integrated communication program in several key ways. It helps launch new products because it provides ways to use the news to announce the products in a credible way that generates excitement. It helps organizations identify key stakeholders, analyze the nature of those relationships, and deliver the messages needed to keep the relationships positive and productive. Corporate advertising, an area where advertising and public relations intersect, requires strong coordination with other marketing communication areas. Planning for a crisis is also crucial to an integrated program, especially when the crisis is precipitated by a product or marketing activity, such as a product that fails or a promotion that goes awry. To ensure integration, public relations specialists must be sensitive to the bottom-line concerns of business managers, and companies must recognize the key role PR can play in relationship marketing.

7. Describe the tools used in public relations programs.

PR managers use many tools. These tools include publicity; corporate advertising; publications, videos, and film for internal and external audiences; special events and sponsorships of events to generate publicity and increase enthusiasm; lobbying; fundraising; meetings; and organized social activities.

POINTS TO PONDER

Review the Facts

1. Distinguish the terms "public relations" and "publicity."
2. Define a public. Differentiate between internal and external publics. Name several types of publics that are of interest to the PR planner.
3. Explain why the concept of *relations* is so important to public relations.

Master the Concepts

4. What steps might a public relations person take to prevent a firm from developing a negative public image?
5. What are the pros and cons of using corporate advertising? Under what conditions would it be appropriate?
6. How does public relations differ from advertising and sales promotion? What advantages does public relations offer that are not available through these other two marketing communication functions?
7. Evaluate the credibility ratings in Table 11.1. Explain why you think public relations is rated so low on the list and why it is rated higher than advertising.

Apply Your Knowledge

8. You are the public relations director for a company that makes children's clothing. Develop a proposal for a public relations issues and crisis management program. What research needs to be done? What kinds of recommendations would this program be likely to address with top management?
9. St. Ignatius Hospital in northern California has experienced a sharp decline in the number of patients admitted. It suspects one reason might be its policy of accepting patients with AIDS. What kind of research would you gather to assess the image of St. Ignatius and determine the nature of the problem it faces in filling its beds?
10. Prepare a set of guidelines for developing a healthy relationship between the news media and the firm's PR department.
11. Assume that you are the public relations director for a bank. Suppose that two people were robbed while withdrawing money from one of your bank's 24-hour automatic teller machines. The president wants your advice on what to say to the news media. What would you recommend?
12. Use the robbery as a rationale for developing a crisis plan for the bank. Develop a draft that outlines various types of crisis scenarios and how they should be handled. Identify the key roles of senior management and those of the public relations office.

SUGGESTED PROJECTS

1. (Writing Project) Review several newspapers and magazines and collect five articles that you feel are based on news releases prepared by a public relations specialist. What do you believe were the objectives of each of these releases? Do you believe the articles helped create or reinforce a positive image of the company? Prepare a one-to-two page memo that describes your findings. Be sure to attach copies of the articles.

2. (Team Project) Divide into small groups of 4 to 6 students. Assume that you are the PR team for the athletic program at your college or university. The NCAA just announced that it is investigating your football (or basketball) program because some team members have been charged with, but not yet convicted of, illegal drug use. Brainstorm ideas and then outline a public relations strategy that will respond effectively to this bad news. Select one group member to present the group's finding to the class.

3. Develop a crisis communication plan for your school, college, or department. What are the possible disasters that might affect your program? What decisions need to be made in advance of that happening? Who should do what?

4. (Internet Project) Assume you are the marketing communication director for an upscale hotel chain based in Cincinnati, Ohio. The business operates around the world. Recently, press reports in the United States and the United Kingdom claim that business managers in several of your hotels in the Caribbean and Asia have relied on child labor for both cleaning and kitchen jobs. Complaints from potential customers are increasing daily; U.S. bookings are declining. You've set up a toll-free customer hotline in response, but you feel you need a Web site to help communicate in a timely manner with customers, travel agents, and other key stakeholders around the world. You decide to turn to an outside PR agency for help with the site and the planning and implementation of a comprehensive PR strategy.

Visit the Web sites of at least three PR agencies to see who you would consider hiring. Some suggested sites include the following:

Burson-Marstellar (www.bm.com)
Edelman Worldwide (www.edelman.com)
Hill & Knowlton (www.hillandknowlton.com)
Porter/Novelli (www.porternovelli.com)

Explore each company's site. Be sure to note where the agency has offices, how much experience it has in developing Web sites, and whether it has aided other clients with similar situations. Describe your findings and recommendations in a two- to three-page memo.

CASE 11: SHAPING UP THE BODY SHOP

The Body Shop operated with an anti-advertising philosophy for years after it was founded in 1976 by marketing maverick Anita Roddick. The company became successful based on its good reputation and its image as a company with a mission dedicated to social change. Roddick believed her high profile would make it possible to keep the company in consumers' minds, relying on public relations rather than traditional advertising. The company's positive image, however, soured when *Business Ethics* ran an article that spotlighted the gap between its image and its practices.

Roddick, the daughter of Italian immigrants, opened her first store in Brighton, England, more than 20 years ago. Within ten years, some 1100 franchises were operating worldwide with 200 in the United States. The number reached 1400 in 1996. More than 90 percent of the stores are independently owned. Roddick outlined her philosophy as follows:

When I opened the first Body Shop in Brighton in 1976, I knew nothing about business....Today the Body Shop is an international company rapidly expanding around the world....[M]y passionate belief is that business can be fun, it can be conducted with love and be a powerful force for good. . . . Passion persuades, and by God, I was passionate about what I was selling.

An outspoken critic of traditional marketing, she claimed to have never spent a cent on advertising, which she considers to be hype—that is, until after the ethics scandal. Instead, she relied on free coverage in the media to tell her story. Body Shop also relied on its front line—employees and customers—to spread the news about the company and its philosophy.

The 1994 *Business Ethics* article, entitled "Shattered Image," damaged the Body Shop reputation. The issues? First, the U.K.–based retailer and cataloger of personal care products was charged with not purchasing as many ingredients from developing countries as claimed. Second, the ingredients used in Body Shop products were not as socially responsible as claimed. The article alleged that Body Shop lotions and creams were not completely natural and that some ingredients were tested on animals. Third, the franchisees complained that the Body Shop treated them unfairly. The company supposedly sold franchisees products at such high prices that the franchisees could not resell products with standard mark-up prices and remain competitive. Franchise owners also claimed they were misled about the earning potential of a franchise.

Until the article, the Body Shop was often cited as a paragon of socially responsible marketing and a paradigm for how to sell to modern consumers. The idea is that customers will be loyal to companies they consider to be responsible corporate citizens.

Following the article, the U.S. House Committee on Small Business disclosed that it had received numerous complaints from Body Shop franchisees, and the Federal Trade Commission announced that it was investigating the situation. The Boston-based Frankly Research Development Corp., one of the largest investment firms focusing on socially responsible investing, gave the Body Shop its top social rating in 1991. After the article ran in *Business Ethics,* the company eliminated the Body Shop from its roster of rated companies. To compound problems, an Amazon chief featured in Body Shop posters in 1996 sued the company for using his image for publicity purposes without permission—again smearing the image of a company that professed to be interested in doing business with love and concern.

So with the negative publicity, the Body Shop faced the ultimate test of its reputation and credibility. How has it done since then? Financial reports in 1995 and 1996 indicated that the company's U.S. business declined noticeably. Company executives claim the decline occurred because of over-expansion and increased competition. However, analysts cite the bad publicity as another factor.

Though the Body Shop saw growth in its Asian market, particularly Japan, revenues continued steady through 1995 but flattened in 1996. Controversy surrounding the company's proposal to introduce Body Shop Direct (a home-shopping-by-party division) triggered bad publicity and strained relations with franchisees in England that fear the division could harm their survival.

The company cannot be considered financially healthy as long as its U.S. stores are in trouble, and questionable ethics continue to tarnish the company's super-green image.

Case Questions

1. If you were public relations manager for the Body Shop in 1994, how would you have handled the *Business Ethics* article fallout?

2. If you were the public relations manager for another company that emphasized its social responsibility, such as Ben & Jerry's or Tom's of Maine, what would you learn from this case and how would you counsel senior management in your company on what the company needs to do to prevent this kind of situation from happening?

3. Do you believe the Body Shop can rebuild its image? What would you recommend?

4. How would you test the idea that customers who are loyal to companies they believe in will stay loyal in spite of bad news? What could be learned from the Body Shop's experience?

Sources: Ardyn Bernoth, "Roddick Faces Franchise Rebellion," *Sunday London Times,* 22 September 1996, B1; "Body Shop Starting to Lose Gentle Touch," *The Daily Telegraph,* 20 June 1996, 22; Michael Durham and Jan Rocha, "Amazon Chief Sues Body Shop," *The Observer,* 3 March 1996, 5; Susan Gilchrist, "Body Blows Wash Over Body Shop," *The London Times,* 14 October 1994, B1.

ROMA'S LITE INTEGRATED CASE QUESTIONS

(Review the Roma's Lite Marketing Plan in the Appendix before answering these questions.)

1. The objective of public relations is to create goodwill and control a brand's image and corporate reputation. Are these goals important in the launch of a new product like Roma's Lite Pizza? How and why?

2. (Writing Project) What are the various types of public relations programs? Write a brief memo of the programs you would use in the introduction of Roma's Lite Pizza and how you would use them.

3. (Team Project) Develop a public relations program for the launch of Roma's Lite Pizza. What are your objectives, and which stakeholders should your program target? Prepare sample materials to be used in communicating with the various important stakeholders. Explain how these materials tie in with the advertising and sales promotion plans you developed in Chapters 9 and 10.

chapter

12

Communicating Through Direct Marketing

CHAPTER OBJECTIVES

After completing your work on this chapter, you should be able to:

1 **Define direct marketing and explain its role in the marketing communication mix.**

2 **Discuss the strengths and weaknesses of direct marketing.**

3 **Outline how to manage, design, and evaluate a direct-marketing program.**

4 **Describe how direct marketers use the tools of direct mail, catalogs, mass media, and telemarketing media.**

CONSIDER this

Where Everybody Knows Your Name

Max Grassfield runs an upscale men's clothing store in Denver, Colorado. Max wanted to set his store apart. After much research and effort he believes Grassfield's is unique because his employees know their customers "better than the other stores know their customers."

For years Max developed a database of customer-provided information that included names, addresses, telephone numbers, sizes, birthdays, and wives' names. Why the emphasis on wives? Max's survey research found that of his married customers, wives made more than half of the clothing decisions.

Armed with these findings, Max developed a program called Invitational Marketing®, based on the idea that business goes where business is invited. Its objective was simple: Show customers they are important by inviting them to come back. Often. But how could he persuade his sales staff to issue written invitations?

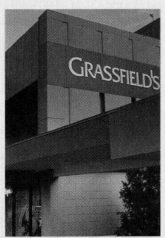

What if . . . the work was done for them? Personal salespeople could link to Grassfield's customer database, create a mailing list, and send personalized invitations to visit the store. Invitations are routinely sent out around the customers' birthdays, when a product the customer likes is available, or for those who haven't shopped in a while. Each note's salutation begins with the name the salesperson uses to greet the customer, and every letter is personally signed by the salesperson who waited on the customer during the last store visit. "We can welcome them, thank them, market to them, show them we know them by name and how much we value their business."

Max divided his customer base into three groups: (1) the active customer, (2) the not-so-active customer, and (3) customers' wives. In addition, he planned three over-sized, four-color postcards showing new fashion styles for the coming season. The results? Sales increased more than 21 percent. The program targeted at wives produced $60,000 in

377

additional business. And 271 of the not-so-active customers became active again.

Max's Invitational Marketing® program worked because it made customers feel they were the most important people in the world. "I want to cement a relationship to such an extent that when our customer thinks of men's clothing they'll think only of Grassfields...." And how does he do that? Max tells us the secret is the theme song of *Cheers*. "Because sometimes you want to go where everybody knows your name."

Max knows that successful marketing also requires a program targeted at new customers—where the names

aren't known yet. To do this Max obtains a regular list of new homeowners in the Denver area and selects only those moving into properties valued at $200,000 or more. Twice a month he mails a welcome letter with a $25 gift certificate. The experience over a ten-month period was quite impressive. Max spent $2957 to acquire 118 new customers who spent a total of $25,845. Assuming a profit margin of 40 percent, Max made a profit of $10,338 on his investment. Hopefully, those 118 new customers will become regular customers known at Grassfield's, of course, by name.

Sources: Arthur Middleton Hughes, "A Tailor-Made Program," *Marketing Tools* (July/August 1996): Internet: www.marketingpower.com/Publications; Murray Raphel, "The Return of Max Grassfield," *Direct Marketing* (April 1995): 30–1; Penny Parker, "Grassfield Marketing Changes with Times," *Denver Post*, Monday, 15 April 1996, 2E.

CHAPTER OVERVIEW

Few areas of marketing have undergone more dramatic change than direct marketing. Until recently, most consumers viewed direct marketing as junk mail and junk products. As Max Grassfield's experience shows, direct marketing can strengthen customer loyalty, target and win new customers, provide consumers with better information more quickly, and can generate more wealth for the company.

In this chapter we first examine the definition and types of direct marketing. Next we explore the strengths and weaknesses of direct marketing in an integrated marketing communication program. Finally, we investigate how to manage, design, and evaluate a direct-marketing program and examine how direct marketers use direct mail, catalogs, and mass media.

THE WORLD OF DIRECT MARKETING

Direct marketing is an interactive marketing communication tool that uses one or more advertising media to effect a measurable response and/or transaction at any location. In addition, **direct marketing** uses a database—a customer file.[1] This definition has five key points.

First, direct marketing is an *interactive system*. That is, the prospective customer and marketer can engage in two-way communication. For instance, Lands' End Inc. may send out a mail-order catalog; the customer can respond by calling for more information, clarifying problems, or even placing an order. Second, as part of the two-way communication, direct marketing always *provides a means for the customer to respond*. Because response is possible, the number and characteristics of those who do not respond have a strong impact on planning.

Third, direct marketing can occur any time and any place. The response does not require a retail store or a salesperson. Instead, the order can be made at any time of the day or night and can be delivered without the customer leaving home. In the case of Max Grassfield, for example, the salesperson can send a picture of the item to the customer (often via fax), and because the salesperson has all the customer's measurements, the item can be express mailed to the customer without a store visit.

Fourth, direct marketing must have a *measurable response*—the direct marketer must be able to calculate precisely the costs of implementing the strategy and the resulting income. Its measurable response represents the primary benefit of direct marketing and is undoubtedly a reason for its recent growth in popularity.

Fifth, direct marketing requires a *database of consumer information*. Through the information in databases, the direct marketer can tailor communications targeted at prospective individual or business customers. The information also allows direct marketers to offer benefits to its consumers: convenience, efficiency, and time savings. For example, when a consumer buys shirts in the mail from Joseph Banks and Company, every step of the process is smoothly executed, from the toll-free conversation with the order-taker to prompt delivery of well-made, fully guaranteed shirts, billed to a Visa card at a cost that is often lower than what many retail stores charge.

Strengths and Weaknesses of Direct Marketing

Many marketing communication activities are better done through direct marketing. To begin with, direct marketing is more targeted than indirect marketing. Direct marketers' ability to tailor a list of prospect names combining several characteristics—for instance, proven mail-order buyers who own VCR machines and take at least two ski vacations a year—allows them to carve out new market segments with profit potential.

Because direct marketers can find out so much more about their prospects and customers, direct marketing is able to address these people in very personal terms. Rather than men or women, marketing communicators can talk to old movie buffs, duck hunters, and tennis players. Also, every dollar spent in direct marketing is measurable. Each call, mailing, and ad contains a call to action that can be counted. This makes direct marketers accountable for every dollar they spend.

Because direct marketers can generate firm numbers that measure the effectiveness of their efforts, it is possible for them to devise accurate head-to-head tests of offers, formats, prices, payment terms, creative approach, and much more—all in relatively small and affordable quantities.

Direct marketing is extremely flexible. This is especially true in direct mail, where there are few constraints on size, color, timing, and format. Other than conformance to U.S. Postal Service standards, a direct-mail marketer can sell with a formula ranging from a postcard to a three-dimensional package. Tremendous growth and poor early management created some problems in the direct-marketing industry. Many of the troubles are symptoms of managerial "nearsightedness"—failure to consider long-term goals and the organization as a whole.

In 1981 Ed Ney, then CEO of Young & Rubicam, was asked whether direct marketing in the future was "an oasis or a mirage." "The difference between general [indirect] marketers and direct marketers," Ney said, "is the difference between the cost of goods sold and the price of success."[2] Ney was referring to brand personality built over the years versus the "one shots" that frequently characterize direct marketing. Examples of the short-term approach crop up daily in consumer mailboxes: mailings that look like telegrams, air-express packages, legal communications, or government documents. Short-term direct marketing does get a response, for a while, until customers become wary. But at what price? This kind of direct marketing creates short-term, disloyal customers who were really fooled into responding.

In contrast, American Express spends hundreds of thousands of dollars a year sending "love letters," communications that might typically congratulate customers on their tenth anniversary as card members. The objective of the communication is to reinforce a customer's relationship with American Express over the long term. Thus, if done correctly, direct marketing can be an effective communication tool that has long-term benefits.

Direct marketing has weaknesses, then, in part because too many aren't using it correctly due to poor training. Companies that would not dream of running an ad in *Hardware Age* or another trade publication without getting professional help let their in-house trainee design their direct-mail piece. Unless direct marketers make the critical changes in strategy, media planning, and creative execution that direct marketing requires, they will fail.

Poorly executed direct marketing creates an environment of distrust. The personalization of direct marketing through sophisticated databases is a case in point. People pay attention when marketers call them by name, and they are flattered if marketers know a little bit about their needs, tastes, and preferences. However, people become upset if they think marketers know too much about them or if marketers seem to be misusing this personal information. The sponsor of such intrusive direct marketing will develop a poor image in the eyes of target audience members.

All too often, direct marketing does not mesh with a company's operations, its distribution systems, communications, research, overall strategy, or even its culture. For example, direct marketers have been part of programs that have failed because they are so successful: catalog companies run out of inventories, costing them not only short-term sales but long-term goodwill, or financial firms generate too many leads for their salespeople to follow up.

Another common weakness is direct-marketing messages that conflict with other marketing communication messages, especially advertising. Conflicting messages occur because the direct-response marketers are not integrated with

Concept Review

STRENGTHS AND WEAKNESSES OF DIRECT MARKETING

1. Direct marketing has the following strengths:
   - More targeted than other forms of marketing communication
   - Ability to personalize approach
   - Results are measurable
   - All elements of a direct-marketing piece are testable
   - Elements are extremely flexible
2. Several weaknesses of direct marketing follow:
   - Ineffective unless used as a long-term strategy
   - Poorly executed direct marketing creates distrust and a poor image
   - Failure to coordinate with operations, distribution, or corporate strategy can lead to decreased goodwill
   - Direct-marketing messages may conflict with other marketing communication messages

other marketing communicators, such as those who do indirect advertising.

Direct Marketing and the Marketing Communication Mix

Direct marketing differs from other marketing communication tools. First, those who use direct marketing go straight to the customer, not to resellers or retailers, for product distribution. Companies such as Kraft General Foods, Ford Motor Co., and Best Foods, for instance, distribute their products through a network of resellers (wholesalers and retailers) who make these companies' products available to customers. Direct marketers tend to skip resellers and contact customers directly. Some direct marketers, such as Harry and David's, have retail stores, but those stores represent a very small part of their business.

Second, direct-marketing communication is designed to generate a response, not create awareness or enhance the company image. Ads for Coca-Cola, Levi's 501 Jeans, and Pert shampoo are not intended to cause an immediate change in behavior. Known as *awareness advertising,* the primary purpose of such ads is to create and maintain brand awareness. Awareness ads reinforce the positive elements of the brand in consumers' minds and can deliver extra value through coupons, rebates, and sweepstakes.

In contrast, direct-marketing communication usually involves **direct-response advertising,** that is, advertising designed to motivate customers to respond with either an order or inquiry. Also, direct marketing communicates directly with customers through targeted media rather than mass media. Examples of such media include direct mail, telemarketing, and point-of-purchase displays.

Direct marketing also differs from personal selling, a marketing communication tool often used to supplement indirect marketing efforts. Direct marketing does not rely on the sales force to spread the sales message. With indirect marketing, the sales force plays a pivotal role by informing and selling to resellers or end users. In contrast, direct marketing primarily relies on media, not a salesperson, to generate a sales lead. It is critical, then, that the direct-marketing piece—such as an ad that contains a toll-free number or a letter that includes a blank order form—contains all the necessary information for the customer to respond.

In direct marketing the message communicated in nonpersonal media makes a measurable contribution to selling. Salespeople, however, are often necessary to complete the sale or provide information in response to inquiries triggered by the direct-mail piece.

For example, the advertisement for *Time for Kids* contains a toll-free number to call for further information and to subscribe to the publication. Salespeople, then, receive the calls and sign up interested educators. This type of direct-marketing advertising has become the primary lead-generating device for many sales forces.

Here is an example of a direct-response ad designed to motivate a response—an inquiry about the product.

The inclusion of an 800 number in this ad provides solid sales leads for this product.

A final difference between direct and indirect marketing is the ease at which
various elements of the media piece can be tested. Because direct marketing leads
directly to sales rather than recall or attitude change (typical goals of indirect marketing), manipulating an 800 number, a special discount, or a product featured as
part of the direct-marketing communication piece can be quickly noted. As a
result, elements that are not working can be readily changed.

Table 12.1 summarizes how direct marketing differs from other marketing communication tools that rely on indirect marketing.

The State of the Industry

The origin of direct marketing goes back many years. Orvis issued its first catalog, offering fishing equipment, in 1844, and the Tiffany catalog made its debut
a year later. Montgomery Ward launched its mail-order business in 1872, and Sears
entered the field in 1886. In the early 1900s L.L. Bean and the Book-of-the-

TABLE 12.1

**Key Differences Between
Direct Marketing and
Indirect Marketing**

Indirect Marketing	Direct Marketing
Reaches a mass audience through mass media	Communicates directly with the customer or prospect through more targeted media
Communications are impersonal	Can personalize communications By name/title Variable messages
Promotional programs are highly visible to competition because mass media is used	Promotional programs (especially pretests) are relatively invisible to the competition
Amount of promotion controlled by size of budget	Size of budget can be determined by success of promotion
Desired action either unclear or delayed	Specific action always requested Inquiry Purchase
Incomplete/sample data for decision-making purposes Sales call reports Marketing research	Comprehensive database drives marketing programs
Analysis conducted at segment level	Analysis conducted at individual/firm level through personalization
Use surrogate variables to measure effectiveness Advertising awareness Intention to buy	Measurable, and therefore highly controllable

Source: Mary Lou Roberts and Paul D. Berger, *Direct Marketing Management* (Englewood Cliffs, N.J.: Prentice-Hall, 1989), 4. Reprinted by permission of Prentice-Hall, Inc.

Month Club came on the scene. It was after World War II, however, that the national magazines turned to the mails as the battleground for their mass circulation wars, and direct mail entered a period of rapid growth and development.

Technology spurred growth in direct marketing even further. The increasing power and decreasing costs of computers enabled businesses to collect and manage databases of information about consumers. The information allowed companies to efficiently and cheaply identify the most likely buyers, segment them, and target them directly. Today marketers can develop or buy sophisticated databases with relevant data about consumers' buying behavior, lifestyle, names, addresses, and so forth. With these lists, marketers can personalize and vary communications, just as Grassfield's was able to personalize and vary its invitations.

Direct marketing is indeed big business. Table 12.2 lists the top 30 direct-marketing agencies of 1994. Ogilvy & Mather Direct was the top agency, followed by Rapp Collins Worldwide. A survey of the top 200 direct-marketing agencies showed billings of $5.1 billion in 1995 compared with $3.4 billion in 1988. The entire direct-marketing industry had billings totaling $187 billion in 1996.

The effect of direct marketing on the economy has been tremendous. In 1995 the Direct Marketing Association (DMA) studied the economic impact of this marketing communication tool. Researchers reviewed 8000 direct-response ads from magazines, newspapers, television, radio, and more than 1000 direct-mail pieces. Here is what the DMA learned:[3]

- When direct-response advertising is used to solicit a direct order, generate a lead, or generate retail store traffic, it will result in nearly $600 billion in annual sales.
- Business-to-business sales from direct order, lead generation, and traffic generation are estimated to reach $500 billion in annual sales.
- Compounded annual growth rates of sales through the year 2000 will be 7.2 percent for consumer (as compared with 5.9 percent in 1992) and 10.2 percent for business-to-business (as compared with 7.5 percent in 1992).
- One in every 13 jobs in the United States today is the result of direct-marketing sales activity.

Types of Direct Marketing

Direct marketing can take three forms: the one-step process, the two-step process, and the negative option.

1. *One-step process.* The consumer responds to an ad in a media vehicle and receives the product by mail. A bounce-back brochure promoting related merchandise may be included with the product.
2. *Two-step process.* The potential customer must first be qualified before ordering the product. Insurance companies use the two-step process when they require a physical exam before enforcing the policy. Similarly, a company selling high-ticket items, such as land or furniture, may require a preliminary credit check. Or a company may charge a fee for a catalog of direct-mail merchandise; the fee can be used as credit toward purchases.
3. *Negative option.* The customer joins a plan such as those offered by record or book clubs to automatically receive unrequested merchandise at regular intervals. The initial merchandise is often offered with a free gift or at a discount price.

TABLE 12.2

Top Direct-Marketing Agencies

Direct Response Agency Ranking by Billings

Agencies	Total Billings (in millions)		U.S. Billings (in millions)		International Billings (in millions)	
	1993	1994	1993	1994	1993	1994
1. Ogilvy & Mather Direct	$928.7	973.0	440.0	413.0	488.7	560.0
2. Rapp Collins Worldwide	833.2	934.4	390.0	461.0	443.2	473.4
3. Wunderman Cato Johnson	708.5	910.5	393.4	430.6	315.1	479.9
4. Kobs & Draft Advertising, Inc.	438.0	493.7	201.2	259.8	236.8	233.9
5. Bronner Slosberg Humphrey, Inc.	305.1	333.5	305.1	333.5	NA	NA
6. Grey Direct International	287.0	312.3	161.0	184.3	126.0	128.0
7. DIMAC DIRECT, Inc.	176.1	271.4	176.1	271.4	NA	NA
8. Barry Blau & Partners, Inc.	204.3	261.6	204.3	261.6	NA	NA
9. McCann Direct	203.0	215.0	53.0	50.0	150.0	165.0
10. Customer Development Corp.	151.3	172.4	151.3	172.4	NA	NA
11. Chapman Direct Advertising	154.2	143.5	154.2	143.5	NA	NA
12. Devon Direct Marketing & Advertising, Inc.	132.0	139.1	132.0	139.1	NA	NA
13. FCB Direct	128.5	135.6	128.5	135.6	NA	NA
14. J. Walter Thompson Direct	126.4	132.4	51.9	59.2	74.5	73.2
15. Clarion Direct	68.9	116.1	68.9	116.1	NA	NA

Source: Direct Marketing (November 1995): 58.

THE PROCESS OF DIRECT MARKETING

Direct marketing uses the planning framework suggested throughout this text. It is unique, however, because its primary objectives are sales-related, and it relies heavily on a high-quality database. It also uses special media to deliver messages and employ a unique creative approach. Finally, there is a reliance on a fulfillment company to deliver the product to the customer. The primary components of the direct-marketing process are shown in Figure 12.1 on page 386. The material addressed in the following sections applies to direct marketing only.

Agencies	Total Billings (in millions)		U.S. Billings (in millions)		International Billings (in millions)	
	1993	1994	1993	1994	1993	1994
16. Bozell Direct—Bozell, Jacobs, Kenyon, & Eckhardt, Inc.	$106.0	114.5	50.0	54.5	56.0	60.0
17. Grizzard Communications Group	83.9	98.7	83.9	98.7	NA	NA
18. Gillespie	76.8	92.7	76.8	92.7	NA	NA
19. GSP Marketing Services, Inc.	65.6	85.1	65.6	85.1	NA	NA
20. Brierley & Partners, Inc.	63.1	75.5	63.1	75.5	NA	NA
21. The Stenrich Group, Inc.	52.9	72.8	52.9	72.8	NA	NA
22. Holland Mark Martin	62.6	70.8	62.6	70.8	NA	NA
23. Russ Reid Co.	64.0	63.0	64.0	63.0	NA	NA
24. The McClure Group	43.7	59.2	43.7	59.2	NA	NA
25. The RTC Group	51.7	55.9	51.7	55.9	NA	NA
26. Williams Television Time	41.3	55.3	41.3	55.3	NA	NA
27. Walther Latham	48.5	49.5	48.5	49.5	NA	NA
28. MHA Carlson (United Kingdom)	42.3	47.2	NA	NA	42.3	47.2
29. Herring/Newman, Inc.	34.7	47.1	34.7	47.1	NA	NA
30. Hill Holliday Direct	39.4	46.3	39.4	46.3	NA	NA

The Database: A Key to Success

The *database* is the essence of direct marketing. A **database** contains information about customers and prospects that has been collected over a considerable time.

Database marketing is the process of building, maintaining, and using customer databases for the purpose of contacting customers and transacting business. Typically, a company can expect to invest anywhere from $100,000 to $750,000 to build and implement a marketing database.

Concept

Review

THE WORLD OF DIRECT MARKETING

1. Direct marketing is an interactive system of marketing that uses advertising media to effect a measurable response or transaction at any location. Every direct-marketing system must have a database.
2. Direct marketing differs from indirect marketing in the following ways:
   - It skips resellers and retailers; direct marketers contact customers directly for product distribution.
   - It relies on direct-response advertising rather than awareness advertising.
   - It communicates through targeted media rather than mass media.
   - It does not rely on a salesperson to generate sales leads, relying instead on customer response to media for those leads.
3. Due to improved technology, better databases, and consumer acceptance, direct marketing has grown to a $190 billion industry.
4. The three types of direct marketing are one-step, two-step, and negative option.

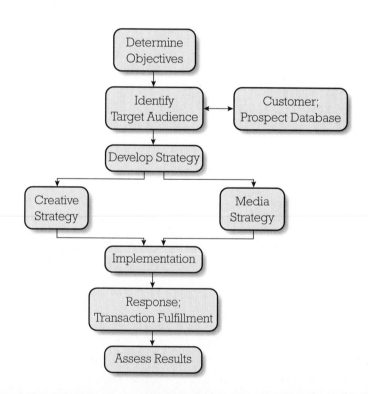

FIGURE 12.1

The Process of Direct Marketing

Most databases are not designed exclusively for marketing but perform several functions within an organization. Although a computer is not required, practically speaking, it is impossible to effectively maintain a database of useful size without one. As an example of questions to ask to build a customer database, Figure 12.2 displays the questionnaire Grassfield's uses to collect internal data.

In the sections that follow, we explore how companies develop, maintain, and use a database.

Developing the Database

Obtaining a *mailing list* is the first step toward establishing a database. A **mailing list** is a list of customer or prospect names, addresses, phone and fax numbers, and e-mail addresses if available. It does not contain any behavioral information, such as purchasing history. The mailing list can be generated internally (through warranty cards, for example) or purchased externally. Once the direct marketer obtains a list, managing the database system involves five additional steps:

1. *Capture, organize, and maintain existing marketing data.* Companies buy or develop mailing lists and continually add to the basic data to keep it current.
2. *Convert the data into useful information that has possible application to company strategies.* Suppose Toyota maintained a database of detailed information about Toyota car users. This year the company hopes to increase sales of a new version of the Camry. Toyota's direct marketers could sort the database information into

GRASSFIELD'S
PREFERRED CUSTOMER

Name ______ (FIRST) ______ (MIDDLE INITIAL) ______ (LAST) Nickname ______

Home Address ______

City ______ State ______ Zip ______

Office Phone ______ Home Phone ______

Suit: ______ ☐ Short ☐ Regular ☐ Long ☐ Extra Long

Trouser: Waist ______ Shoes ______ Are you married? ☐ Yes ☐ No

Shirt: Neck ______ Sleeve ______ Spouse's name: ______

Sweater: ______ Sp. Shirt ______ Your birthday: Month ______ Day ______

FOR OFFICE USE ONLY

Link to ______ Salutation ______ Date ______

FIGURE 12.2

Grassfield's Preferred Customer Form

a list of satisfied Camry owners with cars over five years of age as a target market for the new version.

3. *Apply the database to specific strategies.* The satisfied Camry owner list could then be converted to a mailing list for a direct-mail piece on the new version of the Camry that offers a rebate.

4. *Test results.* Direct marketers have the opportunity to test the wording, design, and message in the direct-mail piece before sending it out to the target market. Toyota could test the direct-mail piece with select customers for feedback. Ultimately, sales of Camrys would be the measure of success.

5. *Capture new data and integrate it into the existing database.* Camry buyers would be surveyed six months after purchase to assess their level of satisfaction and response to specific features.

Companies may develop their database internally or externally, or use a combination of internal and external means. Internal, or in-house, databases are derived from customer receipts, credit card information, or personal information cards completed by customers. The internal approach is cost-effective as long as the company has the expertise and resources.

Many companies have neither the resources nor the expertise to develop in-house database systems. These companies can obtain commercial databases from firms whose sole purpose is to collect, analyze, categorize, and market an enormous variety of detail about the American consumer.[4] Companies such as National Decision Systems, Persoft, and Donnelly Marketing Information Systems are only a few of these firms. From such information as income, education, occupation, and census data, their databases can describe life in individual neighborhoods across the country with amazing accuracy. The ad for RUF suggests the capabilities of one such company.

This ad for RUF Strategic Solutions touts its ability to develop a database of potential customers who fit the profile of the target market.

Maintaining the Database with RFM

Direct marketers continuously refine their databases with information on the **RFM**—the recency, frequency, and monetary value of purchases. Other relevant information that marketers need to maintain a useful database includes the method of customer payment, where they live, what they purchase, how long they have been customers, and their last date of purchase. Each company must consider its own needs when developing its database, given the objective of finding the most profitable customers and prospects. For example, the Remington Arms Co. of Wilmington, Delaware, is developing direct-marketing expertise and building its business by supplementing its retail business with direct marketing. In addition to its standard products, Remington sells accessory products that retailers don't handle. Examples of its direct-marketing products include a line of chemical accessories for maintaining guns and specialty collector knives.

Building Relationships Through CLV

Database marketing is most effective if it focuses on building relationships. In database marketing the Customer Lifetime Value

(CLV) approach is the equivalent of relationship marketing. The CLV approach recognizes that a new customer means not only an immediate sale but additional purchases over the customer's lifetime as a user of your product.

To build a relationship direct marketers must carefully target customers who are most likely to contribute significant sales and profit. Direct marketers often develop customer profiles to target such customers. For example, say a company sells produce to retailers. The company should first know how to meet its customers' needs and wants better than other produce suppliers on the market. Once researched, the company can assess who is most likely to buy from it and how to maintain customer relationships. Frieda's Inc., a produce company based in Los Alamitos, California, learned how to distinguish itself in a crowded market. It consistently sends its customers a "Hot Sheet" bulletin about what's new in the produce industry that is now recognized as a standard information source. The Hot Sheet helps cement Frieda's relationship with management in food chains across the country—they constantly learn what's new in specialty produce trends. More important, they see how Frieda's can satisfy their needs and help them keep up with trends.

Generally, direct-marketing CLV works best when the target market has the means to respond, and the provider supplies sufficient benefits to customers to make it worth their while to respond. The responses can then be measured. The CLV approach requires product research, satisfaction surveys, and personal information to make certain the target market has both the means and motivation to respond. As indicated in the You Decide feature, direct marketers may seek out information that is too personal.

Global Database Management

Before the 1990s database marketing was much more prevalent in the United States than in the rest of the world. Advances in technology and the growing globalization of marketing operations, however, have spurred growth in database marketing in Europe, Asia, and South America. However, differing cultures around the world may require companies to implement global database-marketing methods that are sensitive to others' cultures. Europeans, for instance, tend to distrust organizations that collect and sell personal information, and several countries have passed privacy laws prohibiting such practices. Asians tend to rely on product quality and reputation in their purchasing decisions. Once they try and are satisfied with a particular product, they are often very brand loyal. This tendency suggests that marketers should use database technology to improve relationships with existing customers rather than to constantly prospect for new, one-time buyers.

Designing a Direct-Marketing Strategy

The direct-marketing strategy details the events and methods needed to complete an objective. It includes decisions in five areas: (1) the offer, (2) the medium, (3) the message, (4) timing and sequencing, and (5) customer service.

The Offer

The proposition made to customers is often referred to as the offer. It is the key to success or failure, and the manner in which it is presented can have a dramatic effect. The offer's message and design should be supported by comprehensive

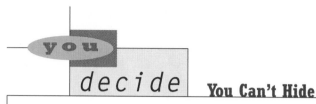

You Can't Hide

For years Lisa Tomaino kept her address secret. She and her husband, Jim, a police officer, wanted to make it as hard as possible for the crooks he put away to find out where they lived. But last year Lisa had a baby. So much for her big secret. Within six weeks she was inundated with junk mail aimed at new mothers. The hospital had sold her name and address to a direct-marketing company, and soon she was on dozens of other lists. Efforts to get their names removed from these lists proved fruitless. "It was a complete violation of our right to privacy," she declares.

Private citizens, private watchdogs, and a handful of lawmakers have railed for years about Big Brotherism by business. But when politicians balance industry's interest in reaching markets against the customer's right to privacy, marketing usually wins. "Existing laws regulating privacy simply aren't effective," gripes Robert Bulmash, president of Private Citizen, Inc., a public advocacy group.

Marketers are keenly aware of the public's reaction to their unwanted attention. After all, it's their job to stay in touch with the preferences of consumers. Vendors of marketing data argue that any intrusion on privacy from selling lists is offset "by the significant potential gain to consumers from the special offers and products offered by direct marketers."

The industry has largely staved off regulation by convincing the federal government that it can police itself. The Information Monitoring Association (IMA), for example, runs a phone number for people who want their names removed from mailing lists. Or, you can register with the Mail Preference Service (MPS), at the following address: Mail Preference Service, Direct Marketing Association, P.O. Box 9008, Farmingdale, New York, 11735-9008.

But relatively few consumers use it, and those who do contend that their names come off some, but not all, lists. Even long-standing laws, such as the 1970 Fair Credit Reporting Act, aren't effective. The statute is supposed to prevent credit agencies such as TRW, Equifax, and TransUnion from releasing financial information about a person except for "legitimate" business needs, such as a credit check. Unfortunately, it doesn't always do so.

As marketing techniques become more sophisticated, the privacy of the Lisa Tomainos of the world will grow increasingly difficult to protect.

You Decide

1. As a direct marketer, how would you justify this perceived invasion of privacy?

2. Suppose the Tomainos started receiving threats from a criminal that Officer Tomaino had apprehended. Suppose also that the criminal had found their personal phone number and address through access to a direct-marketing database. Do you think the Tomainos should have any recourse against the hospital?

3. Now assume that you are the director of a nonprofit hospital. Direct marketers offer hundreds of thousands of dollars for the database you maintain of those who recently had a baby in the hospital. By accepting the money for selling your database, you can lower your delivery and newborn care costs and upgrade medical equipment. However, you're worried about privacy issues. Can you suggest a data collection process that does not violate a patient's right to privacy?

Sources: "American Privacy Watch Offers Personal Choice," *Direct Marketing* (April 1996): 6; "Data, Data Everywhere," *Adweek,* June 10, 1996, 44; Laura Lors, "Privacy Concerns Have Consumers Guarding Data," *Advertising Age,* December 11, 1995, 40; Mark Lewyn, "You Can Run, But It's Tough to Hide from Marketers," *Business Week,* September 5, 1994, 60.

research. When creating an offer, managers must consider numerous factors. Some factors include price of the product, who pays the cost of shipping and handling, what product options to offer, how to motivate customers (greed, fear, goodwill), and how to make it easy for the consumer to respond (for example, use of a toll-free number or postage-paid envelope).

To begin with, there is a *price*. The correct price must not only include a sufficient markup but also reflect what competitors are charging and what consumers expect to pay. Odd-pricing (for example, $7.95), multiple unit pricing (such as two for $29.95), and giveaways (for example, $49.95 plus free steak knives) are common pricing strategies in direct marketing. The components of the price should be stated clearly and concisely.

The cost of *shipping and handling* can be an important part of the offer. Who should pay these costs? Can they be added to the base price of the product without adversely affecting sales? Recent increases in postal rates have shifted this cost burden to consumers in several instances.

Optional features are part of the basic offer. Special colors and sizes, personalization, or large-type editions are a few examples. Certain options can dramatically increase sales, whereas others prove unappealing. This is an area in which research is very important.

Many offers contain a *future obligation*. Book clubs and record clubs are two industries that normally ask for a one- or two-year commitment. The system of sending products at regular intervals and billing automatically allows the marketer to charge a very low price for the first order, knowing there will be a long-term payout. The availability of *credit* may be the most important element of an offer. Research indicates that if either commercial credit (such as Visa or MasterCard) or house credit (for example, an installment plan or Discover) is available, the average order size increases 15 percent.

Extra *incentives,* such as free gifts, discounts, sweepstakes, and toll-free ordering privileges, can all increase the attractiveness of an offer. Yet there is also the risk that the customer will have little interest in the incentive or, more important, that the cost of the incentive will inflate the price.

Time and quantity limits create an urgency in the mind of the customer. Suggesting that an offer will end on a certain date or that a product is a limited edition moves the prospect to action. It is important that the time or quantity limits be legitimate. Limits that are repeatedly extended quickly lose their impact.

The *guarantee* is an automatic part of any direct-marketing offer. Whenever people order products by phone or mail, they perceive risk. They must be assured that they can back out of a mistake. Sometimes there is a "guaranteed buy-back" offer. Some guarantees even pay "double your money back." The free issue wording says simply: I may cancel my reservation after looking at the premier issue.

The Medium and the Message

The choice of medium and the choice of the message are related decisions. The message strategies should consider the needs of the target audience, the company's objectives, and factors such as repetition, memorability, and clutter discussed in Chapter 5. The writing must grab attention through content and design. The media used in direct marketing have been specially developed to accommodate the unique advantages of

Direct marketing requires that the writing and visuals grab attention. This ad uses content, an interesting design, and strong copy to arouse readers' interest.

direct marketing. More will be said about direct-marketing media later in this chapter.

Timing and Sequencing

One difference with direct marketing is the emphasis on the timing and sequencing of the direct-marketing pieces. For example, when should a prospect receive a Christmas catalog or a direct-mail piece? Should the direct-mail piece be followed by telemarketing? Direct marketing must reach the right person at the right time. Direct-marketing experts estimate that 70 percent of the success of direct marketing is contingent on making the correct timing and sequencing decisions.[5] Much of this success depends on the quality of the database and the research behind it.

Customer Service

In direct marketing the importance of service cannot be overstated. The types of customer services offered—toll-free telephone numbers, free limited-time trial, acceptance of several credit cards, and a Web site, for example—are important techniques to motivate consumers to buy via direct-response media. The level of service is equally important. Speed and accuracy in filling orders, careful handling of customer complaints, and guaranteed return policies have been critical to the success of direct marketers such as Lillian Vernon, J. Crew, and Spiegel.

Evaluating Direct Marketing

Direct marketing is the most measurable element in the marketing communication mix. The basic philosophy of direct marketing is quite simple: There is no reason to invest resources in a direct-marketing program unless it has a high probability of success. Because direct marketers have control over both outbound communication to their customers and prospects and inbound communication from customers and prospects (responses), they are able to estimate the probability of success with a fairly high degree of accuracy. In general, direct marketers evaluate profitability and customer characteristics and response.

Profitability Analysis

The bottom line for direct marketing is profitability. Every decision considers how much profit the direct-marketing campaign will generate. If sufficient, the company will proceed with the activity. Essentially, costs and potential revenues are projected for each activity, and a return-on-investment is calculated.

Customer Characteristics and Response

Direct marketers not only want to know if their messages are reaching the right people at the right time, they also want to know if any of the people are responding. Three techniques are used in direct marketing to make this type of assessment: respondent/nonrespondent surveys, tracking studies, and geodemography.[6]

Respondent/Nonrespondent Surveys. As the term suggests, respondent/nonrespondent surveys attempt to identify differences between people who did and did not respond to the direct-marketing program. Because the marketer has a list of both respondents and nonrespondents, this technique entails a follow-up survey by telephone or mail to identify the demographic and psychographic characteristics of both groups and the reasons why they did or did not respond. This information serves as a guide for offering products in the future, for modifying the language in a direct-marketing piece, or for modifying the database.

Tracking Studies. Tracking studies are usually surveys that gather information from a large number of people by simply counting responses over time and collecting some information from a sample of respondents. The purpose is to assess whether purchase patterns and/or purchasers change over time.

Geodemography. This useful technique evolved during the last decade. **Geodemography** analyzes an existing database on the principle that birds of a feather flock together. That is, people who live together in small geographic areas such as blocks and ZIP code units tend to have more similar demographic characteristics than people who live elsewhere. One system, PRIZM, has given its clusters colorful names such as "Blueblood Estates" and "Bunker's Neighborhood." Geodemographic systems can track the demographic quality of respondents or conduct automatic respondent/nonrespondent studies, using only addresses as resources.

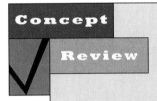

THE PROCESS OF DIRECT MARKETING

1. Database marketing is the process of building, maintaining, and using customer databases for the purpose of contacting customers and transacting business.
2. To manage a database, companies must:
   - Obtain a list of customers or potential customers.
   - Capture, organize, and maintain the existing marketing data.
   - Convert the data into useful information that has possible application to company strategies.
   - Apply the database to specific strategies.
   - Test the direct-mail piece before sending it out to the target market.
   - Capture new data and integrate it into the existing database.
3. Marketers design a direct-marketing strategy by focusing on five components: the offer, the medium, the message, timing and sequencing, and customer service.
4. Marketers use several techniques to evaluate direct marketing, including analyzing profitability and assessing response.

DIRECT-MARKETING MEDIA TOOLS

Direct marketers use many media tools. The six most common direct media are (1) direct mail, (2) catalogs, (3) mass media direct marketing, (4) infomercials, (5) interactive media, and (6) telemarketing.

Direct Mail

Direct mail delivers the message and the product through the U.S. Postal Service or a private delivery organization. Direct mail has been used to generate orders, presell activities before a field salesperson's visit, qualify prospects for a product, follow up a sale, announce special sales in local areas, and raise funds for nonprofit groups. Mail-order sales reached a high of $252.7 billion in 1994, up $32 billion over 1993.[7]

There are a number of advantages associated with direct mail as compared with traditional mass media. First, the medium offers a variety of formats and provides enough space to tell a complete sales story. Second, it is now possible to personalize direct mail across a number of characteristics, such as name, product usage, and income. Finally, direct mail allows the marketer to reach audiences who are inaccessible by other media.

The primary drawback of using direct mail is the widespread perception that it is junk mail. A second disadvantage of direct mail is the high cost per prospect reached. However, a direct-mail campaign may still be less expensive than trying to reach a particular target group through other media. A final drawback is the emergence of new technologies that do the same thing as direct mail. Fax machines are one option. *E-mail* and *voice mail* have also emerged as substitutes for direct mail. E-mail, or electronic mail, is a growing new media for direct marketing. **E-mail** is a message or file that is transmitted from one computer to another. Marketers now send sales announcements, offers, and other messages to e-mail addresses, sometimes to a few individuals, sometimes to large groups. **Voice mail** is a system for receiving and storing voice messages at a telephone address. Some marketers have programs that dial a large number of telephone numbers and leave a voice-mail sales message. The effectiveness of a direct-mail piece depends on the quality of the mailing list, the elements of the package, and the copy.

Lists

To successfully solicit customer orders, managers need accurate and up-to-date lists. Ideally, the lists should include only those who are in a position to purchase. For example, internal lists should include information such as how customers paid, where they live, what they purchase, how long they have been customers, and when they bought last. External lists can be of several types. **Compiled lists** identify people who share some common interest, such as snow skiing, retirement housing, or gourmet cooking. *Lists of inquiry* or *lists of customers from other companies* are provided by both competing and noncompeting companies. Each of these categories can be further refined until the marketer specifies just one characteristic, for example, income or telephone exchange.

Direct-Mail Packages

Everything in a direct-mail package must be designed to work in harmony. The package must stand out from other mail and encourage the receiver to open it. The components of the package should reflect a total design concept. The classic direct-mail package consists of a mailing envelope, letter, circular, response device, and return device.[8]

- *Mailing envelope:* The direct-mail selling process begins with the mailing envelope. Teaser copy of a "flash" (for example, "important, don't delay!") is often used to rouse interest and lead the reader to open the envelope.

As this ad implies, companies such as The Dun & Bradstreet Corp. have become important list providers.

WHAT YOU KNOW ABOUT YOUR CURRENT CUSTOMERS IS JUST THE TIP OF THE... WELL, YOU KNOW...

D&B can help you look below the surface and discover profitable new ways to market to your customer base.

How? We'll match your customer file against our detailed information base of over 10 million companies, and turn it into a rich source of business-to-business marketing knowledge

D&B's Customer File Enhancement Service adds critical information to your records such as Standard Industrial Classification (SIC) Code, sales volume, number of employees, additional contact names, credit and risk indicators, D-U-N-S® Number (a unique business identifier), and more. This knowledge can help you:

- Pinpoint the most productive segments of your customer base
- Profile your best customers to find prospects that match

- Identify corporate links and eliminate duplicate records with our D-U-N-S Number
- Implement more targeted sales and marketing campaigns

Do something with those frozen assets—look into D&B's Customer File Enhancement Service today. Call right away and get a copy of "Finding Hidden Profits in Your Customer Base" absolutely free.

Call **1-800-350-DUNS**, ext. 67, before November 30, 1995.

Dun & Bradstreet
Information Services

A company of
The Dun & Bradstreet Corporation

© 1995 Dun & Bradstreet, Inc.

- *The letter:* The letter should be personalized, speak to the self-interest of the reader, and elicit interest.
- *The circular:* The circular gives the details of the product—the specifications, color, pricing, photographs, guarantees, and endorsements. It presents the primary selling message and can take the form of a booklet, broadsheet (an oversized enclosure or jumbo folder), brochure, flier, or single sheet.
- *Response device:* The response device is the order form, often including a toll-free phone number. It should summarize the primary selling points and be simple to read and fill out.
- *Return device:* This item allows the customer to return the necessary information. It can be an information request form, an order form, or a payment.

Writing Direct-Mail Copy

To write good copy, the direct-mail copywriter needs valid information about the producer, the customer, and competitors. The direct-mail copywriter must know why people buy. Good copy translates selling points into benefits, emphasizes the buyer's self-gratification, and uses crisp, clear language. The offer must be stated immediately and emphatically. Moreover, the writer must convince the customer that what is promised will be delivered. Finally, good copy makes it easy to take the desired action. Requested action should be simple, specific, and immediate.

The large amount of copy space available in direct mail as compared with mass print media presents a temptation as well as an opportunity. There is a tendency to include excess material and use ultracreative formats. But the objective of direct mail is to sell, not to impress. Each word and picture must support that objective.[9] A direct-mail program must often be modified to effectively communicate with different target audiences, as demonstrated in the IMC in Action feature.

Finally, direct-mail expert Murray Raphel lists the most common mistakes made in direct marketing:[10]

1. Forgetting to include a letter in an offer
2. Lack of continuity in identification—the signature looks one way on the envelope, another way on the stationery, and a third on the mailer
3. No benefit indicated on the outside of the mailer
4. No guarantees
5. No testimonials
6. No personal letter from the owner in a newsletter or catalog
7. Too many messages
8. Illegible colors and graphics
9. Doesn't put the offer up front
10. No headlines

Catalogs

Catalog marketers mail over 12.7 billion copies of more than 8600 different catalogs annually. The average household receives at least 50 catalogs per year. In 1996 catalog sales were $75 billion, and by 2001 catalog sales are projected to reach $103 billion. The average consumer catalog buyer is a professional, has

Direct Mail to Asian-Americans

The direct-marketing industry has the ability to target a universe of potential buyers and to customize its messages to a specific culture. Direct mail, then, would seem to be an effective marketing vehicle to Asian-Americans. Here are some pointers for targeting Asian-Americans through direct mail. First, learn as much as possible about each distinct Asian-American demographic group in your target market. Second, become thoroughly familiar with their similarities and differences. Language and cultural ties are two of the most important concerns to examine.

Language

- *Deliver the marketing message in both English and the native language of the target market.* Purchasing decisions in Asian-American homes often involve a bilingual dynamic, so a marketing message in both languages helps reach more of your market.
- *Use both English and the native language on the outside of a direct-mail piece.* The use of both lan-

guages will help break through clutter and increase the chances that a prospect will open the piece.
- *Allow prospects to respond in either language.* To encourage prospects to make further contact with marketers, remove inhibitions about calling a toll-free number, receiving a sales call, or responding to follow-ups by assuring the market they may respond in the language with which they are most comfortable.

Culture

- *Associate the marketing message with traditional symbols, images, and other cultural references.* Asian-Americans have a high regard for their traditions. Traditional symbols and design elements have a high recognition level and will add positive associations to the message.
- *If the design includes traditional symbols and elements, make certain the design is distinctive and tasteful.* The distinctive appeal to tradition will separate packages

from the "junk mail" category, encouraging prospects to open and read the package. A poorly executed design, however, may offend and result in the package being thrown out.
- *Traditional Asian holiday and gift-giving occasions should be incorporated into the marketing strategy, with mailings timed accordingly.*
- *Tie promotions to festivals, celebrations, and other cultural events.*

To reach this diverse audience, marketers must do their homework. The effort, however, can be well worth it.

Food for Thought

1. Find an ad that features or targets Asian-Americans. Evaluate how well it adheres to these suggestions.
2. Now assume you were trying to target Latinos in the southeastern United States. How many of the ideas presented in this feature could you apply to target that market?

children in the household ages 13 to 18, or ages 0 to 3, has some college education, is a homeowner, and is married.[11]

Catalogs have changed dramatically over the last century. Born out of the need to provide products to people living in isolated locations, the catalog has become a shopping and purchase vehicle used by virtually all consumers, employed women in particular. Strapped for time, the modern consumer now accepts catalogs as a reliable and trustworthy alternative for the purchase of all types of products, from doormats to computers to trips around the world.

Catalog developers use sophisticated marketing tools. With the availability of accurate mailing lists, catalogs have become more specialized, both in terms of products carried and consumers targeted. For instance, Lands' End has a specialized "Coming Home" catalog for linens, towels, and other household products that it sends to a specialized target market of homeowners.

There are four general types of catalogs. **Retail catalogs** contain merchandise equivalent to that found in the sponsors' stores. Crate and Barrel has such a catalog. Their intent is to build both store traffic and mail-order sales. **Full-line merchandise catalogs** contain all the merchandise found in a complete department store, plus other products such as appliances and home-related remodeling and installation materials. The Montgomery Ward catalog is such a catalog. **Business-to-business catalogs** contain products that are sold from one business to another to reduce the costs associated with personal selling. Office supply stores are an example. And finally, **consumer specialty catalogs** contain a line of related products that are sent only to those consumers considered potential customers. For instance, the Current catalog of greeting cards and stationery supplies is a consumer specialty catalog.

Everything in a catalog must make a harmonious contribution to the whole. The cover must immediately attract the prospect's attention. The photography must generate interest. The copy should be easy to read, highly descriptive, and concise yet comprehensive. The merchandise selected for sales must create an optimum mix in terms of quality and depth. The order form should be easy to follow and fill out. Finally, the shipping charges should be consistent with the values of the product. For example, shipping charges of $3.75 on a $5.00 item are out of line.

Undoubtedly, the most important change occurring in the catalog industry is the emergence of online services, the Internet and the World Wide Web, as well as other interactive media including CD-ROM and fax-back services. Companies such as Viking Office Products currently have their own home page and are developing the ability to create a different catalog for each customer they service. Although the adoption of this technology by the catalog industry is still in its infancy, expertise is quickly being developed.

The home page for the Internet Mall represents one form of online media.

Elaine Rubix, senior vice president of Interactive Marketing for I Village, Inc., New York, explains three ways to "play" online. They are via Internet Malls, Online Marketplaces, and the Stand-Alone Store.[12] (See the example of an Internet Mall home page.) More will be said about interactive technology later in this chapter.

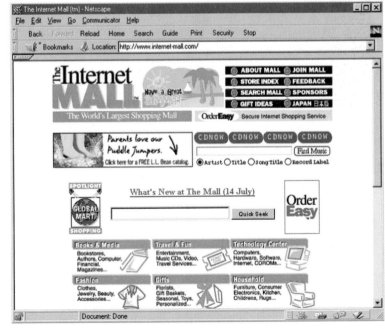

Mass Media Direct Marketing

Television, radio, magazines, and newspapers offer another form of direct-response marketing. The fact that mass media are already classified by demographic and geographic characteristics means that direct-marketing messages can be targeted at certain geographic areas, market segments, or market areas with a history of higher response rates. Direct marketers must weigh the benefit of specific targeting against several disadvantages of using mass media. Unlike direct mail and catalogs, mass media impose time and space limitations on the advertiser. Appeals carried in mass media must compete with the editorial or program content and other ads. And there are extremely high costs associated with mass media.

Because earlier discussion considered only these media and the guidelines for effectively creating ads in each, only considerations unique to direct marketing will be discussed here.

Using Print

Print ads can carry a direct-marketing appeal by simply providing information about the product and an order form or a toll-free number for ordering it directly from the manufacturer. The copy tends to be direct and concise with little emotionalism and few claims. There must be a "call to action." If the reader is not asked to order the product, then the copy should cite other actions—filling out a coupon or calling a number, for instance. The copy should be benefit-oriented, and the design should lead the reader through the ad in logical order. Sufficient space for address information and signature should be provided on the order blank. The terms of the offer, including price, must also be clearly stated. The order form should be keyed or coded so marketers can determine the origin of incoming customer orders or inquiries. The key or code is the most important part of the order card because it indicates the source of sales.

In addition to the standard full-page or partial-page formats, other print ad formats are available. A **magazine insert,** for example, can be a multipage piece or a reply card bound next to a full-page ad. **Bingo cards** appear in the back of magazines and give consumers an easy way to request information on products and services. The publisher prints a designated number for specified literature, and the consumer circles the number of the desired information.

Thanks to new technology, magazines now have some of the same advantages offered by direct mail. Specifically, magazines now offer: (1) selective binding—a computerized binding method to target audience segments with two, three, four, or more ad choices; (2) ink-jet printing—a computerized binding process that can customize individual messages to every subscriber.

Newspaper inserts include single-page direct-marketing pieces, multipage booklets, perforated coupons, or gummed reply envelopes. Sunday supplements, such as *Parade* and *Family Weekly,* are edited nationally but appear in the local Sunday editions of many newspapers. Direct-marketing pieces are placed in these supplements.

Using Television and Radio

Television is well suited to demonstrating a direct marketer's product. Television is used in three major ways: to sell a product or service, to generate leads for a product or service, and to support direct-response advertising in other media (for instance, Publishers' Clearing House or Time-Life books). Marketers provide viewers with toll-free numbers to generate immediate response. In direct-marketing television commercials, at least one-fourth of the broadcast time is devoted to ordering information.

Home shopping on television is booming. Product demonstration as well as price, order, and inventory information are all provided in an entertaining way in the comfort of the living room.

Cable television has become the primary broadcast medium for many direct marketers. It is less expensive, more targeted, and allows longer messages than television. Cable has produced two special forms of direct-message delivery systems. The first is the various types of **home shopping channels,** in which viewers can watch programs that present items for sale, give the price, and explain how to order the item.

Infomercials are the second type of direct-marketing cable delivery system. An infomercial is a "documentary-style" 30- to 60-minute commercial. This format has been criticized because the ads are often written in a manner that makes them sound like regular programming. Nonetheless, the infomercial format has reported sales of $1.2 billion in 1995, and more than 400 new infomercials were aired in 1994. More important, approximately 15 percent of nationally branded advertisers ran infomercials in 1995, with that number expected to double by 2000.[13]

Air and production costs are far lower for direct-radio response than for television. Direct radio can be scheduled quickly and, if live, can be revised at the last minute. Radio is also more efficient than television in attracting particular types of listeners. Radio has its own limitations, however, including the lack of visualization and the fact that many listeners are otherwise engaged when hearing the ad. Because listeners often do not have a pencil and paper handy, the response must be easy to remember.

Using Videotext and Interactive Technology

Videotext ties an individual television set to a remote host computer via telephone line or coaxial cable. Videotext has unlimited capacity to store and deliver information. It is also totally interactive through the same telephone line or cable over which the data are received. By activating a keyboard or keypad, the user can make a request, which then appears on the television screen. The user can obtain product information, order, and pay for the merchandise right at the television set.

Despite the relative uncertainty associated with the profitability of the interactive online medium, companies are spending millions of dollars to become players in cyberspace. Let's look more closely at online marketing. The Internet is a global web of computer networks that allows users to send e-mail, exchange views, research, and shop for products. It also gives direct marketers the chance to reach consumers around the world.

Direct marketers can use the Internet in four ways: create an electronic storefront; place direct-response ads online; participate in forums, newsgroups, and bulletin boards; and communicate via e-mail. For example, if a person types in Sun Microsystem's home page address (www.sun.com), Sun Microsystem's home page appears in full color. It offers several options, including descriptions of its products and solutions, access to sales and service, and information on technology and developers. The key is to entice browsers to visit and then to respond to the company's home page. Web shopping malls are indexes of many product and service providers. Consumer or business shoppers can visit the malls, search via product or service, and link to a company's electric storefront. The shopper can browse offerings and choose the service or product with the click of a mouse. Two examples of shopping malls include The All-Internet Shopping Directory (www.all-internet.com) and The Internet Mall (www.internet-mall.com).

Companies such as Alamo Rent-A-Car can place a direct-response ad online with Prodigy, a commercial online service provider: "Rent a car from Alamo and get up to 2 days free!" Bulletin board systems (BBSs) are specialized online services that focus on a specific topic or group. Thus, a ski equipment manufacturer might want to participate in a BBS that enjoys "extreme skiing." Finally, a company can encourage prospects and customers to send questions, suggestions, information, and even complaints to the company, using the company's e-mail address.

Telemarketing

Another marketing medium is **telemarketing,** which is a direct-marketing technique that combines telecommunications technology, marketing strategies, and information systems. It can be used alone or in conjunction with advertising, direct mail, sales promotions, personal selling, and other marketing communication functions.

There are two types of telemarketing: inbound and outbound. An inbound, or incoming, telemarketing call originates with the customer. Calls originating with the firm are outgoing, or outbound.

Inbound calls are customer responses to a marketer's stimulus, whether a direct-mail piece, a direct-marketing broadcast, a catalog, or a published toll-free number. Because it is almost impossible to schedule customer calls, every effort must be made to ensure that the lines are not blocked. Having numerous lines is costly, however.

Although most inbound telemarketing occurs via toll-free 800 and 888 numbers, the 900 number has also grown in popularity, from a $27 million business in 1985 to $515 million in 1990. Its increased popularity is a direct result of the 1989 introduction of interactive 900 numbers that enable a caller to respond to questions and leave information via Touch-Tone phones. Interactivity has allowed direct-marketing programs to become much more sophisticated. Media and entertainment companies have been in the forefront of promoting via 900 numbers. For example, Phone Programs created a 900 program to promote HBO's *Tales from the Crypt* horror show. For two dollars a call, viewers hear elaborate sound effects and answer horror trivia questions for a chance to win prizes.[14]

Outbound telemarketing is used by direct marketers whenever they take the initiative for a call—for opening new accounts, qualifying, selling, scheduling, servicing, or profiling customers. Wide Area Telephone Service (WATS) is often used as an economic long-distance vehicle. Outbound telemarketing is generally most efficient if the call is directed to a prospect who has been prequalified in some way, because the cost per telephone call is quite high.

Telemarketing has four main applications: order-taking, customer service, sales support, and account management. Order-taking is the traditional use and also an excellent means of possible cross-selling. Olan Mills Studios uses more than 9000 local telemarketers to sell photograph packages, frames, and related items, with a response rate of 3 percent. Customer service usually means handling complaints or initiating cross-selling opportunities by informing customers of new features, models, or accessories. To provide sales support for the field sales force, telemarketers schedule sales calls, confirm appointments, maintain supplies, make credit checks, and sell marginal accounts. Account management replaces the personal contact with customers. If well planned, telemarketing sales specialists can maintain an ongoing relationship with certain customers.

Telemarketing is a viable marketing communication tool, but it must be carefully planned and guided by experts. Although the supposed benefit of telemarketing is cost savings because of its ability to segment the market, it is not cheap. Telephone calls range from three dollars to five dollars for consumer market calls and from six dollars to ten dollars for business market calls. Cost-efficient results will be attained only if the prospect list is targeted and the telephone is not used for random attempts.[15]

Concept ✓ **Review**

DIRECT-MARKETING MEDIA TOOLS

There are several types of direct-marketing tools:

1. Direct mail delivers the message and product through the U.S. Postal Service or a private delivery service. Its success is based on the quality of the lists, the package, and the copy.
2. Catalogs fall into one of four categories: retail, full-line merchandise, business-to-business, and consumer specialty.
3. Mass media used by direct marketing include magazines, newspapers, radio, television, videotext, and online services.
4. Telemarketing includes inbound and outbound calls.

profile

Diana Kronhart-Monninghoff
Account Director for International Accounts
Team Direct/BBDO, Hamburg, Germany

Diana Kronhart-Monninghoff is an account director for international accounts at BBDO's Hamburg, Germany, Team Direct office. Team Direct is an agency that specializes in direct marketing. She is involved in developing and implementing many types of marketing communication strategies such as relationship marketing and specialized direct-marketing programs such as lead generation and direct sales.

Although Team Direct handles its own clients in Germany, the company also works with other offices in the BBDO network to develop communication programs for larger clients involved in more global marketing communication programs such as traditional advertising, sales promotion, and public relations programs.

Team Direct's German clients include Dr. Oetker (similar to Betty Crocker); Allianz Versicherung (Europe's largest insurance company); Hoechst Scherring, AgrEvo (a chemical company); Commerzbank (a large bank); EduScho (a coffee producer); Mercedes-Benz; and the German Telecomm, among others. Some of those clients also do international marketing, as do other BBDO clients handled by Team Direct such as Volkswagen, Barclay's Bank, Wella, and Mars.

In international work an agency is either the "lead agency" or the "local agency." The lead agency works with the client's central headquarters to develop global or regional marketing, including the marketing communication strategy, and coordinates with the local agencies. The local agencies consult with the local client subsidiary and give feedback to the lead agency.

Kronhart-Monninghoff's major clients are Hoechst Scherring, AgrEvo; Wella; and Mercedes-Benz. She also supervises the Delta Airlines account and does extensive work in developing pitches for new business. On the Hoechst Scherring, AgrEvo; Wella; and Mercedes-Benz accounts, her team is the lead agency. It functions as the local agency for the Delta Airlines account.

For all of the clients where her team acts as lead agency, she is responsible for the following:

- Acting as liaison with clients' management team to develop communication programs and to sell these concepts within their organizations
- Developing strategies and managing the research and strategic planning process
- Briefing and coordinating the internal teams in the creative development, client approval process, and project execution details
- Coordinating with the local agencies, using their input in her team's strategic and creative development processes, while ensuring that the global brands and positions are safeguarded
- Overseeing the execution of the programs in Germany with Team Direct staff and in other countries with the help of local agencies
- Controlling budgets and negotiating price with clients

Academic Background and Career Track
A Denver native, Kronhart-Monninghoff received her undergraduate degree in marketing and international business from the University of Colorado in 1987. After graduation, she worked as a retail buyer and department head for two boutique and homeware departments of a large German furniture chain in Regensburg and Ingolstadt, Germany. These jobs gave her initial German business experience. She returned to the United States and worked as an intern at National Demographics and Lifestyles in Denver, a company that specializes in database marketing services. She returned to Germany for graduate study.

Diana received a graduate diploma in marketing from the Polytechnical University of Regensburg in

1991. After graduate school she worked at Andersen Consulting in Frankfurt, Germany, where she was responsible for competitive, industry, and market analyses (including primary market research) and strategic planning. In 1993 she joined Team Direct/BBDO.

Typical Day

Diana groups her days into two types: internal days and external days. An internal day generally means working from 8:30 A.M. until around 7:30 P.M. She spends about 70 percent of her time talking to people—speaking with clients and colleagues on the phone, in staff meetings with the creative team, answering questions, and putting out fires—clients often call with last-minute crises that have to be resolved quickly. Likewise, colleagues often have problems that need to be fixed before they can continue working. She spends some time meeting with colleagues to see how work is progressing.

Diana uses the time after 5:00 P.M. to do conceptual work—developing a strategy, a brief, or a plan. She has found that evenings and weekends are the only times when she can think about something in peace and quiet.

An external day brings travel. Her clients have their German offices in Berlin, Frankfurt, and Munich. She flies to one of these cities once or twice a week to hold presentations or attend meetings. Typically, she leaves on a 7:00 A.M. flight (up at 5:45 A.M.!). Diana returns on the 7:00 P.M. flight to be home by 8:45 P.M. She takes her Macintosh Powerbook with her on these flights so after meeting, presenting, and talking with the client, she can write meeting notes on her return flight. Some clients have European offices in Amsterdam, Paris, and London that she visits about twice a year.

Advice

Diana's foreign language skills have made it possible to work in international direct marketing. She explains: "Try to learn another language. My foreign language skills and ability to adapt to a foreign culture have enabled me to be successful abroad. Going abroad is not for everyone. However, if you have the opportunity, make sure you're properly prepared. Learn about the language and the culture before-

hand. Learn to be open and tolerant of everything different. Learn not to pass judgment on other cultures. Mix in as much as possible and make friends and acquaintances in your new home. Don't live in an isolated American ghetto: many expatriates, unfortunately, do so.

"If you plan to work on an international account based in the U.S., you should seek the opportunity to live abroad first. Until you've seen the world from a different perspective, you cannot truly understand or appreciate your foreign colleagues and their issues.

"I've met many Americans who think they are tolerant and aware of the world, but unfortunately they're not. The U.S. is geographically isolated, so Americans are not comfortable dealing with other cultures and languages away from their 'home turf.' Europeans grow up with a sensitivity to other ways; Americans must learn it later."

In addition to language study and cultural sensitivity, Kronhart-Monninghoff recommends honing your communication skills. "The absolutely most important personal skill for success in the advertising business is your communication ability." She notes that "most people are not strong communicators, especially not in conflict situations, and my colleagues do not stray from that norm." To enjoy a job in marketing communication and excel at it, she says you need:

- Excellent presentation skills: Learn to develop enrapturing and persuasive presentations. Learn to use multimedia properly.
- Strong interpersonal communication skills: You have to motivate and coordinate, negotiate prices and contracts, appraise performance, and listen to and speak to the client's concern.
- Business writing skills: It's truly amazing how many of my clients and colleagues aren't able to write a succinct, comprehensible agency brief, letter, or memo.

Her conclusion about life in marketing communication: "It's fun! I cannot imagine doing anything else with my life. It's often hectic and chaotic, but this atmosphere breeds creativity. The marketing communication industry is exhilarating and bubbling with energy, there's always something new. There's no substitute for agency life!"

SUMMARY

1. Define direct marketing and explain its role in the marketing communication mix.

Direct marketing is an interactive marketing communication tool that relies on a database and uses one or more advertising media to effect a measurable response and/or transaction at any location. It differs from conventional indirect marketing communication tools in two important ways. First, the only way to receive the product is through direct contact with the provider. Second, this direct contact between provider and customer requires some unique adjustments in the marketing strategy, particularly marketing communication techniques.

2. Discuss the strengths and weaknesses of direct marketing.

Direct marketing has several strengths. It is a highly targeted and personal form of marketing communication. It is also easy to measure and test and is flexible. Direct marketing also has some weaknesses. It is not an effective long-term strategy; used ineffectively it can foster consumer distrust, and it is often difficult to integrate with other marketing communication tools.

3. Outline how to manage, design, and evaluate a direct-marketing program.

Database marketing is the process of building, maintaining, and using customer databases for the purpose of contacting customers and transacting business. To manage a database, companies must obtain a list of customers or potential customers; capture, organize, and maintain the existing marketing data; convert the data into useful information that has possible application to company strategies; apply the database to specific strate-

gies; test the direct-mail piece before sending it out to the target market; and capture new data and integrate them into the existing database. Marketers design a direct-marketing strategy by focusing on five components: the offer, the medium, the message, timing and sequencing, and customer service. Marketers use several techniques to evaluate direct marketing, including analyzing profitability and assessing response.

4. Describe how direct marketers use the tools of direct mail, catalogs, mass media, and telemarketing media.

Direct mail offers a choice of formats and provides enough space to tell a complete sales story. It can also be personalized and allows the marketer to reach audiences who are inaccessible by other media. The drawbacks of direct mail are the widespread perception that it is junk mail and the high cost per prospect reached. Catalogs are becoming increasingly more popular and targeted. A shopping and purchase vehicle, catalogs are used by virtually all consumers, especially those pressed for time. Catalogs are available in print format, online, and are offered via other technology such as fax-back services. Direct marketing via mass media is used to reach a wider audience but can be costly. Examples included newspaper inserts, cable home shopping channels, and Internet direct-response ads. Telemarketing is a direct-marketing technique that combines telecommunications technology, marketing strategies, and information systems. It can be used alone or in conjunction with advertising, direct mail, sales promotions, personal selling, and other marketing communication functions.

POINTS TO PONDER

Review the Facts

1. Discuss the primary difference between direct-marketing advertising and general advertising.
2. Compare and contrast inbound and outbound telemarketing.

3. What is database marketing, and why is it important to direct marketing?
4. What are the main differences between direct and indirect marketing?

Master the Concepts

5. "Direct marketing is junk mail that sells junk products. Its popularity is just a fad." Comment on this statement.

6. What types of databases are available to direct marketers? What are the characteristics of a good database? Discuss the issues of privacy.

7. What are the advantages and disadvantages of direct mail?

8. Discuss the four requirements of a successful catalog.

9. Contrast broadcast and print media in terms of their effectiveness for direct marketing.

10. What are the benefits of using online technology for direct marketing? What are the potential risks?

Apply Your Knowledge

11. Select two print ads you consider to be direct marketing, one directed at ultimate consumers and one at businesses. Critique each in respect to how well it makes the offer, includes sufficient information, and provides a mechanism for responding.

12. Select two direct-marketing catalogs and critique each using the criteria you listed in response to Master the Concepts question 8. How well does each catalog satisfy the criteria?

13. As vice president of marketing for a seed company, you are in the process of designing a direct-mail package aimed at experienced gardeners living throughout the United States. Describe the contents of the package and give an example of the copy you might use.

SUGGESTED PROJECTS

1. Select a consumer product that is not normally sold through direct marketing (for example, over-the-counter-drugs, automobiles, pets). Create a direct-marketing plan for this product. Be sure to specify your objectives and indicate the parts of the offer, the medium, and the message.

2. (Writing Project) Contact three mailing-list houses. Compile several consumer profiles and ask for a cost estimate for 100,000 names containing these traits. Also, have the houses indicate the guarantees that accompany the list. Write a brief report summarizing your findings.

3. (Internet Project) The Internet provides an ideal environment for marketing music recordings, books, and other entertainment products. The reason is simple: There are too many titles for a single retail store to stock. Visit at least two storefronts that sell in the same industry. For instance, you may want to visit the following sites:

Music recordings

BMG Music Service	www.bmgmusicservice.com
Columbia House	www.columbiahouse.com
Sony Corp.	www.stationsony.com

Books

Amazon.com Books	www.amazon.com
Books Stacks Unlimited, Inc.	www.book.com
Internet Bookstore	intertain.com

In direct marketing, the offer is crucial. Compare the offers each storefront makes. Which offer is more persuasive? More clear? Does the online store do an effective job convincing consumers that online buying is better than going to a retail store? Does the site make ordering easy? Secure? Based on what you learned in this chapter, what suggestions would you make to improve the offer? Write a brief critique of the two storefronts.

CASE 12: KISS A PIG, HUG A SWINE

Background

The New Pig Corporation, a company that specializes in producing absorbent cleaning materials to soak up industrial leaks and spills, has one of the most creative approaches to integrated marketing communication of any industrial marketer.

The company's name reflects its origins—the product was created in the "pig pen"—a perpetually dirty area of a warehouse dedicated to new product development. The advertising agency that had been hired to choose a name strongly objected to the "pig" name because of its negative connotations. But none of the names the agency proposed had the same cachet, and when test marketed, customers were very positive. "Pigs are really a lot of fun," says Carl De-Caspers, the company's public relations director.

Communication Strategy

The pig theme has been carried throughout the company. Customers are put on hold when calling so that they can hear Ray Stevens' country-western tune, "Kiss a Pig." The title of its catalog is Pigalog®; its most popular sales promotion premium is a pig-snout baseball cap; its business cards, stationery, shipping cartons, and fax covers all are pig-embossed; and its note pads are pig shaped. Here are some other ways the theme is carried throughout the company's business:

Company motto:	No yes, ands, or butts about it … we're out to serve you like no one else!
Address:	One Pork Avenue
Customer fax number:	800-621-PIGS
Customer service survey:	Repork Cards
Trade show mascot:	An 8-foot Mac-the-Pig balloon

Direct-Marketing Strategy

New Pig sells directly to its end-users, whereas many of its competitors use a network of distributors. Consequently, the company has control of its zany image all the way through the pipeline, and its customers are more likely to appreciate the lighthearted approach than would the trade customers in a more traditional distribution channel. Undoubtedly, a few customers are turned off by this approach.

The company markets its products with collateral materials, catalogs, advertising, and trade shows—most of which are produced or managed in-house by its 23-person marketing staff. The company's marketing communication relies mostly on direct mail, where it spends about 85 percent of its total $8.5 million marketing budget. The four-color 250-page Pigalog® catalog showcases some 1500 industrial cleaning products. It is mailed three times a year to 85,000 customers and another 100,000 prospects. In keeping with the company's tone, each catalog also has fun-and-game pages, full-page comic-like photographs, and contests with opportunities to win pig T-shirts and caps. Orders of $50 or more automatically qualify the customer to receive a pig-snout cap.

An important interactive element in the catalog is a mail-in card for customers to share their product ideas in exchange for a pig T-shirt. In addition, a staff of 30 inbound customer service reps take orders and answer questions. Another 20 outbound telesales reps make sales contacts. The company employs no field salespeople.

In addition to the catalogs, New Pig mails monthly "Slim Lines," which are 40-page or less mini-catalogs that focus on one business area, such as safety products, absorbents, or storage and handling products. Because the company has an excellent database, it is possible to mail Slim Lines to heavy buyers of products in each of the company's sales categories, as well as good prospects. Slim Lines is used to lead prospects to other parts of the company's product lines.

As a continuity program to build relationships with active customers, the company also mails a technical newsletter three times a year. Introduced in 1991 as a value-added service, each eight-page issue gives tips and case studies explaining how New Pig's products can help users minimize waste and meet government requirements. Columns include "Ham and Regs," and "Pig Feats."

In addition to the direct-marketing program, New Pig places about 30 quarter-page ads a year in some 13 technical trade publications. It also buys booth space at three trade shows annually and distributes countless sales promotion premiums such as the pig-snout caps, pig-butt hats, pig-shaped pencils, pig-emblazoned boxer shorts, mugs, coloring books, and, of course, T-shirts.

New Pig's philosophy is based on relationship marketing. It focuses less on mass marketing and more on helping each customer as an individual. The individuality of the company's identity program also helps it stand out from its other bigger competitors such as 3M and is the primary way the manufacturer differentiates itself in an industry filled with practical yet mundane products.

Case Questions
1. How would you evaluate the direct-marketing strategy followed by New Pig?
2. What other direct-marketing techniques could New Pig consider?

Source: Ginger Trumfio, "Hamming it Up," *Sales & Marketing Management* (June 1995): 84–5.

ROMA'S LITE INTEGRATED CASE QUESTIONS

(Review the Roma's Lite Marketing Plan in the Appendix at the end of the text before answering these questions.)
1. Why is the database so important in direct marketing? Explain the process of designing a database and how this process could be useful in the launch of Roma's Lite Pizza.
2. Under what conditions would each of the direct-marketing techniques be most effective?
3. (Team Project) Assess which direct-marketing techniques would be useful in introducing Roma's Lite Pizza. Design a direct-marketing strategy for this product and explain how it will tie in with the advertising, sales promotion, and public relations programs you developed in Chapters 9 through 11.

chapter

13

Personal Selling

CHAPTER OBJECTIVES

After completing your work on this chapter, you should be able to:

1 **Define personal selling.**

2 **Describe the strengths and weaknesses of personal selling.**

3 **Discuss how personal selling fits in the marketing communication mix.**

4 **Outline both the types and the process of personal selling.**

5 **Explain the tasks of sales management that relate directly to marketing communication.**

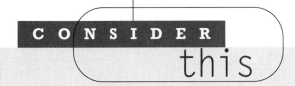

C O N S I D E R this

Integrating Personal Selling: Piece of Cake

Here's the question: Does it make sense for sales reps to spend four days out of five searching for new business prospects? Now the answer: Of course not. They should spend as much time as possible generating sales from current customers and building customer relations. But what's the solution?

Carol Kruse, marketing program manager for Procase Corporation, faced this question while working with the company's 13-person sales force, a highly trained group of engineers. Procase, a young Silicon Valley software company, expanded rapidly due in large part to its SMARTsystem product, a program that enables companies to develop, manage, and upgrade their old software programs.

The Procase sales force was responsible for selling the SMARTsystem software. Because the

product was complex and comprehensive, the sales force often had to sell to top-level systems analysts and to senior management. "A year and a half ago, the direct sales force worked on its own in a vacuum," Kruse says. "They did all their own prospecting. The marketing department provided some assistance, but that was that." More by accident than design, she developed an integrated marketing communication program that helped her company's sales force gain and maintain customers rather than just find potential customers.

Disappointed in the quality of sales leads generated at trade shows and reluctant to spend any of her less-than-$30,000 budget on mass-media advertising, Kruse decided that she could best support the sales force with targeted direct mail followed by a series of carefully timed telephone calls.

To get the most out of each mailing, Kruse provided a variety of ways for prospects to respond: the conventional reply card, a toll-free telephone number, e-mail, and a dedicated fax line. Kruse's follow-up procedures were carefully timed and coordinated with the field sales effort. For instance, once Procase learned through customer response that a prospect's system was technically compatible with SMARTsystem, an information kit was mailed out and a follow-up call was made a week later to assess interest in the product. If the interest wasn't there at that time, explained Kruse, we would "call back in three months or even later."

Procase then added another method of finding new sales leads and building relationships with current customers in a timely manner. It set up a comment site on the Internet for interested customers. The site personnel respond to comments, collect basic information about the consumer—including type of computer system—and pass on viable leads to the sales force.

This just-in-time approach to finding sales leads has two main benefits. First, the technical sales force has more time to demonstrate the software to potential, qualified buyers. Second, virtually all leads given to the field sales force eventually produce some sort of business so more sales result.

Sources: Procase Comment Form (October 1, 1996): Internet (www.sportsite.com/cedro/sia/mgcase/html/mge_comment.htm); Allison Lucan, "Portrait of a Salesperson," *Sales & Marketing Management* (June 1995): 13; Nancy Arnott, "Selling is Dying," *Sales & Marketing Management* (August 1994): 85–6.

CHAPTER OVERVIEW

Procase Corporation's selling efforts illustrate a key point of this text: The most effective way to implement a marketing strategy is to coordinate all marketing communication tools. If advertising, sales promotions, telemarketing, and direct-mail marketing tools are coordinated, the sales job is much easier. Also, customer feedback that salespeople often collect can provide timely and valuable information that marketing communication specialists can use to improve the communication efforts.

In this chapter we investigate what personal selling is, its strengths and weaknesses, and how to integrate personal selling in the marketing communication mix. Then we explore the types and the process of personal selling. We also examine how to manage a sales force effectively. We conclude by analyzing personal selling trends.

PERSONAL SELLING AND THE MARKETING COMMUNICATION MIX

Few companies coordinate marketing communication efforts in support of the sales force as successfully as Procase did. Salespeople are often separated from marketing communication specialists because of both the structure of the business and differences in perspective. Most salespeople view other marketing communication activities strictly as a means to help sell a product or company. Advertisers, sales promotion managers, and public relations experts rarely consider the needs and suggestions of salespeople, and salespeople seldom pay attention to information about a marketing communication campaign.

Integrating personal selling with other marketing communication elements may seriously affect that salesperson's job. Regis McKenna, international consultant, contends that although marketing technology has made salespeople more effective, it may also decrease the need for traditional salespeople who convince people to buy. As we move closer to "real-time" marketing, he believes customers and suppliers will be linked directly so that customers may design their own products, negotiate price with suppliers, and discuss delivery and other miscellaneous concerns with producers rather than salespeople. McKenna suggests that the main role of salespeople will no longer be to "close" the sale. Instead it will be to carry detailed design, quality, and reliability information, and to educate and train clients.[1]

Don Schultz, Northwestern professor of marketing and proponent of IMC, supports this notion of the modern salesperson. "If you create long-term affiliations, then you don't sell. You form relationships that help people buy." He observes that because products have become more sophisticated, the businesses that buy are often smaller than those that sell. "Today, I think the sales force is primarily focused on learning about the product and not about the market. We're talking about flipping that around," he concludes.[2] In short, effective personal selling must focus on customer relationships.

To integrate personal selling with other marketing communication tools to forge strong customer relationships, top management should lead the integration effort. Unless managers understand what salespeople do, however, integration may not be successful. Before considering how to combine selling efforts with other marketing communication tools, we first describe the job of personal selling.

Understanding Personal Selling

Personal selling is a marketing communication tool that is used to increase sales directly through personal contact. Though the other marketing communication mix elements contribute to sales, their impact is often indirect. In contrast, the impact of personal selling is direct—in fact, the salesperson's livelihood depends on making sales. The importance of this direct impact is demonstrated by the number of people employed in the personal selling field. Thousands of people are employed in advertising, whereas millions are employed in personal selling.

Personal selling is the face-to-face presentation of a product or an idea to a potential customer by a representative of the company or organization. This definition highlights a key difference between personal selling and other marketing communication tools: Personal selling involves one-on-one communication rather than the mass communication that characterizes advertising, sales promotion, and public relations. Personal selling also differs from direct marketing, which uses a nonpersonal media to generate a response. In personal selling, information is presented personally, there is immediate feedback, and adjustments to the message can be made immediately.

Personal selling differs from other elements of marketing communication in two other key ways. First, the task and the problems of selling primarily involve interpersonal relations. In selling, the main task is to build relations—between salespeople and customers, between salespeople and their supervisors, and between salespeople and others in the organization. In other marketing communication areas—advertising, for example—the heart of the task is creating a message. Second, even in companies that house their marketing communication specialists in the marketing communication department, most organizations separate the sales force from the other marketing communication areas of a business.

Strengths and Weaknesses of Personal Selling

Personal selling has several important advantages and disadvantages compared with the other elements of the marketing communication mix. Undoubtedly, the most significant strength of personal selling is its flexibility. Salespeople can tailor their presentations to fit the needs, motives, and behavior of individual customers. As salespeople see the prospect's reaction to a sales approach, they can immediately adjust as needed.

Personal selling also minimizes wasted effort. Advertisers typically expend time and money to send a mass message about a product to many people outside the target market. In personal selling the sales force pinpoints the target market, makes a contact, and expends effort that has a strong probability of leading to a sale.

Consequently, an additional strength of personal selling is that measuring effectiveness and determining the return on investment are far more straightforward for personal selling than for other marketing communication tools, where recall or attitude change is often the only measurable effect.

Another benefit of personal selling is that a salesperson is in an excellent position to encourage the customer to act. The one-on-one interaction of personal selling means that a salesperson can effectively respond to and overcome *objections* (customers' concerns or reservations about the product) so that the customer is more likely to buy. Salespeople can also offer many specific reasons to persuade a customer to buy, in contrast to the general reasons that an ad may urge customers to take immediate action.

A final strength of personal selling is the multiple tasks the sales force can perform. For instance, in addition to selling, a salesperson can collect payment, service or repair products, return products, and collect product and marketing information. In fact, salespeople are often best at disseminating negative and positive word-of-mouth product information.

High cost is the primary disadvantage of personal selling. With increased competition, higher travel and lodging costs, and higher salaries, the cost per sales contact continues to increase. Many companies try to control sales costs by compensating sales representatives based on commission only, thereby guaranteeing that salespeople get paid only if they generate sales. However, commission-only salespeople may become risk averse and only call on clients who have the highest potential return. These salespeople, then, may miss opportunities to develop a broad base of potential customers that could generate higher sales revenues in the long run.

Companies can also reduce sales costs by using complementary techniques, such as telemarketing, direct mail, toll-free numbers for interested customers, and online communication with qualified prospects. Telemarketing and online communication can further reduce costs by serving as an actual selling vehicle. Both technologies can deliver sales messages, respond to questions, take payment, and do follow-up.

Another disadvantage of personal selling is the problem of finding and retaining high-quality people. First, experienced salespeople sometimes realize that the only way their income can outpace their cost-of-living increases is to change jobs.

Second, because of the push for profitability, businesses try to hire experienced salespeople away from competitors rather than hiring college graduates, who take three to five years to reach the level of productivity of more experienced salespeople. These two staffing issues have caused high turnover in many sales forces.

Another weakness of personal selling is message inconsistency. Many salespeople view themselves as independent from the organization, so they design their own sales techniques, use their own message strategies, and engage in questionable ploys to create a sale. Consequently, it is difficult to find a unified company or product message within a sales force, or between the sales force and the rest of the marketing communication mix.

A final weakness is that sales force members have different levels of motivation. Salespeople may vary in their willingness to make the desired sales calls each day; make service calls that do not lead directly to sales; or use new technology, such as a laptop, e-mail, or the company's Web site. Finally, overly zealous sales representatives may tread a thin line between ethical and unethical sales techniques. The difference between a friendly lunch and commercial bribery is sometimes blurred. Table 13.1 summarizes the strengths and weaknesses of personal selling.

TABLE 13.1

Strengths and Weaknesses of Personal Selling

	Descriptions
Strengths	
• Flexibility	• Can tailor presentations to suit needs, motives, and behaviors of individual customers
• Minimizes wasted effort	• Unlike mass media marketing communication, the marketing message is only offered to a target audience of likely buyers
• Facilitates buyer action	• The one-on-one interaction allows specific requests for action on a repeated basis, if necessary
• Multiple capabilities	• Collection of payment, servicing the product, accepting returned products, and collecting information are all possible
Weaknesses	
• High cost	• Cost per contact is high due to travel, lodging, and salaries
• Finding and retaining salespeople	• Both salespeople and the company look for alternative ways to maximize personal benefits
• Message inconsistency	• Due to independence of sales force, delivering a unified message is difficult
• Motivation	• Difficult to motivate salespeople to use required sales techniques, make all necessary sales calls, use new technology, and behave ethically

The Role of Personal Selling in the Marketing Communication Mix

In view of the strengths and weaknesses of personal selling, how should managers use this tool effectively in the marketing communication mix? Recall that each marketing communication tool has a unique role to play in reaching communication objectives. For instance, advertising builds awareness, informs the customer about product features, and persuades the customer that the advertised brand is the best choice. Public relations tends to support these objectives indirectly by creating a positive product or company image. Sales promotions, direct marketing, and personal selling all try to prompt immediate action by adding value to the product. Personal selling is the most direct marketing communication tool, enabling salespeople to spontaneously answer questions, establish the key terms of the purchase decision, and make the sale.

As noted in Part I of the text, the IMC approach coordinates the use of all marketing communication tools to create a synergistic effect that optimizes the likelihood of a sale. The best combination of tools depends on several factors. First, it may depend on the market. In general, personal selling is emphasized in industrial markets or in selling to resellers but plays a smaller role in consumer markets. Second, the combination of tools may depend on the type of product. Simple, low-cost products such as cereals and canned vegetables require little personal selling. Mass advertising can provide brand awareness, basic product information, and retail-related information. Sales promotion may provide an extra incentive to buy. In contrast, a technical product such as an automobile or an appliance that requires an explanation, demonstration, or both usually requires a salesperson. Also, products that have a high risk such as real estate or stocks usually need personal selling.

The distribution channel can also influence the role of personal selling. For instance, a Wal-Mart supplier may not need to call on each Wal-Mart store. However, when Hershey Foods Corp. competes against Nestlé Food Company for Wal-Mart's business, Hershey knows personal selling is critical to earn the business. The key is to cement the relationship between the Wal-Mart purchasing agent and the Hershey sales representative. Why? Business relationships are based on a bond of trust between *people,* not between companies. A personal sales call, then, will be much more beneficial than a direct-mail marketing piece in such a case.

Marketing communicators use personal selling when its strengths and the situation prompt its use. In general, when a personal meeting between buyer and seller is important, personal selling dominates. It is unlikely, for instance, that consumers would buy a big-ticket item such as a luxury automobile without a salesperson. Personal selling allows information exchange, adjustments to various types of relationships, and personal persuasive techniques that convince customers to buy.

Ultimately, the marketing director or the marketing communication manager employs four criteria to determine the role of personal selling in the marketing communication strategy:

1. The nature of the information that should be exchanged to promote the product or service
2. The marketing communication objectives

3. The marketing communication mix alternatives available to the organization, with special concern for the firm's capabilities to implement each one

4. The relative cost of personal selling compared with the other marketing communication mix elements

An example of a company that clearly emphasizes personal selling over the other marketing communication mix elements is Artesia Waters, bottler of Artesia water. The company was started in 1979 by Rick Scoville. Artesia bottled water is drilled from the huge Edwards Aquifer, 520 feet below the municipality of San Antonio, Texas. It differs from competitors such as Perrier in that the water does not rise to the surface like spring water, nor does it touch any contaminants in the ground. Artesia relies heavily on one-on-one selling to promote its product. Why? Heavy competition from companies such as Perrier, the need to convince store managers that Artesia is a superior product, and a limited budget mean that personal selling is the centerpiece of Scoville's marketing communication plan.[3]

Integrating Personal Selling

Bringing personal selling and other marketing communication mix elements together remains a major frustration in most businesses, as discussed earlier. Despite the difficulties of such integration, under certain circumstances the benefits outweigh the costs of integrating personal selling with other elements. We examine those instances next.

Personal Selling and Advertising

Under what conditions should personal selling be combined with advertising? Advertising can reach large audiences simultaneously with a vivid message. The message must be quite general and the copy relatively short; opportunity for feedback and adjustment is virtually nil. Because personal selling offers the opposite set of strengths and weaknesses as advertising does, advertising and personal selling tend to complement one another. When audience coverage, vivid presentation, explanation, feedback, and the adjustment are all important to the success of the marketing program, combining advertising and personal selling is appropriate. These factors often arise with the introduction of new products. For instance, when Duncan Hines introduced its low-fat cake mixes, the company ran a great deal of consumer advertising to make consumers aware of this new product. However, it was just as important for the sales force to call on every supermarket manager and explain the product's benefits, show market research results, and offer trade incentives.

Advertising can also provide sales leads when introducing a new product or promoting an existing one. Including a toll-free number or a mail-in coupon in an ad can provide a salesperson with a list of hundreds of prospective customers. Marketers of business-to-business products are particularly effective at this tactic.

In summary, when advertising is needed to create awareness and provide basic information, but personal selling is necessary to complete the exchange process, the advertising–personal selling combination makes sense.

This ad, with its toll-free number and Web site address, helps to generate sales for the company's sales representatives.

Personal Selling and Sales Promotions

Sales promotion is an important tool that can help sales representatives during or in addition to the selling process. Recall from Chapter 10 that salespeople often deliver sales promotion materials to trade members during sales presentations. Price deals, premiums, contests, and other incentives represent part of the repertoire that can make the sales process much more successful. These trade sales promotions are often coordinated with a parallel consumer sales promotion to give both more impact. For example, Dole Pineapple might run a "Trip to Polynesia" sweepstakes with both consumers and resellers.

Sales promotion can work to add additional value to the personal selling process. An IBM salesperson knows that the customer has already been "presold" because the buyer received a direct-mail discount coupon and an opportunity to sample the product. Conversely, salespeople can explain sales promotions more fully or even deliver premiums or prizes to winning customers. Sales promotions add to the value of the product or service. In turn, that extra value makes the product or service easier to sell. The personal selling/sales promotion combination is particularly effective in competitive situations where products are similar and the salesperson needs something extra to create a competitive advantage.

Personal Selling and Public Relations

Some people would argue that the salesperson is the most important public relations strategy in many organizations. If we look at public relations as the shaping and maintenance of goodwill, this is clearly the case. In some instances the role of the salesperson as a public relations provider is informal and revolves around the person's day-to-day activities. The salesperson would probably view activities such as taking a customer out to lunch, remembering the client's birthday, responding to questions or complaints, and treating people with empathy as part of getting the sale rather than public relations.

However, the salesperson can also be involved in more formal public relations activities that help both the salesperson and the public relations manager. For example, salespeople are encouraged to get involved in community activities, head the United Way campaign, join a public service organization, or coach Little League. Salespeople are also excellent at explaining the company's products to people or to organizations that request such information. Leading plant tours or hosting open houses are two other PR activities that salespeople do well. Finally, salespeople are usually an integral part of trade shows, customer meetings, and any other event where customers and the company are together in an informal setting. Top salespeople often staff the booths at trade shows, for example.

Personal Selling and Other Marketing Communication Tools

Personal selling can increase in value when combined with other communication tools such as direct marketing, point-of-purchase marketing, and so forth. Special events, for example, are an effective way for salespeople to generate sales leads, and the event is usually more effective if a salesperson is available to answer consumers' questions.

Direct-marketing techniques such as telemarketing, direct mail, and interactive marketing are also useful in screening customers and generating leads. The benefit works in the opposite direction too. The insights of salespeople who know their customers well can guide the design of direct-marketing tools, point-of-purchase displays, packages, and other promotions. For instance, Lactite, a manufacturer of industrial adhesives, surveys its sales force semiannually for feedback on the company's marketing communication techniques.

Concept ✓ Review

PERSONAL SELLING AND THE MARKETING COMMUNICATION MIX

1. Personal selling is the face-to-face presentation of a product or an idea to a potential customer by a company representative.
2. Compared with other marketing communication tools, personal selling has several strengths: flexibility, minimal wasted effort, sales generation, and multiple capabilities. It also has several weaknesses: high cost, finding and retaining high-quality people, inconsistent messages, and different levels of motivation in the sales force.
3. The role that personal selling plays in the marketing communication mix depends on several factors including the product, the market, the distribution channel, and the available marketing communication alternatives.
4. Integrating personal selling with other marketing communication tools can be beneficial when the tools complement each other.

THE WORLD OF PERSONAL SELLING

Although the sophistication of personal selling has increased over time due to better educated individuals and advanced technology, the selling process has basically remained the same. It still requires a person who has the courage to sell to current and prospective customers daily. Rejection is part of the process. Most people who try to sell, fail. Successful salespeople, however, probably can sell anything. In the sections that follow, we discuss the types of personal selling and the process of personal selling.

Types of Personal Selling

No two sales jobs are exactly alike—even when two sales jobs have identical titles and job descriptions. Nevertheless, we can describe several general types of sales jobs to give you some idea of the range of opportunities. The six following types of sales differ in some important ways.[4]

Responsive Selling

In responsive selling the salesperson reacts to the buyer's demands. Route driving and retailing are two kinds of responsive selling. For instance, route drivers who deliver products such as soft drinks or fuel oil usually do so at the request of the client. Similarly, clerks in an appliance or clothing store sell when the customer asks for their help.

Trade Selling

As in responsive selling, the salesperson is primarily an order-taker, but the job duties place more emphasis on service. Trade selling involves calling on dealers, taking orders, expediting deliveries, setting up displays, and rotating stock. This type of selling is used often in the food, textile, apparel, and household products industries. Special tasks, such as the assembly of point-of-purchase displays, are performed by this type of salesperson. Often this salesperson plays an integral role in maintaining relationships with trade members.

Missionary Selling

A missionary salesperson is normally not an order-taker. Instead, his primary responsibility is to explain a new product (religion) to the market before the total product is available to the public (the "institutional church"). The classic example of a missionary salesperson is the pharmaceutical sales representative who calls on physicians to explain about new drugs offered by the drug company. The missionary salesperson gives physicians free samples of the drug and encourages them to give the sample to patients and to note the results. The salesperson hopes that physicians will specify that particular drug when prescribing to future patients.

Technical Selling

This type of salesperson sells a service—the ability to solve customers' technical problems through expertise and experience. Technical selling is common for industrial goods such as chemicals, machinery, and heavy equipment. The salesperson's ability to identify, analyze, and solve customers' problems is essential. Typically, a technical salesperson calls on prospects who have identified a problem and assume the salesperson's company offers possible solutions.

Creative Selling

This type of selling is usually related to new products or to an existing product that is being introduced into a new market. The salesperson must convince prospects that they have a serious problem or unfulfilled need and that the salesperson's product is the best solution. The salesperson is an "order-getter" who emphasizes and stimulates demand for products. Salespeople working for Procter & Gamble, Compaq Computers, and Arthur Anderson Consulting all sell creatively. For example, a sales representative from the health and beauty aids division of P&G may make several sales presentations to supermarket purchasing managers to demonstrate how a new Head and Shoulders shampoo product satisfies a consumer need better than all other shampoos.

Consultative Selling

This type of selling is a form of relationship marketing. The salesperson first meets with customers, offers little direction, and builds rapport. The salesperson next shifts to directive questions that diagnose customer's needs. Then and only then does the salesperson prescribe the solution with a presentation customized to the customer's needs. She closes the sale, using both direction and support, as she asks for the order and overcomes any of the customer's reservations. After the sale, the salesperson uses support to reinforce the sale, ensure satisfaction, and maintain the relationship.

The Process of Personal Selling

The process of personal selling varies somewhat from company to company, but it typically involves the six steps outlined in Figure 13.1.

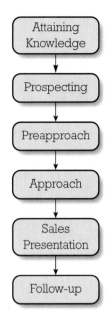

The Process of Personal Selling

Attaining Knowledge

Modern salespeople must be equipped with detailed product information. They need a thorough knowledge of the buyer's motives, characteristics, and behavior. They also need factual information about their own company and the competition.[5] The amount and kind of information required depend on the type of product, product line, characteristics of the customer, organizational structure, and type of selling. If a company has a simple product and few competitors, the level of necessary working knowledge could be quite basic. In contrast, salespeople for companies like Dow Chemical or First Data, which have extensive product lines and many competitors, need technical training to understand their products, how customers use their products, and the strengths and limitations of their competitors' products.

To illustrate how a salesperson attains knowledge, consider Jeff Crown, a 25-year-old who works for Envirotank, a company that makes above-ground storage tanks for oil, gasoline, and used oil products. Jeff spent six months learning about his product and continues to go to seminars about metallurgy and petroleum products. He also collects materials on his four major competitors, visits their Web sites weekly, reads the various trade publications, and talks to prospects and customers as often as possible. He also staffs Envirotank's booth at the two trade shows they attend.

Prospecting

The process of locating potential customers and then obtaining permission to present a sales presentation is called **prospecting.** Prospecting is a continuous task because existing customers are always lost through transfers, retirement, and competition; meanwhile, new buyers constantly enter the marketplace. Surveys estimate that the typical salesperson spends at least 30 minutes each day prospecting and that 20 to 25 percent of sales visits are with new customers.[6]

Prospecting methods vary for different types of selling. The most common methods of prospecting follow:

1. *Inquiries:* Most companies receive a steady supply of sales leads from their advertising, telephone calls, and catalogs.
2. *Endless-chain method:* The salesperson obtains at least one sales lead from each person interviewed.
3. *Center-of-influence method:* This method is a modified form of the endless-chain method. Here, the salesperson cultivates people in the territory who are willing to supply prospecting information.
4. *Public exhibitions, demonstrations, and trade shows:* People attending these events are often already interested in the product so they become prospects that the salesperson meets with at or after the event.
5. *Lists:* Individual sales representatives may develop their own lists of potential customers by referring to such sources as public records, classified telephone directories, club memberships, databases, and hits/inquiries on Web sites.
6. *Friends and acquaintances:* These people are often a source of sales leads for new sales representatives.
7. *Cold-canvas method:* The salesperson makes calls on every individual or company in a target group without any knowledge of their interest level.

To illustrate the prospecting process, let's look again at Jeff Crown of Envirotank. He uses three of the prospecting methods listed. Every Friday afternoon he gathers the inquiries he received from the company's toll-free number. He spends Saturday morning scrutinizing these leads and selecting the top 20 that he will call for appointments on Monday. Jeff also receives leads through trade shows. Finally, he generates a great many leads through Envirotank's Web site. This last source is quickly becoming his most productive option.

In support of Jeff's strategy, there is substantial evidence that leads are increasingly generated through marketing communication alternatives. Figure 13.2 shows the results of a survey conducted by Inquiry Handling Service. The survey asked respondents to estimate the amount of power various communication tools have to generate sales leads. Results indicate that the respondents believe advertising generates 30 to 35 percent of the sales leads, whereas public relations generates between 22 and 24 percent.

Preapproach

Once a prospect has been qualified, the salesperson needs to learn more about the prospect to determine the best selling approach, identify problem areas, and avoid mistakes. This part of the selling process is known as the **preapproach.** During this stage, salespeople gather additional personal and business information about prospects to qualify them further—that is, to determine whether a prospect has the resources to buy, interest in the product, any unique buying conditions, history with the firm, and so forth. Some of this information can be gleaned from

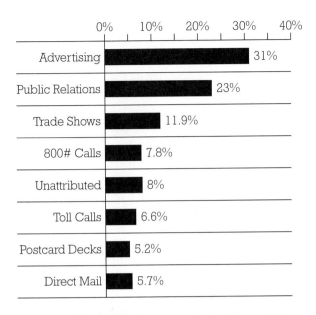

FIGURE 13.2

An Assessment of Sales Leads Through Marketing Communication Tools*

Source: Inquiry Handling Service, Inc.
*Percentages based on the 935,753 leads tracked by Inquiry Handling Service, Inc., 1993.

the prospect directly. Other information may require discussions with knowledgeable people in the industry.

Let's again consider Jeff. He recently evaluated one of his best prospects, DPI Petroleum. DPI would be a new customer with an estimated annual purchase of nearly 500 tanks. Jeff called the DPI purchasing agent, learned that the company is unhappy with its current tank provider, and learned DPI would be interested in receiving a proposal from Envirotank. Further, Jeff had extensive conversations with Jim Barton, a retired engineer/consultant with extensive knowledge of DPI. He also checked the DPI Web site for further information.

Approach

Following the preapproach, the salesperson begins the **approach,** the lead-in to the sales presentation. An approach may have several objectives, but essentially it is the strategy used to gain the prospect's attention so the salesperson can make an effective sales presentation. Some salespeople use phone calls or personal letters to approach prospects. Phone calls save time for salespeople because they reduce waiting time. Letters allow salespeople to include other information—drawings and product specifications, for instance—about the products that cannot be easily communicated. Of course, Web sites provide much of the same information, employing a much more colorful format. All of these methods of approaching prospects have the disadvantage that buyers find it fairly easy to say no over the phone, ignore their voice mail, throw away letters, or refuse to view a Web site.

Regardless of the approach method used, the salesperson must immediately establish a rapport. Establishing a rapport can occur in a number of different ways. In some cases comments about unfinished business from previous sales calls will get the buyer's interest. Another approach is one during which the salesperson informs the buyer of the benefits he or she will gain from the product being sold. Jeff Crown has developed what he calls a "marketing incentive kit" that he sends to prospects. It includes an introduction letter, a set of product fact sheets, testimonials from satisfied customers, and a model of the tank Jeff wishes to sell.

Sales Presentation

A successful sales approach is important in making the transition to the sales presentation, the heart of the sales process. The purpose of the sales presentation is to explain in detail how the product meets customer requirements. The salesperson must inform prospects and customers of the characteristics and benefits of the product and must persuade them that the product will satisfy their needs.

Talking about the weather, the Super Bowl, or business conditions are easy means of starting a sales call. For some salespeople a more effective opener is to start by talking about the organization or person being called on.

Ultimately, every presentation gets to the reason for the salesperson's being there—the product. If the sales presentation is to be effective, the sales representative's claims about the product must be relevant and believable. The salesperson's background knowledge of the account or similar accounts should help establish the most effective presentation.

Sales presentations vary. Here, we see how salespeople can use visual aids and technology to enhance effectiveness.

There are a number of sales presentation categories. All start with an understanding of the customers' needs and wants. They tend to vary in terms of formality. For example, a "fully automated" sales presentation is highly structured, with the salesperson doing little beyond setting up a movie, showing slides, answering questions, and taking orders. This would be used as part of the trade show booth. In the "semi-automated" approach, the salesperson reads from prepared aids such as a flip chart or brochure. If necessary, the salesperson can also add comments. A third technique is the "memorized" or "canned" sales presentation. This is prepared by the company, and very few changes are allowed. In "organized" sales presentations the salesperson has complete flexibility to change the wording of the sales presentation. Finally, "unstructured" sales presentations are designed so that the salesperson and buyer together can more fully explore the product and how it fits the needs of the buying firm. This type of presentation is most effective when the salesperson and buyer stay focused on the buyer's problem or need.[7] Jeff Crown typically uses an unstructured sales presentation technique.

Regardless of the type of sales presentation used, objections are inevitable. Sometimes the objections are irrational or nebulous and have little to do with the product, the company, or the seller. There is also the unspoken objection, which is considered but not expressed. Some objections may, of course, be legitimate. In handling objections there are two basic question to consider: Why do people object? What techniques are available to meet these objections? Table 13.2 depicts some of the more common objections and how they should be handled.

TABLE 13.2

Methods of Handling Objections

Techniques	Description	Example
Direct denial	Defend your company against the criticism.	"Mr. Jones, you simply are wrong about that point."
Indirect denial	Refer to a third party who had a similar objection and state how it was resolved.	"Ms. Smith expressed a similar concern. We called headquarters and had our answer in ten minutes."
Boomerang	The objection is turned back on the user.	"I'm glad you brought that up. That's exactly why I'm here."
Compensation	Admit the validity of the objection and offer compensation.	"Though it's true that we can't promise 72-hour delivery, the quality of our product is twice as good as Brand X."
Pass up	Ignore the objection as invalid.	"Let's go back and talk about some key features."
Question	Ask and listen.	In response to a concern about cost, the salesperson could ask, "How much did you plan to spend?"

Such techniques are not specific, and salespeople often learn how to handle objections through trial and error.

The hardest thing for many salespeople to do is **close**—that is, ask for the business. Yet the good salesperson is always closing. Without a close, the time has been wasted. The close is the ultimate test of sales ability, and a salesperson's income is highly correlated to a successful close.

There are several difficulties associated with closing a sale. Many potentially successful salespeople fail because they are afraid to close. If they never have to ask for the sale, they are never rejected. More often, the close is unsuccessful because the presentation is unsuccessful. Prospects cannot be expected to buy if they do not understand the presentation or if they cannot see how they will benefit as a result of the purchase. Finally, some salespeople do not have good closing skills. They become so fascinated by the sound of their own voice that they talk themselves out of sales they might have had.

A nod of the head, a more relaxed posture, and a smile all may be interpreted as signals of a buyer's readiness to buy. When one of these signals occurs, the salesperson should not hesitate to attempt to close the sale. The basic idea is to incorporate a few *trial closes* in the sales presentation. A **trial close** should be in the form of a question and should ask for an opinion on the part of the buyer: "Do you think this product is within your price range?" or "Does the quality of the product meet your standards?"

Ultimately, the primary reason a person buys is because the salesperson has keyed into one or more motivating factors. Factors that motivate vary by person, company, and situation. Product quality may be pivotal in one case, and price or reliable service or delivery may be critical in another. Successful salespeople know they must identify this hot button.

Follow Up with Postsale Activities

An effective selling job does not end when the order is written up. Postsale service (service after the sale) can build customer goodwill and lay the groundwork for many years of profitable business relations. These services can ensure repeat business and generate leads to other prospects. If product installation is necessary, sales representatives should make certain the job is done properly. Salespeople need to make sure the buyer understands the sales contract and any guarantees fully. In addition, salespeople should reassure customers that they have made the right decision by summarizing the product benefits, repeating why their choice is better than the alternative choices, and pointing out how satisfied they will be with the product's performance. These actions reduce customers' post-decision anxiety.

Style of Communication in Personal Selling

Salespeople must do more than present the right information to buyers. To sell in person effectively, a salesperson must choose the right communication style for the situation. We examine five elements of communication style:[8]

1. *Pace:* The speed at which the salesperson moves to close a sale is known as **pace.** A salesperson must adjust this pace so that the buyer does not feel rushed, offended, or bored.

THE WORLD OF PERSONAL SELLING

1. Six common types of selling are responsive, trade, missionary, technical, creative, and consultative selling.
2. The personal selling process typically involves six stages:
   - Attaining knowledge
   - Prospecting
   - Preapproach
   - Approach
   - Sales presentation
   - Follow-up
3. Five communication style elements in personal selling are pace, scope, depth of inquiry, interactive communication, and the use of supporting materials.

2. *Scope:* **Scope** refers to the variety of benefits, features, and sales terms discussed. Some sales presentations, designed to appeal to all customers, use a broad scope. For high-priced, customized products, the presentation tends to have a narrower scope, focusing on the most important benefit to the buyer.

3. *Depth of inquiry:* The extent of the salesperson's effort to learn the details of the buyer's decision process is the **depth of inquiry.** The appropriate depth is affected by three factors: (a) the salesperson's previous experience with the prospect, (b) the extent to which several people are involved in the purchase decision, and (c) the prospect's feeling about the product before and after the presentation.[9]

4. *Interactive communication:* In personal selling two-way communication must be initiated and maintained. Salespeople must ask questions and listen carefully to match the product with customer needs. They must avoid the temptation to present the product in a manner that discourages customer interaction.

5. *Use of supporting materials:* Many salespeople use materials, such as visual and auditory aids, to support their presentations. Because it is difficult for buyers to visualize intangibles or complex products, flip charts, slides, product demonstrations, written proposals, and the like all help customers visualize product benefits.

MANAGING A SALES FORCE

Most sales executives agree that strong sales supervision is a key ingredient in building an excellent sales force. A typical sales force is composed of men and women with diverse backgrounds and experience levels, often separated from headquarters by thousands of miles. Through necessity, many salespeople become the primary connection between the customer and the company. Consequently, there is a strong tendency for salespeople to be independent and to act as though they are running their own business. In the recent past sales managers made overt attempts to decrease this independence by requiring salespeople to report for weekly meetings. Because of the high cost of travel combined with the communication capabilities of laptop computers, this pattern has changed.

profile

Shellie Harvel
Sales Representative, Van Dahl Engineering

As a salesperson, I often feel like I "do lunch for a living." I represent several factories that supply hi-tech product parts to manufacturers of ultrasound equipment, missiles, satellites, aircraft, locking devices, and microwave products. My job is to sell my clients' products to other businesses.

Most of my products are customized to suit the needs of the buyer. So when I've located a sales opportunity, I bring in my clients' engineers to work with the customer directly. At that point, my goal is to enhance communication and "grease the wheel" by keeping the program moving forward until we finally close the deal.

Academic Background and Career Track

This type of business requires a unique combination of people skills and technical background. I financed my Manufacturing Engineering Technology degree from Arizona State University with a technical degree in Architectural Drafting. I worked as a Welding Engineer for just shy of two years where I encountered a personality conflict with my job … boredom. In desperation, I entered a business partnership as a manufacturer's representative (rep). From that experience I realized I had found my calling and sold a range of services including insurance and investments. I eventually became an Area Branch Manager of a temporary personnel firm. Still not satisfied, I realized I was not using my technical background and went back to where I started, only this time tooled with fourteen years of sales, management, and communications experience.

Advice

Look closely at what you enjoy doing now when you consider your educational direction. And remember, it's not only what you know that counts, it's who you know! Network and talk to people who are living the life you think you want for yourself. Interview the people working at the top of the field you are considering and ask about the up and down sides to their careers. Then, take a good look at yourself. Would you rather spend hours alone with your computer or a great book? Do you study best in a library or a cafeteria? These types of questions are very important in a career choice and even when picking the company you work for. I was at the party and always studied in a cafeteria. Maybe engineering wasn't the best career choice for me.

Typical Day

5:30 a.m.: The alarm goes off and from this point it's anyone's guess. I could be flying to Albuquerque to meet a client at the factory, or I could be driving to Tucson, Arizona, to scout for new sales opportunities. My job is affected by so much human influence I could be overbooked, wondering how I am going to see everyone on my schedule. Then, an hour later, everyone may have called in sick with the flu, so I sit at my desk on the phone for 10 hours. Today I have an early morning appointment with my NordicTrack and

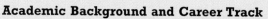

Today salespeople find themselves walking a thin line, splitting loyalties between customers and the company that pays their salary. Salespeople see their customers regularly but may have little contact with the company. In fact, the sales manager may be the only contact the salesperson has with the company.

The sales manager becomes the key link between the company and the sales force. The sales manager defines and interprets business policy, directs the daily efforts of the sales force, coaches the sales force, and helps salespeople resolve problems. The sales manager's task is far more complex than it was 20 years ago.

CNN. So I get up and jump start my day with a cup of coffee.

6:30 a.m.: After sweating through 30 minutes of news, I hit the shower. As I get ready, I boot up the multimedia system and check my e-mail (I get nothing but busy signals after 8:00 a.m.), run my task lists (a list of activities arranged by date, time, and priority) and anything else the computer can do without me.

7:15 a.m.: I put on the head set and start my day by doing my follow-up with known "early birds" like my east coast factories. Next priority is to follow up on any outstanding price quotes. Then, I look over the software-generated task list to start the "cherry picking." My stomach makes that distracting growl sound. Oh yeah, I better get something to eat before my scheduled appointments in the field.

8:30 a.m.: Over a bowl of oatmeal, I finish prioritizing and preparing for the day's sales calls. I get in a few important phone calls between bites of oatmeal and sips of coffee.

9:00 a.m.: Yikes, I'm still in my house coat. Do the superwoman and I'm on the road by 9:15 a.m.

9:30 a.m.: My beeper pages me. It's my 9:45 appointment at McDonnell Douglas who's got the flu and is calling to cancel. Good thing I brought my task lists. I use the time to peel off a few more phone calls in the McDonnell Douglas lobby.

10:00 a.m.: Meet with the Manager of Instrumentation Development and Support for McDonnell Douglas. He gives me a few leads (a warm introduction or referral is worth gold in this business) and a cool Apache Helicopter hat pin. I give him a calendar.

11:00 a.m.: Back in the McDonnell Douglas lobby to access my messages and make some important phone calls.

11:30 a.m.: I race back to my car and I'm off to TRW.

12:00 p.m.: Let the Senior Product Engineer know I'm in the lobby to pick him up for lunch. We go to a nice Italian restaurant and talk about his move from the Midwest and his two kids and wife most of the time. After lunch, he gives me the latest set of drawings for a switch panel, and I'm off to my next appointment.

1:30 p.m.: I have two sequential appointments with a customer who buys everything for a complete program and a customer who buys just a few items. Things go well and I head back to McDonnell Douglas.

3:00 p.m.: My last appointment is with a referral. I have no idea where it will lead. Turns out I get a few more referrals and I'm back on the road. Next stop, the post office to 2nd-day air the TRW drawings.

4:30 p.m.: Back to the office in my home. I look over the mail, scan the new faxes, pull my voice-mail messages, and return calls. I start preparing for tomorrow as I follow up on any urgent business from the day.

5:30 p.m.: OOPS, better get that baked potato in the oven. Back to my desk to finish up.

6 to 7:00 p.m.: My husband tells me he's suffering from hunger pangs. So, I wrap it up and call it a productive day.

Products and services are more diverse and sophisticated. Buyers are more knowledgeable. Consequently, sales managers have had to become proficient at five sets of business activities:

- *Planning:* Planning is the process of forming objectives and strategies for personal selling. Taking into account both internal and external factors, sales managers should organize and plan a firm's personal selling effort so that it is consistent with other aspects of a firm's marketing communication program.

- *Staffing:* Staffing activities are those acts that sales managers take to recruit, hire, train, and maintain a quality sales force.
- *Implementing:* This is the process of taking steps to achieve the firm's sales plans. One step might be to design a program that helps salespeople meet the firm's sales revenue goal.
- *Controlling:* This set of activities is concerned with the performance of salespeople. Performance must be evaluated on a regular basis and must be equitable and consistent.
- *Adapting to change:* Sales managers must develop the ability to adapt to changes in the company, the business world, and technology. Global competition, for instance, may lead to company cost-cutting that forces sales managers to maintain or increase productivity with fewer resources. (The IMC in Action feature discusses cost issues that many sales managers face.) Managers must also quickly master new technology used to support sales efforts. They must often train others and learn to maximize the technology benefits.

Next we examine two sales management tasks that directly support the overall marketing communication effort. These tasks are setting sales objectives and motivating the sales force.

Setting Sales Objectives

The specific objectives for the sales force should be driven by the marketing communication objectives and should complement the stated objectives for the other marketing communication tools (see Figure 13.3 on page 430). Unfortunately, this coordination of objectives is rarely done. Instead, sales managers revert most often to traditional personal selling objectives, such as targets and quotas.

A **sales target** is the desired level of sales for a product or product line during a specified time frame. A **sales quota** is the share of the overall sales goal that is allocated to a salesperson, territory, or some other segment of the company business. Although these traditional sales objectives are relatively easy to understand and implement, they do not necessarily incorporate an integrated perspective. IMC-based personal selling objectives should consider all the contact points between personal selling and all other marketing communication tools. For example, salespeople could have objectives relative to their performance at trade shows, distribution of coupons, or local organizations to which they belong.

Motivating the Sales Force

We've already discussed how difficult it is to tear down the barriers that separate the various marketing communication divisions. This is even more difficult with personal selling, which has traditionally been isolated. Motivating salespeople to sell more may often spill over and create a higher level of cooperation between marketing communication groups. One might assume that salespeople who experience some level of personal and monetary success would not need additional incentives to perform well. In fact, providing such incentives is one of the most time-consuming aspects of the sales manager's job. Motivation provides positive incentives; discipline involves the use of negative incentives.

Sales managers use several methods to motivate. Among the most common are

Balancing the Personal Selling Budget

The personal sales call is no longer the most cost-effective means of satisfying customers' demand for information. In a little over a decade, the average cost of a personal sales call increased 128 percent, from $128 in 1980 to $292 in 1990, according to Cahners Advertising Research Report. Projections indicate these costs will exceed $500 by 2000.

Because of rising costs, marketing communicators can no longer afford to invest as much in the selling cycle. Some major manufacturers now sell directly to the customer. However, they must demonstrate how a product or service provides a cost-effective, competitively superior solution to a prospect's solution. To do that through a series of personal sales calls (one to assess customer needs, one to present a proposed solution, and usually a third to do lunch and close the deal) is often cost prohibitive. It takes 3.7 personal calls to close a sale ($292 × 3.7 = $1080 or $500 × 3.7 = $1850).

Somehow marketing communicators must find a way to generate leads, gather prospect information,

customize presentations, and maintain close contact with the prospect throughout the selling cycle in a cost-effective manner.

Today if you're not spending your salespeople's time exclusively in the interested, you're having an extended going-out-of-business sale. Here are some suggestions:

- *Teleprospecting:* If you can define your target audience by industry, size of company, title, or function, you can generate a prospect list and prequalify prospects over the telephone.
- *Electronic sales call:* If your product lends itself to a demonstration on videotape, computer disk, or the Internet, consider sending a cover letter with a brochure, demo tape, or disk as a first sales call. Or you could send an e-mail that explains how interested prospects can visit a Web site for a demonstration.
- *Selling for bunches:* Assembling ten qualified prospects in a room for a demonstration and sales pitch is a better use of a salesperson's time than calling on them individually.

- *Point-of-sale:* Join forces with other divisions or companies to sell noncompeting families of products. Sharp managers try to maximize sales time and results by giving the sales force a broader base of products that they can sell in one call. The interactive kiosk, for example, may be placed in a central location where prospects can examine alternative sources and seek additional information.

Food for Thought

1. Do you think there will always be some customers who want to talk to a salesperson personally? If so, what are the implications?

2. How could these new cost-effective techniques improve integration of personal selling with other marketing communication activities?

Sources: Andy Cohen, "No Deal," *Sales & Marketing Management* (August 1996): 51–4; Nancy Arnott, "Selling is Dying," *Sales & Marketing Management* (August 1994): 82–6; Richard Van Gaasbeck, "Marketers Can't Afford to Invest More in Personal Sales Calls," *The Marketing News* 27, no. 19 (September 13, 1993): 11.

financial bonuses, security, opportunity for advancement, a meaningful job, status, personal power, self-determination, and pleasant working conditions.[10]

Financial Incentives

Monetary rewards are still the primary means of motivating salespeople. Financial incentives can be divided into two categories: base compensation and extra compensation. Extra compensation includes incentives such as bonuses, optional programs (for example, stock purchases and profit sharing), prizes, and rewards.

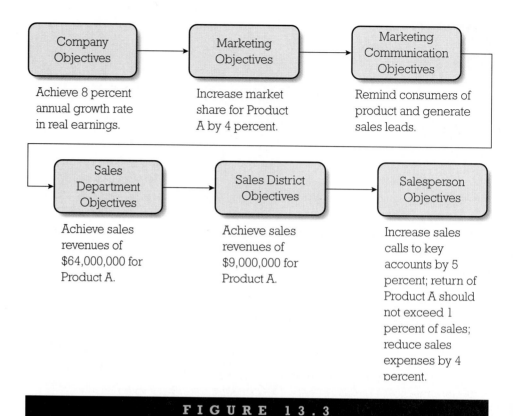

FIGURE 13.3

Company Objectives for Sales Growth Translated into Specific Objectives for the Sales Force

To attract and hold good salespeople, a compensation plan must meet employees' requirements. However, the compensation plan must also be consistent with the company's requirements and must support the overall marketing communication program. Balancing employee and company requirements is not always easy.

The three basic types of compensation for salespeople are *straight salary, straight commission,* and *combination.* **Straight salary** compensates people for time spent on the job. This guaranteed amount provides financial security but provides no incentive to work harder. It is a fixed cost for the company and is a problem only if sales decline severely. Straight salary programs are most appropriate when it is difficult to relate the efforts of individual salespeople to the size or timing of a sale.

Thus, straight salary programs are more common in business-to-business than in consumer product selling, as is the case when several specialists on a team sell complex aerospace products to airlines and the government. Salary is also appropriate in situations where products are presold through advertising or sales promotion and the salesperson primarily takes orders.

The second compensation approach is **straight commission.** Under a commission plan, salespeople are paid a fixed or sliding rate of earnings based on their sales volume or profit contribution. The commission rewards people for getting orders. It also motivates them to exceed established standards of productivity.

Because salary is tied directly to sales productivity, this compensation plan virtually pays for itself. However, it is difficult for salespeople to make a living on a straight commission program if they hit a slow period or take a little longer to get started. For experienced, successful salespeople who wish to have no ceiling on their income, straight commission is a powerful incentive.

Straight commission works best when maximum incentive is needed and when a minimum of aftersales service and missionary work is required. This situation exists for most organizations that sell housewares and cosmetics door to door. Mary Kay Cosmetics, Tupperware, Avon, and Amway use straight commission compensation programs. Other types of businesses that often use straight commission plans include life insurance, real estate, stock brokerage, wholesale clothing, and printing.

The **combination plan** attempts to eliminate the limitations of the straight salary and straight commission programs and maximize their advantages. The salesperson's base salary is usually high enough to provide the financial security that the employee desires. That salary is also low enough so that its fixed cost does not seriously affect the firm in periods of declining sales. In addition to the base salary, an incentive is paid in the form of a commission—usually on sales greater than a set quota.

The primary benefit of combination plans is that they allow the compensation program to be tailored to the needs of a particular firm. For example, if a firm wants a modest incentive, 80 percent of the compensation could be in the form of salary and 20 percent in commissions. Firms that need to give salespeople more incentive to sell products could raise the commission portion of the package to 30 or 40 percent of the total wages. Combination plans are widely used in industrial firms that sell building materials, machinery, electrical supplies, and paper products. This plan is less popular in consumer product companies.

Virtually all organizations also offer *extra incentives* to their salespeople. **Extra incentives** include a variety of awards given to salespeople for achieving specific goals. These extra incentives are in addition to compensation. The awards usually fall into three categories: cash, merchandise, and travel. A recent survey by *Incentive* reports that travel remains the award of choice (36 percent); merchandise is second (33 percent); and cash is third (31 percent).[11] Companies spent $7.9 billion on extra incentives in 1995.

Other Motivators

Security is important to many people. To provide a more secure environment, companies may offer better salaries, better fringe benefits, and an atmosphere that assures salespeople that the company respects and values them.

Opportunity for advancement is another motivating factor. In most companies salespeople tend to follow one of two career paths. Either they want to remain a sales representative with greater compensation and responsibility, or they are using their current job as a stepping stone toward a sales management job. For both career paths, the sales manager must develop a clear and fair set of criteria that a person must meet to be promoted.

Managers also motivate salespeople by making them feel that their job is meaningful. Sales managers must learn to raise the status of selling within the firm on the basis of both its absolute contribution to the firm and to society. In companies where salespeople feel their jobs are meaningful, morale is seldom a problem.

Closely related to the meaning of the sales job is individual status. In many companies status may mean little more than conferring titles and labels that generate personal prestige. Being called a sales representative or a client representative, for example, may seem more impressive than being called a salesperson. Receiving the label CLU (Chartered Life Underwriter) or "member of the million-dollar roundtable" means a great deal to a life insurance salesperson. Status can also be conveyed through the quality of the company car provided, a handsome company-provided briefcase, or the size of an expense account.

Sometimes the incentives provided to salespeople can prompt them to engage in unethical behavior. As noted in the You Decide feature, integrating personal selling with other marketing communication activities may solve this problem.

Increasing salespeople's authority may also motivate, such as giving salespeople the right to make decisions that they were not allowed to make before. Sales managers can also motivate salespeople by giving them more autonomy. Individuals tend to enter the sales field because of the independence it provides. They resent being told what they should do and how they should do it. Although total autonomy is impossible, considerable self-determination can be established by delegating as much authority and responsibility as possible to the sales representatives.

Finally, good working conditions also tend to improve productivity. Many aspects of the sales job (for example, long hours and extensive travel) are unattractive. Intelligent sales managers allow salespeople to live well while traveling by providing a safe, comfortable car and allowing them to eat at good restaurants and stay at pleasant hotels. It is better to economize in other areas than to limit the work environment of the salesperson.

MANAGING A SALES FORCE

1. Sales managers must become proficient at five sets of business activities:
   - Planning
   - Staffing
   - Implementing
   - Controlling
   - Adapting to change
2. The sales manager must also set personal selling objectives and motivate the sales force. Sales managers motivate salespeople through such means as financial incentives, security, and opportunity for advancement.

A CLOSING THOUGHT: THE SALES FORCE OF THE FUTURE

What will the sales force of the year 2020 look like? Will it still consist of independent operators who are assigned a territory and a quota? Will the high costs of competing in a global marketplace change the traditional salesperson? Although we can speculate about dramatic changes in the nature of personal selling, the traditional salesperson will likely remain intact for several decades. Why? Simply

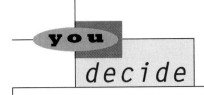

decide | A Different Perspective

Few companies are better candidates for a business-school case study on Murphy's Law than the beleaguered Prudential Insurance Co. of America. When the meter stops, the Pru will probably have shelled out more than $1.5 billion to settle claims from 1980s sales of soured Oil and Gas Limited partnerships by its Prudential Securities, Inc., unit. In 1996, after a joint investigation that had lasted more than a year, a group of state insurance departments concluded that Prudential had improperly urged some customers to cash in or borrow against existing policies to buy new, often more expensive ones. In accepting the findings Prudential agreed to pay a fine of $35 million and to compensate policyholders—a $140 million tab.

Enter Pru senior vice president Martha Goss, who was tapped in 1993 by chairperson Robert C. Winters for a daunting three-year assignment: Install a top-to-bottom system of integral internal controls in every unit, and, along the way, overhaul the corporate culture.

Goss admits that some controls broke down in the late 1980s. To remedy this the company installed a comprehensive, integrated risk control system with the help of Coopers & Lybrand, the Big Six accounting firm. "What's appealing about the approach is that controls are the responsibility of business unit heads and line managers, not support structures," Goss said. Over the next year or so, Goss, with the aid of a small staff, swept through the company, working with managers to identify risks and then building controls to address them. All managers, she said, will be called upon to ask themselves: "What's the worst that can happen, and could I survive it?"

Goss explained that the thrust of the exercise was to make sure that "people know what their jobs are, what's expected of them, and that they're accountable for them." She felt the program could convince employees that they have not only a right but a responsibility to ask questions if they are instructed to do something they don't think is right or don't fully understand. This change in philosophy has a particularly strong bearing on the sales force, who traditionally did what they were told to do, no questions asked. With this integrated approach to the management of Prudential, the risks of salespeople making unethical decisions should have greatly diminished.

However, the 1996 findings of numerous state insurance departments indicated that for more than a decade Prudential's representatives had engaged in improper sales practices that harmed customers.

After Prudential accepted the state insurance findings, it made attempts to reconcile with its customers. The first program is called the Client Acquisition Process. It attempted to reduce the complexity of the application process by instituting the use of a shortened client information form at the point of sale. It connected the client directly with the underwriter and allowed the salesperson more time to build relationships and less time filling out forms. Prudential also agreed to another program—supervised by the Multi-State Task Force, state insurance regulators and independent auditors—in which the firm contacted each person who felt unfairly treated and tried to work through those issues.

You Decide

1. What effect does the sales force behavior have on the other communication elements at Prudential?

2. Do you think the activities Goss undertook could still help Prudential? Explain.

3. Given the latest controversy, which spanned a ten-year time frame, how likely do you think it is that Prudential can reconcile with its customers? What additional steps, if any, should it take?

4. Do you think that Prudential should consider paying its sales force a different form of salary other than straight commission? Explain your answer.

Sources: Joseph B. Treaster, "Prudential to Pay Policyholders $140 Million for Its Sales Tactics," *New York Times*, 25 September 1996, C1; Prudential home page, The Prudential Insurance Co. of America, Newark, N.J. (1996), Internet (www.prudential.com); Philip L. Zweig, "Prudential: Making it Rock-Solid Again," *Business Week*, October 31, 1994, 96.

because many products will still need to be sold personally by a knowledgeable, trustworthy person who is willing to resolve problems 24 hours each day.

Still, major changes in personal selling will occur, in large part due to technology. Though technology has increased selling efficiency, it has also resulted in more complex products so that more sales calls are required per order in many industries. Also, because of the trend toward business decentralization, sales representatives now have more small or mid-sized accounts to service. Currently, companies such as Hewlett-Packard and Fina Oil and Chemical provide laptop computers to all salespeople. Computer-based sales tracking and follow-up systems allow salespeople to track customers.[12] This technology means that salespeople can assess customer-buying patterns, profitability, and changing needs more rapidly. Accessing this information via computer saves the salesperson time and allows customization of the sales presentation.[13]

Sales teams will continue to gain in popularity because customers are looking to buy more than a product. They are looking for sophisticated design, sales, education, and service support. A sales team includes several individuals who possess unique expertise and can coordinate their efforts to help meet the needs of a particular prospect in every way possible. The salesperson acts as the team quarterback, ensuring that the account relationship is managed properly and that the customer has access to the proper support personnel.

Procter & Gamble is one company that has adopted the team approach. P&G has 22 sales executives who coordinate the sales efforts of various P&G divisions in their assigned market areas. Each manager coordinates key account teams composed of sales executives from P&G's grocery division. As many as three key account teams may sell in each market. The marketing manager supervises a logistics team composed primarily of computer systems and distribution executives. The team works closely with retailers to develop mutually compatible electronic data and distribution systems. P&G hopes the team approach will reduce the pressure for trade promotions because the team provides greater service to resellers.[14]

Salespeople of the future will have to adjust to new forms of competition. With the increased capabilities and greater use of direct marketing, for example, salespeople must recognize that some customers will buy a product without contact with a salesperson. Product catalogs that feature everything from computers to classic automobiles are mailed directly to customers or offered on the Internet. These often provide all the information about the product the customer needs to know. Questions can be answered through a toll-free number, an Internet comment form, or e-mail. Salespeople of the twenty-first century should either integrate direct marketing to support the selling process or offer the customer benefits not available through other marketing communication techniques.

On this very small planet, salespeople will also have to adjust to new sources of competition. Companies in Asia, South America, and Eastern Europe are introducing thousands of new products to industrialized nations every year. The salesperson of the future must know how to respond to foreign competitors and how to enter their markets. A program that integrates personal selling with other marketing communication tools will give salespeople more opportunity to act efficiently and have selling success.

SUMMARY

1. Define personal selling.

Personal selling is the face-to-face presentation of a product to a potential customer by a company representative.

2. Describe the strengths and weaknesses of personal selling.

Compared with other marketing communication tools, personal selling has several strengths. First, it is more flexible because salespeople can adjust their presentations to suit customers' needs and motives. Second, salespeople target potential customers rather than a mass audience, so personal selling minimizes wasted communication efforts. Third, the interactive nature of personal selling allows salespeople to make repeated requests for action, often resulting in sales. Fourth, salespeople can perform many jobs on behalf of the company, such as taking orders, collecting information, and offering service. Finally, the effectiveness of personal selling is easy to measure. Personal selling also has several weaknesses. Its cost is relatively high, finding and retaining high-quality people is difficult, the sales force often sends messages inconsistent with other marketing communication and with other salespeople, and sales representatives often have different levels of motivation that can affect product sales.

3. Discuss how personal selling fits in the marketing communication mix.

The marketing communicator must decide how to use personal selling in the marketing communication mix by examining several factors, including the product, the market, the distribution channel, the nature of the information needed to sell the product, the marketing communication objectives, the marketing communication mix alternatives available, and the relative cost of personal selling compared with other marketing communication mix tools.

4. Outline both the types and the process of personal selling.

The six most common types of personal selling are responsive selling, trade selling, missionary selling, technical selling, creative selling, and consultative selling. No matter what type of selling is used, the personal selling process generally follows a pattern of six steps: attaining knowledge, prospecting (scouting for interested customers), preparing for the sale (known as the preapproach), approaching the sales presentation, making the sales presentation, and follow up with activities after the sale (such as service, oversight of installation).

5. Explain the tasks of sales management that relate directly to marketing communication.

To manage a sales force, sales managers must accomplish many tasks, such as planning, staffing, implementing sales objectives, controlling, and adapting to change. Two sales managerial tasks relate directly to marketing communication—setting sales objectives and motivating the sales force.

POINTS TO PONDER

Review the Facts

1. Explain the six steps in the personal selling process.
2. Discuss the strengths and weaknesses of personal selling.
3. The relative importance of personal selling in the marketing communication mix is a function of several factors. What are those factors?

Master the Concepts

4. What styles of communication can salespeople use in personal selling? Explain the key ideas behind each stylistic element.
5. What contributions can personal selling make to a firm that advertising or sales promotion cannot provide?

6. What are the implications of the rapid advances of technology and the high cost of selling on the future of personal selling?

Apply Your Knowledge

7. "Personal selling should be a separate part of the organization. We create the sales, unlike those fools in advertising." Evaluate this statement and explain the problems that result in an organization that has this opinion.
8. What are the problems faced in motivating sales personnel? Identify three types of sales jobs. What type motivation would work best with each?
9. Imagine you were the sales manager for a firm that sells highly complex communication technology systems to businesses. How could you motivate your salespeople? Discuss the major problems of motivating and keeping your salespeople.
10. Now suppose you were the sales manager for a

firm that wants to integrate personal selling more closely with its other marketing communication activities. The business sells nonprescription sunglasses that use a newly patented sun glare protection device that no other sunglasses manufacturer can offer. You've been assigned to work with the marketing director and the managers of advertising, public relations, sales promotion, and direct-marketing. Describe the steps the firm could take to integrate personal selling with the other marketing communication tools, discuss how you might set sales objectives consistent with the marketing communication objectives, and outline how you could motivate the sales force to support the integrated efforts.
11. Consider the process of personal selling. Identify which marketing communication tools could be useful at each stage of the process and explain how those tools would be helpful.

SUGGESTED PROJECTS

1. (Oral Communication) Contact two salespeople (one who sells industrial products and one who sells consumer products). Interview them about the steps they follow in selling their products. How do they differ? How are they alike? Be prepared to present your findings to the class.

2. (Writing Project) Select and research the marketing communication activities of a company of your choice that sells a product or service to other businesses. Write a two-page essay on how personal selling and the other marketing communication techniques could complement one another.

3. (Internet Project) Some experts have predicted that the Internet will replace the traditional sales

force. Others claim that the Web can improve the service a salesperson can offer because it can provide additional support, general information, and a means for reaching customers cheaply at any time of day or night. Take a look at the Web site of at least one direct marketer to see whether the site is designed to help its sales force and, if so, how. Alternatively, does the site seem to encourage ordering directly from the company, rather than putting consumers in touch with a sales representative? Explain. Be prepared to discuss your findings in class. Four suggested sites follow:

Amway — www.amway.com
Avon — www.avon.com
Discovery Toys — www.discoverytoysinc.com
Tupperware — www.tupperware.com

CASE 13: INTERPLAK MAXIMIZES SALES

When Interplak was first introduced to the marketplace, Bausch & Lomb traditionally worked with dentists and hygienists to maximize their sales potential.

The Interplak was distributed primarily through dentists to patients. A revolutionary tool in dental health care, the electric toothbrush featured ten tufts of bristles that rotated 4200 times per minute, reversing direction 46 times each second. It cleaned teeth of plaque and reduced gingivitis so effectively that thousands of dental professionals enthusiastically recommended it to their patients.

The Interplak instrument was then made available at retail stores. Bausch & Lomb salespeople knew that a significant number of consumers bought the instrument because of dentists' recommendations. When consumer demand and retail distribution increased, the sales force wanted to strengthen relationships with dentists who would recommend the Interplak to patients.

Robert LeBoeug, director of professional marketing and sales, described the situation: "One of my first challenges when I joined Bausch & Lomb a year ago was to transition our professional sales force. We needed to move from 'unit sales' strategy to a 'recommendation sales' strategy so dentists would continue to strongly recommend our highly effective product."

To maximize sales Bausch & Lomb needed to minimize the amount of time their professional salespeople spent locating dentists with high recommendation potential. Says LeBoeug, "Most of us who work in an office have a place to start each morning. But because salespeople don't have an office, they have to decide each day where to go and what to do once they get there. The more information we can give them—the stronger our company grows."

So Bausch & Lomb enlisted the help of a company named NDL that could identify areas with the greatest potential. NDL helped Bausch & Lomb develop a way to track their success. First, Bausch & Lomb provided NDL with a list of dentists they wanted to track. NDL created maps of Areas of Dominant Influence (ADIs), broken down by ZIP codes, for each Bausch & Lomb sales territory. On these maps NDL plotted where all dentists were located and highlighted those who were the strongest advocates for the Interplak instrument. Next, NDL developed a consumer profile of existing Interplak users. Finally, by overlaying that consumer profile on NDL's master database, NDL could also map Bausch & Lomb's best prospective Interplak consumers.

What immediate effect did this information have on Bausch & Lomb's professional sales force? "It blew them away," LeBoeug says. "Right away they were impressed that we could give them such detailed information on their territories. That same information also helps Bausch & Lomb motivate its salespeople to increase their productivity. "Before working with NDL, we had a difficult time measuring recommendation sales on a per-territory basis. NDL helped us develop a way to measure the impact of a specific salesperson's efforts, based on the number of recommendations we received within a particular ZIP code. Tracking these numbers tells us how effective our salespeople are in increasing recommendations for our products."

Case Questions

1. What are the benefits of reaching dentists when the primary distribution channel is retail stores?
2. How else could Bausch & Lomb use their database?
3. Assume you sell Interplak for Bausch & Lomb and you have been placed on a marketing communication committee to analyze how to combat competition, including Braun's Oral-B toothbrush. What suggestions would you make to other members of the committee about how the sales force should work with other marketing communication specialists in tackling the competition?

Source: "Interplak Brushes Up on Productivity," *Focus* (Winter 1992): 4–5.

ROMA'S LITE INTEGRATED CASE QUESTIONS

(Review the Roma's Lite Marketing Plan in the Appendix at the end of the text before answering these questions.)

1. Describe the process a salesperson would go through to sell Roma's Lite Pizza to retailers.
2. (Writing Project) Write a brief memo that explains how personal selling should be integrated with the other elements of the marketing communication mix in the Roma's Lite Pizza campaign.
3. (Team Project) Develop a comprehensive strategy that specifies how personal selling will be used to introduce Roma's Lite Pizza to the market.

chapter

14

Marketing Communication that Crosses the Lines

1 **Define and describe the purpose of sponsorships.**

2 **Distinguish between the three main types of sponsorships—event marketing, sports marketing, and cause marketing.**

3 **Explain how marketing communication managers use point-of-purchase and in-store merchandising techniques.**

4 **Describe how specialties and licensing are used to merchandise a product.**

5 **Justify the role and use of packaging and trade shows in the marketing communication mix.**

6 **Discuss the role of marketing support services, customer service, and word-of-mouth marketing in the marketing communication mix.**

CONSIDER this

Virtual Reality Opens Up Immersion Marketing

New and innovative uses of media are immediately of interest to marketers. Virtual reality, for example, which started in the early 1990s as a video game, is now being used to immerse people in product situations and messages. Virtual reality uses interactive technology to create three-dimensional experiences. Through the computer and its 3-D modeling programs, you can see and touch things that really aren't there. Mercedes has even launched a Web site that allows users, through sophisticated graphics that mimic virtual reality, to enter and "look around" the inside of the latest car model. Two companies, a pioneering developer of interactive selling solutions and a virtual reality company, have combined their efforts to produce VisionDome for use at trade shows, dealerships,

exhibits, and other special events. Billed as the industry's most complete immersion in virtual reality, the 3-D viewing environment uses interactive 3-D graphics, high-definition video, and multichannel sound. The dome allows ten or more people to experience virtual reality without goggles, headsets, or glasses.

Bubble Yum Bubble Gum uses virtual reality tours to immerse kids in a Bubble Yum game. The virtual reality game technology creates the illusion of being immersed in an artificial world. Participants wear helmets that are equipped with stereo sound and video screens and travel about in a fantasy world by moving sensor-embedded gloves or joy sticks.

The Bubble Yum Virtuality Tour visits malls with its Virtuality game equipment. The game, which can accommodate up to four players, is set up inside the mall. Kids can play the game free when they present three Bubble Yum wrappers. Those waiting in line can watch the game on giant TV monitors. About 60 people per hour can play the game—about 720 people during a typical 12-hour day at the mall. Although Bubble Yum targets kids ages 8 to 17, the event also attracts the attention of older teens and adults who are curious about virtual reality.

In the Bubble Yum Planet game, players fly over a computer-generated cyberspace of volcanoes, craters, and geysers on bubble gum packs. As they descend to the planet surface, they pass through rings made up of orbiting chunks of Bubble Yum, which they grab and collect in bags. Players can fight off other players trying to steal their bags. They must also avoid giant humming-birds trying to burst their bubbles. Everyone who plays the game gets specialty items such as a purple Bubble Yum sponge ball. The player who collects the most chunks of bubble gum wins a Bubble Yum baseball cap.

The tour is supported by advertising and pre-event announcements on the most popular youth radio stations in each target market. Bubble Yum also works with retailers at each tour stop to display point-of-purchase (P-o-P) materials. Retail personnel are invited to preview the game the evening before the event opens to the public. Each mall's center court is decorated with banners, balloons, and fog machines. Free samples are handed out in the mall during the promotion. The tour is also tied into a Bubble Yum TV campaign that features kids playing a virtual reality game. ◼

Sources: Kathleen Callo, "Advertisers Try to Reach Europe's Internet Users," *Reuters Financial Services,* September 27, 1996; "CWC and Alternate Realities Introduce VisionDome: Virtual Reality Walk-in Kiosk with 3D Graphic, High-Definition Video," *Business Wire,* September 20, 1996; Glenn Heitsmith, "Bubble Yum Launches Virtual Reality Tour," *Promo* (March 1993): 14, 70; David C. Churbuck, "Applied Reality," *Forbes,* September 14, 1992, 486–90.

CHAPTER OVERVIEW

This chapter describes a variety of marketing programs that use a combination of marketing communication tools. The Bubble Yum story, for example, describes a tour that can be used as a sales promotion, a public relations activity, or both. Still other times, some companies consider tours as a special event or part of its event marketing program. In addition to the confusion about how to categorize tours, note that the Bubble Yum tour, just as with all tours, combined a number of overlapping marketing communication activities, such as advertising, public relations, point-of-purchase materials, sampling, and a contest.

This chapter is devoted to marketing communication efforts that defy traditional categorization or may be used in many ways to support marketing communication activities. We begin this chapter by exploring three types of sponsorships: event marketing, sports marketing, and cause marketing. We then investigate marketing communication tools used to merchandise a product (point-of-purchase and other merchandising materials, specialties, and licensing) and marketing services that overlap with marketing communication (packaging, trade shows and exhibits, marketing support services, and customer service). We close with a look at word-of-mouth marketing.

SPONSORSHIPS

A **sponsorship** is the provision of financial support for an activity or organization—sports, art, entertainment, a good cause, or fairs and festivals—so that it can survive. The aim is to polish the sponsor's image in ways that reflect positively on the bottom line. In most cases the company wants to be associated with the positive social values reflected by the person, activity, or organization it sponsors. First we'll talk about sponsorships in general with a special focus on the Olympics.

Then we'll discuss three specific types of sponsorships—event, sports, and cause marketing.

A stadium sponsorship is one of the newest types of sponsorships. For a million bucks or so a year, as Table 14.1 illustrates, marketers buy the opportunity to reach tens of thousands of consumers at every sports event and concert held in the stadium, week after week. That compares favorably with 30 seconds of advertising on *Seinfeld* for $500,000 to $600,000 or half a minute on the Super Bowl for $1.2 million.[1] And the newest corporate drive is to have a stadium or arena named after the company. Corporate spending in this name game has grown from $25 million in the early 1990s to $750 million today.[2]

For signage sponsors, if the local team is strong enough to get national TV coverage, then the sponsor gets national visibility as a bonus. Sponsorships of executive suites—sometimes called skyboxes—in the stadiums are also big business. The new FleetCenter in Boston, for example, has 104 suites that cost about $200,000 a year for a total of $20.8 million split between the team and the Center's owners.

Although many people think sponsorships are used mainly for big-time sports or major causes, sponsorships can be used in other ways. Companies sponsor children's programs at the local symphony, provide materials for schools, and award scholarships for students. Businesses give grants to artists to support their creative work. Some major advertisers, like Hallmark, sponsor their own TV programming, the Hallmark Hall of Fame. As the case study at the end of the chapter demonstrates, the Australian sugar industry sponsored numerous meetings, seminars, scholarships, and research projects to enhance its image.

Under this general heading of sponsorships, companies may affiliate with events, sports and athletes, and good causes in myriad ways. In all cases the bottom-line value of the sponsorship depends on the fit of the business to the affiliation. Does it make sense for a pantyhose manufacturer to sponsor men's tennis? Probably not. It does make sense for Subaru, with its four-wheel-drive feature and its underdog image, to sponsor a women's ski team.

TABLE 14.1

The Stadium Game

Stadium	Location	Sponsorship Terms
Pepsi Center	Denver	$50 million plus over 20 years
3Com Park	San Francisco	$4 million over 4 years
Air Canada Center	Toronto	$14 million over 20 years
Trans World Dome	St. Louis	$26 million over 20 years
GM Place	Vancouver	$20 million over 20 years

Sources: Mark Lewyn, "See a Game, Shop for a Car, Surf the Net," *Business Week,* January 29, 1996, 53; Wendy Tanka, "High-Tech Firms Lift Their Profiles at Sports Venues," *Rocky Mountain News,* 15 August 1996, 16B.

The Olympics

One of the largest sponsorships in the world is the Olympics. The Olympics also combines all three types of sponsorships—it is a special event, it focuses on sports, and it is also a good cause in the sense that donors get to support their country's world-class athletes.

The right to use the Olympic Gold Rings can cost sponsors up to $40 million. For the Atlanta Olympics, approximately 140 sponsors paid the International Olympic Committee (IOC) more than $1.7 billion for the right to the rings. In addition, companies also have hefty budgets for the many promotional activities used in support of the sponsorship. For example, Bell South spent $20 million for a sponsorship, $15 million for advertising, $40 million in marketing support, and $25 million for corporate entertaining in Atlanta. NBC's Olympic ad sales exceeded $680 million from its 55 or so sponsors of television coverage of the events.[3] Table 14.2 provides more details.

Among other things, the Atlanta games had an "official" scoring pad and timepiece, two official game shows (*Jeopardy!* and *Wheel of Fortune*), three official vehicles (a family car, an import minivan, and a luxury sedan for the dignitaries), an official soft drink (Coke), an official computer system (IBM), official fast food (McDonald's), film (Kodak), and an official express delivery company (UPS). The following table illustrates the ways that sponsors use this association.

From a strategic standpoint, the value of such sponsorship depends on the degree to which the sponsoring company can capitalize on the affiliation. It is difficult, for example, for small companies to get any mileage out of an Olympic sponsorship. Why? So many companies sponsor the Olympics that a small company can get lost. A study, for example, found that a majority of respondents sim-

TABLE 14.2

Olympic Sponsorships for Atlanta's Centennial Summer Olympics

Type of Sponsorship	How Many	Price	The Deal
Worldwide sponsors	10	Up to $40 million	Anything they want; the world's priciest club
Centennial Olympic sponsors	10	Up to $40 million	Rights to the Torch, the five rings, and the identifying name "Centennial Sponsor"
Olympic sponsors	About 20	Up to $20 million	Rights to sponsor the games, but not "the Centennial Games"
Licensees	100 or more	Varies	Can use Olympic trademarks on their promotion pieces

Sources: Adapted from Mark Starr and Karen Springen, "A Piece of the Olympic Action," *Newsweek,* January 15, 1996, 58–9; "The Total Cost of the 1996 Olympics Will Be $1,705,000,000," *Fortune,* July 22, 1996, 58–9.

ply said "no" when asked to name three official U.S. Olympic sponsors. The only company that had more than 10 percent awareness was Coca-Cola (19.7 percent). Pepsi, which isn't an official sponsor, was the third-highest named company at 7.4 percent. McDonald's (8 percent) outranked Pepsi but fell behind Coca-Cola. Companies that faced no competition from "ambush" marketers in the same category fared the best.[4] (See the You Decide feature for more on ambush marketing.) And companies that have a single image product, like Coke or McDonald's, do better than companies like 3M with its 60,000 products. 3M quit as a sponsor in 1992.

The Olympics can earn big money from and for sponsors. NBC, for instance, has an agreement with the International Olympic Committee for coverage of the Olympics through 2008. As part of the package, NBC has agreed to pay the IOC $44 million a day—or $92,000 a second— for U.S. television rights to 80 days of Olympics events telecasts, assuming that NBC averages eight hours of coverage every day for the 80 days.[5] Is it any wonder the broadcast charges to advertisers are so high?

The challenge of maximizing the benefits of a sponsorship is to wrap the company's brands in the Olympic image. The company may need to invest in expensive television commercial time for the Olympics at roughly $400,000 per 30-second spot to immerse itself in that image.[6] Sponsors, in other words, pay the steep sponsorship fees and then spend even more money to bask in the reflected glory of the games. Home-town sponsor for the Atlanta Games, Coca-Cola spent upwards of $250 million in such activities as selecting and sponsoring the 2500 Americans who carried the Olympic Torch from coast to coast and sponsoring a traveling sports park, SportsLab. Coke did everything it could to fuse itself to the rings.

Big sponsors, such as Visa and Coca-Cola, are able to leverage massive investments in advertising and other forms of marketing communication to reinforce their connection to the Olympics. Visa, in particular, supports its Olympic sponsorships with programs such as a "Pull for the Team" promotion that involves the card's users in contributions and the "Visa Gold Medal Athlete Program" for up-and-coming athletes. Companies without such deep pockets need to seriously consider the value of the affiliation. That's why Subaru sponsors a ski team rather than the Olympics mega-event.

Some Olympic sponsorships are less visible. A handful of technology companies donated close to $40 million each in goods and services to provide computer services for the Olympic Games in Atlanta.[7] IBM, for example, created an information infrastructure that connected athletes, visitors, and media worldwide. The centerpiece was a system that entered scores from pen-based laptops at each venue into a centralized scoring bank and then fed the information to the press and IBM kiosks scattered throughout the Olympic Village. The kiosks also provided information on officials, athletes, coaches, and everything else a visitor might want to know, such as restaurant picks and other Atlanta activities. Unfortunately, this behind-the-scenes contribution became very visible when organizers, the media, and the public began to complain about the computer system's failures.

Let's now turn to the strategic aspects of the three main types of sponsorships: event marketing, sports marketing, and cause marketing.

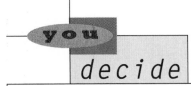

decide   **Ambush at the Finish Line**

Now you can be an Olympic hero just by using your Visa® card. Because Visa will make a donation to help all our Olympic hopefuls every time you make a purchase.

Sponsorships pose an important ethical question, a practice referred to as "ambush" or "parasite marketing." In ambush marketing major companies that are not sponsors send out marketing communication messages to appear as though they are. For instance, a company might advertise during the television broadcast of an event without officially signing on as a sponsor. Because the practice of ambushing erodes sponsorship benefits, it could dry up future pools of sponsors.

Visa, for example, spends no less than $20 million to sponsor the Summer and Winter Olympic Games and millions more promoting itself as the official credit card of the Olympics. American Express TV commercials, however, showed un-named athletes competing in winter sports events and told viewers that they could enjoy "the fun and games" but "they didn't need a Visa." Visa complained that AmEx's ads had the look, feel, and implication of an Olympic sponsorship. AmEx executives say that it wasn't ambush marketing but corrective advertising that needed to explain that AmEx is accepted at most of the shops, restaurants, and hotels where the events are held, even if not at the Olympics ticket window.

In another example, in 1984 Fuji was the official 35mm film sponsor of the games. Competitor Kodak countered by paying considerably less to sponsor the U.S. track and field team and ABC's telecast of the games. At least Kodak sponsored something. In Barcelona, Nike got high visibility at the Olympics without paying a penny in

Event Marketing

Columnist John McManus estimates that the beer, soft drink, car, camera, film, and computer marketers who have pioneered event marketing have made it into a $4.7 billion industry.[8] Following the success of such mega-events as the Los Angeles Olympics, the Statue of Liberty Centennial, and Live Aid, many companies began using event marketing—that is, promoting special events to gain more visibility for their companies. The objective of event marketing is to cut through the clutter of mass media and gain higher levels of awareness by linking with some cause, entertainment, or activity that creates a positive association for the company. Coca-Cola, for example, is involved in about 5000 local, regional, national, and international events a year.

An event staged by Lever Brothers for its products—Dove, Caress, Shield, Lifebuoy, and Lux Soaps—for example, caught the attention of early-morning commuters dashing through New York's Grand Central Terminal. In a stage rigged to look like a shower stall, an amateur singer in Lever's Singing-in-the-Shower contest sang the praises of the product with "My heart belongs to Dovvvvve." Listeners of radio station WNEW-AM also got to listen in on the soapy serenade

sponsorship fees by placing large murals of their spokespersons, Michael Jordan and Charles Barkley, on the sides of buildings. Guess which athletes got substantial press coverage.

The International Olympic Committee, and the coordinating committees of other sporting events, worry that campaigns like Kodak's and Nike's undermine the value of sponsorships. The only thing it can do in retaliation is forbid nonsponsoring companies from running ads or promotions that feature the Olympic rings, mottoes, athletes in Olympic uniforms, or even the word "Olympics."

Now the problem has moved online. Marketers who are not official sponsors but who link themselves in advertising to the Olympics see swift retaliation from the International Olympic Committee, although it is okay to use references in stories and articles. So is an announcement on a Web site a news story or an advertisement? For example, Apple Computer was allowed to set up an ad-supported site focusing on the Olympics, and Nike developed a site called @LANTA under the Nike swoosh home page (www.nike.com), which was designed to offer information on the Olympic games to media, but which also promoted Nike athletes and products.

You Decide

1. What do you think? Should companies like Nike be allowed to engage in ambush marketing? Why or why not? Can it be controlled?

2. Is it a good strategy for companies like Nike (Reeboks is the official Olympic athletic shoe), Wendy's (McDonald's is the official hamburger chain), and American Express (Visa is the official credit card) to be seen as ambush marketers?

3. Imagine you are the Coca-Cola marketing communication director and you believe that Pepsi plans to use ambush marketing during the Sydney Olympics in the year 2000. What steps would you take to prevent or minimize the effects of Pepsi's marketing strategy?

Sources: Jeff Jensen, "Web Brings New Olympic Ambush Threat," *Advertising Age,* June 17, 1996; "Cracking Down on Ambush Marketers," *Marketing Magazine* (July 5, 1996): Internet (mhbiz-link.com/marketing/27.96edit27.total); Bert Roguhton, "Ambush Marketing is American," *Atlanta Journal Constitution* (March 30, 1996): Internet (www.ajc.com/oly/bert/n03bert); Paul Fields and Eric A. Prager, "Ambush Marketing . . . or Astute Marketing? You Make the Call," *Potentials in Marketing* (January 1995): 8–10, 22; Geoffrey Brewer, "Be Like Nike?" *Sales & Marketing Management* (September 1993): 67–74.

as the deejay broadcasted live from the scene and handed out free soap samples. The incentive for participants was a trip to Hollywood and a crack at a $5000 prize. For the sponsor, such events get grassroots involvement, tie-ins with local media, enthusiasm from the sales force, and public relations support, which often translates into free publicity in the news stories on local media.

Public relations programs also use special events to celebrate major happenings such as a groundbreaking, a ribbon-cutting, or an open house after a new building is finished, a political candidate announcement, or a reception for a winning sports team. In marketing public relations (MPR), special events are used to link companies and brands to public events, issues, or ideas that engage the interest of the public.

Special events are not tied to any one marketing communication area. Instead they combine many traditional marketing communication activities—advertising, public relations, and sales promotion among them, as is illustrated in the IMC in Action feature. Furthermore, there are two levels of marketing communication involved in most events—the event itself and the media coverage of the event. In cases like the Olympics, sponsors can also generate

A Ticket to Ride

In late 1995, Apple Corps (no relation to Apple Computer) produced a product aimed at delivering some $100 million in new revenues that year. The product was a newly filmed six-hour documentary, the *Beatles Anthology,* that was shown in more than 40 countries. It was announced with a TV special event that aired in prime time on three nights.

ABC paid Apple nearly $20 million for the U.S. broadcast rights. Over 80 percent of the commercials were sold in the first three weeks, with some 30-second spots fetching more than $300,000. It was the fastest selling special in ABC history. In the United Kingdom the ITV television company outbid the BBC for the broadcast rights with an offer of $10 million.

Ford Motor company bought U.S. broadcast time for 16 commercials during the six hours and was also the exclusive automotive sponsor. Why would Ford be so involved in this project? Ford's advertising manager, Gerry Donnelly, explained that it was a perfect match for the 1995 Taurus launch because the demographics of the audience matched the Taurus target market.

communication through company publicity, advertising, and other forms of tie-in promotions.

Major companies such as RJR Nabisco and Anheuser-Busch and big advertising firms such as Saatchi & Saatchi and DFS Compton have separate divisions or departments to handle special events. Some advertising agencies, such as BBDO and Backer Spielvogel Bates, have spun off or acquired wholly owned subsidiaries to handle events. Major public relations firms such as Burson-Marsteller and sales promotion companies such as Frankel & Co. also have divisions that manage special events. For instance, PR agency Burson-Marsteller used its special events know-how to manage the Frank Sinatra/Sammy Davis, Jr./Lisa Minelli cross-country tour in the 1980s on behalf of its client, American Express. And there has been an

Apple Corps grossed nearly $75 million on the television program alone and another $25 million from record sales. On the day of the television broadcast, record stores were shipped the Volume I CD by overnight express delivery. Itself a major news event, the unusual distribution media event occurred because ABC had the exclusive rights to the first airing of "Free as a Bird," a new Beatles cut adapted from previously unreleased tracks. Because that song was also on Volume 1 of the Anthology, Capitol Records and parent EMI had to find a way to maintain security, comply with ABC's rights, and have the CD available for customers as soon after the broadcast as possible.

Normally it takes about two weeks to move a new album to record stores; the Anthology was drop-shipped overnight. United Parcel Service partnered on cross-promotional media blitzes with Capitol Records, including a TV spot and public relations releases that told the story about how the albums were distributed.

The double-CD set featured never-before-heard Beatles tracks. It also included the new song that was produced by recording the remaining members of the group over an existing John Lennon track. The Anthology meant hundreds of millions of dollars for EMI Records. Not only did EMI reap money from the record-breaking sales of the first volume (855,797 units in its first week). Volume 2 sold nearly 500,000 during its first week and debuted at #1 on Billboard's Top 200 Album chart. Volume 3 of the Beatles Anthology, released in the fall of 1996 along with the rebroadcast of the television special, was also a financial success.

The Anthology media blitz also included an array of unconventional media tactics, including "building wraps" of Capitol's Los Angeles tower and ABC's Century City headquarters. ABC used promo spots in Blockbuster video stores, recorded Beatles messages for patrons on hold on Ticketmaster phone lines, in-movie ads for Screenvision Cinema Network, messages on the Sony Jumbotron screen in Times Square, and thousands of transit ads on buses and bus shelters in New York and Los Angeles. In an attention-getting stunt, ABC commissioned pop artist Peter Max to transform buses in New York and Los Angeles into "Yellow Submarines."

For sheer money-making durability over the years, no one, other than Elvis, comes close to the Beatles.

Food for Thought

1. Can you identify all the MC tools used to promote this event?
2. If you were the EMI event marketing director, what steps would you have taken to integrate the Anthology event's MC messages?

Sources: Peter Newcomb with Robert La Franco, "All You Need is Love . . . and Royalties," *Forbes,* September 25, 1995, 130–33; "Meat the Beatles," *Forbes,* September 25, 1995, 18; Joe Mandese and Jeff Jensen, "Magical Marketing Tour '95," *Advertising Age,* October 23, 1995, 1, 8; Capitol Records, August 13, 1996: Internet (www.hollywoodandvine.com/Anthology/Revised/new2.html).

explosion of new companies that specialize in creating and staging events. Tours, such as the Bubble Yum Virtuality Tour, may also be handled by events specialists.

The growth in event marketing in recent years has been tremendous. Money spent on special events jumped from $850 million at the time of the 1984 Los Angeles Olympics to $4.7 billion in the mid-1990s. And the industry is increasing at a rate of $350 million a year.[9] Three main reasons explain such growth. First, events tend to attract a homogeneous audience that is appreciative of the sponsors of the event. Second, event sponsorship builds support from trade members and employees. The employees who manage the event may receive recognition, and trade members often participate in the event. Finally, compared to producing an advertising campaign, event management is simple because many of the elements can be prepackaged. An organization such as MCI Communications Corp. can use the same group of people and the same plan to manage many different events.

Another strength is that event sponsorship can go where other marketing communication functions, such as advertising, are forbidden or undeliverable. For many U.S. companies marketing in countries abroad, sponsorship of sports or the arts is a requirement as a way of proving commitment to the local culture. In England, where there are only four channels and tremendous demand for advertising space on them, event sponsorships are an important alternative to build corporate or brand visibility. These sponsors are reaching a market that is hard to reach via traditional tools such as advertising.

Three pitfalls to event marketing exist. First, if the match between the event and the company is poor, the benefit to the company may be small compared to the cost. Second, many uncontrollable factors such as weather can influence an event. Third, special events generally reach a smaller audience than mass-media advertising. The events effectively build awareness in a tightly targeted, committed market but are less effective at creating awareness in a broad-based audience.

Companies that jump into event marketing because they have a passion for a sport or a cause, but don't plan or analyze the costs and benefits before providing the sponsorship, often encounter problems. Drew Sheinman, Coca-Cola's event marketing director, observes, "We see more and more people start to foray into event marketing programs that are not founded on a strategic plan [to build] their brands."[10] He concludes that many do not understand how to leverage the value of the association with the brand.

Sports Marketing

The fastest-growing sponsorship category is sports marketing. A company can be engaged in sports marketing in many ways. It may sponsor a sporting event such

World Cup Soccer sponsorships allow marketers to reach audiences around the world with messages about products such as M&M's.

as the Olympics, a bowl game, a golf tournament, a stockcar race, or a 10K run. Alternatively, a company may sign up a star athlete such as Shaquille O'Neal, Ken Griffey, Jr., Katarina Witt, or Cheryl Miller. These athletes use the company's products and appear in its ads and other marketing communication programs. A company may also sponsor a participant in a sporting event, such as Valvoline's sponsorship of a race car driver, or it may sponsor a team. Finally, sports equipment manufacturers who promote their products are also considered sports marketers.

Sports marketing involves a variety of marketing communication activities, ranging from celebrity endorsements to licensed premiums to advertising and public relations activities. There are a number of factors to consider before agreeing to sponsor a sports marketing event. Table 14.3 details some considerations.

Being associated with sporting events can create a positive brand image, but it does more than that. It heightens awareness, improves attitudes about a company and a brand, adds credibility to the company's message, and creates higher levels of confidence in the company.[11] Companies measure changes in audience attitudes to prove the effectiveness of a sports marketing activity. They also consider the investment compared to the potential return. For instance, U.S. Tobacco, Kendall Oil, and Chevrolet sponsor regional tractor pulls at a cost ranging from $50,000 to $150,000 each—a small investment for these major marketers compared to the benefit of reaching nearly three million avid fans who attend these events each year.

Another reason to value sports marketing is the boost such programs give to trade and employee motivation. Visa, for example, uses its sponsorship of sports events like the Olympics to anchor merchant programs (programs in which local retailers cosponsor Olympic tie-in promotions with Visa) and a program for the 18,000-member financial institutions that promote and market Visa cards.[12]

Because of the effectiveness of sports marketing, major companies invest tremendous sums in it. For example, Nike has an all-sports agreement with a number of major universities—Alabama, Colorado, Florida State, Illinois, Michigan, North Carolina, Penn State, USC, Miami, and Michigan. Nike provides the teams with $5 to $6 million in apparel and contributions. In exchange, the teams are required to display Nike's trademark swoosh logo and use Nike shoes, uniforms, and training apparel. Michigan reportedly has the largest deal, worth about $6.3 million over six years. Analysts estimate Nike will likely make back two or three times that amount in exposure, merchandising, and the future endorsement potential of star athletes who move from college to professional ranks.[13]

Sports marketing does have some drawbacks, however. First, not everyone is interested in sports or a particular sport, so finding a match between the target audience and the sports activity audience may be difficult. To avoid this drawback, the sports marketer must understand the company or brand's target audience. That audience must have sufficient interest in the sport to justify the sponsorship. Kraft, for example, sponsors on-pack promotions with its Velveeta Shells & Cheese and Macaroni and Cheese dinners to tie-in with its sponsorship of the USA Basketball Woman's National Team. Kraft will ante up close to $5

In this ad Dallas-based American Airlines celebrates the Dallas Cowboy's NFC Championship and expresses its wish for a Super Bowl win. This ad was a New York Festival winner created by agency Temerlin McClain of Irving, Texas.

TABLE 14.3

Sports Marketing Considerations

The following should be considered before making a deal to sponsor a sport:

- *Does the product match the audience demographic at the sporting event?* Marketing beer at a basketball game makes sense; marketing perfume at a wrestling match doesn't.

- *Does the timing of the promotion match the selling season?* It wouldn't make sense to launch a suntan lotion at a January ice hockey event.

- *Match the locale of the event to the geography of the market.* Don't use a national event for a product that is marketed in only a few regions of the country.

- *Should the promotion be a single event or occur many times in multiple markets?* If the event can go on the road, then it can reach a far larger audience.

- *Match your goal to the audience of the sport.* Do you want stronger trade relations, broader distribution, increased awareness of the brand, or sales increases? Know your goals and make certain the event audience matches your target audience and can deliver on the objectives.

- *Will your sponsorship be a stand-alone effort or integrated into a total communication program?* If so, make it clear who will manage the integration.

- *Do you have the time in the schedule to allow adequate time for merchandising support?* Plan and announce the program at least three months in advance because retailers usually need a 13-week window.

- *Determine what you need to get out of the program before spending anything.* In other words, what is your payout and at what point does it make financial sense—or not make financial sense?

Source: Adapted from Blair R. Fischer, "The Rules of the Game," *Promo* (December 1995): 53–7.

million to leverage this connection, which also includes clinic sponsorships and local tie-ins.

In addition to understanding the target audience, marketers must also understand the size and type of the sports event audience. Only then will they know whether reaching that audience supports the company's marketing communication objectives. A multinational company trying to reach a worldwide audience might sponsor the Olympics instead of a local 10K run. Sports marketers must also consider the type of audience at sporting events. Some sports reach a spectator audience, such as football. Others reach audiences of mainly participants, such as a mountain biking or snowboarding event. Although the participatory sports may reach smaller audiences, those audiences tend to be more committed to the products associated with the sport than are spectators.

A survey found that some sports marketing events are better at inspiring people to purchase sponsored products. Table 14.4 reports the results when people were asked if they buy the product they saw advertised at the event. The interesting finding in this study is the high rating for NASCAR events. This is one

Nike's sponsorship of Tiger Woods requires him to wear the Nike swoosh on his hat or clothing to give the company added exposure and credibility.

TABLE 14.4

Sponsorship Impact on Purchase

Event	% of respondents that said they "almost always" or "frequently" buy
NASCAR	72
World of Outlaws (sprint car racing)	71
Indycar	68
Tennis	52
Pro-cycling	38
NBA	38
Major League Baseball	38
NFL	36
America's Cup	34
Olympics	30

Sources: Blair R. Fischer, "The Rules of the Game," *Promo* (December 1995): 53–7; Chris Roush, "Red Necks, White Socks, and Blue-Chip Sponsors," *Business Week,* August 15, 1994, 74.

of those spectator sports that draws numerous loyal viewers. Their dedication translates into high recall of not only their favorite race car drivers and teams but also the cars' sponsors.

Cause Marketing

When companies run a promotion with a charitable organization and donate a portion of their business profits to the cause, the practice is called cause marketing. The promotion runs for a period of time, briefly boosting the sales and possibly the image of the company.[14] In exchange for the sponsorship, the company earns the right to tell customers that the more of a company's products they buy, the more the cause will benefit. According to the editor of the IEG Sponsorship Report, "the way to sell a product…, whether it's a record or a gallon of gas, is to tie it in to things consumers care about, not differentiating it by price or product attributes."[15] Companies use cause marketing to do something good for society, associate themselves with a positive cause that will reflect well on their corporate image, break through the commercial clutter, and target a group of people interested in that cause.

Cause marketing campaigns usually involve supporting promotional efforts. For example, companies underwrite national advertising and promotional campaigns for the National Breast Cancer Awareness Month during October. Through a direct-mail campaign and ads in *Forbes* and *Fortune* magazines, Lee Apparel sponsors "National Denim Day" on the last Friday of the month, which solicits support of more than 25,000 companies and government agencies. Employees who contribute $4 to the Susan G. Komen Breast Cancer Foundation can wear denim clothing to work that day.

Cause marketing received a boost in the 1990s when companies realized that sales increases could be generated with less investment than needed by traditional sales promotion or advertising programs because of the free publicity and the psychological value from association with a socially responsible cause. After American Express's sponsorship of the Statue of Liberty's restoration in 1983 resulted in favorable publicity and increased credit card memberships, cause marketing took off.

Basically, cause marketing is sales promotion with a public relations spin. In other words, marketing communication managers have found that doing good can be good for business. In a Roper Starch national survey, 2000 U.S. adults reported that when given a choice between two products of equal price and quality, 78 percent said they would be more likely to buy the one that supported a cause that they cared about.[16]

Cause marketing has the strengths and the weaknesses of both public relations and sales promotion. Like sales promotion, it can instantly affect sales by offering something extra. The sales boost is aided further by public relations' ability to break through the commercial clutter. Thus cause marketing helps keep a company or brand top-of-the-mind, but only if the cause and the company are related in some way. For example, Crayola sponsors arts education, and book publisher McGraw-Hill supports literacy programs. But cause marketing has limitations. It is often poorly integrated into a company's overall marketing communication program and may, as a result, be ineffective. As practiced by many companies, it is relatively short term, opportunistic, and seen by more and more people as self-serving and exploitive.[17]

A more strategic way to improve audience relationships through support for socially responsible causes is an approach University of Colorado professor Tom Duncan has dubbed "mission marketing."[18] This approach integrates a noncommercial, socially redeeming value system into a company's business plan and operations. In other words, the cause is not something that is adopted and then forgotten, but an important part of the company's business. Examples of companies that have built significant business activities on mission marketing are Ben & Jerry's ice cream, Tom's of Maine toothpaste, Hannah Andersson's direct-mail children's clothing, and sporting goods company REI.

Mission marketing funnels all of a company's "philanthropy" into a single, long-term commitment that is related to the company's expertise and mission. For example, American Express helped develop tourism in Eastern European countries struggling to find ways to attract hard currency. The company sent executives to work with the Hungarian government's tourism staff, set up a foundation that financed university research on effective ways to publicize the region's museums, and funded tourism educational programs in 23 secondary schools to help prepare students to work in tourism and travel-related businesses. AmEx enlisted local help for these projects from Hungarians in government and in the airline, hotel, and restaurant industries. These government and business contacts with key people in the travel industry will give American Express a strong base when tourism takes off in the countries it has helped.

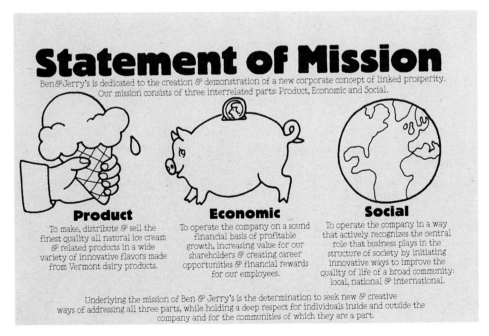

Statement of Mission

Ben & Jerry's is dedicated to the creation & demonstration of a new corporate concept of linked prosperity.
Our mission consists of three interrelated parts: Product, Economic and Social.

Product
To make, distribute & sell the finest quality all natural ice cream & related products in a wide variety of innovative flavors made from Vermont dairy products.

Economic
To operate the company on a sound financial basis of profitable growth, increasing value for our shareholders & creating career opportunities & financial rewards for our employees.

Social
To operate the company in a way that actively recognizes the central role that business plays in the structure of society by initiating innovative ways to improve the quality of life of a broad community: local, national & international.

Underlying the mission of Ben & Jerry's is the determination to seek new & creative ways of addressing all three parts, while holding a deep respect for individuals inside and outside the company and for the communities of which they are a part.

Mission marketing begins with a plan to integrate socially responsible activities in the company's day-to-day operations. Ben & Jerry's mission statement shows its long-term commitment to such a plan.

This "strategic philanthropy" adds an element of trust to the relationship between the company and its customers and other stakeholders. In addition, it provides a tool to create a truly integrated marketing program because it "fosters synergy among business units."[19] When properly done, mission marketing should promote comments such as: "I want to work for this company—or buy its products—because this company stands for something more than just making a profit."

IMC and Sponsorships

Sponsorships of any kind are the ideal place to practice integrated marketing communication because they all involve a variety of messages and media aimed at many stakeholders—all held together by one theme related to the sponsorship. In its sponsorship of World Cup soccer, for example, Sprint's integrated marketing effort used approximately 70 different marketing initiatives targeted at each of Sprint's primary stakeholders: businesses, residences, international customers, business travelers, journalists, and its own employees.[20] Furthermore, sponsorships may affect other areas of the marketing mix as products are designed or redesigned to fit the tie-in, special pricing opportunities are created, and, in some cases new distribution channels are used as part of the event.

Sponsorships are valuable if they provide a meaningful and cost-effective way to build business. They must also fit with the company's mission and help achieve its marketing communication objectives. John Beneath, Visa senior vice president, makes the point that the company's sponsorship of the Olympics would not make sense if the event wasn't integrated into many areas of its communication program beyond just using the Olympic images and symbols. Visa uses Olympic-related activities, for instance, in both employee and trade relations. Employees, customers, and business partners help raise funds for the teams. The key is to leverage the sponsorship throughout the company's business dealings.[21]

Concept Review

SPONSORSHIPS

1. A sponsorship is the provision of a company's financial support so that a sport, event, or cause can survive. The purpose of the sponsorship is to bolster the sponsor's image in ways that reflect positively on the bottom line.
2. Event marketing allows companies to associate their products with everything from jazz festivals to bubble gum blowing contests to cut through the clutter of mass media and gain higher levels of positive awareness.
3. Association with sporting events heightens audience awareness, improves attitudes about a company and a brand, adds credibility to the company's message, and creates higher levels of confidence in the company.
4. Cause marketing occurs when a company runs a promotion with a charitable organization and donates a portion of their business profits to the cause. Mission marketing gives the mission of the company a socially responsible focus.
5. Cause marketing is a complex form of promotion. To keep a cause promotion focused, it is best to manage it with an integrated strategy.

Like all IMC programs, sponsorships often demand some reorganization because the activities cross over so many functional borders. Recognizing the importance of coordination, Kodak, GTE, and Reebok have fully integrated sponsorship departments.

One of the toughest issues is proving that sponsorships are effective. To tackle this issue research firms sich as Yankelovich have teamed with other marketing groups to develop techniques that measure sports and entertainment sponsorship effectiveness. Such techniques analyze how fans react to a promotion at an event. Sponsors learn what fans take away from an event and what image fans have of the sponsor.[22]

MERCHANDISING

Just as with sponsorships, merchandising also requires a variety of marketing communication activities. In this section we examine three merchandising activities: in-store merchandising, specialties, and licensing.

Point-of-Purchase and Other Merchandising Material

A display designed by the manufacturer and distributed to retailers to promote a particular brand or group of products in the store is a *point-of-purchase display* (P-o-P). These displays are often created to support sales promotions and advertising campaigns. Although the forms vary by industry, P-o-P can include special racks, display cartons, banners, signs, price cards, and mechanical product dispensers. More recently, manufacturers are using up-to-date information via computer chips and touch-screen technology. Product visibility is the basic purpose of P-o-P displays. In an industry such as the grocery field, where a consumer spends about three-tenths of a second viewing a product, anything that gives a product greater visibility is valuable. Unfortunately, retailers are often reluctant to use P-o-P displays because they contribute to store clutter.

When all the elements of a sale—the consumer, the money, and the product—come together at the same time, point of purchase is usually the most effective marketing communication technique. As we move toward a self-service retail environment in which fewer and fewer customers expect help from salesclerks, the role of point of purchase will continue to increase. According to the Point of Purchase Advertising Institute (POPAI), 66 percent of purchase decisions are made in the store rather than before entering the store.[23]

Point of purchase is a $15 billion business effort that must be well planned to succeed. Marketing communication planners must start by answering two equally important questions: Is P-o-P appealing to the end user? And will it be used by the reseller? Retailers will use P-o-P only if they are convinced that it will generate greater sales. To ensure greater sales, planners should coordinate the P-o-P with the theme used in other marketing communication, such as advertisements. This consistency not only reinforces through repetition, it also creates a last-minute association between the campaign and the place of decision.

This ad shows how effective point-of-purchase advertising materials can be.

Point-of-Purchase Advertising Perks Up Coffee Sales.

The presence of a P-O-P display increased sales of coffee by an **incredible 567%**. So if you're not using Point-of-Purchase advertising for your brands, it's time to wake up and smell the coffee.

*Joint POPAI/Kmart/Procter & Gamble Study

Other merchandising materials designed for in-store use include signage and displays other than P-o-P. Retailers have become experts in the use of store signage (banners, posters, shelf and cooler signs) and window displays. "Building wraps" like those displayed on Capitol's Los Angeles tower and ABC's Century City headquarters for the *Beatles Anthology* event are a type of large-scale display.

In retail it is through these signs and displays that customers compare prices and selections. In addition, displays may be the main motivator of impulse buying. Given the limited amount of space available, however, the cost of convincing retailers to use these materials may be as great as the cost of designing and producing them.

One issue is whether the retailer charges the manufacturer for placement of these materials. A study of display allowances (see Chapter 10) found that roughly 70 percent of the manufacturers surveyed did not pay for placement. Another 28 percent, however, did report paying these charges, and some of the costs ranged as high as $300,000 or more[24].

Retailers also engage in promotional activities, such as theme promotions, in-store demonstrations, sponsorships of community activities, and support for manufacturers' cooperative efforts—called cross-marketing—where several related products are marketed together. The most common type of event is an in-store theme promotion such as Back-to-School days or White Sales. Theme promotions are supposed to excite consumer interest. A large-scale promotion launched by JCPenney brought together products from India, particularly madras-patterned clothing. Advertising and store decorations reflected the Indian theme.

Specialties

Sometimes called **specialty advertising,** this tool is also considered a form of sales promotion because it usually involves presenting the company's name on something that is given away as a reminder item—calendars, pens, mugs, pencils, match covers, and so forth. During its virtual reality tour, Bubble Yum used specialty items such as purple sponge balls and baseball caps with the Bubble Yum logo. The ideal specialty is an item kept out in the open where a number of people can see it for a long period of time, such as a calendar or penholder displaying the company's name. Other items work well because they are attention-grabbing novelties. Unfortunately, the cost of specialty advertising is often quite high, especially in comparison with the actual value derived. A specialty silk-screened baseball hat may cost as much as $11.00.

The 15,000-plus specialty items manufactured by companies are used for a variety of marketing purposes. They offer stakeholders additional value just as premiums do, except that the consumer does not have to purchase anything to receive that value. The company name and promotional message on the items serve as a reminder. Specialties also build relationships, such as items given away as year-end or thank-you gifts (the calendar hanging in the kitchen). They may also generate sales leads.

Some people question the value of specialty advertising, considering it to be a little tacky, particularly the low-end items like pencils and matches. However, professionals know that if you want to keep the name of your company in front of the customer, give them a calendar or a coffee cup. A fancy chain of theme restaurants in Chicago, owned by the company Lettuce Entertain You, uses artfully designed matchboxes as collectibles to stimulate customers to try other restaurants in the chain. A study sponsored by Specialty Advertising Association of Greater New York suggests these techniques work. Consider this:

1. 83 percent of consumers use such products.
2. 94 percent appreciate receiving them.
3. 94 percent have a positive attitude toward the marketer.[25]

Executive gifts and contest prizes are another area related to specialties, although they usually involve more costly items. Instead of a pencil, an executive gift may be a Cross pen-and-pencil set. For a more important recipient, the company may give a more expensive gift—a Waterman or Montblanc set instead. Prizes for consumer and trade contests can include some inexpensive items like baseball caps. However, prizes intended to motivate or reward extraordinary behavior are often high-ticket items such as electronics (televisions, CD-players) or vacation trips. Even activities like trips often come with related smaller gifts that carry the company or brand identification such as travel cases, luggage, jewelry, and clothing (kimonos, hula skirts, Hawaiian shirts, and so forth).

Licensing

Licensing is the practice of selling the rights to a character or logo or some other image to other manufacturers who use it on their products. Universities make a lot of money by selling their logos to manufacturers of apparel and school-related products. Licensed characters such as the Power Rangers, the Ninja Turtles, and Garfield have made fortunes for their creators. Not just children-focused strategies, the success of the World Cup and various sports team identification efforts can attest to the attraction of these merchandising strategies for adults as well. Such images are powerful merchandising tools and can be an effective strategy for extending the life and impact of popular culture figures.

Disney has amazing success merchandising its characters, particularly with *The Lion King* and *Pocahontas*. The Burger King tie-in with *The Lion King* is one of the most successful promotions ever with the redemption of over 50 million *Lion King* figurines. The eight-week campaign in the summer of 1994 (and duplicated in December following the film's rerelease) increased total sales by 12 percent and store traffic by 19 percent.[26] The chain also gave away Lion King collector cups and extra large fries with the purchase of specified Value Meals. The broad recognition of these promotions usually push sales and awareness, regardless of whether they are based on classic images like Marilyn Monroe or short-term fads like the Lion King figures.

An amazing international success story was the marketing of *Jurassic Park,* one of the highest grossing films of all time.[27] Grossing $344.6 million in the United States and Canada, the international box office sales were $547.5 million. But the revenues from merchandising and the video release were more than twice the box office sales. Compare the total licensing income, estimated at $1 billion, to the $150 million cost to produce, distribute, and market the movie. More than 1000 licenses were granted to manufacture more than 5000 Jurassic Park products, ranging from clothing to toys. Kenner Toys alone earned more than $100 million in

MERCHANDISING

1. A point-of-purchase display (P-o-P) is designed by the manufacturer and distributed to retailers to promote a particular brand or group of products in the store.
2. Specialty advertising, also considered a form of sales promotion, involves presenting the advertiser's name on something given away as a reminder item.
3. Licensing is the practice of selling the rights to a character or logo to other manufacturers who use it on their products.

sales from Jurassic Park. As it swept around the world, the success of the movie and its merchandising made it a "global brand" because the movie transcends language and cultural barriers. For its success, MCA Universal and filmmaker Steven Spielberg's Amblin Entertainment company were named *Advertising Age*'s promotional marketer of the year in 1993. The Jurassic Park team built on its brand image even further with the Jurassic Park sequel, *The Lost World*.

OTHER MARKETING SERVICES

Now that we have investigated how sponsorships and merchandising can extend a marketing communication program, let's explore some areas of marketing that also affect marketing communication and consumer decision making. First we'll look at packaging, then trade shows and exhibits, and various marketing support services. We close with word-of-mouth communication.

Celestial Seasonings uses its distinctive packages to underscore its market position.

Packaging

As we learned in Chapter 2, a package combines a channel of communication and a message. Its presence on a shelf allows the manufacturer to make a final statement about the product and any promotional efforts that support it. This statement should be integrated into the brand's overall "look" and personality so that it is consistent with all other marketing communication messages. Celestial Seasonings' packages, for example, use delicate illustrations, unusual names, soft colors, and quotes about life to reinforce its personality and positioning as a contemporary "new age" tea. Also, the package can tie in with advertising campaigns and seasonal specials.

Packaging is another innovative area. Some marketing communicators use so-called smart packaging—packages with a tiny computer chip that can be programmed to speak to consumers about the product when picked up or opened. Other forms of packaging communication include magnetic strips, bar codes, and electronic chips that can communicate with appliances and computers, as well as consumers.

Package designers feel that their packages have to be entertaining and functional if the product is to get noticed. For instance, when the LifeSavers Company introduced its highly successful new Ice Breakers gum, it used a very "cool," icy blue holographic wrapper designed to stand out on the rack. This was the first use of holography in the gum category. Another example is a package for Philips Media's CD-ROM game *Burn:Cycle,* which incorporates a heat-sensitive liquid crystal. The black package turns to shades of blue, green, and orange when touched.[28]

In the supermarket or discount store, where busy and tired shoppers move quickly down aisles containing as many as 30,000 products, the package has a critical communication role to perform. It works like a billboard on a highway, except that it must attract more than the attention of passersby. It must stop them in their tracks and make the sale, as the Ice Breakers holographic package did.

Packaging is a big business and growing, with the flexible packaging part of the industry reaching $14.7 billion in 1995, according to the Flexible Packaging Association. Fifty percent of the flexible packaging is used for food products and another 25 percent is used to package pharmaceuticals and medical supplies. The remaining 25 percent is used for a vast array of goods, as depicted in Table 14.5.

Tests have found that the package can make a tremendous difference in consumer response to a product.[29] Distinctive packages, such as the Mrs. Butterworth syrup bottle, are important aspects of unusual and memorable products. Murphy's Oil Soap, a furniture-care product with an old-fashioned image, abandoned its cylindrical glass bottles during the 1980s and moved to larger sizes with handles. The sales of the products shot up in response. Sometimes package improvements—dripless spouts, lids that serve as cups for pouring substances like detergents—are themselves the focus of an advertising campaign.

TABLE 14.5

Uses of Flexible Packaging

Food (50%)	Medical (25%)	Other (25%)
Frozen food	Pharmaceuticals	Diapers
Meat and cheese	Medical supplies	Clothes
Bread		Garden supplies
Pet food		Retail shopping bags
Candy		Cosmetics
Cookies		Household goods
Snack food		Condiments
School milk pouches		Industrial and agricultural products
Cereal		
Prepackaged, precut fresh produce		

Source: Sam Bradley, "Packaging . . . By the Numbers," *Brandweek,* October 16, 1995, 43.

For heavily advertised brands the package and the advertising should have an obvious connection. The package should appear in the advertising and the package should carry "flags" that remind consumers of key advertising points and important product features highlighted in advertisements. Packaging is even more important for brands that do little or no advertising because the package has to carry the bulk of the promotional message. Well-designed packages help consumers quickly identify a brand's unique selling points with phrases such as "low-fat," "caffeine free," or "cleans hard water stains." Even an advertised brand like Windex may not promote its individual lines, therefore the packages for the blue, green, "vinegar," and potpourri-scented lines sell their differences.

Packaging experts believe that new package concepts can do much to attract the consumer's attention, stimulate a trial purchase, and even strengthen brand loyalty. Brand equity, especially for brands that have many product lines, resides in the graphic elements that link the various product types together. For instance, all Pepperidge Farm product packages have graphics that tie them to the overall brand image.

Packaging, also called *trade dress,* has some limitations, however, in that designs are easily copied. To illustrate, note how the bright pink Sweet 'n Low package design has been copied by house brands in some discount stores. As one expert says, "In an age where private-label clones that ape the packaging of national brands are routine . . . the marketer that ignores packaging . . . risks having his or her brand's most intimate contact with the consumer become irrelevant, outdated, or surpassed by a competitor."[30] However, a copycat package design may reinforce the branding of the original product because it signals that the copycat is trying to imitate the original—a sign that the original is worth emulating.

As discussed in Chapter 2, another problem occurs when packaging is excessive. Such packaging is criticized for its environmental impact. More and more products are being redesigned with less packaging. In Germany manufacturers are responsible for recycling all the packaging from their products, so minimalist packaging has become fashionable. Furthermore, some packaging techniques, such as clear cellophane windows in boxes, are not allowed. In this case the glue used to attach the plastic to the cardboard means the box can't be recycled. Although such laws do not exist in the United States, package design changes still happen because of consumer concern about the environment and because reduced packaging is often more cost-effective.

Trade Shows and Exhibits

Thousands of businesses present and sell their products at exhibits and trade shows that allow them to demonstrate the product, provide information, answer questions, compare competing brands, write orders, and generate sales leads. A **trade show** is a big fair where the makers of various products in an industry exhibit their wares to buyers, as well as others in the industry. Exhibits in corporate lobbies and other special events are particularly good at meeting public relations objectives of creating goodwill and providing information. The ideal exhibit is colorful, pictorial, and unusual. If possible, it fosters viewer participation. If viewers can push buttons, see pictures, and answer questions, all the better. Businesses also use displays to promote their products. Displays include parade floats, museum exhibits, historical exhibits, mock-ups of new products such as new automobiles, and models of buildings and other developments under construction.

Companies spend more than $9 billion annually on trade shows. In exchange, trade shows generate over $70 billion annually in sales.[31] Some companies, particularly those in the entrepreneurial end of the high-tech market, direct most of their planning efforts and marketing budgets at trade shows.

Trade shows allow companies to show products to their target audience, generate leads for follow-up contact by the sales staff, permit manufacturers to gather a great deal of information about their competition, and build relationships. The atmosphere tends to be relaxed; free products are distributed; and many businesses sponsor parties. In an environment where all the companies attempt to give a clear picture of their products to potential customers, however, competitors can easily compare quality, features, prices, and technology.

Booth design and booth staffing are important factors for successful trade shows. The design of many booths at trade shows, for instance, features interactive technologies—audio and video text, CD-ROMs, telephone services, corporate TV networks, conference computer networks, and virtual reality. Chrysler has used jeep simulators at auto shows to increase booth traffic and create excitement about the jeep's new design features. Booths are usually staffed by the manufacturer's top salespeople who make personal contact with top executives representing various middle agents. Importantly, the selling costs at a trade show are low compared to the costs of advertising or personal sales calls.

Trade shows also rely on a variety of advertising media, such as print ads and direct mail, to drive attendance. Specialties are also used before, during, and after trade shows to attract prospects to an exhibit, increase awareness and recall of a company, and increase attendees' preference to do business with a company. Pre-show marketing is particularly important to guarantee the success of an exhibit. Studies have found that a pre-show promotional gift can increase exhibit traffic nearly three times as much as a pre-show invitation.[32] Creative contests such as drawings for interesting prizes also encourage and increase booth traffic. Pre-show mailings may tie in with the contest to entice people to stop by.

Marketing Support Services

The marketing services that support a product may have marketing communication implications. For example, if you purchase a bike at Sears, you might be offered the use of Sear's credit, assembly for a small fee, delivery, an explicit guarantee or warranty, a return policy, a hotline, product use information, and a maintenance and repair program. Many supermarkets now provide both in-store shopping and home delivery services. Some stores can be accessed by e-mail for online ordering. Stores have always provided credit programs, but many of them are now using credit as more than just a service for the customer. It is also a way to build a database and engage in dialogue with regular customers. The service part of automotive marketing is almost as important as the car itself. Likewise, GMAC, which handles financing for GM cars, is as big a business as car sales. Leasing has also become popular in automotive marketing, and that gives a dealer a strong basis for a continuing relationship with a customer.

In this world of commodity products, the availability of support services may be the primary reason to select a particular brand. IBM, for instance, is famous for its 24-hour service policy and a willingness to "take care of customers, no matter what the costs." An important role of marketing communication is to inform consumers about these support services and prove that they are important.

Customer Service

The cornerstone of all marketing and marketing communication programs is customer satisfaction. Satisfying customers is the objective of every strategic decision in the marketing mix and essential to building a strong relationship program. Customer service programs should be designed to manage the customer satisfaction function, although many are set up just to handle complaints. Complaints are important, of course, but are only one part of a customer service program—a program that monitors all types of customer suggestions, inquiries, and complaints.

Toll-free numbers used by customers to ask questions and to make arrangements for repair and returns are absolutely critical to good customer service programs. The idea is to make it as easy as possible to engage in dialogue. That also means that toll-free numbers have to be adequately staffed so callers don't have to endure long waits, and the people staffing the line have to be well informed so they can answer questions. Should they not be able to provide an answer, then there should be a policy that the staff person will call back with the answer.

In Chapter 1 we introduced relationship marketing as a key part of an integrated marketing communication program. Customer service is one of the two foundations on which relationship marketing programs are built, as Christopher, Payne, and Ballantyne argue in their book, *Relationship Marketing*.[33] The other factor is quality. Companies that recognize the central role of communication in marketing—and particularly word of mouth—will serve and service their customers better. Word of mouth is an important part of many public relations activities. Financial relations, media relations, and employee relations all rely on face-to-face communication.

Concept Review

OTHER MARKETING SERVICES

1. A package combines a channel of communication and a message. Its presence on a shelf allows the manufacturer to make a final statement about the product and the promotional efforts that support it.
2. Businesses present and sell their products at trade shows and exhibits that allow them to demonstrate the product, provide information, answer questions, compare competing brands, write orders, generate sales leads, and build customer relations.
3. Behind every product is a set of supporting services that may also have communication implications—credit, assembly, delivery, an explicit guarantee or warranty, a return policy, and maintenance and repair programs.
4. Customer service programs are the basis for relationship marketing and should be designed to satisfy customers by monitoring customer suggestions, inquiries, and complaints.

A CLOSING THOUGHT:
WORD-OF-MOUTH MARKETING

As discussed in Chapter 8, word of mouth is the most powerful form of communication. Word of mouth is another marketing communication tool that crosses the line and contributes highly persuasive messages to an integrated marketing communication program. The Starbucks discussion in Chapter 8 illustrates how many marketing communication tools had to be used to create positive word of mouth. In a new book on word-of-mouth marketing,[34] author Ivan Misner describes it as the forgotten advertising medium in marketing. But it is more than just advertising: it is the heart of a relationship marketing program.

Word-of-mouth marketing stimulates recommendations and referrals by people who are trusted and whose opinions are respected. Investing in the strategic use of word-of-mouth marketing means building and strengthening referral networks and creating spheres of common business interest. A sphere of business interests brings together a group of professionals who can provide full service to a customer, but only by working together. Networking and teamwork are two other concepts related to common interests. A referral network generates sales leads and alerts a company to potential problems that customers and field staff discuss.

A key audience for a word-of-mouth marketing program is employees. Employee relations, no matter who manages it, must communicate marketing plans to employees and elicit their insights.

The reason word-of-mouth marketing is important in this chapter is that it brings us full circle to the notion expressed in the first chapter that all forms of communication are important in a marketing communication program. Even something as basic as word-of-mouth messages should not be left to chance.

SUMMARY

1. Define and describe the purpose of sponsorships.

A sponsorship is a contribution (financial aid, equipment, or services) provided by a company to support an event, organization, person, or good cause. A company may act as the single sponsor of an activity, organization, or person. In other cases, such as the Olympics, companies may be one of many sponsors. Companies use sponsorships to enhance their image in ways that reflect positively on the bottom line. They do this by associating with activities that are of interest to their target audience.

2. Distinguish between the three main types of sponsorships—event marketing, sports marketing, and cause marketing.

Event marketing, the sponsorship of a special event, creates visibility and positive feelings for the company. Sports marketing is a type of sponsorship that permits companies to tie in with high-visibility sports and athletes. Companies that participate in cause marketing adopt a good cause in which their target markets believe to create a more positive company image.

3. Explain how marketing communication managers use point-of-purchase and in-store merchandising techniques.

Merchandising involves maximizing the promotional value of a product's image or activities. Point-of-purchase displays are in-store displays used to present the product in a highly visible way at the point of purchase. Often P-o-P displays are created to tie in with some other promotion or advertising campaign.

4. Describe how specialties and licensing are used to merchandise a product.

Specialties are free merchandise with the company, brand, or campaign identification given to people in the target audience to remind them of the company or event. Licensing is an arrangement made with a manufacturer who wants to reproduce an organization logo, slogan, or a person's image to place on their merchandise.

5. Justify the role and use of packaging and trade shows in the marketing communication mix.

Packaging is the last message a consumer sees before making a purchase decision. For some products it is the primary message carrier. To be effective the message conveyed by a package should be consistent with other product marketing communication messages, such as those in advertising or sales promotion. Trade shows provide a way to display the product to the trade, demonstrate it, and explain its features in a one-on-one communication environment. It's one of the cheapest ways to sell to important buyers in the industry, as well as make them aware of product improvements and new products.

6. Discuss the role of marketing support services, customer service, and word-of-mouth marketing in the marketing communication mix.

Marketing support services include a variety of marketing tools that are used to convince the customer to trust the product and its manufacturer or to assist in making the sale possible. Customer service is one such support service that focuses on smoothing out problems in the customer relationship and using every possible opportunity to create a dialogue with customers. It uses word of mouth, one of the most powerful forms of communication and an entirely new area for marketing communication planning.

POINTS TO PONDER

Review the Facts
1. Define sponsorship and explain how it is used strategically by a company to create positive associations.
2. What is ambush marketing? What are its pros and cons?
3. Why are special events a useful marketing communication tool?
4. What are three important considerations you need to decide before you advise your company to sponsor a sport?
5. What does the phrase "strategic philanthropy" mean?

Master the Concepts
6. Review the discussion of sponsorships, event marketing, sports marketing, and cause marketing and compile a list of their strengths and weaknesses. Identify when you would use each of these various strategies.
7. What are the similarities and differences between event marketing, sports marketing, and cause marketing?
8. People who attend NASCAR events report the highest level of loyalty to the products advertised on the cars. Why do you suppose that is so?
9. What are the similarities and differences between cause marketing and mission marketing?

Apply Your Knowledge
10. You own a souvenir shop in a tourist area. Explain how point-of-purchase displays, specialties, and licensing might be apparent in your shop. How do they impact on your business?
11. Visit a drugstore and find a product that you think has some packaging problems. Write an analysis of the problems and develop a set of recommendations that would solve the problems.
12. Interview the owner of an electronics store or a bookstore in your town. Does he or she attend trade shows? Why or why not?
13. Research the marketing support services offered to support the sale of your favorite computer. How many are manufacturer based and how many are retailer provided? Can you think of any services that either manufacturer or retailer might provide that would make your purchase and use of the computer easier?
14. Visit the customer service center in a major discount retailer such as Kmart, Target, Wal-Mart, or Venture. Identify all the different ways the retailer attempts to satisfy customers. Is there anything missing that you might recommend to improve the store's customer service program?

SUGGESTED PROJECTS

1. You are in charge of merchandising for the launch of the next Beatles Anthology set and video series.
   a. Design the P-o-P display that will be distributed to music stores and build a mock-up to present in class.
   b. Develop a proposal for a booth to use at the next music industry trade show. Include in your proposal answers to the following questions: What are the booth's objectives? What would the booth look like? What would people do who visit it? What would your staff do? What could you do to increase booth traffic?

2. You are the new customer service manager for a Saturn dealership and have been asked to develop a word-of-mouth marketing program. Develop a list of recommendations on how this valuable tool might be used more effectively in automotive marketing.

3. (Internet Project) Research several Web sites to find at least three businesses that are using marketing communication that crosses the lines (such as cause, event, or sports marketing; innovative merchandising or packaging; and so forth). Describe in a brief memo what the activities are and critique them based on the information you have learned in this and previous chapters.

CASE 14: SWEETENING THE SUGAR INDUSTRY IN AUSTRALIA

In the 1980s sugar in Australia was in a very difficult situation. After 80 years of stability, per capita consumption was rapidly declining. Fifty percent more people had negative attitudes to sugar than positive. Criticism had gone past dental issues into questions of general health and nutrition, including cardiovascular disease and diabetes.

The Australian Sugar Industry (ASI) responded by developing a plan with the following objectives:

1. Change the negative attitudes held about sugar, not only by the general public but also health professionals, government, politicians, and the media.
2. Assist nutrition education of the public via the key consumer influencer groups.
3. Slow down and then halt the decline in per capita sales by improving attitudes and changing behavior.

A strong, central big idea was created to anchor the effort. The campaign used a multitude of communication opportunities to deliver the sugar message. The line "Sugar. A natural part of life" became the focus of the campaign. The idea, in other words, is that sugar has a legitimate role to play in our lives.

A variety of traditional and nontraditional marketing communication activities were used to reach a wide range of stakeholders:

1. Health professionals—this communication included the sponsorship of seminars and mailing of a regular publication detailing research findings.
2. The media—this included an information kit; criticism about sugar through the media was monitored and countered with factual information from the Australian Sugar Industry.
3. Government relations—an information kit was produced on the industry and health concerns, and efforts were made to talk to federal and state government officials.
4. The food industry—the ASI worked closely with a number of key associations in disseminating balanced information about nutrition, and conferences both in Australia and overseas were attended and contributed to.
5. Employees—sugar industry employees were also kept well informed by presentations in all the key cane-growing areas and through newsletters.
6. Communities—community involvement in nutrition via athletic sponsorships was used to generate millions of dollars that were spent to encourage young people to take up healthy athletic activities.
7. Schools—a school Nutrition Education Program, anchored by education kits that were distributed to all schools in Australia, provided knowledge about nutrition and health.
8. The scientific community—a great deal of money was spent funding scientific research by various independent bodies.

Perceived negative attributes of sugar stabilized at half the original levels. As a result of this campaign, public opinion was changed. A majority of Australians came to see sugar as essential to a healthy diet. From a situation where a majority had not seen sugar as a natural ingredient, the vast majority now knew it was. Per capita consumption also moved up to a new level.

The ASI discovered that integrated communication tactics focusing on a single idea can be highly effective. In a column reporting on this case, PR expert Alan Kuczynski concludes that it's the way of the future and is the key to success for businesses big and small.

Case Questions

1. How many different events and sponsorships did the Australian Sugar Industry use in its image turnaround campaign?
   a. Explain who you think the target was for each.
   b. Explain what you think the objectives might have been for each.
2. Analyze the big idea that held this effort together. How well did it address the concerns of each stakeholder group?
3. If you were assigned next year's marketing communication campaign for this association, what would you recommend?

Source: Alan Kuczynski, "Beyond Advertising Towards Integration," *Marketing* (June 1992): 50–3.

ROMA'S LITE INTEGRATED CASE QUESTIONS

(Review the Roma's Lite Marketing Plan in the Appendix at the end of the text before answering these questions.)

1. (Writing Project) What kind of sponsorships would be appropriate for New Roman Foods to use in the product launch of Roma's Lite Pizza? Develop a proposal for the marketing director that explains your ideas on how best to use sponsorships.

2. (Writing Project) What kind of merchandising materials would be useful in launching Roma's Lite Pizza? Develop a written proposal and sketch examples of the materials that you think need to be created.

3. Investigate the design of frozen pizza boxes in your local supermarket. What would you recommend for the design of this package for Roma's Lite Pizza? Develop a sketch or a mock-up of your best idea.

4. (Team Project) Roma's Lite Pizza will be featured at the big food trade show in Chicago for the first time this year. Your boss has asked you to design the booth for this launch. Write up a proposal and sketch your ideas.

video case   Nike's Secret Weapon?
Its Marketing Communication Tools

Nike is a world leader in sports footwear and plans to expand to sports fitness in general. It is a product and marketing communication innovator that centers its identity around the "Just Do It" theme and its "swoosh" trademark (which represents the wing of the Greek goddess of victory).

How did Nike become a multi-billion-dollar company? Its success is due in large part to its cutting-edge marketing communication. First, it relies heavily on advertising that incorporates the "Just Do It" theme. It also uses other marketing communication tools, including product placement, specialty items, sports marketing, sponsorships, and the public relations generated by the athletes it sponsors. The key, however, is that Nike combines these tools to create a recognizable image of top-notch quality, currency, and a bit of magic.

Author Donald Katz credits Nike co-founder Philip Knight with the marketing insight that drove the company to great heights. In Katz's book *Just Do It: The Nike Spirit in the Corporate World*, Katz claims

that Knight believed that if "the general public could be helped to imagine great athletes as he imagined them—as having implications of the very best that the human spirit had to offer—then those athletes would become heroes like the heroes of old." Knight wanted Nike's marketing effort to create customers who were like fans. "Nobody roots for a product."

Take Nike's Air Jordans as an example of Nike's marketing communication prowess. Nike signed basketball star Michael Jordan in his first year as a professional player. Nike's first endorsement contract with Jordan was a good deal for the company and the player—$2.5 million over five years plus a royalty for each pair of shoes sold. However, the contract also contained several escape clauses, including a provision allowing the company to drop the Air Jordan line if sales were low or if Jordan failed to make the All-Star team in his first three years as a professional player. Nike's fears were unfounded. In 1985, the year the Air Jordan line was launched, the line generated revenues of

$100 million. By the mid-1990s, annual sales in the U.S. athletic shoe market had grown to $8 billion.

Nike designed the Air Jordan for the young athlete in unconventional black-and-red colors that were devised to grab attention. In the NBA, black shoes were not permitted. Jordan was fined every game because of his footwear, but the extra controversy generated free public-relations exposure that boosted product sales.

The television ad campaign that introduced the Air Jordan is industry legend: In one ad, Jordan soared aloft in slow motion while the soundtrack pulsed with the roar of a jet engine at takeoff. The ad captured Jordan's athletic grace and had a profound effect on television audiences and the marketing communication industry. As Steve Friedman, Ammirati & Puris/Lintas advertising executive, explained, "These ads changed the economics and mechanics of everything we do. They redefined what is celebrity."

Today, demand for Air Jordan sneakers is so high that Nike no longer advertises when a new model appears in stores. In fact, Jordan has achieved so much success as both an athlete and a celebrity endorser that a backlash of sorts has set in. In addition to fulfilling his duties with the world champion Chicago Bulls, Jordan has appeared on Wheaties boxes, in commercials for McDonald's, and co-starred with Bugs Bunny in a Warner Brothers movie. Fashion designer Bijan recently launched a new Michael Jordan cologne. Couple this amount of exposure with increased public awareness of the salaries superstar athletes like Jordan command, and it's not hard to see why some consumers don't want to root for Jordan.

Some negative publicity has cropped up, too. Critics point out that the actual cost of producing a typical pair of Air Jodans is about $20. Some stories indicate that this low cost is attributable to the use of child labor in lesser-developed countries. Consumers have started to ask why Nike prices the shoes at $140 or more—far beyond the means of many youngsters who idolize Jordan. Reports in the media describe how young people

have been mugged—even killed —for their Air Jordan sneakers.

What does Jordan say about the controversies? He notes that in some instances youthful materialism and the lust for a pair of sneakers have replaced more important values. He notes, however, that a young person's desire for Air Jordans can provide a parent with a motivational tool that can reward good performance or teach children how to save money to buy what they want. Nike's response to the criticisms is to launch a less expensive line of Air Jordans.

Because Nike has learned the hard way about the ups and downs of sponsorships, it wields considerable control over the athletes who endorse its products. For instance, Nike now insists that the athletes it sponsors sign management contracts with Nike Sports Management to ensure that they won't sign sponsorship deals with too many other companies.

Discussion Questions

1. Do you think Michael Jordan is being overexposed as an en-

dorser? How does this affect Nike?

2. Review the end-of-chapter case for chapter 1 on Tiger Woods' relationship with Nike and the product life cycle material in chapter 2. Given that Woods and Jordan play in two different sports and the products they sponsor are different life cycles, do you think some marketing communication tools are more effective for the products Woods sponsors as compared to Jordan's?

3. If you were in charge of marketing the Air Jordan product line, what marketing communication tools would you use and why?

Video Source: "Michael Jordan—The Selling of an Idol," *Nightline,* 7 February 1997. *Additional Sources:* Lynn Hirschberg, "The Big Man Can Deal," *New York Times Magazine,* 19 November 1996, 46–51; Bob Greene, "When Athletes Endorse, Why Does Anyone Listen?" *USA Today,* 8 April 1997, 15A; Kenneth Labich, "Nike versus Reebok: A Battle for Hearts, Minds, and Feet," *Fortune,* 18 September 1995, 90–92+; "Popcorn Tins, Aprons, Valentines and Bandages All Look Like Mike," *Wall Street Journal,* 15 November 1996, B1; Linda Himelstein, "The Soul of a New Nike," *Business Week,* 17 June 1996, 70, 72.

chapter

15

IMC Media

CHAPTER OBJECTIVES

After completing your work on this chapter, you should be able to:

1 Explain the comparative strengths and weaknesses of the various media alternatives.

2 Describe the characteristics, buying process, and strengths and weaknesses of the primary print media—newspapers and magazines.

3 Describe the characteristics, buying process, and strengths

and weaknesses of the primary broadcast media—TV and radio.

4 Describe the characteristics, buying process, and strengths and weaknesses of the primary out-of-home media—outdoor and transit.

5 Explain the role that supplemental and new media play in the overall media strategy.

CONSIDER this

The Future of Mass Media

The similarities between the early days of TV and the current evolution of interactive media are striking. Some observers view it as part of a natural business cycle. "All radically new technologies are met with huge skepticism. This was true about television and it's true about interactive media," says George Gilder, author of "Life After Television." "The people who've learned the old technology are afraid to learn something new. People's knowledge is really their resource." Others see it as being indicative of marketing communication firms' underlying fear of the unknown and unwillingness to encourage companies to take risks.

Today, with passive TV a dominant force in people's lives, many question whether viewers will want to interact with TV, or whether they'll want to sit in front of a computer to do tasks, such as banking and shopping, that they now do outside the home. Part of what drew marketers to TV in the early days,

despite their fears, was the belief that early adopters of new technologies represent more desirable, affluent, and educated consumers. The same belief is drawing marketers to interactive services today.

Eugene Kummee, chairperson emeritus of McCann-Erickson Worldwide, indicates that advertisers "were reluctant to give up the efficiency of radio and print until they were absolutely sure [TV] was coming.... I think the same thing is happening today." *Newsweek* vice chairperson Don Durgin notes, "Nobody's pooh-poohing interactivity, like they did TV. . . . They're simply saying nobody knows how to place the bets on how all of this will come out."

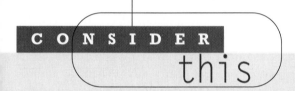

Based on the growth of Web sites alone one would have to assume that interactive media is here to stay and that it is only a matter of time before it reaches critical mass. Already the Internet has become the ultimate narrowcasting vehicle: Everyone from UFO buffs to New York Yankees fans have a Web site (or a dozen) to call their own—a

471

"dot-com" in every port. The featured Web-TV Network ad suggests the next stage of evolution: interactivity via your TV.

No one has taken a more aggressive look at interactive media than Edwin Artz, chair of Procter & Gamble. He envisions a P&G–produced CD-ROM, for example, titled: "Are You Getting a Cold?" The CD-ROM's program would follow a cold's average five-day cycle, demonstrating the patient's need each day for a new P&G product, from Vick's VapoRub to NyQuil. This kind of detailed, tailored pitch can't be done today, notes Artz, even in print ads. P&G is now experimenting with a CD-ROM ad for its Cover Girl cosmetics.

Sources: Richard Zoglin, "The News Wars," *Time,* October 21, 1996, 58–63; Scott Donaton, "The Next 50 Years," *Advertising Age* (Spring 1995): 54; "P&G's Artz: TV Advertising in Danger," *Advertising Age,* May 23, 1994, 34, 40; Mark Rebuchaux, "Despite Many Claims for 500-Channel TV, Long Road Lies Ahead," *Wall Street Journal,* 29 November 1993, A1.

CHAPTER OVERVIEW

Regardless of how well designed and targeted a marketing communication message is, it will not succeed unless it is transmitted through the most appropriate medium. What is an appropriate medium? One that complements the message, one that target audience members use consistently, and one that can deliver the message at the right time—that is, when the target audience is most receptive.

Selecting and combining appropriate media effectively is a complex process. It requires that marketing communication managers plan a comprehensive combination of media suitable for both the marketing communication message and the target audience. This combination of media—known as the media mix—must suit both the message and audience to increase the chance of a successful marketing communication program.

Though media planning—the process of selecting media objectives for the marketing communication program and devising a strategy to reach those objectives—is a key part of marketing communication, few students begin their college careers with media planning in mind. The job requires a penchant for numbers, detail, and organization as well as an ability to see the big picture and to generate creative solutions. Media planning also requires two kinds of knowledge. First, **media planners** (those who make decisions about the media mix and implement those decisions) must have a thorough understanding of all types of media—of their capabilities, limitations, trends, and technology. Second, media planners must understand the media planning process, such as how to select media objectives and evaluate whether the media suits the target markets, the schedule, and the budget. **Media buyers** actually purchase the media selected. This job is usually an entry-level position that leads to media planning.

In this chapter we explore five different types of mass media: print, broadcast, out-of-home, supplemental, and new media. The supplemental category includes specialty media, the Yellow Pages, telemarketing, and direct mail. The new media section deals with recent trends, including online technology. Total 1995 spending for all of the primary media is shown in Table 15.1.

TABLE 15.1

Media Spending in the Communications Industry (1995–2000)*

Industry	1995 Spending (in billions)	Growth Rate (1995–2000) (percentage)	2000 Spending (in billions)
Television broadcasting	$ 30.6	6.1%	$ 41.2
Radio broadcasting	11.3	7.0	15.8
Basic cable systems	16.8	7.5	24.1
Cable advertising	5.3	13.0	9.9
Filmed entertainment	31.4	5.5	41.1
Recorded music	12.3	8.1	18.2
Newspaper publishing	50.4	5.5	65.8
Daily papers—advertising revenue	36.0	5.6	47.4
Book publishing	24.9	5.3	32.2
Magazines	23.4	6.2	31.5
Consumer magazine advertising	8.7	7.5	12.5
Business magazine advertising	5.9	6.9	8.3
Interactive digital media (all)	7.6	21.6	20.3
Consumer online/Internet service	3.2	28.2	10.9
Total spending	**267.8**	**7.0**	**353.3**

*Combined communications industry media gross expenditures (in billions) and compound annual growth rate (projected).

Sources: Keith J. Kelly and Chuck Ross, "Bright Prospects Seen for Cable TV, New Media," *Advertising Age,* August 19, 1996, 8; Growth rate projections from Veronis, Suhler & Associates.

MASS MEDIA DEVELOPMENTS

A **mass medium** must meet two requirements: (1) it can reach many people simultaneously, and (2) it requires the use of some technological device to connect the marketing communicator with the audience. Thus the interactive media discussed in earlier chapters, such as interactive television, is mass media because it can reach many audience members at the same time and uses technology to do so.

Marketing communicators strive to find the most effective mass media for their messages, given the target audience, schedule, and budget. Understanding of the capabilities of each type of mass media can help marketing communicators find the most effective mix. Table 15.2 summarizes the capabilities of many types of

TABLE 15.2

Strategic Capabilities of Mass Media

Tyes of Media	Market Coverage	Cost	Cost per Thousand	Flexibility	Emotional Impact	Targetability	Reputation	Clutter	Message Length	Frequency	Immediacy	Creativity	Reseller's Support	Production
National newspapers	—	—	+	—	0	+	+	—	+	+	+	+	—	+
Local newspapers	+	+	+	+	0	+	+	—	+	+	+	—	+	—
Magazines	—	0	—	—	+	+	+	—	+	0	+	+	+	+
Network television	+	—	+	—	+	0	+	+	0	0	+	+	+	+
Cable television	0	+	+	+	0	+	0	+	+	+	+	+	+	+
Network radio	0	—	+	0	—	—	+	+	—	+	+	0	+	+
Local radio	+	+	+	+	0	+	0	—	—	+	+	0	+	0
Out-of-home	—	+	+	—	—	—	—	—	—	0	—	0	—	0
Yellow Pages	0	+	+	—	—	+	+	—	—	—	—	0	—	0
Online	—	0	—	+	+	+	—	0	+	+	+	+	0	+

— Weak Capability   0 Moderate capability   + Strong capability

mass media. In the following sections we detail the strengths and weaknesses of each media type.

Media planners must also understand the cost of each medium. The tremendous cost and waste associated with traditional mass media, such as network television commercials, have pushed many marketing communicators toward media that is less expensive, better targeted, and easier to track. Media planners are also becoming more aggressive in dealing with the media by dictating rates, demanding greater service, and asking for guaranteed results. Competition from U.S. and global competitors, spurred by technological advances, has forced many media suppliers to respond to marketing communicators' demands or else run the risk of lost revenues.

Media alternatives are also being analyzed as part of an integrated marketing communication program. Media planners evaluate which combination of media can best deliver the marketing communication message in a way that builds relationships with stakeholders. In integrated programs, then, media intended for the masses are often modified to appeal to the individual. For instance, a media planner might choose to run a print ad in *Newsweek* that is personalized through a computer selection process, includes a toll-free number or Internet home page address, and is placed in a demographic edition modified to speak to the needs of the mature target audience. Or the media planner for STP might opt for a commercial on ESPN that would not only sell STP gas treatment but would also inform viewers of both local dealers who sell the product and an STP-sponsored racing event.

Throughout this chapter and the next, we view media and media planning as part of an integrated marketing communication program. Media that complement one another and facilitate one-to-one communication usually aid integration more than media that cannot do these things. We look carefully at these types of media, beginning with print media. The order of discussion has nothing to do with the relative importance of the media alternatives. Employing an integrated approach means that a media strategy starts with a blank slate.

PRINT MEDIA

Before the emergence of television and radio, print media dominated our society. However, since that time we have become a broadcast-based society. CNN and the nightly TV news have surpassed the daily newspaper as the primary source of information. Catalogs, telemarketing, and infomercials are gradually supplanting magazines as the media through which niche markets learn about products. Still, print media can accomplish some objectives better than broadcast media, as shown in Table 15.2. IMC strategists must understand the capabilities of print compared with other types of media, such as radio and TV. For instance, a recent study of 2000 consumers conducted by Video Storyboard shows that consumers consider print ads more informative, more entertaining, and less offensive than broadcast commercials.[1]

Newspapers

Media historians suggest that the first significant newspaper in the United States was the *New England Courant,* founded by James and Benjamin Franklin in 1721. From that time until the introduction of television, newspapers were the primary source of news for Americans. Today the role and appearance of newspapers have changed. Legions of newspapers are taking their cue from *USA Today,* which uses four-color presses and includes eye-catching charts and weather maps. Newspapers are also emphasizing "soft news" such as entertainment, sports, and travel over the traditional "hard news" (that is, politics, social issues, and world events).

Newspapers are changing the way they deliver the news. In the near future newspapers will link customers through telephones and cable television hookups. Many papers are moving online in more accessible ways, including through the electronic catalogs now in wide use in public libraries. Daily papers are also adding new technology to allow readers to interact in different ways with the papers' information databases. One such example is *The Kansas City Star,* where an audio-electronic link allows callers to access recorded information, including musical selections related to articles in the paper. In addition, daily and national papers are adding more phone-accessible fax delivery of articles and special reports. There are even companies that offer a totally customized daily supply of information. "I'll take the Washington headlines, please, plus the health news, NFL scores, updates on AT&T's stock price—and anything on Madonna."

The Industry and Its Audience

More than 9000 newspapers are published in the United States today. These publications may be classified in several ways: by their physical size (standard or tabloid), intended audience (for example, financial, Spanish-speaking), and type of circulation (for example, paid or controlled). Most newspapers are "paid," that is, subscribers pay for them. A **shopper,** such as *Thrifty Nickel* or *Real Estate Guide,* is usually distributed free to certain homes in certain neighborhoods, or through supermarket racks. The primary way of classifying newspapers, however, is based on their frequency of publication, either daily, weekly, or on Sunday. Table 15.3 lists the top 25 newspapers by circulation.

Over 1530 daily newspapers and over 8000 weeklies are published in the United States today. Most Sunday papers are published by dailies; few papers publish Sunday editions only. The Sunday paper is considered the centerpiece of newspaper advertising. Fat with news, features, and ads, it offers the biggest package of the week on the day that people have the most time to read. The average reader spends 62 minutes on the Sunday paper, 17 minutes more than on the weekday edition.

Who is this reader? The main source for information about newspaper audiences is the Audit Bureau of Circulation (ABC), formed in 1914 by advertisers, agencies, and publishers. Its objective is to establish standard and acceptable methods of measuring circulation of member publications and to audit circulation figures. Newspapers that do not submit to an audit from a firm such as ABC may instead provide potential advertisers with a publisher's statement supported by a sworn affidavit or a *post statement*. A **post statement** is a statement of the newspaper's claimed circulation figures given once each year to the post office. These two types of statements are viewed as equivalent to ABC figures.

ABC and various trade organizations provide information that help media planners understand the readership patterns of subscribers. For instance, market research shows that readers have gotten more selective about what they read in the newspaper. To maintain subscribers many newspapers have become more responsive to the needs and interests of their readers. Such information is quite useful to the marketing communication strategist, who can then determine whether a product would fit the newspaper.

Buying Newspaper Space

A newspaper's audience size, demographic characteristics of readers, and advertising rates are among the characteristics media planners must consider. Most daily newspapers offer *classified advertising* (including regular and display) and *display advertising.* **Classified ads** include all types of messages arranged by classification of interest, such as Help Wanted, Cars for Sale, and so on. Classified display ads allow more flexibility than regular classifieds because advertisers may use borders, large type, white space, photos, and occasionally color.

Display ads are found throughout the newspaper and generally use illustrations, headlines, white space, and other visual devices in addition to the text copy.

TABLE 15.3

Top Newspapers by
Circulation

Rank	Newspaper	Circulation	Change (percentage) 1995–1996	Sunday Circulation	Change (percentage) 1995–1996
1	Wall Street Journal	1,841,188	+1.0%	None	—
2	USA Today*	1,617,743	+3.0	2,009,223	+1.5%
3	New York Times	1,157,656	−1.1	1,746,707	−1.3
4	Los Angeles Times	1,021,121	−3.5	1,391,076	−4.6
5	Washington Post	834,641	−0.7	1,140,564	−1.1
6	Daily News	758,509	+4.5	1,010,504	+3.7
7	Chicago Tribune	667,908	−3.4	1,066,393	−2.9
8	Newsday	555,203	−17.1	643,421	−13.7
9	Houston Chronicle**	551,553	+33.3	764,443	−25.6
10	Dallas Morning News†	518,402	−3.8	803,610	−2.2
11	Chicago Sun-Times	501,115	+0.1	469,161	−4.9
12	San Francisco Chronicle	493,942	−1.1	646,171	−2.1
13	Boston Globe	486,403	−2.8	777,902	−1.0
14	Philadelphia Inquirer	446,842	−5.1	901,891	−1.9
15	Newark Star-Ledger	433,317	−3.8	641,393	−5.1
16	New York Post	418,255	−2.5	None	—
17	Phoenix Republic A.B.	407,195	+1.9	597,255	−2.4
18	Cleveland Plain Dealer**	398,398	−1.5	528,818	−2.9
19	Minneapolis Star-Tribune A.B.	380,569	−6.0	682,318	−1.9
20	Miami Herald**	378,195	−5.0	500,654	−4.0
21	San Diego Union-Tribune**	376,511	−1.6	453,891	−0.9
22	St. Petersburg Times**	364,810	−2.1	462,103	−1.9
23	Orange Co. Register**	358,173	+0.1	419,401	−0.3
24	Portland Oregonian	349,193	−0.5	445,293	−0.2
25	Baltimore Sun A.**	337,292	+19.3	488,562	−1.2

*USA Today's Friday circulation is listed in Sunday column. **Rank based on Monday–Saturday circulation. †Figures adjusted by *Advertising Age* to indicate weekday average circulation. A = change in publication plan and/or frequency. B = figures adjusted by *Advertising Age* to indicate comparable Monday–Saturday figures for 1996 compared with 1995.

Source: Keith J. Kelly, "Dailies Hold Their Own As Circulation Stabilizes," *Advertising Age,* May 6, 1996, 52.

They can be of any size. For display ads the infrequent advertiser usually pays a standard rate per column inch. An advertiser who uses significant amounts of space pays a discounted bulk or contract rate based on the total amount of space purchased. Advertisers and newspapers frequently sign annual contracts for a given space commitment. When it comes time for a tally, if less-than-agreed-upon space was purchased, a **short rate** that is higher than the contract rate is applied. If more space was purchased, a rebate is provided.

Determining Costs. Sources such as a newspaper's rate card, the *Editor and Publisher's Yearbook,* and the *Standard Rate and Data Service* list the newspaper's line rates. The rates vary depending on circulation, costs of operation, labor costs, qualitative factors, and type of newspaper. Media buyers refer to Standard Advertising Units (SAUs) to compare the cost of one newspaper with another. The SAU system means that all newspapers (actually about 90 percent) use column widths, and standard papers have six columns. The column inch is the standard unit of measurement.

Most newspapers offer a lower rate to local advertisers than to national advertisers. The national rate averages 75 percent higher than the local rate. Newspaper publishers claim that this rate difference is justifiable because retailers, particularly a few leading retailers, use far more space than national advertisers in local papers. They also claim that local retail advertising is news that has inherent interest. Another reason for the differential is that local retail advertising is usually prepared and placed directly by the retailer, without the intercession of an advertising agency. To combat the higher rate, national advertisers use cooperative advertising. They cooperate with local dealers by financing advertising that the local dealer places at the local rate. Newspapers also create "hybrid" rates (that is, rates customized for certain customers) to attract advertising by airlines, car rental companies, hotels, and resorts.

Specific Marketing Communication Options. Advertisers can usually order specific pages or positions for an extra charge. For example, if an advertiser using the *Chicago Sun-Times* wants to insure ad placement at the very top of the page and next to reading matter along one of its vertical sides (called full position), the advertiser may have to pay as much as 33.3 percent more. However, certain advertisers may be able to negotiate for the same position without paying extra.

Newspapers may also offer special production capabilities for additional charges. For instance, run-of-press color (black plus one color) costs 17 to 35 percent more than black and white for a full-page ad. If full color (black plus three colors) is used, surcharges average from 29 to 62 percent extra.[2]

Color preprint is a service offered by almost all daily newspapers. In this process color ads are preprinted on a roll of paper that is fed into the presses. Color preprints provide the national and local advertiser with many of the "quality" advantages of magazine color while allowing each retailer to place imprinted copy next to the national advertiser's four-color ad on the same page.

A final option offered by newspapers is the supplement. Each of the syndicated supplements is compiled, edited, and printed by a central organization that then sells it to newspapers all over the United States; it offers group-rate advertising charges. Printed on paper that is heavier and better finished than newsprint, supplements offer surprisingly low rates.

Newspaper Strengths and Weaknesses

As noted earlier, a primary strength of newspapers is that they serve as a trusted source of local information for many consumers. Sales promotion information (such as price discounts and coupons) and public relations information (such as open house announcements and special events) can all be delivered through newspapers. More important, consumers seek out this information.

Market flexibility is another advantage of newspapers. Gone are the days when one general newspaper served a particular market. Today newspapers have the capability of reaching special-interest groups, unique ethnic or racial groups, or even people living in isolated parts of the world (for example, *The Stars and Stripes* is mailed to all military personnel). Miami's *Diaria Las Americas* is a Spanish-language newspaper with a circulation of over 70,000.

Lead time flexibility is a third advantage of newspapers. Lead time is the amount of time between when an ad must be delivered to the medium and when it is actually run. For example, the lead time for a newspaper ad is quite short, often 48 to 72 hours. Ads can therefore be changed at the last minute, or new ads can be inserted to meet an unforeseen circumstance, such as a dramatic change in the weather.

Newspapers also provide the advantage of a large pass-along audience. Not only do members of a family share the same newspaper, but newspapers are also read by people at fast-food chains, diners, railroad stations, and professional offices.

Furthermore, newspapers effectively combine local ads or sales promotions with national promotions. A local retailer can easily tie in with a national campaign by using a similar ad. For example, Computerland stores tend to run ads that appear similar to those produced by IBM and Compaq. Newspapers also allow preprinted ads and freestanding inserts (FSIs) to accommodate national promotions.

The most serious weakness of newspapers is clutter. With 65 percent or more of a typical newspaper filled with ads, it is difficult to create awareness. Clutter is also a problem with the freestanding inserts that now deliver more than 50 percent of consumer coupons. FSIs are now so thick and bulky that sorting through them all is a task that many readers reject, choosing instead to remove the entire packet and put it aside.

Concept ✓ **Review**

PRINT MEDIA (NEWSPAPERS)

1. Media planners rely on circulation and rate information provided by the Audit Bureau Circulations, the primary source of such information as where to place ads.
2. Classified and display advertising in newspapers are sold on the basis of either a line rate or a bulk or contract rate. Newspapers charge a higher rate to national than to local advertisers.
3. The strengths of the newspaper medium are its credibility as an information source, the flexibility of its market and lead time, a large pass-along audience, and the local tie-in to national promotions.
4. The weaknesses of the newspaper medium are clutter, short life, technical quality, and high extra rates for national advertisers.

Other limitations of newspapers include the one-day life of a paper, which means that a message has a very short time in which to work. The technical quality of newspapers is another problem. Porous paper and poor reproduction of print and photography often mean that an ad is difficult to read. A final weakness is the high advertising rates for national advertisers. Until the rates are reduced, newspapers will just remain an attractive alternative for national advertisers.

Magazines

Today magazines (known as **books** in the industry) are the most specialized of the mass media, dramatically demonstrating the fact that the mass audience is becoming increasingly segmented. For example, *Writer's Market* lists more than a hundred magazines that deal with farming, soil management, poultry, dairy farming, and rural life. Farming magazines are one example of **special-interest** publications, which account for more than 90 percent of the total number of magazines published today.

Magazines and Their Audiences

Special-interest magazines have flourished partly as a result of the high advertising rates charged by mass-circulation, **general-interest** magazines such as *Reader's Digest, TV Guide,* and *People.* This division into special- and general-interest magazines is just one of several ways of classifying magazines.

Magazines may also be classified by frequency of publication and the audience to which they are directed. Monthly magazines are the largest category, followed by the weeklies, semi-monthlies, bi-monthlies, and quarterlies. On the basis of the audience served, there are three types of magazines:

1. *Consumer magazines,* which are edited for people who buy products for their own consumption.
2. *Farm magazines,* which are circulated to farmers and their families. They can be general (for example, *Successful Farming*) or specialized (for example, *Beef*).
3. *Business magazines,* which are directed at business readers. These may be further divided into trade papers (read by retailers, wholesalers, and other distributors), industrial magazines (read by manufacturers and service providers), and professional magazines (read by such groups as physicians and lawyers).

Table 15.4 displays the total circulation of the top 25 consumer magazines, and Table 15.5 lists the top nonpaid magazines.

The magazine industry applies three other possible classifications to each of the three just discussed. Consumer, farm, and business magazines can also be classified by geographic, demographic, and editorial content.

1. *Geographic content:* Sectional or regional editions of national publications (for example, *Time* and *Southern Living*) may be circulated in an area as large as several states or as limited as one city.
2. *Demographic editions:* Many magazines offer special editions for subscribers of a certain age, income, occupation, and so forth (for example, *Time* and *Newsweek* have special student editions).
3. *Editorial content:* Magazines are defined by interest category such as general editorial, women's services, and business.

TABLE 15.4

Top 25 Consumer
Magazines by Paid
Circulation

Rank	Publication	Circulation	Change (percentage)
Top paid circulation magazines for the first half of 1996 (compared with the same period in 1995) based on Audit Bureau of Circulations and BPA International figures. ABC and BPA also audit nonpaid circulation.			
1	Modern Maturity	20,673,063	−3.0%
2	Reader's Digest	15,150,822	−1.2
3	TV Guide	13,076,790	−5.5
4	National Geographic	9,184,878	1.1
5	Better Homes and Gardens	7,616,270	1.1
6	Good Housekeeping	5,032,901	−1.8
7	The Cable Guide	5,022,477	13.4
8	Family Circle	5,003,227	−0.6
9	Ladies' Home Journal	4,705,020	−5.0
10	Woman's Day	4,501,612	−0.1
11	McCall's	4,284,939	−6.9
12	Time	4,131,676	0.9
13	Sports Illustrated	3,384,328	1.4
14	People	3,364,252	−0.5
15	Prevention	3,251,851	−7.6
16	Playboy	3,233,170	−4.9
17	Newsweek	3,228,231	1.6
18	Redbook	2,851,493	−13.4
19	The American Legion Magazine	2,792,067	−1.9
20	Avenues	2,738,634	1.6
21	National Enquirer	2,614,332	−2.3
22	Cosmopolitan	2,559,853	−0.5
23	Southern Living	2,483,337	0.8
24	Motorland	2,350,888	4.0
25	Home & Away	2,330,886	6.7

Source: Keith J. Kelly, "Magazines Stay On Downward Course In 1st Half," *Advertising Age,* May 6, 1996, 25.

The magazines with the largest paid circulation in 1995 were *Modern Maturity, Reader's Digest, TV Guide, National Geographic,* and *Better Homes and Gardens. Modern Maturity* is the official magazine of the American Association of Retired Persons (AARP); it reaches all its members and is included as part of their annual dues. Note also that the magazine industry has its version of the newspaper industry's

			Change
Rank	**Publication**	**Circulation**	**(percentage)**

TABLE 15.5

**Top Nonpaid
Circulation Magazines**

Top magazines with 1 million or more nonpaid circulation for the first half of 1996 (compared with the same period in 1995) based on Audit Bureau of Circulations and BPA International figures. ABC and BPA also audit paid circulation.

Rank	Publication	Circulation	Change (percentage)
1	The Disney Channel Magazine	5,356,962	−4.3%
2	Rx Remedy	2,022,988	0.2
3	U-The National College Magazine*	1,570,138	0.2
4	Healthy Kids	1,503,856	−0.0
5	American Baby	1,393,637	13.4
6	Fantastic Flyer Magazine	1,173,128	2.7
7	Baby Talk	1,101,066	9.6
8	Microsoft Magazine	1,091,178	N/A

*The following magazines also reported paid circulation: *U-The National College Magazine,* 59; *American Baby,* 261,987; *Baby Talk,* 2,688; and *Microsoft Magazine,* 19,212.

Source: Keith J. Kelly, "Magazines Stay On Downward Course In 1st Half," *Advertising Age,* May 6, 1996, 25.

shopper (see Table 15.5). For instance, nonpaid magazines such as Disney's *The Disney Channel Magazine* are distributed to children for free.

Information like that in Figure 15.1 comes from the Audit Bureau of Circulations, which collects and evaluates data about magazines as well as about newspapers, as discussed earlier. A magazine's total circulation is just one of the significant pieces of data. For example, some media buyers regard news-stand sales as a good criterion of the quality of a magazine's circulation, because purchases at a news stand are completely voluntary. By paying more per copy and taking the initiative, news-stand buyers are viewed as more serious readers. Information relating to which subscribers renew their subscriptions is also important. Many media analysts carefully watch the trends in subscription sales of various magazines, especially the rate at ABC.

Audience profiles are invaluable to media buyers because reliable buyers can see how closely the magazine audience matches the target audience. In general, magazine readers are better educated, better read, and better paid than other members of the population.[3] However, the trend is definitely moving away from general-interest magazines and toward specialty titles. With consumers having less time to themselves, they're more interested in indulging in their personal interests. "If people are going to do something superficial, it might as well be fun," notes Gene DeWitt, president of media-buying service DeWitt Media, New York. Accordingly, one reason so many niche magazines are a big hit with readers and advertisers is because their missions are "clear, simple, and desirable."[4]

Many magazines provide reader profiles to their advertisers to influence them to buy space. A media buyer may find that the audience profile for a magazine

ANALYZED PAID CIRCULATION
PROTOTYPE
Anytown, State Zip

FIELD SERVED: Edited for the home-owner and providing guidance, repair maintenance and improvements of his house and property. All articles presented in "Do-it-Yourself" step-by-step format and profusely illustrated.

1. AVERAGE PAID CIRCULATION FOR 12 MONTHS ENDED DECEMBER 31, YEAR:

Total Average Paid Circulation:		**799,105**
Advertising Rate Base:	to 02/01/YR	800,000
	since 02/01/YR	900,000
% Above/Below Rate Base (+/–)		-10.4
Total Average Non-Analyzed Non-Paid Circulation:		26,492

		% of Total
Subscriptions: Individual	762,245	95.4
Single Copy Sales:	36,860	4.6
		100.0

1a. AVERAGE PAID CIRCULATION of Regional, Metro and Demographic Editions:

None of record

2. PAID CIRCULATION BY ISSUES:

Year Issue	Subscriptions	Single Copy Sales	Total Paid	Year Issue	Subscriptions	Single Copy Sales	Total Paid
Jan.	767,086	30,765	797,851	July	760,345	48,150	808,495
Feb.	759,881	35,917	795,798	Aug.	762,113	36,366	798,479
Mar.	757,771	42,632	800,403	Sept.	754,401	43,626	798,027
Apr.	760,434	36,867	797,301	Oct.	768,419	29,422	797,841
May	760,038	32,632	792,670	Nov.	767,402	35,602	803,004
June	761,024	33,726	794,750	Dec.	768,023	36,619	804,642

AVERAGE PAID CIRCULATION BY QUARTERS for the previous three years and period covered by this report:

Calendar Quarter Ended	YEAR	YEAR	YEAR	YEAR
March 31	764,239	762,208	785,204	798,017
June 30	766,830	759,076	779,475	794,907
September 30	777,645	759,862	814,349	801,667
December 31	764,036	755,788	808,084	801,829

AUDIT STATEMENT

The difference shown in average paid circulation in comparing this report with the Publisher's Statements for the period audited is 4,129 copies per issue deduction.

To Members of the Audit Bureau of Circulations:

We have examined the circulation records and other data presented by this publication for the period covered by this report. Our examinations were made in accordance with the Bureau's Bylaws and Rules, and included such tests and other audit procedures as we considered necessary under the circumstances.

In our opinion, the total average paid circulation for the period shown is fairly stated in this report, and the other data contained in this report are fairly stated in all respects material to average paid circulation.

May, 1997   **Audit Bureau of Circulations**
(04-0000-0 - #000000 - 000 - 000)

Copyright © 1997 Audit Bureau of Circulations. All rights reserved.

FIGURE 15.1

A Sample Audit Report from the Audit Bureau of Circulations

is attractive enough to override the fact that its circulation is smaller than that of a competitor. Careful media buyers need a complete picture of the magazine audience before purchasing advertising space. As a minimum, they should consider the following factors:

- Total circulation
- The percentage of the publication read completely
- Reader loyalty
- Reader demographics
- The magazine's past ability to generate high response in mail-order ads
- Special sections
- Number of pass-along readers

Buying Magazine Space

Besides considering the characteristics of readers, media buyers must also consider the cost of magazine space. Only a handful of marketers can afford to pay $30,000 to $85,000 for a full-page pull-out in a mass-circulation magazine. As a result, many smaller companies have turned to less expensive special-interest magazines, where their messages will be seen by fewer but more receptive readers.

Advertising Rates. Magazine space is sold primarily on the basis of pages or some increment of a page. For example, the rate card for *Time* demographic editions is shown in Figure 15.2. Note that the rates are based on the purchase of a full page or some part of a page, converted into columns and some portion of a column. Also, four-color ads will cost considerably more than black-and-white ads.

A number of publishers, especially those with geographic or *demographic editions,* sometimes find themselves with extra space in some editions when they are ready to go to press. Rather than run an empty space, the publisher often offers this **remnant space** to advertisers at a big discount.

Marketing Communication Options. In most cases the double-page spread is the largest unit of space sold by magazines, although larger books such as *Better Homes and Gardens* and *People* also offer a three-page *gatefold.* Magazines allow

TIME NATIONAL 4.0

The world's most influential, most authoritative and largest-circulation newsmagazine. Available weekly.

Rate Base: 4,000,000	B&W	B&1 Color	4 Color
Page	$111,000	$139,000	$162,000
Cover 4	NA	NA	207,500
2 Columns	83,300	104,300	129,600
1/2 Page Horizontal*	66,600	83,400	105,300
1/2 Page Horizontal Spread*	133,200	166,800	210,600
1 Column	44,400	55,600	72,900
1/2 Column	27,800	34,800	NA

* Subject to availability.

TIME BUSINESS

Offers the largest U.S. all-business circulation and reaches only subscribers qualified individually by job title or qualified business households. All circulation verified by ABC. Provides in-depth reach to top, middle and technical management and professionals in all 50 states. Available every other week.

Rates are based on subscription circulation only.

Rate Base: 1,635,000	B&W	B&1 Color	4 Color
Page	$68,000	$84,000	$101,000
2 Columns	51,000	63,000	80,800
1/2 Page Horizontal Spread*	95,200	117,600	141,400
1 Column	27,200	33,600	45,500
1/2 Column	24,500	29,400	NA

* Subject to availability.

TIME DIGITAL

TIME's first selective editorial feature, TIME Digital explores how new technology is reshaping our lives at work and at home. Circulation is 100% professional/managerial, 80% own home PCs, and is based on TIME Business subscribers matched for qualifying characteristics within the Time Warner database. Available six times in 1997.

Rate Base: 900,000	B&W	2C/4 Color
Page	$36,000	$52,000
2 Columns	27,100	41,600
1/2 Page Horizontal Spread	50,500	72,800
1 Column Vertical or Square	16,300	23,400
1/2 Column	10,800	15,600
Cover 2 & 3	NA	62,000
Cover 4	NA	67,000

Source: CIMS IntelliQuest Home Influencer Study v2.1

TIME WOMEN SELECT

A demographic edition that delivers affluent, professional women who are hard to reach through traditional women's magazines. Circulation is comprised of employed women who qualify for TIME Business and/or TIME Top Management, and female subscribers in high-income households. Each subscriber is individually identified. Available 11 times a year.

Rates are based on subscription circulation only.

Rate Base: 975,000	B&W	B&1 Color	4 Color
Page	$29,000	$36,200	$42,200

FIGURE   15.2

A Rate Card for *Time* Demographic Editions

one-page or double-page ads to be broken into a variety of units called **fractional page space:** vertical half-page, horizontal half-page, double horizontal half-page, island position (surrounded by editorial matter), half-page double spread, and checkerboard.

Sometimes a magazine cover or an inside page opens to reveal an extra page that folds out and gives the ad a big spread. Advertisers use these **gatefolds** on special occasions to make the most spectacular presentation in the magazine, usually to introduce a colorful product like a new model car or beautiful flooring. They are an additional expense that requires advance planning.

An example of an unusual gatefold was partnered by *Elle* magazine and Elizabeth Arden Co. *Elle* agreed to split the cover of its March issue down the middle to hide an ad for Arden's Sunflowers fragrance beneath the flags. To keep the cover from tearing, *Elle*'s March issue was wrapped in a clear plastic bag. The wrap also kept readers from seeing the split cover until after they bought the magazine.

The physical size of a magazine can be either **standard** ($8'' \times 10''$), **small** ($4\frac{3}{8}'' \times 6\frac{1}{2}''$), or a size unique to a particular magazine. These measurements are approximations; when ordering plates, advertisers must get the exact page size from the publisher.

The front cover of a magazine is called the **first cover page.** The inside of the front cover is called the **second cover page,** the inside of the back cover the **third cover page,** and the back cover the **fourth cover page.** Depending on the magazine, these covers may cost 10 to 60 percent more than a page inside the book.

The cheapest magazine rate is **run-of-book** (ROB), which means that the ad can be placed anywhere in the magazine. A **bleed ad** means the color runs to the edge of the page. It often costs an extra 15 to 20 percent.

Many magazines also offer space for inserts. Examples are return cards (usually blown in—that is, unattached), coupons, receipt booklets, product samples, and other kinds of outside material bound or blown into the magazine in connection

This Pentax ad shows a four-color bleed ad.

with an adjoining ad. Inserts are never sold separately. Negotiating and creating such inserts is the job of the marketing communication manager. A special type of insert that appears to be growing in popularity is called an **advertisorial.** It is a set of consecutive pages on a single product or advertiser that is glued or stapled into the magazine. Pick up *Fortune* magazine and you are likely to see an advertisorial of 6 to 12 pages long, sponsored by a foreign country, for example.

Other features are offered by mass-circulation magazines in an effort to meet the competition from special-interest magazines. For example, magazines such as *Time* offer local companies reduced rates for regional **breakouts,** messages that will appear only in copies sent to a specific geographic region. Reduced regional rates give smaller companies a chance to appear in a national magazine at a rate they can afford. *Time* also offers advertisers the opportunity to target subscribers who are doctors, members of top management, students, educators, or even those who live in special high-income ZIP code areas. Editions that are sent to these subscribers are known as **demographic editions.**

Purchasing Procedures. Magazine advertisers are ruled by three dates. The **closing date** is the last date on which a magazine will accept advertising materials for publication in a particular issue. The **cover date** appears on the issue's cover. The **on-sale date** is when the issue goes on sale. Thus a magazine with a January cover date could go on sale December 15. The on-sale date is important because it tells when most issues reach the reader.

Desktop publishing and satellite transmission have shortened the lead time for magazines. Computer-processed magazine pages are sent directly to the printing operation via satellite, thus shortening the time it takes to produce the magazine. *Vanity Fair* closes some pages just hours before press time, using totally electronic page composition and satellite transmission to its printer.

Magazine Strengths and Weaknesses. The ability to reach highly segmented target audiences is clearly the main advantage of magazines. As a result, the absolute cost for magazine promotions is fairly low, but not as low as broadcast costs, discussed in the next section. Allowing the ever-increasing audience specialization of magazines, personalized editions are the next logical step.

Through selective binding (a computerized process that allows for the creation of hundreds of editions of a magazine in one continuous sequence and personalization of advertising) consumer magazine publishers will be able to offer ultranarrow targeting previously available only through trade magazines. Ink-jet imaging is a special computer-controlled printing process that allows parts of the message to be changed by the program. Ink-jet imaging also enables the advertiser to address readers personally. You can tell a reader, "If you're interested, Mr. Jones, you can buy this product at Leroy's Hardware at 39th and Elm." Sophisticated database management allows even greater segmentation. Publishers can match subscriber lists against various public and private lists—census, auto registration, catalog lists, and so forth—and transfer that information to subscriber lists.

As indicated in the IMC Concept in Focus feature, the ability of magazines to reach clearly segmented markets can sometimes get out of hand. "Generation X" may appear to be a profitable segment, but it can only purchase a limited number of magazines.

Another advantage of magazines is their excellent visual quality. Magazines are printed on good paper and provide excellent photo reproduction in either black and white or color. Also, thanks to computer software such as Imagic and Quantel, photocompositing systems can bring together a studio photo and several ad stock photos to create a striking visual.

Magazines also provide coupon distribution, special editions, and print ads of various sizes. In fact, the willingness of magazines to accommodate advertisers' needs and wants remains one of the main attractions. Recently, magazines have led the way in joint programs with other media. Examples are tie-ins with other media outlets such as direct mail and cable. *Sports Illustrated* and ESPN, for example, joined together to entice marketing communicators such as Gatorade and Budweiser to advertise in both media.

Another advantage offered by magazines is reader involvement. People subscribe to magazines because they are interested in their content. The time

focus

Too Many Mags for Generation X

Many publishers are desperate to persuade advertisers and readers that they fill a particular Generation X niche. But with so many Gen X magazines groping for ad dollars, media buyers easily get confused. "I think these magazines are kind of hard to differentiate," says Felix Wong, senior media planner at Citron Haligman Bedecarre, which handles Kenwood America's Corp.'s audio account. "You can reach all the same people using some of the bigger publications, like *Wired, Rolling Stone, Spin,* and *Details*. . . . They are not incredibly different from one another, and you get a lot of magazines covering the same ground." Case in point: In New York *Project X* identifies its readers as young, mostly male club hoppers, whereas *KGB* targets young, mostly avant-garde males.

Indeed, jumping on the bandwagon of prior success seems inevitable, not just among media buyers looking for places to position ads but also among new magazines looking for readers and ad dollars. "Everybody's wooing the same advertisers," says Brian Solis, publisher of Southern California's free tabloid *Reality.* "Nobody is creative enough to create their own niche. Magazines may have their own angles in mind, but that doesn't mean they are actually creating them—and you have to do

that before you can get a national advertiser."

Luke Barr, coeditor and copublisher of *KGB,* agrees. "If magazines can't convey that they do have a niche to the advertiser, they are not going to get ads. Everyone already knows there's the 'Gen X' market now," he says. "It's no longer unique to approach a media buyer/planner and say, 'you need to sell to Generation X.' It's too broad; you have to differentiate within the Gen X marketplace."

Most titles, many less than a year old, already are showing the strain of the crowded market. Many titles first appeared in odd shapes and sizes to help create their identities but now are printing with more conventional and cheaper paper. At least three titles are handing out free advertising to selected national marketers. And some can't pay their employees.

Food for Thought

1. Why do you think so many magazine publishers are targeting Generation X?

2. What kinds of magazine elements would work best for Generation Xers?

3. Let's say you were trying to start

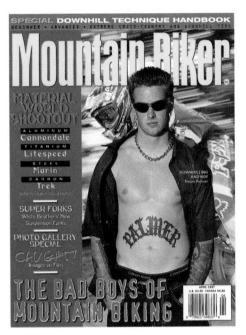

a new magazine aimed at the demographic group labeled Generation X. Knowing that much of your revenue would ultimately come from those who buy space to advertise from you, what steps would you take to insure that your magazine could earn the needed revenues? What image would you try to create and how?

Sources: Karen Cooperman, "Marketing To Generation X," *Advertising Age,* February 6, 1995, 27; Laurie Freeman, "Advertising's Mirror Is Cracked," *Advertising Age,* February 6, 1995, 30; Todd Pruzan, "Advertisers Wary of Generation X Titles," *Advertising Age,* October 24, 1994, S22–S24.

spent reading the magazine, according to research, is active involvement. Also, readers do not seem to view magazine ads to be as intrusive as ads in other media.

The key weakness of magazines is the difficulty of reaching a mass audience.

Advertising in mass-audience magazines, such as *People* and *Reader's Digest,* leads to wasted circulation, high costs per contact, and limited premium locations.

Also, such magazines often have high clutter. Magazines such as *GQ* and *Seventeen* often will consist of 70 percent ads and 30 percent editorial material. In addition, many of these ads are for direct competitors.

Print Goes Online

Clearly the major trend affecting both newspapers and magazines is their move to online technology. (We have already discussed the online option in the direct-marketing chapter, and will not repeat that information.) Both newspapers and magazines are employing the World Wide Web and online services to create home pages and repackage information. For example, publishing giants Advance, Cox, Gannett, Hearst, Knight-Ridder, Times Mirror, Tribune Co., and the Washington Post Co. formed a consortium called New Century Network that has produced a series of Web sites featuring their various newspapers.[5] The privately held Newhouse chain, while pouring money into its newsroom operation at New Jersey's *Star-Ledger* and the Cleveland *Plain Dealer,* is also giving its online services a push. "What we are trying to do is reinvent the paper to the extent it is necessary to come up with a product that people in the '90s think is valuable and essential," says *Star-Ledger* editor Jim Willse.[6]

The first issue of *Salon,* for example, offers a thoughtful interview with author Amy Tan, a criticism by essayist Camille Paglia, and a discussion about race in America by seven prominent thinkers and activists. *Salon* is one of the latest efforts to create virtual magazines on the Internet—magazines without paper, postal muss and fuss, or limitations of length. Even more recently, Microsoft Network hired Michael Kinsley, former editor of *The New Republic* and cohost of CNN's *Crossfire,* to launch an online magazine of commentary on news, politics, and culture. An old-timer, *HotWired,* is a stepchild of the print-based *Wired* magazine and has 289,000 registered readers.[7]

Although there is a great deal of excitement about print going online, many are skeptical about its future. Most point to the "bathroom factor." Simply, you

Concept Review

PRINT MEDIA (MAGAZINES)

1. Magazines are the most specialized of the mass media, as verified by the growth of special-interest magazines.
2. The three types of magazines are consumer, farm, and business. These types can be further classified by geography, demographics, or content.
3. Careful media planners must understand the complete picture of a magazine's readership before buying space.
4. The primary strengths of magazines are their ability to target the audience, high-reproduction quality, flexibility of services, and reader involvement.
5. The main weaknesses of magazines are that some promotional efforts are wasted, they provide limited premium locations, and are sometimes cluttered.
6. Print media have moved to online technology in the hope that readers will accept this form of media.

can't take a computer to bed very comfortably. You can't read it in the tub. Critics argue that magazines and newspapers have existed for several hundred years in their current format because they provide interesting reading that is portable and answers the "why" questions. The Web is most certainly not that, which begs the question: Will people really want their newspapers and magazines online in condensed form? This is a question media planners must answer as well.

BROADCAST MEDIA

Historically, broadcast media referred to radio and television—both media that were developed during the mid-twentieth century. Today some experts prefer the term "electronic" in favor of the term "broadcast" because they believe it reflects the technology in a more accurate manner and broadens its scope to include computer-generated messages that are broadcast to mass audiences. However, as is the case with online newspapers and magazines, "electronic" media can also deliver traditional print messages. To avoid confusion, we retain the term "broadcast," recognizing that many of the media we discuss in this section are now delivered electronically.

Television: A Changing Industry

For most of its brief history, the structure of the television industry was straightforward. The United States had three big commercial networks and hundreds of local stations. In the past twenty years, however, the industry has been shaken up by the emergence of new networks, the increased popularity of cable television and VCRs, changes in public television systems, and popular shows going into syndication. We discuss each of these developments next.

Local Stations and Networks

Local stations can be either independent or affiliated with a network. The Federal Communications Commission (FCC) defines a network as a program service with 150 or more hours of prime-time programming. Accordingly, there are currently four networks: Columbia Broadcasting System (CBS), National Broadcasting Company (NBC), American Broadcasting Company (ABC), and Fox.

Systems such as ESPN, CBN, CNN, and Metromedia are considered regional networks in that they offer programming during certain times of the day and/or in certain regions of the country. More recent systems such as Warner Bros., Paramount, MCA, Columbia, and King World are seeking a network designation so that they can sign contracts with local stations as *affiliates*. This is important because most viewing is still done through network stations via local affiliates.

Networks produce very few of their own programs, relying instead on individual production companies such as Tandem and Lorimar to produce prime-time shows. Networks sign contracts with local stations to carry their programming. Each of these stations then becomes an **affiliate.** The networks buy the program from a production company, provide a means to distribute the program through local affiliates, and make their money by selling commercial time to national advertisers. If the networks pay too much for a program, or if ratings are low, they cannot make a profit.

The networks pay a fee (called **compensation**) to local stations to carry their programming. The networks pay this compensation at a rate of approximately 20 to 30 percent of the advertising revenue, and the remaining 70 to 80 percent is kept by the network to pay for the program and for the costs involved in getting the program to the affiliates. In turn, the affiliates sell their own advertising time. Approximately 30 percent of this revenue is sent to the network to pay for programming. In general, affiliates make most of their income by selling local advertising. In fact, network compensation has become less important to local stations since the increased popularity of cable television.

Compensation aside, network affiliation is crucial to local stations because it allows stations to fill up airtime with diverse, high-quality programming and generates strong lead-ins for local news and syndicated programs. Stations can also piggyback on the considerable promotion and public relations value of the networks and their leading stars.

Each of the major networks has approximately 220 affiliates. When a station carries a network program, this is called **clearance,** because the local station clears the time for the network show. A network should have as high a clearance as possible (that is, from 95 to 100 percent) so it can offer advertisers total market coverage. Affiliates are not required to show specific network programs, but they may lose network affiliation if they do not carry enough.

Cable Television

Cable television originated because obstacles such as tall buildings, forests, and mountains prevented normal television broadcast signals from reaching potential viewers. Initially, the cable service built a community antenna on a hill or tall structure to pick up signals from conventional television stations. The cable company did not pay for the pickup but simply delivered the signals by means of a wire or cable to subscribers. By the 1990s about 60 percent of American households subscribed to cable television.

Today the cable industry is in a state of constant flux. Part of the change is due to new legislation. In 1992 the FCC abolished a ruling restricting telephone companies from carrying other types of signals. This has not only opened the door for cable via telephone lines, it has also prompted cable TV companies to counter the new competition by offering rival telephone service through coaxial cable originally installed to transmit TV programming. Also, the Financial Interest and Syndication Rules, which have limited the networks' ability to produce or own an equity stake in the shows they air, was abolished in 1995. This action prompted a series of mergers—Disney and ABC, Westinghouse and CBS, Time Warner and Turner, just to name a few. This trend clearly puts the advantage on the side of the networks and greater pressure on cable to develop or buy programming.

Finally, in 1996 the passage of the Telecommunications Act essentially allowed all communication companies to engage in all aspects of the business. Eventually, there will be little distinction between telephone, cable, and networks.

Cable companies, such as TCI and Jones Cable, make money through subscriber fees and advertising revenue. In addition, they also earn money by offering programming only to subscribers who are willing to pay a monthly fee (such as HBO, Showtime) or a one-time fee (pay-per-view). TCI also owns Primetime, which offers cable service to rural subscribers who cannot obtain normal cable. These subscribers pay a monthly fee to rent an 18-inch satellite dish and receive up to 150 channels. There are also independent companies that provide direct-to-home satellite systems. Thanks to a technology called digital compression, 500 stations are on the near horizon.

Public Television

A few years ago it would have been inappropriate to discuss the public television system in a text like this because public television contained no advertising. But this is no longer the case due to two changes that occurred during the 1980s and 1990s. First, because of federal funding cuts in 1988 and cuts of 15 percent in 1996 and 30 percent in 1997, public television looked for new sources of funding, including advertising. One option would allow stations to air up to three minutes of ads an hour between prime-time programs. For a PBS station such as KUHT-Houston, this type of arrangement would provide net revenues of $2 million.[8]

Second, the FCC changed the guidelines for marketing communication messages on public television. According to current FCC guidelines, messages on public television can include corporate and product logos if they are nonpromotional; business locations and telephone numbers if not used for direct-response selling; and brand names, service marks, and logos. Products or services may be described in a way that is "value neutral" when shown in use. FCC (and station) guidelines prohibit the corporate message from including product promotion, price, calls to action, inducements to buy, comparative statements, competitive claims, or a program host selling program-related merchandise. The messages can be shown only during the two-and-a-half-minute program breaks, preceded by a station-produced announcement that identifies a company's support but does not specify that the support is applied toward any one program.[9]

However, what the FCC will allow and what public stations will accept are not always the same. Each station maintains its own guidelines, and some are looser than others. In fact, some public stations run the same spots aired by commercial stations. Public television is well suited for image campaigns that do not make comparative claims, and even campaigns that do so in a subtle manner are occasionally accepted.

Syndication

A network program that has run its course can be sold to a local station in syndication. Actually, syndicated programs (also called strips because they appear everyday, much like comic strips) are either network shows that may still be running *(Seinfeld),* former network shows that are still produced for syndication only *(Jeopardy),* or original programs produced for syndication, such as *Baywatch.* Even public television has a separate division that develops and provides programming needed by networks, independents, and cable systems. The emergence of **off-network syndication** has become a multibillion dollar industry.

An original program cannot go into syndication until 88 episodes are produced. Typically, the original producer does not make money until the program goes into syndication. For example, Viacom, the syndicator for *The Cosby Show,* sold the show to 174 stations for approximately $600 million for four years. In 1996 Columbia Tri-Star Television Distribution sold *Mad About You* to 200 stations with ad rates starting at $100,000 per 30-second spot. Stations are expected to air *Seinfeld* and *Mad About You* back to back. Procter & Gamble spent more than $200 million advertising on syndicated shows in 1995. *Friends* went into syndication in 1998 at an approximate cost of $5 million per station.

The syndicated show usually includes commercial time for the producer who provided the show as well as time for national or local commercials. The problem with advertising on syndicated shows is that those shows often appeal to older, less-educated viewers and are often shown at times that don't match the target audience. Also, syndicators rarely provide good research information.

Methods of Measuring Broadcast Audiences

Different methods of measuring audiences can yield different results. Four basic techniques are used to measure broadcast audiences: *audimeter, telephone coincidence, diary method,* and *roster recall.*

The first technique uses an electronic recorder commonly called an **audimeter.** The A.C. Nielsen Company, which uses this technique, attaches the audimeter to the television set to measure not only which show is being watched but also who is doing the watching. For example, the Nielsen electronic "people meter" is a small box with eight buttons—six for the family and two for visitors—that is placed on top of the television. Each member has his or her own button. A remote control makes it possible to make entries from anywhere in the room, and a sonar device sends out an alert to log in or out. The four networks pay Nielsen approximately $20 million annually for this information. The machine measures only which shows people watch.

A second technique uses **telephone coincidence.** An interviewer calls households chosen at random and asks which program is being watched. Up-to-date data can be collected quickly, but not all times of the day or days of the week may be covered completely.

The **diary method** is the third technique. Preselected homes are mailed **diaries** in which each viewer writes down the stations and programs watched. A separate diary is provided for each television in the home and a cash award is given for cooperating.

A.C. Nielsen has about 250,000 households keeping viewing diaries that also ask why they watch a program. The diaries are supplemented by research from 5000 household viewing meters Nielsen has installed in homes. Nielsen uses the information from these two sources to compile the Nielsen Television Index (NTI) reports. These resources are then used by national advertisers to determine their CPM, or cost per thousand. Thus CPM indicates what advertisers paid for and what they received. The formula is stated as follows:

$$CPM = \frac{Ad\ cost \times 1000}{Circulation\ (audience\ size)}$$

If *Friends* has an audience size of 21 million and a 30-second spot costs $316,000, then the cost per thousand would be

$$CPM = \frac{\$316,000 \times 1000}{21,000,000} = 1.5047619$$

The fourth method, called **roster recall,** uses door-to-door interviews. The interviewer carries a roster of programs that were broadcast the day before and lets the person look at the roster while answering questions. Several demographic questions are also asked.

The four methods of measuring audiences provide a wealth of information. Perhaps their most significant information is the Nielsen weekly rankings of program rating and share. A program rating is the percentage of television households in an area tuned to a specific program during a specific time period. Thus if 21 million people watched *Friends,* of the 106,300,000 total television households, the rating for *Friends* would be

$$\frac{21,000,000}{106,300,000} = 19.8$$

A rating point (RP) is extremely important to the network and the media planner because it dictates the price charged per 60 seconds. It also provides a basis for comparing one program with another. This is referred to as cost per rating point (CRP) and is calculated as follows:

$$CRP = \frac{Cost}{RP} = \frac{\$310,000}{19.8} = \$15,656.57$$

Share is the percentage of households with their sets on that are watching a particular program at a particular time. It is calculated by dividing the number of households (HH) tuned to a particular show by the number of "households using television" (HUTS). If 70 percent of television sets were on during *Friends,* then 74,320,000 sets were actually on, of which 21 million were watching *Friends.* The program's share would be 28.3 (21,000,000 ÷ 74,320,000). Typically, the rating services report the two numbers: *Friends*: 19.8, 28.3. Research on the local audience is used to define *television markets.*

A **television market** is a rigidly defined geographic area in which stations generally located in the core of the area attract most of the viewing. Each county is placed in only one television market to avoid overlap, although there may be several counties in a market. There are approximately 200 television markets, accounting for more than 3000 counties.

Buying Television Time

Television is an extremely costly medium. With an average prime-time cost of $193,000 for a 30-second commercial, the range can run from a low of $60,000 for a new show scheduled opposite a top-rated show to a high of $500,000 and up for *Seinfeld.* These rates are directly related to the rating and share scores discussed earlier. There is also a match-up factor. Some shows, such as the new *Cosby,* are a perfect match with companies that have targeted the family audience. Consequently, *Cosby* can demand a higher rate even though the scores do not necessarily support this price. There are also alternatives to prime-time network commercials.

Key Purchasing Options

If media buyers decide to use television, they then face many decisions about how to use it well. Among the key choices are whether to buy time on a network or from a local station, what the level of commitment should be, and what time periods and programs should be selected.

Network and Cable Time. For mass coverage, a network buy is the best option. Placing an ad with ABC, for instance, means that all the ABC affiliates will show the commercial, thus reaching several million people simultaneously. The networks still tend to offer the most popular programs, and purchasing time on a network is relatively simple. However, the absolute cost of network advertising is very high, as is the waste. Also, a large portion of prime time is sold during the up-front market, a buying period (usually in May) when the networks sell a large part of their commercial time for the upcoming season.

For marketing communicators with limited funds or limited market coverage, two alternatives to network buys may be attractive. First, the major networks offer regional networks; that is, marketing communicators can select a region of the country for their promotion and pay the network a proportional rate plus a nominal fee for the splitting of the network feed. Second, marketing communicators may turn to the smaller networks and cable television networks. These outlets charge less and can provide more targeted coverage than the major networks.

Currently, time on cable television can be purchased by negotiating rates with independent cable system operators in each market or by buying time from broadcast stations that make their signals available to cable operators via satellite. Time on special-interest networks like ESPN or MTV may be purchased separately from the cable system, without having to buy the other programs or networks carried by the cable system. An advertiser can also purchase time through interconnects. The interconnect technology allows the cable system to carry different ads on separate parts of their system. Thus local advertisers can show their ads on the part of the system that reaches their target market.

Spot and Local Advertising. Television advertising is divided into three categories: network, national, spot, and local spot. We have already discussed the advantage of network advertising—simultaneous coverage of a mass market. However, the other two options offer certain advantages as well. When time is bought directly from local television stations, it is called **spot advertising.** Because local stations usually cannot sell time in the middle of network programs, most spot ads occur adjacent to network programs, but local stations also show them during their own programs.

When a national company buys local time, it is called **national spot advertising.** In contrast, spot advertising bought by local firms is called **local advertising.** As a result, local advertising is virtually a synonym for retail advertising. The major spenders on local advertising include department and discount stores, financial institutions, automobile dealers, restaurants, and supermarkets. To illustrate, a national car manufacturer such as General Motors Corp. buys network television advertising to reach the entire U.S. market. Chrysler Corp. buys national spot advertising for the Jeep Cherokee campaign because it only wants to reach markets where off-road vehicles are popular. And McDermott Chevrolet buys local spot advertising because the Gainesville, Florida, market is its primary target audience.

For the marketing communicator, buying time from local stations rather than national networks provides flexibility. An advertiser can select particular markets at particular times on particular programs. National marketing communicators might use spot ads to supplement a regional network campaign; to test new products, a media mix, or a creative strategy; or to obtain a cost-effective alternative in markets with high sales.

Still, using spot promotions has three key drawbacks. First, the likelihood of clutter is increased, because unless network advertisers have bought all of the commercial time on a program, local stations can sell time on network-originated shows only during station breaks between programs. Second, spot promotion is cumbersome for the national promoter. The marketing communicator must communicate with stations in many markets to select a station, determine airtime, negotiate the price, and check the promotion's appearance. And finally, if the cost per thousand is calculated, local television turns out to be much more expensive than national television. Hence, national companies prefer to purchase network time; when necessary, they supplement those purchases with messages on local television.

Sponsorship, Participation, Spot Announcements, and Barter. When buying television time, promoters must also determine their level of commitment. In the early days of television, it was very common for a single advertiser to sponsor an entire program, paying for production, salaries, and airtime. The *Kraft Music Hall* and *Hallmark Hall of Fame* are two examples of programs that showed only the ads of the sponsor and had a very pronounced impact on the viewing audience. Today, **sponsorships** are too expensive for most advertisers who are unwilling to devote the majority of their budget to one 30- or 60-minute slot. Nevertheless, for highly seasonal products (for example, holiday toys and greeting cards), using sponsorships is still a viable strategy.

Because most advertisers cannot afford sponsorships, they opt for **participation.** In fact, almost 90 percent of all network time is sold under this format. It means that several advertisers buy spots on a particular program. An advertiser can participate in a particular program once or several times on a regular or an irregular basis. Advertisers often split major sporting events, leading to an announcement that "this portion of the U.S. Open is brought to you by. . . ."

We discussed a third option earlier. National **spot announcements** are purchased from local television stations and appear during the adjacent time periods of network programs.

The final option is called **barter.** Barter is the exchange of goods without money, and it takes two forms. In the first and simpler form, a marketing communicator exchanges goods for time. This exchange typically occurs at the local level and could entail a local furniture store exchanging office furniture for ten 30-second spots. The second and more formal form of barter is **barter by syndication.** In this case the promoter supplies a syndicated show to the television station at no cost. Usually, some part of the advertising time is presold to national advertisers and the rest is available to the local advertiser. This not only benefits the national advertiser but also gives the local station free programming, plus profit through the sale of the remaining time to local advertisers. *Jeopardy* and *Oprah* are often sold this way.

Times and Programs. Those who buy television time must consider the time of day and the program broadcast because both affect the size and nature of the audience reached and, as a result, the rate charged for the television time. Although these time frames vary somewhat across time zones, the standard time periods in television are the following:

Early morning	6 A.M.–9 A.M.
Daytime	9 A.M.–5 P.M.
Early fringe	5 P.M.–7:30 P.M.
Prime	7:30 P.M–11 P.M.
Late news	11 P.M.–11:30 P.M.
Late night	11:30 P.M.–1 A.M.

Each time period reflects different audience size and characteristics. For example, early morning audiences are fairly small and represent upscale men and women getting ready to leave for work, children, and specialty audiences, such as viewers of exercise shows. Prime time has the largest audience and represents the family more than any other time.

To schedule purchases of television time, media buyers look at **gross rating points,** or GRPs. GRPs measure the viewing audience of a group of programs. Nielsen ratings provide the basis for GRPs. To demonstrate, let's look at a Tuesday night buy in 1996, which included *Full House* (11.4), *Home Improvement* (21.0), *NYPD Blue* (13.2), *Wings* (9.8), and *Frasier* (10.2). These would deliver a total of 65.6 GRPs. We take a close look at GRPs in the next chapter.

Purchasing Procedures

A media buyer has three main ways to buy television time: prime-time network buys, national spot buys, or local buys. The heavyweights of the television industry—corporate advertising directors and agency media executives—make prime-time network buys. The major buying period for network buying is in the early spring. That time period has three stages:

1. *Up-front market:* Advertisers make full-season commitments of approximately $5 million shortly after the announcement of the fall prime-time schedules. Advertisers usually limit up-front buys to prime-time shows, some sports programming, and popular daytime shows.
2. *Scatter market:* After the up-front market advertisers make their purchases, the scatter market buys time. As the name implies, this market does not buy spots on one show but negotiates for spots scattered throughout several shows. In this stage fewer good time slots are available because the up-front market has taken most. Also, the prices are generally higher than in the up-front stage because of the smaller number of spots purchased, though some deals can be made because of the poor initial ratings or other unknowns, especially at the end of the year when stations become desperate to sell remaining time.
3. *Opportunistic markets:* This last stage is essentially the remnant segment, composed of week-to-week purchases of unsold time. Remnant space may be space that was never sold because of its low desirability or space that was sold and then canceled.

To purchase local advertising, the media buyer must contact each station to obtain proposals and request rates and commercial position. The **avail** request is a formal request for information about available times and dates, prices, program ratings, total households, and GRPs. The station draws up several proposals based on the avail request.

Both network and local television time may be bought on a fixed, preemptible, or immediately preemptible basis. A fixed spot is the costliest because it cannot be displaced by another advertiser's commercial. Preemptible spots are bought with the understanding that if another advertiser will pay more, the original advertiser will be preempted. When this happens, the station gives the original advertiser enough notice so that another arrangement can be worked out. The cheapest spots are the immediately preemptible spots, which the station can move as it sees fit.

Discount plans can be negotiated between the marketing communicator and the station. Networks prefer advertisers who contract for year-round package plans because this arrangement provides guaranteed income to the network long before the promotion airs.

Television Strengths and Weaknesses

No medium has a greater potential to create an impression on consumers' minds than television. Combining moving pictures, voices, music, and convincing acting, television has the capability to run the entire gamut of human emotions. Television allows the audience member to learn more about the product, the spokesperson, and the message because the consumer is more personally involved.

Television also offers wide market coverage flexibility. Network television allows the marketing communicator to reach the entire country. Cable, public television, and interconnects bring a message to highly focused markets. As indicated in the IMC in Action feature, it also reaches other countries.

A third advantage of television is the important role it plays in our culture. For many people, television is the primary, most reliable source of entertainment, news, and sports. People count on television and hold a favorable attitude toward it.

Another advantage of television stems from its ability to deliver well-defined audiences. Research shows that there are remarkable similarities in the characteristics of viewers. *Home Improvement* delivers the family audience to advertisers such as Kraft Foods, Procter & Gamble, and Coca-Cola week after week. MTV delivers an audience of young people.

Television, usually thought of as a medium for delivering advertising messages, can also deliver sales promotion, public relations, and personal selling–related messages. For example, television can make sweepstakes exciting, highlight the value of a premium, or add urgency to a temporary price reduction. Many public relations efforts benefit from advertising. The "Just say no" anti-drug campaign is much more powerful on television than in print. Finally, because of its emotional impact, television does an excellent job of preselling a product, thus simplifying the job of the sales rep.

Television has weaknesses that can deter some marketing communicators from choosing this medium. Television's absolute cost is still high. *Seinfeld* costs about $500,000 for one 30-second spot. With production costs of $150,000 to $1,000,000, it is apparent that few promoters can afford national television. Clutter, especially on network television, exists. As many as 25 separate spots can be shown during 30 minutes of prime-time programming. Finally, television does not

IMC in action

MTV as an International (Local) Medium

MTV Europe's access to 59 million cable and satellite homes has made it one of the few successes in pan-European TV. In September 1995 MTV Networks introduced VH1, its first channel with programs tailored to a local market. But it has not abandoned its more than 300 pan-European advertisers, some of whom are also buying airtime on VH1 UK. The latter is aimed at 25-to-49-year-olds in more than three million British cable and satellite homes. VH1 aims to complement MTV Europe, a plan that appeals to jeans marketer Levi Strauss & Co. "Although VH1 is for an older audience, we've learned that one-third of its audience is from the [jeans-buying] MTV age group," says Steve Clark, group media manager at Levi Strauss' agency, Bartle Bogle Hegarty, London.

When the Media Centre, London, buys airtime for Anheuser-Busch's Budweiser beer, it uses VH1 to circumvent regulatory obstacles that could be caused by advertising alcohol on a pan-European network, according to Andrew Smith, the Media Centre's head of TV buying.

VH1 UK now claims more than 200 advertisers, including Nestlé, Procter & Gamble, Unilever, Nissan, Volkswagon, and Compaq. MTV's next move will be a tailor-made VH1 channel for other countries. "I see no reason why we won't consider VH1 for other European markets," outside the UK, Smith says. "It would have been difficult to introduce a pan-European version for VH1 because there aren't that many similarities in the lifestyles, culture, or history of TV's older viewers in the different European countries."

The advent of digital compression technology in Europe will enable MTV Europe to transmit different versions of MTV and VH1 using the same signal. Advertisers will be able to run commercials simultaneously in local languages in any combination or assortment of countries. "MTV Europe has been seen to be a very successful blueprint for advertisers in other parts of the world," notes Smith, who is moving to Singapore to introduce MTV Asia and MTV Mandarin.

The success of VH1 and MTV Europe is a rarity. Since the breakup of state-controlled broadcasting

monopolies in 1992, the general trend in much of Europe is to develop home-grown programs and shy away from American hits, such as *Dynasty* and *Dallas,* that once dominated. In Italy the top five shows are all Italian. In France seven of the top eight are French. Part of this trend is cultural, part is economic. Since 1991 American programs have more than tripled in price. That has given independent producers in Europe an opening for their lower-cost—and now more popular—shows.

Media planning in Europe is clearly a mixed bag. No longer should U.S. advertisers assume that European consumers will prefer U.S. programs. Instead, familiarity with local preferences should become the norm.

Food for Thought

1. What are the risks a media planner would assume by concluding that the success of MTV Europe is the norm?

2. Is international MTV possible?

Sources: John Tagliabue, "Local Flavor Rules European TV," *New York Times,* October 14, 1996, C1, C4; Juliana Koranteng, "MTV: Targeting Europe Market-by-Market," *Advertising Age,* March 20, 1995, 113, 120.

work with products that are unattractive (for example, industrial fluids), that cannot be demonstrated (for example, Preparation H), or that do not have inherent emotional characteristics or emotional associations (such as table salt).

The popularity of cable television is based partly on the fact that it eliminates most of the weaknesses of network and local television. Cable is very targeted, has little waste, and is also relatively inexpensive. Unfortunately, these strengths are balanced by the fact that cable has tremendous clutter, the quality of programming is sometimes suspect, and it takes multiple station buys to reach a mass audience. Nor can cable stations usually provide the research support given by networks.

<table>
<tr><td>

Concept

Review ✓

</td><td>

BROADCAST MEDIA (TELEVISION)

1. Television comes in four forms: network, local, cable, and public.
2. When advertising on television, marketing communicators can buy network, spot, or local advertising, or can also opt for sponsorship, participation, or spot announcements.
3. Television market size is assessed through four techniques: audimeter, telephone coincidence, diary method, and roster recall.
4. The size of a program audience is assessed through rating points and share. The weight of the schedule is determined by the total number of gross rating points (GRPs) delivered.
5. Market coverage and emotional involvement are the primary strengths of television.
6. High absolute costs and clutter are the major weaknesses of television.
7. Cable television is targeted and less expensive but often lacks quality programming and has little audience research.

</td></tr>
</table>

Radio: An Old Standard

More than 10,000 radio stations are now operating in the United States. Two types of stations exist: those than transmit signals via amplitude modulation (AM) and those that transmit via frequency modulation (FM). The primary difference is the distance covered by the signal. AM signals can travel up to 700 miles, whereas FM signals travel about 40 or 50 miles. However, the clarity of the signal across the maximum FM distance is better for FM stations than for AM. FM accounts for 75 percent of all radio listeners and 60 percent of all radio advertising. Today there are more than 600 million radios in America, with the average U.S. household owning nearly six radios.

The term **network radio** applies only to the traditional line networks interconnected (wired) by AT&T circuits, for example, ABC and CBS. A major trend in network radio is consolidation. Experts suggest there are now only four major radio networks: Westwood One (the parent company of NBC Radio and Mutual Broadcasting System), CBS Spectrum, ABC, and Unistar. ABC has the largest number of affiliates (1565).

Radio networks operate differently from television networks, most noticeably in the small amount of programming supplied for local stations. Because network programming is limited in time, stations may belong to more than one network, each providing specialized programming to complete a station's schedule. Thus a local station may be an affiliate of NBC and Mutual, taking sports programming and news from NBC and classical programming from Mutual. There are also special networks, such as the National Black Network (NBN), whose 90 affiliates are targeted toward the African-American population. Today radio talk shows (such as that hosted by Larry King), call-ins, advice shows, and the creation of local radio celebrities draw listeners everywhere. In turn, these deejays and local radio celebrities play an important role in sales promotion activities such as grand openings and special events.

Buying Radio Time

Years ago nearly all radio programming was live. As radio has become a more local medium, there has been a greater use of recorded shows, with little live programming except the news and on-the-spot broadcasts. This change has reduced the costs of commercials while improving the quality.

Advertising Rates. Radio rate cards are usually broken down into six time periods:

Morning drive time	6 A.M.–10 A.M.
Midday	10 A.M.–3 P.M.
Afternoon drive time	3 P.M.–7 P.M.
Evening	7 P.M.–Midnight
Late night	Midnight–6 A.M.

The cost of radio time primarily depends on four classifications:

1. *Drive time:* Drive time refers to the periods in which the population is moving around, in transition between sleep and the activities of the day or in transition from daytime activities to the events of the evening. These are the periods in which radio listening is at its highest levels and during which the adult population is least likely to be attending to television.
2. *Run-of-station (ROS):* This means that the radio station can move a commercial at will within the time period, wherever it is most convenient; preemptible ROS has the lowest rates.
3. *Special features:* This time slot is adjacent to weather signals, news reports, time signals, traffic reports, or stock reports.
4. *Demographics:* Demographics in the listening area also determine the cost or rate charged.

As is true in other media, advertisers pay less per commercial when they purchase spots in larger volume. Radio stations refer to volume purchases in several ways: 6- and 13-week flights, package plans (the station puts together an assortment of times), and scatter plans (a collection of spots in drive time, daytime, evening time, and weekend time).

Marketing Communication Options for Radio

Radio commercials may be 10, 30, or 60 seconds long. Radio time may be bought on a network, a group of stations, or an individual station.

Network radio is available in virtually every market. It is efficient and relatively inexpensive. A media buyer can, with one buy, distribute an advertising message to several hundred affiliates. For example, Dr. Pepper can buy five 60-second spots on *Dick Clark's National Music Survey* (Mutual Broadcasting System) and reach its 950 affiliates. Prices vary by day part and depend on the number of affiliates, the competitive situation, the amount of the network's available time, and the audience size and demographic characteristics.

There are several groups of unconnected local stations that offer a group discount on the advertising rate for purchasing time from the stations separately. These groups include McGavern Internet, Forbett Supernet, Katz Radio Group, Blair Radio Network, and Keystone Network.

FRANKLIN BANK
"THE WIZARD"

SFX:	OZ SFX (Loud)
OZ:	I am the huge bank! The great and powerful! Who are you?
DOROTHY:	I have a small business account here and I was….
OZ:	Silence! The great and powerful knows why you have come. Step forward insignificant one!
ANNCR:	Some banks, it seems, consider small business accounts a nuisance.
DOROTHY:	Please sir, I'd like some personal service.
OZ:	Oh, you'd like personal service huh! You bungling, bumbling beggar of benevolent banking!
ANNCR:	At Franklin Bank, we know what small businesses really need. That's why Franklin Bank gives you the lowest fees on commercial checking. And special services like a separate business branch, longer daily hours and account executives that make it their business to know you.
OZ:	Bring me a giant business account worth millions and I'll grant you personal service. Now go!
ANNCR:	Call Franklin Bank. The new thinking in banking for business. 358-5170. Member FDIC
SFX:	Music (Somewhere Over the Rainbow Intro)
DOROTHY:	There's no bank like Franklin. There's no bank like Franklin. There's no bank like Franklin (fade out).

This ad script for "The Wizard" is an example of a 20-second commercial.

Spot radio is available through all 10,000-plus stations. This means buying individual spot ads (usually 30 or 60 seconds) on a station-by-station basis. Spot radio is an excellent means to supplement a national campaign that is running locally in other media. However, buying spot radio, like spot television, means dealing with nonstandardized rate structures.

Who Listens to the Radio?

Arbitron, the chief measurement service for radio audiences, reports that nearly everyone (96 percent of all persons aged 12 and older) tunes in to a radio station at least once a week. People listen to the radio while cooking, reading, jogging, eating, driving, and working. This unusual participation makes radio a powerful means of reaching lifestyle segments and demographic groups. Age and sex are still the basic demographic measures, and radio stations divide the population by these characteristics. Young men under age 25 are the most likely to listen to classic rock stations. Teenagers and women under age 30 commonly choose contemporary hit stations. Both rock and contemporary hit stations are usually

FM stations. The music is constant and flowing; the deejays seldom intrude with more than a funny line, the time of day, and the name of the song.

Young people and older people seldom listen to the same kind of radio stations. Whereas most young people like rock, rap, or country, the stereotypical radio format for older people is "beautiful music"—instrumental versions of favorite songs. But not all mature adults prefer this kind of so-called elevator music. Men and women aged 55 and older are the primary listeners of news and talk stations. In markets where separate news and talk stations exist, men aged 55 and older prefer talk, and both men and women listen to all-news stations.

Radio Research

For radio, an Arbitron "book" is the equivalent of the Nielsen ratings of television programs. Although several smaller companies such as Media Statistics Inc., Mediastat, and RAM Research compete with Arbitron, Arbitron ratings generally determine how a radio station is doing. An Arbitron book can run up to 300 pages or more, filled with thousands of numbers estimating how many and what kind of listeners are tuned in to a given station at a specific time of day. Arbitron Radio uses the diary method of gathering data, which enables the company to report not only listening levels but also the demographics of the audience.

Arbitron randomly selects households in its 263 markets and first contacts a member of the household on the phone. If the household agrees to participate in the survey, Arbitron then mails a diary. The "diarykeeper" is supposed to write down exactly what stations their family listens to, for how long, and at what times. When the completed diary is mailed back to Arbitron, the household is usually financially compensated with a few dollars for their time.

The Arbitron book delivers data in two broad categories: quarter-hour estimates and cumulative (cume) estimates. Quarter-hour figures indicate how many people are listening at any given moment (for example, between 10 A.M. and 11 A.M. on Saturday morning); cume estimates indicate the total number of people tuned in during a specific period (for example, on Saturdays and Sundays from 6 A.M. to midnight).

Radio Strengths and Weaknesses

One of the main advantages of radio is that it can deliver a highly selective audience at a very low cost. Therefore, it is one of the few media that can allow market penetration and high repetition. KQEO-KMGA Albuquerque, for example, can deliver 15 percent of the Albuquerque market with ten daily repetitions of a message for less than $400 per day. Second, radio is a very flexible medium. A radio station is tolerant of last-minute changes, unusual formats, mobile hookups, and so forth. This adaptability makes radio appealing to a wide variety of companies and businesses. A small manufacturer, a local insurance agent, and a Kroger supermarket can all use radio. Third, radio provides immediacy because it is constantly delivering the latest news, time, and weather. The audience actively listens to the radio, so an ad sandwiched between news announcements is given attention. Finally, if the marketing communicator encourages imagination and imagery, radio can do an excellent job of creating high interest and involvement. When using radio, a humorous tactic tends to work best.

Radio has three main weaknesses. First, it is viewed as a passive medium because it provides only sound, and people tend to have the radio on while they are doing

BROADCAST MEDIA (RADIO)

1. There are AM and FM radio stations and four major radio networks.
2. Radio stations sell their time as drive time, run-of-station, and special features.
3. Radio markets are measured through the Arbitron book.
4. Radio offers excellent local coverage at a low cost, it is a flexible medium that has immediacy, and it can create high interest and involvement.
5. Radio is a passive medium that does not work well with some products.

other things (driving, eating, or studying, for example). Compared with television messages, people have low recall of radio messages. Recall, however, increases when messages of high interest are on the radio (for example, news, weather, a favorite song, or a popular deejay). Finally, radio is not appropriate with certain products that are difficult to visualize or that are used infrequently (for example, medical products) or to reach a national audience simultaneously.

OUT-OF-HOME MEDIA

The term **out-of-home** includes outdoor (outdoor boards and billboards) and transit media. It refers to all media that carry messages where the message or the consumer is on the move or mobile. It is a relatively minor medium that usually supplements print or broadcast.

Outdoor Media

In a sense outdoor advertising represents the oldest medium because it is a distant cousin of the sign. It is virtually impossible to go anywhere in this country without being exposed to outdoor advertising. Perhaps because of this constant overt exposure, outdoor advertising remains the medium most criticized by the public for desecrating the natural beauty of our country.

Types of Outdoor Vehicles

There are three primary types of outdoor advertising: posters, painted bulletins, and electric spectaculars. The advertising message on posters (highway billboards) is usually lithographed on sheets of paper and then posted on some structure. The standard-size posters in the United States are the 24 sheet (8 feet, 8 inches high by 19 feet, 6 inches long), the 30 sheet (9 feet, 7 inches high by 21 feet, 7 inches long), and the bleed poster (10 feet, 5 inches high by 22 feet, 8 inches long). The bleed poster extends the artwork right to the frame of the panel and is about 40 percent larger than the 24-sheet poster.

Each poster is mounted on a standard poster structure that is 12 feet by 25 feet long. Most posters are printed on 10 to 15 individual sheets, not on 24 or 30 separate sheets. There is no difference in promotion costs for the three sizes, although production costs are greater for the larger types. In some markets smaller posters are available. These posters are generally used for pedestrian traffic and are often placed in shopping center parking lots or on the sides of buildings.

This eye-catching bulletin was painted on a wall in Manhattan's Upper East Side.

Painted bulletins usually measure 14 feet by 48 feet. The message is changed two or three times a year. Painted bulletins can also be painted on walls as opposed to structures such as billboards. Wall bulletins cannot be standardized in size because the shape and area on the side of a building are unpredictable. Some bulletins have cutouts that provide a three-dimensional effect. Most bulletins are illuminated.

Spectaculars are large, illuminated, and often animated signs in special high-traffic locations. Examples include the spectaculars located on Broadway in New York City or on Chicago's Michigan Avenue and scoreboards at athletic stadiums. Spectaculars are custom designed and are sold for time periods of one year or more.

Because outdoor is such a visual medium, everything must be kept simple. People should be able to grasp the message clearly and completely in a maximum of five seconds. There should be one dominant design; five or so words of copy; bright, warm colors; and crisp lettering. Physical factors are also important. For example, the longer the poster or painted bulletin is visible to passing travelers, the better. Slower traffic is also beneficial. Obviously, it is preferable if the outdoor ad stands alone.

Buying Outdoor Media

During the last decade, an attempt to make the outdoor industry more professional and thereby more competitive with other media led to the adoption of the gross rating points (GRPs) system, the gathering of more data on audience segments, and the emergence of organizations such as Out-of-Home Media Services (OHMS). OHMS conducts research on the industry and provides a national buying service for outdoor and transit advertising.

If an advertiser purchases a hundred GRPs daily, the basic standardized unit is the number of poster panels required in each market to produce a daily effective circulation equal to 100 percent of the population of the market. As used by the outdoor industry, a rating point is 1 percent of the population one time. GRPs are based on the daily duplicated audience as a percentage of the market. If three posters in a community of 100,000 people achieve a daily exposure to 75,000 people, the result is 75 GRPs.

Posters are rented for 30-day periods. Painted bulletins and spectaculars are bought on an individual basis, usually for one-, two-, or three-year periods. On an illuminated bulletin, the original design is painted, and twice during the year it can be repainted with entirely new copy. On unilluminated locations, one extra painting is usually provided without extra cost. In many cities cutout displays can be rotated every 30, 60, or 90 days among certain choice locations.

Outdoor Media Strengths and Weaknesses

For certain marketers, such as restaurants, motels, and gas stations, outdoor media can provide some real benefits.

1. By combining color, art, and short copy, outdoor ads can quickly create an association with a particular brand.
2. This medium provides repetition. If a product or service is advertised at a busy crossroad, audiences see the ad again and again. The more often the idea is repeated, the more likely it is to be retained.
3. Billboards also have immediacy and can be located in the neighborhoods that are most relevant to the marketing communicator. A local bank can be quite sure that the majority of consumers who pass its billboard are potential customers.
4. The cost is reasonable. The cost per billboard in a major metropolitan area is quite low.
5. Outdoor advertising gains attention through sheer size.

Outdoor advertising also has the following limitations:

1. Outdoor copy must be brief because it is perceived while the audience is on the move. For certain types of products, it is impossible to effectively deliver the message or demonstrate the product.
2. A great many uncontrollable factors may lessen the effectiveness of outdoor ads. Signs, trees, structures, traffic signals, or a hazardous part of the highway may distract the consumer. An ad placed next to others that are controversial or in poor taste could damage the image of the company.
3. Good locations may be limited. In some communities there may be just one spot that has a high traffic count.
4. Many people view outdoor ads as an ecological nuisance.

Transit Media

Transit media can be considered a minor medium compared with those already discussed. Still, total annual expenditures amount to approximately $25 million. Transit advertising is carried by more than 70,000 vehicles, including buses, subways, rapid transit, and commuter vehicles. The consumer has a relatively longer time to look at transit messages compared to outdoor advertising, and the marketing communicator can get a more complete story across. There are three primary types of transit advertising.

1. *Car cards:* Typically, a car card is 11 inches by 28 inches, although widths of 42 inches by 56 inches are often available. These cards are placed inside the vehicle along each side above the windows. In some vehicles larger, different-shaped cards are placed at the middle or end of the vehicle. Inside displays are purchased on the basis of full-, half-, or quarter-fleet showings.
2. *Outside displays:* Exterior traveling displays are located on buses and taxis. Again, these ads are bought on the basis of showings—100, 75, 50, or 25.
3. *Station posters:* These mini-billboards are located at bus, railroad, subway, and air terminals. The most common units are the two-sheet poster (46 inches by 60 inches) and the one-sheet poster (46 inches by 30 inches).

Transit media offers several advantages:

1. Most notably, transit posters offer a relatively inexpensive medium for reaching a variety of people, repeatedly, in a variety of locations (for example, sidewalks and shopping centers) closest to the point of sale.
2. Several techniques make the medium flexible and attractive, including backlighted displays, curved frames, optical effects, and the take-one poster.
3. Transit promotion can serve as a type of reminder ad in conjunction with other media.

The limitations of transit media, similar to those of outdoor media, follow:

1. Transit cards must carry relatively short and concise messages.
2. Viewers' attention may be hard to attract and retain because of the many distractions (for example, crowded cards, traffic, noise, marked and torn signs).
3. Transit space is not available in all markets.

SUPPLEMENTAL AND NEW MEDIA

In every media plan several supplemental and new media are used to support primary media such as newspapers, magazines, TV, radio, and out-of-home. Their intent is to reinforce the primary idea and reach the target audience at times when primary media cannot. In many instances these media provide marketing commu-

This transit ad shows how flexible and attractive the medium can be.

OUT-OF-HOME MEDIA

1. There are three main types of outdoor advertising: posters, painted bulletins, and electric spectaculars.
2. The three transit media include car cards, outside displays, and station posters.
3. Outdoor and transit promotions can reach the market with a reminder message at a low cost.
4. Both outdoor and transit promotions have a relatively short time to deliver their message and must contend with many uncontrollable factors.

nicators with an affordable, effective, and targeted media supplement. The list is quite lengthy, and many were fads that lasted a very short time. We highlight the dominant forms of supplemental and new media in the following sections.

Supplemental Media

Specialty advertising and in-store media are two of the more popular alternatives of supplemental media. Discussed in Chapter 14, these media forms are both intended to create last-minute reminder information, through a pen or a sign. Telemarketing and direct mail are also supplemental and were discussed in Chapter 12.

Directories represent an important supplemental medium, especially to local businesses. Directories can be industry specific, product specific, or target-market specific. The aerospace industry has its own directory, as does the electric motor product category. The Silver Yellow Pages are targeted at consumers over the age of 55. The messages often tie in with advertising on television or in the newspaper. Undoubtedly, the Yellow Pages is by far the largest directory. Many advertising agencies have specialists who work on their clients' Yellow Pages advertising. The primary purpose is to establish the trademark as the reference point and then list all the local dealers under that trademark. The dealer may then run their own ads separately.

Other supplemental media that have achieved a level of acceptance include: ads spliced onto viedotaped movies, ads on videocassettes (usually in the form of an infomercial), ads sent via fax, ads shown in movie theaters or in in-flight movies, ads on computer disks or CD-ROM, ads that are implicit by placing a product in a movie or TV show (who can forget Reese's Pieces in *E. T.*?), and ads found in changing rooms, bathroom stalls, and brochures hung on your door knob. All these choices tend to be less expensive than primary media but lack market coverage and, in the case of fax and changing room placements, may irritate the consumer. They should be considered when there is a need to fill in the blanks and when spending limited dollars on such media makes sense.

New Media

As noted earlier, the most dramatic breakthroughs in media development during the last decade have come through the emergence of digital interactive technology. Early adopters of this technology consider it the wave of the future. To these individuals the "conventional" ad world is becoming irrelevant, and the large ad shops are either dinosaurs soon to become tar pits or, more charitably, are being led by managers who "just don't get it." But most media directors feel that the digital future may be further away than the advocates think. The projection is that interactive advertising will amount to $7.5 billion worldwide ($2.1 billion in the United States) by the year 2000. That amount would represent less than 2 percent of media spending.[10] Ken Auletta, media correspondent for *The New Yorker,* says the overriding issue today is whether interactive technologies will open up new opportunities for TV as we know it, or will lead to the death of the boob tube.

Still, the technology is not going to stop. Some experts suggest, for example, that the differences between cable television and personal computers will become increasingly irrelevant. Others predict that manufacturers will have their own channels, catalog companies could deliver products almost instantaneously, anyone could sell anything on the Internet or via interactive TV, costs will decrease, and penetration will multiply. The IMC in Action feature shows how some businesses are responding to the effects of new media.

It's fun to speculate about the interactive media that will exist in the future. For example, Xerox PARC chips could be carried around in our pockets, and they will "talk" to other chips by means of video, radio, or infrared signals. These chips can also be embedded in the walls, desks, light sockets, and practically every other square foot of your workplace and home. They will communicate with one another via the information highway. All the chips would have the capability to carry marketing messages. How would you like every room in your home wired and capable of talking to you?

New media is being introduced every day. Media planners must be able to gauge its place in the media mix.

SUPPLEMENTAL AND NEW MEDIA

Supplemental media are used to reach other target audiences or primary target audiences at other times. The supplemental media currently employed are

1. Speciality advertising
2. In-store media
3. Directories
4. Ads on videotaped movies, on videocassettes, sent via fax, shown in movie theaters and in in-flight movies, on computer disks and CD-ROMs, and product placements.
5. Most new media relate to interactive digital systems. It is still uncertain how relevant this media will be in the immediate future.

A CLOSING THOUGHT: PUTTING IT ALL IN PERSPECTIVE

Despite the excitement about interactive digital media, media planners must be aware of the fact that consumers only have 24 hours in a day and old habits die hard. It is more important to view interactive technology as one element in an integrated marketing communication strategy. By combining media into a unified effort that encompasses sales and trade promotion as well as public relations and direct mail, the marketing communicator reaps the benefits of a campaign that provides a coordinated communication effort against his or her target audience.

Historically, agencies viewed media as a "necessary evil." Now it's treated with respect and as an important part of the agency function, and it will become even more important in the future.

SUMMARY

1. **Explain why marketing communicators must understand the comparative strengths and weaknesses of the various media alternatives.**
A mass medium reaches many people simultaneously and requires the use of some technological device to connect the marketing communicator with the audience. Media planners must understand the strengths and weaknesses of each medium, as well as its costs, to find the most effective media mixes, especially in light of an integrated approach.

2. **Describe the characteristics, buying process, and strengths and weaknesses of the primary print media—newspapers and magazines.**
Primary print media include newspapers and magazines. There are a number of characteristics unique to each. Newspapers are the number-one local medium, whereas magazines are highly segmented. Both are willing to carry a variety of sales promotion elements. Print has gone online during the last five years. There is a mixed review as to the role online technology will play in the future.

Newspapers offer both classified ads and display ads. For the latter, ads are sold based on a rate per column inch, the rate based on rate cards or rating services. Magazines are sold based on a page or some increment of a page. Advertisers must also comply with three lead dates.

The primary strength of the newspaper medium is its acceptance as a local news source. It also is quite flexible and carries sales promotions. Newspapers and magazines suffer from clutter. Magazines are highly targeted and possess excellent reproduction quality.

3. **Describe the characteristics, buying process, and strengths and weaknesses of the primary broadcast media—TV and radio.**
Primary broadcast media include television and radio. Television includes a number of classifications, including network, local, cable, and public. Each offers certain advantages and disadvantages and is purchased in different ways. Mostly, television reaches a mass audience with a limited message at a low cost per contact. Cable television is much more targeted. Radio, like newspapers, is an important local medium. It is targeted and an excellent reminder medium, although it lacks a visual component, greatly limiting its use. TV media buyers have three options: prime-time network buys, national spot buys, or local buys. Radio offers the same buying options.

4. **Describe the characteristics, buying process, and strengths and weaknesses of the primary out-of-home media—outdoor and transit.**
Out-of-home media include outdoor and transit. It is an excellent reminder medium and is best used in close proximity to the product or service. However, there are many disadvantages, especially limited locations and poor image. This type of media is purchased based on GRPs or through buying services such as OHMS.

5. **Explain the role that supplemental and new media play in the overall media strategy.**
Supplemental and new media are used with audiences and in places that are not fully reached by primary media. Examples include specialty advertising, in-store, direct mail, telemarketing, directories, videocassettes, infomercials, product placements in movies and TV shows, and so forth. The most important new media is interactive digital technology. This media will allow greater targeting and may dramatically change the nature of print and broadcast media.

POINTS TO PONDER

Review the Facts

1. What is interactive digital technology?
2. List the strengths and weakness of radio as a media alternative.
3. What are the strengths and weaknesses of directories as a media alternative?

Master the Concepts

4. Why would a manufacturer of high-quality running shoes probably select magazines as its primary medium?
5. What techniques are used by rating services to gather and provide data concerning television viewership?
6. What are the implications of cable interconnect systems?

7. Under what circumstances would spot television advertising be more appealing than national television advertising? Network versus cable?

Apply Your Knowledge

8. Prepare an argument in favor of the use of radio instead of television as the primary medium for an integrated marketing communication strategy.
9. "Any ad agency that hasn't wholeheartedly accepted the interactive revolution is going nowhere." React to this statement.
10. Think of the college or university you attend as a product. Considering the characteristics of the product, develop an evaluation process that would allow you to assess media alternatives.

SUGGESTED PROJECTS

1. (Writing and Oral Communication Project) Contact an ad agency that has an interactive media department. Interview the director and determine the role this media will play. Write a three-page report on your findings.

2. (Writing and Oral Communication Project) Interview a media buyer for a local department store. Assess what he/she views as the pros and cons of the various media. Write a two-page report that summarizes your findings.

3. (Internet Project) Visit three Web sites for magazines or newspapers that also have print versions. Examples of such sites include the *Los Angeles Times*, the *New York Times*, *Business Week*, or *Fast Company*. Compare the print version with the online version of each magazine or newspaper. If you were the marketing communication media specialist for a kitchen appliance manufacturer, would you prefer to buy ad space in the print or online version of each magazine or newspaper you examined? Explain your answer. What if you were the media specialist for a software developer? Do your conclusions change? Why?

CASE 15: *SPORTS ILLUSTRATED* INTEGRATES WITH MULTIMEDIA

The gamble that *Sports Illustrated* took in 1993 when it integrated its marketing communication efforts and focused on multimedia appears to be a solid hit, if not a grand slam. In 1994, *Sports Illustrated*'s 40th anniversary, the weekly reversed a three-year ad page slide to finish up at 19.4 percent, with 2415 pages. Since that time, with an increased TV presence through its own production arm, ad pages have risen even more.

A memorable example of a successful multimedia

thrust is The "Sports Illustrated" Swimsuit Special: Class of 1995. NBC aired the show on Valentine's Day. All 16 30-second ad packages sold out for $297,000 each. The price tag included two ad pages in Sports Illustrated magazine editions: one in the 5.1 million circulation swimsuit edition plus another page in the 3.1 million circulation regular edition. For the swimsuit issue itself, which went on sale on February 15, ad pages jumped 20 percent.

"We were surprised at how quickly advertisers responded to the multimedia opportunity," comments Mike Dukmejian, director of sales development for the magazine. "With a mature title, you always have to reinvent yourself," notes Donald Elliman, president of Sports Illustrated since 1992.

The designation of Elliman as Sports Illustrated president was the first hint Time, Inc., was changing its mind on centralizing selling. Yet the integrated marketing approach that flopped at the corporate level appears to have worked like a charm at Sports Illustrated. "Time, Inc., made a big switch about a year and a half ago and gave individual power back to the publishers. As a result, Sports Illustrated is branching out into other media to bring greater value to advertisers," says Ellen Oppenheim, senior vice president, media director of FCB/Liber Katz Partners, New York. Today that includes everything from ten-minute sports vignettes that appear as part of ABC's Wild World of Sports to monthly poster giveaways at Foot Locker shoe stores.

It all translates into bottom-line gains. One program links advertisers such as Procter & Gamble's Old Spice and Nissan to monthly advertisorial features tied to local sports figures. The strong advertisorial programs did not exist a few years ago, but today they account for $10 to $15 million in revenues per year.

In another integrated marketing push, footwear-maker Fila gave away posters of NBA star Jamie Mashburn at 1400 Foot Locker stores for one month. Six other clients also used the month-long promotion: Champion Products, American Express Co., the National Football League, Reebok International, Starter Corp., and the National Basketball Association.

To date, Sports Illustrated ranks as the best in putting together these various media components for advertisers.

Case Questions

1. What are some of the marketing communication strategy implications of the multimedia approach discussed?
2. What are potential problems with this approach?

Source: Keith J. Kelly, " 'SI' Scores by Using Integrated Strategy," Advertising Age, February 13, 1995, 16.

ROMA'S LITE INTEGRATED CASE QUESTIONS

(Review the Roma's Lite Marketing Plan in the Appendix at the end of the text before answering these questions.)
1. Under what conditions would print media be more effective than broadcast media?
2. Evaluate out-of-home media as an alternative to major mass media.
3. (Team Project) Evaluate the various media alternatives for introducing Roma's Lite Pizza to the U.S. market.

chapter

16

Developing the Media Plan

CHAPTER OBJECTIVES

After completing your work on this chapter, you should be able to:

1 **Explain how marketing communication and media interface.**

2 **Describe the procedure for producing a media strategy.**

3 **Discuss the tactics that are part of a media strategy.**

4 **Explain how computer technology affects media planning.**

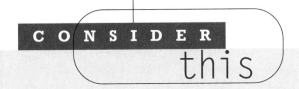

CONSIDER *this*

A New Brand of Media Planner

When United Parcel Service wanted a bite of the home-office and small-business delivery market, Doug Ray and his team created a plan outlining how the shipping company could find these customers. What Ray, a media planner at Ammerati & Puris/Lintas, New York, and his media department colleagues spearheaded was not a market research project but a media plan.

For media planners, product marketing knowledge is often part of the job description. Ray is one of a new breed of marketing-based media planners—known at Ammerati as "marketing planners specializing in media." The forte of this new type of planner is creating low-cost, high-reach media plans and investigating and using the proper media (traditional or unconventional) needed to reach a marketing objective. "Because of the multiple media options available today we needed people who were much more marketing-oriented," says

David Martin, president and CEO of PentaCom, the Michigan-based division of BBDO North America dedicated to Chrysler Corp.'s media planning and buying. "The creative people and the media people must intertwine their work as much as possible. They have to understand that the overall project is part of a targeting process."

This marketing orientation is a decided trend at smaller agencies. "Every account is run differently . . . and it's going to be a long time before the big ones cross over to integrated media-client relationships," says Erica Joseph, a senior media planner at Culver Moriarty and Glavin (CMG) in New York. CMG staffers say accounts from smaller clients such as Pivot Rules, an athletic apparel company, are ideal for marketing-based media planning. "The traditional ad agency for Pivot Rules would plan to spend a certain amount in 'X' media category and execute that," says Hope Ross, CMG's director of marketing and media services.

To extend the brand's reach

513

beyond a Father's Day campaign targeting women, CMG's media department developed plans involving in-store promotions and a partnership between *McCall's* and the Ladies Professional Golf Association. The marketer donated apparel in exchange for print, TV, and on-site ads, she says.

Even academics recognize how the media department's demands have changed. "These days agencies are thinking of media as part of the creative and marketing mix," says Lynda Maddox, assistant professor of marketing and advertising at George Washington University. "In the past, we could all shy away from accountability. But now clients want to link the creativity and placement of the campaign to sales."

Sources: "UPS Delivers at the Speed of Business With New Campaign," UPS home page (February 1, 1995): Internet (www.ups.com/news); Jane Hodges, "Say Hello to a New Breed of Planner," *Advertising Age,* July 24, 1995, S12.

CHAPTER OVERVIEW

To be effective, a marketing message must reach a particular audience in an optimal manner. It must attain **aperture**—that point in place and time when the audience is most likely to use the message. From Ray's team, the strategy for UPS was to target small and home-based businesses. That decision led to a campaign running in small-business magazines such as *Inc.* and *Entrepreneur.*

Finding aperture is becoming more difficult for the marketing communication manager. The average consumer has more than 30 television channels from which to choose. Some 11,500 magazines are in print. Boston alone has 14 AM and 16 FM radio stations. Catalogs, direct-mail advertising, and out-of-home media bombard consumers at their homes, offices, and all points in between. Although the number of media choices is expanding, the time consumers have to spend with media is not.

Keith Reinhard, chairperson and CEO of DDB Needham Worldwide, describes the task facing the media strategist: "In the future, the most important part of the promotion strategy will be to identify which media vehicles attract which consumers, and what media patterns those consumers follow through a day or week or month, and then to intelligently program messages on the consumers own personal 'media networks'."[1]

Media strategists have a tremendous amount of factual information about media, including information about circulation, audience characteristics, buying patterns, rates, and competition. But because of the great difficulty in comparing media and the virtually unlimited number of media combinations possible, selecting the appropriate media plan is still quite arbitrary and somewhat subjective. In addition, as noted in the chapter opener, the modern media planner must also have a thorough understanding of marketing. Moreover, the planner must be capable of integrating the two.

This chapter discusses the process of developing a media plan. We explore the relationship between marketing and media planning first. Next we will examine the two stages in the media planning process: creating a strategy and implementing the media plan. We then look at the use of computer technology as a tool for media planners and close with an investigation of IMC's role in media planning.

MARKETING AND MEDIA PLANNING

The **media plan** is a blueprint that maps out the best ways to send the marketing communication message to the target audience. To create the plan, media planners must evaluate and choose the channels of communication that will deliver the marketing communication message to the target audience at the right time, in the right place, and for the right cost.

Recall from Chapter 4 that marketing plays a critical role supporting a company's marketing program. Media planning, in turn, plays a key role in the marketing communication program. Just as the marketing communication plan and objectives are based on the firm's marketing plan, the media plan depends on the marketing communication plan and objectives. A simplified version of this relationship is shown in Figure 16.1.

Who is responsible for media planning depends on the size of the business and the size of the agency. For example, in a small manufacturing business with a marketing communication budget of $100,000, the vice president of marketing is likely to plan the entire marketing communication effort, including the media plan. For Intel Corp., a director of marketing communication (under the vice president of marketing) is responsible for all the facets of communication, including the media plan. However, Intel has the media plan designed by the media

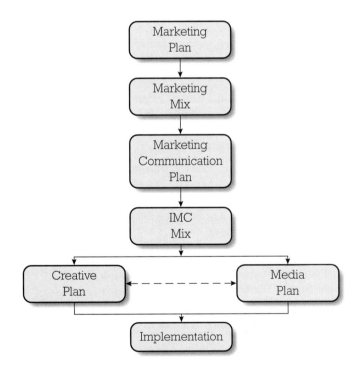

FIGURE 16.1

The Place of Media Planning

planning department at J. Walter Thompson, an outside agency. We see, then, that people with very different titles may be engaged in media planning. Likewise, media buying may be the job of the marketing vice president or the media buyer working under the agency's media planner. A media buyer is typically the entry-level job in media planning.

We first look at seven marketing factors that affect media decisions: the firm's marketing objectives, the product, its profitability, its channels of distribution, the IMC strategy, marketing resources, and the target audience.

1. *Marketing objectives:* The media plan should support the firm's overall marketing objectives. Because the objectives should drive media decisions, the media plan must wait until those objectives are outlined in enough detail to support media direction. Most marketing objectives relate directly to market share; others relate to communication objectives. For example, a market-share objective for Keebler Cookies might be to increase market share of the fancy cookie market to 12 percent by attracting the Hispanic consumer in the southwest region. A marketing communication objective might be to increase the overall awareness of the Keebler brand name in regions that account for two-thirds of sales.

Both objectives provide insights into the type of media plan to use. The market-share objective indicates that a media planner should choose media that appeal to Hispanics. For example, the planner could choose Spanish-speaking radio and television and Spanish-language newspapers and magazines that are released only in the southwestern United States. The marketing communication objective suggests a much broader media strategy that would reach target areas where sales are high—a far more expensive strategy than the first.

2. *The product:* The product also influences the media effort. The price of the product, its newness, stage in the life cycle, and means of distribution suggest the type of consumer who purchases the product. This information also suggests what media mix will present the product to the right audience. A product such as an expensive fishing boat implies a unique group of media and a particular schedule. For instance, this product probably appeals to a prestige-conscious market segment, so it would not be promoted in *Reader's Digest* or the *Enquirer.* It is also a seasonal product, so it would be best to promote it in the spring issues of *Sports Afield, Field & Stream,* and *Bass.*

3. *Product profitability:* Closely related to the influence of the product in media is the product profitability. It is difficult to justify expensive network television for a product that has a small profit margin. A small margin may also affect the amount of retailer support for a marketing communication program. A lack of local retail advertising support can shape the media strategy. A company such as Jimmy Dean sausage, for example, has concentrated on regional television because retailers do not feature its product and because a small profit margin dictates little waste in the media strategy. Jimmy Dean also distributes coupons through various distribution companies.

4. *Channels of distribution:* The channels of distribution influence the media plan in several ways. First, it is wasteful to buy media in markets where the product is not available. Second, certain kinds of resellers are better able to use particular media. For example, wholesalers tend to be good at using direct mail and catalogs, which usually include a great deal of detailed information and require a good mailing list. Retailers are best at using local newspapers and radio. Third, particular resellers may be impressed by manufacturers who use certain media, such as national television. Fourth, consumers who buy the product at particular kinds of outlets may expect to locate product information in certain media. Consumers who purchase groceries at supermarkets, for instance, expect to find product information and coupons in both print media and direct mail.

5. *IMC strategy:* The media plan should take into account the other elements of the IMC strategy. In particular, the amount of effort devoted to advertising, personal selling, and sales promotion helps form the media plan. For instance, if personal selling is emphasized, then trade publications might be the only medium used. But if the marketing communication strategy relies on mass advertising, then planners should create a comprehensive media mix. If the strategy calls for coupon promotions, then media planners must include a print medium, such as newspapers, to distribute the coupons.

6. *Resources:* Obviously no business has all the resources it needs. This is particularly true in media planning where the cost of a comprehensive media plan is beyond the reach of most companies. Although Sprint may spend $60 million on its long-distance campaign, that is a far cry from AT&T who spends about $370 million. In addition to a limited budget, another marketing constraint is lack of human resources. Some companies do not have a sales force or the media talent to discern a good media choice from a bad one.

7. *Target audience:* Though the factors discussed so far strongly influence the media plan, in an integrated marketing communication program the most critical factor is the target audience. Traditionally, media planners' knowledge of the target audience is limited to secondary research (discussed later in this chapter). Although this type of information is useful, it does not insure that the media planner has in-depth knowledge of that audience. In integrated marketing communication programs, media planners must assess exactly how the target audience wants to receive information and how media are best combined to reach the target audience, including nontraditional media. This assessment may require a company to conduct media-related research on its target audience. As noted in the IMC Concept in Focus feature, understanding the customer is a prerequisite for integrated media planning.

Concept

Review

MARKETING AND MEDIA PLANNING

A media plan must consider the following marketing factors:

- Marketing objectives
- Product
- Profitability
- Channels of distribution
- Marketing resource constraints
- IMC strategy
- The target audience

It Begins with the Consumer

Media planners face a serious problem: how to integrate media. IMC expert Don Schultz contends that the real question is how to integrate *from the view of the consumer.* Why is an integrated media plan a problem? Most media planners think about media from the marketer's viewpoint, not the buyer's. They talk about target markets and media weights, effective reach, and cost per thousand. These concepts have little meaning for the prospective purchase or the loyal buyer of a brand.

Taking the marketer's view of media planning creates another terminology problem. Just what is "media"? Only those delivery vehicles that can be measured, such as radio, TV, newspaper, magazine, and outdoor? Or are "media" all systems that can deliver a message or an incentive to a consumer? For example, is packaging a medium? Is a T-shirt or key chain? That's a problem for many media planners who do not consider the buyer's perspective. From the buyer's point of view, anything that delivers the message is the medium.

Can planners integrate media without shifting their view from the marketer to the buyer? Probably not. What to do? Here's a modest proposal: Let's start over. Let's start with the understanding that integration needs to be done from the

consumer's or customer's view. That means planners should no longer talk about media. Instead, they should talk about delivery channels or delivery systems. Delivery channels are any method marketers can use to deliver either a message or an incentive to a customer, prospect, gatekeeper—anyone the marketing communication program tries to influence. Second, planners should recognize that most consumers don't know the difference between advertising and sales promotion, direct marketing and public relations, and all those other functional activities. Consumers don't talk in terms of receiving a direct-mail promotion or seeing a brand-image advertising campaign. They talk about seeing or hearing or learning something about a brand, product, or company. And in most cases they think in terms of only two things: They receive a message, or they receive an incentive.

The message is something they put away in their heads, generally for later use. The incentive is something they have in their hands and can use right now: a coupon or discount or a key chain—yes, even a T-shirt.

Finally, media planners should forget all those nifty media terms such as "reach" and "frequency" and "gross rating points." Those

are marketer's concepts. Instead, they should look at message delivery from the view of the consumer. When is the message or incentive most relevant to the consumer? Delivering a coupon to me on the reverse side of a magazine article I want to save is not relevant. If marketers want to talk to loyal coffee buyers, probably the best time is when they are making coffee in the morning. That suggests packaging and in-pack premiums and maybe some radio commercials. That's when the consumer is receptive.

How would this kind of message delivery approach work? Quite simple. Start with the consumer, then determine whether to deliver a message or an incentive to get a response. Then decide when and where and under what conditions the message or incentive would be most relevant and when the consumer would be most receptive.

Food for Thought

1. What problems could emerge if a company adopted this approach to media planning?
2. Is the consumer a reliable source for such information?
3. What would be the benefits of such an approach? Explain.

Source: Don E. Schultz, "Integration and the Media: Maybe Your Approach is Wrong," *Marketing News,* June 21, 1993, 15.

CREATING A STRATEGY

The two stages of media planning are (1) creating the media strategy and (2) developing tactics to implement that strategy. The first includes a series of basic discussions about the situation, objectives, and the media strategy. The tactical part of media planning involves detailed directions for implementing the media strategy. The primary components of the entire process are shown in Figure 16.2. We describe the two stages in detail in the sections that follow.

The first stage of media planning, creating the media strategy, begins with a situation analysis and then moves to setting media objectives. Once the objectives are set, planners can outline a strategy that suggests specific activities to achieve objectives. In this section we examine these first steps.

Assess the Situation

Marketing exists in a very dynamic world that requires constant reassessment. Therefore, at the beginning of any planning process, planners need to take a measure of the situation in which the product will be marketed. The situation analysis includes an identification of factors relevant to the media plan, followed by a determination of the relative importance of each. A natural starting point is to address the seven marketing factors discussed in the previous section. Planners also need to assess environmental factors outside the business. Examples include the economic situation, the regulatory situation, and cultural and social factors. For instance, regulations virtually eliminate television advertising in Middle Eastern countries. Finally, the situation analysis should consider the activities of your competition. Virtually all the major computer software manufacturers advertise in the same set of media. Although it may not be strategically sound to copy the media strategy of a competitor, it may be necessary to be located in the same medium so that customers can make comparisons.

A great deal of this situational information may be available through the manufacturing department. In other cases research must be conducted. Once the media planner gathers the pertinent information, the next step is to identify which

STAGE 1: Creating a Strategy

STAGE 2: Choosing Tactics

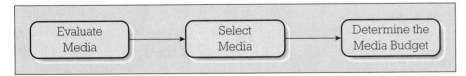

FIGURE 16.2

The Two Stages of the Media Planning Process

situational factors will have the greatest bearing on the media plan. Some companies, for instance, follow the lead of their competitors. In such a case a great deal of effort will be devoted to gathering additional information about their competitors' media plans, including a spending analysis across media categories. Planning for media in foreign countries presents other problems. A media strategist entering the Chinese market quickly realizes that cultural mores and regulations prohibit a host of media alternatives. Billboards cannot be used, for instance, and radio will not carry contest or sweepstakes messages.

Horror stories abound of media planners who did not do their homework. For example, when Honda introduced the Acura Legend, the company assumed the car would appeal to white male executives making over $75,000. The initial media plan emphasized business magazines, direct mail, and early morning television. In fact, the product appealed to a much broader target audience, and Honda had to expand its media plan accordingly. This cost Honda millions of dollars in wasted media placement and wasted time.

Conversely, some agencies have become so paranoid about collecting all relevant information that they risk crossing the line into potentially unethical behavior (see the You Decide feature).

Set Media Objectives

As in any aspect of business, a media plan must begin with specific objectives, given the conclusions drawn from the situation analysis. **Media objectives** are quantifiable statements of what the plan intends to accomplish. Objectives must be specific enough to provide guidance, realistic, measurable, and sufficiently achievable to be practical within the available budget.

Media objectives are determined by the marketing communication objectives, which in turn are dictated by the marketing objectives. Media objectives may be stated implicitly in terms of *reach, frequency, continuity,* and *cost*. They may be explicitly stated in terms of *geographic distribution* and *target audience*. Implicit objectives suggest that these goals are not directly tied to a particular target audience. Explicit objectives indicate a direct connection with the audience.

For example, the marketing objective for American Greeting Cards is as follows: Introduce a new brand to an existing category and establish it as the dominant brand in the category with a 30-percent market share. The resulting media objective might read as follows: Allocate a disproportionate percent of reach and frequency weight in the first 13 weeks of the introductory period to achieve rapid awareness and induce early trial. This assumes that the target audience and geographic dispersion remain the same.

Having introduced the terms "reach," "frequency," "continuity," and "cost" as media objectives, let's turn now to a more thorough discussion of these concepts. Reach and frequency are often discussed together—that is, an objective might set a goal of desired monthly reach and frequency.

Reach and Frequency

Reach is the number of people or households exposed to a particular media vehicle (such as a specific magazine or TV program) or media schedule (the total number of vehicles across a period of time) at least once during a specific time

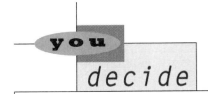

you

decide ### The CIA Is Alive and Well

I help conduct competitive media warfare. My tools aren't firearms or explosives but strategic media ideas. I don't arrange clandestine meetings with operatives, but we conduct our business with the secrecy of the CIA. Our mission: to respond to competing brands' media strategy maneuvers and to maintain and improve our clients' market share.

It's not easy being part of a competitive media "SWAT team." You can't tell anyone about that part of your job, let alone admit that this function exists. But it's a task which is becoming increasingly important in this era of strategic media planning.

In the old days the lowest man on the media department totem pole was assigned the competitive responsibility: How much did our competitor spend? What [TV time slots] and publications did they use? That's nice. Come back again next year and tell us the same thing. The inherent problem with this was that these analyses were not action plans. Brand managers would listen to your findings, smile, say "Thank you," and that's it—nothing more than an information presentation. But today more clients need to know the [strategy underlying the competition's media mix,] as well as the . . . execution. The emphasis a competitor puts on a certain execution tells lots about its marketing strategy. Any drastic or quick changes in a mix can say a lot about what they have in mind.

Here at FCB we have a dedicated group of strategists called the "Chess Team," whose job it is to act as the competitor and "live" two to three moves out in the future. The media department advises the "Chess Team" on media intelligence, weight levels, messaging mix and trends, as well as their strategic implications. . . . We can predict their moves and identify our client's opportunities and vulnerabilities.

Thanks to technology we seem to be moving to a world of real-time competitive monitoring. At FCB, we spend quite a bit of time analyzing competitive data. As technological advances are made, we can only be placed in a stronger position to outmaneuver our competitors.

You Decide

1. Do you feel this type of work is ethical? Is it useful? Explain.
2. What risks do businesses face if they rely on media warfare tactics? What risks do they face if they don't?

Source: Excerpted from Julie Chan, "A View From The Media War Trenches," *Advertising Age,* July 24, 1995, S2.

period (usually weekly or monthly). If *60 Minutes* is seen at least once in a four-week period by six out of ten homes, the reach is 60 percent (6 ÷ 10 = 0.6 or 60%). Although determining reach is complicated when dealing with several media vehicles, a variety of manuals and mathematical techniques exist to make the necessary calculations.

High reach goals are appropriate when the communication goals are very broad or cognitive—for example, if the goal is to achieve consumer attention, awareness, or knowledge. When reach goals are high, media planners need to choose a wide range of media vehicles that minimize the duplication between vehicles and media categories. That is, they should avoid media, such as women's magazines, where the same consumer may read several publications in the same category.

Frequency is the number of times within a given period that a consumer is exposed to a message (usually figured on a weekly and/or monthly basis). If a Reebok ad is given a total of 21 exposures during a one-week period, the total frequency is 21 and the average frequency is 3 (21 ÷ 7 days = 3 exposures per day).

High frequency goals make sense when the marketing communicator aims to change attitudes and behavior. When frequency goals are high, the media plan should provide a great deal of duplication within and between media vehicles and categories. The media strategy then should focus on the continuous use of a group of media categories, subcategories, and vehicles. For example, Healthy Choice frozen dinners are advertised in all the traditional women's magazines, such as *Redbook* and *Woman's Day,* on daytime television, and advertised cooperatively with local supermarkets.

Calculating GRPs. The two measures, reach and frequency, can be combined to reflect the total weight of a media effort. This combined measure is called **gross rating point** (GRP) and is derived by multiplying reach times frequency. All the viewers together are also called **gross impressions.** Say, for instance, that *The Simpsons* has an audience of 250,000 viewers, then each time the marketer uses that program, the value in impressions is 250,000. If Nestlé showed a Nestlé's Crunch candy bar ad four times during a program, the number of gross impressions would be 1,000,000 (250,000 × 4). The term **gross** is used because the planner has made no attempt to calculate how many *different* people view the show. Because rating points are equal to gross impressions, it is easier to use GRPs. To illustrate, assume three 30-second IBM spots were shown each day on *Wheel of Fortune* and the weekly rating was 29.3, the GRP would be as follows:

$$GRP = 29.3 \times (3 \times 7) = 615.3$$

This number is not necessarily good or bad. The experience and judgment of the IBM media planner play a big part in assessing whether 615 GRPs is adequate. Of course, GRPs would be calculated for the total media schedule, not just three 30-second spots. Table 16.1 gives an example of GRP calculations for a total media schedule. Note that without more information we cannot assess whether the total GRP figure of 883 in Table 16.1 is satisfactory.

The media planner must compare this figure with the media plan objectives to judge whether the number exceeds or falls short of the stated media objectives. This may be the least scientific aspect of media planning. In fact, based primarily on experience, media planners often rely on rules-of-thumb to determine minimum GRPs to make an impact in a particular market. For example, Los Angeles may be 5700 GRPs, New Orleans 2200 GRPs, and Gary, Indiana, 680 GRPs.

GRPs include the total audience and do not account for the wasted reach (that is, people seeing the message who are not in the target audience). A better estimate is **target rating points** (TRPs) because it includes only the numbers of people in the primary target audience who are reached by the message, as well as the number of times. This adjustment is a much more accurate reflection of the desired media schedule. Suppose the TRPs that Lennox China & Crystal desires is 1250 (50 percent of the target audience, 25 times). However, to produce a TRP of 1250, a much higher GRP number might be required because several of the media choices would contain waste circulation (people not in the target audience).

Effective Reach and Frequency. Suppose a total media buy or schedule has a GRP of 1100. Does this media buy have more total weight than the example

TABLE 16.1	Ratings × (Reach)	Number of Messages (frequency)	= GRPs
Calculating GRPs			
Television			
E.R.	21	4	84
NYPD Blue	12	2	24
General Hospital	2	1	2
Seinfeld	18	5	90
Friends	19	4	76
Today Show	10	8	80
Evening News	14	12	168
Magazines			
Field and Stream	11	4	44
Time	19	10	190
Playboy	23	3	69
Fortune	28	2	56
Total GRPs			**883**

given in Table 16.1 of a GRP of 883? Yes is the tentative answer, but the specific reach and frequency levels must be appraised relative to one another. Gross rating points do not account for the varying impact of certain exposure levels (reach) combined with certain frequencies. Two measures, *effective frequency* and *effective reach,* try to adjust for these calculations.

Effective frequency is the number of marketing messages needed to affect individuals in the way the marketer desires. That is, what is the number of times the prospect should receive the message to insure the most effective communication? The answer is often a judgment call. Although no one knows exactly what the optimum number of exposures is, three general approaches help solve the problem: linear, decreasing return, and learning curve. We summarize these approaches in Table 16.2.

The **linear approach** suggests that each exposure adds as much purchase probability as the one preceding it. If each exposure produces a purchase probability of 2 percent, then 4 exposures produce an 8 percent probability and 10 exposures produce a 20 percent probability. The linear approach supports greater frequency as being better.

The **decreasing return approach** assumes that the first exposure is the most powerful, and each ensuing exposure is less effective. Advocates of this approach opt for low frequency. The **learning curve approach** suggests that the effectiveness of each exposure increases more than an equal amount up to a certain point and that subsequent exposures add little. Exposure 1 produces a 2 percent

TABLE 16.2

**Approaches for
Determining the
Optimum Number of
Exposures**

Approach	Description	What the Associates Say
Linear	Each exposure is as powerful as the previous one	The more frequency the better
Decreasing returns	First exposure is most powerful; all others are less and less effective	Low frequency is better
Learning curve	Up to a certain point, successive exposures are increasingly more powerful; after that point, the exposures have little power	Search for the optimum frequency

probability, exposure 2 increases the probability to 5 percent, exposure 3 produces 9 percent, and so forth, up to 7 exposures. This approach searches for the optimum number of exposures and does not advocate frequency for its own sake.

When measuring effective frequency, *impact* should also be analyzed. **Impact** is the intrusiveness of the message. That is, was the message actually perceived by the audience? Being in the room with the television on does not mean that the viewer actually sees every ad on the screen. Media planners use several research techniques to tell whether impact has actually taken place.

Effective reach builds on the concept of effective frequency. However, in contrast to effective frequency, which measures *the average number of times a person must be exposed to a message* before communication occurs, **effective reach** measures *the number of prospects who are aware of the message.*

Recall that reach counts the percentage of people who are exposed to the message at least once, and perhaps only once. However, it is not enough to expose an audience to a message once; to insure success, people must be aware of the message. For each marketing communication message, then, there are two reach components: empty reach (those in the audience exposed to a message who still have no awareness of it) and effective reach (those exposed enough times to be aware of the message).

Continuity

One key media plan objective concerns the timing of media messages. Media planners must determine how and when media dollars should be allocated throughout the campaign and plan the timing of the message. Should the message be delivered continuously and uniformly? Or should there be times when no media are purchased and other periods when a large part of the media budget is allocated? Product characteristics, market size, budget, and a number of other considerations determine the answers to these questions. For example, Mattel Inc. might allocate 10 percent of its budget in September, 20 percent in October, 20 percent in November, 40 percent in December, and 10 percent during the rest of the year. These allocations correspond to products that are seasonal, with the peak purchasing time preceding the winter holiday season.

Typically media planners consider three continuity options: continuous, pulsing, and flighting. The continuous pattern is one in which the planner schedules media at the same level throughout the year. Pulsing is media on an erratic schedule, timed to coincide with some factor (for example, a seasonal product). Flighting is a media schedule within a "flight," such as a 13-week period of time. These terms will be discussed in more detail when we consider scheduling later in the chapter.

Cost

Cost considerations represent a final media objective. Media planners usually receive a specific budget and must plan accordingly. They must be aware of factors such as unit costs (for example, the cost of a 30-second television ad on a prime-time network), production costs, available discounts, and the various trade-offs between cost, production quality, size, and location. As a bottom-line cost figure, media planners normally use the **cost per thousand** (CPM) computation, the cost of reaching 1000 people in the medium's audience. The CPM figure allows the planner to compare vehicles within a medium (for example, one magazine with another or one program with another) or to compare vehicles across media (for instance, the CPM of radio compared with that of newspapers). Although the analyses can be done for the total audience, it is more valuable to base it only on the audience segment that has the target characteristics.

To calculate the CPM, two figures are needed: the cost of the **unit** (for example, per page or per 30-second spot) divided by the unduplicated reach:

$$\text{CRP} = \frac{\text{Cost of unit} \times 1000}{\text{Reach}}$$

Some media planners prefer to make cost comparisons on the basis of rating points instead of reach. This is called **cost per rating point** (CPRP), and the calculation is parallel to CPM:

$$\text{CPRP} = \frac{\text{Cost of unit}}{\text{Rating point}}$$

As noted in Table 16.3, CPMs vary tremendously across countries and across mediums. These cost considerations will be discussed further in the section on the media mix.

In conclusion, the media planner can use reach, frequency, continuity, and cost as a basis for expressing goals. In addition, summary measures such as GRP, TRP, and CPM can be produced through these goals in order to make comparisons. For example, a local Ford dealership wants to develop a media plan to support an end-of-the-model-year short-term campaign to rid itself of inventory. The media objectives are to reach a relatively small number of prime prospects as many times as possible, on a daily basis, with a low CPM. Local television and radio would probably achieve these objectives. However, if a manufacturer were introducing a new, nondurable consumer product, and the marketing communication objective was to create a 75 percent level of brand awareness in the target market, the related media goal might be to achieve a high level of reach with moderate frequency levels.

TABLE 16.3

**Ad Costs Vary by
Medium and Country**

Country	TV Peak Time	Radio Peak Time	Newspapers	Magazines
CPMs for adults 15 and older				
France	$ 9.49	$ 7.00	$21.63	$ 5.33
Germany	13.31	2.20	7.41	6.91
Italy	11.62	3.24	5.80	4.89
Japan	4.91	N/A	2.25	4.08
Netherlands	11.68	N/A	4.84	5.04
Spain	7.99	5.39	6.63	4.14
Switzerland	23.72	15.46	9.28	18.64
United Kingdom	6.82	N/A	4.16	4.88
United States	6.66	1.53	11.26	4.91

Sources: Young & Rubicam Europe; Jeff Jensen, "TV is Advertisers' Big Pick in Europe," *Ad Age International*, June 21, 1993, I19.

Design the Media Strategy

Once the determination of the media objectives has been completed, the media planner must next develop a comprehensive strategy that specifies how these objectives will be reached. This detailed document addresses several questions. To whom should the message be targeted? Are there multiple targets? When should the targets receive the message? Does the selected media meet the unique requirements of the strategy? Next we discuss four elements that are part of a comprehensive media strategy: the target audience, dispersion and concentration requirements, qualities the media must have, and the media implications of the message content.

Describe the Target Audience

Although the overall marketing plan describes the target market, this information must be translated into a format for the media plan. Media strategists need information that will allow them to pinpoint the most effective means for delivering the message to the appropriate audience. Whereas creative strategists attempt to understand those for whom they will create marketing communication messages, media strategists make sure that a particular media audience matches the intended target audience. Media strategists want to select media that are most efficient in delivering messages to people who are in the target market and to avoid media that deliver a high proportion of messages to those outside that market.

   Media strategists, then, are interested in information that helps them relate certain consumer characteristics to particular media. They are most concerned about media audience characteristics—especially product buying and usage. To make valid comparisons among media, media planners must have information about the audience characteristics. The two most widely used syndicated research resources for providing this information are published by Simmons Market Research Bureau (called SMRB, or Simmons) and Mediamark Research, Inc. (MRI).

Simmons Market Research Bureau reports the results of an annual probability survey of 19,000 adults and households. This report—called the Study of Media and Markets—spans 43 volumes and provides data on product usage, publication audiences, and multimedia audiences.

Mediamark parallels the information found in Simmons in both product and media volumes. The data are derived from a survey of 20,000 adults and cover more than 450 products. The fundamental difference between MRI and Simmons is one aspect of their research techniques. MRI's technique, **recent reading,** relies on the use of "flash" cards containing magazine logos, which the respondents sort into those magazines they have read recently and those they have not. The results then become the basis of subsequent questioning. Simmons' technique, **through the book,** utilizes stripped-down or skeleton copies of magazines as the basis of its research.

Why is it important that media strategists have useful and comparable data? Suppose a media planner promotes a hot cereal that has two primary target markets—children and senior citizens. The manufacturer decides to deliver the advertising message to senior citizens. The media planner would want to know the characteristics of senior citizens. People in this age category tend to have lower incomes, have no children at home, live a more sedentary lifestyle, and have poorer health. Thus the media planner might identify lifestyle, health, and age characteristics.

This task completed, the media planner must consider which of the many ways of describing consumers is most appropriate to the particular product. A general guideline will help: Limit the number or criteria to no more than three or four. For example, media planners for Clairol hair products might be most interested in demographics such as gender, occupation, income, and age. If more criteria are considered, comparing media across these characteristics becomes almost impossible. The more criteria included in the definition of a consuming group, the fewer the people who will meet all the criteria.

Note that the media planner can set audience objectives only in terms of those audience characteristics that have been measured. Although it would be desirable to collect demographic, psychographic, and product usage data from media sources, typically only demographics are available.

Determine Dispersion Requirements

Many people believe that the primary objective of a media plan is to deliver a message to as many consumers as possible. **Dispersion** refers to a media policy that places the message in as many different programs and spots as possible to avoid duplicating the audience. The request for **maximum dispersion** means that reach has priority over frequency. In this case the media buyer should avoid duplicating programs as much as possible. Using different shows increases the opportunity for different or unduplicated audiences. For instance, a media planner might describe comparable strategies as follows:

- Plan I: Ten nighttime television appearances in a three-month period. This plan guarantees that 60 percent of the national television audience will see the message at least once during the three-month period.

- Plan II: Eight daytime television announcements during a three-month period. This plan guarantees that 50 percent of the television market will see the message at least once.

Because both plans cost the same amount, it appears that Plan I is superior to Plan II, but several other considerations should be examined before making this decision.

First, the coverage should be compared not only in gross impressions but in terms of the specific target audience as well. For example, although Plan II appears inferior, if the target audience is women between the ages of 25 and 44, they are the main recipients of the daytime message in Plan II. Dispersion of messages means dispersion among the target audience, as defined by the marketer.

A second consideration is to specify more clearly what the phrase "at least once" really means in a given situation. Although a certain percentage of the audience will see the message at least once, a percentage of that group will also see it more than once. For example, an advertiser might follow Plan I and purchase a nighttime television scatter plan, which means that 24 messages appear in a variety of programs to achieve maximum dispersion.

The marketing communication message appears in six television programs (PGM) during the three-month period, and the total audience for these six programs is 51.5 million (PGM 1 = 6.3 million, PGM 2 = 9 million, PGM 3 = 4.7 million, PGM 4 = 11.2 million, PGM 5 = 9.4 million, and PGM 6 = 10.9 million). This total figure of 51.5 million is often referred to as **gross impressions**. However, because some of these audience members receive the message more than once, an adjustment must be made to determine how many *new* viewers are actually added by each additional program. That is, even though the first program delivers 6.3 million and the second 9 million, 3.1 million are the same people. After removing this redundancy from all six programs, the actual number of people exposed to the message is 12.8 million. This number is referred to as the **net coverage**. Dividing the total number of homes reached by a media plan by the net coverage of that plan produces the **average frequency of contact.** Average frequency of contact provides media planners with another basis for comparing plans:

Plan I: Average frequency of contact $= 51,500,000 \div 12,800,000 = 4.02$
Plan II: Average frequency of contact $= 43,600,000 \div 16,500,000 = 2.6$

The smaller the number, the better the coverage of the plan. Based on average frequency of contact, Plan II is the better plan.

A third consideration is the distribution of frequency of exposures. Research results indicate that the most effective media plan tends to concentrate message delivery at the middle of the frequency range rather than at the extremes (see Figure 16.3). Rather than achieving one exposure to many people and many exposures to a few people, it would be best for the majority of households to receive two or three advertising exposures, with the balance receiving only one or two. Media planners may wish to make such frequency distribution goals explicit in their media strategy statements so that these goals are included in the criteria established to evaluate alternative plans.

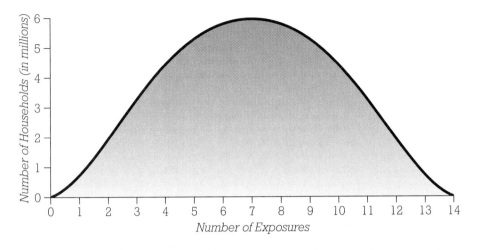

F I G U R E 1 6 . 3

Distribution of Frequency of Exposures

Ideally the majority of households should be subjected to three or more exposures.

Determine Concentration Requirements

Marketers of products such as toys, turkeys, snow skis, and cold remedies face some special problems related to the continuity objective. Marketers must concentrate their message at a particular time of the year or in a particular part of the country. Under these conditions, the media planner must deal with a series of decisions. When should the campaign start? When should it peak? How should the budget be distributed? Can the same campaign be run in various geographic areas? The answers reflect not only traditional spending patterns but also pressures from retailers and the direct sales organization.

Identify Inherent Qualities Required of Media

Many media exert qualitative effects on the messages they carry. The **qualitative media effect** is what the medium does to enhance or depreciate a message after the medium has delivered the message. As an example of this effect, some companies avoided advertising during the evening news at the time of the Gulf War because of the negative association with "bad news." In contrast, the *Washington Post* might enhance the quality of a message because of the high-quality reputation of its editorials.

A media planner may want to place a message anywhere on this qualitative continuum. For example, a media planner might not be concerned with minimizing cost and may have little concern with the quality of the medium. Consider the products advertised in supermarket tabloids. These are often questionable, low-quality products. Consequently, the media planner could place a message about such a product on the sides of abandoned buildings, taxicabs, and matchbook covers. At the other extreme, promoters of high-fashion women's clothing

CREATING A MEDIA STRATEGY

1. The process of media planning begins with a situation analysis. Gathering primary and secondary information and determining which information is pertinent to the media plan are first steps.
2. Media objectives determine direction and control for the media plan and are stated in four ways:
   - Reach: number of people or households exposed to a media vehicle at least once during a specified time period
   - Frequency: number of times within a given period that a consumer is exposed to a message
   - Continuity: the timing of media insertions
   - Cost considerations: several cost factors must be considered
3. The design of the actual media strategy includes the following factors:
   - Describe the target audience
   - Determine dispersion requirements
   - Determine concentration requirements
   - Identify inherent qualities required of media
   - Analyze implications of message content

may feel it is critical that their messages appear in fashion magazines such as *Glamour* and *Vogue*. The perceived quality of these publications by the large target audience should enhance the message.

The important factor is that the interaction between the medium and the message should be complementary. Although Franco-American may wish to sponsor opera and ballet programs, the consumer might have trouble associating the San Francisco Ballet Company with Spaghettios. If media planners cannot derive significant qualitative value by placing a message in a particular medium, they probably should not do so. Perhaps the qualitative goal can be met through some other means than the media strategy.

Analyze Implications of Message Content

A final consideration for the media planner is to match the medium with the message. Creative directors produce specific messages with a variety of factors in mind. We have previously discussed the influence of the product on message content. In turn, the resulting message content has a bearing on the medium selected to deliver it. Messages that carry a great deal of detailed information suggest print over broadcast. Messages with a strong emotional appeal suggest broadcast over print.

The possibility also exists that the medium will be selected first, and the message will be created with television or magazines in mind. By law, cigarette marketers can use only print. Media strategists plan knowing the essence of the message that their media plan will deliver and adjust the plan accordingly.

CHOOSING TACTICS

Once a media strategy is in place, what does a media planner do to implement it? Most of the tactics are carried out by the time and space buyers in the media department of advertising agencies. The process of selecting tactics usually consists of three stages:[2]

1. Evaluate media.
2. Select media.
3. Determine the media budget.

Evaluate Media

A thorough evaluation of all the media relevant to a particular strategy is an important aspect of any media plan. Chapter 15 described the strengths and weaknesses of the various media. And we have already discussed the objective and subjective factors to consider. Collecting the necessary information to appraise these factors may require extensive primary research by the sponsoring firm or its agency. This research is both expensive and time consuming. As a result, many media planners rely heavily on research findings provided by the medium, on experience, and on subjective appraisal.

Every media planner should follow two guiding principles when evaluating media. The first is to realize that the medium simply carries the message; it is not the instrument that accomplishes the final effect. The medium should be evaluated not in terms of whether it will sell the product but in terms of how effectively it will deliver the message.

The second principle is to recognize that the total audience attracted to a particular medium may be much larger than the target audience actually reached. That is, fewer people see a particular marketing message within the newspaper than see the newspaper. Media planners must do the best they can to develop information or estimates of the relation between exposure opportunity and actual exposure. Effective reach is one measure of this process.[3]

Sometimes, as noted in the IMC Concept in Focus feature, technology has made the separation of media types even more complex.

Select Media

Once media planners have considered the media objectives and the qualitative and quantitative characteristics of various media, they must make several important decisions. These decisions can be divided into two general categories: mix decisions and timing decisions.

Before beginning this discussion, it is important to note that these decisions are always restricted by the size of the budget. Budgets are never large enough to accomplish all that the media planner has in mind. The media planner must work within the budget provided, even though the media plan may turn out to be a compromise that may not totally satisfy the established objectives.

The Media Mix

The media planner faces a series of decisions when selecting a medium or combination of media—the **media mix.** Media mix decisions are usually made in conjunction with timing decisions. That is, the scheduling possibilities of a medium such as network television may dictate the need for an additional medium to meet reach and frequency objectives. In this section we examine some of the key questions a media strategist should consider when drawing up the media mix.

Multimedia Clouds the Water

Depending on who you ask, the term "multimedia" can mean almost anything. Multimedia is fairly new to the marketing world, which explains why there is so much confusion surrounding its definition and capabilities. This new technology can combine nearly all the elements of other media and use sophisticated software to display this information on a computer screen. More than that, the program can be made interactive. The user can touch a button and jump to other sections of the program, rewind, fast forward, or pause. With multimedia, you can integrate graphics, photography, animation, type, sound effects, voice, music, video, slides, special effects—almost anything—and weave it into a single interactive program.

The uses of this new technology seem endless. For example, *Mar-* *keting Etcetera* recently crafted a multimedia program touting the merits of Hewlett-Packard ScanJet scanners. The program fit neatly onto two computer diskettes, which were distributed with other information to Hewlett-Packard's resellers. The resellers simply loaded the program onto their computers and let the customized screen saver run to attract consumer attention. By touching any button, the core of the multimedia program would be activated, leading the viewer through the ScanJet's benefits. At certain points, the viewer could choose to skip ahead to other points of interest. Absolutely no computer knowledge was required to interact with the presentation. The users were also given the options of performing an actual scan, simulating a scan, and printing out a list of software they could use with ScanJet.

The entire program is a slick, entertaining presentation incorporating animation, music, graphics, type, and photography.

The interactivity of multimedia makes it ideal for trade shows, sales seminars, point-of-sale solutions, electronic catalogs, product updates—anywhere where computers can tell the sales story. And because a live body doesn't have to be present to walk the viewer through the program, it can expand a firm's sales capability relatively inexpensively.

Food for Thought

1. Can you think of other communication applications for this technology?
2. Are there any risks?

Source: Elizabeth Weisiger, "Multimedia: Shaking Up the Marketing Mix," *A&M Review* (April 1995): 6–8.

Number of Insertions. One key question for media strategists is determining the ideal number of insertions they should use in a particular medium in a given period of time. Armed with this information, media planners should be able to set up usage guidelines for different media and build an estimate of the cost of implementing various media mix plans. Say that the media planner for Subaru determines that the ideal number of insertions during a year for magazines is 550 and the ideal number of TV insertions is 315. Given the rates for each medium, the planner knows the company must spend at least $5 million on print and $12 million on TV to launch a successful campaign.

As noted earlier, there is little agreement and no well-developed general knowledge about how many insertions in a particular medium are ideal. That number is likely to depend on the media objectives, the marketing communication program, and the ability of the message to connect with the audience. For example, if the objective is to reach a large number of people and have them recall the message in the short run, then it would probably be best to concentrate the messages during a 13-to-15-week period, to spread these exposures across a large group of consumers, and to reduce the exposure frequency as time progresses.

Experience and research often guide planners' decisions about the number of insertions given the particular situation. Many sophisticated practitioners have developed their own rules for particular situations through continuous testing in the marketplace, through continuous analysis of sales patterns, or both. Of course, it doesn't matter how many insertions you buy if the message is not on strategy.

Relative Efficiency. Even if media planners have some research knowledge or arbitrary rules for determining patterns of media usage, they still need to know about the relative efficiency of each media type. Is television more efficient for my product or is radio? They will also want to know the efficiency of one media vehicle compared with another. Will an ad in *Sports Illustrated* reach the same objective for a lower cost than an ad placed in *Sports Afield*?

The standard measure of relative efficiency within media is the cost per thousand (CPM) computation explained earlier. Suppose that a media planner wished to reach bank executives 24 to 34 years old and is considering three magazines: *Bankers Magazine, Bank News,* and *Bank Systems & Technology.* The media planner would start by learning the one-page cost (black-and-white or four-color) and enter it into the numerator of the equation. For the sake of illustration, let us assume that the insertion costs for a black-and-white, full-page ad in the three publications are as follows:

Bankers Magazine	$1420
Bank News	930
Bank Systems & Technology	3670

Calculating the denominator of the equation is more difficult. One approach is to use the circulation of each magazine. This information is available and reliable. However, this figure does not reflect actual people, because it includes businesses, libraries, and other institutional subscribers. So the media planner may use some measure of the people reached by the particular vehicle as the denominator. The audience measure employed is contingent on the target audience characteristics specified in the media objectives. This type of information may be available through the medium itself or through private research companies such as Simmons Media Studies. In our example the relevant audience is males, 24 to 34 years of age. Suppose the total audience fitting this description for each magazine is as follows:

Bankers Magazine	9511
Bank News	9279
Bank Systems & Technology	5692

The cost-per-thousand computations for a black-and-white, full-page ad for each magazine are as follows:

$$Bankers\ Magazine = \frac{\$1420}{9511} = \$14.930$$

$$Bank\ News = \frac{\$930}{9279} = \$100.23$$

$$Bank\ Systems\ \&\ Technology = \frac{\$3670}{5692} = \$644.76$$

These values are referred to as the **cost-per-thousand–target market** (CPM-TM) because it includes an audience adjustment. A comparison of three daytime soap operas in terms of CPM-TM is shown in Figure 16.4. Note that the information in Figure 16.4 is sufficient to calculate the **cost per rating point** (CPRP), another indicator used to evaluate media alternatives. With this technique many vehicles can be compared. The only limiting factor is whether the necessary audience information is available.

Comparing the efficiency of different types of media is quite different. The key question is whether the audience data are truly comparable from medium to medium. The answer is usually no, for three reasons. First, the audiences of different media are measured in different ways. For example, A.C. Nielsen measures audiences based on television viewer reports of the programs watched; outdoor audience exposure estimates are based on counts of the number of automotive vehicles that pass particular poster locations. Second, each of these measurements deals with different aspects of consumer involvement. The measurements for an outdoor poster audience assume that every passing automobile contains an attentive passenger. Electronic measurements of national television audiences assume that the set is on and the person is probably in the room, but the measurements do not assume that the viewer is watching the program. Third, comparisons based on audience exposure do not reflect the potential value of the medium, which depends on how well the promoter exploits the medium's ability to attract consumers. The ability to attract cannot be reflected in cost-per-thousand computations.

Despite these limitations, many media planners still resort to the cost-per-thousand computation. Table 16.4 displays other criteria a media planner can employ in comparing media categories.

Effects of Multiple Media. Finally, to select the appropriate media mix, media planners should gauge the pros and cons of using multiple media. Above all, they

No. 1 daytime show "The Young and the Restless" (CBS)	No. 2 daytime show "General Hospital" (ABC)	No. 3 daytime show "All My Children" (ABC)
Rating—8.0	Rating—7.4	Rating—6.5
Cost per 30-second spot—$17,200	Cost per 30-second spot—$19,200	Cost per 30-second spot—$17,800
CPM women, 18 to 49—$6.51	CPM women, 18 to 49—$6.22	CPM women, 18 to 49—$5.70

FIGURE 16.4

A Comparison of Three Daytime Soap Operas

Source: Advertising Age, May 28, 1990, 36. Used with permission.

TABLE 16.4

Some Criteria for Comparing Media

Audience Factors/Data	Television: Network	Spot	Cable	Radio: Network	Spot	Newspapers: National	Local	Supplemental	Magazines: Consumer	Business	Farm	Out-of-home	Direct Mail
Typical adult rating (%)	16	16	2	2	2	14	40	25	20	20	20	60	2+
Reach*	H	M	L	L	L	L	H	H	H	L	L	H	M
Frequency*	M	H	H	H	H	M	M	L	L	L	L	H	L
Selectivity		X	X	X	X			X	X	X	X		X
Seasonal usage				X	X						X		
Controlled circulation										X	X		X
Geographic flexibility		X	X		X		X		X	X	X	X	X
Local coverage		X	X		X		X		X			X	X
Ethnic appeal		X			X		X		X			X	X

*H = high, M = medium, and L = low.

Message Factors/Data	Television: Network	Spot	Cable	Radio: Network	Spot	Newspapers: National	Local	Supplemental	Magazines: Consumer	Business	Farm	Out-of-home	Direct Mail
Typical adult rating (%)	80.0	72.5	62.5	40.0	37.5	35.0	35.0	35.0	52.5	52.5	52.5	47.5	65.0
Vehicle audience weight										X	X	X	
Long message life								X	X	X		X	
Simple message	X	X		X	X								
Emotional appeal	X	X	X	X	X				X	X			X
Immediacy				X	X	X	X						
Control ad placement	X	X	X	X	X							X	X
Editorial association	X		X	X		X	X	X	X	X	X		
Supporting medium		X	X	X	X	X	X	X		X	X	X	X
Good response measures						X	X	X	X	X	X		X
Good ad reproduction								X	X	X	X	X	X

should consider the possible benefit of placing a message once in two media versus twice in the same medium. Some people see no media at all, and others concentrate on one medium to the exclusion of others. Both of these factors suggest greater coverage if media planners use a media mix instead of one medium.

A second benefit of a media mix program is its tendency to even out the frequency of exposure within the total audience. When 12 messages are played on two different media (for example, radio and television), the heavy users of each medium receive a lower, more even dose of the message than they receive when all 12 are played on radio. Finally, a mix of media allows media planners to send slightly different messages to those audience segments that are exposed to several media. An individual listening to the radio version of a message, for example, will pick up on different cues than those in the television version of the message. The person perceives two unique messages even though a large percentage of both messages are identical. Some media companies have tried to make all of this a little easier by selling media packages.

The Timing of Media

The timing of media refers to the actual placement of marketing messages. Timing includes not only the scheduling of promotions but also their size and positions. Timing decisions are dictated by the media objectives. For instance, the media objectives state that the target audience must receive the message at a particular time or with a certain level of impact.

Scheduling. The effectiveness of a media schedule depends in large part on four considerations.[4]

1. *Exposure:* How many exposures are created by the media schedule? As discussed earlier, evaluating this aspect of a media schedule entails counting the number of exposures that can be obtained. In the case of magazines, the number of exposures is the circulation figure converted into a CPM number; for television, the basic unit of counting is the GRP. In addition, this figure should reflect exposure to the advertising rather than to the media vehicle. If there is any reason to believe that readership for some vehicles is higher than for others, the basic CPM figures should be adjusted accordingly.

2. *Segmentation:* Who is exposed and what percentage represents members of the target audience? Delivering a message to people who are not in a target segment has little value. Data to consider in evaluating this aspect of a schedule might include demographics, lifestyle profiles, and product usage. Describing segments in terms of factors such as these allows further adjustment in the CPM and GRP figures.

3. *Media-option source effect:* Does exposure in one vehicle have more impact than exposure in another? The media-option source effect provides three qualitative measures of media alternatives. The first is the **media-class source effect,** which compares different types of media (for example, television ads versus magazine ads). The second qualitative measure, **media-option characteristics,** examines the effect of variations in size (full page or half page), length (30 seconds or 60 seconds), color (black and white or color), and location. Finally, the **vehicle source effect** compares the impact of a single exposure in one vehicle with a single exposure in another vehicle. A Pioneer Stereo ad in *Rolling Stone* might make a greater impact than the same ad in *Time,* even if the audience were the same.

4. *Repetition effect:* What is the relative impact of successive exposures to the same person? Although it may take a minimum number of successive exposures to penetrate the consumer's mind, beyond this point the value of successive expo-

sures is uncertain. The key is to make the correct assumptions about the value of successive exposures. Such assumptions must consider the timing of the exposures (that is, people forget between exposures), differences in appeals, interest level, month, product characteristics, and so on. Some campaigns make a strong impact quickly; others take a long time to create awareness.

Some people conclude that three exposures within a purchase cycle are all that are needed to induce attitudinal or behavioral change.[5] Advertising theorist Herbert Krugman suggests that each of the first three exposures has a different purpose. The first exposure elicits a "what is it?" response. The second exposure continues the evaluation and information-gathering process. The third exposure provides a reminder that the audience member has not acted on the message. Exposures beyond the third simply repeat the process and serve no real benefits.[6] Of course, this rather simplistic explanation does not account for many other considerations.

The media planner sets the schedule after assessing the four considerations of exposure, segmentation, source effect, and repetitious effect. The schedule should specify the time and date of messages in each media vehicle. It should be based on the continuity objectives discussed earlier.

Recall that one of three continuity patterns may be followed, as Figure 16.5 illustrates. The first is **continuous.** This pattern is called for if the audience needs to be exposed to the message constantly because of the nature of the product (that is, it is purchased frequently and regularly) and excessive competition. A continuous pattern also assumes that the media budget is very large.

A second pattern, **flighting,** calls for heavy scheduling during shorter time periods in order to increase reach and frequency in the hopes that these effects will carry over into longer time periods. A media planner may therefore concentrate media buys in a 13-week period rather than over 52 weeks. This strategy allows the media planner to buy media at better rates. Compared with a more diluted schedule, flighting also may create a much better impact on the consumer. This advantage is still debatable because a short-run impact may not carry over through the rest of the year. If impact does not carry over, the entire effort could be wasted. On the other hand, if the company has limited promotional funds, this strategy could be the most effective. Flighting might also prove appropriate for seasonal products whose season fits the 13-week time frame.

A variation of flighting is **pulsing,** which is a combination of continuous advertising and flighting, with continuous advertising "emphasized" during the best sale months. Because this approach tends to minimize waste (that is, delivering messages when the consumer is not in the market), it represents the best of both of these techniques. Not all marketers should use pulsing, however. It best fits products that are sold year-round but that have heavy sales at intermittent periods such as stationery products, hot dogs, beer, and linens and towels (often featured as white sales).

Size and Position. Timing of the media effort also involves determining the size and position of a particular message within a medium. Although a great deal of research has been conducted in this area, the results are not conclusive.

CONTINUOUS

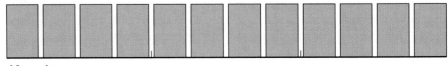

12 weeks
100 GRPs/week

FLIGHTING

4 weeks   *4 weeks*   *4 weeks*
150 GRPs/week   150 GRPs/week

PULSING

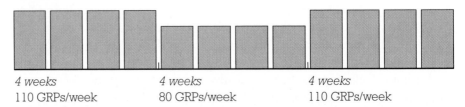

4 weeks   *4 weeks*   *4 weeks*
110 GRPs/week   80 GRPs/week   110 GRPs/week

FIGURE 16.5

The Three Scheduling Alternatives

We do know that simply doubling the size of an ad does not double its effectiveness. Although a larger promotion creates a higher level of attraction and greater opportunity for creative impact, the extent is still undetermined. Equivocal results have been reported for print media of various sizes and for television and radio commercials of various lengths. Depending on what advertisers have to say and how well they can say it, a 30-second commercial may do the job much better than a 60-second commercial. Bigger or longer may not always be better. Still, the media planner must consider the possible positive effects. The size or length chosen should also be related to the objectives.

Guidelines regarding positioning are only slightly more enlightening. In general, there is some evidence to suggest that within a print medium (1) the inside cover and first few pages get a slightly better readership, (2) placement of compatible stories adjacent to an ad may enhance its effect, and (3) having many competing ads on the same page detracts from effectiveness. Findings related to broadcast media are almost nonexistent.

Determine the Media Budget

How much to spend on media is a strategic decision. It depends on sales potential, objectives, and affordability. The IMC budget must be viewed as a function of the marketing of the brand or company. It is not possible to reconcile ambitious marketing goals with a modest budget. Conversely, it makes no financial sense to have an ambitious budget if the marketing goals are modest. A comprehensive discussion of budgeting is given in Chapter 17. In most instances, because media represent 80 percent of that budget, they are carefully considered.

The media planner's role in this decision making can vary greatly. When top management gives the total dollar amount to the media planner, the media planner's control tends to be limited, especially when management gives the media planner a dollar figure that is insufficient to implement the media strategy. Ideally the media planner is allowed to gather and present media cost information to management, which is considered part of the budget determination process. This information includes marketing communication expenditures by the competition, the cost of media, and the audience delivery affordable at given budget levels. Table 16.5 shows an example of a media budget.

Media planners must cope with several timing problems related to the budget. They cannot always abide by the budgetary schedule used by the rest of the business, which often begins on January 1 or July 1. Due to product seasonality, media availability, and several other factors, media budgets can start or end on any date.

Another timing issue has to do with lead time. Media planners often have to move quickly to make media buys. Corporate executives may take weeks or months to evaluate and approve budgets, so it's best if the company gives the media planner some flexibility to make quick budget decisions.

A final issue related to timing is rooted in the dynamic nature of media planning. Media buying has often been compared with buying and selling stocks. Every day media buyers negotiate with hundreds of media about such factors as rates and special discounts. Media representatives are constantly putting together media packages and desperately trying to sell unsold space or time in minute-by-minute contact with media planners. Media buyers without adequate budgets or contingency funds are unable to engage in this negotiation process and may wind up spending millions of extra dollars on media. Again, flexibility is a crucial tool for managing the media budget.

CHOOSING TACTICS

Three tactical decision areas are associated with the media plan:

1. Evaluation of how media will facilitate the delivery of the message and what the actual exposure of a particular medium will be
2. Media selection, which is based on the following:
   - The media mix—determining which media work best together
   - The timing of media—entailing scheduling and selecting size and position
3. The media budget

TABLE 16.5				

**A Media Budget for
Luxury Automobiles**

**Brand Report No. 170
Luxury-Car Expenditures
January–December 1989**

	Media Total	BAR Network Television	BAR Spot Television	BAR Cable Television
Cadillac DeVille/Fleetwood	$14,780.9	$10,371.5	$259.6	$330.6
Lincoln Town Car	13,592.8	6,303.6	2,484.7	246.3
Buick Electra	6,666.2	1,935.9	144.8	86.5
Acura Legend	47,916.7	23,647.5	7,409.5	1,306.8
Lincoln Continental	6,131.4	1,128.1	754.4	—
Volvo 740	5,853.6	—	186.4	202.5
Cadillac Brougham	2,697.8	912.5	73.5	4.7
BMW 3 Series	14,944.5	2,909.9	4,345.3	458.9
Cadillac Eldorado	1,562.8	1,100.2	141.5	46.2

Note: Figures are in millions of dollars.

BAR   Arbitron's Broadcast Advertiser's Report
LNA   Leading National Advertisers
RER   Radio Expenditure Reports
MR   Media Records

Source: Marketing & Media Decisions (May 1990): 87. Used with permission.

COMPUTER TECHNOLOGY AND MEDIA PLANNING

Undoubtedly, computer technology has simplified media planners' jobs in some ways. However, several issues limit practitioners' use of technology. First, there is no satisfactory way to compare several media simultaneously because each medium differs in its costs, ratings, size, and so forth.

For instance, media space and time offer quantity discounts, but these discounts

Brand Report No. 170
Luxury-Car Expenditures
January–December 1989

BAR Syndicated Television	RGR Spot Radio	LNA Magazines	MR Newspapers	LNA Sunday Magazines	LNA Outdoor	BAR Network Radio
—	$54.2	$3,384.3	$334.5	$48.2	—	—
$9.4	154.5	4,322.5	—	—	$69.5	—
—	42.2	—	188.0	—	—	$714.4
—	1,921.9	12,978.7	652.3	—	—	—
576.4	—	2,907.5	706.5	—	—	—
—	—	5,096.6	366.1	—	—	—
—	—	1,472.7	234.4	—	—	—
—	—	5,552.5	2,725.6	62.7	—	—
—	—	292.0	52.2	—	—	—

may not be comparable. Similarly, the value a particular medium can deliver varies with the time and place. For example, the value of network television is much greater when programs are being shown for the first time (as compared with the rerun period of the summer, when television viewing goes way down). Finally, the value delivered by a particular medium also depends on the media objectives. A software manufacturer specializing in banking might have a high-reach objective and value a magazine such as *Bank Systems & Technology* over *Business Week*.

Another issue is that creating the best media schedule requires some judgment about how to combine all the elements—including message form, placement in time, and media vehicles—to produce the greatest effect. Ultimately, designing a media schedule is more art than science.

Because of these issues and others, practitioners have limited their acceptance of computer technology. Steve Farella, executive vice president and director of corporate media services at Wells Rich Greene advertising, explains: "There are some departments that see [the computer] as a very integral part of the media planning process. We don't do that. . . . We still think that media thinking can be done independent of the machine."[7] In fact, many practitioners have developed a good deal of specific knowledge about how media work for their products, services, or institutions on the basis of market testing. Other practitioners have reached conclusions about how best to use media based on their own extensive experience. Many practitioners readily accept the results of their own experience over the results produced by management scientists.

Still, there is a definite trend toward technology. Computerization has brought about many improvements and made things available that were not even possible before in media buying. For example, merely a dozen years ago it was not unusual for a buyer to spend a day or more manually rating the programs that the television stations offered. Today these estimates can be made in seconds.

There have been four main lines of development: retrieval and estimation models, optimization models, simulation models, and media buying models. All four suggest that students interested in media as a career must be proficient in a broad range of computer software.

Retrieval and Estimation Models

The computer allows vast amounts of data to be stored and retrieved in a meaningful format. Companies collect a great deal of information about their customers. They can also purchase data about consumer characteristics, behaviors, and lifestyles. Some computer programs can combine this data, along with media usage data, to create alternative media schedules or campaigns and compute the relevant cost per thousands. These computer models can also estimate the potential reach for individual media or for various media combinations. Virtually all the syndicated research firms, including MRI and SMRB, make data available in computerized forms, which can then be combined with other software to create a media schedule.

Optimization Models

Optimization models attempt to modify data on audience characteristics, measures of reach and frequency (in order to eliminate problems or irrelevant relationships), and so forth. The modified data can then be compared and the best plan selected. It is impossible for research to produce "perfect" information; its purpose is to produce better information than was previously available.

Simulation Models

These models compare media plans by simulating their effects on typical consumer behavior such as purchase, store visits, coupon redemption, and information requests. The models allow media planners to compare many plans without committing to an actual plan. The models can even specify particular market segments and make comparisons for each.

Simulation models cannot eliminate the difficulty of comparing media. Selecting the appropriate consumer characteristics is not easy. Nor does this technique account for the impact of multiple combinations of media or the deterioration of media effect.

Media Buying Models

The actual processing of media buys, along with invoicing, remains one of the most archaic dimensions of media planning. However, the barriers to efficient media buying are not technological. They are human. Media sales reps want to keep their jobs, users are reluctant to give up a paper trail of transactions, and companies do not want to foot the bill for developing the standards necessary for interchanging data electronically. There are a few breakthroughs, however.

With Media Management Plus, for example, agencies can explore "what if" scenarios with narrow audience segments, giving them as much if not more information than their reps have. Agencies can also do post-buy analyses and line-by-line comparisons of orders and affidavits. With this system, Pizza Hut monitors its 26 regional agencies buying in 160 television markets.

Another product that links buyer and seller is Hot-Net, a system sold by Info-Edge. Hot-Net lists avails and last-minute inventory. It also makes electronic mail possible through CompuServe, a public bulletin board and data exchange service.[8]

Few people would disagree that computers are playing an increasingly important role in the media planning process. The use of computers saves time and frees the planner from a great deal of lengthy computations and routine paperwork that were formerly required. Some experts, however, are concerned about the possibility that planners could develop a blind acceptance of computerized data to such an extent that it could lessen the amount of judgment that goes into planning. These experts point out that no matter how valid formula models are, they do not justify uncritical acceptance of the data without being modified by experience and judgment.

Concept ✓ **Review**

COMPUTER TECHNOLOGY AND MEDIA PLANNING

Several types of computer technology can aid media planners.

1. Retrieval and estimation models collect vast amounts of audience and media data, combine them into alternative media schedules, and estimate the effectiveness and cost of each.
2. Optimization models provide a systematic way of selecting and modifying media-related information.
3. Simulation models allow the testing of various media strategies without committing actual resources.
4. Media buying models can make the specific media purchases, accounting for all possible contingencies.

profile

Lisa Fleischman
Media Planner and Buyer
Karsh & Hagan Advertising

Academic Background and Career Track

I graduated from the University of Colorado at Boulder in May of 1992 with a communications degree. When I graduated from college, I didn't know much about advertising, but I was fortunate to find a three-month internship at a local agency, Karsh & Hagan. I then secured a full-time position as a media coordinator with the Thomas & Perkins advertising agency in Denver. I was in this position for $1\frac{1}{2}$ years, during which I was responsible for checking media invoices, billing clients, and assisting all the media planner/buyers. This was my first real exposure to media.

I then moved to Karsh & Hagan to advance my career. This change greatly increased my responsibilities. For the next year I was an assistant media planner/buyer. That experience helped me learn

more about the different types of media. I did some print buying in Denver and broadcast buying for small markets (Colorado Springs, Grand Junction, and others). I began to realize how rapidly the markets changed, and how much there is to learn in the media field. The more I learned, the easier it was for me to advance. Over the course of the year, I became familiar with national magazine buying for one of our clients. That experience eventually led to a promotion, my current job.

I worked very closely with our media director on several accounts, and my work was soon highly visible. My role and duties continue to expand. I am currently involved in national and local accounts that use print and broadcast media. I work on five different accounts, some of which I am the only media contact and others where there are multiple planners and buyers.

A CLOSING THOUGHT: KEEPING MEDIA UNDER ONE ROOF

Media is a different colored "horse" than it was a few years ago. Once only accountable for a "low cost per thousand," media buyers are now required to run faster, jump higher, and get more "bang for the buck." Moreover, media planners must cope with new media forms that spring up almost daily and contribute to growing clutter. Some sources estimate that a person may now see as many as 2000 advertising impressions per day.

How can a media planner become an expert on all these choices? In fact, the solution appears to be absorbing special media areas (such as direct mail, telemarketing, and online) under one roof. The full-service agency now includes a full range of media specialists as well. This phenomenon is referred to as "splintering." Perhaps as a result of splintering, the most important question media buyers will address in the future will be "What percentage of the marketing communication dollar should be allocated to mass versus target marketing (and how should this ratio change as a product matures)?"

Typical Day

My typical day is nothing like most people expect it to be. Advertising is usually not the glamorous life that we see on television. I usually get to work by 7:30 A.M., so that I am caught up before other people arrive and the phone starts ringing. I try to decide every day whether I am going to answer my phone or not, because answering the phone and returning calls can be an all-day project. I receive an average of 40–50 calls per day.

Most of our clients have different fiscal years, which usually determine when the busiest times of the year are. Planning is extremely busy because of the different stages that we must go through to get the annual plan approved. Once the approval is finalized, the execution begins. This usually includes weekly status meetings with the agency to make sure that everything is going as planned. No matter what type of media is included, there is always maintenance to be handled after the plan is implemented. All of our print ads must be checked to see that the materials are reproduced to an acceptable quality, and all our broadcast invoices must be checked to see that the spots ran as they were ordered.

Although my days are usually planned perfectly, there are times that meetings run late or are scheduled at the last minute. In these situations you have to be able to change your schedule immediately. Throughout the day there are always emergencies that come up, such as publications not receiving ad materials on time, radio or television stations running the wrong spot, or clients calling directly (rather than going through their account executive).

I'd like to think that coming into the office early would allow me to leave on time, but that is not the case. My day usually wraps up around 6:30–7:00 P.M. I find that in a typical day I get the most accomplished between 7:30 and 8:30 A.M. and between 5:00 and 7:00 P.M.

Advice

The career advice that I would give to anyone starting a media or marketing communication career is to be patient. Take the time to observe your supervisors because their experience is the best learning tool available. You truly have to love your work to succeed because it is a very stressful, demanding career. Also, remember that the marketing communication community is very small—try not to burn any bridges.

At the same time that media is splintering, there is also a trend toward media moguls. Walt Disney Company's merger with Capital Cities/ABC is a prime example. To assess how well of this media giant could reach its key demographic (adults, ages 25 to 54, with kids), DDB Needham Worldwide—using its media planning software program Personal Media Mapping Process, data from A.C. Nielsen Co., Media Research, Inc., and proprietary agency studies—determined that 86 percent of this demographic can be reached in a six-month period. This figure means that Disney (and other media giants) can offer a powerful media mix package, with all the appropriate supportive data, to prospective clients. Although this may make media planning and buying more efficient, there is also a risk that such strong competitors will eliminate legitimate media choices.

At risk, as a result of these mergers, may be the independent media buying services. Rather than allowing the advertising agency to handle the media buying, independents offer advertisers significant cost benefits if they provide that service rather than the agency. However, agencies have fought back, and independents are looking for ways to compete other than price. Many are moving into strategic planning. Media giants may negate the limited advantages offered through independents.

This leads to another important media question. Is a global media buy possible? In addition to the difference in culture, laws, and availability that make global media planning very difficult, the prospect of a global media buy appears unlikely. The biggest impediment to global media buying deals is the lack of centralized client control. Most clients are decentralized by continent or by country. As a result, no one person has the authority to combine budgets across countries.

Finally, the most important question many media planners will address is how, given the tremendous growth in media choices, an integrated media plan will be possible. Rather than coordinating five or six major media alternatives, today's media planner is faced with hundreds of choices. Undoubtedly this task represents one of the more serious roadblocks to accepting IMC. It will mean that biases are eliminated and media planners will have to start with the target audience—their communication needs and wants.

SUMMARY

1. Explain how marketing communication and media interface.
Finding aperture, the optimum point in time and place to reach the target audience, is the primary purpose of media planning and buying. If this is not done correctly, all the other marketing communication tasks performed will be diminished or doomed to failure.

2. Describe the procedure for producing a media strategy.
The media plan is a blueprint that maps out the best way to send the marketing communication message to the target audience. It is dependent on the marketing communication plan and the creative plan. There are several issues that influence the media plan: marketing objectives, the product, product profitability, the channels of distribution, the integrated marketing communication mix, resource limitations, and the target audience. The

media planning process includes a set of strategic considerations—situation assessment, media objectives, and strategy.

3. Discuss the tactics that are part of a media strategy.
The media planning process includes several tactical considerations—how to evaluate, select, and budget for media. Each one of these tasks has many subactivities that are crucial to implementation.

4. Explain how computer technology affects media planning.
Computer technology has evolved to assist in all facets of media planning and buying. Despite the technological advances, experience and judgment are still the most important factors in the media planning process.

POINTS TO PONDER

Review the Facts
1. Describe the two levels of a media plan.
2. Define reach, frequency, continuity, and waste circulation.
3. Define what is meant by effective reach and effective frequency.

Master the Concepts
4. What are some problems that a media planner may encounter when executing the media strategy?
5. Explain the concept of gross rating points and demonstrate how it is derived.
6. How many repetitions are enough? Explain.

Apply Your Knowledge
7. Assume that you are on a committee to choose the best media plan from several alternatives. The other members favor Plan A because it reaches more people at least once at approximately the same cost as the other plan. What might you say to convince them that a judgment based on that criterion alone is erroneous?
8. How would you evaluate whether reach, frequency, or continuity is the appropriate media strategy?
9. Many practitioners rely on media-supplied information, experience, and their own subjective appraisal to evaluate media. Can you explain why more objective considerations are not used?
10. Perform the following calculations:
    a) Calculate the GRPs for a daily soap opera with a weekly rating of 3.8 for three 30-second spots that are run during the program five days a week. How would you evaluate this number?
    b) Now calculate the CPM for this show. How does the resulting figure help your media planning process?

SUGGESTED PROJECTS

1. (Oral Communication) Contact a local business, interview the people involved in media planning, and devise a one-year media schedule for the business.

2. (Writing Project) Survey the media department of five advertising agencies. Ask them about their use of computers in media planning. Write a report on your findings.

3. (Internet Project) Suppose you were the media planner for a compact disc producer that markets alternative rock bands from Central Europe. Market research indicates that your target audience (men and women aged 18–27) spends approximately 5–7 hours per week on the Internet. You want to investigate whether buying advertising space on the Web will fit your marketing communication budget. For background information, you may want to investigate the AdSpace Locator at the Web site for Jupiter Communications Webtrack Information Services (www.jup.com/webtrack).

That service helps media planners select the appropriate Web advertising vehicle.

Visit three sites at which you think your company might want to advertise. Find out the advertising rates and other information that your marketing communication director might wish to know before authorizing the media buy. For instance, at Netscape, advertising space costs vary (as do CPMs) depending on where a company's ad appears. Some suggested sites include:

Netscape	www.netscape.com
Excite	www.excite.com
HotBot	www.hotbot.com
CD Club Web Server	www.hirschhorn.com/cdclubs

Compile your findings in a memo to your marketing communication director. Be sure to make recommendations about where you think the company should advertise and why.

CASE 16: CRAYOLA ON THE COMEBACK TRAIL

Background

What do you do when your chief product seems to be at the end of its product life cycle, when your customers have turned to newer, more modern substitutes, and when your brand name seems destined to evoke feelings of nostalgia rather than excitement? Some companies let the product die and try to succeed with new and different ones. Others rethink their approach and try to broaden their appeal.

That's what Binney & Smith, makers of Crayola crayons, decided to do in 1990. The company had done well for years by selling its products to parents. Parents bought crayons because they viewed them (and the company promoted them) as an educational tool and because the parents remembered what fun crayons were when they were kids. But our culture changes so fast that today's kids often have no use for toys that delighted their parents. And though parents still make most of the buying decisions for their kids' toys, children today have both more spending power and more influence over their parents' spending than did previous generations.

Targeting Different Markets

So now Crayola is marketing its product to both children and parents. Its first ad aimed directly at kids was called "Crayola Rock 'n Rolls." Borrowing its approach from MTV, the commercial used rock music, eye-catching colors, and hip kids and was aired at times when young kids were most likely to be watching TV.

At the same time, the company began a new campaign aimed at parents. The slogan emphasized nostalgia, trying to elicit fond memories of the parents' own early years: "Crayola. Childhood isn't childhood without it." But the copy, running in parents' and women's magazines, stressed how little effort crayons require from parents, allowing children to play independently.

With the two ends of the age spectrum covered, Crayola also reached for the middle. It now makes ColorWorks—colored pens, pencils, and erasable crayon sticks, all aimed at a teenage audience. Traditionally, kids gave up crayons at about the age of 7, but Crayola is hoping that teens will decide that coloring can be cool and will make posters with their Color-Works pens.

Color Change Controversy

The company's most controversial move was to change colors for the first time in 32 years. A survey showed that kids, no doubt influenced by the popularity of loud, artificial colors in the culture at large, wanted brighter colors. So Crayola replaced eight of the older, subtler colors with more brilliant, eye-opening shades. The response was similar to that which greeted the production of New Coke. Many parents were outraged at the loss of their favorite colors, even though their kids preferred the new ones. So attached were Americans to their favorite colors that protest groups were formed, including the RUMPS (Raw Umber and Maize Preservation Society) and the national campaign to save Lemon Yellow. So Crayola, taking its cue from Coca-Cola, reintroduced its classic colors, pleasing everyone and basking in the free publicity.

It's too soon to tell how well crayons can survive in a world of Nintendo and Sony Play Station, but by rethinking its audience and developing a varied media campaign, Binney & Smith has given its most important product a fighting chance.

Case Questions

1. Given the information provided in this case, outline the strategic and tactical considerations to evaluate in developing Crayola's media plan.
2. What other media alternatives might have worked for Crayola?

Sources: Crayola Web site (May 6, 1996): Internet (Crayola.com.80/trivia/triviasheet); Cara Applebaum, "Bright Ideas for Crayola Ads," *Adweek*, September 10, 1990, 64.

ROMA'S LITE INTEGRATED CASE QUESTIONS

(Review the Roma's Lite Marketing Plan in the Appendix at the end of the text before answering these questions.)

1. Discuss the pros and cons of the possible media objectives for this product.

2. What situational criteria should be considered as part of media planning?

3. (Team Project) Based on the process provided in this chapter, develop a complete media plan for Roma's Lite Pizza.

Carson Pirie Scott & Co. Adds TV to Its Media Mix

Television advertising has rarely been the choice of fashion-oriented retailers. The conventional wisdom about displaying merchandise and generating store traffic from the downtown shopping corridors to the megamalls has been to rely on the newspapers, freestanding circulars, or glossy magazines. However, in early 1996 this approach changed somewhat when Carson Pirie Scott & Co. contracted with the Television Bureau of Advertising (TVB) to test the effectiveness of television advertising with its customers. The TVB offers free marketing consultation to companies interested in using broadcast TV advertising.

As a member of TVB's Television Retail Advisory Committee (TRAC)—a committee comprised of retail, agency, and television-station executives formed to strengthen the relationships between the industries—Ed Carroll Jr., Executive Vice-President for Sales Promotion and Marketing for Carson Pirie Scott & Co., was aware of past successes with TVB's television impact studies. The retailer determines impact study goals. TVB then designs a study to measure whether the goals are achieved.

After emerging from Chapter 11 in 1994, Carson Pirie Scott & Co. felt that the time was right to reestablish its image with customers and build customer loyalty. Its objective was to make their store a destination for something other than price. Carson felt that it was an excellent opportunity to measure the effectiveness of television and partnered with TVB to conduct such a test. Mr. Carroll was aware of the need to create a partnership with TV broadcasters that could not only solve the problems at hand but could also blossom into an ongoing relationship in the key markets where Carson does business. Over time he hoped to provide print-oriented retail merchants with the informa-

tion and tactics needed to use TV advertising to its best advantage.

By selecting September for the test campaign, the store capitalized on the "back-to-work" attitudes of their key markets, Chicago and Milwaukee. TVB organized member stations in both markets to assist in executing the TV ad campaign and the pre- and post-awareness studies. Member stations WBBM, WGN, WISN, WITI, WLS, WMAQ, and WTMJ funded the test. A decision was made to concentrate on a category of merchandise for one week at a time to test TV's imaging-making and traffic-building capabilities. Each week Carson aired 300 target rating points (TRPs) in Chicago and in Milwaukee.

TVB also formed a partnership with Laughlin/Constable, Carson's advertising agency, to understand and achieve the store's objectives. In this case the agency, the client, and the broadcasters shifted the conventional adversarial paradigm. They worked as partners focused on designing a fair and reasonable test that could obtain the desired results. The objectives were stated as follows.

- To increase the percentage of customers who believe Carson offers a superior shopping experience.
- To increase sales revenue for Men's Better Sportswear, Misses' Better Sportswear, and Petites with profitable margins.

Beta Research Corporation, a leading marketing research company, was hired to establish baseline awareness and to measure the effects of advertising. They conducted 200 pre- and 200 post-commercial random-dial phone surveys in each market.

The perceptual research results of this partnership were positive. Awareness of ads for business attire on TV increased. More importantly, consumers' intention to shop at Carson stores for business attire increased while scores for key competitors dropped. TV advertising improved consumers' perception of Carson stores as classy (+8%), sophisticated (+9%), and suitable for well-dressed professionals (+4%).

Best of all, by applying TV advertising to the media mix, Carson saw a huge increase in business. For Men's Better Sportswear, sales increased 35 percent in Chicago and 92 percent in Milwaukee. Misses' Better Sportswear sales jumped 40 percent in Chicago and 45 percent in Milwaukee. Petites' sales skyrocketed 122 percent in both markets. These increases were much stronger than other markets that had print-only programs.

Discussion Questions

1. Assess the extent to which these test results are valid. Are there alternative explanations for the increases?

2. What does the expanding cable network system offer a retailer like Carson Pirie Scott & Co.?

3. What risks would Carson Pirie Scott & Co. assume if they committed to cable TV?

4. If you were the media planner for a Carson Pirie Scott & Co. competitor, what types of media would you include in your media plan? Why? Would the size of your media budget affect your choice of media? Explain.

Video Source: "Niche TV Channels and Advertising," *Wall Street Journal Report (TV),* 13 July 1996. *Additional Sources:* "The Carson Pirie Scott & Co. TV Impact Study," *Adweek,* 2 June 1997, vol. XLVII, no. 22, 18–19; "Cable Inching Ever Closer to Parity," *TV Upfront,* 2 June 1997, 10–11; Junu Bryan Kim, "Cable Creating Another Niche," *Advertising Age,* 13 June 1996, S-14, S-15; Laurel Wentz, "Stay Tuned for the Future of TV," *Ad Age International,* March 1997, 13; David Leonhardt, "Bright Lights, Big Stores," *Business Week,* 17 March 1997, 43; Edward T. Pasternack, "Retail Advertising Effectiveness," *Direct Marketing,* May 1996, 36–38.

part five

IMC APPROPRIATION, EVALUATION, AND CAMPAIGN PLANNING

chapter 17

Developing the IMC Appropriation

Planning for Marketing Communication and Budgeting

- Preliminary Considerations
- Assessing the Situation
- Sales and Cost Forecasts
- Setting Objectives
- Strategic Decisions

Determining Appropriations for Advertising

- Predetermined Budgetary Methods
- Strategy-Based Budgeting Approaches

Determining Appropriations for Other Forms of Marketing Communication

- Sales Promotion Budgeting
- Public Relations Budgeting
- Direct-Marketing Budgeting
- Personal Selling Budgeting

Marketing Analysis: The Budgetary Ideal

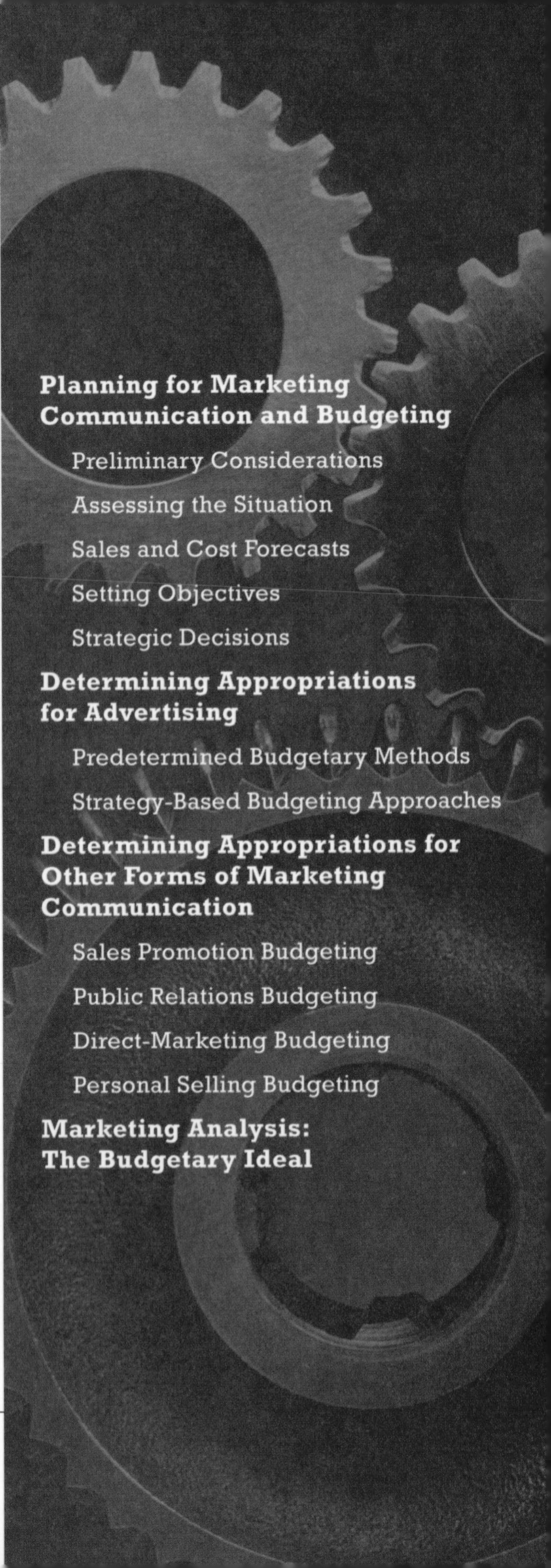

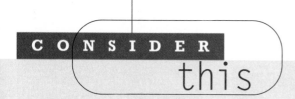

CONSIDER this

Raving About the RAV4

The RAV4 is one of the hottest sport utility vehicles (SUVs) to hit the U.S. market in recent years. Since Toyota launched the RAV4, it has earned numerous awards (including *Automobile Magazine*'s 1997 Automobile of the Year) and its sales have exceeded expectations. The vehicle has been successful thanks to the combination of a unique product and a carefully executed marketing communication plan backed by sufficient appropriation.

First, the RAV4's design is more carlike than trucklike. Using a body frame similar to that of a Camry, the vehicle offers the versatility of an SUV without sacrificing comfort, safety, or style. Second, it was the first SUV priced under $20,000. Third, the product had been launched successfully in Japan and Europe, so Toyota knew that consumers liked its product. Finally, although it would be natural to target Generation X, Toyota's marketing research showed that a broad range of people were potential RAV4 buyers—from people looking to buy their first car to sports enthusiasts to older consumers looking for a second vehicle. To reach this target market, the creative concept of the campaign ("It's Out

There") was purposefully broad. The tagline for initial print and television ads—"Dream Your Own Dream"—built on this broad theme.

To determine the dollar amount allocated for the RAV4 campaign, Toyota had to look at the objectives of its IMC plan, analyze the competition and other situational factors, and consider the tasks required to implement the IMC objectives. The twin marketing communication goals were to develop name recognition and to communicate the vehicle's features. The competitive analysis was tough because there was no comparable vehicle on the market. The RAV4 team looked at sport utility vehicles, entry-level cars, and cars that families might choose as a second vehicle. The team also considered how much competitors spent on comparable launch budgets. (Some spent as much as $40 to $60 million.)

The RAV4 marketing communication team also considered three key internal factors. First, Toyota launched a new version of the 4Runner about a month before the RAV4 launch. To ensure that proper resources were allocated to both launches, the RAV4 and 4Runner launches were closely coordinated and timed. Second,

553

after considering the market and the product, Toyota targeted first-year sales of 30,000 vehicles. Third, Toyota examined the cost savings it could realize by taking an IMC approach. For instance, the footage used for the television ads was also used in dealers' point-of-sales displays. Artwork for the print ads was used in sales brochures, and so on. This approach resulted in substantial savings.

Once the goals were set and the marketing situation analyzed, the RAV4 team examined all the tasks needed to implement the marketing communication plan. To meet the goals, the team developed a marketing communication mix that reached market segments in the most efficient manner. The mix included TV and print advertising, direct marketing to select Toyota owners, Internet advertising, press kits, sales brochures and CD-Roms, point-of-purchase dealer materials, outdoor advertising, and event marketing. To create initial name recognition, the team planned a heavy national TV advertising blitz for a three-week period, then a more balanced mix between advertising and other marketing communication tools, and finally another big push on national TV.

The Toyota team then asked its outside agency, Saatchi & Saatchi Pacific, to obtain price estimates for implementing its IMC plan. Saatchi's specialists relied on the marketing communication task list, targeted sales volume, and the media plan to set a preliminary budget. Once Toyota approved the estimated budget, the marketing communication plan was put into action.

How did the RAV4 do in the United States? It has been one of the most successful product launches in Toyota's history. Actual sales were 50 percent higher than forecasted, a tremendous feat for a brand-new product.

Sources: Interview with Mr. Irving A. Miller, Vice President of Sales and Dealer Development, Toyota Motor Sales U.S.A., Inc., Lexus Division, 11 July 1997; Interview with Mr. Ian Beavis, formerly Group Account Director of Saatchi & Saatchi Pacific, 29 January 1997.

CHAPTER OVERVIEW

The Toyota RAV4 situation suggests that allocating dollars to any business strategy, especially marketing communication, is a combination of careful analysis, experience, and luck. Toyota will never know whether the dollar amount it selected was just enough, too much, or too little. Toyota does know, however, that the RAV4 was a success.

Many company executives still want assurance that marketing communication expenditures will improve the firm's bottom line. Even with these assurances, the most experienced and sophisticated executives are never sure whether they have allocated the right amount to marketing communication. Some marketing communication managers' solution? Ask for twice as much as your budget requires and hope that you will get half. Although all the major players may play this budgeting game, such an approach is certainly not strategically sound.

In this chapter we investigate the planning process for marketing communication *appropriation* and *budgeting*. An **appropriation** is the maximum amount of dollars that management allocates to a specific purpose. In contrast, a **budget** is the nuts-and-bolts details of how this sum of money will be used. Usually the marketing communication manager asks for an appropriation and creates a related budget that reflects the marketing communication strategy.

Often the marketing director gives the marketing communication manager an appropriation amount and then the manager allocates these monies. Ideally the manager's allocation takes an integrated approach. That way, opportunities for saving money or producing more from the same amount would be more likely to occur. Unfortunately this integration rarely happens and budgeting tends to be done for each communication tool independent of the others. Thus the advertising manager fights for her share of the pie, as does the director of sales promotion, the PR manager, the national sales manager, and the vice president of direct marketing. Throughout this chapter we present separate budgeting criteria for each marketing tool, but keep in mind that the integrated approach taken by Toyota and Saatchi & Saatchi is the ideal, as shown in the opening vignette.

PLANNING FOR MARKETING COMMUNICATION AND BUDGETING

Figure 17.1 shows the planning framework used for marketing communication appropriation and budgeting using a strategic orientation. As noted, we present this as an ideal, recognizing that few companies approach budgeting this way. Note also that a prerequisite of determining an appropriation is forecasting both sales and cost. As we see later, decision makers must make appropriations based on accurate sales and cost estimates, so this element is integral to the appropriation decision.

Also, both cost forecasts and objectives are made at the marketing communication tool level. This suggests an objective-task approach (a technique discussed later), which means that the appropriation should be made by looking at the objectives of each marketing communication tool, and budgets built from the bottom up.

Preliminary Considerations

Though the appropriation and budgeting process relies on numerical information, the process is more art than science. It is usually based on educated guesses, tradition, or the financial condition of the company. One industry expert observed: "Of all the decisions marketing managers must make, questions concerning marketing communication allocations are thought to be most difficult."[1] To understand how appropriation and budgeting decisions are made, then, marketing communication should identify how the organization approaches the appropriation process, who the primary decision makers are, and how the marketing manager allocates marketing communication costs.

Most businesspeople recognize that marketing communication is important to corporate growth and health. Still, many businesspeople act as if marketing communication were an expense of selling rather than an investment in strong consumer relationships that generate higher sales. They often estimate sales for some ensuing period, establish the manufacturing, administration, direct-selling costs, and acceptable profit levels, and then determine the marketing communication budget with whatever money remains.

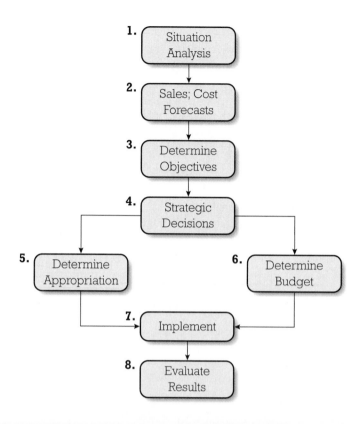

1. Situation Analysis
2. Sales; Cost Forecasts
3. Determine Objectives
4. Strategic Decisions
5. Determine Appropriation
6. Determine Budget
7. Implement
8. Evaluate Results

FIGURE 17.1

The Planning Process for Marketing Communication Appropriation and Budgeting

A company's marketing communication appropriation is often based on what is traditional for a company of its size in its industry. The general level of marketing communication expenditures within an industry tends to settle into a competitive equilibrium. That level remains more or less undisturbed until one firm finds a more successful or efficient manner of spending marketing communication dollars or settles on a marketing mix that is distinctly different from the industry pattern. Why? Many managers are afraid to depart from the normal range of marketing communication spending for similar products. They fear that if they reduce the percentage of dollars spent on communication, they will lose market share; if they increase it, they invite an equal and damaging response from competitors.

Instead of thinking about how marketing communication works to achieve objectives, then, marketing communication managers often set marketing communication appropriations by routinely applying a set of decision rules year after year. For example, in the cosmetics industry 5 percent of forecasted sales often go to marketing communication. Chrysler Motors allocates $70 toward advertising for each unit forecasted. Like any business decision, the marketing communication appropriation is shaped by some established decision-making process. Whether the appropriation is wise and effective depends in part on who decides the amount of the appropriation and how the appropriation is defined and applied.

The Appropriation Decision Makers

A wide range of individuals can help determine the marketing communication appropriation. In a small mom-and-pop hardware store, virtually everyone working in that business might express an opinion about how much to spend on communication. As that store grows and becomes a True Value franchise, the folks at True Value may offer several guidelines and even mandate expenditure through the lure of cooperative dollars. There are also differences between companies that sell consumer products versus those that sell to other businesses. For instance, in a large consumer goods company such as Kraft Foods, the product manager has a strong impact, as does the advertising manager, the promotion manager, and the director of field sales. Because Kraft has a great deal of confidence in its primary advertising agency, Foote, Cone, and Belding also offers advice.

In a business-to-business company such as Prestige Electronics, the decision is made by the director of marketing in conjunction with general advice from the CEO. In general, the greater the number of decision makers and the more removed those decision makers are from the marketing communication strategy, the more likely they will be to make conservative appropriations. Likewise, one shouldn't assume that larger companies are better able to make effective marketing communication appropriation decisions.

The Marketing Communication Appropriation: Expense or Investment?

Companies vary in their view of the marketing communication appropriation. For instance, many businesses charge any expense item relating to the consumer to 1) the cost of producing sales (such as personal selling), 2) the cost of creating the product (including research), or 3) the cost of communicating with the consumer. This last category would include all facets of communication, including letters to irate consumers, but most facets would have a strategic basis. Table 17.1 lists the marketing communication activities in this third category along with percentage allocations.

For companies that view marketing communication appropriations as a short-term expense, the strategic approach tends to be shortsighted as well. Communication efforts are viewed as 12 months long, with a tendency to start from scratch each year. For companies that adopt an integrated perspective, marketing communication appropriations are considered an investment, equivalent to machinery or a building, that pays off for many years. This perspective supports the notion of a campaign, which requires a much longer time frame than an individual ad or coupon drop. Rather, the integrated approach acknowledges that it may take time to achieve communication objectives, and that the payoff may be later than sooner. It represents a change in attitude and suggests that you don't give up on a brilliant communication idea simply because the results aren't immediately evident.

TABLE 17.1

**Change in Marketing
Communication
Budget Allocation for
1995**

	Increase	Decrease	Same	Don't Use
Customer database marketing	61%	1%	21%	18%
Public relations	61	4	32	3
Advertising in trade publications	51	10	33	6
Promotional marketing efforts to end users	49	5	26	19
Existing customer communication (e.g., newsletters)	49	4	35	13
Direct mail (using outside lists)	48	7	32	13
Electronic marketing (e.g., online, diskette)	48	1	15	36
Distribution activities	47	10	19	24
Promotional activities for channel	47	3	30	19
Advertising in specialized publications (e.g., computer, leisure publications)	45	11	25	18
Telemarketing	42	4	24	29
Cooperative advertising	36	16	26	22
Trade shows	24	33	40	4
Advertising in general business publications	23	7	28	42
Advertising in consumer publications	19	10	10	61
Newspapers	16	2	26	56
Television advertising	10	3	9	78
Radio advertising	9	2	15	73

Source: Advertising Age, September 5, 1994, B14.

Appropriation Issues

Although the marketing communication appropriation includes several communication areas, such as advertising, public relations, direct marketing, personal selling, and sales promotion, the majority of appropriation research comes from the advertising area. For example, researcher Gary Lilien suggests three important issues confront the executive who makes national advertising appropriation decisions:[2]

1. *Economies of scale:* Is there some relevant range in which increments of advertising yield increasing returns?
2. *Threshold effects:* Is there some minimum level of exposure that must be exceeded for advertising to have a discernible effect?

An IMC Approach Toward Budgeting

Managers from restructured and downsized companies often have scarce resources—and little energy—to develop, implement, and evaluate corporate initiatives. This has been particularly true for marketing communication managers. Too often, top management equates IMC with lower cost. Instead, corporate management should reevaluate how and why they allocate money to marketing communication.

Many organizations rely on microeconomic analysis as the basis for managing their operations, taking a stated corporate goal and using it as a basis for planning. Using this approach, the firm allocates a percentage of expected sales revenues for marketing communication. If the sales goal for the coming year is $1 million, the costs and desired profit are deducted from that amount, then the leftover funds are earmarked for various functional activities such as marketing communication. If sales revenues drop or management believes they soon

will, management trims the budget for the functional areas.

Some firms, however, use an ROI (return-on-investment) approach to marketing communication spending. With this approach, the business focuses on the return it will reap from marketing communication spending. If the marketing communication manager can prove that the IMC meets the organization's ROI financial goals, then as long as cash flow is adequate, the organization should make the investment. Under an ROI approach, IMC dollars would no longer be treated as a fixed cost, that is, taken in the current accounting period. Instead, they would be treated as a variable cost that will provide returns in the future. Just like any other sound investment, the more you spend on IMC, the more you get back.

Don Schultz explains that he once calculated a projected ROI of about 200 percent for a proposed IMC program in a service company. If the company invested $10,000 in the program, then it

would have to generate $40,000 in additional sales. Could the IMC program do that? Historically, marketing communication programs generated incremental sales of 23 percent—much lower than the projected 200 percent. In that case the general manager's decision was easy: Don't invest.

If marketing communication expenditures are a variable, not a fixed cost, the marketing communication manager must track and evaluate marketing communication returns to see if they comply with the firm's required ROI. The problem with this approach is that such returns have been hard to measure. Today, however, technology and continuous improvement processes make measuring communication programs not only possible but practical.

Sources: Don E. Schultz, "How to Generate an Unlimited IMC Budget," *Marketing News,* June 5, 1995, 7; Don E. Schultz, "Trying to Determine ROI for IMC," *Marketing News,* January 3, 1994, 18; Don E. Schultz, "Spread Sheet Approach for Measurable ROI for IMC," *Marketing News,* February 28, 1994, 12.

3. *Interaction effects:* Does advertising interact with each element of the marketing mix (especially personal selling) to produce effects that are greater than the sum of their separate effects?

Unfortunately executives tend to respond to these issues in a manner that is not strategic. Instead they often use mechanical decision rules that are routinely applied to make appropriations year after year. This mechanical process both excuses executives from careful thought about the task of determining just how marketing communication affects sales and insures that the appropriation will fall neatly into the financial structure that exists within the company.

Of course, some businesses strive to apply an IMC approach to make strategic appropriation decisions. As indicated in the IMC Concept in Focus feature, this approach can be difficult to implement.

Assessing the Situation

In deciding the amount of money to allocate to marketing communication, the astute decision maker should evaluate the key situation factors. Which factors are influential depends on whether the marketing communicator is a manufacturer, a retailer, or a direct marketer.

Situational Factors Influencing the Manufacturer

Manufacturers consider the following six factors when determining the marketing communication appropriation:[3]

- The product, including its type, stage in the life cycle, and strategic components
- The market
- The competition
- The financial condition of the company
- Research guidelines
- The distribution system

The Product. Certain product elements have a tremendous impact on the marketing communication appropriation. We examined these elements in Chapter 2 when we discussed how the type of product, the stage in its life cycle, and its strategic components affect both the need for marketing communication and the effectiveness of particular types of marketing communication. For instance, it takes a larger amount of marketing communication dollars to launch a new product than to keep an old one selling. The same is true for convenience products compared with durable products. Marketing communication for consumable products such as milk, cigarettes, and soft drinks use mass selling techniques to presell the product. Consumer durables, such as furniture and appliances, require an emphasis on personal selling because sales representatives can differentiate the products for consumers, tailor the presentation to meet prospects' needs, and use persuasive tactics to convince buyers to make such a high-cost purchase. Also, emotion-based products such as cosmetics, perfumes, and cars profit more from advertising than do products bought for primarily rational reasons, such as industrial machinery.

The Market. Both the size and nature of the market influence the marketing communication appropriation. Manufacturers who expect to cover a national market rather than a regional one will obviously spend more money. Maxwell House Coffee directs all its marketing communication efforts at coffee drinkers, whereas Gallo Winery tries to turn nonwine drinkers into wine drinkers. These opposite strategies require different marketing communication tactics and different dollar requirements to support them. Characteristics of the market, including demographics and psychographics, the attitudes and perceptions of the consumer toward the manufacturer, the amount of brand loyalty toward the firm and its competitors, and the amount of product use should also be considered in the appropriation process.

The Competition. Many companies monitor the expenditure of their competition and match these amounts either directly or proportionately. Expenditure information is available through observation or industry statistics. As we discuss later in this chapter, matching is usually an ineffective strategy. There are instances, however, when a major competitor dramatically increases the budget for a particular brand, and the only recourse is to match this increase.

The Company's Financial Condition. When a company faces falling profits or during a general economic downturn, marketing communication budgets, especially advertising and public relations, are often cut first in firms that view marketing communication as a cost, not an investment. Then, when business booms, marketing communication is usually reinstated. This strategy can backfire. As mentioned in Chapter 5, firms that continue their marketing communication spending during poor economic conditions do better in the long run than firms that decrease or eliminate such spending.

Realistically, however, the marketing communication allocation is limited by what a company can afford. As a practical matter, a ceiling on the allocation always exists. The marketing communication manager should be aware of this approximate dollar limit before beginning the planning process.

Research Guidelines. Some companies, such as small companies in furniture manufacturing fields, use little research to guide their decisions; they rely instead on experience and tradition. For the more sophisticated organization, marketing surveys, media data, census material, forecasts, and many other types of research are available.

The Distribution System. A channel of distribution can be quite long and include many intermediaries (that is, wholesalers and retailers). Or it can be quite short and direct, as it is for a manufacturer who uses a catalog and the mail to distribute products. A long, complex channel may require a large marketing communication appropriation to support the product because of the divided efforts of the intermediaries. For example, Coca-Cola Enterprises Inc. follows an intensive distribution policy because its products must be available in every possible outlet. Because these outlets usually carry competing brands of soft drinks as well, Coca-Cola cannot expect the intermediaries to carry much of the marketing communication effort. A retailer may engage in some cooperative advertising, but little more. Consequently, Coca-Cola must make use of extensive mass marketing communication, especially advertising and couponing, that will pull the product through the channel.

In contrast, clothing manufacturer Hart, Schaffner, and Marx distributes its suits through an exclusive dealership arrangement. Because the retailers are guaranteed the sole right to sell the brand, they in turn provide certain efforts for the manufacturer. The retailer will engage in extensive personal selling as well as local advertising. Much of the marketing communication effort and cost, then, is taken off the shoulders of the manufacturer.

Although these factors are all important in determining the marketing communication budget, the manager must never lose sight of the fact that all communication tactics must be considered for possible funding. Take, for example, Lange Watches, a famous German luxury watch manufacturer whose factory was destroyed by Russian bombs at the end of World War II. Relaunched in October 1994 after the destruction of the Berlin Wall, great-grandson Adolph Lange plays the heritage benefit in his marketing. It began with a reception at a castle in

Dresden and a print ad campaign. The print ads featured old and new Lange time-pieces with the copy, "The economy in East Germany starts to tick differently. A Lange & Sohne has returned. A legend has become a watch again." Large watches sell for $10,600 to $106,400. Swiss agency GGK Basil, which handles Lange's $700,000 account, has also produced a 60-page catalog titled, "When Time Came Home," detailing the history of the Lange family and their watches. The company prints 10,000 copies of the catalog in German and recently added English and Italian versions. By the end of 1995, the company had sales of $14 million, and 700 watches were snapped up.[4]

Situation Factors Influencing the Retailer

Many of the factors just discussed have a direct bearing on the marketing communication budget for retailers as well as for manufacturers. However, retailers who engage in budgeting must also consider a variety of factors unique to retailing. Seven key factors follow:

- Age of store: New stores require more advertising.
- Location of store: Bad locations may require more promotion.
- Merchandising policies: Discount stores usually need a greater amount of mass selling to turn over product.
- Competition: The greater the level of competition, the more promotion is needed.
- Media availability: The size of the community often dictates the type and extent of the media that can be employed.
- Size of the trading area: Marketing communication tends to increase with market size.
- Support from the manufacturer: Manufacturers may provide retailers with advertising support, point-of-purchase displays, sales training, and other promotion support that will reduce the expenditures required of the retailers.

Situational Factors Influencing the Direct Marketer

There are also a number of situational factors that affect the direct marketer's budget allocation.

- The database: The more specific and the more frequent the update of the database, the more it will cost.
- The role of technology: Using new technology, such as interactive and artificial intelligence, will add risk and expense.
- Legal implications: Several direct-mail techniques, especially telemarketing and direct mail, are heavily legislated. Compliance with these laws add greatly to the expected expense.
- Location of the target audience: Delivering a direct-marketing message usually is more costly the further it has to travel or the more isolated the recipient.
- Direct marketing via retailing: Factory outlets are like direct marketing and must consider the same factors found with retailing.

Sales and Cost Forecasts

A sales and cost forecast is a necessary part of the budgeting and appropriation process. Sales for the coming year can never be known exactly and therefore require a managerial estimate or "forecast." This estimate may be based solely on judgment (for a completely new product) or may be supplemented by previous experience with similar situations. A variety of techniques are used to produce this forecast. **Executive judgment** bases the sales estimate on the intuition of one or more executives. It is also possible to survey customers, the sales force, or experts in the field. Two techniques that are far more complicated are *time series analysis* and *market tests*. **Time series analysis** uses the company's historical data and tries to discover a pattern or patterns in the firm's sales over time. The method assumes that past sales patterns will continue. **Market tests** involve making a product available to buyers in one or more test areas and then measuring purchases and consumer responses to marketing tactics. These results lead to projections for the project in the total marketplace.

Sales forecasts are used to determine the appropriation in at least two ways. First, the general trend in sales (that is, up, stable, down) provides a general guideline for the direction the appropriation should take. Second, many companies set their appropriation as a percentage of projected sales. (This method will be discussed in more detail later.)

Cost forecasting also affects budget decisions. Costs *must* be forecasted to justify a budget request. Agency-related costs, media costs, production costs, special events costs, entertainment costs, and coupon distribution costs all must be estimated and totaled. Most of this information about costs is available either through secondary sources or through the provider of the service or product. References such as the **Standard Rate and Date Service** give media costs for a specified period of time. Production houses readily provide cost estimates. Several calls may be necessary before all the cost information is gathered, but it can be done. There are also computer databases that provide a great deal of cost information. The databases usually guarantee information for a given period of time, note rate increases or decreases, and provide dates for revised cost information. Buying broadcast media during the up-front market, for instance, is one way of controlling ever-changing media costs.

Setting Objectives

A strong relationship exists among the marketing communication objectives, the appropriation/budget objectives, and the expenditure of funds required to meet the marketing communication objectives. Assuming that an organization has specific marketing communication objectives, it should be a fairly straightforward matter to estimate the marketing communication expenditure necessary to reach these objectives. However, the appropriation and budgeting objectives also affect the appropriation process. These objectives provide an important link between the marketing communication objectives and the resulting appropriation. Essentially, appropriation/budgeting objectives tend to be either *quantitative* or *qualitative* (see Figure 17.2).

Quantitative objectives are concerned with the appropriation's ability to maximize profit, sales, or market share. (The theoretical foundation for these quantitative objectives is marginal analysis, discussed later in the chapter.) Maximization of profits suggests that the goal of marketing communications would be to contribute to profitability. The amount of profit depends on the costs associated with each

FIGURE 17.2

How Marketing Communication Objectives Lead to Appropriations

marketing communication element. Complying with the profit maximization objective would emphasize keeping costs low or making sure that high-cost items have very high payoffs. For example, media would be chosen that had a low CPM, or markets would be targeted that produced high profit margins.

Sales-based objectives attempt to maximize expected sales. A special concern is to avoid *overspending*. **Overspending** means that continued spending would produce sales at a decreasing rate. The saturation point has been reached and further spending is wasteful. **Underspending** is also a concern. If sales are below their expected minimum, marketing communication spending is too low. Forecasting and tracking sales are mandatory to achieve sales-based objectives.[5] Because constant monitoring of the market is part of this process, budget flexibility is important. That is, money should be available at a moment's notice to take advantage of sales trends.

Reaching market-share objectives is similar to maximizing sales in that the company has to estimate competitors' sales curves which, together with the firm's, comprise the market. Estimating a competitor's sales curve is difficult because it also requires estimating how the competitor's sales will respond to a particular level of spending. This difficulty in making estimates is possibly why so many false budgets are leaked to marketing communication trade publications; either a high appropriation intimidates competitors altogether or a low appropriation induces competitors to underspend. Maintaining market share means matching competitors' spending, and gaining market share means outspending the leading competitors.[6]

Qualitative objectives address the subjective issues achieved through the appropriation rather than the quantitative issues of profit, sales, and market share.

In this context the goal is to assess the extent to which the dollars spent achieve the qualitative objectives associated with the marketing communication plan discussed in earlier chapters. In the case of media selection, for instance, qualitative objectives focus on whether the medium selected matched the image of the company, whether the tone of the medium was appropriate, or whether the right people understood the message in the manner intended. Qualitative appropriation and budget objectives indicate the extent to which the dollars allocated will achieve these marketing communication objectives at the most effective level.

Strategic Decisions

Despite the fact that billions of dollars are spent on marketing communication every year, the majority of the companies spending these dollars use decision processes that are based on little if any strategic thinking.[7] Although this pattern has not proven detrimental to many of these companies, there is growing evidence that marketing managers are using more sophisticated techniques in setting marketing communication appropriations and budgets. Traditional subjective methods are gradually being replaced by data-driven approaches. These approaches may provide an additional competitive advantage to those willing to commit to them. First, however, we will discuss the subjective methods of appropriation for the main marketing communication areas.

Concept
Review

PLANNING FOR MARKETING COMMUNICATION AND BUDGETING
1. Distinction should be made between appropriation and budgeting.
2. The planning framework for marketing communication appropriation and budgeting determination includes the following:
   - Preliminary considerations
   - Assessing the situation
   - Sales and cost forecasts
   - Setting objectives
   - Strategic decisions

DETERMINING APPROPRIATIONS FOR ADVERTISING

The budgetary approach used by a particular advertiser typically varies with the product, the size of the appropriation, and tradition. Table 17.2 lists some of the key techniques for determining the size of the appropriation and indicates their popularity among advertisers. In the following sections we describe the advantages and disadvantages of some of these methods.

Predetermined Budgetary Methods

Earlier, we suggested that marketing communication budgets are often handed down to the marketing communication manager by management fiat, with little or no input from the marketing communication manager. Next we examine four common budgetary techniques used under these conditions: the percentage-of-sales, unit-of-sales, competitive parity, and all-you-can-afford methods.

TABLE 17.2

Methods Used to Help Set Advertising Budgets

Regularly Use	1987 Survey (n = 1204) (%)	1982 Survey (n = 1700) (%)	Z-Score	Significance Level
Objective and task	50	(40	5.35	0.001
What we can afford	50	(49)	0.53	ns
Percentage of sales (previous or expected year)	25	(38)	7.58	0.001
Experimentation and testing	20	(14)	4.20	0.001
Match the competition	8	(8)	0.00	ns

n = Number of responses
Z-score = Statistical difference between two dates
ns = Not significant
Source: James E. Lynch and Graham J. Hooley, "Increasing Sophistication in Advertising Budget Setting," *Journal of Advertising Research* (February-March 1990): 67–74.

Percentage of Sales

The percentage-of-sales technique is probably the most popular of the marketing communication budgetary methods. Management bases the marketing communication appropriation on a fixed percentage of sales of the previous year, of an anticipated year, or of an average of several years. To illustrate, if sales were $3 million on average for the last three years, management using this technique might pick 5 percent of that average and allocate $150,000 to marketing communication. One advantage of this method is that expenditures are directly related to funds available—the more the company sold last year, the more it presumably has available for marketing communication this year. Another advantage is its simplicity. If businesspeople know last year's sales and have decided what percentage they wish to spend on advertising, the calculation is easy.

The percentage-of-sales method suffers from several serious limitations, however. Most notably, it assumes that marketing communication is a result of sales rather than a cause of sales. It does not take into account the possibility that sales may decline because of underspending on marketing communication. Also, this method does not include the possibility of diminishing returns—meaning that after a certain point additional dollars may generate fewer and fewer sales. In short, using the percentage of sales may mean underspending when the sales opportunities are high and overspending when the potential is low.

Perhaps the most effective manner in which to use the percentage-of-sales technique is to examine both past sales and forecasted sales. This examination also assures that market potential is accounted for when the forecast is considered. Regardless of its limitations, the percentage-of-sales method will no doubt remain popular.

Unit of Sales

The unit-of-sales method is very much like the percentage-of-sales technique. Instead of dollar sales, though, the base is the physical volume of either past or future sales. Toyota, for example, would base their appropriation for Camry on the 38,000 units they expect to sell in the United States next year rather than the value of those 38,000 units. This unit value is then multiplied by a fixed amount of money (for example, $125) to derive a total marketing communication appropriation of $4,750,000. This method exhibits the same strengths and weaknesses as the percentage-of-sales method, and the same solutions apply. It is commonly used for high-ticket items such as automobiles and appliances.

Competitive Parity

Many marketing communicators base their allocations on competitors' expenditures. Information on expenditures is available readily through sources such as *Advertising Age,* A.C. Nielsen, and government reports. This technique is rarely the sole determinant of the appropriation but normally complements other marketing communication methods.

The competitive parity technique has three advantages. First, it recognizes the importance of competition in marketing communication. Second, it often helps minimize marketing communication battles between competitors. Because competitors are all spending about the same on marketing communication, they tend not to try to outspend one another. Finally, this approach is simple to use because the only information required is the dollar amount expended by competitors.

The fact that this technique is based on a simple dollar amount also suggests a limitation. Important competitors may vary widely in the size and direction for their budgets, so comparisons may be hard to make. Another drawback is that competitive parity assumes that a company's marketing communication objectives are the same as its competitors, and this can be a treacherous assumption. It also assumes that competitors' allocations are correct. Finally, information on competitive advertising expenditures is available only after the money has been spent, so it may not indicate future selling.

All You Can Afford

With the all-you-can-afford method, the amount left over after all the other relevant company expenditures are made is allocated to marketing communication. Companies of all types and sizes use this method. It is particularly popular when introducing a new product. As unsophisticated as the approach appears, it often produces effective results. If a company is doing a good job allocating to the other elements of its business, it may not be surprising that the amount left over for marketing communication fits the needs of the company.

Strategy-Based Budgeting Approaches

In contrast to the predetermined budgeting methods that are based on simple rules of thumb and industry traditions, several budgeting techniques are based on the marketing communication strategy itself. These bottom-up approaches begin with the input of people implementing the marketing communication strategy, continue on to the marketing communication manager, and ultimately reach top management, accompanied with documentation supporting the budget amount requested. Admittedly, these techniques are more difficult to use but insure that the marketing communication plan will be implemented effectively. We explore four strategy-based budgetary methods: the objective-task, mathematical model, experimental, and payout planning methods.

Objective-Task

The most popular strategic technique is the objective-task method. With this method, the marketing communication manager first studies the market and product thoroughly to set logical marketing communication objectives. Then the marketing communicator defines specific objectives (such as creating consumer awareness and increasing coupon redemption) for a particular time period. After setting the objectives, the marketing communicator determines how much money will be necessary to achieve them. If the associated costs are greater than the money available, then either the objectives are adjusted or more funds are found. This method is equivalent to the zero-based budgeting method discussed in Chapter 4.

The main advantage of this method is that it develops the budget from the ground up, so that objectives are implemented strategically. It does not rely on factors outside the control of the decision maker, such as past sales or competitors' spending. The second advantage is that the task method works well for new product launches such as the RAV4, when advertising must be developed more or less from scratch or when the firm makes major changes in the marketing communication program for established products. In these "change" situations, historical and competitive information do not provide useful budgeting guidelines. The objective-task method has one key drawback: Its results are only as good as the stated objectives and the accuracy of the dollar amounts assigned to each objective. Setting objectives and assigning accurate dollar amounts are difficult tasks. If done poorly, the budget and the marketing communication fare poorly.

Mathematical Models

During the last several decades, the use of quantitative techniques in marketing communication budgeting has grown but has not found wide acceptance in the industry. These quantitative methods may apply mathematical models from other fields, such as physics or psychology, or may use models developed specifically for marketing.

Mathematical models have not been widely accepted for a variety of reasons. First, they require experimental and formal analysis techniques beyond the capabilities of many companies. Second, the process is time-consuming and expensive. Third, models from other fields have not been successfully modified to apply to marketing, and little agreement exists as to the reliability of the marketing communication budgeting models. Although new quantitative budgeting models are being proposed, their extensive use in actual practice will probably be slow in coming.

The Experimental Approach

The experimental approach is an alternative to modeling. The marketing communication manager uses tests and experiments for different marketing communication budget options in one or more market areas and uses the results to guide budget decisions. For instance, a product might be tested simultaneously in several markets with a similar population, brand usage level, and brand share. Varying advertising and budget levels would be determined for each market. Before, during, and after the expenditure, sales and awareness would be measured in each market. By comparing the results, marketing communicators can estimate how the varying budget levels might perform nationwide. The budget that produced the best results would then be used.

To a great extent, this technique eliminates the problems associated with the other budgetary approaches. The major drawbacks of this approach are the time and expense (in the low six figures annually) involved in getting the data and the difficulty of controlling the environment. Dow Chemical Co. has used the experimentation approach for many years. The company has increased total sales and profits while decreasing advertising costs.

Payout Planning

The payout plan is often used with other budget-setting methods to assess the investment value of the marketing communication. It projects future revenues generated and costs incurred, usually for a two- or three-year period. Its purpose is to show what level of expenditures needs to be made, what level of return might be expected, and what time period is necessary before the return will occur. Payout planning is a useful budgetary technique when a new product is introduced with a commitment to invest heavily in marketing communication to stimulate awareness and product acceptance. It acknowledges the likelihood that this situation will diminish company profits for the first year or two. Management naturally wants estimates of both the length of time that marketing communication dollars must be invested before sales occur and the expected profit flow once the brand has become established.

Table 17.3 illustrates a payout plan for a chain of bagel shops operating in the United States. In its first year the bagel shop chain spent $2 million of its $2.18 million in profit on marketing communication, plus $4 million on corporate investment, producing an operating loss. The second year the company invested $3 million on marketing communication and $1 million on corporate investment, producing a cumulative loss of $3.6 million. The third year showed a net profit of $1.28 million and a cumulative debt of $2.3 million. The fourth year of operation the organization profited after investing $4.1 million in marketing communication; the gain was $3.3 million, with a payout of $990,293.

The key to the payout plan is the accuracy of the forecasting. Forecasts must be made of sales over time, factors affecting the market, and costs. A successful brand typically grows in its early years and then levels off at a stable market share. Investment in marketing communication is high in the beginning and low later on. As indicated in the IMC in Action feature on page 581, ad production costs can make a dent in any budget.

The payout plan is a useful planning tool, but it has limitations. Most notably, it cannot account for all the uncontrollable factors that may affect the plan. New competitors, legislation, natural disasters, and new technologies are just a few of the contingencies influencing the plan. Also, the assumptions underlying the plan

TABLE 17.3

Example of a Payout Plan for a Bagel Shop Chain

		Year 1	Year 2	Year 3	Year 4
Sales		$ 9,461,053	$16,588,017	$21,650,000	$37,200,000
Ingredient cost	29%	2,743,705	4,810,524	6,278,500	10,788,000
Labor cost	21%	1,986,821	3,483,483	4,546,500	7,812,000
Materials cost	7%	662,273	1,161,164	1,515,500	2,604,000
Overhead	20%	1,892,270	3,317,634	4,330,000	7,440,000
Total operational costs	77%	7,285,070	12,772,733	16,670,500	28,644,000
Gross profit	23%	2,176,042	3,815,243	4,979,500	7,440,000
Marketing communication costs		2,000,000	3,000,000	3,700,000	4,100,000
Organization profit		176,042	815,243	1,279,500	3,340,000
Corporate investment		4,000,000	1,000,000	0	0
Corporate profit/loss		(3,823,958)	(194,757)	1,279,500	3,340,000
Cumulative profit/loss		(3,823,958)	(3,629,207)	(2,349,707)	990,293

tend to be optimistic. What happens if the product has no competitive advantage or the marketing communication is not effective? Clearly, top management would react badly to a payout plan that is two or three years behind the projected break-even point.

Concept Review

DETERMINING APPROPRIATIONS FOR ADVERTISING

The following methods are used for determining appropriations for advertising:

1. Predetermined budgetary methods
   - Percentage of sales: fixed percentage of last year's or forecasted sales
   - Unit of sales: fixed dollar amount of each unit sold
   - Competitive parity: proportionate match of the amount spent by competitors
   - All you can afford: amount left over after all other relevant expenditures are made
2. Strategy-based budgetary methods
   - Objective-task: costs budgeted to achieve objectives
   - Mathematical models: application of mathematical models to budgetary decisions
   - Experimental approach: tests of various budget allocations in various markets
   - Payout planning: projects future revenues generated and costs incurred

Production Costs Skyrocket

Commercial production costs, on the upswing since the ad industry began formally tracking them, have broken through the roof. For the first time, the average cost of making a national TV commercial has exceeded the $200,000 mark. Equally significant is that the inflation rate for commercial production has nearly doubled in the past year.

"There's no intelligent reason for it," says David Perry, chairperson of the Four A's (American Association of Advertising Agencies) broadcast production committee. "The trend has been that we are making fewer commercials as an industry. Therefore, we must be investing in fewer slots." Although many advertisers and production houses take exception with some of the Four A's methodology, all sides agree that it's a useful barometer of cost trends. Everyone is miffed. "Why do we accept these [increases] as a given? We let it [happen]. We don't demand other-

wise," bemoans Jan Soderstrom, senior vice president of advertising and promotion at Visa. "It's part of the old thinking and the fact that there's no incentive to agencies from a compensation standpoint to come in with lower prices."

Many major national advertisers have taken steps to control the process. Procter & Gamble, for example, switched from a traditional cost-plus-fixed-fee system that it had championed for years to a fixed-bid system. Under a fixed-bid system, a production company agrees to produce a commercial on a budget unless major revisions are made to specifications by advertiser and agency. If the commercial shoot runs over cost, it comes out of the production company's margin. However, George Bragg, president of George Bragg & Associates, a Darien, Connecticut-based advertising production cost consultant, explains: "The firm bid is increasing, yet prices are go-

ing up. It's not saving any money by shooting with firm bids if nobody holds the production company to it." Meanwhile, production company margins have been slipping. In addition, many advertisers are seeking to control production costs by farming work out.

Just about every side of the issue agrees that more discipline on the part of advertisers, agencies, and production companies could go a long way toward reducing production costs.

Food for Thought

1. Why are agencies and commercial production companies reluctant to save money?
2. What are the long-term risks if they continue to follow this strategy?

Sources: Joe Mandes, "Cost to Make TV Ad Nears Quarter-Million," *Advertising Age,* July 4, 1994, 3; "Oddly Enough, Commercial-Production Costs Don't Fall," *Adweek,* August 23, 1993, 17.

DETERMINING APPROPRIATIONS FOR OTHER FORMS OF MARKETING COMMUNICATION

The methods we have described for determining the appropriations for advertising are also used to set appropriations for other elements of the marketing communication mix. Most companies use more than one of these methods. In fact, the method used may vary from division to division or even between functional areas. For example, a company might use competitive parity to set its personal selling budget, percentage of sales to establish the advertising budget, and all-you-can-afford for the other marketing communication activities. Or a company might use mathematical modeling for new products and a percentage of sales for mature products. In the following sections we examine appropriation techniques used with the other marketing communication elements: sales promotion, public relations, direct marketing, and personal selling.

Sales Promotion Budgeting

One serious difficulty associated with sales promotion is the vast number of activities that fall under this marketing communication tool. As a result, there is ongoing uncertainty about which activities should be the financial responsibility of sales promotion. *The Dartnell Sales Promotion Handbook* offers the following list of activities that should be covered by the sales promotion budget:[8]

1. Research
2. Travel
3. Sales education
   a. Training literature
   b. Films and visuals
   c. Housing and administration
4. Promotional literature
5. Dealer services
6. Sales tools and equipment
7. Fairs and exhibits
8. Educational material for schools
9. Sales contests and campaigns
10. Dealer and other meetings
11. Community relations
12. Speaker's bureau
13. Publicity
14. Trade associations

When these activities overlap with the other marketing communication elements, the costs should be shared. For the most part, the extent to which sales promotion is allowed to share its financial burden depends on who is in charge of sales promotion. Most large companies use a brand management system, and the brand manager is responsible for determining the total amount to be invested in sales promotion. Because this individual usually has the responsibility for the total marketing budget, it is likely that the sales promotion budget will be dealt with fairly.

When the brand management system is not used, the marketing communication manager usually develops a total sales promotion budget for the department that includes all expected expenses. Salaries, sales promotion activities, department expenses, ongoing costs, and similar charges are individually budgeted. Either approach benefits from an internal accounting system capable of providing budgetary control.

Most of the budgetary methods discussed in determining advertising appropriations are also used with sales promotion. Five primary techniques are used to allocate funds to sales promotion:[9]

1. *Predetermined ratios:* These ratios involve rules of thumb based on company policy or historical precedent, possibly modified by the strategic position of the brand.
2. *Objective-task method:* Objectives for sales promotion are stated and plans are developed to accomplish these objectives at minimum cost.
3. *The build-up approach:* The budget begins with the necessary marketing communication expenses and successively adds the less important ones.
4. *Competitive parity:* The budget mirrors that of a close competitor, scaled up or down as needed.
5. *Optimal modeling:* A sales response model is used to find the budget that will maximize profits. The model is either solved analytically or by using a simulation approach. The "optimal" budget becomes a guideline or starting point for other budgets.

Although senior managers often specify predetermined ratio guidelines, historical precedent (that is, last year's allocation) is the most commonly used method of allocation in sales promotion.[10] This use of historical precedent is discouraging because the objective-task and theoretically optimal expenditure methods have much more intuitive appeal. Part of the problem may be that sales promotion is a relative newcomer to the marketing communication mix, so businesses do not use more complicated budgetary techniques.

As indicated in earlier chapters, an ongoing concern of marketing communication managers is how to allocate dollars between advertising and sales promotion. The following factors influence this allocation decision:[11]

- Characteristics of the decision maker (preferences and experience)
- Power and politics in the organization
- The organization's structure (centralized or decentralized, formal or complex)
- Use of expert opinions
- Approval and negotiation channels
- Pressure on senior managers to produce an optimal budget

Public Relations Budgeting

Compared with the other areas of marketing communication, public relations uses the least sophisticated budgeting techniques. Essentially, public relations managers follow one of four strategies in setting budgets. The first is equivalent to the all-you-can-afford technique. Because public relations is often at the end of the line when funds are allocated, the amount given to public relations is typically much lower than that given to advertising, sales promotion, or other types of marketing communication.

Competitive parity is the second technique. However, because the amount that competitors spend on public relations is very difficult to gauge, the amount chosen is often based on an approximation of what competitors are spending on public relations. Because many public relations costs are hidden, however, budgeters often make serious miscalculations in their estimates.

A version of the objective-task method is a third budgeting technique used in public relations. This budgeting technique usually depends on the objectives established for the other marketing communication elements. For example, a sales promotion program such as a special event is also the responsibility of public relations. The objective established for the special event by sales promotion dictates the public relations objective, which in turn can be assigned a cost figure.

The final budgeting technique follows a cost accounting approach. Simply stated, the public relations manager develops a list of activities and events that he or she would like to implement in the upcoming year. The manager then creates an itemized list of costs that is compared with a budget ceiling or submitted to top management for approval. Adjustments then follow.

Direct-Marketing Budgeting

For the most part, direct-marketing budgets employ a cost-based approach tied to the techniques discussed in advertising. Direct-mail marketers, for instance, can estimate to the partial penny the cost of mailing out a direct-mail piece to a given number of people. The cost of the database, printing, sorting, bundling, postage, and so forth are well-known numbers. The same is true for a telemarketing campaign, a catalog, or designing a Web site. Although there is no available information to support a particular budgeting approach, one might safely conclude that an all-you-can-afford strategy is predominant. Alternately, because a primary benefit of direct marketing is accountability, an objective-task approach makes the most sense, with a typical objective being response rate.

Personal Selling Budgeting

In most businesses the dollar figure allocated to personal selling is calculated independently from that of the other marketing communication functions. That is, the sales manager and the marketing director determine the personal selling budget with little concern for what the other mix elements are spending. This tendency toward having a separate selling budget is a major reason why coordinated personal selling with advertising, sales promotion, direct marketing, and public relations has been so difficult.

The two cost categories associated with personal selling are (1) **direct selling expenses,** or field selling expenses; and (2) **indirect selling expenses.** This latter category includes moving expenses, special entertainment expenses, and special marketing communication expenses. Many companies have drastically reduced

Preparing a Sales-Costs Budget

1. Metro areas	2. Projected sales	3. Lodging costs	4. Meal costs	5. Auto rental	6. Misc. expenses	7. Entertainment	8. Transportation	9. Promotional	10. Total metro expenses
11. Metro totals									
12. Projected total territory									
13. Percent of total	%	%	%	%	%	%	%	%	%
14. Budgeted salaries									
15. All-metro total									
16. Actual expenses									

FIGURE 17.3

Preparing a Sales-Costs Budget

this cost area in recent years. Moving expenses have become prohibitive; tax law changes, costs, and attitude changes have also decreased the popularity of the seven-course expense account lunch and other entertainment expenses. This discussion will concentrate on direct-selling expenses.

Figure 17.3 shows a suggested process for developing a personal selling budget. The 15-step process begins with a list of the location of each sales territory, followed by a sales forecast for each metro area. Steps 3 through 9 indicate all the direct-cost items associated with each metro area. These cost items are totaled under step 10. Step 11 totals the specific cost items for all metro areas. Step 12 projects sales of the territory. Step 13 calculates the percent of the territory's sales that will be accounted for by total sales of the metro area listed. Step 14 enters the budgeted salaries. Step 15 enters total forecasted expenses for the metro areas from column 10. Step 16 adds steps 14 and 15 for a total budget figure. The derivation of the dollar amounts placed in each of the cost categories can be percentage of sales, objective-task, all-you-can-afford, or some combination of these methods. Here again, the simpler methods prevail.

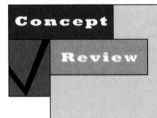

Concept Review

DETERMINING APPROPRIATIONS FOR OTHER FORMS OF MARKETING COMMUNICATION

1. Sales promotion, public relations, and direct marketing use many of the same budgeting techniques as advertisers.
2. Budgeting for personal selling considers two categories:
   - Direct selling expenses
   - Indirect selling expenses

MARGINAL ANALYSIS: THE BUDGETARY IDEAL

Hundreds of approaches are used to determine how much to spend on marketing communication. However, the theoretical basis for determining the size of the marketing communication budget is **marginal analysis.** In theory it means that a business adds to the budget as long as the marginal revenues from the expenditures exceed the amount of the expenditures. The point at which the marginal revenue and marginal costs are equal shows the optimal budget level.

This model is illustrated in Figure 17.4. The optimal level of marketing communication expenditure is that level that will maximize profits. To find that level, we must start by assuming that the only determinant of dollar sales *(S)* was the amount spent on marketing communication *(MC)*. So, sales is a sole function *(F)* of marketing communication.

$$S = F(MC)$$

Also, assume that the general shape of the sales curve is represented by the top line in Figure 17.4. In addition, the expenditure on marketing communication is represented by the upward sloping linear line labeled *(MC)*. The line designated as *MF(MC)* represents the relative difference between the projected sales and marketing communication expenditures, that is, gross margin. Gross margin is also

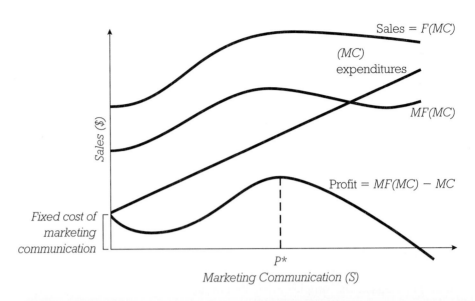

Sales = F(MC)

(MC) expenditures

MF(MC)

Profit = MF(MC) − MC

Sales ($)

Fixed cost of marketing communication

P*

Marketing Communication (S)

FIGURE 17.4

Illustration of Marginal Analysis

reflected as a profit curve in the lowest line. Accordingly, the most profitable point of expenditure is $P^\star$. Any expenditures beyond this point would provide a lower and lower level of profitability. As long as sales exceeded costs, it would be wise to continue a budget increase. However, a dollar invested in marketing communication above the level $P^\star$ would yield less than $1 profit.

Although the $F(MC)$ is portrayed as being S-shaped (see Figure 17.4), the shape and parameters determining the curve can vary tremendously. However, at least in the case of advertising, there are several reasons why an S-shaped curve seems justified: (1) there is always some sales return for additional advertising investment, but the rate of return declines as more money is spent, (2) no amount of advertising investment can push sales above some limit imposed by the culture and the competitive environment, (3) there are threshold levels of advertising such that expenditures below the threshold have no effect on sales, and (4) some sales will be made even with no advertising investment. These conclusions are depicted in Figure 17.5.

Marginal analysis has also been applied to budgets for personal selling. Although the primary benefit of marginal analysis in this context is to determine the optimum size of the total sales organization, it has a secondary advantage of providing a basis for making adjustments in the sales force throughout the year. Both decisions have a direct impact on the personal selling budget. The application of marginal analysis is straightforward. If an additional salesperson is hired, total sales should increase as should total selling costs. If a person is let go, sales will decline and so will expenses. In general, the manager will hire another person if the gross margin on the additional sales raises more than the selling cost increases—that is,

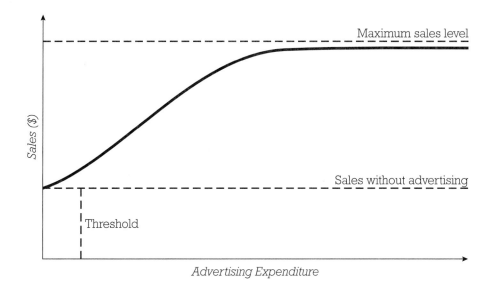

FIGURE 17.5

Advertising Expenditure

Source: Figure from *Advertising* by Kenneth A. Longman, copyright © 1971 by Harcourt Brace Jovanovich, Inc., reproduced by permission of the publisher.

if the extra salesperson will contribute more in gross margin than in cost. When replacing salespeople, the opposite reasoning applies. That is, salespeople will be replaced if they don't contribute marginally.

This decision-making process is illustrated in the following example. Suppose that a company currently has 50 salespeople at a total cost of $800,000 and a total profit of $1,060,000 (see Table 17.4). One of the salespeople has announced the intention to quit and the personnel manager has reported that three qualified people are available as replacements. The information found in Table 17.4 can be used to evaluate the following alternatives:

1. Do not replace the salesperson.
2. Replace the salesperson.
3. Expand the force by one or more.

If the salesperson is not replaced, the gross margin will drop by $70,000 and $20,000 will be saved. Hiring one person to replace the departing salesperson will generate a $40,000 differential, hiring two people will increase net profits by $30,000, and hiring three people will generate another $20,000 and a larger market share. Thus, 52 salespeople represent the optimum sales force size because the marginal profit is still greater than the marginal cost.

Although there are no examples of marginal analysis applied to sales promotion or public relations, there is no reason why this rationale would not work. In sales promotion the applicable units relate to levels of couponing, sampling, or

TABLE 17.4	Profit Contribution		Selling Cost	
Number of Salespeople	Total	Marginal	Total	Marginal
49	$ 900,000		$780,000	
50	1,060,000	70,000	800,000	20,000
51	1,120,000	60,000	820,000	20,000
52	1,170,000	50,000	840,000	20,000
53	1,210,000	40,000	860,000	20,000

Marginal Analysis of Sales Force

price discounting. For public relations, the units of input are information releases, special events, or participation in open houses. The marginal unit sales from any given increase in these inputs can be calculated, producing a similar curve to that in Figure 17.4. With the exception of the threshold level, most of these propositions have been widely accepted in the advertising industry.[12]

Although marginal analysis reflects an important ideal, applying it in practice has been difficult, if not impossible. The first problem relates to the assumption that sales are a direct result of marketing communication expenditures. This assumption may be valid in the case of direct-mail promotion, but it is questionable in most other types of marketing communication. The assumption that sales are determined solely by marketing communication expenditures is obviously faulty in practically all situations. Even if a researcher could isolate and control all the relevant variables for one time, there is no guarantee that the derived response curve would be valid in the future.

Second, marginal analysis ignores how the sales-response relationships change if copy strategy, media strategy, or other elements of the marketing mix are changed. Some changes can cause the response relationship to become more or less efficient by making dollars work harder or easier.

Third, marginal analysis does not account for the cumulative effect of past marketing communication effort on future sales. A consumer who buys a microwave oven in February could be affected by marketing communication seen in December and an encounter with a salesperson six months earlier. There is also the possibility that marketing communication might attract buyers who become loyal customers for many years. To date, marginal analysis is not able to accommodate this **lag effect** of marketing communication.

There are continuing efforts to adjust the marginal analysis technique to reduce these limitations. Some researchers have developed sophisticated experiments in which the various budget variables affecting sales are manipulated and the results are compared. Elaborate statistical regression models are added to these experiments to provide even greater predictability. However, the high level of expertise required to implement these techniques has discouraged their use. Instead, marketing communication managers opt for simpler budgetary methods.

Concept

Review

MARGINAL ANALYSIS: THE BUDGETARY IDEAL

1. Marginal analysis is a theoretical basis for setting a marketing communication budget.
   - A business continues to supplement the marketing communication budget as long as the incremental expenditures are exceeded by the marginal revenue that they generate.
   - The optimal level of marketing communication expenditure is the level that will maximize profit.
2. Marginal analysis is difficult to implement because of the following reasons:
   - It is impossible to judge whether sales are the direct result of marketing communication.
   - It does not consider changes in different elements of marketing communication strategy.
   - It does not account for the cumulative effect of past promotions.

SUMMARY

1. Explain how a strategic budgeting planning process works.

An appropriation is the maximum amount of dollars that management allocates to a specific purpose, such as marketing communication. A budget is the nuts-and-bolts details of how this sum of money will be used. The budgetary planning process includes the following steps: situation analysis, sales and cost forecasts, communication objectives, determining the appropriation, determining the budgets, implementing, and evaluating results. Key preliminary issues to consider are (1) who are the appropriate decision makers, (2) whether the appropriation is viewed as a cost or investment, and (3) theoretical considerations.

In assessing the situation the budget planner should consider aspects of the product, the market, the competition, the financial condition of the company, research, and distribution. There are a number of techniques used to forecast sales and costs, such as executive judgment, market tests, and secondary information sources. Relevant objectives to consider can be quantitative or qualitative.

2. Describe the budgeting techniques used in advertising, sales promotion, public relations, direct marketing, and personal selling.

Using advertising as a reference model, appropriation approaches can be considered as predetermined (percentage of sales and units, competitive parity, all-you-can-afford) or strategy-based (objective-task, mathematical models, experiments, payout planning). Sales promotion, public relations, personal selling, and direct marketing all use one or more of these appropriation approaches. Marginal analysis represents the budgetary ideal in that your budget should maximize profits.

POINTS TO PONDER

Review the Facts

1. Differentiate between the terms "appropriation" and "budget." What is the role of each?
2. Discuss the factors that influence the absolute size of the appropriation.
3. What factors influence the promotion allocation of the retailer?

Master the Concepts

4. Describe both the marginal analysis and the objective-task methods of determining the appropriation. How are the two methods comparable?
5. What is the problem with using the competitive parity approach when developing the appropriation for a new product? Suggest an alternative approach.
6. In addition to selecting the method of budgeting

and subsequently determining the size and allocation of the budget, what other factors should the manager consider?

7. Describe the experimental approach to budgeting. What are the drawbacks associated with this method?
8. There are several difficulties in appropriating a budget for sales promotion. Discuss them.

Apply Your Knowledge

9. What are the first two budget decisions that a marketing communication manager must make? How is the manager influenced by competition when making these decisions?
10. What procedure would you use to develop a payout plan for a new product?

SUGGESTED PROJECTS

1. (Oral Communication) Interview two local businesspeople (one retailer and one manufacturer), and ask them to discuss the method they use to establish their marketing communication budget. Compare your findings from the two interviews.

2. (Writing Project) Write a two-page memo defending the use of predetermined budgeting methods.

CASE 17: UNITED WAY CHANGES ITS WAYS

Few business organizations have gone through more changes than the United Way. The organization began in Denver in 1887 when the first United Community Campaign was organized. It was known as the Community Chest from the 1920s through the 1940s. Then the organization became known as the United Fund or the United Givers. It was not until the 1970s that United Way took its current name.

The intent of the United Way remains consistent—to raise money simultaneously for several worthwhile causes, thus cutting down on duplication of fund-raising drives and saving time and frustration for donors.

Individual charities within local United Ways receive on the average one-fourth of their funding from the annual United Way campaigns. The remainder of funding comes from grants and bequests, from government agencies in fees for contracted services, and from supplemental fund-raising drives.

As one would expect, the marketing program for United Way to date has been very simple. The national office was responsible for coordination, long-range planning, and providing some services to the approximately 2100 local United Ways in the United States and Canada. Headquarters furnished the local organizations with technical support for local campaigns and tried to build and maintain good relations with large corporations. More specific activities had to do with the development and production of films and other materials for use by voluntary solicitors and the media, development and production of planning and budgeting manuals, review of national agency programs, publication of various newsletter series, training of locals in management techniques and fund-raising, maintenance of a lending library of pertinent reports, and the execution of public opinion and market research. For example, one research effort found a direct correlation between contributor knowledge of United Way and support.

All the advertising for the United Way has been through the support of the Advertising Council, a social marketing organization formed for the purpose of supporting selected nonprofit causes with the creation and placement of donated professional advertising. Advertising agency Bozell & Jacobs, International, volunteered to create the advertising, and the National Football League agreed to support the United Way on its televised games. Later, the National Hockey League and National Basketball Association agreed to similar arrangements. The entire cost to United Way for the NFL series was $200,000, the cost of production.

Marketing communication efforts at the United Way have changed, however. The United Way is planning to develop a series of print, television, and radio ads that will be targeted at the general public. These ads will run the entire year, not just during campaigns. United Way faces one other unusual problem. Because the money spent on marketing communication has been donated and should go to the various charities, the public is very critical about spending on other programs.

Top management at United Way has never had to develop a marketing communication budget before, so there is a great deal of confusion as to where to begin and what the process should look like. There appear to be two camps thus far. One group simply wants to come up with a total appropriation based on the experiences of for-profit businesses with comparable revenue and cost figures. This group has identified six such businesses and has estimated that $11 million would be necessary to support a one-year advertising program. The allocation of money to the various components of the advertising strategy would be based on cost figures submitted by the people responsible for each component.

The second group, headed by staff economist John Blair, wishes to employ a marginal analysis approach in deriving the appropriation. The group argues that having detailed support for such a large financial decision is particularly important when an organization is spending donated money. Admittedly, there will be some problems making all the necessary forecasts that are part of the marginal analysis approach. In the worst case scenario, intelligent assumptions can substitute for hard data.

Case Questions

1. Given the situation faced by United Way, assess the appropriateness of the two appropriation techniques suggested.
2. Are there other techniques United Way should consider? Which ones? What advantages are offered by these alternative techniques?

ROMA'S LITE INTEGRATED CASE QUESTIONS

(Review the Roma's Lite Marketing Plan in the Appendix at the end of the text before answering these questions.)

1. What are the planning considerations you must consider when developing a marketing communication appropriation?

2. How does budgeting differ for the various marketing communication activities? Is there one appropriation technique or combination of techniques that might work for all of them?

3. (Team Project) Design a strategy-based appropriation process for Roma's Lite Pizza. Simulate a proposed budget.

chapter

18

Measuring IMC Performance

CHAPTER OBJECTIVES

After completing your work on this chapter, you should be able to:

1 **Address the main issues in measuring the performance of marketing communication.**

2 **Explain the specific testing methods used with advertising, sales promotion, public relations, direct marketing, personal selling, and other IMC tools.**

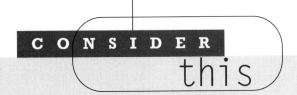

CONSIDER this

What's in Store for AT&T

In 1996, AT&T was on top again in the long-distance telephone advertising wars, causing rival MCI Communications Corp. to lose its cool. AT&T's "True" theme and campaign reversed its fortunes. For the first time in a decade, it regained customers. Second-place MCI was so perturbed by its rival's success that it dropped its humorous advertising attitude in favor of attack ads. In one newspaper ad the copy read: "Shame on you, AT&T." The ad accused AT&T of promoting "half-truths" in "[o]ne of the most expensive and nastiest advertising campaigns in history." A three-page print ad offered a "true-false" test attacking True USA and True Voice, with the tagline: "AT&T. It just doesn't ring true." This same theme was translated into a $40 million TV campaign.

AT&T's turnaround began in 1994. The company plugged the "True" campaign theme into a broadly integrated marketing communication strategy for several well-targeted long-distance calling products. Those

products included the True Rewards loyalty program offering frequent flier points; the True USA discount calling plan; and the True Voice product that offered superior sound quality to subscribers. AT&T's internal records show 1 million customers signed up for one of these programs in 1994, including thousands previously wooed away by the discounts and innovative marketing and advertising efforts of MCI and Sprint. In 1995, its consumer market share was 76 percent. "We have recovered from market share losses in previous years and we're on a roll," reported Dick Martin, AT&T's vice president of corporate advertising.

MCI sniped privately that AT&T "bought" its market share gains with an incessant barrage of network, spot, and cable TV spots; hefty print ads; and direct mail that offered large cash rewards to customers who switched back to AT&T. For the first nine months of 1994, AT&T spent $491 million on measured media and MCI spent $238 million.

Of course all of this changed in November 1996 when President Clinton signed the Telecom Act, which essentially deregulated the entire communications industry and opened up a new wave of intense competition. It has also unlocked some new opportunity. For instance, AT&T is in the local telephone business again. In addition, AT&T has made a dramatic effort to become an all-in-one communications provider. It has become the market leader in product bundling, such as local and long-distance calling, wireless service, and Internet access service. AT&T re-

searchers estimate that AT&T customers spend an average of $27 per month on long-distance calling and $100 to $200 a month on all their electronic communication needs. With bundling, AT&T aims to get all, or at least most, of this monthly bill. The opportunities are tremendous, as are the risks. Success will be difficult to assess accurately because the marketing effort has become much more complex for AT&T.

Sources: Mark Landler, "AT&T: A Bold Plan Has Turned Sour," *New York Times,* 13 April 1997, F1, F7; Catherine Arnst, "AT&T: Will The Bad News Ever End?" *Business Week,* October 7, 1996, 122–8; Seanna Browder, "AT&T Faces Hard Calls," *Business Week,* September 2, 1996, 40–1; Kate Fitzgerald, "AT&T's 'True-ly' Effective Campaign," *Advertising Age,* January 2, 1995, 10.

CHAPTER OVERVIEW

One of the most difficult problems marketing communication managers face is determining whether they have met their objectives. For marketing managers and product managers, the measures of success are often quantifiable, such as sales, market share, or profits. The marketing communication manager, however, must assess qualitative results that are difficult to gauge and are less concrete. Is communication performance best measured through awareness, recall, attitude change, coupon redemption, sales, or some other indicator? AT&T measured the success of its long-distance communication strategy by the number of new sign-ups. Should it also assess the retention of these new sign-ups? Or the cost of creating this new customer, relative to the profits generated? (Checks enticing customers to switch to AT&T cost the company $1 billion in 1996.)[1]

Clearly this measurement process will become much more difficult when product bundles are offered to subscribers. Should communication messages feature all the products in the bundles? Should different messages be targeted at different segments? What types of sales promotion strategies will prove most effective? What will be the role of direct marketing?

Simply stated, marketing communication managers want to be guaranteed that the measurement of marketing communication performance is done accurately and responds directly to the marketing communication objective. This mandate is constant regardless of the type, size, or location of the business.

Complying with this request has been neither easy nor universal. There are serious and unresolved questions regarding what to measure, how to measure, and what the measurements mean. Two similar companies can take entirely different paths in measuring performance but may make equivalent findings. There are also pragmatic issues. Conducting state-of-the-art research is quite expensive. It requires new technology, training, and time. Nevertheless, this research should be the goal of any marketing communication manager who wishes to plan and implement strategies. In this chapter we address the philosophical issues related to the evaluation of marketing communication performance. We also examine specific evaluation techniques for advertising, sales promotion, public relations, direct marketing, personal selling, and other IMC tools.

MARKETING COMMUNICATION IN PERSPECTIVE

Before we can sensibly address the problem of measuring performance, it would be helpful to reconsider what marketing communication is and what it is supposed to do. Recall from Chapter 1 that all marketing communication is driven by one or more objectives, such as creating brand awareness or increasing market share. The objectives, however, are meaningless unless some mechanism can measure the extent to which they have been reached. Marketers' objectives range from the very subtle to the definite (for example, market share). Generally, the task of marketing communication is to dispose people to change their attitudes, their behavior, or both as requested by the marketer.

In this chapter we examine evaluative research, which measures the effectiveness of the marketing communication planning process. It differs from the research conducted to analyze target markets or to select media, which we discussed in earlier chapters. Though evaluative research may take place at various times throughout the marketing communication process, it is carried out with the specific purpose of assessing the effects of various strategies. Thus, evaluative research allows the marketing communication manager to evaluate the performance of specific program elements and provides input into subsequent situation analyses. It is a necessary ingredient of a continuing planning process.

To conduct evaluative research the marketing communication manager should ask four related questions: What should be tested? Should we test? If so, when? And how? We investigate the answers to these questions next.

What Should Be Tested?

The basic problem in assessing marketing communication is to show that a specific effort produced specific results. Did the new Tylenol ad increase the viewers' understanding of the drug's benefits? Did the 25-cent coupon for Chef Boyardee Chicken and Spirals increase its sales? Whether the effort caused the results is difficult to discern.

Several other factors may have contributed to increased understanding or a change in behavior. An increase in product quality or the deletion of a competitor may offer a better explanation. In addition, controversy surrounds the question of which results to measure to assess marketing communication—short-term or long-term effects, the change in sales level, or some other benchmark. Top management often argues, for instance, that unless dollars spent on marketing communication generate sales, then they have been wasted. Still others argue that too many uncontrollable factors affect sales and market share for marketing communication to be held accountable for them.

The hierarchy of effects model, discussed in Chapter 4, provides one way of resolving this debate. The model assumes that consumers move through seven steps to the point of purchase: unawareness, awareness, knowledge, liking, preference, conviction, and purchase. Because marketing communication helps move consumers through these steps, each step, then, suggests a legitimate objective for a marketing communication strategy. Figure 18.1 lists some appropriate marketing communication activity for each step, and corresponding ways to measure effectiveness.

In this text we categorize all results and efforts into just two components: communication and behavior. That is, we assume that the effectiveness of marketing

	COMMUNICATION Source, Message Media		**BEHAVIOR** Pseudo-purchase, Purchase
PRETESTS	• Focus groups • Checklists • Split-run • Readability	• Physiological • Direct mail • Theater • On-the-air	• Test marketing • Single-source
CONCURRENT	• Recall • Attitude • Tracking • Coincidental		• Single-source • Diaries • Pantry checks
POSTTESTS	• Readership • Recall • Awareness	• Attitude • Association • Audience assessment	• Single-source • Split-cable • Inquiry • Sales counts

FIGURE 18.1

A Matrix of Evaluation Measures Used in Marketing Communication

communication equals the extent to which the communication worked and, if appropriate, changed behavior.[2]

To see whether the communication worked, managers should consider the marketing communication objectives. For example, assume that a manager wanted to evaluate the effectiveness of a 20 percent discount in a line of children's play clothes. Say that discount was offered to move 70 percent of the company's out-of-season merchandise. In measuring the effects of the discount, counting inventory before and after the discount would provide reliable sales results. Although sales-related objectives are appropriate for sales promotion and personal selling, they are not usually appropriate for advertising and public relations.[3] These marketing communication tools are more closely linked to other marketing communication objectives, such as building product awareness and knowledge and changing attitudes and preferences. Sales promotion and personal selling provide the impetus to take action. The impetus provides the necessary motivation (conviction) to get up and dial a toll-free number, visit a store, sign on the dotted line, pay cash, or hand over a Visa card (purchase).

Communication Factors

Recall from Chapter 8 that persuasive communication depends on the proper manipulation of the message, the source, the means of delivery, and the control of noise. Given the importance of these communication factors in effective marketing communication, we must determine the measurable elements of each factor and choose the best way to make these measurements. Next we explore how to find the measurable elements of each factor. Later we discuss the measurement techniques.

Message Variables. There are numerous elements in a typical marketing communication message. Words, music, color, visuals, layout, headlines, and the logo can all affect the outcome of a marketing communication message. All these message elements are more or less important to the various individuals involved in the message creation. For example, the marketing manager or product manager who initiates the communication and provides the primary direction for its design is most concerned that the *focal concept* is delivered clearly through the message. A **focal concept** is the key idea that the message contains. Sometimes the focal concept is very specific, such as product safety in the case of Volvo. In other cases the focal concept is a general mood or attitude that the message is supposed to deliver. Coke ads suggest that drinking Coke and having fun go together.

The copywriter or commercial director may have an entirely different set of message variables to test. The copywriter is concerned with whether the headline attracts attention. Is it understood as intended? Are funny words perceived as funny? Is the long technical copy interesting to the reader? Is "25% off" easier to understand than "now $1.99"? The art director wants to know if the photograph works better than the line drawing. Is the red background more soothing than the yellow? The television commercial director is concerned with whether the 1950s rock-and-roll background music turns some people off. Does the fast pace of the commercial distract the viewer from understanding the message? There are literally hundreds of questions such as these that are asked during and after the creative process. Because of testing and retesting every important element of a marketing communication message, it often takes weeks or months to produce positive results.

Source Variables. The source could be a celebrity, an animated character, a background voice, an actor, or someone singing a jingle. Key questions include whether the source that delivers the message creates the desired result. Factors to evaluate might include the following: the attitude change produced through the source, the trust or credibility associated with the source, the likability of the source, and the possibility that the source will dominate the message (that is, the consumer will not remember the name of the sponsor). Once these source-related variables have been identified, there are a number of techniques available to measure attitude, likability, credibility, wearout, and so forth.

Delivery Variables. Marketing communication messages can be delivered in a variety of ways. Advertising messages are normally delivered through the mass media. A tremendous amount of research is available to support mass media decisions. This research not only aids in placement decisions but also provides measures of effectiveness. The marketing communication manager can compare the effectiveness of one medium class with another (for example, newspaper versus television), specific vehicles within a class (station WTBS versus WGN, for example), size or length of the ad, and position in the vehicle. The marketing communication manager can specify very precise media objectives and be fairly sure that the measures are available to assess these goals.

Sales promotion messages can be delivered through conventional mass media as well as nonconventional media. For example, Campbell Soup Co. can deliver a coupon for its new soup through print advertising, a freestanding insert, or a direct-mail coupon drop. The company can also offer samples of the product at the point of sale by setting up a soup kettle at the end of a supermarket aisle and having a person pass out cups of soup. How is this variable evaluated? Campbell's marketing communication objective is to get the new product into 50 percent of U.S. kitchens within 30 days of market entry. Speed of coupon delivery, coupon redemption, and product trial are the responsibility of sales promotion. Measuring these factors is quite complicated, and sales figures are often considered a result of the strength of sales promotion.

The process becomes even more confusing when we consider public relations. In the case of publicity, counting the number of lines and/or stories appearing in the popular media is often considered an indicator of success or failure. But how does one compare the relative goodwill produced through a story in *Time* to a plant tour with elementary students to the sponsorship of a 10K run? Goodwill is a vague phenomenon: Public relations still finds it difficult to develop objectives and measures that help select the best delivery mechanisms. More will be said about measuring public relations later in the chapter.

Even personal selling has the capability to compare delivery mechanisms. Issues such as the timing of message delivery, who should deliver the message, and the size of the message are all considerations. Typically, the measure of performance is sales. However, other intermediary measures might also be considered. Examples include the number of sales calls made, the percentage sold, the type of products sold, the cost per sale, and the profit per sale. A good sales manager is constantly taking measures such as these and making adjustments as needed. Paine Webber Investments, for example, discovered that it is very important that high-dollar accounts be serviced by older, successful investment advisers.

Behavioral Factors

The behavioral factors associated with marketing communication include intent to buy, purchase, and brand loyalty. In the hierarchy model, these factors lead to conviction and purchase. We have already alluded to the difficulties in integrating advertising with sales. Nevertheless, advertisers are faced with increasing pressure to produce sales. In some cases advertisers are willing to opt for action measures that suggest an intent to buy but fall short of actual purchase. Among these action measures are brand choice, store visits, and contact (such as calls or written responses). These action measures are appropriate early in the product life cycle, when creating awareness or educating the consumer is a prerequisite to commitment. There may also be historical evidence showing a strong correlation between intent to buy and actual purchase, as is the case with high-involvement products such as automobiles and expensive clothing.

Where these action measures prove unsatisfactory, advertisers have turned to sales tracking companies such as Nielsen Marketing Research, Information Resources, Inc., SAMI Market Segmentation Service, and D.H. Macey & Associates. Companies such as these use three primary methods of obtaining sales data: monitoring warehouse shipments to resellers, cash register scanning at the stores, and conducting household diary panels. The ultimate sales test is to set up specific controls so that the advertiser can manipulate the ad, control who receives it, and then determine the results. Experiments can be done by the advertiser: Test cities with comparable characteristics are found, and one city receives the ad and the other one does not, then sales are measured. Experiments can also be done by research firms such as BehaviorScan, which has the capability of combining split-cable television (that is, different people on the cable system receive different versions of the ad or no ad) with checkout scanning equipment that is also tied to the specific cable subscribers.

Some companies assign market share as an advertising objective. However, the connection between advertising and market share is usually tenuous. Advertising is considered only one of several variables that contribute to market share changes.

Sales promotion and personal selling consider all the behavioral variables just discussed, including sophisticated sales tracking. For example, sales promotion often considers incremental sales rather than sales. **Incremental sales** are the additional sales produced by the sales promotion. The calculation of these sales eliminates people who would have purchased the product anyhow, regardless of the availability of a coupon, rebate, or price reduction. Personal selling often considers sales figures relative to profitability. In other words, the costs associated with producing one dollar in sales are just as important as the sales themselves. Likewise, the cost of gaining 1 percent of market share may be greater than the benefits. As indicated in the You Decide feature, sometimes test results can be misleading.

Should We Test?

Several benefits come from testing communication efforts. First, testing increases the efficiency of marketing communication by helping managers eliminate unproductive alternatives. The Nissan Motor Corp. USA found this to be the case when it introduced the Infiniti through a series of ads entitled "the rocks and trees approach" by critics. Initial tests showed that an automobile ad that does not show the car raises curiosity but does not give reasons to buy. The campaign was changed. Second, information from testing can help managers avoid disasters that can destroy the campaign or even the organization. A controversial ad for the new wide-mouth Coors beer can was dropped because parts of the creative copy were considered disgusting. In addition, testing gives a basis for future planning. Finally, tests provide feedback to those who create and implement the marketing communication campaign.

There are also problems that may preclude testing. First, testing costs a great deal of money. A complete testing program for one year ranges from $100,000 to $500,000. Second, windows of opportunity for marketing communication can be very short and may not allow enough time for testing. Third, the adequacy of the testing instruments and the meaning of the results are often questionable. High recall scores may be more a reflection of an unusual appeal than effective communication. Fourth, testing can create internal tensions and squabbles. People may disagree about what to test, especially because management is reluctant to support tests that are not related to sales. Creative people, especially copywriters,

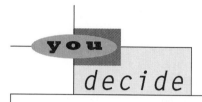

The Mystery of Online Ads

When people buy magazines, they leaf through the pages, getting impressions of ads. When people watch TV, they see ads on the screen. If they take car trips, they see billboards along the road. Thanks to researchers in each medium, marketers can more or less tell how many and what kinds of people will see the message, based on circulation, viewership, or traffic.

The Internet, however, combines elements of all the above media: As nothing less than integration of print and broadcast—an interactive text-and-picture magazine, catalog, or billboard delivered on-screen at the consumer's request—it's no wonder the advertising and publishing communities are having trouble pinning it down. But without a standardized method of tabulating audience exposure and impact, much less a way for marketers to know who's on the other end of the mouse, companies that advertise on the Internet still do so largely on the basis of trust.

"There has to be some standardization for the Internet to move forward," says Alison Smith, a spokesperson for Next Century Media, a Web audit service. "It's going to be an advertiser-supported medium, and it needs to have more advertiser support. Look at it from the advertiser's perspective. You want to know what rate of return you are getting and how you can actually make money on this."

There remains a general disagreement as to what to measure. Collecting raw data on Web site use is easy. When users log on to the Internet server, software tracks "hits" and "click-throughs." Sometimes it even tracks time spent at a site. But counting alone can be misleading, and the fact that much of the data is collected by Internet providers themselves makes it questionable as a basis for rate assessment.

Internet content providers already set rates according to the available figures, even based on numbers of hits. "We haven't gotten any further in quantifying the Web," says Charles D'Ogly, director of online research at Yankelovich Partners. "There are companies out there that manage to sell ad space using CPMs. *Playboy* charges something like $5 per thousand hits. Figures like that encapsulate the need for third-party advertising. There's a degree of trust that will last for awhile, but once you have large sums of money online, advertisers will feel much better with an audited site."

Better tools could eventually solve the problem of building demographic information about Internet users. Web content providers already know the characteristics of what D'Ogly calls the high-value cyber citizen: pioneering Web users who typically are male, educated, and more likely to read newspapers than watch TV. Beyond that, little user information can be distilled from this anonymous medium. Until effective measures are developed, the Internet remains the mystery medium.

You Decide

1. What are the risks associated with using the Internet as a message delivery mechanism?
2. What changes would have to be made to make advertising on the Internet reliable?

Sources: Laura Rich, "Measure For Measure: What Is The Web Worth?" *Adweek,* November 11, 1996, 32–3; Ian P. Murphy, "On-Line Ads Effective? Who Knows For Sure?" *The Marketing News,* September 23, 1996, 1, 38; Michael Schrage, "The Internet's Promise," *Adweek,* June 3, 1996, 36.

resent having research dictate the words they must use. Finally, testing encourages people to engage in activities that increase ratings but have little to do with objectives. For instance, a designer knows he can improve recall scores by simply including a cute baby or puppy in the ad.

To decide whether to test, managers should weigh the costs and benefits of testing. Unfortunately, most marketers tend either to ignore this step or to concentrate on just one or two key factors. The decision to test is often based on the testing capabilities offered by the marketer's agency.

When Should We Test?

If testing is worthwhile, the next question concerns the timing of the testing process. The possible answers may be classified as *pretesting, concurrent testing,* and *posttesting.* Ideally, all three would be employed.

Pretesting (also known as evaluative research) is research conducted before the audience is exposed to the marketing communication. Pretests are useful when managers need to examine possible problems before resources are spent on the actual message. For example, a manager may want to know whether a potential spokesperson is credible. A survey might satisfactorily answer the question before the commercial is actually produced and distributed.

Concurrent testing evaluates the marketing communication effort while it is running in the marketplace. This form of testing may be the most difficult to implement and maintain, but it has several advantages. It allows the researcher to quickly determine to what extent the message is reaching the desired target market. Concurrent testing may also indicate whether the message is being interpreted properly and may measure the effects of the message. Most important, this technique allows adjustments to be made immediately.

Posttesting is research conducted after the audience has been exposed to the message, medium, or spokesperson. It is designed to determine to what extent the marketing communication objectives have been attained. It allows researchers to evaluate how well they did and then to make appropriate changes.

How Should We Test?

Hundreds of specific tests can be used to evaluate marketing communication. However, all these measurement devices can be placed into three categories: *experiments, surveys,* and *mechanical measurement* techniques.

Experiments give individuals a controlled exposure to the message and change their opinion, attitude, or cause some other action. Experiments may take place in the laboratory or in the field. For example, an advertising agency designs three print ads in which the copy, illustrations, size, and other factors are all kept the same. The only difference among the three ads is the spokesperson; one is African-American, one is Caucasian, and one is Asian. The experiment's objective is to measure the effect of these manipulations on attitude toward the product. A thousand names are randomly selected from a master list. (In randomization, everyone has an equal chance of being selected or assigned.) Then these people are randomly assigned to view only one of the ads. All the people fill out an attitude questionnaire. Finally, the evaluator conducts statistical tests to assess the difference in attitude among the three groups.

An experimental design is valuable because it provides results that can be evaluated through the most advanced statistical tests. Such tests determine the *validity* and *reliability* of the results. **Validity** means the concept is confirmed to be what it claims to be. **Reliability** means that the same results are repeated time after time. Companies balk at using experimental designs because of their high costs.

In a **survey** interviews or questionnaires are used to obtain information about people's exposure to a particular message, medium, or person, and the resulting changes in their attitudes or actions. People are simply asked what they think, feel, remember, or do. Statistical analysis of the responses yields a measure of correlation between the reports of exposure and the changes in attitude or action.

Like the experimental approach, the survey method requires that the researcher deal with conceptual and technical matters. If a survey is to have any use at all, the researcher must take care that the design of the sample, the questionnaire construction, and the interviewing methods do not bias the results. Surveys are much easier and faster to conduct than experiments. However, the fact that surveys do not control for unknown variables means that alternative factors could be producing the measured results.[4]

Mechanical measurement techniques collect information through a device. Physiological devices, the most common type of mechanical techniques, will be discussed later. These devices usually measure involuntary responses of the automatic nervous system; thus these techniques offer objectivity. The use of these techniques tends to vary by agency size and commitment to this type of research technology.

Concept Review

MARKETING COMMUNICATION IN PERSPECTIVE

1. Evaluative research helps determine whether marketing communication has reached its objectives and suggests ways to improve communication efforts.
2. The evaluative process requires answers to four questions:
   a. What should be measured?
      - Communication factors, which include message variables, source variables, and delivery variables
      - Behavioral factors, which include intention to buy, purchase, and brand loyalty
   b. Should we test?
   c. When should we test?
      - Pretesting
      - Concurrent testing
      - Posttesting
   d. How should we test?
      - Experimental approach
      - Survey design
      - Mechanical measurement

MEASURING ADVERTISING PERFORMANCE

Until the 1920s, copy and media testing were practically unknown in advertising. Today they are a common part of the research efforts of most medium- and large-sized agencies. In addition, syndicated researchers conduct independent research. Because most of the performance research techniques were developed in the advertising industry, it is not surprising that most of the discussion will be in an advertising context. Essentially, managers in sales promotion, direct marketing, and public relations have adapted these techniques for their respective fields.

Syndicated media research may be purchased directly by the advertiser, or it may be sold to agencies and provided to the clients. Usually done on a regular basis, media research is designed to meet the needs of current as well as potential clients. The television rating services of A.C. Nielsen and the radio rating services of Arbitron Ratings Co. are well-known examples. Publication and audience research are done by companies such as the Simmons Market Research Bureau (SMRB) and Mediamark Research, Inc. (MRI). Media trade associations such as the Newspaper Advertising Bureau (NAB), Audit Bureau of Circulations (ABC), and the Advertising Research Foundation (ARF) conduct syndicated research as well.

Tables 18.1 and 18.2 summarize studies of practices in advertising research. Table 18.1 reports on a survey of 94 of the top ad agencies. The respondents were asked to indicate their usage patterns in areas of advertising research: (1) media factors, (2) sources of audience data, and (3) methods for evaluating communication effects. The percentage reported reflects the number of people using each technique or measure. The results indicate that these top agencies measure media performance in terms of reach, gross rating points, CPM to target, average frequency, effective reach, and frequency distribution. The top three sources used when assessing audience data were Arbitron, A.C. Nielsen, and Simmons. Finally, communication effectiveness is measured primarily through recall, advertising exposure, awareness, and attentiveness.

In contrast to the general research-related findings shown in Table 18.1, the information in Table 18.2 reports on the specific type of television copy research used by a survey sample of 112 advertising agencies. The second column shows the percentage of those surveyed that use a particular method. The top three reported tests were evaluating finished ads (93.8 percent), undertaking preliminary background or strategic research in preparation for advertising commercials (92.9 percent), and evaluating rough commercial execution of other formats prior to finished commercial (91.1 percent). It is interesting to note that two of the three techniques were pretests, and the top-rated test was a posttest. This fact suggests a strategic orientation in at least this facet of advertising. Correctly, advertising copy should be evaluated before being implemented.

The sophistication of advertising performance tests has grown dramatically over the years, especially since the advent of the computer. Many of the techniques discussed can be employed in more than one area of marketing communication.

Pretesting: Communication and Behavior

The appeal of testing an ad before running it in the media is obvious. The test gives some assurance of success before money is spent. Although there is no sure-fire way of predicting success, certain methods of pretesting can give helpful information if used intelligently.[5] These methods include tests of consumer opinion or awareness, physiological measurements, readability tests, and test marketing. These methods and their descriptions are summarized in Table 18.3, p. 596.

Tests of Opinion or Awareness

Opinion methods is a catchall classification for the simplest method of evaluating ads. People readily give their opinions. When shown a proposed ad, they will state whether they think it would get their attention, how interesting they think it is, which advertising claims they believe, and how likely they believe it

TABLE 18.1

Report on Media, Audience, and Communication Measures Used in Advertising Research

Factors Evaluated in Media	Percentage
Reach	90.4%
Gross rating points	89.4
CPM to target	88.3
Average frequency	87.2
Effective reach	86.2
Frequency distribution	75.5
Quintile distribution	43.6
Others	30.8
Sources of Audience Data	
Arbitron Ratings Co.	92.6
A.C. Nielsen	78.7
Simmons Market Research Bureau	76.6
Mediamark Research, Inc.	63.8
RADAR	52.1
Media Records	45.7
The Birch Report	22.3
Monroe Mendelson	10.6
Others	40.5

TABLE 18.2

General Findings Regarding Copy Research

Type of Copy Research	Percentage
Evaluate finished commercials.	93.8%
Undertake preliminary, background, or strategic research in preparation for advertising campaigns.	92.9
Evaluate rough commercial execution of other formats prior to finished commercial.	91.1
Evaluate television campaigns.	90.4
Evaluate copy ideas, storyboards, and other formats prior to rough commercial.	88.7
Test competitive commercials.	56.1
Test commercials for wearout.	42.9

Source: B. Lipstein et al., "Television Advertising Copy Research: A Critical View of the State of the Art," *Journal of Advertising Research* 24, no. 2 (April/May 1984): 21–5. Used with permission.

Communication Effects Evaluated	
Recall	58.5
Advertising exposure	52.1
Awareness	47.9
Attentiveness	43.6
Purchase	31.9
Recognition	24.5
Preference	18.1
Attitude toward brand	18.1
Prepurchase behavior	17.0
Comprehension	16.0
Interest	16.0
Knowledge	14.9
Intentions	12.8
Attitude toward ad	11.7
Conviction	8.5
Others	9.6

Source: P.J. Kreshel, K.M. Lancaster, and M.A. Toomey, "How Leading Advertising Agencies Perceive Effective Reach and Frequency," *Journal of Advertising* 14, no. 3 (1985): 32–8. Used with permission.

would cause them to buy the product or service. They will also compare ads on the basis of all of these functions and give opinions at any stage of an ad's development. Most opinion methods are simple, fast, and inexpensive.

Opinions may be solicited from any member of the general public—from the prospective consumer to the creative person to the advertising expert. However, researchers must watch out for pitfalls associated with each of these sources. People associated with the advertising business are usually prejudiced. This prejudice may be unconscious, based on allegiance to client brands or on conviction regarding the superiority of particular techniques. Conversely, when consumers give their reactions to ads, rather than explain how the ad influenced them, they frequently try to give "expert" opinions on ads. This reaction may occur because people assume the researcher expects them to be experts, or they believe everyone is an expert on advertising because it so pervasive and simple. In either case it is common for individuals to want to report what they think other people like or dislike rather than to speak directly for themselves.

Opinions about behavior entail a special problem: They are likely to be speculative. When respondents are shown ads and asked such behavioral questions as

TABLE 18.3

Pretesting Methods for Assessing Advertising Effectiveness

Method	Description
Tests of opinion or awareness	People express their opinions about different characteristics of an ad or their awareness of its existence.
Focus groups	A focus group, consisting of eight to ten potential buyers, evaluate the ad's copy, creative concept, product name, or campaign.
Program analyzer/ mechanical voting	Designed for broadcast media, it allows audience members to continuously record their likes and dislikes of a program and the associated commercials.
On-the-air tests	Viewers see a test commercial in selected markets and are asked to express their attitudes toward the brand, their ability to play back the commercial, and their brand knowledge.
Anteroom trailer method	A trailer is parked near a mall, and volunteers are asked to view test commercials and are then interviewed as to their effectiveness.
Physiological measures	This series of techniques is designed to assess physiological responses to an ad.
Readability tests	A variety of tests assess the general readability and understandability of the ad.
Test marketing	Different versions of an ad are placed in different markets, and the results are compared.

whether the ads would catch their attention or motivate them to send in the coupon, the respondents can only guess.

Opinion ratings are usually made by interviewing respondents individually. When a sufficient sample has been obtained, the total is called a **consumer jury.** In a variation respondents are brought together to get the benefits of group discussions and judgments. Specific procedures used to obtain ratings include focus groups, program analysis, and on-the-air testing.

Focus Groups

A typical focus group consists of eight to ten people who are potential users of the product. A moderator usually supervises the group, providing direction and control. The format depends on what is being evaluated. For example, when Kellogg Co. wanted to test the concept "Corn Flakes are a high-fiber alternative," it conducted nearly a hundred focus groups of people from 40 to 55 years old living throughout the United States. Some groups were all male, some all female, and some mixed. Groups were videotaped, and management evaluated the tapes.

Usually focus groups serve as a pretest device, but they are also useful for concurrent and posttesting. They may be used to evaluate copy, a concept, a product name, or a campaign. To compare ads for the same product, two or more ads are presented, and members of the group are asked, "Which of these ads do you like least?"

The rating given by focus groups appears to have a high positive correlation with the success of the ad. Therefore, there is general agreement that focus groups do reflect the consumer's point of view. Focus groups are also relatively inexpensive, and they can be organized and completed quickly.

Still, research reveals problems with some focus groups. Foremost is the inability to draw concrete conclusions from focus groups. These groups often view only parts of a marketing communication. Some are asked to make value judgments that are beyond their capabilities. For example, it would be impossible for members of a focus group to determine whether a particular ad would prompt them to buy the product without a great deal of additional information. It is therefore important not to have expectations of a focus group that are beyond its capabilities. Also, focus groups are small and may not be representative of the target market. Careful selection and evaluation of focus group participants can lessen this problem. Finally, because members are being paid, they tend to say what they think the researcher wants to hear.[6] The group moderator must always be sensitive to this problem.

Program Analysis

Paul F. Lazarsfeld and Frank Stanton designed a technique specifically for broadcast media called the **program analyzer.** It allows members of an audience to indicate likes and dislikes continuously throughout a program, including the commercials. Each seat in a room or auditorium is equipped with right-hand and left-hand switches for signaling likes and dislikes as the presentation proceeds. When neither control is operated, the evaluators assume the person is indifferent.

Other types of mechanical voting equipment have been developed, but some investigators find paper ballots satisfactory. Schwerin Research Corporation, for example, uses a procedure in which people mark their reactions on a ballot when numbers are flashed on a screen. Each critical point in the script has a number assigned to it, and the ballot has corresponding places in which to indicate favorable or unfavorable reactions.

Like many other procedures, program analysis permits researchers to apply a variety of approaches. Investigators usually go beyond collecting ballots. In order to test a group's memory of commercials, they may ask the members to write down all the sales points they can remember. Then the group is likely to be invited to discuss its reactions to the program and commercials at any selected point.

On-the-Air Testing

Another method of pretesting opinions, called **on-the-air testing,** analyzes a new commercial by comparing it with an existing commercial. The test commercial is aired in one or more cities, either in place of the regular commercial or in a new time period. Viewers who saw the new commercial are interviewed by telephone to determine their brand attitudes, their ability to recall the commercial message, and their brand knowledge. This information is compared with the responses of people who saw only the existing commercial.

Other Methods

Another popular way of pretesting opinions is the **anteroom trailer** method. A mobile home or recreational vehicle is parked near a shopping center. People are invited into the trailer and may be offered some incentive for participating. They enter a comfortable room that contains easy chairs, magazines, and a television set showing a prerecorded program. Test commercials are interspersed throughout the program. After the commercials have been shown, the subjects are interviewed and the effectiveness of each commercial is ascertained.

Opinion tests with standardized formats are readily available to any advertiser who has the necessary resources. However, agencies and advertisers have designed many opinion pretests to meet special needs. For example, the McCann-Erickson agency originated the **sales conviction test.** In this test the agency asks heavy users of a particular product which of two ads would be most likely to convince them to buy the product. Then the interviewer asks them how they came to their decision and whether they disliked any part of the ad. Each test involves at least 1800 interviewees in New York, Chicago, Los Angeles, and in a distant suburb of each city. The final score comes from an analysis of the respondents' comments.

Physiological Measures

Over the years, advertisers have experimented with assessing people's physical reactions to ads to measure effectiveness. Of the many techniques tried, five are worthy of special note:

1. *Eye movement tracking:* Participants are asked to look at a print ad or television commercial while a sensor aims a beam of infrared light at their eyes. A portion of the light reflected by the cornea is detected by the same sensor, which electronically measures the angle between the beam reflected by the cornea and the center of the eye's pupil. This information can be processed to show the exact spot in the ad or on the television screen where the eye is focused.
2. *The pupillometer:* This device measures pupil size when a person is exposed to a visual stimulus such as an ad or a package. The assumption is that pupil size increases with interest.
3. *The psychogalvanometer:* This device is part of the lie detector apparatus. Two zinc electrodes are attached to the subject, one on the palm of the hand and the other on the forearm. When the subject is exposed to an ad, emitted perspiration on the palm results in lower electrical resistance, which is recorded on a revolving drum.
4. *The tachistoscope:* This device controls exposure to a print message so that different parts of the ad can be shown without revealing the other parts. That way, the tester can tell at what point each part is perceived. Advertisers can thus find out how long it takes respondents to get the intended point of an illustration or headline.
5. *Brain waves:* Through the use of the electroencephalograph (EEG), data can be collected from several locations on the skull. Several electrical frequencies at each location are checked up to 1000 times per second. By measuring the electrical activity in various parts of the brain, this technique can tell the researcher when the subject is resting or when there is attention to a stimulus.[7]

These physiological tests suffer from several limitations. First, because respondents may feel threatened by these devices, the validity of the results is questionable. Second, there is a great deal of uncertainty as to what this machinery actually measures. Increased perspiration may provide a measure of emotional arousal, but is it a meaningful reflection of advertising effectiveness?

Readability Tests

An ad must be readable before it is set in final form. The length of the words and sentences and the impersonality of the writing are some of the elements that influence readability. Short words and short sentences make for easier reading.

The Flesch formula, developed by Dr. Rudolph Flesch, is a widely accepted technique for measuring readability. The formula uses four elements as they appear in 100-word writing samples:

Average sentence length
Average number of syllables
Percentage of personal words
Percentage of personal sentences

For example, Flesch contends that "fairly easy" sentences average 14 words in length and have 139 syllables per 100 words. The Flesch formula cannot be used for radio and television writing because a good announcer can make difficult copy sound very simple.[8] The ad for Hong Kong Bank is considered very readable.

Test Marketing

A **test market** might be used to test some elements of an ad or a media mix in two or more potential markets. The test markets should be representative of the target market. Some cities, such as Buffalo, Indianapolis, and San Antonio, are considered excellent test markets because their demographic and socioeconomic profiles are very broad. That is, they have virtually all income, race, ethnic, and education categories represented within the city. In a typical test market, one or more of the test cities serve as controls while the others are the test. In the control markets the researcher can either (a) run no advertising or (b) continue to run the old ad. The new ad is used in the test cities. Before, during, and after the advertising is run, sales results in the test cities are compared by checking inventories in selected stores.

In addition, test markets can measure communication variables such as recall, awareness, and correct message interpretation. Kraft Foods conducted a rather sophisticated market test. Two versions of a cross-promotion print ad were tested. One version contained the headline, "Super Choices Sweepstake" and the other, "The More Super Choices Coupons You Redeem, the More Chances You Have of Winning." Coupon redemption was used as the performance measure.[9] The second headline won.

Materials for Pretesting

Even if an ad has been completed, it may still be pretested before being distributed in case some elements have the potential for

The copy for this ad is clear, simple, and easy to read.

Everything has changed. Except the relationship, and the barbecued duck.

In Asia, there are always new markets and new opportunities. And there are always new ideas, new products and new technologies. But there are also old ties and long relationships.

HongkongBank
The Hongkong and Shanghai Banking Corporation Limited
Member HSBC Group

causing problems. To preview print ads, advertisers use several types of special material. In folio (short for *portfolio*) testing a cross section of consumers examines a portfolio of ads, usually at home. A dummy publication is specially prepared by a magazine or newspaper for testing purposes. It includes editorial material and 15 to 20 ads. Copies of the dummy publication are distributed to a sample of consumers who are told to read the publication in a normal fashion. A tip-in is a page that is glued to the binding of a real magazine in such a way that a reader cannot tell it from the regular pages. Some copies will have the tip-in ad, some will have the regular ad. Later, people who have read the publication with the tip-in page are questioned.

For broadcast commercials it is often too expensive to produce several completed commercials for testing. In such cases animated or live-action roughs fill in. An artist draws key frames of the commercial in sequence, then the drawings are photographed and a sound track recorded. Finally, a film is made of the drawings. Admittedly, a live-action rough does not contain all the elements of the finished commercial, but the essence is there. This technique is best suited for researching brand awareness and recall.

Concurrent Testing: Communication and Behavior

As mentioned earlier, concurrent testing takes place while the advertising is actually being run. There are three primary techniques: coincidental surveys, attitude tests, and tracking studies. The first two techniques assess communication effects. Tracking studies evaluate behavioral results.

Coincidental Surveys

This technique is most often used with broadcast media. Random calls are made to individuals in the target market. By discovering what stations or shows are being seen or heard, the advertiser can determine whether the target audience is hearing the message and, if so, what information or meaning the audience members receive. This technique can be useful in identifying basic problems.

Attitude Tests

In Chapter 6 we discussed the relationship between an attitude—an enduring favorable or unfavorable disposition toward a person, thing, idea, or situation—and consumer behavior. Researchers measure consumers' attitudes toward elements of an ad or toward a brand being advertised either concurrently or as a posttest. The measurement techniques for print and broadcast are virtually identical. Researchers survey individuals who were exposed to the ad, asking questions about the spokesperson, the tone of the ad, its wording, and so forth. Results that show strong negative attitude scores may prompt the advertiser to pull an ad immediately.

There are five techniques to measure attitudes in this context:[10]

1. *Direct questions:* Respondents express how they feel toward a particular brand, ad, or element of the ad through an open-ended format.
2. *Rating scales:* Respondents indicate their feelings on a progressive scale (for example, from "strongly agree" to "strongly disagree" or from "easy" to "very hard to use").

3. *Checklists:* Respondents check characteristics or feelings considered appropriate. For example, in response to the question "Which is the primary benefit of Gold Medal Flour?", participants might list price, quality, or convenience.

4. *Semantic differential:* Characteristics of concern are displayed as bipolar opposites on a seven-point scale. For example, "Would you say the Jeep Cherokee is economical to drive? Expensive to drive?" "How does it compare with the following competitors?"

5. *Partially structured interviews:* Rather than getting feedback on ads, the interviewer asks broad questions that allow respondents to discuss the product in general and reveal attitudes.

Attitudinal tests are considered more valuable than survey opinion evaluation because they tend to reflect a direct emotional reaction. Recall that people have opinions about a great many things but hold strong attitudes about relatively few. There is also the assumption, right or wrong, that a favorable attitude indicates that the person is more likely to purchase a brand than if she has an unfavorable attitude. There is little solid evidence that this correlation is always accurate. In addition, many experts in the field claim it is nearly impossible to accurately measure attitudes.

Tracking Studies

Studies that follow the purchase activity of a specific consumer or group of consumers over a specified period of time are **market tracking studies.** These studies combine conventional marketing research data with information on marketing communication spending. Compared with other tests, tracking studies provide fuller integration of data and a more complete view of the market.

Researchers use market tracking for both concurrent testing and posttesting. It may serve two basic objectives: (1) to show how the marketer's product sales or market share compares with the competition, at a point in time after implementing some marketing communication, and (2) for reassessment, that is, to help the marketer understand how the market responds to changes he made in the marketing communication strategy.

Tracking studies evaluate copy media and changes in sales. Higher sales for one strategy, compared with those produced by an alternative strategy, implies that the former strategy is better. Tracking studies have had an impact on many decisions, ranging from pulling advertising to changing copy to altering a campaign strategy.

Because spending information is integrated into the analysis, much of the impact of tracking studies deals with the target market, the selection of media vehicles, the schedule, the marketing communication mix, and the media mix.

Marketing communicators use several methods to collect tracking data: wave analysis, consumer diaries, pantry checks, and single-source tracking.[11]

Wave Analysis. This technique assumes that the effects of advertising over time and multiple measures provide a clearer picture of this process. Wave analysis involves a series of interviews during a campaign. The tracking begins with a set of questions asked of a random sample of consumers on a predetermined date. The first questions usually qualify the person as someone who remembers hearing or seeing the ad. Once the person is qualified, a series of follow-up questions is asked. The answers serve as a benchmark and allow adjustments in the message content, media choice, and timing. Perhaps two months later, another series of random calls is made and the same questions are asked. The second wave is compared with the first. The periodic questioning may continue until management is satisfied with the ad's market penetration.

Consumer Diaries. Sometimes advertisers, such as Frito-Lay, ask a group of representative consumers to keep a diary while a campaign is being run. The consumers may be asked to record activities such as brands purchased, brands used for various activities, brand switches, media usage, exposure to competitive promotions, and use of coupons. The advertiser can then review these diaries and determine factors such as whether the message is reaching the right target audience and if the audience is responding to the message as intended. Although the technique is limited by the amount and accuracy of the information obtained, it can serve as an early warning system. One common unfavorable finding from consumer diaries is the indication that no attitude or behavioral change occurred because of exposure to the campaign.

Pantry Checks. The pantry check provides much of the same information as the diary method but requires little from the consumer. A researcher goes to homes in the target market and asks what brands or products have been purchased or used recently. In one variation of this procedure, the researcher counts the products or brands currently stocked by the consumer. The consumer may also be asked to keep empty packages, which the researcher then collects and tallies. The purpose is to correlate product use with the introduction and completion of the campaign.

Single-Source Tracking. Thanks to scanners, combined with computer technology and data and the use of electronic media, researchers are very close to showing a causal relationship between advertising and sales. To set up a **single-source tracking system,** researchers first recruit people living in a particular market to join a consumer panel. The system has four elements:

1. Participants receive a card (with an identification number) that they give to the checkout clerk each time they make a purchase in a supermarket. Scanners identify the person and record his purchases so researchers know who they are and what they buy.
2. The panel members (who are all cable subscribers) are split into matched groups, with each group receiving a different version of a television ad. Electronic test market services transmit the appropriate commercial to the appropriate home so the advertiser knows which household sees which commercial.
3. Meters record the television viewing by panel members. Thus researchers know whether members saw the commercial, when they saw it, and how many times they saw it.
4. Print advertising, coupon distribution, and other marketing communication activities are all controlled. Researchers therefore know what else influences a household's decision to buy or not to buy.

The possibilities for isolating single variables in electronic test markets are almost limitless. Researchers can increase the frequency of advertising or try a different media schedule. They can see whether an ad emphasizing product convenience will stimulate sales to two-career families. They can try an ad that plays up the product's fiber or vitamin content or compare the effectiveness of a two-for-one promotion and a cents-off coupon.

There are only three electronically-based single-source services: Arbitron's Scan America, Nielsen's Scan Track, and Information Resources' Info-Scan. In early tests Arbitron reported that Scan America improved the efficiency of advertising (in terms of reaching the client's target audience) by an average of 43 percent.[12]

Critics contend that current single-source data systems are just fancy versions of the old paper-and-pencil diary and provide little insight into which elements in the marketing communication mix are making a difference and why the consumer reacts in a particular manner to particular cues. In fact, current single-source methods provide a great deal more information than traditional methods.

Table 18.4 summarizes these concurrent testing measurement techniques.

Method	Description
Coincidental surveys	Random calls are made to assess whether people are watching a commercial while it is actually running and what they understand.
Attitude tests	Researchers survey individuals who were exposed to the ad, asking questions about the spokesperson, the tone of the ad, its wording, and so forth.
Tracking studies	These studies follow the purchase activity of a specific consumer or consumer group and correlate this with spending on marketing communication. Techniques include wave analysis, consumer diaries, pantry checks, and single-source tracking.

TABLE 18.4

Concurrent Testing Methods for Assessing Advertising Effectiveness

Posttesting: Communication

More testing occurs after the advertising has run than before, even though resources have already been spent on the ad. The popularity of posttests is explained in part by the limitations of pretesting. In addition, posttests indicate who listened to the message and can thereby provide a basis for planning future messages. The most widely used methods of posttesting fall into three categories: readership, recall, and attitude change.

Readership (Recognition)

Daniel Starch is credited with being the primary developer of readership (recognition) tests. Readership tests provide a mechanism for breaking a print ad into its more important components (that is, headline, visuals, body copy, logo) and then measuring how these elements are remembered by a sample of readers. The intent of the test is to show advertisers that the mere presence of an ad does not mean that readers notice it. The test procedures follow:

1. The Starch organization sends copies of a recent issue of a magazine or newspaper to a certain number of interviewers.
2. The interviewers find a certain number of people who saw the publication (within ten days after the date of publication for weeklies).
3. The interviewer goes through an unmarked copy of the publication with respondents and asks them to indicate the ads they read. When the ads are a half page or larger, the interviewer asks respondents which components they saw.

To assure high-quality results, no respondent is asked to view more than 100 ads, and each respondent starts at a different point in the publication.

Starch regularly covers most of the major magazines. The expense of the readership tests is borne partly by the publishers, which use the results to bolster advertising sales, and partly by ad agencies, which use the results to indicate the impact of an ad. The agencies receive copies of the magazine with a set of stickers on each ad showing what percentage of men and women observed each part; the Timberland ad shows an example. Each ad is evaluated in terms of several criteria: (1) *noted* includes the percentage of people who remembered seeing the ad, (2) *associated* includes those who not only noted the ad but also saw or read some part of it that clearly indicated the brand or advertiser, and (3) *read most* includes the percentage who read half or more of the written material.

Readership tests allow the advertiser to compare ads across several dimensions, such as color, size, and copy. This technique also suggests which elements are most successful in gaining attention. Against these strengths, three weaknesses should be

(Courtesy: Timberland and Roper Starch.)

The Starch scores are shown on the labels for this Timberland ad.

Courtesy: Timberland and Roper Starch.

weighed. First and foremost, the Starch test measures readership, but readership does not necessarily translate into sales or penetration of an idea. Second, readership scores may lead advertisers to use trick means of getting high readership. Finally, results can be misleading because readers are frequently confused. They are often unsure whether they saw a particular ad in one magazine or another, or if they really saw it at all.

Recall Tests

Like the readership test, the *recall test* depends on the memory of the respondent. In readership tests researchers show specific ads to respondents. In contrast, **recall tests** give little or no aid to respondents because the object is to measure the penetration of the ad.

Perhaps the most famous recall test is the Impact service offered by Gallup and Robinson, a prominent research firm. Before respondents are interviewed, they must answer questions to prove that they have read the magazine. After being accepted, they receive cards showing the names of all the products advertised in full or double pages in the issue. After respondents have listed each ad they think they have seen, they are asked to tell what the ad looks like. They are next asked to tell all they can about what the advertiser said—what the sales points were, what message the advertiser tried to get across, and the like. Respondents are also asked to tell the interviewer what they got out of the ad. Next they are asked whether the ad made them want to buy the product or find out more about it. And finally the interviewer asks questions to find out whether the respondent is a prospect for the product advertised.

The Impact method is designed to measure the depth of impression an ad leaves on the reader's mind. Three dimensions of an ad's impression are reported: proven name registration (the percentage of qualified readers who can recall the ad and describe it with the magazine closed), idea penetration (the respondent can describe the contents of the ad), and conviction (the respondent wants to see, try, or buy the product).

To evaluate television commercials, Burke Research Corporation has developed a **day-after recall** test. The day after a commercial is aired, interviewers conduct telephone interviews with a sample of television viewers to determine the extent of brand-name recognition as well as recall of various selling points communicated by the commercial. Typical scores range from 15 to 30 percent recall.

Recall tests do a good job of providing information on the penetration of copy. They also help gauge the extent to which a message provides the correct impression. On the negative side, there is not necessarily a relationship with sales. Recall tests are also quite expensive, and not all companies can afford them. There is also the problem that some people have better memories than others. Recall tests cannot account for these differences. Also, various elements that are part of general communication (for example, stories adjoining the ad, poor reproduction quality) can become confused with the advertising message.

Attitude Change Measures

When used for posttesting, attitude measurement tests generally try to assess the effectiveness of advertising or other marketing communication in changing the consumer's evaluation of the company and/or its brands. As noted earlier, it is assumed that a favorable change in attitude predisposes people to buy a product. Recall and attitude tests are often combined to determine if there are major differences between consumers who remember the advertising messages and those who do not. Attitude tests at this stage in the process are also used to measure changes in consumer perceptions of a brand or measure degrees of acceptance of various claims made in the advertising.

Because attitude change is perceived to have more bearing on purchase than recall, attitude measures are highly regarded and heavily used by many marketing communication managers. In addition, testing attitudes can be done with ease and minimum expense. Nevertheless, there are serious problems associated with attitudes and their measurement. Although marketing communication managers assume that they are measuring brand attitudes toward ad execution, a host of other factors are often being assessed instead.

Posttesting: Behavior

Although most marketers feel the ultimate payoff from advertising should be a change in behavior—phone response, store visit, or direct sales—measuring advertising's contribution to sales has proven extremely difficult and expensive. Researchers have two key testing methods that try to measure advertising's effect on sales: inquiry tests and sales tests.

Inquiry Tests

Inquiry tests check the effectiveness of ads by asking those who have seen them to respond to questions. The advertiser runs a certain number of ads and offers some inducement to reply to them. The offer may be a booklet, a sample of the product, a toll-free number, or something else of value. The marketing communicator finds the cost per inquiry by dividing the cost of the ad by the number of inquiries.

Inquiry testing may be used to check media, individual ads, or campaigns. To check the effectiveness of two ads, a promoter might run ad A one day and ad B the next in the local paper. The ad that produces the most inquiries per dollar is deemed more effective.[13]

Another version of the inquiry test is the split-run test. Split-run refers to the practice of testing ads by running two or more versions of the same ad on the same issue date but in different editions of a newspaper or magazine. The different ads appear on the same day in identical positions. Each version of the ad may change only one element—copy, illustration, headline, coupon redemption, or readership. Or the advertiser might run four entirely different ads.

Split-run is also available on cable television. The cable system is able to show different commercials for the same product in different households simultaneously. Later, viewers' opinions are surveyed by phone, mail, or personal interview.

Split-run testing can be used as a pretest or posttest. Sometimes a split-run test is conducted on alternative versions of an ad for different market segments and wants to find out whether a standardized ad would suffice; posttesting with a split-run may provide the answer.

There are several advantages of inquiry testing. The results indicate that the person not only read or saw the ad but also took some action (that is, responded to the inquiry). Action is a much stronger indicator than recall or awareness. More-over, there is fairly good control of the variables that influence action, especially if split-run is used; the only variable that changes is the ad itself. However, one can question the sincerity of a person who expresses an interest in the product or service being offered. Also, unless one element is being modified, one is never sure why one ad is better than another. Finally, inquiry tests are time-consuming. It may take three or four months before replies are measured.

Sales Tests

Several posttests presumably reflect a relationship between a particular ad and a particular sale. Comparing past sales with current sales is a common approach, particularly with the big catalog houses like Spiegel and Montgomery Ward. These businesses assume that a particular ad placed in a catalog is responsible for the sales generated. If sales increase from year to year, the ad is given credit.

Field tests are also used to examine the impact of ads on sales. For example, various ads may be run in several comparable markets, targeted to different market segments. Then evaluators compare the sales in each test market or segment.

Although these various measures of advertising effectiveness provide important insights, the ultimate question is, "Does advertising work?" If we go back to the assumption that every ad has a different objective, ranging from creating awareness to purchase, then the answer is yes—advertising works. The IMC in Action feature offers support for this position. The same conclusion can be drawn for the other communication mix tools.

Table 18.5 provides an overview of the posttesting measurement techniques just discussed.

Method	Explanation
Readership (recognition)	An ad is broken into its more important components, and researchers determine how these elements are remembered by a sample of consumers.
Recall tests	Recall tests give little or no aid to respondents because the object is to measure the penetration of the ad.
Attitude change measures	This measurement assesses the effectiveness of advertising or other marketing communication tools in changing the consumer's evaluation of the company and/or its brands.
Inquiry tests	An advertiser runs a certain number of ads and offers some inducement to reply to them in order to check media, individual ads, or campaigns.
Sales tests	Sales are compared before and after an ad is run.

TABLE 18.5

Posttesting Methods for Assessing Advertising Effectiveness

Can Marketing Communication Create Sales?

There remains a great deal of controversy about the ability of marketing communication to cause sales. Take a look at the following sample of studies. All suggest that a causal relationship exists.

- To find out just how effective business-to-business advertising is, the Association of Business Publishers and Advertising Research Federation designed a study in which two products (a $10 portable safety product and a $10,000 commercial transportation component package) were advertised for a year in similar business publications. The study proves through the tracking of actual product sales that business publication advertising produces more sales than would occur without advertising. It also proves that increased advertising frequency can increase product sales. Results also suggest that a single advertising campaign may be effective for a full year or longer.

- Gerald Tellis conducted a study in which 250 volunteers in Eau Claire, Wisconsin, were each given an identification card that notified a grocer's computerized checkout counters to track all the items they bought. The subjects' TV sets were outfitted with a device that continuously monitored which channels were being watched and hence which commercials the family was seeing. Daily newspapers were monitored for coupons and store specials. Tellis found that in the case of laundry detergent, television advertising's effect on sales was minimal; lowering prices through coupons and store specials, however, resulted in a large boost in sales.

- According to a ten-year study of data from Information Resources' BehaviorScan, TV advertising produces long-term sales growth even two years after a campaign ends. Also, a shift from a daytime media schedule to prime time produced better sales results; a bigger ad schedule worked better during a new-product introduction; and better results were produced by concentrating increased advertising into fewer weeks than by a sustained but lower-level effort.

- *Family Circle* tracked the supermarket purchases of its readers before and after an issue of the magazine was released. Scanner-derived data from Citicorp POS Information Services made it possible to track the sales of 22 products advertised in that issue. Sales differences between *Family Circle* households and control households increased for 15 of the products advertised, with an average increase of 20 percent.

- According to John Philip Jones, who researched and authored the book *When Ads Work: New Proof that Advertising Triggers Sales,* advertising has a real but temporary short-term effect in 70 percent of the products he studied. Further, the average market share of all advertised brands is higher than that of unadvertised brands. Prices of advertised brands are also higher, and sales growth of advertised brands is 3 percent above unadvertised ones.

Food for Thought

1. Armed with this information, do you think it would be tough to convince a CEO to spend money on marketing communication if the business was suffering from financial trouble? Why?

2. If you were attempting to prove that marketing communication caused sales (and money for research was plentiful), what methods would you use? What if your funds were limited?

Sources: John P. Jones, *When Ads Work: New Proof that Advertising Triggers Sales* (New York: Lexington Books, 1995); "Print Advertising Proves Itself," *American Demographics* (January 1992): 16; Howard E. Potter, "IRI Study Confirms Some Conventional Wisdom," *Marketing News,* January 6, 1992, 22; Gary Levin, "Ads Outperform Promotions in Profits Study," *Advertising Age,* April 17, 1989, 4; "Science 1, Advertisers 0," *U.S. News & World Report,* May 1, 1989, 60–1; Jerome W. Vozoff, "Ad Effectiveness: A New Study," *Adweek,* May 16, 1988, 56; "On the Effectiveness of Advertising," *Adweek,* May 26, 1987, 19.

MEASURING THE PERFORMANCE OF SALES PROMOTION

Measuring the effectiveness of sales promotion can be just as complicated as measuring the effectiveness of advertising. Part of this complexity is a result of the nature and diversity of sales promotion objectives. Recall from Chapter 10 that these objectives can range from stimulating immediate action to enhancing product value and brand equity to match the competition. Several sales promotion objectives are directly related to sales, and many of the same sales-based measurement techniques discussed in earlier sections are also used with sales promotion. Intermediate objectives, such as trial purchase, trading up, and multiple purchases, are more difficult to measure and require customized methods developed by sales promotion managers. Sales promotion also attempts to accomplish communication objectives. Coming up with valid ways to measure these responses while separating the effect of the media has proven very difficult.

A second reason for the complexity in measuring sales promotion performance revolves around the organizational structure supporting sales promotion. Two dimensions of the structure are particularly relevant. First, sales promotions are often delivered to the end user through one or more resellers. The effectiveness of a sales promotion, then, depends on the abilities of the reseller as well as on the marketing communication strategy. Wholesalers and retailers who actively support a marketer's sales promotion can greatly enhance its performance. The opposite is also true.

Another organizational problem is the diversity of sales promotion service agencies. Some service companies build trade show booths or supply audiovisual equipment for sales promotion events. Others plan or implement marketing communication strategies. No matter how broad or narrow their scope of operations, all these suppliers are known as sales promotion agencies. This generic title often confuses potential or current clients because they are unaware that an agency may have expertise in only one facet of sales promotion and is incapable of measuring effectiveness of the other areas.

Despite these limitations, a great deal of effort has been devoted to improving the quality of sales promotion performance measures. Simple measures, such as counting the number of coupons redeemed, are still used and provide valuable information. Advanced mathematical models have recently found their way into sales promotion testing. For example, elaborate regression models are able to determine the contribution of various sales promotion tactics on sales. Sales promotion has borrowed heavily from advertising measurement techniques as well. For instance, the pretest, concurrent test, and posttest framework is also used in sales promotion. There is one major difference, however, between the evaluation of advertising and the evaluation of sales promotion. Evaluations of advertising tend to emphasize communication measures. For sales promotion, evaluation tends to focus on behavioral measures. As the field of sales promotion grows in sophistication, the evaluation of communication variables will increase.[14]

Pretesting Sales Promotion

In general, sales promotion managers are reluctant to pretest. Short lead time and concern for alerting competitors are two reasons for this hesitation. Instead, managers tend to rely heavily on experience ("What worked before will work again") and determine that sales promotion is best evaluated through sales, its ultimate goal. Although experience and sales are important, there are benefits in pretesting before spending the money or committing unresolvable strategic mistakes. Pretests consider communication and behavioral variables. Because many of these measurement techniques were discussed earlier, only brief mention will be made in the discussion that follows.

Pretesting Communication

There is a wide variety of measures used to pretest the communication elements of sales promotions. In addition to the typical communication elements found in advertising (that is, headline, copy, and visuals), an overriding communication element contained in most sales promotions is *perceived value.* **Perceived value** is the calculation the consumer makes in her mind of the extra value contained in the sales promotion compared with the risks in accepting the offer. For example, a consumer may weigh the benefit of 40 percent off on an unkonwn brand of shoes compared with the risk of buying an unfamiliar product. Measuring perceived value is complicated because consumers are not sure what these promotions are worth. Some promotions—price-offs, bonus packs, rebates and refunds, and trade coupons—provide an immediate value. Others, such as premiums and continuity programs, give gifts to enhance value. A third group—samples, demonstrations, warranties, contests, and sweepstakes—provides a promised or implied value. Consumers might be asked to evaluate the trade-off through a survey questionnaire. Or the researchers can vary the type of value offered and assess how consumers respond to each.

This assessment can be done through several different devices. Focus groups and consumer panels are common. Other techniques include the *ballot method, portfolio tests,* the *jury method,* and *mall intercepts.* The **ballot method** consists of mailing a printed ballot to a list of consumers. The sales promotions to be evaluated and some additional information are given about each one. Consumers are asked to vote for the one they like best and return the ballot to the research firm. **Portfolio tests** are similar to the ballot method except a portfolio of sales promotions is developed and shown to consumers in person. Although portfolio tests are more expensive than the ballot method, the information obtained is considered more accurate. The **jury method** is a combination of the previous two techniques except the jurors are paid for their evaluation and may be knowledgeable about sales promotions. The **mall intercept** technique involves stopping people at random in a mall and showing them the various promotions for evaluation. Although print and television can be tested, it is the most expensive device.

Pretesting Behavior

The most common device used to pretest the behavioral response to sales promotion is the market test. Depending on the specific sales promotion technique, the behavioral response considered could be trial purchase, purchase, repeat purchase, incremental purchase, and so forth. We have already discussed the process of market testing. In sales promotion pretesting, market tests usually consist either of testing two separate markets against each other or matching several stores in the same market against one another. In either case the sales promotion device or program being tested is the only variable manipulated. All else is kept constant.

Pretesting Sales Promotion with Resellers

If resellers are unhappy with the sales promotion effort, they will either reject it outright or give it only partial support. It is therefore important to get the evaluation of resellers before implementation. It is possible to pretest some aspects of sales promotion programs with resellers—particularly materials that are used in-store or that rely on the reseller's cooperation to make them work. The easiest way to pretest a sales promotion program is simply to go to several key retailers or wholesalers and discuss the plan with them. It is occasionally more efficient to contact a third party, such as a marketing organization, that has strong ties with the retailer.

Concurrent Testing of Sales Promotion

Concurrent testing is evaluating the performance of sales promotion while it is still running. As noted in the advertising section, this testing allows the marketing communication strategists to modify the sales promotion to increase performance or eliminate it to reduce negative consequences. For sales promotion, essentially all concurrent tests measure changes in sales or some variation of sales in response to the promotion. Thanks to advances in scanner research capability, sales information can be combined with consumer information to provide a very elaborate analysis of a specific sales promotion device or program. For marketers who do not have access to such technology, traditional sales comparisons (actual and forecasted sales figures or sales among competing stores, for instance) are still employed.

Posttesting Sales Promotion

Because the main objective of sales promotion is to stimulate immediate action, it is not surprising that the most valid and reliable measures of performance are posttests. Although sales and market share remain the predominant areas of interest, researchers also measure communication and behavioral factors.

Communication Posttest Measures

Usually the information sought to measure the effectiveness of communication elements relates to consumer awareness and attitudes. The information-gathering devices, however, are much simpler than the techniques used in advertising research. For example, the most common methods for measuring consumer awareness and attitudes are telephone calls, mailed questionnaires, and personal interviews. Direct mail is the least expensive method, and personal interviews are by far the most expensive. The information sought is usually related to changes in consumer awareness, attitude, or actions in reference to a specific sales promotion event.

Posttesting is also done through in-store observations and interviews and in follow-up survey interviews with responders and nonresponders to a promotion. In-store observations and intercept interviews with shoppers at the point of purchase are particularly relevant for store-distributed promotions such as samples and premiums.

Behavioral Posttest Measures

Techniques are available that assess the extent to which sales promotion affects the behavior of resellers and consumers. Monitoring sales is the most common technique. Data-gathering techniques include market testing and tracking studies. The interpretation of these figures varies. For example, traditional break-even analysis can be employed. First, fixed costs and variable costs of the promotion are determined; second, the variable contribution margin of the brand is determined; and finally, break-even sales volume for the promotion is calculated. Multiple regression analysis is a statistical technique that estimates the contribution of several variables acting jointly on a single dependent variable—sales. By its basic nature, the analysis of sales promotions tends to fit this technique well. Finally, there are statistical models built into the scanner systems that can provide a very detailed analysis.

MEASURING THE PERFORMANCE OF PUBLIC RELATIONS

Ascertaining the results of a public relations effort is, for several reasons, the most neglected branch of the art. Such evaluation deals with the most difficult thing to measure—changes in human opinion. Public relations' contribution is difficult to measure because it is used along with other marketing communication tools. If PR is used before the other tools come into action, its contribution is easier to evaluate.[15] Because evaluation of the results of public relations is difficult, it is also expensive. However, once an organization feels that a public relations effort is reasonably successful, it is usually inclined to spend a lot of money to estimate the degree of success.

This evaluation process may be informal or scientific. It may involve a few people seated around a table or a massive survey. It can take a few hours or a few weeks. Basically the process seeks to answer the question, "How did we do?" As is the case with all marketing communication elements, public relations needs to understand to what extent its programs achieved the objectives.

In Chapter 11 we described some of the primary methods used to evaluate a public relations effort: focus groups, content analysis, monitoring, and informal observations. These methods can be used to measure exposure, psychological change, or behavioral change.

Exposures

The easiest measure of PR effectiveness is the number of exposures created in the media. Publicists supply the client with a clipping book showing all the media that carried news about the product and a summary statement such as the following:

> Media coverage included 3500 column inches of news and photographs in 350 publications with a combined circulation of 79.4 million; 2500 minutes of airtime on 290 radio stations and an estimated audience of 65 million; and 660 minutes of airtime on 160 television stations with an estimated audience of 91 million. If this time and space had been purchased at advertising rates, the cost would have amounted to $1,047,000.

This exposure measure is not very satisfying. There is no indication of how many people actually read, heard, or recalled the message, nor what they thought afterward. There is no information on the net audience reached since publications overlap in readership. Because publicity's goal is reach, not frequency, it would be useful to know the number of unduplicated exposures. Nor does this exposure measure indicate whether these figures reflect positive or negative coverage. However, there is evidence that better exposure measures are on the horizon.

Change in Awareness, Comprehension, or Attitude

A better measure is the change in product awareness, comprehension, or attitude resulting from the PR campaign (after allowing for the impact of other marketing communication tools). For example, how many people recall hearing the news item? How many told others about it (a measure of word of mouth)? How many changed their minds after hearing the news item? The Potato Board learned, for example, that the number of people who agreed with the statement "Potatoes are rich in vitamins and minerals" went from 36 percent before the campaign to 67 percent after the campaign, a significant improvement in product comprehension.

Sales and Profit Contributions

Sales and profit impact, if obtainable, are often the most satisfactory measure of the results of public relations. For example, sales of 9-Lives increased 43 percent at the end of the "Morris the Cat" PR campaign. However, advertising and sales promotion had also been stepped up, and their contribution was considered too. Suppose total sales increased $1,500,000; based on experience, management estimates that PR contributed 15 percent of the total sales increase. Then the return on PR investment is calculated as follows:

Total sales increase	$1,500,000
Estimated sales increase due to PR (15%)	225,000
Contribution margin on product sales (10%)	22,500
Total direct cost of PR program	−10,000
Contribution margin added by PR investment	$12,500
Return on PR investment ($12,500 ÷ $10,000)	125%

MEASURING THE PERFORMANCE OF DIRECT MARKETING

Direct marketing has been around for a long time and has developed evaluation techniques unique to that industry. For example, an outgoing telemarketer such as AT&T or MCI keeps careful records of calls made, characteristics of people called (those that reject/accept the marketing pitch), and the general conversion rate. Telemarketers know that a conversion rate of 2 to 4 percent is average and can actually test various scripts to determine which message is producing the best results. Likewise, a direct-mail company now has the capability of carefully controlling its database, so that it can customize direct-mail pieces to reach specific audiences. Analysis of response rates is then fairly easy. In addition, direct-mail experts know that previous buyers are far more likely to buy again and require different messages. Earlier we discussed the current difficulty of assessing the performance of online direct marketing. New technologies will have to be developed to bring this area into the realm of valid and reliable testing.

MEASURING THE PERFORMANCE OF PERSONAL SELLING

Because of the typical organizational separation, the performance measures developed in personal selling are quite different from those found in other areas of marketing communication. To begin with, the personal selling function is evaluated by the sales manager and the marketing manager. Their task is twofold: (1) to evaluate the sales production of various sales territories and (2) to evaluate the performance of the salespeople responsible for that territory. Performance standards are compared with actual performance and adjustments are made. It is unlikely that the performance of personal selling as part of the total marketing communication strategy would be of interest to or the responsibility of the sales manager. Therefore marketing communication managers need to evaluate the relative performance of personal selling in the marketing communication mix, as opposed to sales performance. Each level of evaluation will be discussed.

Evaluating the Salesperson

The goal of this evaluation is to determine appropriate corrective action. To do that managers must assess the factors that affected performance and determine which ones the salesperson could or could not control. The three most important controllable factors are volume, activities, and quality.[16]

Volume Analysis

Sales volume is the simplest type of sales performance measurement and probably the most often used. Volume analysis can be appraised in terms of both effectiveness and efficiency. In terms of effectiveness, actual sales performance of a particular spokesperson can be compared with the previous year's sales, the present year's budget, the sales performance of other salespeople, the number of sales closed, the number of accounts in the territory that are inactive, and the concentration on sales of special merchandise.

As with effectiveness, sales efficiency can be measured in many ways. Experience suggests four measures: gross margin on sales, contribution to profit, expense-to-sales ratio, and market share. The employment of basic accounting procedures quickly provides the appropriate data to run these tests for an individual salesperson, across salespeople, or across territories.

Activity Analysis

A manager's understanding of salespeople's performance has often been increased by examining their activities as well as their sales volume. Again, the possibilities are numerous.

The effectiveness of the sales force can be evaluated with respect to the number of sales calls, new accounts opened, and complaints received. The precision of these analyses might be improved by looking at both efficiency and effectiveness. For example, calls per day and costs per call might provide more useful information than just the raw number of calls. It might also be interesting to look not just at the number of new accounts opened but at the size of each account. Perhaps the number of complaints should be balanced by the number of sales. Finally, sales representatives may be putting in long hours, but they may not be selling hours. A look at the ratio of selling time to total time can also provide useful insights.

Evaluating Personal Selling as a Part of Marketing Communication

Poor cooperation between sales management and marketing communication management has meant that this type of evaluation is rarely performed. Personal selling is often reluctant to provide the information requested by the marketing communication manager because of distrust and a sense of separateness. Consequently, the quality of the information tends to be poor.

However, a more inherent problem is that there is little evidence that companies actually have objectives that specify how personal selling should contribute to the overall marketing communication effort. The nature of the evaluation therefore relies heavily on subjective criteria developed by the marketing communication manager. For example, a marketing communication manager may be very concerned with whether the salesperson uses the sales promotion materials provided, including point-of-purchase displays, catalogs, brochures, pamphlets, and cooperative advertising programs. It might also be important to know whether these materials were used correctly. How is this information gathered? Surveys of the sales reps is one possibility, although the reps are reluctant to answer such surveys. Another possibility is to monitor the sales force—but that is costly and creates more distrust. Consequently, the validity and reliability of this information are suspect.

The other area in which salespeople might be evaluated is communication. Do salespeople provide feedback from customers about programs, competition, market information, or program effectiveness? This information is difficult to quantify, and the results may produce simple yes-or-no categories. This facet of evaluation remains the weakest in promotion. It is unlikely that the situation will improve until the organizational and perceptual boundaries separating personal selling from the other marketing communication elements are removed.

EVALUATING OTHER TYPES OF MARKETING COMMUNICATION

As indicated throughout this text, there are many elements or techniques that fall under integrated marketing communication. Trade shows, point-of-purchase, packaging, sports marketing, and licensing are just a few of these communication techniques. Many cross over into the more traditional communication areas and rely on the same evaluation tools. For example, marketers often view event marketing and sports marketing as part of public relations and evaluate them accordingly.

However, the demand by marketers to hold events more accountable has prompted the development of new measures to evaluate sponsorships.[17] The beauty of event promotions is that results easily can be measured against sales by counting retail displays and impressions via pre- and post-event attitude surveys. For example, Yankelovich Partners, Inc., and Lifestyle Marketing Group (LMG) have launched a service called Yankelovich Express Lifestyle Tracking. YELT measures and evaluates sports and entertainment sponsorships, events, and related promotions through the use of optically-scannable "Tech Cards," short survey forms that break lengthy questionnaires into groups of questions that appear on separate cards. The cards take from 30 to 90 seconds to complete and can double as sweepstakes entries, which increases response rates.[18]

Also, there are a number of research companies that specialize in measuring employee satisfaction and customer satisfaction. This can be done through focus groups, personal in-depth interviews, or the survey technique. These measures assume that satisfaction is a result of good customer service, so strong satisfaction implies good service.

As the number of communication techniques grow, it will be even more important to develop evaluation tools that are appropriate for each technique. More important, it would be best to have evaluation tools that work across all these communication techniques simultaneously.

Concept

✓ **Review**

MEASURING THE PERFORMANCE OF SALES PROMOTION, PR, DIRECT MARKETING, PERSONAL SELLING, AND OTHER TYPES

1. Sales promotion uses pretest methods, concurrent testing methods, and posttesting methods, similar to those used in advertising, to measure performance.
2. Techniques used to measure the performance of public relations include: focus groups, content analysis, monitoring, and informal observation.
3. Direct-marketing techniques to assess performance are unique for each direct-marketing tool.
4. Personal selling performance is measured through volume analysis, activity analysis, and analysis of selling qualities.
5. A number of other communication techniques, such as trade shows, point-of-purchase, packaging, and so forth, are beginning to develop their own performance measures.

A CLOSING THOUGHT: THE SEARCH FOR A UNIVERSAL MEASURE

One of the key issues in successfully integrating marketing communication is to be able to measure the effectiveness of a communication strategy simultaneously. That is, how do the individual components blend together to achieve objectives? Although we have techniques and technologies that have been applied to each of the mix components separately, a universal measure that applies across all communication tools does not yet exist.

Scanner and single-source techniques are capable of assessing advertising and sales promotion simultaneously but have not incorporated public relations and personal selling as well. Until this challenge of a cross-functional measurement system is met, total integration remains quite difficult.

SUMMARY

1. **Address the main issues in measuring the performance of marketing communications.**
In conducting evaluative research, four preliminary questions should be answered: What should be tested? Should we test? If so, when? And how?

2. **Explain the specific testing methods used with advertising, sales promotion, public relations, direct marketing, personal selling, and other IMC tools.**
Measuring advertising performance can be done as a pretest, concurrent test, or posttest. Common pretest methods include: tests of opinion/awareness, focus groups, program analysis, on-the-air tests, physiological methods, readability tests, and test markets. Concurrent testing methods include coincidental surveys, attitude tests, and tracking studies. Posttest methods include: readership (recognition), recall tests, attitude change measures, inquiry tests, and sales tests. Techniques used to assess the effectiveness of sales promotion include measuring perceived value, market testing, sales, tracking studies, and in-store observations. Techniques used to assess the effectiveness of public relations include focus groups, content analysis, monitoring, and informal observations. Analysts use specialized techniques for each area of direct marketing to assess direct marketing's effectiveness. To measure the effectiveness of personal selling, researchers use volume analysis and activity analysis.

POINTS TO PONDER

Review the Facts
1. What prominent decisions should the marketing communication manager consider when measuring promotional performance? Elaborate.
2. What are the most common measures of advertising effectiveness?
3. What information would you require to assess public relations performance?

Master the Concepts
4. What are the major limitations in measuring the effectiveness of the sales promotion program?
5. Explain the utility of the model for measuring advertising effectiveness. What are the stages involved in the model?
6. Why were inquiry tests developed? In what ways can they be utilized?

7. What mistakes are made by sales managers who use sales volume alone to measure sales performance?

Apply Your Knowledge

8. The marketing manager for a large cereal manufacturer wishes to increase sales by 10 percent through a massive communication effort including television, print, coupons, a sweepstakes, and event sponsorship. Evaluate whether the sales objective is an appropriate way to evaluate performance of this promotional strategy.

9. Select an advertising objective and create several rough ideas for ads that relate to the objective. Finally, devise an experiment that can measure the relative effectiveness of those ads.

10. Assume that a severely limited budget motivated your firm's marketing communication manager to reevaluate the methods used to test advertising. Pretests, concurrent tests, and posttests were used in the past. In light of the budget constraints, your associates feel that only posttesting should be considered. Do you agree? Explain.

SUGGESTED PROJECTS

1. Outline a performance evaluation program for a fast-food retailer such as McDonald's, Burger King, or Kentucky Fried Chicken.

2. (Oral Communication) Visit an advertising agency and discuss its techniques for measuring effectiveness with an account executive or top-level manager. How does the agency's approach compare with the techniques discussed in this chapter?

3. (Writing Project) Go to your campus library and identify five or six secondary research sources that

provide companies with assistance in measuring performance. In a brief one- to two-page memo, describe the type of information they provide.

4. (Internet Project) Conduct some research on the Web to find at least two sources that provide companies with assistance in measuring Internet advertising performance. In a brief one- to two-page memo, describe the information the sources provide. Be sure to note how each source measures performance.

CASE 18: ADVERTISEMENTS THAT ARE GOOD FOR YOUR HEALTH

People who work for advertising agencies have to get used to negative public perceptions about the work they do. Consumer advocates charge agencies with subliminally coaxing people to buy products they can't afford or don't want or need. Public service ads have a reputation for being unrealistic and preachy, and even the anti-drug ad campaigns get criticized for using inaccurate information and ignoring deadly but legal drugs.

A Healthy Victory for Ads

But ad agencies around the country have been feeling a little better about public acceptance of their

work as a result of the state of California's anti-smoking campaign. The campaign's ads have won the respect of viewers and media critics and have apparently done their job—getting people to quit smoking.

The anti-smoking campaign is the result of a taxpayer referendum in 1988. California voters approved a 25-cents-per-pack tax on cigarettes, with the money to be used to warn citizens, particularly those in high-risk groups, of the perils of smoking. The state wanted at least half of its 30.5 million residents to be aware of the ads, a goal that was quickly reached. Ten years later, the campaign is still a success story.

Targeting Minority Groups

Part of the success of the ads is attributed to their specific targeting of young people, pregnant women, Spanish speakers, Asians, and African-Americans. A Los Angeles advertising agency, Keye/Donna/Perlstein, was the lead agency, but Muse Cordero/L.A. and The Hispanic Group/Santa Monica, two minority-owned shops, get credit for the effectiveness of ads directed at ethnic markets. Early studies showed that 78 percent of California's African-Americans, 85 percent of its Spanish-speaking population, and 65 percent of its Asian population had seen or heard at least one of the campaign's television or radio spots.

The Results

Within six months of the start of the campaign, three out of four California residents indicated that they were aware of the ads. Almost half of the adult smokers who had seen the ads said they intended to quit, as compared with 39 percent of those who hadn't seen the ads. The ads have led to more positive attitudes toward good health among both adults and students, and early surveys showed a slight drop in smoking by students.

The ads break the stereotype of bland, unrealistic public-service messages. Rosemary Romano, director of public information for the Federal Office on Smoking and Health, says they "are hard-hitting, the quality is excellent, and they cover a range of issues."

Although the tobacco industry fought hard against the original referendum, it had no plans to organize a counterattack. The industry trade group, the Tobacco Institute, disputes claims of success by the anti-smoking campaign, pointing out that tobacco sales had fallen 14 percent statewide in 1989, before the campaign began. Some people may, in fact, be quitting more because of the extra cost of smoking than because the ads are having the desired effect. But judging from the requests from around the nation and around the world to borrow or buy the ads, the particular agencies involved, and the entire industry, should view the California anti-smoking campaign as a major sign that ad agencies can do effective work for the public good.

Unfortunately, some of this success diminished due to cut-backs in the appropriations for these anti-smoking educational programs. Initially, funding from 1990 to 1995 showed a decline of nearly 25 percent. Not coincidentally, youth smoking rates climbed by nearly 20 percent during that same time period, whereas adult smoking rates declined by 42 percent. This outcome caused such an uproar by Californians that the campaign budget was reinstated in the 1996–1997 budget. Perhaps these monies will create the same high level of success achieved in 1989 and 1990.

Case Questions

1. What are the problems associated with the effectiveness measures mentioned in this case?
2. Suggest a measurement process that would better meet the assessment objectives cited.

Sources: California Cancer Institute home page (September 4, 1996): Internet (www.CA.cancer.org:80/Prop 99/wewon); California State Government Health Statistics (February 3, 1996): Internet (www.ao.ca.Gov1CgHlth3); Pat Hinsberg, "Anti-Smoking Ads Capture An Audience," *Adweek*, November 5, 1990, 18.

ROMA'S LITE INTEGRATED CASE QUESTIONS

(Review the Roma's Lite marketing plan in the Appendix before answering these questions.)

1. Consider the four preliminary questions to be answered when measuring the effectiveness of marketing communication. How would you answer them when considering Roma's Lite Pizza?

2. How would you measure the effectiveness of the other message-delivery methods discussed in Chapter 14?

3. (Team Project) Develop a comprehensive system for measuring the effectiveness of the communication strategy proposed for Roma's Lite Pizza.

chapter

19

Campaign Planning

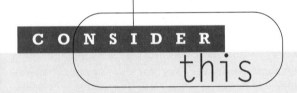

CONSIDER *this*

Saturn: A Different Kind of Car Company

Saturn believes that everything it does sends a message. General Motors launched the Saturn car in 1990 as a separate "nameplate" (a line of cars, such as General Motors' Chevrolet car line). The product launch was intended to be an all-out effort to beat the Japanese in the small-car market. Along the way, the car company earned a reputation for how it treats its employees, neighbors, dealers, and, of course, its customers, who have given it near-cult status. What's important, however, is that the initial strategic vision that guided the development and launch of Saturn has continued to provide direction for ten years.

Saturn is a good example of relationship marketing based on an understanding of the importance of all stakeholders, company actions, and product performance. The integrated marketing communication program started in 1988 at the

same time the car was being designed. The case study used throughout this chapter illustrates not only how communication can remain consistent and true to a company vision across all types of communication but also across a long period of time.

Saturn's initial launch communication emphasized that it was "a different kind of company, a different kind of car," a position maintained in marketing communication to all its stakeholders—employees, suppliers and vendors, dealers, the community, the media, and its customers. This approach was demonstrated not only in its launch advertising but also in its revolutionary new dealer-customer relationship and a ground-breaking new union relations program.

Saturn's approach to its advertising agency was revolutionary too. The agency, called a "communications partner," was selected by a committee of Saturn managers and union representatives. Hal Riney & Partners, the agency that masterminded the launch, was involved from the beginning of the car's planning in 1988. Its performance was so outstanding that Hal Riney was named Agency of the Year in 1992, the year after the launch, because of its work on this integrated marketing communication program.

Sources: Information for this case study was provided by Greg Martin, Director of Corporate Communications, Saturn. Other sources for this discussion and throughout the rest of the chapter include "Pitch Man," *Sales & Marketing Management* (January 1995): 124; "Smile on Saturn—Don't Change What's Working," *Advertising Age,* March 28, 1994, S24; Bruce Horovitz, "Saturn Hopes Folksy Image Isn't Lost in Shuffle," *USA Today,* 6 December 1994, B1–B2; Eric Hollreiser, "To Haggle or Not to Haggle? Dealers, Makers Roll the Dice," *Brandweek,* November 21, 1994, 18–19; Warren Brown, "Saturn Homecoming Draws 30,000 Back to Spring Hill," *Boulder Camera,* 16 June 1994, 4A; Barry Meier, "Engine Fires Prompt G.M. to Issue Recall of 80% of Saturns," *New York Times,* 11 August 1993, A1, A10; Lindsay Chappel, "Dealers Return Profit to Raise Saturn's Total," *Automotive News,* June 14, 1993, 1; Alice Z. Cueo and Raymond Serafin, "With Saturn, Riney Rings Up a Winner," *Advertising Age,* April 14, 1993, 2–3; Greg Hassell, "The New Deal," *The Houston Chronicle,* 7 February 1993, 2; Raymond Serafin, "The Saturn Story," *Advertising Age,* November 16, 1992, 1, 13, 16; James B. Treece, "Here Comes GM's Saturn," *Business Week,* April 9, 1990, 56–62; Raymond Serafin, "GM's Saturn Breaks Mold: UAW Helps Select Ad Agency," *Advertising Age,* March 7, 1988, 1.

CHAPTER OVERVIEW

This chapter introduces the campaign planning process. It shows how everything we have discussed thus far can be used to produce a consistent, creative set of messages that accomplishes various objectives. More important, the campaign process provides a framework for integrating all the marketing communication elements into one coordinated whole. Even though the concept of a campaign is most commonly used in the context of advertising, the marketing communication manager must view the entire communication effort as a campaign that extends across time, across different message delivery systems and functional areas, and across different target audiences.

The Saturn story is one of a complex integrated campaign whose strategy has been maintained with consistency throughout the car company's history. We use this campaign case study throughout this chapter to illustrate how an IMC campaign is planned and managed.

PLANNING A CAMPAIGN

A *campaign* is not created in a vacuum; it is guided explicitly by the realities of the situation and implicitly by the marketing and corporate business plans. Campaign planners create a blueprint for all messages delivered over time, across various media, and to various audiences. A **campaign** is a series of marketing communication messages designed to meet a set of objectives based on a situation analysis and delivered over time (at least one year), through several marketing communication activities, and through various media. By taking a campaign approach, marketing communication planners increase the likelihood that the communication efforts will create synergy.

In contrast, companies that create one marketing communication message at a time (such as one TV or print ad, one direct-mail piece, or one billboard) are not involved in a campaign planning process. This one-message-at-a-time strategy is called the one-shot approach and can lead to problems with inconsistent messages.

In Chapter 4 we discussed general approaches to planning. In this chapter we consider the specific process used to develop a comprehensive campaign, from the situation analysis to creating the message to the media plan to the final evaluation. Table 19.1 describes eight steps that are important in campaign planning.

The end result of the campaign planning process is a document—called a **campaign plan**—that summarizes all the campaign planner's recommendations. The main sections of the campaign plan are similar to the steps in the campaign planning process. In other words, the outline in Table 19.1 can also be used as an outline for the campaign plan document. This document is reviewed by everyone who will execute the campaign. The review usually generates feedback, the document is revised, and ultimately it must be approved by the external agency's top management (if developed out of house) and the client.

1. Situation analysis
   - Conduct appropriate research
   - Identify stakeholders
   - Analyze the strengths, weaknesses, opportunities, and threats (S.W.O.T.s)

2. Strategic decisions
   - Set message objectives
   - Define target audiences
   - Target the competition
   - Develop a positioning strategy

3. Marketing mix decisions

4. Marketing communication tool selection
   - Match strengths and weaknesses of marketing communication tools to the objectives
   - Identify which tool(s) should lead the effort; and which will be used to support it

5. Budget planning
   - Determine the appropriation
   - Decide how it is to be split among the various marketing communication activities

6. Message design
   - Develop a "big idea" or campaign theme
   - Develop the creative strategy for the various targeted stakeholders
   - Write and design the messages (for each marketing communication area)
   - Pretest the messages

7. Media/message delivery system
   - Identify the contact points and message sources
   - Select vehicles that deliver to those points
   - Schedule the media activities
   - Estimate the costs; compare against the budget

8. Evaluation
   - Develop a research proposal to evaluate whether the campaign met its objectives
   - Evaluate retention

When the campaign plan is developed by an external agency, it is presented to the client in a formal business presentation that may last several hours. The presenters usually provide listeners with a campaign book that details the recommendations and "leave behinds"—handouts used during the presentation that call attention to key proposals. Presentation skills are extremely important for people who plan and manage campaign efforts because the agency's recommendations have to be "sold" to the client.

This "selling" can take several forms. Agencies that have a longtime relationship with a client may still make a formal campaign presentation if they are working on an annual or campaign project assignment. The relationship between the account executive and the client's management staff, however, is an important factor in determining how well received the ideas are and how differences of opinion are negotiated. This is how the client/agency partnership takes on meaning.

The personal relationship doesn't exist when presenting to a potential client. Consequently, winning the account depends on both the quality of the presentation and the brilliance of the ideas. *Where the Suckers Moon,* a book by Randall Rothenberg, chronicles how this process happened for the Subaru account.[1] The winning agency, Wieden & Kennedy, proposed an understated postmodern approach that satirized car advertising. Once the client selects the agency, the difficult task of building a quality working relationship begins. In Subaru's case the Wieden & Kennedy campaign didn't work, and the agency was subsequently replaced.

Marketing communication programs don't run by themselves. And integrated marketing communication programs are even more complicated to steer because, instead of one leader from the client and the agency, the operation is usually managed by a team of people from different functional areas—advertising, public relations, and so on—who plan, implement, and monitor the work. Managing and working with this team often require tremendous effort, but, as the Saturn example demonstrates, the payoff can be great—a creative, cohesive campaign that can last for years.

Concept Review

PLANNING A CAMPAIGN

1. A campaign is a series of messages that are disseminated in a variety of different ways, that are designed to meet a set of objectives, and that are based on an analysis of the marketing communication situation.
2. There are eight steps in the campaign planning process:
   - Analyze the situation.
   - Make strategic decisions: objectives, targeting, competitive positioning.
   - Analyze the communication dimensions of the marketing mix.
   - Identify the best marketing communication functional areas.
   - Establish and allocate the budget.
   - Design the message: big idea, creative strategy, executions.
   - Design the media or message delivery system.
   - Evaluate the success of the campaign effort.

SITUATION ANALYSIS

The situation analysis summarizes everything that's known about the marketing situation—the economy, trends in the industry, the competition, the company's strengths, and the buyer's decision making, among other information. These facts are gathered through formal primary and secondary research and informal marketplace assessment. Once all the information is gathered, planners look for windows of opportunity in their analysis.

Research

Although research cannot substitute for careful analysis or creative solutions, sound research can provide insight into difficult marketing communication problems. A framework for determining the types of research needed is illustrated in Table 19.2. The table suggests, for example, that concept testing research would be useful in selecting an appropriate campaign theme. A concept test employs a focus group format: Eight to ten people are gathered in a room and asked to assess whether they understand and like various message approaches such as "saving money," "personal safety," and so forth.

TABLE 19.2

Campaign Planning Research

To make this decision	One must choose/identify	Using
Key S.W.O.T.s	Internal/external factors; competitive situation; sociocultural factors	Industry studies; economic studies; primary and secondary consumer research
To whom	Stakeholder groups; prioritize to target	Stakeholder analysis; segmentation studies; attitude, opinion, and behavior studies; ethnographic analysis
What to say	Theme; copy platform; appeals; selling points; position	Concept tests; perceptual mapping and positioning studies; likability studies
How to say it	Marketing communication activity	Zero-base analysis of strengths and weaknesses; effectiveness analysis
How often	Frequency of exposure	Repetition studies; memorability and irritation analysis
Where	Media/delivery systems	Media models; syndicated data; readership/viewership studies
How much to spend	Budget level	Sales analysis; payback/break-even analysis
And afterwards		
Did it work	Objectives to be measured	Copytesting (awareness, attitude, behavior, comprehension, likability)

Five general types of research are particularly important in campaign planning:

1. *Corporate/brand:* Analyze the strengths and weaknesses of the organization for whom the campaign planning is being developed. Which strengths can be leveraged?

2. *Industry/competition:* Analyze the industry's growth and downturns to determine its economic health. Within the industry, who are the leaders and who are the followers? What are the market shares? What marketing communication programs are being used by the competition, and how much are they spending? Where are the threats and opportunities?

3. *Product:* Review the product (goods, service, idea) in terms of its uses, packaging, quality, price, unit of sale, brand image, distribution, competitive positioning, and product life cycle.

4. *Consumer behavior:* Describe the consumer demographically and psychographically so that campaign planners can answer the following kinds of questions: Who buys—or doesn't buy—the product? In particular, who isn't buying the product and why? If one in ten people buy the product or brand, what is going on in the minds of the other 90 percent? (This tells what product or service features should be improved, changed, or deleted.) What other related products do they buy? What other activities or lifestyle associations relate to this product? When do they buy? How frequently do they buy? How do they use the product? Who else is involved in the purchase decision? What factors are most important in the purchase decision? Why do they repurchase or not repurchase the product?

5. *Target markets:* Analyze the stakeholder groups that affect and are affected by this situation and what kind of influence they have on the success of this program. How do you define the various stakeholder groups and estimate their size? How do you prioritize them in terms of their importance? Where are the best prospects in terms of demographic/psychographic characteristics, geographic location, and degree of product usage? How accessible are the target markets? If the company thinks it might use direct-mail advertising, for example, the availability of an accurate database is critical.

Communication Audit

One key factor that affects the success of an IMC program is whether the messages being sent are consistent, focused, and on strategy. This information is best gained by doing either a formal or informal **communication audit** that collects all communication materials, sorts them, compares them, and finally determines if they are working to support a set of integrated objectives.[2] Content analysis of the messages is a useful tool for this exercise.[3] A formal IMC audit, as described by University of Colorado professor Tom Duncan, also looks at the processes and organizational structure used to create marketing communication and the materials produced.[4]

Analysis

The objective of the research is to identify key problems and opportunities, or if you are using a S.W.O.T. analysis—to identify those strengths, weaknesses, opportunities, and threats that should be either leveraged or minimized. Not every problem uncovered in a situation analysis can be solved with a communication campaign; nor are all of them equally important. So a key aspect of a situation analysis is the *analysis*—the assessment of which factors are important enough to affect the success of the marketing program and which of those factors can be addressed by marketing communication.

Saturn's Situation

In Saturn's case GM wanted a small, relatively inexpensive but well-designed car that would compete with imports and turn around GM's long seasons of lost market share. Research showed that in the five years between 1985 and 1990, GM's share of the U.S. passenger-car market dropped 11 points to 33 percent while Japanese car makers' share climbed seven points to 26 percent. Furthermore, according to a study by J.D. Power and Associates, 42 percent of all new-car shoppers in 1990 wouldn't even consider buying a GM car. Clearly GM needed a new philosophy. Saturn's goal was to reverse these buying trends and sell 80 percent of its cars to drivers who otherwise would not have bought a GM car.

Organized as a separate corporation, Saturn's management was given a tremendous amount of independence from GM. The intention was to distance itself from GM's perceived weaknesses at that time—its impersonal image and reputation for low productivity, high absenteeism, defective products, and mediocre after-sales service. The opportunity it saw was the absence of a U.S. automotive organization known for top-notch quality and superior customer service. This orientation is stated in Saturn's philosophy: "To be truly successful, our sights must be aimed beyond providing customer satisfaction: we must exceed customer expectations. . . ."

Starting from scratch, GM hoped to reinvent itself by slashing production costs, boosting quality, and using the best technology and organization in the industry. Saturn, in other words, was conceived by then GM chairperson Roger Smith as a laboratory for achieving automotive excellence. It took seven years—from

---

Concept **✓ Review**

SITUATION ANALYSIS

1. The situation analysis is based on both primary and secondary research.
2. It gathers information from five key areas:
   - Corporate/brand
   - Industry/competition
   - Product
   - Consumer behavior
   - Target market
3. Conclusions are drawn in terms of problems and opportunities or S.W.O.T.s—strengths and opportunities that can be leveraged and weaknesses and threats that need to be addressed.
4. The key to a situation analysis is the *analysis*—determining which factors are important enough to affect the success of the marketing effort and which of those factors can be addressed by marketing communication.

November of 1983 when Smith publicly announced the Saturn project to late 1990 when the first car rolled off the assembly line—and approximately $4.5 billion in investments to make Saturn a reality.

One of Saturn's objectives was to make inroads on the Japanese car-buying market. It did this by appealing to the predominately middle-age college graduates with a household income in the $50,000 range who make up the bulk of the Japanese car market. This market also tends to include more female and single buyers than the traditional U.S. car-buying market.

STRATEGIC DECISIONS

The strategic direction of an integrated campaign depends on decisions about objectives, positioning, and targeting. Strategic marketing communication planning can be handled in a number of different ways. First, the client can do all the planning and let the agency implement these decisions. In this kind of an approach, the agency is more of a service provider than a partner. A second approach is to allow the agency to do more of the strategic planning for the communication activities. If strategic planning is the agency's responsibility, an account planner or an account executive and the account management team handle the planning.

Account planning is a British marketing communication concept that has found some acceptance in the United States. An account planner is a person skilled in both research and account management who has the insights to speak with authority about the customer's needs and wants. In most marketing communication efforts, the traditional partners are the agency, represented by an account executive, and a client, represented by a marketing or advertising manager. Account planning adds a third viewpoint to the strategy development—that of the customer.[5]

What the account planner brings to the table is a wider range of research tools, including an emphasis on more qualitative research methodologies used to develop deeper consumer insights. As Lisa Fortini-Campbell explains in her book, *The Consumer Insight Workbook*, today's marketing communication demands that brands connect with consumers. To create that connection, planners must go beyond just knowing and describing the consumer and develop deeper insights that lead to understanding, respect, and empathy.[6] The account planner takes on that responsibility by proactively recommending strategies that are thought to be more customer-focused and by reacting to creative ideas from the customer's viewpoint—will that message speak to customers in a meaningful way?

The account planner role has been slow to develop in the United States because most U.S. marketing communication agencies believe that account executives can handle this customer-advocacy function. Some agencies, however, use account planners in the strategy stage of campaign development to extend and deepen the customer focus. Chiat/Day, Goodby Berlin & Silverstein, and Deutsch, Inc., are three U.S. agencies that have used account planners successfully.

Objectives

Every campaign should be guided by a clear, precise, and measurable statement of objectives. Objectives serve three functions.[7] First, they are a communication device. That is, campaign objectives are a practical method of informing all levels of management about goals and tasks. Second, objectives act as a decision-making guide for management. Objectives indicate the anticipated results of the campaign. Planners can evaluate the objectives to identify feasible approaches to tackle weaknesses and take advantage of opportunities. Finally, and most important, campaign objectives can be used to measure the specific results of the program so the company can learn from the experience.

Although marketing communication managers realize that setting objectives is a key part of planning a campaign, there is still a great deal of confusion about what objectives are appropriate for various types of marketing communication. Ultimately, the measure of success for any marketing communication campaign is its ability to increase sales and market share for the company. However, there are some steps leading to the result of increased sales that also must be considered. Although the Red Roof Inn motel chain, for example, wants occupancy rates to increase dramatically because of its $6 million investment in mass advertising, its agency knows that customers need time to develop the awareness and trust necessary to foster these increased levels of sales. So marketing communication is used first to build awareness and trust. Sponsors naturally want every dollar they spend to trigger increased sales, but, as discussed in previous chapters, some areas of marketing communication (sales promotion, direct marketing) are better at that than others (advertising, public relations).

Planners should set objectives for a campaign as well as for each marketing communication tool used. In designing the campaign objectives, the components of a campaign should build on each other and create a positive synergy, thereby improving the chances that the consumer will select the company's brand. Planners refer to this sequence as movement from awareness to direct action—in other words, from communication objectives to sales objectives.

The plan's objectives also move from general to specific. The marketing plan objectives are the most general; the marketing communication plan objectives are more specific, especially in each subsection that focuses on a communication activity such as advertising or sales promotion. When the objectives are aligned like this, they "cascade" from one level to another, as shown in Figure 19.1.

Consider the AT&T campaign to introduce a universal credit card. Because the universal card represented a new product category in a new market, AT&T had to start from scratch. It began with awareness ads followed by other marketing communication intended to accomplish different objectives. Telemarketing and direct marketing, for example, were used to make final sales.

In contrast, when Procter & Gamble introduced new Tide in 1990, it concentrated on direct-action advertising. Because P&G's Tide has a powerful brand name and the product did not represent a new category, P&G did not need to spend resources on awareness advertising. The introductory print campaign included coupons so that consumers could try the product at a reduced price. This ad campaign was driven by a massive sampling program.

Many types of stakeholders—customers, creditors, employees, suppliers, the media, community members, shareholders, and governmental agencies—are concerned with the operation of the firm. The process of objective setting must

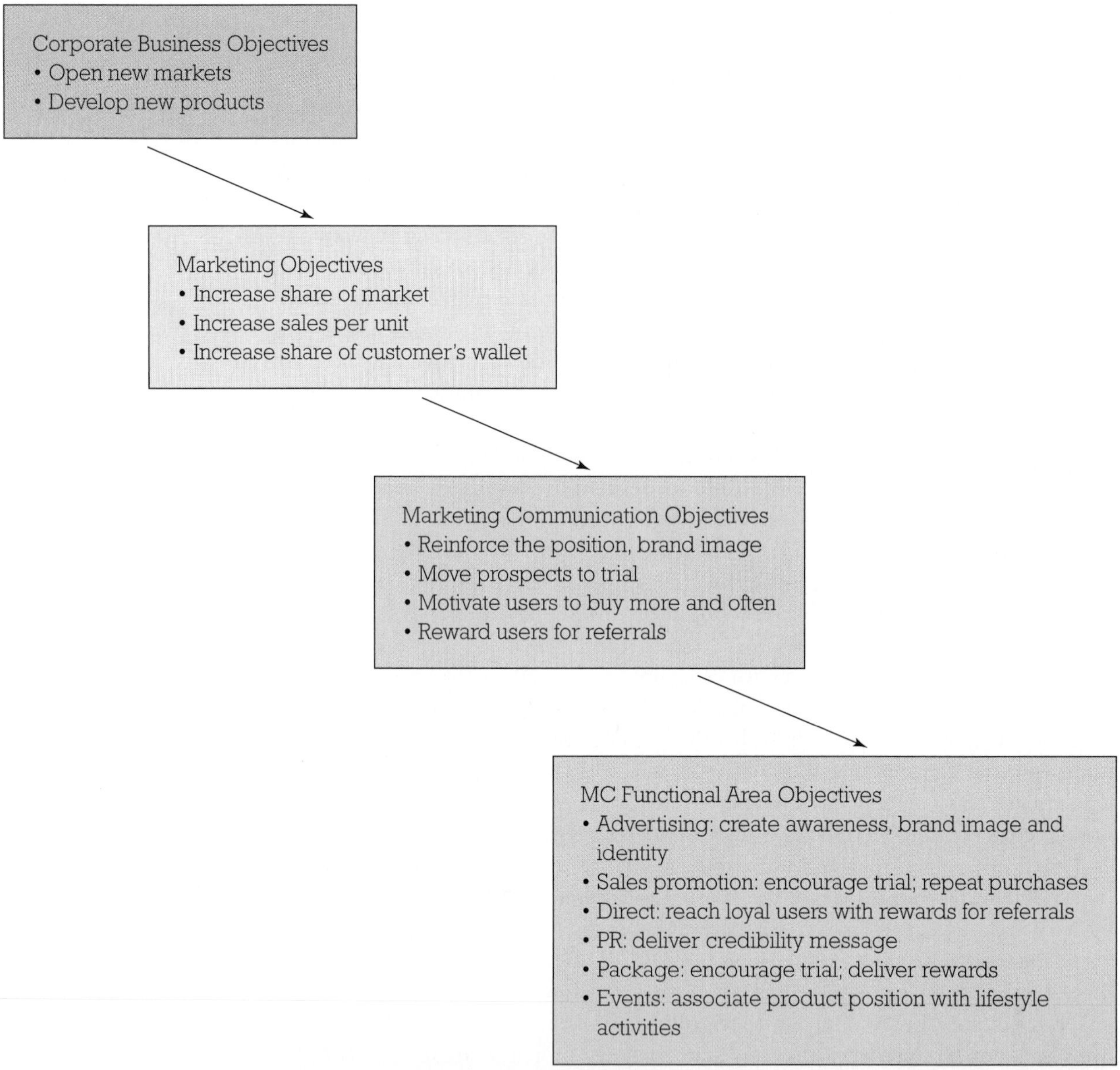

Corporate Business Objectives
• Open new markets
• Develop new products

Marketing Objectives
• Increase share of market
• Increase sales per unit
• Increase share of customer's wallet

Marketing Communication Objectives
• Reinforce the position, brand image
• Move prospects to trial
• Motivate users to buy more and often
• Reward users for referrals

MC Functional Area Objectives
• Advertising: create awareness, brand image and identity
• Sales promotion: encourage trial; repeat purchases
• Direct: reach loyal users with rewards for referrals
• PR: deliver credibility message
• Package: encourage trial; deliver rewards
• Events: associate product position with lifestyle activities

FIGURE 19.1

Sample Campaign Objectives

recognize the relative importance of these groups, and plans must incorporate and integrate their interests. Determining the relative weight given to any particular interest group is usually the campaign planner's responsibility, with the approval of management.

Stating Objectives

Objectives must be stated in terms that are understood and acceptable to those who will work to achieve them. Unrealistic goals, for instance, would not be acceptable to all involved. Therefore, planners should develop objectives with the input of all those expected to implement them. The campaign planner should set up a system to provide feedback during the planning process from all relevant people—both inside and outside the organization.

Furthermore, the objectives should be clear and specific. Precise wording enhances clarity. A campaign objective should specify who is to be affected, by what, how, when, and exactly what the result should be. In the following example, objectives for an ad campaign for Campbell's Chunky Soup are put in the context of the campaign's overall strategic directions:

- Who? Caucasian men, ages 35 to 55, blue-collar occupations, with incomes under $50,000; Campbell's Soup wants to reach 40 percent of this target audience with this message
- By what? An appeal to the virtue of obtaining the hearty taste of homemade soup by buying a premium-price canned soup
- How? Through a greater understanding of the product's benefits
- When? During the next six months
- Objectives/results? Awareness of the product benefits increases by 20 percent from 40 percent to 48 percent; and an increase of 12 percent in sales
- Supporting communication objectives? The attitude score of the benefits of Chunky Soup versus homemade soup should reach 3.5 on a 6-point attitude scale after the individual has seen the ads

Planners assign numerical values to as many components as possible so they are measurable. Furthermore, the starting point and anticipated results are necessary for measuring change or impact. For example, the awareness result for Campbell's Chunky Soup listed the current awareness level of 40 percent as a point of comparison for the anticipated result of 48 percent. Then the percentage difference was calculated (an 8-point change equals 20 percent) to give a sense of the magnitude of the change.

Concept ✓ **Review**

STRATEGIC DECISIONS (OBJECTIVES)

1. Campaign objectives may be classified as either sales objectives or communication objectives.
2. Planners should set both marketing communication objectives for each marketing communication activity and campaign objectives that link the campaign to the ultimate goal of increasing sales or market share.
3. Objectives must be stated in terms that are understandable and acceptable to all those who must meet them. They must be specific and state who is to be affected and by what; they must be measurable; and they must be assigned a time duration.

Saturn's Objectives

Saturn's overriding objective is to become America's best-liked car company. Another Saturn objective is to reintroduce U.S. car buyers to General Motors. In particular, GM wanted the Saturn name to attract new buyers who owned or might otherwise buy import cars. Furthermore, for those who buy Saturns and would like to "move up," an objective was to increase their consideration of other GM products. And, of course, Saturn's marketing communication is expected to contribute every year to meeting GM's sales and marketing share objectives.

Competitive Positioning

Campaign planners usually target competitors to see how their brand compares with the competition. To target the competition, planners identify all the other options a consumer considers when making a product decision. A position statement identifies the core characteristics of the brand that differentiate it from the competition and summarizes its appeal to consumers. IMC expert Tom Brannan states that "without a clear positioning, there can be no true integration." He believes that positioning "is an essential prerequisite to integrated communication since it provides the single focus around which every aspect of our communication will be constructed."[8] Positioning strategies are developed when a brand is new, but they are also reinforced in every campaign. Strategic planning means using your messages and vehicles to outflank the competition by creating a more attractive position or making your position more appealing. One strategic purpose for a campaign, as is illustrated in Figure 19.2, is to create, reinforce, or reposition a brand.

Saturn was entering the highly competitive and import-dominated small-car

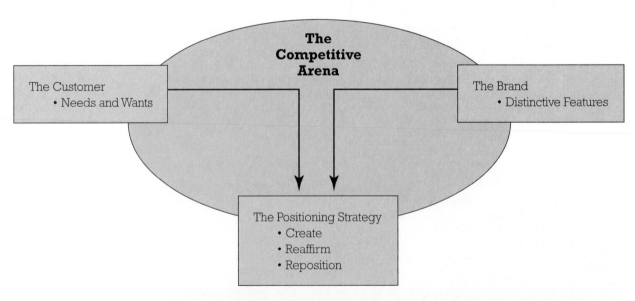

FIGURE 19.2

Positioning Strategies

market. Saturn's target competitors were Honda Civic, Nissan Sentra, Toyota Corolla, and other small cars in the $15,000 to $20,000 range (later this category also included the Dodge/Plymouth Neon). The price for a Saturn initially started at $9,000 but during the early 1990s ranged from $11,000 to $17,000.

Positioning strategies are built on an understanding of the competitive situation. You will remember from Chapter 4 that a position is the location the product holds in the mind of the consumer relative to the competition. In other words, it is always comparative—this beverage tastes better, is sold cheaper, is more nutritious, or is more easily available, for example.

Although GM had taken the rap for years about the quality of its products in comparison to Japanese cars, its development research for Saturn showed that only 25 percent of a customer's buying decision was based on perceptions of a car's quality; three-quarters of the decision was based on price and service. A Saturn marketing manager explained that when customers were asked in research what they like and don't like, "by far and away the most overriding concern was that they don't like the hassle in the showroom. They don't trust car salesmen."

The strategy for Saturn was to position the new car as an affordable, quality small car and to provide an automobile ownership experience that went beyond mere satisfaction. The idea was to make the quality high for the category, have a competitive price, and beat everyone else in the marketplace on service and customer relations. Saturn's goal was to make car buying such a pleasurable experience that its customers would bond with the company for life.

Concept Review

STRATEGIC DECISIONS (COMPETITIVE POSITIONING)

1. Targeting the competition is done by identifying all the other options a consumer considers when making a product decision.
2. Positioning strategies are built on an understanding of the competitive situation; a position is the location the product holds in the mind of the consumer relative to the competition.

Targeting Stakeholders

Once the objectives have been identified, every campaign should have a clear sense of who the important stakeholders and the targeted audiences are for the various messages. It is necessary to decide the relative importance of each stakeholder group, of segments within each group, and how these groups can best be reached by various types of marketing communication activities.

How the target audiences are defined has a substantial impact on other campaign decisions such as the message and media strategies. To illustrate, if a cafeteria chain decides to offer a special menu for senior citizens, the creative approach would probably emphasize senior discounts, show people of the same age group in the visuals, and use contact points that would best reach this age group. However, if the chain wanted to increase business among families, then it would offer kids' meals, and the creative approach would focus on family pricing strategies, show families in the visuals, and use media vehicles that would reach parents.

Figure 19.3 illustrates a stakeholder targeting worksheet that could be used in an IMC campaign. In a planning document like this, you would identify the key stakeholder groups and diagnose what they think about the brand and what motivates them. It's also useful to note the ways they can be reached through their contact points. Finally, you would decide how important the various stakeholders are for this campaign and prioritize them.

Saturn's Targeted Stakeholders

The Saturn approach represents a well-rounded program of integrated marketing communication. One of the most important aspects of an IMC program is the recognition that all stakeholders are important, and they should be considered in planning the company's total communication program. Furthermore, stakeholders often overlap, so the messages must have a consistent theme, style, look, and feel—

Stakeholder	Perceptions of Brand	Wants and Needs	Contact Point	Priority

FIGURE 19.3

Stakeholder Worksheet: Evaluation Tool

even if the messages themselves vary according to the needs of the different stakeholder groups.

Saturn's approach is to build partnerships with important stakeholders. Two of the most important Saturn stakeholders are its marketing communications agency, Hal Riney & Partners, and its union, The United Auto Workers. These partnerships result from Saturn's recognition of the stakes and vested interests of everyone involved in the business venture. With the help of the union, Saturn established a program of employee partnerships in sales, service, and marketing. The marketing initiative involving the union members portrays a message that together, a workforce's standard of living can be maintained or enhanced if the company is a world-class competitor. Saturn's relationship program for its marketing communication agency is detailed in the IMC in Action discussion.

The Customer Target

Saturn sales efforts have been targeted at the 25-to-48-year-old upscale professional. Women count for 60 percent of the customers. Its target market includes car buyers with an average age of 40, 55 percent of whom are college graduates and whose average household income is $54,000 and whose median household income is $50,000. In Saturn's market 62 percent are female and 48 percent are single. For 28 percent of the buyers, the Saturn car is the first new car purchase. Saturn's market matches almost perfectly with that of its primary competitors—Honda Civic, Nissan Sentra, Toyota Corolla, and Dodge/Plymouth Neon.

The following is a discussion of other important stakeholder targets in Saturn's IMC program.

Suppliers and Dealers

Stakeholders besides customers are also important to Saturn and are treated with respect. Vendors, for example, purchase a certain software that links them to Saturn through computer networking. All purchasing activities are carried on electronically, which saves the company—and its suppliers—millions of dollars annually. Suppliers are chosen based on their belief in the Saturn philosophy and a willingness to work in an environment of integrated decision making. They are involved in a number of Saturn teams that design and manage production.

Dealers are also important in automotive marketing. The Saturn division has a relatively small number of franchises now totaling around 320 dealers, giving each control over a broad geographic area. The Saturn Information System (SIS) links dealer sites via satellite with the production facilities and Saturn headquarters in Spring Hill, Tennessee. The system allows dealers to receive news about new products and practices as they transmit business data such as sales and customer demographic information. Management can react to market trends quickly. SIS also handles payroll, title transfers, a sales and purchasing management system, and sales trend analyses.

The dealer can also connect to other dealerships and search their inventories for desired cars and features with another service called SALESLINE. This service is also used for inventory management, particularly in the parts area, where dealers only have to carry minimum levels of parts because they can connect directly to the parts factory and receive necessary items quickly and efficiently, just when dealers need it. This type of inventory control is called "just-in-time" inventory management.

Selecting a Marketing Communication Partner

Riney's agency was not even on the list of some 50 agencies that had initially applied for Saturn's account. A team of GM and Saturn executives contacted Hal Riney, the agency's chairperson and CEO, and traveled to San Francisco to interview him and the agency. Riney impressed them by asking probing questions and convincing them that his strong views on automobile advertising were valid. Riney was selected as Saturn's "communications partner" in 1988, 29 months before the first car went on sale. From the beginning it was clear that the agency would be concerned with more than just advertising.

The agency was involved in every aspect of the car's launch. Hal Riney was even instrumental in naming the car lines. A consultant recommended that the various lines have distinctive names like Lumina or Wrangler. Riney argued against that, feeling that these would dilute the Saturn name and identity. Thus, the Saturn coupe is simply the Saturn SC, and various sedans are named Saturn SL-1 and Saturn SL-2. The agency (or communications consultant in Saturn terms) handled every aspect of the marketing communication.

The agency even wrote the classified ads for Saturn retailers to use in hiring sales representatives and service advisers. The ads had an astonishing response, according to Saturn representatives, and they will pay off for years because the dealers have such a solid relationship with their sales teams that there is virtually no turnover.

Even before the car was available, the Riney agency was involved in producing internal communication pieces about the company. Linda Bradford, co-design director for Riney's spin-off design subsidiary, went to Spring Hill, Tennessee, to interview workers. She discovered an "incredible emotional involvement" at the plant that is conveyed in a number of marketing communication pieces. The most important is a Riney-produced 26-minute film, "Spring, in Spring Hill," documenting the start-up of the Saturn project. The film played an important role in communicating the Saturn story. It has been used to train and help explain the company to new employees, suppliers, and the press. Executives use it when they make speeches. And the film eventually aired as an infomercial on several cable networks. "Spring" works because it lets Saturn team members explain, often emotionally, what the project was all about and what it meant to them.

Many ad agency personnel are not interested in doing anything but big-budget commercials. However, the Riney team was involved in a wide variety of marketing communication materials including client letters, merchandising signage, hang tags, brochures, and other collateral materials, such as sales literature, and even the company's annual holiday greeting card. The Riney agency did not actually write the owner's manual, though it was involved in the design, graphics, writing style, and choice of paper. Many of these collateral materials were produced by Riney, Bradford & Huber, a subsidiary graphic design shop.

Joe O'Neill, Riney's national creative director, explains that "[y]ou have to have quite a few senior people in the agency who understand the real needs of the client and take pride in creating a communication program rather than TV ads." That same philosophy holds true even in the agency's billing procedures. Tony Houghton, president of the agency, explained that the agency doesn't distinguish between the time a creative person spends on a recall letter or a TV commercial. He notes that everyone works on everything not for the sake of efficiency, but for consistency.

Employees

Employees are another important stakeholder group. One of Saturn's biggest accomplishments is the positive relationship between union members and Saturn management. The innovative employment contract eliminated nearly all the rigid job classifications traditional to manufacturing. Workers in return get lifetime job guarantees (under most circumstances) and a bigger say in the company—such as a voice in choosing the marketing communication agency. In fact, all decisions are made by consensus. Employees were recruited on the basis of their willingness to work as a team and shed their old habits. The applicants had to be approved by a Saturn panel of union members and company management.

Union members are part of business teams, and it's not uncommon to find union representatives working next to company executives, a phenomenon showcased in one of the original launch advertisements. The team approach is apparent in production and also guides the development process, which is called "simultaneous engineering." New products and the means to make them are established at the same time by teams of designers, factory engineers, line employees, marketers, accountants, service people, and vendor representatives.

Communities

Neighbors are also an important stakeholder for Saturn. The construction of the Spring Hill, Tennessee, plant had tremendous implications for the size and resources of the population of Spring Hill. The effect on this tiny rural community of a big company like Saturn has to be carefully managed. Saturn considered Spring Hill residents in all decisions that could affect the community. Because environmental issues are important to Saturn, it decided to locate the plant and its parking lots in sites that would not dominate the view. In addition, Saturn created an environmental advisory council involving local Spring Hill citizens to help the company understand local values and to get community participation in the company's decision making.

This Saturn ad features a Saturn retailer working side by side with production workers, showing the importance Saturn places on teamwork between sales and production. The ad also spotlights UAW community service.

Saturn and its dealers sponsor numerous community activities such as the Saturn Playground project featured here.

Saturn is also part of a larger community. As a new initiative for 1996, Saturn sponsored the EBONY/JET guide to Black Excellence, a multifaceted program designed to promote self-awareness and build self-esteem among black youth. The program works with key African-American entrepreneurs, leaders, and entertainers. As part of the program, Saturn donated program materials to inner-city school districts. More recently, Saturn dealers have undertaken programs in their own communities. The 15 dealers in New York, for example, are working together to create new playgrounds for children.

Concept Review

STRATEGIC DECISIONS (TARGETING)

1. Targeting involves identifying and prioritizing the key stakeholder groups, then targeting specific audience segments within these stakeholder groups.
2. How the target audiences are defined has a substantial impact on other campaign decisions such as the message and media strategies.
3. The various audiences are addressed with a central theme, but separate messages address each target group's particular concerns.

THE MARKETING MIX

In Chapter 3 we described how the marketing mix can communicate messages and dictate message strategies. How the product is designed, priced, distributed, and serviced are some of the most important factors in developing a message strategy. In the case of Saturn, a number of marketing mix factors communicated messages about the car and its personality.

Quality

The Saturn Information System (SIS) keeps track of the history of every car from the moment it is assigned a VIN number to its last service. Service records follow the car throughout the car life though it may change owners. This makes it quick and easy to notify dealers and owners of any defects or potential problems. In 1991, for example, Saturn was able to inform owners about potential problems so they could bring in their cars for a part replacement.

Customers are contacted about a problem before they are even aware of it. This makes the customers feel that Saturn cares about them rather than being angry at the inconvenience. The big challenge came in 1993 when engine fires prompted GM to recall 80 percent of its Saturns. The customer-satisfaction level was so high, however, that even this major recall did not damage the company's reputation for quality, and it continued to be one of the highest-rated cars in customer-satisfaction surveys.

Selling and Pricing

Saturn sales consultants are not stereotypical "car salespeople." One customer described them as more like birthing coaches—soothing, funny, and informed. The sales consultants make a point to be informed about how Saturn compares with other cars and about educating their customers so they are informed buyers. This approach has been so successful, it has spawned a new buzzword in the car business. The process of improving customer sales and service at a car company is now being referred to as "Saturnization."

One of Saturn's marketing breakthroughs was its no-haggle, low-pressure sales style. Initial research during development showed that potential buyers felt they could not get trustworthy information about vehicles from dealers, they didn't believe in the trade-in value given for their old cars, and they preferred a fixed price. Armed with this information, Saturn decided to set its price using a fixed pricing strategy that is perceived as fair. It doesn't offer rebates, price-cutting specials, or artificial discounts on the sales lot. Trade-in values are based on Blue Book value. The company believes that by not negotiating prices, it creates a win-win situation for the company as well as its customers. No-haggle pricing has since become a trend in the market as more and more dealers are finding out that customers have negative feelings about negotiable prices.

The end of the sales process is a celebration. When a customer buys a Saturn, the dealership has a ceremony where the dealer's staff assembles to cheer the customer. Buyers receive a Polaroid photo of the ceremony.

The no-haggle pricing strategy is shown on Saturn's Web site where potential buyers can see how much a Saturn will cost before they step into a showroom.

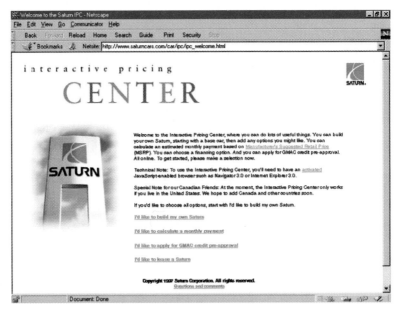

The Dealerships

Saturn has used the design of its dealerships to make a statement since it opened its first 26 retail sites. All of the dealerships have a consistent design and theme. The stark white Saturn sign and facility stand out amidst the multicolored, carnival-like mega-dealers and auto malls. The unique design and construction emphasize crisp, clean lines and an uncluttered and spacious front and layout. The objective is to project an image of a warm, inviting retail experience based on trust. The design of the facility, in other words, is being used to underscore Saturn's commitment to quality and service.

Customer Service and Aftermarketing

Saturn service, based on individual customer care and convenience, is a cornerstone of the car's customer enthusiasm. Saturn, its field team, customer assistance center, and retailers are fully committed to insuring that each owner is satisfied and that customer concerns are addressed quickly and correctly the first time. Because of such care, Saturn has been the top-rated domestic nameplate, first among all small cars for customer satisfaction, and ranks third overall in the prestigious J.D. Power and Associates' Customer Satisfaction and Sales Satisfaction surveys.

Both new and used Saturns have been rated among the top vehicles for reliability and resale value in the annual *Consumer Reports' Auto Issue. Consumer Reports'* research shows that Saturns represent an outstanding value in the marketplace. For example, on a scale of 1 to 5 (5 being much better than average), Saturn scored a 5 in depreciation and a 4 in reliability, joining the Acura Integra as top vehicle in the small-car class.

Studies have shown that service after the car purchase is as important as the quality of the car itself. From the moment of purchase on, customers are part of the Saturn family. They are invited to weekend barbecues and car clinics, and they are encouraged to bring friends to the clinics. After getting their cars serviced, they receive surveys by mail to determine their satisfaction. Saturn owners believe they are part of a special relationship. They wave to each other when they pass on the highway, and some have even volunteered to work at Saturn displays at auto shows.

If a new owner is not satisfied with his car, Saturn also has a no-quibble return policy that not only solves the problem of an unhappy owner who says bad things about the car but also turns a potentially negative situation into a positive one. Even those people who were not happy with the car become advocates for the company because they were treated with respect. Word of mouth from a satisfied Saturn owner or ex-owner is the company's most persuasive form of marketing communication.

Saturn publishes a newsletter for Saturn owners and "team members." It also sponsors an online service that allows customers to receive information promptly about anything that has to do with their car—availability of a car with specific features and availability or price of a part. The sales/service staff process these requests through the Saturn Information System to provide immediate answers to the customer.

This ad stresses the special relationship that Saturn owners have with their cars.

Certified Used Cars

Saturn is doing for the used-car business what it did to change the shopping and buying experience for new cars. The company recognizes that all customers, regardless of whether they buy a new or used vehicle, should be treated in the same honest, straightforward manner. That's why Saturn and participating retailers added a certified used-car process in 1996 to give used-car buyers peace of mind. Each Saturn Certified Used Car must pass a stringent 150-point inspection that tests not only how the car runs but how it looks. As an added measure of security, each used car comes with a limited warranty and an unprecedented 3-day money-back and 30-day/1500 mile trade-in guarantee. Customers have a variety of used cars, both Saturn and other makes, to shop for in the no-hassle environment for which Saturn is noted.

MARKETING COMMUNICATION TOOLS

The next step in campaign planning is to decide which marketing communication tools to use to develop the campaign and which one should lead the effort. In Chapter 4 we presented general strengths and weaknesses for the key marketing communication areas. The decision about which area to use depends on the problems to be solved and the stated objectives. The planning process involves analyzing the objectives, strengths, and weaknesses of the various marketing communication tools and then matching objectives to the tools that can best deliver success.

Advertising, for example, is particularly good for reminding people of established brands and their positive past experiences. If you have an announcement to make, then public relations and advertising can work hand in hand as shown in the Gillette case examples highlighted in this text. Public relations is also good at building or rebuilding credibility, particularly when there is a believability problem. If you want to build excitement and enthusiasm, then an event may target your market and involve the right audience in your message. Many times, a number of different areas can be employed, so the lead area becomes the one that generates the best "big idea."

For example, to reposition Black Gold, a Scandinavian beer, from an older market to a younger, yuppie market, the local DDB Needham agency used an event—a film noir festival—as the centerpiece of the campaign. The event may not seem to be the strongest marketing communication activity to lead a repositioning, but the strength of the creative idea—film noir and its association with the product name—made the event a winner. The festival was supported with advertising to announce the event, publicity, collectors' posters, postcards, and tabletop cards in bars.

Some marketing communication activities work together naturally. For a new product launch, for example, public relations will often lead to take advantage of the news angle, and then the advertising kicks in to build high levels of awareness and motivate people to look for the product. In most cases advertising and sales promotion also interact closely; advertising is used to build excitement for sales promotion, and sales promotion is used to reinforce an action message carried in the advertising. Other than the obvious differences in technique, the major differences between advertising and sales promotion are expectation and accountability. Recall from Chapter 10 that the intent of sales promotion is to provide an incentive to action through the addition of some kind of extra value. Thus, sales promotion is tied to immediate sales or response. In contrast, advertising tends to have several intermediate objectives leading to sales, such as creating awareness and building brand equity, and accomplishing these objectives takes time. Advertising relies heavily on the other mix elements, especially personal selling and sales promotion, to close the sale. The proper blending of advertising with sales promotion has proven to be very effective. A print ad containing a coupon, for example, has shown to increase recall scores eightfold as compared with the same ad without a coupon.

Saturn's Marketing Communication Mix

Saturn's marketing communication is dominated by advertising, a natural medium for relaying the stories that bring its homespun approach to life. But advertising is only one of the marketing communication tools used to build the program. The Saturn philosophy is that car makers and customers not only learn more about each other but also build and maintain long-term relationships through various forms of two-way communication such as word of mouth, personal sales, and other forms of interactive marketing communication. Personal selling, of course, is important in car marketing, but customer satisfaction leading to referrals through word of mouth is another important part of Saturn's communication strategy.

To stimulate word of mouth and cement customer relationships, Saturn established a CarClub in 1996. When members join, they get to meet other Saturn aficionados and receive a package of goodies from the Saturn company including a road atlas, travel services packet, window decal, key fob, CarClub T-shirt, and a membership handbook. The CarClub is supported by a special section on the Saturn Web site (www.saturncars.com), as well as a newsletter and free travel planning services, similar to that provided by other automobile clubs.

Special events are also important because they provide ways to involve Saturn's stakeholders—customers, employees, dealers—in participatory activities that fuel the car company's extraordinary level of loyalty. As an indication of how successful Saturn has been at building the important stakeholder relationships, 44,000 owners journeyed to the company's headquarters in Spring Hill for a three-day homecoming in June 1994 to celebrate the company's first five years. Not only did they come, they paid $34 for adults and $17 for kids to attend. Saturn's director of consumer marketing, Steven Shannon, explained that the idea came from the owners, many of whom had contacted the company and asked to see the plant.

All owners were sent brochures and personal invitations. TV spots showed national parks empty because of the Saturn homecoming. Saturn owners enjoyed a barbecue, toured the plant where their Saturn was built, met employees, and were entertained by country singer Wynona Judd; children enjoyed Camp Saturn's kids activities. Reporters described the feeling of the event as akin to a revival meeting. There was even an impromptu wedding ceremony. Shannon explained, "It's a way to say thank you to the owners and foster a closer relationship."

The Riney agency engineered the move into electronic marketing with the establishment of a Prodigy site and then a Saturn World Wide Web home page. The Saturn Web site mirrors an actual retail facility with a welcome area, an electronic showroom featuring the Saturn line, and a Saturn magazine filled with customer and employee stories highlighting their experiences. Although users can't take a Saturn out for a test drive, the site's locator feature will let them know where their nearest Saturn retailer is located. Since its introduction in June 1994, more than 200,000 people have accessed the many interactive applications in the Saturn Web site. With over 30 million online users, Saturn recognizes that these programs give them additional means to increase brand awareness and build relationships with consumers.

THE BUDGET

As discussed in Chapter 17, the appropriation governs all proposed activities by placing upper limits on what can be spent. Often the overall marketing communication appropriation is set as part of a marketing plan, so the problem becomes fitting the campaign into this framework. One of the truisms of the business is that there is never enough money to do it right, so the planner is always trying to make the greatest impact with less money than he or she feels is needed. Once the appropriation level is determined, then the budget is developed, which determines how the money will be allocated.

Most important, campaign planners have to decide how to allocate the money among different marketing communication activities and different types of message delivery systems.

The success of the Saturn Homecoming prompted similar events such as the Saturn Owner Appreciation Day described in this invitation.

Television commercials, for example, are expensive to produce and run. However, they reach large audiences and their per-impression cost is quite low. Personal sales is extremely expensive on a per-impression basis, and yet in some industries—particularly business-to-business marketing—a personal sales call on a limited number of key buyers may be the only way to do business. Campaign planners constantly juggle costs and reach as they try to decide where to best put the money.

The campaign budget is developed by estimating the costs for all the various elements in the plan. Once those estimates are totaled, then the planner compares that amount with the appropriation. Inevitably the campaign plan will then have to be adjusted to keep the activities on budget and the expenses aligned with the available money.

Purely financial decisions by top management often stop campaigns that appear to offer excellent potential. In the case of the "1984" commercial that launched the Macintosh, for example, the cost of producing the commercial and the cost to play it during Super Bowl led the board of directors first to reject and then to reapprove airing the commercial. It has since been identified as one of the most effective commercials of all time in terms of exciting consumer interest.

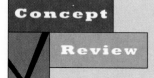

Concept Review

MARKETING MIX, MARKETING COMMUNICATION TOOLS, AND BUDGET

1. The marketing mix decisions communicate important information and contribute to the message strategy.
2. The decision about which marketing communication activities to use is based on the problems to be solved and the objectives to be achieved.
3. The lead marketing communication activity is often the one that can contribute the most to support the big idea. Many, if not all, of the other marketing communication tools can be used in support of the big idea once the lead activity has been chosen.
4. The budget level has to be established if it is not a given, and then the total budget has to be allocated among the various marketing communication activities.

MESSAGE DESIGN

Message design is the creative side of marketing communication planning. You are trying to determine what to say and how to say it. Every campaign is focused on a central big idea that holds the communication efforts together. The DDB Needham film noir idea, for example, was the central idea behind the Black Gold campaign. Without a coherent concept, there is no way to make a complex set of messages mesh together.

Once the big idea has been decided, then the *creative strategy* can be designed. The **creative strategy** outlines what to say to the various target audiences who may have different message needs. Trade members, for example, will want to know how they can make money by supporting this promotion. Employees need to be informed about the campaign so they can reinforce its messages. Sales representatives will need a variety of sales support materials to use in their sales calls to buyers. They will also need motivational programs to encourage them to work hard in support of the campaign. Finally, the targeted consumer audience will need a different set of messages that get attention, build awareness, and lock the information in memory. All of these messages are different in terms of what they say. However, their overall theme and tone should reflect and reinforce the general campaign theme.

In advertising the creative strategy is translated into a **copy platform,** a document that specifies what will be said to whom and with what effect. It often gives direction about the executions. For instance, the copy platform might describe the tone of voice and product personality for the ad. Other elements might include a statement of the product position, the psychological appeal, and the selling premise.

There are many different approaches to creative strategy, as discussed in Chapters 3, 4, and 9. Generally, the approaches focus on information, argument, image, emotion, or entertainment. In a marketing communication campaign plan, these various strategies may relate to the different audiences. For example, employees may respond most effectively to information, the trade to reason or argument, sales personnel to an emotional appeal, and consumers to entertainment.

Creative tactics provide the details of the executions in all the various areas. What will the ads say and look like? What will the press releases focus on? How will the events be organized? What sales support materials are needed, and what will they say and look like? The campaign plan will spell out as many of these details as possible, so the managers who are approving the plan will have some idea of the scope and scale of the effort. Budgets will also be estimated for all of the individual execution activities.

Evaluation

With rapidly rising costs, overwhelming numbers of advertising messages, and more and more advertising voices seeking to be heard, most authorities agree that advertising should be pretested. Pretesting is done to avoid costly mistakes; to predict the relative strength of alternative concepts, strategies, and tactics; and to increase the efficiency of the campaign effort. Posttesting is done to determine if the campaign met its objectives.

Companies concerned with whether their campaign messages will be heard and understood will do concept testing to check the power of the big idea as it is being developed. They will also test various message strategies to compare their impact on the target audiences and do execution testing to evaluate various approaches to the actual construction of the messages. In the final analysis pretesting is done to select the best appeals and provide benchmarks against which the communications can be measured. The basic advantage of campaign pretesting is to gain some measure of assurance in the creative product for a rather modest investment. The cost-benefit ratio seems favorable when compared with the media investment, particularly for advertising. For example, a media investment of $5 million may require a pretesting investment of $50,000. It seems much wiser to invest creative research funds before using the material rather than to conduct lengthy posttests to determine if the material was successful. Indeed, if sufficient pretest information could be gathered, the need to posttest extensively would be lessened. In the end, however, the campaign planner must appreciate that good pretest results simply mean that the likelihood of success is good, not guaranteed.

Posttesting involves developing research methods to test whether or not the campaign reached its objectives. Copytesting services can provide information about levels of awareness, comprehension, attitude, and likability. Sales tracking can provide sales data, and other behavioral responses can be measured by tracking inquiries, coupons returned, phone calls, and Web page hits. The methods used in pretesting and posttesting were described in detail in Chapter 18.

Saturn's Campaign Theme

In the case of Saturn, the theme is focused on a homespun tone that personalizes the car and the company. The objective is to present the car in such a way that customers and other stakeholders feel strongly about being identified with it. It uses touching stories to establish bonds and build relationships. All this is embodied in the somewhat understated slogan: "A different kind of company, a different kind of car." Because Japanese cars were making such an inroad into GM's market share, naturally they were perceived as the primary competition. The campaign strategy, however, avoided overt flag waving and instead used Spring Hill and the Saturn employees and owners as a symbol for the values of America.

Campaign Development and Evolution

What is interesting about the Saturn campaign is that it has maintained a consistent theme and tone throughout three different periods as the campaign has evolved over time from the pre-launch, the launch in 1990, and the continuing campaign since then.

An award-winning pre-launch video talked about Spring Hill, Tennessee, and what the company was doing to protect its rural small-city atmosphere. Pre-launch ads ran in local markets for six weeks before the car was available and focused on employees as a symbol of the company and its philosophy of quality. One commercial told the story of a St. Louis native who moved to Spring Hill to make a difference in building a different kind of car. Another showed how an executive and a union member formed a bond in traveling around the world researching new ideas for building the car.

The initial launch advertisements focused on the people who build, sell, and service the car consistently. The ads stressed that Saturn is made by people who really care and whose number-one priority is to satisfy customers and build a long-term relationship with them. In a particularly heartfelt spot, an employee described his pride as the first Saturn models left the plant. It was a unique advertising approach because most car advertising focuses on styling and handling of the vehicle.

In terms of public relations, Saturn was named one of "The Year's 100 Greatest Achievements in Science and Technology" in December 1990 by *Popular Science*. A month later *Popular Mechanics* gave Saturn a "Design and Engineering Award" for "manufacturing processes that result in exceptionally high quality for an all-new vehicle." These events gave the new car a reputation for being well engineered.

Pre-launch

Launch

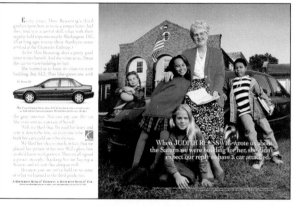

Post-launch, 1992

Post-launch, 1997

These ads show the three phrases of the Saturn campaign: the pre-launch, launch, and post-launch. They use a consistent format, style, and tone. Do you think the consistency helps Saturn's image? Why?

After the launch was over, advertising strategy shifted to feature satisfied owners explaining why they like the car. This shift in storytelling from Saturn employees to Saturn owners, who are selected through their letters or anecdotes passed on by dealers, marks the third stage in the campaign; however, the ads maintain the same folksy image and tone—real people talking about their experiences with the car and their feelings about it.

These stories include a small-town police chief who orders two Saturns as patrol cars; a golfer showing off a photo of "two things I miss a lot, my son (who monopolizes my car) and my Saturn"; a young man describing how he faced a barrage of questions from another motorist at every stoplight; and an older woman who uses her Saturn to pick up friends for bingo. Even though the last one depicts someone outside the target market, its popularity comes from its authentic story that, Riney executives feel, transcends demographics. In a spot about a third-grade teacher who sends a school picture so employees know who they are building the car for, an employee at the factory tapes the photo to the rearview mirror on the assembly line. That commercial demonstrates all the Saturn values—the enthusiastic customer, the caring employee, the bond between them, and the pride in a quality product.

The honors and awards continued as Saturn sales developed momentum. The following list cites some of the awards the car won in its first five years as it made a name for itself and redefined notions of quality for U.S. small cars, as well as GM. Each award was a publicity opportunity that dovetailed with the marketing communication strategy of promoting Saturn's quality.

1990
- A car with a stock Saturn engine won a four-hour endurance race at Sears Point Raceway—the first victory for an all-new vehicle since Mercedes-Benz won in 1954.
- *Popular Science* named Saturn one of "The Year's 100 Greatest Achievements in Science and Technology."

1991
- *Home Mechanix* named Saturn the "Easy Maintenance Car of the Year."
- The Automobile Association of America named the Saturn Coupe "Best Car" in the $10,000–$15,000 category.
- *Motorweek*/PBS gave Saturn the "Driver's Choice Award for Best Small Car" in both 1991 and 1992.

1992
- *Motor Trend* named the Saturn SL among the "Top Ten Domestic Buys."
- The Saturn SL was named "Best in Class" by *Kiplinger's Personal Finance Magazine.*
- Saturn is the highest-ranking domestic nameplate in the J.D. Power and Associates Customer Satisfaction Index.

1993
- *Automobile Magazine* gave Saturn the "Technology of the Year" award for its affordable and innovative traction control system.
- *Consumers' Digest* named the Saturn sedan and wagon among the "Best Buys in Compact Class."

1994
- *Intellichoice* selected the 1993 Saturn SL as the "Best American Car Value" and the "Best Overall Value in the Compact Class."
- *Kiplinger's Personal Finance Magazine* rated the Saturn SL-2 as "Best in Class" and "First for Safety." The SC-2 was "Tops in Resale Value."

Saturn was also earning a reputation as a good citizen. Saturn received two Silver Anvil Awards from the Public Relations Society of American in 1991 for outstanding achievements in community relations and internal communications. Department of Labor Secretary Lynn Martin gave Saturn the EVE (Exemplary Voluntary Efforts) Award for its work to recruit women and minorities.

Campaign Tone and Style

The understated advertising was not product-focused; instead, it had a folksy, homespun tone. It was badly misread by industry experts when it was initially launched. Bob Garfield, the advertising critic for *Advertising Age,* apologized for not understanding its power to stand out among the amorphous, nondistinctive car ads used by others in the industry. Riney executives point out, however, the last thing they could do was boast about the quality, reliability, or durability of cars that were unproven. Their strategy was to sell Saturn the company rather than the product. GM chairperson John Smale has stated that he believes the advertising worked. He reports that studies show that the consumer's image of Saturn is of the "caring" car company.

Unlike other car manufacturers that do well in customer-satisfaction surveys, Saturn has chosen not to advertise its high J.D. Power ranking, letting its satisfied customers carry that message instead. In fact, it has even shown commercials featuring a recall order. In that spot a Saturn representative travels to Alaska to fix the seat in a Saturn owned by Robin Millage, a real customer who had ordered her car sight unseen from a dealer in the continental United States.

But the stories aren't the only type of advertising done by Riney. For the first several years, the product could not keep up with demand. New owners had to go on a waiting list. On one hand, that was a positive occurrence because it made the car more valuable; on the other hand, it was a nuisance. Riney used that phenomenon to create radio and newspaper ads that apologized for the shortage and turned it into a positive message by explaining that Saturn wouldn't speed up production and risk quality.

This Saturn ad tells the story of a satisfied customer who spreads the word to colleagues. Do you think it's effective?

MESSAGE DESIGN

1. Every campaign is held together by a central big idea.
2. Creative strategies describe the general message approaches to be used with the various stakeholder audiences, including the targeted consumer audience.
3. Executions are the actual ads and other materials produced by the various functional areas involved in the campaign.
4. Pretesting is used to determine if campaign messages will be heard and understood. Concept testing checks the power of the big idea. Pretesting is also used to test various message strategies and executions to evaluate alternative approaches.
5. Posttesting is used to determine if the campaign met its objectives.

MEDIA/MESSAGE DELIVERY SYSTEM

The media—or message delivery—plan is just as important as the creative plan. The two plans are usually developed simultaneously. Sometimes the campaign planner may have already decided that a certain medium—such as direct mail—must be used, and the creative effort is designed accordingly. Media planning involves the following steps:

1. Selecting the best vehicles to reach the audience
2. Deciding on the frequency—the level of repetition the message needs
3. Scheduling the media efforts across time
4. Estimating the costs and allocating the budget among the various vehicles

Because the world of media planning is extremely complex, a media planner's ability to select a media mix that blends perfectly with the creative effort is both an art and a science. In advertising media selection computers can now perform media-related data analysis in seconds that formerly took hours. In addition, the information available about consumer media habits and behavior has made media selection far more exact and less wasteful.

Still, the choices appear endless and the costs enormous. Even large marketers such as the Clorox Company, maker of Clorox Bleach, have found it difficult to find the right media to reach the elusive working woman. Traditional daytime television and women's magazines have given way to specialty magazines and direct mail. And college students, a favorite target for many clothing and sports manufacturers, are even more difficult to reach with conventional media. That's why special programs such as on-campus and spring break events are used so extensively. As discussed in Chapters 15 and 16, choosing the media plan has become a major undertaking.

In Saturn's case the customer stories run both on TV and in some three dozen magazines on Saturn's media schedule. Its 1996 media selection follows:

- 9 national commercials
- 20 regional commercials
- 9 national print ads (plus gatefolds and pages)
- 80 regional print ads

- 40 information boxes (kiosks)
- 16 radio ads
- 12 outdoor boards (plus regional)
- 3 brochures (Full-Line, Auto Show, Customer Assistance Center)
- 150 pages on the Saturn Web site

Media Creativity

Saturn commended the Riney agency's media department for its innovative use of message delivery systems, particularly the use of the "Spring" documentary as an infomercial. Saturn has also staged "Media Days" at the Spring Hill factory for media representatives, who mostly come from big cities. One creative connection was to link Saturn with bicycling sponsorships and publications. The media department's research found that people who cycle often drive an import in the same price range as Saturn. They concluded that Saturn's image fits right in with cycling's environmental and health benefits. In 1992 Saturn sponsored a cycling team that represented the United States in the Olympic games, a tie-in that was intended to appeal to its cycling-minded target market.

Even though Saturn's initial ad budget, at an estimated $100 million, wasn't large by automotive standards, one media goal was to seek preferential treatment from media. For example, media buyers bought space from a select group of 35 magazines and used frequent insertions in each to develop a connection with those magazines' readers. In exchange for the number of insertions, the magazines often gave Saturn prime locations to run its ads. As a further incentive to secure the prime location for a print ad, Saturn media buyers told magazines that any back cover sold to Saturn would be in addition to Saturn's existing page commitment. Saturn, then, often bumped other advertisers out of the back cover position. Saturn was also one of the first advertisers to take a substantial position on the now-popular Fox network.

In a similar deal Saturn also became the largest out-of-home advertiser in California, the number-one out-of-home market and the largest auto market in the country, where commuting times are long and the highways are frequently clogged. For less than 10 percent of the total advertising budget for California, Saturn dominated the state's outdoor boards and used outdoor advertising to reinforce its national TV, radio, magazine, and newspaper advertising messages. Tracking study research found that of the people aware of Saturn without promoting (unaided recall), 56 percent recalled seeing Saturn's outdoor advertising, which is an incredibly high response rate.

EVALUATION

Evaluation is the final and, in some respects, most important step in developing a campaign because it is the point where a company learns from its experiences. Many companies overlook this step, which is unfortunate because that makes it difficult to develop progressively more effective communication plans. Campaign evaluation is concerned with questions of effectiveness: Does the campaign work? Does it do what needs to be done? What were the results? It is also concerned with questions of taste and judgment: Is the campaign fair and accurate? Does it mislead?

Two problems make evaluation particularly difficult. First, despite the best efforts of campaign planners, many marketing communication programs are disjointed. This is especially true when people executing the plan in the various areas do not work together closely. The disjointed efforts may lead to inconsistency at best and at worst may lead to a disaster. A second problem is that there is little agreement on how to measure the success of a campaign—how much emphasis should be placed on communication effects and how much on sales? Though it is true that most managers understand, for example, that advertising does not necessarily lead directly to sales, the expectation is still there.

Finally, it is sometimes difficult to diagnose the nature of the problem. Pepsi-Cola, for example, experienced tremendous success with campaigns featuring Michael Jackson, Lionel Ritchie, and Ray Charles; a campaign that featured Madonna, however, was a disaster. With the former campaigns, recall, awareness, attitudes, and sales increased; with the latter, only letters of protest increased. Why the difference? Sometimes it takes a sophisticated research effort to deconstruct a campaign to find out what went wrong.

Nevertheless, evaluation must take place. Essentially, two types of evaluations may be made: ongoing evaluation—tracking studies—while the campaign is running, and post-evaluation at the end of the campaign. The former allows the advertiser to make adjustments before the problems become too severe. Maxwell House Coffee discovered that consumers were afraid that its new coffee was a potential health risk, so it opted for an ongoing evaluation. Using the information collected, Maxwell House was able to quickly develop print and broadcast ads that carefully explained the controversial issues. Had Maxwell House been concerned only with evaluating sales rather than communication effectiveness during the campaign, it would have been too late to solve the problems as they were uncovered.

Post-evaluation allows marketing communicators to make major adjustments so that mistakes will not be repeated. Cadillac Motors, for example, went through a period where its campaigns were changed every six months because post-evaluation indicated that the target audience was having a difficult time determining the primary idea in Cadillac ads.

Saturn's Success

Saturn has been successful in many ways. Its cars consistently receive a rating of best small car in customer satisfaction. It has the most loyal owner base of any small North American car, and it has achieved the status of having the best resale value in the industry.

Saturn also met its objective to take business away from imports, as the following 1995 company data indicate:

- 72 percent "plus business" to General Motors—Translation? Had it not been for Saturn, 72 percent of customers say they would not have purchased a GM product.
- Nearly 50 percent of Saturn owners say that but for Saturn they would have purchased an import, with most buying a Honda or Toyota.

- As a result of their Saturn ownership experience, approximately 40 percent of Saturn owners say they will consider a GM product as their next purchase.
- Saturn's demographics closely mirror those of its key import competitors.

In terms of meeting sales and marketing share objectives, consider 1994 results reported in July of 1995. Sales for 1994 represented a 26.7 percent increase over 1993. That year also saw 11 record sales months with the streak continuing into 1995. Saturn was number two in overall retail sales in the country and number one in overall retail sales in California, which has always been a lucrative market for imported cars. Share of the small and sport market segments increased from 7.7 to 9.5 percent (an increase of 23 percent), and overall share of the total new-car market increased from 2.7 to 3.18 percent (an increase of 18 percent). Retailers led the automotive industry for the third consecutive year with 899 sales per facility.

Was the company a financial success? Auto industry experts will argue forever about whether the $4.5 billion investment was worth it. Originally planned to deliver 120,000 cars a year, demand outpaced production. Saturn sold 196,126 cars in 1992, its second year, an increase of 236 percent over its first-year sales of 76,375 cars. Business publications at the time praised the company for selling more Saturns per dealership than any other car, domestic or foreign, accounting for 7 percent of all small cars sold in the United States. In 1993 sales were up nearly 30 percent with sales targets of 300,000. In 1994 sales increased 21 percent compared with gains of about 11 percent for the rest of the industry.

The company's goal was to break even in 1993 and make a profit in 1994. In a reversal of usual industry relations, dealers gave 1 percent of their margin back to the factory in 1993 to help the company turn a profit during that year, which would move the company ahead of its schedule. Saturn also earned a 2.1 percent share of the U.S. car market, beating out Hyundai, Subaru, Volkswagen, and Mitsubishi. Saturn finished third that year in buyer satisfaction, behind only Lexus and Infiniti. Its price, which started at $9195, was only a fraction of what a Lexus or Infiniti costs.

No matter how experts view the company's financial success, there's no doubt that Saturn is a successful marketing communication case study on how to build a brand by focusing on how customers and other stakeholders relate to both the product and the company behind it.

Concept ✓ Review

MEDIA/MESSAGE DELIVERY SYSTEM AND EVALUATION

1. Media planning involves:
   - Selecting the best vehicles to reach the audience
   - Deciding on the frequency of the message
   - Scheduling the media efforts across time
   - Allocating the budget among the various vehicles
2. Campaign evaluation is concerned with questions of effectiveness.
3. Evaluation is the point where a company learns from its experiences, either through ongoing evaluation or post-evaluation.

CONTINUING THE CONSISTENCY

Saturn and its marketing communication campaign was launched by GM president Roger Smith, and continued by subsequent GM presidents, even in the face of jealousy and backbiting by other GM divisions. The fact that Saturn has stayed true to its positioning and message strategy has kept it in the success column. GM chairperson John Smale told a meeting of Saturn dealers in 1994 that he felt Saturn's strong image was largely attributable to its determination to keep its message strategy consistent. He explained, "the advertising has been effective because the same message and the same 'look and feel' are carried through in print copy as well as television—and because [Saturn] hasn't varied from that message of its 'look and feel.'" The result is a strong brand personality built in a very short time. Smale acknowledged that, "You've built a brand equity of great value. Every time the consumer sees a Saturn ad, you increase the strength and value of that equity." He admonished the dealers not to give in to pressures to detour from this established marketing communication strategy.

Even the local dealer association advertising, contrary to most automotive brands, does not dilute or contradict the national advertising and brand image. Because the retailer advertising is also developed by Hal Riney, it carries the same message, look, and feel. That management strategy insures the retailers' message will be consistent in tone and content with the rest of the campaign.

As an example of how consistent the advertising remains, one of the most successful ads that ran in 1994 and 1995 featured Dean Koontz, a satellite dish salesperson in Spokane, Washington. Since 1991 Koontz has been driving his Saturn SL-1 four-door sedan an average of 250 miles a day over bumpy, wet, snowy, icy rural roads that only four-wheel drive vehicles can handle. He has accumulated more than 185,000 miles and generated a wealth of leads for the Spokane Saturn dealership. He explains that many of the people he calls on aren't familiar with Saturn, so they ask about the car as he demonstrates his satellite dish. When asked, he gives them his Saturn dealer's card and a testimony about the car's durability and handling. So far his word-of-mouth marketing has produced at least six sales.

In 1994 GM folded Saturn into its small-car division, causing analysts to fear that Saturn's autonomy and distinctive image would be lost. Saturn executives, however, fought to keep its independence. Saturn's president, Richard "Skip" LeFauve, was placed in charge of GM's revamped Small Car Group. GM executives said the change was made so that Saturn thinking would dominate the small-car unit and other models could learn from its experiences, although critics feared that Saturn's brand image and quality would be diluted with the merger. GM's position? Saturn was set up as a model from which to learn; it was time for Saturn to teach its successful techniques to the rest of the corporation. Both Saturn and GM executives admit that its marketing communication campaign has played a big role in the car's success, and there is no reason to jeopardize that.

This homespun ad featuring satellite salesperson Dean Koontz is a testimony to the power of customer satisfaction.

A CLOSING THOUGHT: A SUCCESS STORY

The Saturn story is about how a company, through planning and action, can create positive relationships with its key stakeholders. Saturn understood the total range of communication contact points that deliver a company's message and worked hard to send a consistent message from all those points. Finally, the Saturn experience shows the organization necessary to manage communication messages delivered in a variety of ways over a long period of time. The Saturn integrated marketing communication program helped develop a strong brand image, one of quality cars made by a quality U.S. company that cares about its customers, their sales experience, and their long-term satisfaction with the product.

Saturn has been able to create a successful marketing communication platform and hold it together for close to ten years, an uncommonly long time for an integrated communication program to stay intact. It remains to be seen whether the program will continue now that Saturn has lost its separate status. It also remains to be seen if it is time for Saturn to move to a new marketing communication approach. What would you recommend for the future if you were the new marketing communication director for Saturn?

SUMMARY

1. Distinguish between a campaign and a one-shot marketing communication effort.

A campaign is a series of marketing communication messages designed to meet a set of objectives based on a situation analysis and guided by the marketing and corporate business plans. Campaign messages are delivered over time, through different media and message delivery systems, and to various audiences. Campaigns normally mean a commitment to a message strategy that will last at least one year. In contrast, companies that create one marketing communication message at a time—such as an advertisement, a public relations press release, or a direct-marketing piece—are not involved in a campaign planning process. This one-message-at-a-time method is called the one-shot approach.

2. Outline the steps in the campaign planning process and explain the campaign planning document.

Planning a campaign involves eight steps: analyzing the situation, deciding on a set of key strategic decisions (objectives, targeting, and competitive positioning), analyzing the communication dimensions of the marketing mix, identifying the best functions to lead and support the effort, determining and allocating the budget, designing the creative strategy, designing the media or message delivery system, and evaluating the success of the campaign. These are also the major sections in the campaign plan document.

POINTS TO PONDER

Review the Facts

1. What is a one-shot approach, and how does it differ from a campaign?
2. What is a campaign plan?
3. What is a marketing communication audit, and how can it be used in campaign planning?
4. What is account planning, and what does it add to the campaign planning effort?

Master the Concepts

5. Why do you think many marketing communication professionals regard campaign planning as a complicated task?
6. Discuss how campaign objectives are set. How would campaign objectives differ from objectives for an individual ad?
7. Explain the difference between creative strategies, message strategies, and creative tactics.
8. Explain how a planner should select the marketing communication activities used in a campaign. What is one way to determine the marketing communication activity that will lead the effort?
9. Explain what is meant by the notion that the marketing mix (other than marketing communication) can deliver messages.

10. "A company should evaluate a campaign to learn from its experiences." Explain what might be learned from such an exercise.

Apply Your Knowledge

11. Assume that you are working on the campaign to launch a new Wish-Bone Cheddar and Bacon dressing. What research would have to be done to support this campaign?
12. In planning the media or message delivery systems to be used in a campaign, what are the four decisions a planner has to make? Suppose you are the media planner for the launch of a new Wish-Bone Cheddar and Bacon dressing. Develop a set of recommendations demonstrating that you understand how these four decisions are applied to a campaign.
13. Adopt a nonprofit association in your community and develop a marketing communication budget for it. Identify its most important activities, the expenses associated with them, and its income sources. How much money needs to be raised through donations to make the income cover the expenses?

SUGGESTED PROJECTS

1. (Writing Project) Find an example of at least one print and one broadcast ad that belong to the same campaign. Compare and contrast the ads. Do they seem to follow the same campaign strategy in a consistent theme? How are they similar and how are they different? Write a brief report that explains what you think the reasons are for the differences.

2. (Team Project) Break into small groups of four to six students. Each member should find one article about a current campaign in any of the trade magazines—*Advertising Age, Adweek,* or *Brandweek,* for example. As a group, discuss each campaign article and select the one the group would like to evaluate. Using the information available in the article, outline the campaign using the eight sections in a campaign plan. Then critique the campaign and assess ways to improve it, if any. Select a group spokesperson to present your findings to the class.

3. (Writing Project) Based on the Saturn case discussed in this chapter, outline the different types of marketing communication activities used in this car's marketing program. Explain how they are integrated. Is there any marketing communication area that wasn't discussed? In that area, or any other area that you feel was underutilized, what might you recommend that Saturn marketing communication planners include in next year's campaign plan? Write your proposal.

4. (Internet Project) Assume that you are the new media communication specialist for Saturn. Visit the Saturn home page (http://www.saturncars.com) and investigate the site. Assess whether the current site sends the same message as other Saturn advertising in print, TV, or through other methods. What stakeholders does the site target? Is the site easy to navigate? Is it engaging? Does it provide enough information? Write a brief memo analyzing the current site and making recommendations for next year.

Case Questions

1. Explain the evolution of the creative message used by Saturn during its three periods: pre-launch, launch, and post-launch.
2. Watch for some current Saturn advertising on television and in magazines. Explain the strategy behind these new ads and how they link (or don't link) with the previous campaign efforts discussed in this chapter.
3. If you were a strategic planner on the Saturn account, where do you think the message strategy should go next year?
4. How many different ways are being used to communicate the Saturn message? Develop an analysis of the Saturn message delivery system.
5. If you were in charge of Saturn's current campaign, how would you evaluate its success? Develop an evaluation plan that will help you determine if the Saturn marketing communication program is effective.

ROMA'S LITE INTEGRATED CASE QUESTIONS

If you have been working with the Roma's Lite Pizza project throughout this text, then you have almost developed a comprehensive campaign plan. Compile all your work to date into a formal campaign plan. You should have enough of the work completed to make an impressive campaign plan document.

1. (Writing Project) What rewriting needs to be done to make the sections work together and flow nicely as a business report? Do the rewriting and prepare this document as a campaign plan for the launch.

2. (Team Project) Break into small groups of two to four students. Develop a presentation for the rest of the class that will explain the highlights, key strategic decisions, and the most important details of your marketing communication recommendations. Use as many visuals as possible presented either on overheads or using one of the computer graphic presentation programs such as PowerPoint.

video case Procter & Gamble Gets the Word out about Olestra

Procter & Gamble has long enjoyed a reputation for cutting-edge marketing practices. Every move P&G makes is closely scrutinized by industry observers. In recent years, for example, the company has streamlined its pricing policies, reduced the number of product variations that it offers, and experimented with eliminating coupons.

Now, P&G faces one of its most formidable marketing challenges —successfully commercializing olestra under the P&G brand name Olean®. Olestra is a fat substitute that has been in product development for over 25 years at a cost of $200 million. According to P&G, its development program included more than 150 studies of over 20,000 people. Wendy Jacques, a corporate communications executive at P&G, acknowledged that those pre-market tests showed that olestra could produce a "modest gastrointestinal effect" in some people.

In January 1996, the FDA ap-proved olestra as an additive in snack foods. The approval, however, required P&G to conduct additional market surveillance tests that the FDA would review in June 1998. The FDA also required that P&G add vitamins to its olestra products and include the following warning label: "This product is made with olestra. Olestra may cause abdominal cramping and loose stools. Olestra inhibits the absorption of some vitamins and other nutrients. Vitamins A, D, E, and K have been added." Critics, such as the Center for Science in the Public Interest (CSPI), The American Public Health Network, and the National Women's Health Network vocally opposed the FDA approval of olestra.

P&G immediately began test-marketing fat-free potato chips fried in olestra. Health concerns raised by critics, however, presented a marketing communication challenge. On the eve of the FDA's decision, the olestra controversy was featured as the cover story in *Time* magazine. In a press conference, CSPI executive director Michael Jacobson denounced olestra as "unfit for human consumption." Jacobson called olestra "the first food additive with negative nutritional value." In response, P&G touted the value of helping Americans reduce fat in their diets, the addition of vitamins to the products, the relatively small number of people that experienced cramping or loose stools, and positive word of mouth from those who tested its products.

Market tests of potato chips made with olestra began in September 1996. In Columbus, Ohio, P&G passed out thousands of samples of Fat Free Pringles at a farmer's market near the Capitol, in Kroger's supermarkets, and other locations. From September to December, according to P&G, more than three million servings of chips made with olestra were sold or sampled. P&G and Frito-Lay, the other chip maker testing olestra products, set up a toll-free number (found on the product packages) that consumers could call to voluntarily report complaints. P&G claimed that there was less than one complaint for every 3,000 servings of chips sold or sampled.

Aside from conducting tests to overcome critics' health concerns, P&G has taken two other steps to aid its marketing communication efforts. First, it set up a Web site (www.olean.com) for people to learn about olestra, read expert opinions and press releases, and link to other related sites. In a P&G press release found in the site, the company reported that sales continued to exceed expectations in the Columbus market. Second, P&G reported asked the FDA to permit use of a less-graphic warning label on olestra products after market tests showed consumers reacted negatively to the FDA's wording. A *Wall Street Journal* article reported that P&G suggested dropping references to abdominal

cramping and loose stools, and saying instead that olestra may cause intestinal discomfort or a laxative effect.

Why all the effort? Industry watchers speculate that P&G's sales of olestra could exceed $300 million annually.

Discussion Questions

1. Review Part II (Chapters 5–8). What factors in the marketing communication environment affected P&G's test launch of olestra snack foods? Do you think that the test findings will help P&G's national product launch?
2. Review Part III (Chapters 9–14). What marketing communication tools did Procter & Gamble use to test market its Fat Free Pringles products?
3. Now assume that the FDA has reviewed P&G's additional tests up through June 1998. Based on the company's findings and ad-

ditional scientific research, the FDA has agreed to let P&G modify the olestra warning label. Outline the steps you would need to take to develop an IMC campaign for the Fat Free Pringles line of snack foods made with Olean and what additional information you would need to develop that campaign.

Video Source: "People Are Talking About . . . Olestra" *Primetime Live,* 17 January 1996. *Additional Sources:* Procter & Gamble Olean® Web site, Procter & Gamble Press Releases, September 1996–February 1997, Internet: www.olean.com; Ruji Narisetti, "Down the Drain: Move to Drop Coupons Puts Procter & Gamble in Sticky PR Situation," *Wall Street Journal,* 17 April 1997, A1, A10; Ruji Narisetti, "Too Many Choices: P&G, Seeing Shoppers Were Being Confused, Overhauls Marketing," *Wall Street Journal,* 15 January 1997, A1, A8; Nanci Hellmich, "Consumers Sink Teeth into Olestra Chips," *USA Today,* 30 September 1996, 6D; "P&G Seeks Less-graphic Warning Labels for Olestra," *CNNfn Archive,* 9 April 1996, Internet: www.cnnfn.com/news/9604/09/olestra; "FDA Approves Fat Substitute, Olestra," *HHS News,* 24 January 1996, Internet: www.fda.gov/bbs/topics/news/new00524; Michael D. Lemonick, "Are We Ready for Fat-Free Fat?" *Times,* 8 January 1996, 53–55+.

Getting a Slice of the Pie:

A Marketing Plan for Roma's Lite Pizza*

Pizza is one of the most popular foods in North America. On average, people in the United States eat about 20 pounds of pizza per year. They eat pizza in restaurants; they take out pizza from restaurants and grocery stores; they make their own at home; and they buy frozen pizza for quick, convenient meals. Sales of pizza products are increasing at a rate of 11 percent annually and sales top $30 billion, up from $17 billion in 1994. However, pizza is a highly competitive, cluttered market. It is also one of the most intensive battlegrounds in the "healthy" food category. As a result, developing and introducing a new pizza product requires sophisticated marketing and marketing communication.

New Roman Foods is taking a market-driven approach to a new healthy pizza product by developing its product based on significant consumer input. The strategy behind this new product is detailed in this marketing plan, prepared by the Director of Marketing, who analyzes the market, recommends a set of strategies, and coordinates the marketing-mix activities necessary for a successful launch of Roma's Lite Pizza—a premium, low-calorie, "healthy" pizza.

Situation Analysis

In this situation analysis, we examine corporate goals and background information; the product category; sales trends, distribution, and pricing practices in this product category; relevant competitive information; consumers in this market; and key problems and opportunities.

Corporate Review

New Roman is a 12-year-old company with three business units: pizza, snacks, and entrees—all sold primarily through food stores. A larger consumer study done last year indicates that consumers perceive that our products are a good value but are not necessarily top quality or great tasting.

*This is a real case, but the company identity has been disguised.

In evaluating the success of new products, New Roman's corporate financial guidelines require new products to have at least an 18-percent return on investment (ROI). Business unit managers adhere to these guidelines because only then can the company continue the annual ten-percent or more increase in net profits that the company has enjoyed since 1988. To ensure such financial success, the launch of this new product must be carefully planned and well executed. A review of New Roman's channels of distribution and research and development for the new product follow.

Because New Roman Foods frozen products have national distribution and authorization for its products in major grocery stores, we will have leverage to obtain authorization for this new product line with our distributors across the country.

This new healthy pizza product, Roma's Lite Pizza, fits a relatively untapped niche with a potentially large growth opportunity. In 1990, New Roman Foods began investing heavily in research and development to develop the sauces, low-fat meats, low-fat cheeses, and pastas necessary to introduce low-fat, low-calorie, low-sodium, and low-cholesterol Italian food products. An entree product line was introduced in 1993 and succeeded beyond original sales projections. The company's two other business units continued to develop healthy versions of their products. The snacks line was introduced in late 1995. Research on the pizza line began in earnest in 1995, and now, after extensive development, the company is ready to launch a line of premium, low-calorie (low-cal), "healthy" pizzas.

Product Category Review

Although premium low-cal pizza may appear to be a niche product, we are operating in a complex category. Though our most direct competition comes from the frozen pizza category, competition will also come from such categories as other frozen entrees, in-store "deli-fresh" pizzas, home-delivery and restaurant take-out pizzas, and, of course, restaurants that serve pizzas.

These categories, subcategories, and niches can also be compared in terms of their estimated share of retail pizza sales. That information is provided in the following chart.

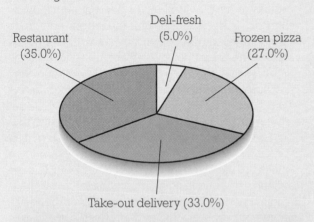

Restaurant (35.0%)

Deli-fresh (5.0%)

Frozen pizza (27.0%)

Take-out delivery (33.0%)

FIGURE A.1

Estimated 1998 Share of Retail Pizza Sales

To best understand this competitive environment, we review four market segments: general frozen entrees, low-cal and healthy, frozen pizza, and the specific niche of low-cal "healthy" frozen pizzas.

1. Frozen Entrees

The frozen-entree category is a mature, highly competitive category. Although the number of frozen-food entrees has increased over the last ten years, the outlook for this category is still positive. A supermarket trade publication, *Supermarket News*, has stated that both the economy and "growing interest in nutrition have helped increase sales of frozen dinners and entrees." Other important considerations regarding frozen entrees follow.

Trend Toward Low-Priced Items The economic situation during the last five years seems to have attracted people to the lower-priced entrees. The moderate growth of the economy in the last five years has led to conservative consumer purchasing patterns. Shoppers seem attracted to lower-priced frozen entrees for convenience meals, rather than the more expensive ready-to-eat products, as evidenced by buying patterns in the first few months of this year.

Fastest Growth in Microwave Products Microwaves are available in 70 percent of the nation's workplaces and in even more homes. It is estimated that 50 percent of all cooking is now microwave cooking. The challenge to the microwave food industry (and consequently the frozen-food industry) has been to come up with healthy microwavable foods that also taste good. Substantial R&D investments have been and are being made by frozen-food leaders, and this category is developing into one of the hottest growth areas in the freezer case.

Growth in Snacks and Mini-Entrees Another fast-growing frozen-food product category is the meal/snack-type item. These are single-serving items such as hamburger and fries, chicken tidbits, pita-style stuffed sandwiches, mini-hotdogs, and small pizzas. This category is exploding, according to Ed Russell, director of market research at Campbell Soup Company, who was quoted in *Progressive Grocer* as saying that it is partly the result of the trade's desire to compete with fast food and the consumer's desire for convenience.

2. Low-Calorie, Healthy Foods

The Weight Watchers International line of low-calorie foods has dominated this market for years even though it is perceived as a line of diet products—a slightly different category than low-calorie foods that have broader appeal to all kinds of people concerned about their health.

- In most supermarkets in the 1990s, low-calorie food products account for roughly one-third of the merchandise sold and 40 percent of the gross sales volume
- A supermarket trade publication reports that "with the nation's growing health-consciousness. . . manufacturers are realizing that offering low calories is not enough; many are now flooding the market with new, reformulated, and expanded lines that combine low calories with low sodium, low cholesterol, and low fat."
- There is increasing demand for space in supermarket freezers due to the growing demand for low-calorie and microwavable versions of existing frozen-food lines.

- Low-calorie frozen foods are growing 350 percent faster than frozen dinners as a whole.

3. Frozen Pizza

The frozen-pizza category accounts for more than $1.5 billion in retail sales in 1997. The frozen-pizza category, however, is a mature category, and as the established lines seek niches to increase competitiveness, the hottest growth items in the frozen-pizza section are microwavables and single servings.

Gourmet pizzas are also beginning to appear in the frozen-food case, although they have been slower to take off, due to the lingering "gut-filler" image of this product category. Experts predict that as good-tasting and healthier products enter the market, the gourmet-pizza market will develop just as gourmet lines developed in the frozen-entree category. The gourmet frozen pizza is definitely an undeveloped category and possibly a quite profitable niche.

4. Low-Calorie, Healthy Pizza

In 1982, Cornell University researchers, along with egg industry officials and an Iowa agricultural consultant, began to market a low-calorie pizza crust; the crust was made primarily from egg whites and contained about two-thirds the calories of traditional wheat-flour pizza crust. Importantly, the crust didn't become soggy when baked in the microwave. With continuing R&D, the industry has been improving on this low-calorie, microwavable crust throughout the 1980s and early 1990s. The push is now on to develop and market a low-cholesterol, low-calorie crust that is microwavable.

- At the same time in the early 1980s, Jeno's experimented with a line of low-calorie frozen pizza. The line, however, never made it to market because Jeno's was bought out shortly thereafter by Pillsbury.
- In 1986, the first low-calorie pizzas began showing up in pizza chains. Pizza Inn was one of the first to test this concept.
- The market for low-calorie frozen pizza took off in the late 1980s with the introduction of pizzas in the Weight Watchers line and that of a smaller enterprise, Gilardi's. The Weight Watchers line of low-calorie French-bread pizzas was similar to Stouffer's already-existing French Bread Pizzas.

- "Healthy" food product claims require pizza makers to rethink their ingredients and substitute low-fat pepperoni and sausage. However, that practice only moves the calories down a notch; to move into the "healthy" list, makers must also substitute chicken and turkey for pepperoni and sausage, use more vegetable toppings and spices to enhance the flavors, and add vitamins, minerals, and fiber to the ingredients.
- Figures from the *Supermarket Business* annual consumer-expenditures study show annual gains of three to four percent in grocery sales of frozen pizzas through the 1980s and 1990s. Diet and low-calorie frozen products played an increasingly significant part in the growth of the frozen-pizza category.

Sales Trends

Frozen pizza is sold throughout the year with little seasonal fluctuation. The highest period of sales is during the fall and winter months, with January, February, March, April, October, November, and December being the months in which sales exceed the average monthly share of 8.33 %.

Share of Market   Pillsbury, through its Totino's, Jenos, Pillsbury, and regional Pappalo's lines, leads the frozen-pizza market nationally with a 23.5 percent share of unit volume for the 52-week period ending July 13, 1997, according to industry research. The share of the frozen-pizza category follows.

Share of Major Frozen-Pizza Brands

1. Pillsbury (Totino's, Jenos, Pillsbury, Pappalo's)   23.5%
2. Tony's Pizza (Tony's and Red Baron lines)   18.3
3. Kraft General Foods Tombstone   10.0
4. Stouffer's   7.7
5. Quaker Oats Celeste   5.9
6. McCain Ellio's   3.7
7. Others   30.0

Geographic Trends

Regional category development index (CDI)[1]—breakdowns indicate the frozen-pizza purchasing levels for different parts of the country. As you can see from the table that follows, the swings between high-

and low-CDI areas are not dramatic. The north central and northeast regions are areas of opportunity in terms of their generally high levels of pizza consumption; the southeast, southwest and northwest regions have lower CDIs.

CDI Based Geographical Review

1.	northeast	151
2.	southeast	93
3.	north central	121
4.	south central	102
5.	northwest	95
6.	southwest	87

An analysis of frozen-pizza sales by city, however, demonstrates more variable regional purchasing patterns. The product-category performance levels as indicated by CDIs are high in such cities as Milwaukee, Philadelphia, Boston, Baltimore, Chicago, Los Angeles, Phoenix, Albany, Miami, and Denver. Unfortunately, there are no clear regional delineations in such data. The same pattern holds in the cities with low CDIs.

It should also be noted that New Roman's Italian foods also have above-average sales levels in all the cities with high CDIs. Los Angeles, Boston, Baltimore, Phoenix, and Philadelphia are particularly important markets for New Roman Foods.

Category Distribution

Frozen pizzas are distributed through major supermarket chains, independents, and convenience stores. Some are also sold as prepared foods in such locations as bars, amusement parks, and movie houses. Low-cal products are primarily sold through supermarkets.

Category Pricing

A relevant pricing analysis of the frozen-pizza category, as well as the new low-cal healthy pizza niche, is largely based on the single-serve size, which is the product formulation in which Roma's Lite will be competing. Store price checks indicate that these single-servings range in size from $6\frac{3}{4}$ to 12 ounces, with the most common packages found in the 7–9 ounce size. Single-slice pizzas are in the 4–5 ounce range. Prices for the single-serving items range from $1.89 to $2.89.

One interesting finding from store checks is that most brands seem to be using one price per product line no matter which topping variety is offered on the product. The supreme, for example, may be priced the same as the cheese pizza even though the cost of the ingredients is higher for the supreme. The cost differential is accounted for by manipulating the amount of the product offered. For instance, a sausage-and-pepperoni item may weigh only 7.25 ounces while the extra cheese item may weigh 9.15 ounces. They would both, however, be priced the same.

Competitive Review

Weight Watchers, the market leader, has more than $500 million in food sales including $279 million from frozen dinners and entrees. Its primary competitors are ConAgra's Healthy Choice, Stouffer's Lean Cuisine, and Campbell's Le Menu line. The newest competitor is Slim-Fast, the largest seller of liquid-diet meals in the United States, which is introducing an extensive line of low-calorie food products, including soups, pastas, salad dressings, sodas, fruit juices, and variations on the original diet drink. The new products will all be enriched with vitamins, minerals, and fiber, and the company's president claims that "neither Healthy Choice nor Weight Watchers offers the same healthy nutrients."

Frozen Pizza Product Lines Two "healthy" pizzas are already on the market: Pillsbury's Totino's brand and Kraft General Foods Tombstone pizza. The Tombstone entry was introduced in 1990 with a light version of its regular line claiming 50 percent less fat. H.J. Heinz Co.'s Weight Watchers and Stouffer's Lean Cuisine have marketed pizza since 1982 and 1988, respectively. The offerings are considered "diet" products and may not even be found in the same part of the freezer case with the more traditional pizza brands. In 1990, both companies lowered sodium and fat in their offerings to keep up with the health claims of the new offerings by the more traditional pizza companies.

New entries in the healthy frozen-pizza category are coming on the market at this time. Because these lines are still under development, the only thing we know about them is what is being written in the trade press. Kraft General Foods is introducing a new healthy line called Eating Right and McCain Ellio's is launching a line called Healthy Slice.

Product Offerings and Pricing

Although these lines and offerings change weekly, the following is an average based on store and price checks in six high-CDI Midwestern markets. There are many single-serving and microwavable offerings, but only one company, Tombstone, has a low-cal product on the shelf. There is also one gourmet pizza line routinely on the shelf.

Product and Price Comparisons

Brand	Type	Size (in ounces)	Price
Celeste Pizza For One	pepperoni supreme deluxe	$6\frac{3}{4}$–9	1.89
Red Baron Super Single	sausage sausage & pepperoni	11.25	2.10
Red Baron	sausage pepperoni supreme Mexican	12	1.59
Stouffer's Microwave	sausage pepperoni sausage & pepperoni extra cheese deluxe	$7\frac{1}{4}$–10	2.89
Tombstone Singles	sausage pepperoni sausage & pepperoni Italian sausage supreme ranchero deluxe	12.5 9.15	2.79 2.29
Tombstone Microwave	pepperoni sausage & pepperoni Italian sausage three cheese supreme taco	7.17–8.95	2.19
Tombstone Light	sausage pepperoni sausage & pepperoni chicken deluxe vegetable	8–9.2	2.29
Totino's Singles	sausage pepperoni combination	4.2	1.19
Totino's Crisp Crust Microwave	sausage pepperoni	4.2	1.19
Tony's Microwave	sausage pepperoni sausage & pepperoni supreme Canadian bacon cheese	8.75–9	1.89–2.09
Wolfgang Puck's	spicy chicken sausage & herbs chicken & turkey sausage	10.5	2.29

Positioning and Marketing Communication

The four main competitors' positioning and marketing communication strategies follow.

- Le Menu. This line is offering what is believed to be a first in marketing communication campaigns for frozen-food products—a money-back taste guarantee. The campaign promotes the Le Menu Healthy line as the best tasting of the healthy choices in the frozen-food segment and its ads feature a toll-free number to call for a refund. The budget is approximately $5 million.
- Healthy Choice. The line is being incorporated into a $50-million umbrella campaign that also includes Pillsbury's other pizza products; handled by Campbell-Mithun Esty, Minneapolis. Position—pizza is also good for you; Healthy Choice's marketing communication budget is around $26 million, nearly five times the budget of Le Menu's healthy line.
- Eating Right. Features brand spokeswoman Chris Evert; handled by Foote, Cone & Belding, Chicago;

budget unknown. Position—pizza for people who care about their bodies.

- Healthy Slice. Will spend about $4 million for the launch of its new low-cal pizza line; TAB, New York, created the campaign using the theme, "Bite into a Healthy Slice of Life."

Consumer Analysis

Consumers of frozen pizza have varying demographic, psychographic, and lifestyle characteristics, which we analyze next. We also examine consumer trends in this market segment.

Demographics   Frozen-pizza buyers tend to be mothers of young families, single men, and teenagers. Heavy use is by teenagers, young singles, particularly young men, and children old enough to prepare their own food.

Health foods, however, skew to an older and/or more upscale audience. The 40-plus market has been described as a "growing segment of the population looking for healthy, low-cal foods." With increasing age, calorie needs decrease for most men and women. Furthermore, this segment is the leading edge of the baby boomers, who are now in their middle-age years. This fact represents a significant bump in the U.S. population profile. The 40-plus market is growing and is a key market to tap into for premium food products because they are used to a relatively good life and have the discretionary funds to spend for upscale and gourmet lines. Le Menu's target, for example, is females 45 and older.

The targeting decision involves balancing the frozen pizza market (younger, male) against the healthy foods market (older, female).

Psychographics/Lifestyle   The lifestyle of the typical frozen-pizza user is different from the lifestyle of the healthy-food user. The frozen-pizza market is primarily seen as downscale, with most of the product sold to people who are concerned about price but less concerned about health or taste. The image of frozen pizza is not generally as good or as high as that of restaurant pizza or fresh pizza purchased at a supermarket to take home and bake.

In contrast, people who are concerned about their health tend to be more upscale. They are often scornful of frozen pizzas because of their "gut-filler" im-

age. However, while these people are leery of high-fat and high-cholesterol ingredients such as processed meats and cheeses, they do like pizza. Selling a healthy pizza, then, necessitates reducing the amount of high-fat ingredients, using a more upscale marketing approach, and creating a product with a quality-pizza taste experience. It can't taste like cardboard and reach this group of consumers. The following summarizes what is known about the psychographics of healthy food buyers.

- Nearly half of the U.S. population engages in at least one athletic activity every day (or almost every day), and 71 percent participate in physical exercise at least once a week

- A *Marketing and Media Decisions* article reports that "If the 1990s was the decade of diets and 'going for the burn,' the decade of 2000 promises a decade of health and good-for-you food."

- *The New York Times* reports that in the 1990s consumers began turning away from the drive to be instantly skinny and focused more on foods that appear healthful in the long run rather than products that promise a quick shortcut to shedding pounds that always seem to return.

- A Roper Poll confirms that this trend is long running. During the 1980s, the opinion-research firm asked consumers if they were careful about what they eat mainly because they wanted to lose weight or because they wanted to be healthy. In 1983, 35 percent cited weight and 35 percent cited health; in 1987, 25 percent said weight and 41 percent said health. Although this survey hasn't been updated, a Roper vice-president has said that other research confirmed that this trend continued through the 1990s.

- Stephen Hughes, vice-president of new ventures at ConAgra, maker of Healthy Choice frozen dinners and entrees, reported that in the 1990s, while 29 percent of the population couldn't care less about what they eat, another 20 percent of Americans are restricted dieters, and a surprising 30 percent are so-called health-conscious people who watch what they eat: "They're younger, mainstream consumers, who are realizing they'd better start thinking of some of these things."

Consumer Trends in Low-Cal Frozen Pizzas   In terms of pizza eaters, the market for healthy products is new and relatively small at this time. The director of marketing for Pillsbury's pizza division says that, "our consumers are telling us they want a pizza, not a diet or health food."

The questions are these: How many traditional pizza eaters will respond to a healthy claim and, likewise, how many consumers of healthy foods, who have avoided this category before because of its image as a fattening product, will eat a healthy pizza?

Problems and Opportunities

This new-product launch faces several problems that must be considered in strategic planning. They are as follows.

- Roma's Lite will be a late entry.
- Frozen-food space is at a premium.
- Cost of entry will be high.
- Company image is not "high quality."
- Frozen-pizza image is not "healthy."

However, Roma also has some advantages and opportunities with the new-product launch. The opportunities include the following.

- The product is in tune with a consumer trend toward more healthy food.
- Pizza, especially frozen pizza, continues to be popular.
- Competitive brands are more expensive.
- Although the competition has low-calorie entries, no one yet owns the healthy position.

Strategic Plan

This strategic plan is being developed for the launch of a new low-calorie healthy pizza. The plan for introducing the product is to test-market for six months, followed by a one-year rollout that will reach 27 percent of the U.S. market in the initial launch year.

Marketing Objectives

The objectives of this effort are to accomplish the following during the first year rollout period.

- Achieve 20 percent share of healthy/low-calorie frozen-pizza category in the first-year markets.
- Achieve 40 percent trial of target market.
- Achieve a minimum of 60 percent distribution in all targeted markets.
- Establish sales level of $5.5 million and case sales of 821,240 units.
- In each market receiving support, be the number-one frozen, low-cal, healthy pizza within 18 months.

Marketing Strategies

Some general strategic decisions guide the direction of this marketing plan.

- Price is a less-important decision factor for this consumer segment than healthy features—low-calorie, less fat, low-cholesterol, low-sodium—and taste.
- Although aligning this product with the gourmet pizza category will signal that it is different from the "gut fillers," because the market for a gourmet line is still undeveloped, the emphasis should be clearly focused on the healthy features. The gourmet concept can be signaled by upscale packaging and a few flavor options like tomato and basil.
- For Roma's Lite to get a major piece of the frozen, low-cal, healthy pizza business, we must create a strong consumer brand franchise that will *pull* the product through the channel.
- To develop a successful pull strategy, a complete consumer marketing communication plan is needed for several reasons.
  1. The majority of consumers are not aware of frozen low-cal healthy pizza and no one knows that Roma's Lite has an entry in this niche. In Boston, we recently found that only 22 percent of consumers are aware of the Roma's Lite brand frozen pizza, and only 9 percent are aware of frozen low-cal pizza—and Boston is one of our better pizza markets.
  2. Nearly every major chain has had frozen-pizza niche items at one time (some more than once) and watched as they just sat on the shelf. The trade, as well as sales, recognizes that new frozen-pizza offerings must be advertised and promoted to the consumer if items are to move.
  3. The trade is well aware that many lines don't make it, even when supported by consumer

advertising and promotion. Therefore, to take up warehouse and case space with an unadvertised line is often considered too high a risk. Several major supermarket chains now have a policy that they will not even consider adding a line unless it is backed by a consumer-pull program.

4. Not only must our consumer marketing communication program be strong, it must also have continuity—it must be more than a few weeks of TV and one or two newspaper-coupon ads. The program must be front loaded to ensure that items are moving at least a third of a case a week after 90 days.

- To verify demand and continue strategy development, it is recommended that we use a six-month test market.
- To minimize costs, it is recommended that we put a consumer-pull program in only selected markets and use a rollout plan that staggers the introduction of the product in six cities every three months in the first year of the launch.

Targeting and Segmenting

- Primary consumer target market: older teens and adult women 18–35 in high-CDI premium-pizza markets.
- Secondary market: aging baby boomers, 35–49.
- Trade market: buyers for major food-store chains, independents, and convenience stores.

Consumer Profiles Unlike Weight Watchers, which targets people on a diet, our target will be broader and aimed at older teens and adults who eat frozen pizza and who are concerned about their weight and appearance. These people regularly drink reduced-calorie beverages and/or eat other reduced-calorie foods. People who regularly buy low-calorie foods are more upscale, willing to pay more, and are more interested in gourmet items than the typical buyer of the lower-priced "gut-filler" frozen pizza.

Competitive Advantage

- Priced slightly below the competition.
- More emphasis on quality healthy ingredients.

Positioning

"A delicious-tasting frozen pizza for health-conscious pizza lovers"

The cuisine leader of low-cal pizza. In other words, while the taste is better than the typical low-priced frozen pizza, the ingredients are more healthful. The position will edge close to gourmet—without trying to make that claim directly—because the ingredients will be different from those of the typical frozen pizza, but not as exotic as those of the typical gourmet pizza. The more upscale audience will be able to appreciate this feature.

Marketing Mix

The marketing mix of product, channels of distribution, pricing, and marketing communication for this product launch are analyzed next.

Product

We review three key components of the product: the development process, the proposed product line, and the product name.

Development Four testing stages were conducted during the development phases to test consumer reaction to the product. All respondents were screened to see whether they bought frozen pizza and low-cal food and/or beverages within the last 60 days to determine if they were in the target market.

1. A 100-sample consumer test was conducted at the food lab's headquarters in California. Costs were included in the development contract.
2. Concept and bite test against competition conducted in California. Our objective was to have at least a 40 percent taste preference against the market leader; respondents were not told that the test product was low-cal until after tasting. Cost: $38,000.
3. Focus-group discussions and one-on-one interviews for feedback on product concept, usage, appearance, packaging, name, and advertising. Cost: $12,000.
4. A three-city taste test that gave the supporting documentation for our advertising claims. This test was conducted in consumers' homes against the market leader. Cost: $6,000.

All tests have been conducted, results analyzed, and product reformulated as needed in response to consumer tests.

The Product Line The prototype line includes seven single-serving frozen pizzas that average 8.0 ounces and between 250 and 260 calories—half the calories of the average pizza of similar size. The pizzas will be 8 inches in diameter. The line includes seven varieties.

The exact calories, as well as the weight, will vary with the ingredients. Although we will still offer such traditional pizza flavors as pepperoni and sausage, the calorie count for that offering will be 270; the calorie count for tomato and basil is 230, the lowest calorie count in the line.

Deluxe	280
Pepperoni & sausage	270
Canadian bacon & pineapple	265
Italian turkey & sausage	250
Spicy chicken	250
Italian veggie	240
Tomato & basil	230

- Ingredients will be part-skim mozzarella cheese, a special low-cal sauce that we are calling the "M" sauce, pork and beef products that are at least 90 percent fat free, and a self-manufactured low-cal baked crust made from a secret recipe. Spices will be used to maintain the quality pizza taste.
- In addition to a single-serving concept, we will also be introducing in the fourth quarter a 10-ounce, $8\frac{3}{4}$-inch double-serving product. This item would allow us to say "under 300 calories per serving," which is comparable to Lean Cuisine's claim.
- Flavor profile is "juicy" (because the product has the same ration of sauce as the average extra-toppings cheese pizza) and "sweet" due to the special reformulation of the "M" sauce. Both of these characteristics will help overcome the diet-food stereotype of dry, bitter, and/or tasteless.
- The caloric claim will require nutritional labeling and testing that will cost approximately $30,000 a year. This cost includes the addition of one part-time lab technician and the required annual outside analyses costs.

Naming The recommended name is ROMA'S LITE PIZZA. Based on a memo from legal dated October 18,

there is no problem using the term "lite" as long as there is a legitimate one-third calorie reduction. The fact that "lite" is not a registered trademark was again confirmed by counsel last week. Therefore, by using this word, which has been well seeded, it will help clearly and quickly communicate our product benefit. Other names that have also been consumer tested include ROMA'S HEALTHY PIZZA, ROMA'S LOW-CAL, ROMA'S DIET, and ROMA'S LITE AND CRISPY.

Distribution

After the test market, the first stage of the rollout will reach 27 percent of the country in 17 cities during the initial launch year. The markets that have been selected meet at least one of the following criteria:

- a frozen-pizza category development index (CDI) of 75 percent or more,
- current pizza distribution of 60 percent or more,
- a strong Roma's franchise.

The following markets, which include 27 percent of the United States, are recommended for the first year rollout.

Group A (program starts in January)

Albany	St. Louis	Syracuse
Milwaukee	Minneapolis	Detroit

Group B (program starts in March)

Denver	Salt Lake	Seattle
San Francisco	Los Angeles	San Diego

Group C (program starts in May)

Miami	Atlanta	Phoenix/Tucson
New Orleans	Kansas City	Chicago

These markets currently account for 70 percent of our pizza volume and 47 percent of our entree volume. Even though frozen-pizza sales in the northeast are far above average (CDI of 151), we recommend that we do not initially compete with the strongly established northeast brands. Syracuse, a relatively small northeastern market, has been included as a test to determine how well we can do against these established pizza brands. It should also be noted that the northeastern regional brands have not yet established footholds or dominance outside that region. If we are to get there first, we should begin now.

Pricing

Costs for the eight-ounce prototypes, based on a self-manufactured baked crust, result in a line price of $16.55 per case, which would be $1.98 at retail, assuming a 30-percent retail gross margin. (See attached pro forma.)

This cost would include 14 percent for sales promotion, ten percent for advertising, and six percent for overhead and profit.

Because our individual item costs are not that far apart, and because cheese, which is on all of the items, is our second-highest cost, it is recommended that we line price; in other words, that we offer all items at the same price. This practice is favored by the trade and will help earn their authorization. It also is in line with pricing practices within the industry.

Marketing Communication

The budget, schedule, and the strategies for marketing communication follow.

Budget   Above-normal marketing communication dollars must be budgeted for the following reasons.

- Because of Roma's Lite's initial low volume, dollars generated at the company's usual 10.5 percent for advertising and 14 percent for promotion are not sufficient for launching even a minimum consumer-pull program. Therefore, we must use NIBT (net income before taxes) and overhead allocation for marketing communication budgeting (16.5 %).
- A strong consumer program throughout the first year of introduction is necessary to protect low-cal healthy pizza from becoming a commodity item like pizza.

Schedule   Begin the consumer-pull program in August for the following reasons.

- Frozen-pasta sales are highest in the fall and winter.
- The Roma's Trade Presentation schedule for July is a perfect time to sell our entire program to the trade and ask for authorizations, displays, and features.

Advertising   When most consumers hear the words "frozen pizza," they think of "gut-filler" products. TV is needed to demonstrate clearly that our products are significantly different from the average frozen pizza, taste much better (that is, they are "good enough to serve to friends"), and are more upscale.

Copy Strategy   Convince women 18–49 who buy frozen pizza that Roma's Lite Pizza has one-third fewer calories than Roma's Extra Topping Pizza, is a healthy product, and tastes better or as good as (depending on research results) the leading frozen premium pizza.

Media Strategy   The media strategy is primarily based on local media buys because of the rollout schedule.

1. Spot television is recommended as the primary medium for the following reasons.
   - It reaches over 90 percent of targeted households, more than any other advertising medium; as our target-audience demographics show, the target market is broad based and therefore requires a broad-reach medium.
   - In many markets today, TV costs no more per point than radio.
   - All markets would receive, in the first 12 months, 1,800 GRPs in prime, early-fringe, and daytime
2. Spot-TV buys will be reinforced with spot-radio and coupon ads delivered through newspapers.
   - Cost-per-coupon redeemed is cheaper with newspaper than with either direct mail or magazines.
   - Newspaper coupon ads provide space to explain the product and show the package, thereby reinforcing the TV message.
   - Because newspapers are the primary way the trade advertises, the trade can be more easily persuaded to run a tie-in feature with a newspaper coupon than with any other kind of advertising.

Consumer Promotion

- The pull campaign will be reinforced by seven quarter-page newspaper ads carrying 35-cent coupons. The lead time required for free-standing inserts and direct mail makes them high risks for test markets, as we learned from our last product introduction.
- In-store demonstrations will also be used, especially in high-volume stores.

- Tie-ins cut media and product-promotion costs in half. A quality tie-in brand is an endorsement of our quality and taste. Because awareness of Roma's Lite pizza is nonexistent, tie-ins with brands such as Diet Coke and Diet Pepsi will help make believers out of the trade.

Trade Promotion

Limit the number of cases sold at a quantity discount ("on-deal") to 65 percent for the following reasons.

- As another check to prevent Roma's Lite from becoming a deal-only item, a limit must be set.
- Deals are essential for trade support; for the last 13 periods, 81 percent of entrees and 78 percent of pizza have been sold on deal.
- Ten percent will be spent on trade promotions (the other four percentage points in the promotion budget will be for consumer-coupon redemption); limiting discounted volume to 65 percent will allow us to offer as high a discount as 15 percent.

Packaging

The consultant's prototype design with the light background will be used to distinguish Roma's Lite from the darker background on our other pizza items. Design research found that consumers perceived a light background to connote lesser quality. This perception will have to be counterbalanced by upscale typefaces, graphics, and accent colors that communicate quality. The front panel will have a large flag saying "only 350 calories" or "one-third fewer calories." Complete nutritional information will be on the back panel.

Sales (This particular company's organization had sales located in a separate department. The sales manager developed a separate plan for that department in cooperation with the marketing director.)

Control and Evaluation

This section details both the test market and the national rollout implementation plan, as well as other dimensions of marketing scheduling and program evaluation.

Test Market

We recommend that test marketing be conducted in three cities—Milwaukee, Syracuse, and St. Louis—

for three months preceding the Group A rollout in January. Before test marketing begins, we will need to design and print packages and produce a television spot and related print ads.

Also, to make sure that we have a viable product and to provide us with the hard-selling product-superiority claims that we want to use in the test market, we need to do a "national" consumer taste test against the market leader.

Test Market Cities We recommend that we test in two high and two average New Roman markets. The following markets have been selected because of their size, distribution opportunities, and CDIs.

Strong Markets	New Roman	Competition
Albany	125	157
Milwaukee	198	113
Average Markets		
Syracuse	105	114
St. Louis	115	98

Test Market Costs To evaluate our test market effort accurately, we will need to do tracking studies in at least two of the markets. Our budget for the test market follows.

Package development (includes design, photography, separation, production)	$40,000
Production of TV spot, sales kit, promotional ads, and related materials	150,000
TV air time	298,000
Two coupon ads (850 lines)	36,000
Two FSI coupons	3,100
Coupon Redemption (1,430,000 × 4% × .25 × 4)	57,200
Market research (national taste test study and test market tracking study)	50,000
Total	**$634,300**

Test Market 12-Month Forecast and Costs Estimates of sales and costs are based on the following assumptions:

- 60 percent ACV (All Commodity Volume) of three items
- .5 case per item per week per store
- supermarkets with $2 million-plus in sales.

Test Markets	Number of supermarkets	Annual cases
Milwaukee	427	20,000
St. Louis	449	21,000
Albany	174	8,200
Syracuse	191	9,000
Total		**58,200**

Test Market Payout Analysis   The following costs are predicted for testing marketing in the four cities for three months: Based on the 12-month forecast of 58,200 cases at $16.50 per case, payout would take 16 months.

National Rollout

The budget and payout plan for the first stage of the national rollout will be based on projections that will be tested in the test market. Based on these estimates, the following dollars-per-case figures are available for marketing communication:

	dollars per case	percent
Advertising	$1.79	10.50
Sales Promotion	2.32	14.00
Overhead & Profit	2.72	16.47

At projected sales of 1,121,239 cases × 6.78 per case = $7,602,000 for marketing communication. Of that total, $3,250,000 will be spent on advertising; $3,750,000 will be spent on sales promotion, $602,000 will be spent on other merchandising and point-of-purchase materials.

Scheduling   The schedule for the national rollout has four phases.

Phase I: Do consumer taste test and advertising concept-evaluation test week of March 21; results available by April 18.

Phase II: If consumer tests are positive, issue approval for second stage of development, $175,000, which will include:

- package design
- copy for print and television advertising
- three-city test against Celeste.

This will allow us to have a finished product in printed packages along with a rough-cut television spot for our sales meeting in June

Phase III: Begin the test-market program that will be conducted during the third and fourth quarters. Test-market sales would begin immediately after sales meeting, with first shipment during the week of June 25.

Phase IV: Begin the national rollout in January with sales initially directed at the Group A cities, followed by sales to the Group B cities two months later; and then sales to the Group C cities two months after that.

Ongoing Consumer Evaluation

As we move into the launch of this new product line, the following are issues that we must continue to investigate from the target market who buy diet/reduced-calorie products and frozen pizza as part of our ongoing consumer research program:

1. How are low-calorie, microwavable, and low-cholesterol features perceived by buyers of frozen pizza?
    - Is the feature believable? If not, why not?
    - Assuming that taste reception is not high for this type of product, what areas of taste/texture are liked and not liked?
    - Single-serve versus double-serve—which is preferred and why? (For instance, how many in the family are watching weight and do they eat together?)
    - How is the product used: snack, lunch, or quick dinner?
2. Is there a market for a healthy, low-calorie frozen pizza among consumers who are not currently frozen-pizza buyers? Will health-conscious consumers believe that pizza can be healthy and will they buy a frozen pizza?
3. In addition to the targeted market, is there also a market among men who buy frozen foods and/or among children—that is, will mothers buy healthy pizza for their children?
4. How do product image, appearance, and taste compare to competitors in the minds of consumers?

[1]A Category Development Index (CDI) is a consumption index (per household sales) that compares tha average sales for a particular market with the total country average sales. In other words, a market that consumes a lot of frozen pizza will have a CDI that is over 100; a market that consumes less than the country's average will have a CDI that is less than 100.

NOTES

Chapter 1

1. "A Well-Tailored Corporate Culture," *Business Ethics* (November/December 1995): 55.
2. Don E. Schultz, Stanley I. Tannenbaum, and Robert F. Lauterborn, *Integrated Marketing Communications* (Chicago: NTC Business Books, 1993), xvii.
3. NPO Group. Reprinted with permission from *Advertising Age,* 22 March 1993: 3. Copyright, Crain Communications, Inc. 1993.
4. Tom Duncan, "A Macro Model of Integrated Marketing Communication," American Academy of Advertising Annual Conference, Norfolk, Va., 1995.
5. "Southwest Airlines Fact Sheet," and "Southwest Historical Advertising Gallery," (January 1996): Internet (www.iflyswa.com); Michael Wilke, "Southwest to Break Out of Low-fare Positioning," *Ad Age,* October 7, 1996: Internet (www.adage.com).
6. Jeffrey E. Barnhart, "Small Firms Look to Integrated Marketing," *Sales and Marketing Strategies & News* (July/August 1994): 13, 15.
7. William Weilbacher, *Brand Marketing* (Lincolnwood, Ill.: NTC Business Books, 1993).
8. Regis McKenna, *Relationship Marketing* (Reading, Mass.: Addison-Wesley, 1991): 4.
9. Terry G. Varva, *Aftermarketing* (Homewood, Ill.: Irwin, 1992): xiii.
10. Frank K. Sonnenberg, "If I Had Only One Client," *Sales & Marketing Management* (November 1993): 4–107.
11. Frederick E. Webster, Jr., "The Changing Role of Marketing in the Corporation," *Journal of Marketing, 56* (October 1992): 1–17.

Chapter 2

1. Quoted in Frederick Webster, Jr., *Market Driven Management* (New York: John Wiley & Sons, 1994): 7.
2. "AMA Board Approves New Marketing Definition," *Marketing News,* March 1, 1985, 1.
3. Kurt Eichenwald, "U.S. Inquiring Into Texaco's Action in Suit," *New York Times,* 5 November, 1996, C1, C2.
4. Tom Duncan and Sandra Moriarty, *Driving Brand Equity* (New York: McGraw Hill, 1997); Don

E. Schultz, Stanley I. Tannenbaum, and Robert F. Lauterborn, *Integrated Marketing Communication,* (Lincolnwood IL: NTC Business Books, 1993), 45.
5. Theodore Levitt, "Exploit the Product Life Cycle" *Harvard Business Review* (November/December 1965): 81–94.
6. John Markoff, "Microprocessor Boom Dooms Cray," *The Sunday Camera,* 26 March, 1995, 15.
7. Margaret Isa, "Consultants with Tender Faces," *New York Times,* 8 August 1996, C1.
8. Larry Armstrong, Bruce Nussbaum, and Robert D. Hof, "Winners: The Best Product Designs of the Year," *Business Week,* June 5, 1995, 88–101.
9. David W. Stewart, Gary Frazier, and Ingrid Martin, "Integrated Channel Management: Merging the Communications and Distributions Functions of the Firm," in *Integrated Marketing and Consumer Psychology,* Esther Thorson and Jerri Moore ed. (Hillsdale, N.J.: Lawrence Erlbaum Associates, 1996).

Chapter 3

1. Michael Hammer and James Champy, *Reengineering the Corporation* (New York: HarperCollins, 1993), 28.
2. Tom Duncan and Steve Everett, "Client Perceptions of Integrated Marketing Communications," *Journal of Advertising Research* 33 (May/June 1993): 30–5.
3. Hammer and Champy, *Reengineering the Corporation,* 28.
4. Polly Labarre, "This Organization is Dis-Organization," *Fast Company* (July/August 1996): Internet (www.fastcompany.com).
5. John McManus, "Think Like a Peasant to Reap Regal Rewards," *Brandweek,* October 17, 1994, 16.
6. Tom Duncan, "The Concept and Process of Integrated Marketing Communication," *IMC Research Journal* 1, no. 1 (spring 1995): 3–10.
7. Lynn Sharp Paine, "Managing for Organizational Integrity," *Harvard Business Relations Review* 17, no. 3 (1991): 106–7.
8. William C. Taylor, "At Verifone It's a Dog's Life (And They Love It!)" *Fast Company* (November 1995): Internet (www.fastcompany.com).

9. Tom Duncan, "The Concept and Process of Integrated Marketing Communication," *IMC Research Journal,* 1:1 (Spring 1995): 3–10.
10. Glen M. Broom, Martha M. Lauzen, and K. Tucker, "Dividing the Public Relations and Marketing Conceptual Domain and Operations Turf," *Public Relations Review* 17, no. 3 (1991): 219–26.
11. Dan Logan, "Integrated Communication Offers Competitive Edge," *Bank Marketing* 26 (May, 1994): 63–6.
12. Anders Gronstedt, "Integrating Up, Down and Horizontally: Lessons from America's Leading Total Quality Corporations," *Integrated Marketing Communications Research Journal* 1, no. 1 (spring 1995): 11–5.
13. Michael McCarthy, "GM to Redefine Agency Roles, Fees," *Brandweek,* October 17, 1994, 3.
14. Manjot Kochar, "A Study of Advertising Agencies Providing Integrated Marketing Communications," *Integrated Marketing Communications Research Journal* 1, no. 1 (spring 1995): 16–27.

Chapter 4

1. David Whitford, "The Snack Food That's Packing America," *Inc. Magazine,* October 1996, 50.
2. Ibid.
3. John D. Leckenby, "Conceptual Foundations for Copytesting Research," University of Illinois Advertising Working Papers, No. 2 (February 1976).
4. Russell Colley, *Defining Advertising Goals for Measured Advertising Results* (New York: Association of National Advertisers, 1961).
5. Michael L. Ray, "Communication and the Hierarchy of Effects," in *New Models for Mass Communication Research,* P. Clarke, ed. (Beverly Hills, CA: Sage Publications, 1973): 147–75.
6. Robert C. Lavidge and Gary A. Steiner, "A Model for Predictive Measurements of Advertising Effectiveness," *Journal of Marketing* (October 1961): 59–62.
7. Sandra E. Moriarty, "Beyond the Hierarchy of Effects: A Conceptual Model," in Current Issues and Research in Advertising, 1 (1983): 45–56.
8. David W. Stewart, "The Market-Back Approach to the Design of Integrated Communication Programs: A Change in Paradigm and a Focus on Determinants of Success," AAA Special Conference on Integrated Marketing Communication, Norfolk, WV (March 1995).

Chapter 5

1. David Shef, "Levi's Changes Everything," *Fast Company* (June-July 1996): Internet (www.fastcompany.com/fastco/issues/third).
2. Milton Rokeach, *The Nature of Human Values* (New York: 1973), 5.
3. J. Michael Munson and Edward F. McQuarrie, "Shortening the Rokeach Value Survey for Use in Consumer Research," in *Advances in Consumer Research,* vol. 15 (Cambridge, Mass.: Association for Consumer Research, 1988), 381–6.
4. Leon G. Schiffman and Leslie Lazar Kanuk, *Consumer Behavior,* 3rd ed. (Englewood Cliffs, N.J.: Prentice-Hall, Inc., 1987), 506.
5. Martha Farnsworth Riche, "Psychographics for the 1990s," *American Demographics* (July 1989): 25–6, 30–2.
6. Philip Cateora and John M. Hess, *International Marketing,* 4th ed. (Homewood, Ill.: Irwin, 1979), 90.
7. Hazel Kaban and David Mulryan, "Out of the Closet," *American Demographics* (May 1995): 40–7.
8. Nancy Coultun Webster, "Playing to Gay Segments Opens Doors to Marketers," *Advertising Age* (May 30, 1994): 5–6.
9. Theodore Levitt, "The Globalization of Markets," *Harvard Business Review* (May-June 1983): 92.
10. Ibid., 94.
11. Philip Kotler and Gary Armstrong, *Marketing: An Introduction* (Englewood Cliffs, N.J.: Prentice-Hall, Inc., 1990), 477.
12. Rupa Chatterjee, "A McDonald's Outlet Opens in New Delhi," *India Abroad* (October 18, 1996): Internet (indiaworld.com/openbin/show/ia/subscribe/961018/economy-index).
13. Peter Francese, "America at Mid-Decade," *American Demographics* (February 1995): 23–31.
14. Laurie Feeman, "No Tricking the Media Savvy," *Advertising Age,* February 6, 1995, 30.
15. Laurie Feeman, "Advertising's Mirror is Cracked," *Advertising Age,* February 6, 1995, 30.
16. Jennifer Steinhauer, "Making Bucks as a Guide to

Baby Busters," *New York Times,* 16 September 1996, C1, C9.

17. Diane Crespill, "Generations to 2025" *American Demographics* (January 1995): 4.

18. Robert B. Settle and Pamela L. Alreck, *Why They Buy: American Consumers Inside and Out* (New York: John Wiley & Sons, 1986), 129.

19. Schiffman and Kanuk, *Consumer Behavior,* 318.

20. Settle and Alreck, *Why They Buy,* 171.

21. Alvin Toffler, *The Third Wave* (New York: William Morrow, 1980), 248.

22. Stephanie Shipp, "How Singles Spend," *American Demographics* (April 1988): 22–8.

Chapter 6

1. C. N. Coffer and M. H. Appley, *Motivation: Theory Research* (New York: John Wiley & Sons, 1964).

2. K. Levien, *A Dynamic Theory of Personality* (New York: McGraw-Hill, 1935), 88–91.

3. Barnaby J. Feder, "At Motorola, Quality is a Team Sport," *New York Times,* 21 January 1993, 15.

4. Meryl Gardner, Andrew Mitchell, and J. Edward Russo, "Strategy-Induced Low Involvement with Advertising," paper presented at the first Consumer Involvement Conference, New York University, June 1982.

5. Richard Petty and John T. Cacioppo, "Issue Involvement as a Moderator of the Effects on Attitude Advertising Content and Context," in *Advances in Consumer Research,* ed. K. B. Monroe, vol. 8 (Ann Arbor, Mich.: Association for Consumer Research, 1981): 20–4; Richard E. Petty and John T. Cacioppo, Attitudes and Persuasion: Classic and Contemporary Approaches (Dubuque, Ia.: William Brown Co., 1983).

6. L. Festinger, *A Theory of Cognitive Dissonance* (Stanford, Calif.: Stanford University Press, 1957).

7. Feder, "At Motorola, Quality is a Team Sport," 15.

8. Susannah Baker, "College Cuisine Makes Mother Cringe," *American Demographics* (September 1991): 10–11.

9. Henry Assael, *Consumer Behavior and Marketing Action,* 3rd ed. (Boston: Kent Publishing, 1987), 84.

10. R. Kelly, "The Search Component of the Consumer Decision Process—Theoretic Examination," in *Marketing and the New Science of*

Planning, ed. C. King (Chicago: American Marketing Association, 1968), 273.

11. James Bettman, *An Information Processing Theory of Consumer Choice* (Reading, Mass.: Addison-Wesley, 1979).

12. Richard E. Petty, John T. Cacioppo, and David Schumann, "Central and Peripheral Routes to Advertising Effectiveness: The Moderating Role of Involvement," *Journal of Consumer Research* 10 (September 1983): 135–46.

13. F. H. Nothman, "The Influence of Response Conditions on Recognition Thresholds for Taboo Words," *Journal of Abnormal and Social Psychology* 65 (1962): 154–61.

14. Peter H. Webb and Michael L. Ray, "Effects of TV Clutter," *Journal of Advertising Research* 19 (June 1979): 7–12; Thomas J. Madden and Marc G. Weinberger, "The Effects of Humor on Attention in Magazine Advertising," Journal of Advertising 11, no. 3 (1982): 8–14; Michael A. Belch, Barbara E. Holgerson, George E. Belch, and Jerry Koppman, "Psychophysiological and Cognitive Responses to Sex in Advertising," in *Advances in Consumer Research,* vol. 9, ed. Andrew Mitchell (Pittsburgh: Association for Consumer Research, 1982), 424–7.

15. Junu Bryan Kim, "Generation X Gets Comfortable with Furnishings, Housewares," *Advertising Age,* January 10, 1994, S-2.

16. Bruce G. Posner, "The Future of Marketing Is Looking at You," *Fast Company* (October-November 1996): 108–9.

17. William Keenan, Jr., "Surveys as a Sales Tool," *Sales & Marketing Management* (January 1996): 65.

18. Michael D. Hutt and Thomas W. Speh, *Industrial Marketing Management* (Chicago: Dryden Press, 1981), 15–6.

19. William A. Dempsey, "Vendor Selection and the Buying Process," *Industrial Marketing Management* 7 (1978): 257–67.

20. Donald R. Lehmann and John O'Shaughnessy, "Difference in Attribute Importance for Different Industrial Products," *Journal of Marketing* (April 1974): 36–42.

21. Stephanie Gruner, "Customer Relations: Image Building," *Inc. Magazine,* August 1996, 87.

Chapter 7

1. Robert E. Wilkes and James B. Wilcox, "Recent FTC Actions: Implications for the Advertising Strategists," *Journal of Marketing* 38 (January 1974): 55–6.
2. Willy Stern, "Throwing Collectors a Curve," *Business Week*, December 18, 1995, 95.
3. Letter to Congress Explaining FTC's New Deception Policy," *Advertising Compliance Service* (Westport, Conn.: Meckler Publishing, November 21, 1983).
4. Ray O. Werner, "Legal Developments in Marketing," *Journal of Marketing* (July 1991): 66.
5. Michael Durham and Jan Rocha, "Amazon Chief Sues Body Shop," *The Observer*, March 3, 1996, 5.
6. M.D. Bernacchi, "Substantive Advertising Standards: Discretion and Misinformation by the FTC," *Journal of Advertising* 5 (spring 1976): 26.
7. John F. Cady, "Advertising Restrictions and Retail Prices," *Journal of Advertising Research* 16 (October 1976): 29.
8. Gary J. Ford and John E. Calfee, "Recent Developments in FTC Policy on Deception," *Journal of Marketing* 50 (July 1986): 82–103.
9. Martin J. Cohen, "The Internet: A Whole New Set of Rules," *Promo* (May 1996): 33.
10. Scott Donation, "Publishers Bracing for Smoke-Free Pages," *Advertising Age*, March 12, 1990, 3.
11. William H. Bolen, *Advertising* (New York: John Wiley & Sons, 1984), 59.
12. Nancy A. Reese, Thomas W. Whipple, and Alice E. Courtney, "Is Industrial Advertising Sexist?" *Industrial Marketing Management* (1987): 231–9.
13. National Science Foundation, *Research on the Effects of Television on Children* (1977): 45.
14. Michael J. Miller, "The Web Wore Black," *PC Magazine*, March 26, 1996; Fritz Messere, "Analysis of the Telecommunications Act of 1996" (September 11, 1996): Internet (www.oswejo.edu/~messere.telcom2).
15. Rory J. O'Connor, "Parents Now Must Control Their Kids' Net Traffic," *San Jose Mercury News*, 13 June 1996; Miller, "The Web Wore Black," *PC Magazine* (March 2, 1996): Internet (www.pcmag.com).
16. John B. Broder, "The Chairman of the F.C.C. Starts a Crusade Against Hard Liquor Ads on Television," *New York Times*, 9 April 1997, C7; Sally Goll Beatty, "Seagram Again Challenges Ban on TV Advertising," *Wall Street Journal*, 24 September 1996, B16; Chuck Ross, "FCC Taking Look at Seagram Ads," *Advertising Age*, September 30, 1996, 2, 63.
17. Steve Gelsi, "Benz Revs Up New Pitch," *Brandweek*, March 18, 1996, 20–1.
18. Wendy Bounds, "Fuji Considers National Campaign to Develop All-American Image," *Wall Street Journal*, 1 October 1996, B8.
19. Marcus W. Brauchli, "A Change of Face: China Has Surly Image, But Part of the Reason is Bad Public Relations," *Wall Street Journal*, 16 June 1996, A1.
20. Barbara Crossette, "Globally, Majority Rules," *New York Times* 8 August 1996, S4, P1.
21. Ray E. Hiebert, "Advertising and Public Relations in Transition from Communism: The Case of Hungary, 1989–1994, *Public Relations Review* (Winter 1994); 364.
22. "Read All About It: Western Magazines Find Way to Russian Women's Hearts," *Wall Street Journal*, 11 November 1996, A10.
23. David Lieberman, "Wired Up or Beamed In, It's Coming Cheaper, Faster," *USA Today*, 11 June 1996, 2B.
24. Darren McDermott, "Singapore Unveils Sweeping Measures to Control Words, Images on Internet," *Wall Street Journal*, 6 March 1996, B8.

Chapter 8

1. "Communicating Differential Advantage is Essential," *Marketing News* 25 (October 1985): 26.
2. Frank X. Dance and Carl E. Larson, *The Functions of Human Communications: A Theoretical Approach* (New York: Holt, Rinehart and Winston, 1976).
3. Werner J. Severin and James W. Tankard, Sr., *Communication Theories: Origins, Methods, Uses* (New York: Hastings House, 1979).
4. Frank Rose, "The End of TV as We Know It," *Fortune*, December 23, 1996, 66.
5. C. David Mortensen, *Communications: The Study of Human Interaction* (New York: McGraw-Hill, 1972).

6. B.S. Greenberg and G.R. Miller, "The Effects of Low-Credible Sources on Message Acceptance," *Speech Monographs* 33 (1966): 127–36.

7. Jon B. Freiden, "Advertising Spokesperson Effects: An Examination of Endorser Type and Gender in Two Audiences," *Journal of Advertising Research* 24 (1984): 33–41; Denis McQuail, *Mass Communication Theory* (Beverly Hills, Calif.: Sage, 1984).

8. Barry L. Bayers, "Word-of-Mouth: The Indirect Effects of Marketing Efforts," *Journal of Advertising Research* 25, no. 3 (June/July 1985): 31–9; Blaine Goss, *The Psychology of Human Communication* (Prospect Heights, Ill.: Waveland Press, 1989).

9. Ibid.

10. Alice Z. Cuneo, "Starbucks' Word-of-Mouth Wonder," *Advertising Age,* March 7, 1994, 12.

11. Albert Hirschman, *Exit, Voice, and Loyalty: Response to Decline in Firms, Organizations and States* (Cambridge, Mass.: Harvard University Press, 1970); Roobina Ohanian, "The Impact of Celebrity Spokespersons' Perceived Image on Consumers' Intent to Purchase," *Journal of Advertising Research* (February/March 1991): 46–54.

12. Jagdip Singh, "Voice, Exit, and Negative Word-of-Mouth Behaviors: An Investigation Across Three Service Categories," *Journal of the Academy of Marketing Science* (Winter 1990): 46–54.

13. Stephen Weitz, *Nonverbal Communication,* 2nd ed. (New York: Oxford University Press, 1979).

14. R. Buck, "Nonverbal Behavior and the Theory of Emotion: The Facial Feedback Hypothesis," *Journal of Personality and Social Psychology* 38 (1980): 811–24; Christy Fisher, "Wal-Mart's Way: No. 1 Retailer Relies on Word-of-Mouth, Not Ads," *Advertising Age,* February 16, 1991, 3, 48.

15. Elizabeth C. Hirschman, "The Effect of Verbal and Pictorial Advertising Stimuli on Aesthetic, Utilitarian, and Familiarity Perceptions," *Journal of Advertising Research* 15, no. 2 (1986): 27–34.

16. James MacLachlan, "Making a Message Memorable and Persuasive," *Journal of Advertising Research* 23, no. 6 (December 1983/January 1984): 58–9; Paul M. Herr, Frank R. Kardes, and John Kim, "Effects of Word-of-Mouth and Product-Attribute Information on Persuasion: An Accessibility-Diagnosticity Perspective," *Journal of Consumer Research* 17 (March 1991): 454–62.

17. Larry Percy, "A Review of the Effect of Specific Advertising Elements Upon Overall Communication Response," in *Current Issues and Research in Advertising,* vol. 2., ed. James H. Leigh and Claude R. Martin, Jr. (Ann Arbor, Mich.: University of Michigan, 1983), 77–118.

18. C. Hovland, *The Order of Presentation in Persuasion* (New Haven, Conn.: Yale University Press, 1957).

19. Michael Ray and Alan Sawyer, "Repetition in Media Models: A Laboratory Technique," *Journal of Marketing Research* 8 (1971): 20–9.

20. Betsy D. Gelb, Joe W. Hong, and George M. Zinkhan, "Communications Effects of Specific Advertising Elements: An Update," in *Current Issues and Research in Advertising,* vol. 11, ed. James H. Leigh and Claude R. Martin, Jr. (Ann Arbor, Mich.: University of Michigan, 1985), 75–98.

21. George W. Booker, "A Comparison of the Persuasive Effects of Mild Humor and Mild Fear Appeals," *Journal of Advertising* 10 (1981): 29–40.

22. I.L. Janis and S. Feshback, "Effects of Fear-Arousing Communications," *Journal of Abnormal and Social Psychology* 48 (1953): 1, 78–92; B. Sternthal and C.S. Craig, "Fear Appeals: Revisited and Revised," *Journal of Consumer Research* 1 (9174): 22–34; J.J. Burnett and R.E. Wilkes, "Fear Appeals to Segments Only," *Journal of Advertising Research* 20 (1980): 21–4.

23. B. Sternthal and C.S. Craig, "Humor in Advertising," *Journal of Marketing* 37 (1973): 12–8.

24. Donald L. Duncan and James Nelson, "Humorous Advertising in Radio," *Journal of Advertising Research* 25, no. 4 (October/November 1985): 84–7.

25. William B. Beggs, Jr., "Humor in Advertising," *Link* (November/December 1989): 12–5.

26. Gelb, Hong, and Zinkhan, "Communications Effects," 75–98; Herbert Fried, "Humor Is Our Best Fool," *Advertising Age,* April 8, 1991, 26.

27. Judith A. Wiles and T. Bettina Cronwell, "A Review of Methods Used in Measuring Affect, Feelings, and Emotion in Advertising," in *Current Issues and Research in Advertising,* vol. 13, ed. James H. Leigh and Claude R. Martin, Jr. (Ann Arbor, Mich.: University of Michigan, 1990), 261.

28. J. Nunally and H. Bolerex, "Variables Concerning the Willingness to Receive Communications on Mental Health," *Journal of Personality* 27 (1959): 38–46.

29. W.J. McGuire, "Resistance to Persuasion Confirmed by Active and Passive Prior to Refutation of the Same and Alternative Counter Arguments," *Journal of Abnormal and Social Psychology* 63 (1961): 326–32.

30. Joan Meyers-Levy and Brian Sternthal, "Gender Differences in the Use of Message Cues and Judgments," *Journal of Marketing Research* 28 (February 1991): 84–96.

31. Diane McGuinness and Karl H. Pribram, "The Origins of Sensory Bias in the Development of Gender Differences in Perception and Cognition," *Cognitive Growth and Development,* ed. Morton Bortner (New York: Bruner/Mazel Publishers), 3–56.

32. P.S. Raju and Subhash C. Lonial, "Advertising to Children: Findings and Implications," *Current Issues and Research in Advertising,* vol. 12, ed. James H. Leigh and Claude R. Martin, Jr. (Ann Arbor, Mich.: University of Michigan, 1990), 231–74.

33. Mary Ann Strutts and Garland G. Hunnicutt, "Can Young Children Understand Disclaimers in Television Commercials?" *Journal of Advertising* 16, no. 1 (1987): 41–6.

34. Leslie Isler, Edward T. Popper, and Scott Ward, "Children's Purchase Requests and Parental Responses: Results from a Diary Study," *Journal of Advertising Research* 4 (October/November 1987): 28–39.

35. Ibid.

36. Jessica M. Bailey, "The Persuadability of Elderly Consumers: A Study of Focus on Control and Responsiveness to Fear Appeals," in *Current Issues and Research in Advertising,* vol. 10, ed. James H. Leigh and Claude R. Martin, Jr. (Ann Arbor, Mich.: University of Michigan, 1987), 213–47.

Chapter 9

1. Peter D. Bennett, *Dictionary of Marketing Terms* (Chicago: American Marketing Association, 1988), 4.

2. "Does Advertising Pay? The Impact of Advertising Expenditures on Profits for Consumer Business" (San Francisco: The Strategic Planning Institute and the Ogilvy Center for Research and Development, 1986).

3. "How Advertising in Recession Periods Affects Sales" (New York: American Business Press, Inc., 1979); McGraw-Hill Research Report No. 5262.1, Laboratory of Advertising Performance (New York: McGraw-Hill, 1985).

4. Chuck Ross, "Marketers Fend Off Shift in Rules for Ad Puffery," *Advertising Age,* February 19, 1996, 41.

5. "Remington Finds the Numbers Don't Lie," *Focus* (NDL magazine) (Winter 1992): 10–11.

6. Kathy Haley, "In the Changing '90s Market, the Infomercial 'Here to Stay'," *Advertising Age,* March 11, 1996, 2A.

7. Steve Lohr, "The Great Mystery of Internet Profits," New York Times, 17 June 1996, D1.

8. Jane Hodges, "CMR Takes Ad Tracking Service to the Internet," Advertising Age, March 4, 1996, 24.

9. Tom Duncan and Sandra Moriarty, "Global Advertising: Issues and Practices," *Current Issues and Research in Advertising* 13, nos. 1 and 2 (1990): 313–42.

10. Tara Parker-Pope, "Ford Puts Blacks in Whiteface, Turns Red," *Wall Street Journal,* 22 February 1996, B5.

11. Joan E. Rigdon, "Hip Advertisers Bypass Madison Avenue When They Need Cutting-Edge Web Sites," *Wall Street Journal,* 28 February 1996, B1.

12. Dave Vadehra, "Budweiser's New Menagerie Hops to the Top of the Ad Charts," *Advertising Age,* March 18, 1996, 40.

13. Gina Buglieri et al., "The Best and Worst of 1996," *Time,* December 20, 1996, 77.

14. Stuart Elliott, "Commercial Use and Abuse, 1996," *New York Times,* 27 December 1996, C1.

15. Marilyn Much, "New Research Quantifies the Effect of Ads," *Investor's Business Daily,* 24 April 1995, A4.

16. Ruth A. Wooden, "Ad Council Action," (letter to the editor), *Adweek,* January 1, 1995, 9.

17. Raymond Serafin, "GM Will Standardize Assessment of Ad Work," *Advertising Age,* December 18–25, 1995, 1, 30.

Chapter 10

1. John F. Luick and William L. Ziegler, *Sales Promotion and Modern Merchandising* (New York: McGraw-Hill, 1968), 11.

2. "Shaping the Future of Sales Promotion," Council of Sales Promotion Agencies (1990): 3.

3. J. Brian Robinson, "Promotion is a New Way to Make Brand Contact With Buyers," *The Marketing News,* April 12, 1994, 2, 16.

4. Scott Hume, "Rallying to Brands' Rescue," *Advertising Age,* August 13, 1990, 3.

5. Scott Hume, "Brand Loyalty Steady," *Advertising Age,* March 2, 1992, 19.

6. Michael Schrage, "Reinventing the *Wheel,*" *Adweek,* April 6, 1993, 23.

7. Sally Goll Beatty, "IBM Combines In-Store Promos Seemingly Out of the Big Blue," *Wall Street Journal,* 23 February 1996, B4.

8. "Carol Wright Survey: 'Trade Promotion Still Dominates'," *Promo* (June 1996): 107.

9. Betsy Spethmann, "Crowning the New Brand Kings," *Brandweek's Superbrands '96,* special edition, October 19, 1995, 25–8.

10. R. Craig MacClaren, "Creativity Can Burst the Trade Spending Balloon," *Promo* (October 1995): 54.

11. "Our Favorite Incentives," *Adweek,* October 19, 1992, 20.

12. Kevin T. Higgins, "Sales Promotion Spending Closing in on Advertising," *Marketing News,* July 4, 1986, 8.

13. Jack Neff, "This Space for Rent," *P-o-P Times* (September 1993): 36–42.

14. Kerry Smith, "Cents-Off Currency: The Case for Chaos," *Promo* (April 1992): 29–32.

15. Bob Gatty, "Consumers Using Fewer Coupons," *Promo* (June 1993): 85.

16. Betsy Spethmann, "Coupons Shed Low-Tech Image," *Brandweek,* October 24, 1994, 30–1.

17. Scott Hume, "Coupon Use Jumps as Distribution Soars," *Advertising Age,* October 5, 1992, 3.

18. Glenn Heitsmith, "Rebates are Getting a Bad Rap," *Promo* (March 1993): 10, 42.

19. Glenn Heitsmith, "Prosecutors Eye 'No Purchase' Claims'," *Promo* (March 1993): 1.

20. Pam Weisz, "Body Shop, in Lieu of Ads, Hits the Road," *Brandweek,* April 24, 1995, 42.

21. Alison Fahey and Bradley Johnson, "Frequent Shopper Programs Ripen," *Advertising Age,* August 6, 1990, 21.

Chapter 11

1. Walter W. Seifert, "The Outlook for Public Relations: Brighter Than Ever," *Public Relations Quarterly* (summer 1973): 18–30.

2. "Careers in Public Relations," Public Relations Society of America (New York, 1989): 2.

3. "Good Times. Is It Deja Vu All Over Again?" *Inside PR,* March 25, 1996, 2.

4. "Applying PEW Typologies to an Issue: Big Business," *PR Reporter,* April 8, 1996, 2.

5. "Kekst, Fleshman, Burson Tops in Harris Survey of PR Firm Clients," *Inside PR,* September 9, 1996, 1, 3.

6. Mark Landler, "Corporate Insurer to Cover Cost of Spin Doctors," *New York Times,* 10 September 1996, C1.

7. "Case: When You're Wrong, the Best Course is To Say So," *PR Reporter,* January 15, 1996, 1.

8. "Management Wants Integrated Communication and Impact Measurement," *IABC Communication World* (November 1994): 32.

9. Ibid.

10. William D. Novelli, "Stir Some PR into Your Communications Mix," *Marketing News,* December 5, 1988, 40.

11. Yustin Wallrapp, "How Advertising-PR Partnership Can Succeed," *Advertising Age,* September 18, 1989, 40.

12. Mark Maremont, "Ben & Jerry Tell on Themselves," *Business Week,* June 26, 1995, 8.

13. Doug Newsom, Alan Scott, and Judy Van Slyke Turk, *This is PR: The Realities of Public Relations,* 4th ed. (Belmont, Calif.: Wadsworth Publishing Co., 1989), 61.

Chapter 12

1. *Direct Marketing* (July 1995): 4.

2. Herbert D. Hennessey, "Matters to Consider Before Plunging into Telemarketing," *Marketing News,* July 8, 1983, 2.

3. "WEFA Study Measures Direct Response Ad," *Direct Marketing* (November 1995): 6.

4. Rich Roscitt and I. Robert Parket, "Direct Marketing to Consumers," *Journal of Consumer Marketing* 5, no. 1 (Winter 1988): 5–14.
5. "DM Marketplace," *Direct Marketing* (August 1986): 8.
6. Robert Kestanbaum, "Growth Strategies for Direct Marketers," *Direct Marketing Association,* Release 110.2 (January 1984).
7. *The 1994 Guide to Mail Order Sales,* Marketing Logistics, Inc., Highland Park, Illinois, 1995.
8. Robert Stone, *Successful Direct Marketing Methods* (Lincolnwood, IL: National Text Book Co., 1986), 2.
9. Ibid.
10. Murray Raphel, "Common Direct Mail Mistakes," *Direct Marketing* (September 1994): 28–9.
11. Debra Ray and George Reis, "Catalog Sales Projected to Reach $74.6 Billion By Year End," *Direct Marketing* (August 1996): 20–6.
12. Ibid.
13. Kim Cleland, "More Advertisers Put Infomercials Into Their Plans," *Advertising Age,* January 18, 1995, 50.
14. Anita Brown, "Pay to Play," *Marketing and Media Decisions* (September 1990): 16–17.
15. "Behavior and Attitudes of Telephone Shoppers," *Direct Marketing* (September 1987): 50–1.

Chapter 13

1. Regis McKenna, *Relationship Marketing* (Reading, Mass.: Addison-Wesley Publishing Co., 1991).
2. Nancy Arnott, "Selling is Dying," *Sales & Marketing Management* (August 1994: 84.
3. "Rick Scoville Tests the Waters," *Sales & Marketing Management* (July 1990): 30–1.
4. Ben M. Enis, *Personal Selling: Foundations, Process and Management* (Santa Monica, Calif.: Goodyear, 1979), 1.
5. G.D. Bruce and B.M. Bonjean, "Self-Actualization Among Retail Sales Personnel," *Journal of Retailing* 44 (Summer 1969): 73–83.
6. J. W. Thompson and W. W. Evans, "Behavioral Approach to Industrial Selling," *Harvard Business Review* 47 (March–April 1969): 69–83.
7. Marvin A. Jolson, "Should the Sales Presentation be 'Fresh or Canned'?" *Business Horizons* 16 (October 1973): 83–5.

8. John I. Coppett and William A. Staples, "A Sales Mix Model for Industrial Selling," *Industrial Marketing Management* (1980): 32.
9. Ibid.
10. Stan Kossen, *Creative Selling Today*, 2nd ed. (New York: Harper & Row, 1982), 423–24.
11. "Sales Incentives," *Incentives* (September 1990): 55–8.
12. Nancy Arnott, "Paying the Piper," *Sales & Marketing Management* (August 1995): 58–68.
13. Shawn Clark, "Sales Force Automation Pays Off," *Marketing News,* August 6, 1990, 9.
14. Laurie Freeman, "P&G Rolls Out Retailer Sales Teams," *Advertising Age,* May 21, 1990, 18.

Chapter 14

1. Mark Lewyn, "See a Game, Shop for a Car, Surf the Net," *Business Week,* January 29, 1996, 53; John Riley, "Fields of Green," *Newsday,* 18 August 1996, A4; "NBC's 'Seinfeld,' 'ER' Bag $1 Mil per Ad Minute," *Advertising Age* (April 18, 1997): Internet (www.adage.com/bin/viewdataitem.cgi.articles&articles418); Wendy Tanka, "High-Tech Firms Lift Their Profiles at Sports Venues," *Rocky Mountain News,* 15 August 1996, 16B.
2. Michael Hiestand"Creative Packages Spur Stadium Sponsorship," *USA Today,* 8 October 1996, 7C; Mark Kreidler, "The Naming Game is All About Money," *Sacramento Bee,* 8 September 1996, CI.
3. Mark Starr and Karen Springen, "A Piece of the Olympic Action," *Newsweek,* January 15, 1996, 58–9; "Sponsorship is an Olympic Tradition," Time Official Olympic Web Site (July 5, 1996): Internet (www.com.au/time/site/olympicz/tradition.titu/); Matthew Grim, "Olympic Grab Bag," *Brandweek,* June 10, 1996, 26–34; Melanie Wells, "Games Could Provide Biggest Ad Blitz Ever," *USA Today,* 15 July 1996, 1, 2; "The Total Cost of the 1996 Olympics Will Be $1,705,000,000," *Fortune,* July 22, 1996, 58–9; Matthew Grimm, "The New Olympic Gold," *Brandweek,* September 11, 1995, 27–32.
4. "Can You Name Three Official U.S. Olympic Sponsors?" *Adweek,* February 21, 1994, 14.
5. John McManus, "The Ring Cycle of Richard Pound," *Brandweek,* February 26, 1996, 30–4.

6. Karen Benezra, "Ring Ding," *Brandweek*, November 20, 1995, 1, 6.
7. Nicole Harris, "The Game's Afoot—and It's Marketing," *Business Week*, January 22, 1996, 95.
8. John McManus, "Despite Its Huge Economy and Growth, Event Marketing is Still Evolving," *Brandweek*, April 17, 1995, 16.
9. McManus, "The Ring Cycle."
10. McManus, "Despite Its Huge Economy."
11. Thomas L. Harris, *The Marketer's Guide to Public Relations* (New York: John Wiley & Sons, 1993), 199.
12. John Bennett, "Shopping for Sponsorships? Integration is Paramount," *Brandweek*, February 14, 1994, 18.
13. Brian Metzler, "Swoosh! CU Deal Boon for Nike," *Daily Camera*, 24 December 1995, 1E, 4E.
14. Kristen Traeger, "Mission Marketing: The Next Strategic Step on the Philanthropy Continuum," *IMC Research Journal* 1, no. 1 (spring 1995): 35–8.
15. Jane L. Levere, "National Breast Cancer Awareness Month Has Inspired Extensive Corporate Advertising," *New York Times*, 3 October 1996, C6.
16. Paul Carringer, "Not Just a Worthy Cause," *American Advertiser* (spring 1994): 17.
17. Goeffery Smith and Ron Stodghill, "Are Good Causes Good Marketing?" *Business Week*, March 21, 1994, 64.
18. Tom Duncan, "Why Mission Marketing is More Strategic and Long-Term than Cause Marketing," in *1995 Winter Educator's Conference*, vol. 6, ed. David W. Stewart and Naufel J. Vilcassin (Chicago: AMA), 469–75.
19. Craig Smith, "The New Corporate Philanthropy," *Harvard Business Review* (May–June 1994): 107.
20. Alex Nieroth, "Success Takes Strategic, Olympic Effort," *Brandweek*, August 21, 1995, 22.
21. Bennett, "Shopping for Sponsorships?"
22. Howard Schlossberg, "New Service Helps Measure Impact of Sponsorships," *Marketing News*, January 3, 1994, 24.
23. Cyndee Miller, "P.O.P. Gains Followers as 'Era of Retailing' Dawns," *Marketing News*, May 14, 1990, 2.
24. Jack Neff, "This Space for Rent," *P-o-P Times*, September 30, 1993, 36–42.
25. "Consumers Notice Specialty Items," *Promo* (June 1992): 74.
26. Blair R. Fischer, "The Top 10 Premium Promotions of the Past Ten Years," *Promo* (May 1995): 17–21.
27. Mark Bubula, Kevin McClure, and Manjot Kochar, "International Marketing of U.S. Films: A Case Study of Jurassic Park," unpublished paper, University of Colorado, 1994.
28. Pam Weisz, "Packaging 2000," *Brandweek*, October 16, 1995, 40–2.
29. Greg Erickson, "New Package Makes a New Product Complete," *AMA Marketing News*, May 8, 1995, 10.
30. Thomas Hines, "Ignore Packaging . . . At Your Own Risk," *Brandweek*, October 16, 1995, 24–43.
31. "The Power of Trade Shows," *The Trade Show Bureau* (1993): 2.
32. "Study Shows Effectiveness of Promotional Products at Trade Shows," *Potentials in Marketing* (July 1992): 27.
33. Martin Christopher, Adrian Payne, and David Ballantyne, *Relationship Marketing: Bringing Quality, Customer Service, and Marketing Together* (London: Butterworth-Heinemann, 1993).
34. Ivan Misner, *The World's Best Known Marketing Secret: Building Your Business with Word-of-Mouth Marketing* (1995).

Chapter 15

1. Kevin Goldman, "Consumers Like Print Ads Better Than Those on TV, Study Says," *Wall Street Journal*, 6 June 1995, B9.
2. *Advertising Age Yearbook* (January 1982): 173.
3. "Study of Media Involvement," *Audits and Surveys* (March 1996): 14.
4. William Spain, "In General, Where Are The Readers?" *Advertising Age*, October 14, 1996, S6.
5. Michael Schrage, "Newspapers are Jointly Venturing On-Line, But The Flaw Is In Themselves," *Adweek*, May 22, 1995, 14.
6. Elizabeth Gleick, "Read All About It," *Time*, October 21, 1996, 66–9.
7. Elizabeth H. Weise, "On-Line Magazines: Will Readers Still Want Them After The Novelty Wears Off?" *Marketing News*, January 29, 1996, 1, 14.

8. Alan Guttesman, "A Bright Future For A Change," *Adweek,* September 9, 1996, 6–9.

9. Joe Mandese, "Going Public: A Proposal to Ease Advertiser Access to Public TV Stations Could Open the Medium to More Messages," *Marketing and Media Decisions,* September 1990, 34–5.

10. Scott Donaton, "The Next 50 Years," *Advertising Age* (Spring 1995): 54.

Chapter 16

1. Bickley Townsend, "The Media Jungle," *American Demographics* (December 1988): 8.

2. Anthony F. McGann and J. Thomas Russell, *Advertising Media,* 2nd ed. (Homewood, Ill.: Irwin, 1988).

3. J.M. Agostine, "How to Estimate Unduplicated Audiences," *Journal of Advertising Research* (March 1961): 11–14.

4. David A. Aaker and John G. Myers, *Advertising Management,* 4th ed. (Englewood Cliffs, N.J.: Prentice-Hall, Inc., 1990).

5. Michael J. Naples, *Effective Frequency: The Relationship Between Frequency and Advertising Effectiveness* (New York: Association of National Advertisers, 1979), 79.

6. Herbert E. Krugman, "What Makes Advertising Effective?" *Harvard Business Review* (March/April 1975): 96–103.

7. Dennis H. Gensch, "Computer Models in Advertising Media Selection," *Journal of Marketing Research* 5 (November 1968): 423–4.

8. Cathy Madison, "Media Buyers Plug into Electronic Deal-Making," *Adweek,* April 30, 1990, 27.

Chapter 17

1. Donald C. Marschner, "Theory Versus Practice in Allocating Advertising Money," *Journal of Business* 40 (July 1967): 286–302.

2. Gary L. Lilien et al., "Industrial Advertising Effects and Budgeting Practices," *Journal of Marketing* 40 (January 1976): 16–24.

3. Leonard M. Lodish, *The Advertising and Promotion Challenge* (New York: Oxford University Press, 1986), 92–4.

4. Dagmar Mussey, "Selling Esteemed Watch With Limited Ad Budget," *Advertising Age,* February 12, 1996, 18.

5. John Philip Jones, "Ad Spending: Maintaining Market Share," *Harvard Business Review* (January–February 1990): 38–42.

6. Nigel F. Piercy, "The Marketing Budgeting Process: Marketing Management Implications," *Journal of Marketing* 51 (October 1987): 45–59.

7. James E. Lynch and Graham J. Hooley, "Increasing Sophistication in Advertising Budget Setting," *Journal of Advertising Research* 30 (February/March 1990): 67–75.

8. Ovid Rio, *The Dartnell Sales Promotion Handbook,* 7th ed. (Chicago: The Dartnell Corp., 1987), 91–2.

9. Paul W. Farris and John A. Quelch, *Advertising and Promotion Management: A Manager's Guide to Theory and Practice* (Radner, Penn.: Chilton, 1983).

10. Roger A. Strang, *The Promotional Planning Process* (New York: Praeger, 1980).

11. George S. Low and Jakki J. Mohr, "The Budget Allocation Between Advertising and Sales Promotion: Understanding the Decision Process," AMA Educators' Proceedings, Chicago, Ill. (Summer 1991): 448–57.

12. Julian L. Simon, "Are There Economies of Scale in Advertising?" *Journal of Advertising Research* (June 1965): 15–20.

Chapter 18

1. Mark Landler, "AT&T: A Bold Strategy Turns Sour," *New York Times,* 13 April 1997, F7.

2. Charles Ramond, *Advertising Research: The State of the Art* (New York: Association of National Advertisers, 1976).

3. Robert J. Lavidge and Gary A. Steiner, "A Model for Predictive Measurements of Advertising Effectiveness," *Journal of Marketing* 25 (October 1961): 59–62.

4. Johan Arndt, "What's Wrong With Advertising Research?" *Journal of Marketing Research* 16 (June 1976): 9.

5. H. D. Wolfe, J. K. Brown, S. H. Greenberg, and G. C. Thompson, *Pretesting Advertising Studies in Business Policy,* no. 109 (New York: National Industrial Conference Board, 1963).

6. David W. Stewart, "Measures, Methods, and Models in Advertising Research," *Journal of Advertising Research* (June/July 1989): 54–60.

7. Michael L. Rothschild, Ester Thorson, Judith E. Hirsch, Robert Goldstein, and Byron B. Reeves, "EEG Activity and the Processing of Television Commercials," *Communication Research* (April 1986).

8. Rudolph Flesch, *The Art of Readable Writing* (New York: Harper & Row, 1974).

9. Julie Liessee, "KGF Taps Data to Target Consumers," *Advertising Age,* October 8, 1990, 3, 88.

10. Don E. Schultz, *Strategic Advertising Campaigns,* 3rd ed. (Lincoln, Ill.: NTC Business Books, 1990), 550.

11. James F. Donius, "Market Tracking: A Strategic Reassessment and Planning Tool," *Journal of Advertising Research* (February/March 1985): 15–19.

12. Wally Wood, "Update: Single Source," *Marketing and Media Decisions* (September 1989): 116–17; Laurence N. Gold, "TV Ad Testing Enters New Generation," *Marketing News,* October 23, 1989, 2.

13. Simon Broadbent, *Spending Advertising Money* (London: Business Books, 1975).

14. Robert C. Blattberg and Scott A. Neslin, *Sales Promotion: Concepts, Methods, and Strategies* (Englewood Cliffs, N.J.: Prentice-Hall, Inc., 1976), 377.

15. Robert L. Dilenschneider and Dan J. Forrestal, *The Dartnell Public Relations Handbook* (Chicago: The Dartnell Corporation, 1987), Chapter 6.

16. Richard B. Still, Edward W. Cundiff, and Norman A.P. Govoni, *Sales Management,* 3rd ed. (Englewood Cliffs, N.J.: Prentice-Hall, Inc., 1976), 377.

17. David Barboza, "Research Firms Say They Can Tell Companies if Sponsoring an Event Is Worth the Money," *New York Times,* 18 November 1996, C11.

Chapter 19

1. Randall Rothenberg, *Where the Suckers Moon* (New York: Alfred A. Knopf, 1994).

2. Ian Linton and Kevin Morley, *Integrated Marketing Communications* (Oxford, U.K.: Butterworth Heinemann, 1995), 43; Chris Fill, *Marketing Communications* (London: Prentice-Hall, Inc., 1995), 172–3.

3. Audrey Ward and Jeremy Hebert, "The IMC Audit Content Analysis," *IMC Research Journal* 2, no. 1 (spring 1996): 28–31.

4. Tom Duncan, "Is Your Marketing Communication Integrated?" *Advertising Age,* January 24, 1994, 24.

5. Shelly Garcia, "The Knights of New Business," *Adweek,* July, 1992, 21–2, 24, 26–7; Warren Berger, "The British Reinvasion," *Creativity* (June 1993): 36–7.

6. Lisa Fortini-Campbell, *The Consumer Insight Workbook* (Chicago: The Copy Workshop, 1992), ii.

7. David A. Aaker and John G. Myers, *Advertising Management: Practical Perspectives,* 3rd ed. (Englewood Cliffs, N.J.: Prentice-Hall, Inc., 1987), 85.

8. Tom Brannan, *A Practical Guide to Integrated Marketing Communications* (London: Kogan Page, 1995), 23.

GLOSSARY

account managers, or **account executives** Advertising agency employees who work as liaisons and work out strategies and details of the assignment with the clients' marketing communication managers.

account planner The person who analyzes consumer trends and buyer decisions.

adese The use of hyperboles by advertisers to pump up their claims with such terms as "astounding," "stupendous," and "amazing."

advertising Any paid form of communication by an identified sponsor that promotes ideas, goods, or services.

advertising allowance A common promotion technique in which the manufacturer pays the wholesaler or retailer a certain amount of money for advertising the manufacturer's product.

advertisorial A set of consecutive pages on a single product or advertiser that is glued or stapled into the magazine.

advocacy advertising A type of corporate advertising that expresses the viewpoint of the company on selective issues.

affective component Feelings expressed toward the object advertised.

affiliate A local station that has signed a contract with a network to carry its programming.

AIDA model Describes the effect of marketing as beginning with awareness, then moving to interest, then to desire, and finally to action.

annual report An official document required by the Securities Exchange Commission (SEC) for publicly held companies which contains financial information.

anteroom trailer A pretesting opinion method in which people are invited into a comfortable room, in a mobile home or recreational vehicle usually parked in a busy shopping area, and are shown test commercials interspersed with a prerecorded show. These people are then interviewed and the effectiveness of each commercial is ascertained.

aperture The point in place and time when the audience is most likely to use the marketing message.

approach The lead-in to the sales presentation.

appropriation The maximum amount of dollars that management allocates to a specific purpose. Also, the use of private pictures without permission.

art The visual elements, which include illustrations or photographs, the type, logotypes (logos, or brand symbols), signatures (how the brand name is written), and the layout (how all the elements of the ad are arranged) in print.

aspirational reference group A group in which a person does not hold membership or with which he or she does not have face-to-face contact, but to which this person wants to belong.

at least once The use of different shows to increase the opportunity for reaching different or unduplicated audiences, guaranteeing that a percentage of the audience will see the message *at least once* in a given period of time.

attention When the consumer must devote mental resources to stimuli in order to process them.

attitude An enduring disposition, favorable or unfavorable, toward an idea, a person, a thing, or a situation.

audimeter An electronic recorder used to measure broadcast audiences.

audio The sound.

avail A formal request for information about available times and dates, prices, program ratings, total households, and GRP's.

average frequency of contact This is determined by dividing the total number of homes reached by a media plan by the net coverage of the plan; it provides media planners with another basis for comparing plans.

avoidance group A group in which a person does not hold membership or with which he or she does not have face-to-face contact, and whose values, attitudes, and behavior he or she disapproves of.

awareness Implies that the message has made an impression on the viewer or reader, who can later identify the advertiser.

bait advertising An alluring but insincere offer to sell a product or service that the advertiser does not really intend or want to sell.

ballot method A pretesting process that consists of mailing out sales promotion to be evaluated. The sales promotions to be evaluated and some additional information are given about each one. Consumers are asked to vote for the one they like and return the ballot to the research firm.

banded pack A pack that offers one or more units of a product sold at a reduced price compared with the regular single-unit price.

barter The exchange of goods without money, usually occurring at the local level.

barter by syndication When the promoter supplies a syndicated show to the television station at no cost. Usually, some part of the advertising time is presold to national advertisers and the rest is available to the local advertiser.

behavioral component Actions taken toward the object of an attitude.

belief An opinion that reflects a person's particular knowledge and assessment of something.

believers Conservative and predictable consumers who favor established brands. Their lives are centered on family, church, community, and the nation.

benefit Identifies the basis on which the product can best serve a consumer to fill a need.

benefit segmentation The grouping of consumers according to the benefits they seek from a product.

bingo cards Appear in the back of magazines and give consumers an easy way to request information on products and services. The publisher prints a designated number for specified literature, and the consumer circles the number of the desired information.

bleed ad The color runs to the edge of the page, often costing an extra 15 to 20 percent.

bonus packs Contain additional amounts of the product free when the standard size of the product is purchased at the regular price.

books Name by which today's magazines are known in the industry. Books are the most specialized of the mass media, dramatically demonstrating the fact that the mass audience is becoming increasingly segmented.

bottom-up approach The communication-management approach where managers are in close daily contact with customers and other stakeholders and where cross-functional teams cooperate across departmental boundaries.

brand The name, design, symbol, or any other feature that identifies the good, service, institution, or idea sold by a marketer.

brand loyalty The result of involvement with the product decision.

brand manager The business leader for a brand who has ultimate responsibility for coordinating sales, product development , budget, profits, and marketing communications.

brand mark, or **logo** The part of the brand that cannot be spoken, such as a symbol, picture, design, color combination, or distinctive lettering.

brand name That part of a brand that can be spoken, such as words, letters, or numbers.

branding strategy The process of developing and selecting brand names, brand marks, and the supporting marketing campaign.

breakouts Messages that will appear only in copies sent to a specific geographic region.

budget The details of how an allocated sum of money will be used.

business plan A long-range plan that outlines the objectives and specific actions the organization will take to reach its goals.

business segment The portion of the population that buys the product to use in its business or to make products.

business-to-business catalogs Contain products that are sold from one business to another to reduce the costs associated with personal selling.

business-to-business marketing Organizations selling exclusively to other organizations and never coming in contact with consumer buyers.

buying allowances A type of trade deal in which a manufacturer pays a reseller a fixed amount of money for purchasing a certain amount of the product during a specified time period.

buying loaders A gift given for buying a certain order size.

campaign A series of marketing communication messages designed to meet a set of objectives based on a situation analysis and delivered over time (at least one year), through several marketing communication activities, and through various media.

campaign plan A document that summarizes all the campaign planner's recommendations and is the end result of the campaign-planning process.

centrality A measure that depends on the degree to which an attitude is tied to values.

cents-off deal A reduction in the normal price charged for a good or service.

channel of distribution All the institutions, processes, and relationships that help the product from the manufacturer to the ultimate buyer, either industrial or consumer.

classical conditioning A response learned as a result of the pairing of two stimuli.

classified ads Include all types of messages arranged by classification of interest, such as Help Wanted, Cars for Sale, and so on.

clearance When a local station carries a network program.

close To ask for and secure the sale.

closing date This is the last date on which a magazine will accept advertising materials for publication in a particular issue.

cognitive component Includes beliefs and knowledge about the object of the attitude.

cognitive dissonance When consumers typically experience some postpurchase anxiety after all but routine and inexpensive purchases.

combination plan The combination of salary and commission program aimed at maximizing its program's particular benefits.

commercial bribery The act of influencing or attempting to influence the actions of another company's employee by giving the employee money or a gift without his or her employer's knowledge.

communication A process in which two or more persons attempt to consciously or unconsciously influence each other through the use of symbols.

communication audit A formal or informal process that collects all communication materials, sorts them, compares them, and finally determines if they are working to support a set of integrated objectives.

community relations The management of relations with stakeholders from the local community.

comparison advertising The comparison of two or more specifically named or recognizably presented brands of the same generic product or service class in terms of one or more specific product or service attributes.

compensation A fee paid by the networks to the local stations to carry their programming.

competitive advantage When consumers believe that a product satisfies their need better than a competitor's product.

competitive positioning strategies These focus on claims made by other brands, thus providing a frame of reference for the consumer.

compiled lists These lists identify people who share some common interest such as skiing, retirement housing, or gourmet cooking.

complex decision making   A search for information and an evaluation of alternatives leading to a decision.

comprehension   A person's ability to understand information.

concurrent testing   Evaluation of a marketing communication effort while it is running in the marketplace.

conditioned response   That which has been learned as a result of the pairing of stimuli.

conformity   Obedience to group norms and rules.

consumer jury   The collective sampling of opinion ratings obtained by interviewing respondents individually.

consumer products   Products purchased for personal or family consumption with no intention of resale.

consumer promotion   A promotion directed at consumers.

consumer sales promotion specialists   Those whose role is to understand how and when to use price deals such as sales, coupons, samples, contests and sweepstakes, refunds and rebates, loyalty programs , and premiums or gifts that encourage purchase.

consumer segment   The portion of the population that buys the product for its own personal or household use.

consumer specialty catalogs   Contain a line of related products that are sent only to those consumers considered potential customers.

consumer-focused position strategies   These emphasize the target market, the type of appeal it responds to, and how and when it uses the product.

contest   Promotion that requires consumers to compete for a prize or prizes on the basis on some sort of skill or ability; that is, participants must perform some task. The guidelines for stating the chance of winning, the considerations for entering, and the nature of the prize are governed by the FTC.

continuity-coupon plan   A type of mail premium that requires the customer to save coupons or special labels attached to the product that can be redeemed for merchandise.

continuous   A continuity pattern called for if the audience constantly needs to be exposed to the message because of the nature of the product and excessive competition.

contractual reference group   A group in which a person holds membership or with which he or she has regular face-to-face contact; this person approves of the group's values, attitudes, and standards.

cooling-off directive   When a company is required to give consumers a three-day period to reconsider their product purchase.

cooperative advertising   An advertising program in which a manufacturer supplements a retailer's advertising, either financially or through technical expertise.

cooperative advertising allowance   A contractual arrangement between the manufacturer and the retailer in which the manufacturer agrees to pay part or all of the advertising expenses incurred by the retailer.

copy   The text of an advertisement or the words that people say in a commercial.

copy platform (workplan)   In advertising, the translation of the creative strategy into a document that specifies what will be said to whom and with what effect and that gives directions about the executions.

copytesting   Research in advertising used to decide whether an ad should run in the marketplace and to help guide execution decisions.

copywriters   Those responsible for creating the copy for an advertisement.

core values   Dominant cultural values.

corporate advertising   Advertising used by the company, and managed by corporate public relations, to create positive attitudes and goodwill toward the company.

corporate public relations High-level counseling with senior management about the company's overall reputation, its image in the eyes of various stakeholders, and its response to issues that may affect the success of the company.

cost per rating point An indicator used to evaluate media alternatives.

cost per thousand (CPM) The cost of reaching 1000 people in the medium's audience.

cost-per-thousand-target market (CPM-TM) Cost computations that include an audience adjustment.

coupons Legal certificates offered by manufacturers and retailers that grant specified savings on selected products when presented for redemption at the point of purchase.

cover date Date appearing on the issue's cover.

creative staff The copywriters, art directors, and broadcast producers who design and produce the advertising for media.

creative strategy An outline of what to say to the various target audiences who may have different message needs.

creative tactics The details in the execution of the creative strategy.

credibility The extent to which the receiver perceives the source to be truthful or believable.

crisis management Public relations staff anticipates the possibility of disaster and develops a plan to manage communications during the crisis.

cross-functional management, or **boundary spanning** The process by which teams oversee "horizontal functions," such as PR, sales promotion, packaging, and so forth.

cue Persuades the direction the individual will follow to satisfy the goal of the ad.

culture The sum of learned beliefs, values, and customs that regulate the behavior of members of a particular society.

customer service A program designed to deal with customers' ongoing needs after they have bought the product.

customs Overt modes of behavior that constitute culturally approved ways of behaving in specific situations.

databases Files of information that include names, addresses, telephone numbers, e-mail addresses, and demographic and buying-behavior data.

database marketing The process of building, maintaining, and using customer databases for the purpose of contacting customers and transacting business.

day-after recall A test in which people conduct telephone interviews with a sample of television viewers the day after the commercial is aired to determine the extent of brand-name recognition as well as recall of various selling points communicated by the commercial.

dealer loader A premium that is given to a retailer by a manufacturer for buying a certain amount of a product.

decode To interpret a message.

decreasing return approach The assumption that the first exposure is the most powerful, and each ensuing exposure is less effective.

defamation Any untruthful communication to at least one person (other than the person or entity defamed) that tends to damage a reputation.

demographic editions Editions sent to target subscribers who are doctors, members of top management, students, educators, or even those who live in special high-income zip code areas.

demographics The observable characteristics of individuals living in the culture.

departments The marketing functions are divided up into departments to achieve internal control and to organize marketing communication activities.

depth of inquiry The extent of the salesperson's effort to learn the details of the buyer's decision process.

diaries Preselected homes are sent diaries in which each viewer writes down the stations and programs watched. A separate diary is provided for each television in the home and a cash award is given for cooperating.

diary method See **diaries.**

direct marketing An interactive system of marketing that allows the consumer to access information, purchase the product through a variety of media, or both.

direct premiums A type of premium that provides an immediate incentive at the time of purchase.

direct selling expenses, or **field selling expenses** One of the two selling cost categories. These expenses arise from activities directly connected to personal selling.

direct-mail advertising Ads in print and broadcast media that offer a product and a means to respond to the ad with an order.

direct-response advertising Advertising designed to motivate customers to respond with either an order or an inquiry.

directories An important supplemental medium, especially to local businesses. Directories can be industry specific, product specific, or target-market specific.

directory advertising Occurs in books that list the names of people or companies, their phone numbers, and addresses.

disclaimant group A group in which a person holds membership or with which he or she has face-to-face contact, but this person disapproves of the group's values, attitudes, and behavior.

dispersion A media policy that places the message in as many different programs and spots as possible to avoid duplicating the audience.

display ads Found throughout the newspaper, they generally use illustrations, headlines, white space, and other visual devices in addition to the text copy.

display allowance A direct payment of cash or goods to the retailer if the retailer agrees to set up the display as specified.

display loaders A display that is given to the retailer as a reward after supporting a promotion.

domains model The idea that changing perceptions, providing education, and persuading consumers are the primary objectives for marketing communication.

dyad Two people of two distinct groups.

e-mail A message or file that is transmitted from one computer to another.

effective frequency The number of marketing messages needed to affect individuals in the way the marketer desires; that is, the number of times the prospect should receive the message to ensure the most effective communication.

effective reach A measure of the number of prospects who are aware of the message.

emotional appeal A message directed toward the individual's feelings and intended to create a certain mood, such as guilt, joy, anxiety, or self-pride.

emotional motives Are characterized by feelings that may emerge without careful thought or consideration of social consequences.

employee relations Programs designed by a company's human resources or public relations specialists to motivate employees to do their best work.

encoding The process of transforming thoughts into a sequence of symbols.

exchange The act of obtaining a desired object from someone by offering something of value in return.

executive judgment The intuition of one or more executives.

experiments Giving individuals a controlled exposure to a message to change their opinion, attitude, or cause some other action.

exposure The point at which information processing starts, usually with some source of stimulation such as watching television, going to the supermarket, or driving past a particular billboard.

external agency Communication expert that provides a service to a company for a contractual fee.

external flow Marketing communication that is directed outside the business: to past, present, and potential customers; to resellers, wholesalers, and retailers; to other companies; and to government agencies, private agencies, and experts in the field.

external publics People with whom an organization communicates but does not have regular or close ties, such as community neighbors, government officials, regulators, special-interest groups, media, and financial communities.

extra incentives A variety of awards given to salespeople for achieving specific goals.

fair use An exception to the copyright law that allows the use of a part or parts of a work in criticism, comment, news reporting, teaching, scholarship, or research without seeking permission from the copyright holder.

feedback Process through which the receiver communicates with the sender.

financial relations A public relations field in which specialists who understand finance work with the financial community and comply with government financial regulations for public companies.

first cover page Name given to the front cover of a magazine.

flighting A continuity pattern that calls for heavy scheduling during shorter time periods in order to increase rate and frequency with the hope that these effects will carry over into longer time periods.

focal concept The element in a marketing communication message that becomes the key idea that is delivered.

forward buying When retailers buy more merchandise at the discounted price than they need during the deal period.

fourth cover page Name given to the back cover of a magazine.

fractional page space One-page or double-page ads broken into a variety of units.

free goods allowance A certain amount of product offered to wholesalers or retailers at no cost if they purchase a stated amount of the manufacturer's product.

free-in-the-mail premium A type of premium that requires the customer to mail the advertiser a purchase request and proof of purchase.

freelancer Self-employed specialist who is hired by a company to work on a specific project, but is not on the company's payroll.

frequency The number of times within a given period that a consumer is exposed to a message (usually figured on a weekly and/or monthly basis).

fulfilleds Mature, responsible, well-educated professionals who are consumers. Their leisure activities center on their homes, but they are well-informed about what goes on in the world, and they are open to new ideas and social change.

full-line merchandise catalog Contains all the merchandise found in a complete department store plus other products such as appliances and home-related remodeling and installation materials.

game A type of sweepstakes. It differs from a one-shot sweepstakes drawing in that the time frame is much longer. A continuity is established, requiring customers to return several times to acquire additional pieces (such as bingo-type games) or to improve their chances of winning.

gatefold A magazine cover or inside page that opens to reveal an extra page that folds out and gives the ad a big spread.

general contractor An interpublic agency who, for a fee, develops an overall strategy and retains outside specialist agencies needed to carry out the plan.

general interest publications Mass circulation magazines such as *Reader's Digest, TV Guide,* and *People.*

geodemography Analyzes an existing database on the principle that people who live together in small geographic areas such as blocks and zip code units tend to share more demographic characteristics than people who live elsewhere.

goods Tangible products such as toothpaste, cookies, cars, and bicycles.

gross The term used to describe the total number of viewers taken as a whole. The planner has made no attempt to calculate how many *different* people view the show.

gross impressions The impressions of all viewers taken together.

gross rating point (GRP) The combined measure of reach and frequency that reflects the total weight of a media effort. It is derived by multiplying reach times frequency.

group Two or more people who interact to accomplish either individual or mutual goals.

habit The act of a consumer making a decision without the use of additional information or the evaluation of alternative choices.

halftone An image that converts a full range of tonal values to a screen pattern that can be printed.

heterogeneous The type of market composed of separate, smaller groups known as segments.

hierarchy of effects This provides a general framework for analyzing the impact of communication.

high-involvement decisions Those decisions that are important to the consumer.

home shopping channel A television show that presents items for sale, gives the price, and explains how to order.

homogeneous The type of market that marketers treat as a single, large unit.

image positioning strategy This focuses on the tangible and intangible characteristics of the product that cannot be duplicated easily by competitors.

impact The measure of whether the audience actually perceived the message.

in-house agency A group of internal marketing communication specialists that operates as its own profit center and handles all the marketing communication work for its primary client—the company to which it is affiliated.

incremental sales The additional sales that are produced by a specific sales promotion.

indirect selling expenses Those expenses associated with personal selling but not directly associated with the product (such as moving expenses, special entertainment expenses, and special marketing expenses).

industrial products Products purchased by an organization or an individual that will be used to make another product, will be distributed to an industrial customer for a profit, or used to meet some other business objective.

inertia The condition when a consumer is not highly involved in the initial decision to buy a product and makes no commitment to the product but simply responds to the positive reinforcement it provides.

instrumental conditioning A response learned or strengthened because it has been associated with certain consequences.

integrated marketing The process of understanding the needs of the customer (and other stakeholders), orienting the firm's manufacturing and sales processes to meet these needs, and applying integrated thinking to all marketing and management decisions.

integrated marketing communication (IMC) The practice of unifying all marketing communication tools—from advertising to packaging—to send target audiences a consistent, persuasive message that promotes company goals.

integrated strategy The combination of the right information, the right people, the right sources, and the right time into marketing communication strategy.

intensity A measure that depends on the affective component of an attitude.

interactive communication system   The use of computer technology, allowing marketing communicators to send persuasive messages while simultaneously allowing the receiver to react, modify, and customize the message and the response.

interference   Environmental factors that distort the communicators' relationship or the communication process.

internal flow   Marketing communication that occurs within the organization.

internal publics   People with whom an organization normally communicates in the ordinary routine of work, such as employees, investors, suppliers, dealers, and regular customers.

interpersonal communication system   Communication system that may consist of as few as two people and as many as can interact face-to-face so that the participants have the opportunity to affect each other.

involvement   Refers to the intensity of the consumer's interest in a product, medium, or message.

issue management   The corporate public relations practice of planning a company's response to important issues.

jury method   A combination of the ballot and portfolio methods of pretesting, except the jurors are paid for their evaluation and may be knowledgeable about sales promotions.

key visual   An image that conveys the essence of the message and can be easily remembered.

lag effect   The cumulative effect of past marketing communication effort on future sales.

latent motives   Emotional motives people are often unwilling to admit openly.

learning   A process of taking in information, processing it along with existing information, and producing new knowledge.

learning curve approach   This approach suggests that the effectiveness of each exposure increases up to a certain point and that subsequent exposures add little.

libel   Written defamation.

licensing   The practice of selling the right to use a company's character or logo on another company's products.

linear approach   This approach suggests that each exposure adds as much purchase probability as the one preceding it and supports the notion that greater frequency is better.

lobbying   A type of public affairs activity aimed at influencing policy decisions by government officials.

local advertising   Spot advertising bought by local firms.

logo   The imprint that is used for immediate identification of a business.

lottery   A payment or other legal consideration in exchange for a chance to win a prize.

low-involvement decisions   Those that are not important to the consumer.

lower class   The traditional view of the working class.

magazine insert   A multipage piece or a reply card bound next to a full-page ad.

mail premiums   A type of premium that requires the customer to take some action before receiving the premium, such as sending in proof-of-purchase seals.

mailing list   A list of customer or prospect names, addresses, phone and fax numbers, and e-mail addresses if available.

mall intercept   A pretesting method that involves stopping people at random in a mall and showing them the various promotions for evaluation.

manifest motives   Motives that people are conscious of but are often unwilling to acknowledge.

marginal analysis   The theoretical basis for determining the size of a marketing communication budget.

market   An aggregate of people who, as individuals or organizations, have needs for products and have the ability, willingness, and authority to purchase the product.

market aggregation strategy Deciding that the market is homogenous, marketers promote a single product through a single marketing program designed to reach as many customers as possible.

market segmentation strategy A strategy in which marketers divide the market into several market segments.

market strategy A strategy that identifies how the marketers will approach the market.

market tests Making a product available to buyers in one or more test areas and then measuring purchases and consumer responses to marketing tactics.

market tracking study Research that follows the purchase activity of a specific consumer or group of consumers over a specified period of time.

marketing The process of planning and executing the conception, pricing, promotion, and distribution of ideas, goods, and services to create exchanges that satisfy individual (customer) and organizational objectives.

marketing communication The process of effectively communicating product information or ideas to target audiences.

marketing communication mix The activities (or tools) used to achieve the marketing communication objectives.

marketing intelligence Information from internal or external sources that is useful in developing the marketing strategy.

marketing mix The use of marketing communication to showcase important features of product, price, and distribution to increase the odds that the consumer will buy a product.

marketing plan A document that analyzes the current marketing situation, identifies market opportunities and threats, sets objectives, and develops action plans to achieve objectives: the central instrument for directing and coordinating the marketing effort.

marketing public relations (MPR) The public relations field that seeks positive publicity of products.

marketing services A department of people that specialize in managing various marketing communication tools, such as advertising and sales promotion.

marketing strategy The process of evaluating the options for achieving the marketing goals.

mass communication A system of communication characterized by delayed feedback and no direct contact.

mass medium It can reach many people simultaneously, and it requires the use of some technological device to connect the marketing communicator with the audience.

maximum dispersion The situation occurring when priority is greater than frequency; the media buyer should avoid duplicating programs as much as possible.

mechanical measurement Information collected through a device that measures involuntary responses of the automatic nervous system.

media buyers People who negotiate the deals for media time and space.

media mix The combination of media.

media objectives Quantitative statements of what the marketing communication plan intends to accomplish. They must be specific enough to provide guidance, realistic, measurable, and sufficiently achievable within the available budget.

media plan A blueprint that maps out the best ways to send the marketing communication message to the target audience.

media planners The people who make decisions and implement the media mix that best fits the client's marketing strategy.

media relations The public relations function primarily responsible for publicity.

media-class source effect A qualitative measure that compares different types of media.

media-option characteristics   A qualitative measure that examines the effect of variations in size, length, color, and location.

message presentation source   The person, animated character, or voice-over who delivers the actual message.

message strategy, or **creative strategy**   A plan that outlines what type of message needs to be developed.

message variables   The specific elements used to communicate an idea and the way these elements are organized.

middle class   The social class falling between the very wealthy (upper class) and the lower, working class. People in business and the professions.

motivational promotions   Promotions designed to encourage salespeople to work harder.

motive   An inner drive or pressure to act in order to eliminate tension, to satisfy a need or want, to solve a problem, or to restore a sense of equilibrium.

multi-attribute attitude model   Helpful with message strategy, it systematically predicts individuals' attitudes toward an object by examining their reactions to specific object attributes.

national spot advertising   Local advertising time bought by a national company.

need   A state or feeling of deprivation, such as hunger, the need for affection, knowledge, or self-expression.

negative reinforcement   A negative response to a cue.

net coverage   The number of people exposed to the message.

network radio   Applies only to the traditional line networks interconnected (wired) by AT&T circuits (for example, ABC and CBS). Experts agree there are now only four major radio networks.

news release   A form of publicity that commits a story to paper or video in the style acceptable to the medium for which it was intended.

newspaper inserts   Single-page, direct-marketing pieces, multipage booklets, perforated coupons, or gummed reply envelopes.

niche marketing   An approach that assumes market segments exist that require customized strategies.

norms   Expectations about what behavior is appropriate.

nuclear family   Two adults of the opposite sex, living with their own or adopted children.

off-network syndication   A network program that has run its course and is sold to the local station in syndication.

on-sale date   The day the issue goes on sale, which is when it reaches the reader.

on-the-air testing   A method of pretesting opinions that analyzes a new commercial by comparing it with an existing commercial.

one-sided message   Presents an argument for the sponsor without mentioning counterarguments.

opinion method   A simple method of evaluating an advertisement by showing members of the general public a proposed advertisement and asking their opinion of it.

organizational communication system   A system composed of a large collection of subsystems organized around common goals.

out-of-home   Out-of-Home Media Services (OHMS) conducts research on the industry and provides a national buying service for outdoor and transit advertising.

out-of-home advertising   Advertising that reaches audiences in their daily external environment.

overlay   A sales promotion combined with other marketing communication tools and delivered together.

overspending   A saturation point at which continued spending would produce sales at a decreasing rate.

pace   The speed at which a salesperson moves to close a sale.

pacing   The speed at which the action develops.

packaging   Both a container for a product and a display for a marketing communication message.

participation   When several advertisers buy spots on a particular program. Almost 90% of all network time is sold under this format.

perceived value   The calculations that consumers make in their minds of the extra value contained in a sales promotion compared with the risks in accepting the offer.

perception   The assignment of meaning to stimuli received through the senses.

personal selling   The face-to-face presentation of a product or an idea to a potential customer by a representative of the company or organization for the sake of making a sale.

pleasant appeal   A message that creates a positive experience and product likability.

point-of-purchase or merchandise materials   Materials that deliver marketing communication messages at the point of sale and facilitate the consumer's likelihood to purchase.

portfolio test   A pretesting method that is conducted in person and consists of showing consumers sales promotions to be evaluated and some additional information about each one. They are then asked to vote for the one they like the best. Considered more accurate than the ballot method.

position   The image that the product projects relative to competing products.

positive reinforcement   A positive response to a cue.

post statement   A statement of the newspaper's claimed circulation figures given once each year to the post office.

posttesting   Research that is conducted after the audience has been exposed to the message, medium, or spokesperson.

premium   A tangible reward given to consumers for performing a particular act, usually purchasing a product or visiting the point of purchase.

press conference   An event held by an organization to make a significant announcement to representatives of the press.

press kit   A collection of supporting material distributed at a press conference to representatives of the press.

pretesting, or **evaluative research**   Research that is conducted before the audience is exposed to the marketing communication.

price   The value assigned to the product by the seller and the buyer.

price bundling   The practice of selling multiple units of a product or combination of complementary products for a lower total price than if sold separately.

price copy advertising   Advertising that touts price as the dominant marketing mix element.

price fixing   The illegal act of setting prices in concert with competitors.

price-pack deal   A method of price discounting which provides the consumer with something extra through the package itself.

primary information   Information collected for the first time.

product differentiation   The process of creating a difference in the mind of the consumer between one product and other products.

product placement   The practice of having a product appear in a news show or movie to generate valuable visibility.

product positioning   Determining how the company can best market its product based on the customer's view of the product compared to the competition.

program analyzer   A technique designed specifically for broadcast media that allows members of an audience to indicate likes and dislikes continuously throughout a program, including the commercials.

promise A type of benefit statement that looks to the future and pledges that something good will happen if the consumer uses the product.

prospecting The process of locating potential customers and then obtaining permission to present a sales presentation.

psychographics A tool that combines consumer characteristics, such as attitudes and motives, that may bear on a consumer's response to products, packaging, advertising, sales promotion, and public relations efforts.

public affairs Public relations programs that focus on government relations by working closely with federal, regional, state, and local government agencies.

public communication system A verbal exchange from one person to a large group of people, as occurs when a person gives a speech to an audience.

public relations A coordinated attempt to create a favorable product image in the mind of the public by supporting certain activities or programs, publishing commercially significant news in a widely circulated medium, or obtaining favorable publicity on radio, television, or stage that is not paid for by the company selling the product.

publicity A tool of public relations that is used to provide the media with information disseminated as news stories or mentions in news stories.

publics All audiences that a marketing communicator targets to receive messages about the company or who are perceived as influencing opinions about the company.

puffery Advertising or other sales representations that praise the product or service with subjective opinions, superlatives, or exaggerations, vaguely and generally, without substantiation.

pull strategy A promotional strategy that directs most marketing efforts at the ultimate consumer and is usually implemented with large advertising expenditures.

pulsing A combination of continuous advertising and flighting, with continuous advertising emphasized during the best sale months. This continuity pattern tends to minimize waste and thus represents the best of both techniques.

push money An extra payment given to salespeople for meeting a specified sales goal.

push strategy A promotional strategy that directs most marketing efforts at resellers and the sales force to stimulate personal selling efforts.

qualitative media effect What the media does to enhance or depreciate a message after the medium has delivered the message.

qualitative objectives An organization's objectives that address the subjective issues achieved through the appropriation rather than the quantitative issues of profit, sales, and marketing.

quantitative objectives An organization's objectives that concern an appropriation's ability to maximize profit, sales, or market share.

rational appeal A message that contains both factual and logical appeal.

rational motives Are supported by a reasoning process that consumers perceive as being acceptable to their peers.

reach The number of people or households exposed to a particular media vehicle (such as a specific magazine or TV program) or media schedule (the total number of vehicles across a period of time) at least once during a specific time period (usually weekly or monthly).

reason why Another form of a benefit statement that explains with logic or reasoning why the user will benefit from a product feature.

rebate Essentially, a refund.

recall To remember the content of the advertising message.

recall test A test that measures the depth of impression an advertisement leaves on the reader's mind.

receiver The recipient of a message (an individual, a group, or an institution).

recent reading Medimark Research, Inc.'s research technique that relies on the use of "flash" cards containing magazine logos. Respondents sort these cards among various magazines.

recognition To remember having seen information about some product creating top-of-mind awareness.

reengineering A process that businesses use to break down rigid, departmentalized structures to create more fluid and flexible organizations that can respond quickly to marketplace challenges.

reference group Any person or group that serves as a point of comparison (or reference) for an individual in the formation of general or specific values, attitudes, or behavior.

refund An offer by the marketer to return a certain amount of money to the consumer who purchases the product.

reinforced The resulting condition of a behavior when a consumer has a positive or negative response to a product.

relationship marketing A type of marketing that builds long-standing positive relationships with customers and other important stakeholder groups.

reliability When the same test results are repeated time after time.

remnant space Publishers, especially those with geographic or demographic editions, sometimes have extra space in some editions when they are ready to go to press. Publishers usually offer this space to advertisers at a big discount.

researcher A person who conducts consumer research on a particular segment of the population with a specific product or brand in mind.

reseller source The wholesaler or retailer that cosponsors advertising with the product's manufacturer.

resellers Wholesalers, brokers, and retailers.

respondent/nonrespondent surveys This type of survey attempts to identify differences between those who did and those who did not respond to the direct-marketing program.

response How an individual reacts to a cue.

retail catalogs Contain merchandise equivalent to that found in the sponsors' stores.

retail salespeople Employees of a retail business who sell products to customers and are retained and managed by the retailer.

retailers Those who receive products from wholesalers, or possibly from manufacturers, and then sell those products to the ultimate users.

retention The storage of information for later reference.

retrieval The process by which information is recovered from the memory storehouse.

RFM The recency, frequency, and monetary value of purchases.

role A prescribed way of behaving based on the position of the group member in a specific situation.

roster recall Door-to-door interviews whereby the interviewer carries a roster of programs that were broadcast the day before. The interviewee answers questions about these programs and responds to demographic questions.

run of book (ROB) Means the ad can be placed anywhere in the magazine.

S.W.O.T. (Strengths, Weaknesses, Opportunities, Threats) analysis An investigation into market conditions to determine how strengths, weaknesses, opportunities, and threats affect strategy.

sales conviction test A test in which a heavy user of a particular product is asked which of two ads would be most likely to convince them to buy the product.

sales kits Packages containing sales manuals with background information, details about other elements of the promotional effort, or detailed product specifications.

sales meeting   An educational meeting that can bring together a local, regional, national, or international sales force.

sales promotion   Marketing activities that add to the basic value of the product or service for a limited time and directly stimulate consumer purchasing, the cooperation of distributors, or the effort of the sales force.

sales promotion managers   People who set objectives and budgets and evaluate the success of promotions.

sampling   Allowing the customer to experience the product or service free of charge or for a small fee.

scope   The variety of benefits, features, and sales terms discussed.

second cover page   Name given to the inside of the front cover.

secondary information   Information that already exists.

secondary values   Impermanent values that can sometimes be influenced by marketing communication.

self-liquidator   A type of premium that requires consumers to mail in a payment before receiving the premium.

selling premises   The ideas that touch people's lives and feelings. Also referred to as "hot buttons."

sender (source)   An individual, a group, or an institution that wishes to transmit a message to a receiver or target audience.

services   Intangibles that are represented by activities of people.

share   The percentage of households watching a particular program at a particular time.

shopper   Publications such as Thrifty Nickel or Real Estate Guide usually distributed free to certain homes in certain neighborhoods or through supermarket racks.

short rate   A rate higher than the contract rate that is applied if less-than-agreed-upon space was purchased.

simple decision making   A minimal information search and evaluation of alternatives leading to a decision.

single-source tracking system   The use of computers and scanners to monitor participants in a study that evaluates the relationship between advertising and sales.

situation analysis   A section of the marketing plan that identifies and appraises all environmental factors that affect the marketing program.

slander   Oral defamation.

slotting allowance   A fee that retailers charge manufacturers for space the new product will occupy on the shelf.

small group   A collection of more than two but fewer than twenty people.

small magazine size   Generally accepted physical size of $4\frac{3}{8}$ inches by 6 inches or a size unique to a particular magazine.

social accountability position strategy   This tries to establish goodwill by positioning the organization as a good community citizen.

social class   A position on a social scale based on criteria such as occupation, education, and income.

societal issues   When the marketing communication activities of a business appear to violate widely held values and, as a result, part of society wants to change the offending actions.

sociocultural environment   Those factors beyond the individual's personal world.

source   A reference group.

special interest publications   Target a special interest such as farming, travel, and so on. These publications account for more than 90 percent of the total number of magazines published today.

speciality advertising This tool is a form of sales promotion. It usually involves presenting the company's name on something that is given away as a reminder item (calendars, pens, pencils, mugs, match covers, and so forth).

specialties Free gifts used as reminder items because they carry the brand or corporate identification.

sponsor source The manufacturer who pays for the message delivery and is usually identified somewhere in the message itself.

sponsorship A company's financial support of an event or cause in exchange for an affiliation with the organization or event sponsored; can create goodwill and positive associations that companies can feature through other communication tools such as advertising.

spot advertising Advertising time bought directly from local television stations.

spot announcements Purchased from local television stations, these announcements appear during the adjacent time periods of network programs.

stakeholder Anyone who has a stake in the success of a company or its products.

standard magazine size Generally accepted physical size of 8 inches by 10 inches.

standard rate and date service A service that provides media costs for a specified period of time.

stereotyping Ignoring the differences among individuals and presenting the group in an unvarying pattern.

storyboard A drawing of the key scenes in the commercial.

straight commission Compensation paid to salespeople on a fixed or sliding rate of earnings based on their sales volume or profit contribution.

straight salary The compensation of people for time spent on the job.

strategic alliances Agreements between firms of different marketing specialties to complement each others' services and provide referrals.

strategic consistency Tailoring the message to each market segment that is targeted while staying consistent with the central themes of the marketing communication program.

strategic planning The process of developing and maintaining a viable fit between the organization's objectives, its resources, and its changing market opportunities.

subculture A group of people who share a set of secondary values.

subliminal message A message that is sent in such a way that the receiver is not consciously aware of receiving it.

supportive programs Programs that prepare salespeople to do their jobs.

survey Interviews or questionnaires that are used to obtain information about people's exposure to a particular message, medium, or person, and the resulting changes in their attitude or actions.

sweepstakes Games of chance that are lawful only if there is no charge or obligation of any kind for participation. The guidelines for stating the chance of winning, the considerations for entering, and the nature of the prize are governed by the FTC.

taglines A phrase used in a memorable way at the end of an advertisement to summarize the point of the message.

talent The people or animals in the commercial.

target audience A group of people who receive marketing messages and have significant potential to respond to the messages.

target rating points (TRPs) An accurate reflection of the desired media schedule, this estimate includes only the numbers of people in the primary target audience who are reached by the message, as well as the number of times.

telemarketing A direct-marketing technique that combines telecommunications technology, marketing strategies, and information systems. It can be used alone or in conjunction with advertising, direct mail, sales promotions, personal selling, or other marketing communication functions.

telephone coincidence   Households are called at random to discover which programs are being watched.

television market   Rigidly defined geographic area in which stations generally located in the core of the area attract most of the viewing.

test market   One or more cities that serve as a test area for an ad or media mix.

think-feel-do model   Presumes that we approach a purchase using the following sequence of responses: We think about the cue, then we form an attitude or opinion about it, and finally we take action and respond to it.

third cover page   Name given to the inside of the back cover.

through the book   A technique that use stripped-down or skeleton copies of magazines as the basis for research.

tie-in   A promotion that links one product to another, so that the marketer can take advantage of the brand strength of another product.

time series analysis   The use of a company's historical data to discover a pattern or pattern's of the firm's sales over time.

top-down management   Management approach where top-level executives control various marketing communications programs and manage their integration.

tracking study   Survey that gathers information from a large number of people by simply counting responses over time and collecting some information from a sample of respondents.

trade deals   Allowances, discounts, goods, or cash given to a retailer in return for handling a special promotion.

trade promotion   A promotion directed at resellers and sales forces.

trade promotion specialists   Experts who know how and when to use point-of-purchase displays and other in-store merchandising materials, dealer and salesperson contests and sweepstakes, and trade shows and exhibits.

trademark   A brand name or brand mark that is legally protected through registration with the Patent and Trademark Office of the Department of Commerce.

traffic managers   Those who schedule and track an ad as it is produced and hire production specialists.

trailers   Filmed commercials shown in movie theaters before the feature. These advertisements are similar to television commercials but are generally longer and better produced.

transit advertising   Primarily an urban advertising tool that uses vehicles to carry the message throughout the community.

trial close   A question that asks for the potential buyer's opinion of a product or service.

two-sided message   A message sponsored by a company that presents both the argument and the counterargument.

tying arrangement   When a seller forces a buyer to purchase one product to obtain the right to purchase another.

underspending   Low marketing communication spending resulting in sales below their expected minimum.

unique selling proposition   A selling premise based on a product formula, design, or feature that is both unique and important to the user.

unit   A measure used in calculating the cost per thousand (for example, per page or per 30-second spot).

unplanned messages   Elements associated with a company or brand that are capable of delivering implicit messages to consumers.

upper class   The wealthiest social class.

validity   When a concept is confirmed through testing to be what it claims to be.

value-added Providing additional value to a product through speed of delivery, maintenance, warranties, return policy, and the like.

values General statements that guide behavior and influence beliefs and attitudes.

vehicle source effect A qualitative measure that compares the impact of a single exposure in one vehicle with a single exposure in another vehicle.

vice president of marketing, or **director of marketing** The top executive in charge of the marketing effort.

video The images.

videotext Ties an individual television set to a remote host computer via telephone line or coaxial cable.

voice mail A system for receiving and storing voice messages at a telephone address.

wearout Excessive repetition of a message that results in a negative consumer response.

wholesaler A distribution channel member who receives products from a manufacturer or other wholesaler and distributes them to a retailer or another wholesaler.

willingness to comply The degree to which a person can be persuaded.

word-of-mouth source A source that does not benefit from the acceptance of the message and is not under the control of the sponsor.

CREDITS

Chapter 1

3 Reproduced with permission of PepsiCo, Inc., 1997, Purchase, New York

Chapter 2

29 Courtesy of Hanna Andersson, Inc. **32** UPS and UPS Shield Design are registered trademarks of United Parcel Service of America, Inc. Used by permission. **36** Courtesy of Boehringer Ingelheim Pharmaceuticals **40** Courtesy of SAS Institute, Inc. **48** Courtesy of The Coca-Cola Company **51** Courtesy of Brooks Brothers **52** Courtesy of Tandy Corporation

Chapter 3

65 Courtesy of Arthur Anderson **67** Courtesy of Xerox Corporation **68** © 1994 Lotus Development Corporation. All rights reserved. Used with permission of Lotus Development Corporation. **77** Courtesy of Harris Drury Cohen **81** Courtesy of The Dannon Company, Inc.

Chapter 4

91 Courtesy of Fleishman Hillard, Inc. **95** Courtesy of Tom's of Maine, Inc. **103** Courtesy of Imation Corp. and Jett Titcomb/Liaison Intl. **105** Courtesy of Sony Electronics, Inc. **115** Courtesy of The Gillette Company **135** Courtesy of *Out* **141** Courtesy of Mastercard International **142** Courtesy of Ford Motor Company **143** "The Club Chair," Courtesy of Crate and Barrel Furniture Store **147** Courtesy of Jhane Barnes **148** Courtesy of Sanrio **156** Courtesy of GE Capital Assurance

Chapter 6

163 Courtesy of Frank Herholdt/Tony Stone Images **168** Courtesy of Boxell Worldwide, Inc. as agent for National Fluid Milk Processor Promotion Board **173** Courtesy of Qantas **177** Courtesy of Room Plus Furniture, Inc. **185** Courtesy of Westin Hotels & Resorts **192** Courtesy of General Accident Insurance and Steve Belkowitz Photography

Chapter 7

201 Copyright © 1996 by The New York Times Co. Reprinted by permission. **210** Reprinted by permission of NIKE, Inc. **212** Courtesy of Harvard Industries **217** Reproduced with permission of the International Advertising Association **218** Copyright American Association of Advertising Agencies. Reprinted with permission. **221** Courtesy of the Campbell Soup Company **223** Copyright American Association of Advertising Agencies. Reprinted with permission. **230** Courtesy of Black Star and Dennis Chamberlin

Chapter 8

239 Copyright © 1996 Gateway 2000, Inc. Reprinted with permission. **250** Reproduced courtesy of Chesebrough-Pond's, Inc. **251** Courtesy of MetLife and United Feature Syndicate, Inc. **259** Courtesy of SallieMae **263** Courtesy of United Colors of Benetton **269** Courtesy of Peter Blakely/SABA

Chapter 9

279 Courtesy The Gillette Company **285** Courtesy of United Colors of Benetton **286** Ad provided by Foote, Cone & Belding/New York. Reprinted by permission of British Virgin Islands. **287** Courtesy of PETA **288** Courtesy of Comsat **295** Reproduced with permission of PepsiCo, Inc., 1997, Purchase, New York **299** Courtesy of Tom's of Maine, Inc.

Chapter 10

311 Courtesy of Binney & Smith, Inc. **332** Courtesy of Fleishman Hillard, Inc. **336** Reprinted with the permission of AT&T

Chapter 11

343 Courtesy The Gillette Company **352** Courtesy of The Prudential Insurance Companies of America **355** Courtesy The Gillette Company **363** Courtesy The Gillette Company **366** Courtesy of State Farm Insurance Companies **367** Courtesy Ben & Jerry's **369** Courtesy of the National Trust for Historic Preservation

Chapter 12

377 Courtesy of Grassfield's **381 bottom** Used with permission from *TIME for Kids* magazine, copyright 1996 **387** Courtesy of Grassfield's **388** Courtesy of RUF Strategic Solutions **394** Copyright 1996, Dun & Bradstreet, a company of The Dun & Bradstreet Corporation **397** Courtesy of The Internet Mall **399** Courtesy of Black Star and David Graham

Chapter 13

409 Photo courtesy of Andy Freeburg Photography. © Andy Freeburg. **419** Courtesy of H&R Block Tax Services, Inc. **426** Copyright © Todd Buchanan

Chapter 14

448 Courtesy of Allsport **449** Courtesy of American Airlines/Dennis Murphy **453** Courtesy of Ben & Jerry's **455** Courtesy of Point-of-Purchase Advertising Institute

Chapter 15

471 Courtesy of WebTV Networks, Inc. **484** Courtesy of *Time* Magazine **485** Courtesy of Pentax **487** Courtesy of *Mountain Biker* **501** Courtesy of Franklin Bank and Solomon Friedman Advertising **504** Steve McCurry/National Geographic Society **506** Photo courtesy of Ed Quinn Photography

Chapter 16

513 Courtesy of Doug Goodman Photography

Chapter 18

599 Courtesy of Hong Kong Bank **604** Courtesy of Timberland and Roper Starch

Chapter 19

621 Copyright © Saturn Corporation. Used with permission. **637** Copyright © Saturn Corporation. Used with permission. **638** Copyright © Saturn Corporation. Used with permission. **639** Copyright © Saturn Corporation. Used with permission. **641** Copyright © Saturn Corporation. Used with permission. **643** Copyright © Saturn Corporation. Used with permission. **647** Copyright © Saturn Corporation. Used with permission. **649** Copyright © Saturn Corporation. Used with permission. **654** Copyright © Saturn Corporation. Used with permission.